The Police and the Community

Third Edition

Louis A. Radelet
Professor, School of Criminal Justice
Michigan State University

Research and Complementary Materials Prepared by
Hoyt Coe Reed
Associate Professor Emeritus
Department of Social Science, University College
Michigan State University

MACMILLAN PUBLISHING CO., INC.
New York
Collier Macmillan Publishers
London

The first edition of this text was dedicated to my students, as was the second; I see no reason to change this for the third. This book was originally inspired by my students, and they remain the most important yardstick by which its usefulness is measured. If education were a corporation, they would be the stockholders.

Copyright © 1973, 1977, 1980 by Louis A. Radelet

Printed in the United States of America

GLENCOE PUBLISHING CO., INC.
17337 Ventura Boulevard
Encino, California 91316
Collier Macmillan Canada, Ltd.

Library of Congress Catalog Card Number: 78-71744

ISBN 0-02-470680-9

2   3   4   5   6   7   8   9   10   83   82   81

LOUIS A. RADELET

Louis A. Radelet is professor of Criminal Justice and coordinator of the under-graduate criminal justice program at Michigan State University, where he has taught since 1963.

He founded and directed the National Institute on Police and Community Relations at Michigan State University from 1955 to 1970, and coordinated the National Center on Police and Community Relations at MSU from 1965 to 1973. He has directed the Michigan Statewide Institute on Community Relations and the Administration of Justice since 1970.

Professor Radelet is a member of the Academy of Criminal Justice Sciences, the International Association of Chiefs of Police and the Michigan Association of Criminal Justice Educators. He is a Fellow of Phi Kappa Phi and of the Society for Values in Higher Education. He was a consultant to the President's Commission on Law Enforcement and the Administration of Justice (1965–1967), and to the National Advisory Commission on Civil Disorders (1967–1968). He has directed workshops in human relations at the University of Michigan, the University of Notre Dame, Adelphi University, and the University of Montreal.

Besides writing numerous articles, monographs, and reports on intergroup relations and police-community relations, Professor Radelet is the author of *Police and the Community: Studies* (Glencoe, 1973) and coeditor (with A. F. Brandstatter) of *Police and Community Relations: A Sourcebook* (Glencoe, 1968).

HOYT COE REED

Hoyt Coe Reed was a cofounder, secretary, and editor of the *Proceedings* of the National Institute on Police and Community Relations at MSU from 1955 to 1968. He also acted as secretary of the National Center on Police and Community Relations during those years. Since 1970 he has been serving in a similar capacity for the Michigan Statewide Institute on Community Relations and the Administration of Justice. Professor Reed taught social science at what is now Fairleigh Dickinson University from 1935 to 1945, and at Michigan State from 1945 to 1968. He currently serves as Librarian for the James J. Brennan Memorial Library of the School of Criminal Justice at Michigan State.

ROBERT H. SCOTT

The coauthor of Chapters 14 and 15 is Robert H. Scott. Mr. Scott graduated from Yale in 1931, then earned the LL.B. (later J.D.) degree in 1934 at Albany Law School, Union University. While practicing law in the following years, he served for a time as a justice of the peace and as a special probate judge. In 1948, he moved to Michigan State University as an associate professor in the School of Police Administration and Public Safety, and in 1955 directed the first National Institute on Police and Community Relations. He shifted to the Michigan Department of Corrections as director of its Youth Division and was appointed Deputy Director for Program Serviecs of the department in 1966. Mr. Scott was later appointed a member of the State Parole Board, remaining in this capacity until December, 1973, when he retired. He is currently on part-time appointment as a professor in the School of Criminal Justice at Michigan State University.

Glencoe Criminal Justice Texts

Allen/Simonsen: **Corrections in America: An Introduction** (Second Edition)

Bloomquist: **Marijuana: The Second Trip**

*Brandstatter/Hyman: **Fundamentals of Law Enforcement**

*Coffey/Eldefonso: **Process and Impact of Justice**

*DeAngelis: **Criminalistics for the Investigator**

Eldefonso: **Issues in Corrections**

Eldefonso: **Readings in Criminal Justice**

*Eldefonso/Coffey: **Process and Impact of the Juvenile Justice System**

*Eldefonso/Hartinger: **Control, Treatment, and Rehabilitation of Juvenile Offenders**

*Engel/DeGreen/Rebo: **The Justice Game: A Simulation**

*Gourley: **Effective Municipal Police Organization**

*Kamm/Hunt/Fleming: **Juvenile Law and Procedures in California** (Revised Edition)

*Lentini: **Vice and Narcotics Control**

*Melnicoe/Mennig: **Elements of Police Supervision** (Second Edition)

*Nelson: **Preliminary Investigation and Police Reporting: A Complete Guide to Police Written Communication**

*Pursley: **Introduction to Criminal Justice** (Second Edition)

*Radelet: **The Police and the Community** (Third Edition)

*Radelet/Reed: **The Police and the Community: Studies**

*Roberts/Bristow: **An Introduction to Modern Police Firearms**

*Simonsen/Gordon: **Juvenile Justice in America**

*Waddington: **Arrest, Search, and Seizure**

*Waddington: **Criminal Evidence**

Walton: **Laboratory Manual for Introductory Forensic Science**

*Wicks/Platt: **Drug Abuse: A Criminal Justice Primer**

*Glencoe Criminal Justice Series
G. Douglas Gourley, General Editor
Former Professor Emeritus and
Former Chairman
Department of Criminal Justice
California State University, Los Angeles

CONTENTS

FOREWORD

Throughout the nation, crime has become a paramount concern of urban dwellers. Their property and personal safety are constantly threatened, and as the victimization rate has increased, so has their fear. Many citizens have become paranoid, altering their lifestyles, arming themselves, investing in security devices, and barricading their homes.

In response, law enforcement agencies have employed additional manpower, expanded in-service training, initiated crime prevention programs, utilized advanced technology, and purchased sophisticated hardware.

In spite of this combination of effort and expenditure, crime continues to escalate, because it is a social problem, not a police problem. Therefore, it can be resolved only when prevention and suppression become a joint social enterprise. In concept, uniformed officers are merely a visible symbol of the authority and responsibility of citizens to self-police their own community. However, without mutual commitment to the same set of goals, a self-policing society is doomed to remain merely a concept instead of becoming a reality.

To transfer the concept into reality, law enforcement must cultivate and motivate public good will, cooperation, and involvement through viable "police-community relations," which are variously defined as community services, public information, cross-cultural relations, and public relations. The term actually encompasses all four definitions and Louis A. Radelet's text, *The Police and the Community*, has long been recognized for its excellent treatment of this complex subject.

Now in its third edition, this text provides an important resource for the training of both recruits and experienced officers. It can greatly assist in developing each officer to his or her fullest potential, not only by increasing competence on duty but also by expanding each officer's capacity for total community awareness. This educational enrichment is essential to expand police capability to meet the challenges of an ever-changing society and develop appropriate modes of response to these changes.

Professor Radelet's experience and expertise guide his readers into full development of these interpersonal skills that foster communication and cooperation between police and the citizens they serve. Through interaction with all segments of the population, the officer becomes an integral part of the community. He or she can thereby establish the credibility to promote willing compliance with the laws and encourage fellow citizens to vigorously participate in their enforcement. Together, with officers and citizens sharing a sense of common purpose, barriers will give way to a participatory partnership in which crime suppression and reduction can be transformed from abstract ideal into viable reality.

E. Wilson Purdy

Former Director, Metropolitan Dade County, Florida Department of Public Safety

Former Commissioner, Pennsylvania State Police

Former President, Police Executive Research Forum

PREFACE

This text is about the relationship between the police and the people they serve. It also examines the interactions among the criminal justice system, the community, and the processes of social control, in response to changing views of crime both inside and outside the criminal justice system.

Just as our views of crime and criminals have changed, our concept of police-community relations has changed, too. One healthy sign of this change is that some PCR programs, such as community-based crime prevention and neighborhood watch programs, have been created in response to requests from the community. People who today say that PCR is an outmoded concept are perhaps still thinking in terms of the sixties.

True, many PCR programs of the sixties disappointed us. But if they did, it was because our idea of PCR during those years was incomplete: we simply didn't realize how central the *community's* role and responsibility in police matters really was. PCR was something the police did, something they themselves saw as a low-priority public relations effort, an activity on the fringes of "real police work."

The key, I feel, is still the community, and if I read the signs correctly, PCR today is moving in that direction. The active and responsible involvement of the community will enable us to develop a new concept of PCR and improve the processes of criminal justice in the future.

Organization. The Police and the Community is divided into five parts, allowing students to explore the main issues in police-community relations from several perspectives. Part One explores the scope of the police-community relations problem, examining the history leading to the need for PCR programs, the concept of PCR as it has existed to the present, the role of the police in today's society, police professionalism, and the discretionary use of police power.

Part Two explores PCR from a psychological perspective, discussing the self-image of the police officer, the public image of the police, and perceptions and prejudice involving the police and the people they serve.

In Part Three PCR is explored from a sociological perspective, including such topics and issues as social processes, population trends, and the urban environment; the police and minority groups; collective behavior, terrorism, and civil disobedience; youth, women, and the elderly; and complaints and the police.

Part Four considers other forces and systems in society that affect police-community relations. These include the relationship of the police to the other elements of the criminal justice system—courts and corrections. Part Four also examines the media, politics and the police, and crime prevention.

Part Five is devoted to PCR programs. In three chapters PCR programs of the past, the present, and the future are discussed and evaluated.

Changes in the Third Edition. Changes in the third edition reflect suggestions from users, suggestions earnestly solicited and gratefully received.

This edition has been tightened and condensed, so instructors will find it easier to present the material in a semester. Chapters 8 and 9 of the second edition (the first covering attitudes and values, the second prejudice and rumor) are now combined into the new chapter 8, "Perceptions and Prejudices." This new edition also has a format that makes it easier for students to read.

New material has been added on crime prevention programs, public attitudes towards the police, terrorism, and the relationships of the police with such groups as women and the elderly. More attention has also been given to the discretionary use of police power, the conflict-repression school of criminology, demographic trends, women in police work, crime and the elderly, stress among police officers, and program analysis and evaluation.

Part Five has been completely revamped to focus on PCR programs of the past, the present, and the future.

Learning Aids. Students will find a summary at the end of every chapter and also at the end of each part.

The Police and the Community includes one of the most comprehensive bibliographies available on PCR. This bibliography has been annually updated and maintained for use in Michigan State's National Institute on Police and Community Relations. The bibliography in this third edition contains a new feature: annotated entries for the most important books published during the last five years.

Instructor's Manual. The instructor's manual that accompanies this edition of *The Police and the Community* has been prepared on the basis of extensive classroom experience—forty years of teaching at the college level. This manual includes schedule breakdowns for teaching the course during a quarter or a semester, chapter summaries for teacher use, and a list of audio-visual teaching aids. Also included are case studies and two types of questions—discussion questions and multiple-choice test questions—for each chapter.

Acknowledgments. No book of this scope can be written without the assistance of many generous people. Hoyt Coe (Dick) Reed has been my collaborator from the beginning, doing research and preparing supplementary materials. Thanking him is a little like time thanking a clock for making it all possible. Bob Scott is the coauthor of two chapters of this text and the third member, with Dick Reed and myself, of a team that has been doing PCR work together since the first National Institute at Michigan State in 1955. My thanks to Bob have long since been too great to express.

My wife, Grace, and Anne Reed have been typing manuscript for us since 1970. That's a lot of words—and a lot of gratitude. My son Mike, now assistant professor of sociology and psychiatry at the University of Florida, has rewritten his section of the chapter on the public image of the police for this edition. His dad wishes he could write as well as Mike.

Special thanks to E. Wilson Purdy, director of the Dade County, Florida, Department of Public Safety, who wrote the foreword for this edition. Thanks also to Dr. Mladen Kabalin, director of the Science division of the Michigan State University library, who has done a masterful job on the index.

To all the writers who have graciously granted permission for me to borrow their ideas and incorporate them in these pages, my heartiest thanks. And finally, the editors join me in thanking the reviewers for their many suggestions, which greatly contributed to the quality of this text. Reviewers who contributed suggestions for the third edition include Dr. Hugh J. B. Cassidy of Adelphi University; Dr. John Thomas of Indiana University of Pennsylvania; Dr. Robert W. Stearns, head of the criminal justice department of Miami-Dade Community College; Dr. Rana A. R. Khan of Grambling State University; and Dr. Sloan T. Letman of Loyola University in Chicago.

Writing a book, like any other team task, is a lesson in interdependence. That's really what this book is about.

Louis A. Radelet

Jewels Among Swine

(Drawing from *Harper's Weekly,* June 13, 1874)

The police authorities, that do not enforce the laws against the liquor traffic, that do not suppress gambling or houses of ill repute . . . distinguished themselves on Saturday by arresting forty-three women, who went on the streets to sing and pray, and marching them to the station house.

———*Cincinnati Gazette*

From Morton Keller, *The Art and Politics of Thomas Nast* (New York: Oxford University Press, 1968), plate 70.

PART 1

The Scope
of the Problem

1

BACKGROUND

The police and the processes of criminal justice are part of the main body of orderly society—the *community*. This text deals with the scope of this proposition. The idea is hardly a recent discovery. Its history parallels the history of police organization and related functions of society.

The origins of the modern-day municipal police department can be traced back to 1829, the year in which Sir Robert Peel managed to secure approval by an apprehensive English Parliament of his bill for a metropolitan police.[1] There was considerable opposition to Peel's idea, as some members of Parliament were concerned that such a force might become a mechanism of political tyranny. A parliamentary committee had reported on an earlier Peel proposal "that forfeiture or curtailment of individual liberty which the creation of an effective police system would bring with it would be too great a sacrifice on behalf of improvements in police or facilities in detection of crime."[2] However, Sir Robert's bill finally became law, and the "Peelers," or "Bobbies," set the stage for our city police of today.

It is interesting to contrast Peel's principles of law enforcement with law enforcement today, particularly because of the difference in emphasis given the part the ordinary citizen plays in police services (see Table 1-1, page 4). This contrast points up the modern American misconception that the police are paid to do what civilians would prefer not to do—one expression of contemporary police-community separatism.

Why have the police been viewed as "pigs" since the founding of the first police force? (See frontispiece.) Clearly, the reference is not indicative of a love affair between police and public. While most people seem to have a favorable view of the police most of the time, many people frankly prefer to avoid contact with the police if at all possible, and the outright hostility of some groups toward the police is a well-established reality. There seems to be something peculiar about the police relationship with the community that makes it the object of special study by scholars interested in such social processes as human and intergroup relations, governmental operations, bureaucratic organizations, and the administration and management of public service agencies.

Police-community relations is a subject that has come to the forefront of social concern in the United States during the past two or three decades. The idea of equal protection under the law for all citizens advocated in the civil rights movement and the recognition of the uniformed police officer by minorities as the most visible representative of the establishment are reasons for this interest.

3

We hear it said that successful police work depends on the cooperation of the public with the police. In fact, in a democracy, every citizen has a serious *obligation to do police work*, and the existence of a paid police force does not alter this duty. Some historical background is useful to put the subject into perspective.

TABLE 1–1
Peel's Principles of Law Enforcement

1. The basic mission for which the police exist is to prevent crime and disorder as an alternative to the repression of crime and disorder by military force and severity of legal punishment.
2. The ability of the police to perform their duties is dependent upon public approval of police existence, actions, behavior, and the ability of the police to secure and maintain public respect.
3. The police must secure the willing cooperation of the public in voluntary observance of the law to be able to secure and maintain public respect.
4. The degree of cooperation of the public that can be secured diminishes, proportionately, the necessity for the use of physical force and compulsion in achieving police objectives.
5. The police seek and preserve public favor, not by catering to public opinion, but by constantly demonstrating absolutely impartial service to the law, in complete independence of policy, and without regard to the justice or injustice of the substance of individual laws; by ready offering of individual service and friendship to all members of the society without regard to their race or social standing; by ready exercise of courtesy and friendly good humor; and by ready offering of individual sacrifice in protecting and preserving life.
6. The police should use physical force to the extent necessary to secure observance of the law or to restore order only when the exercise of persuasion, advice, and warning is found to be insufficient to achieve police objectives; and police should use only the minimum degree of physical force which is necessary on any particular occasion for achieving a police objective.
7. The police at all times should maintain a relationship with the public that gives reality to the historic tradition that the police are the public and that the public are the police; the police are the only members of the public who are paid to give full-time attention to duties which are incumbent on every citizen in the interest of the community welfare.
8. The police should always direct their actions toward their functions and never appear to usurp the powers of the judiciary by avenging individuals or the state, or authoritatively judging guilt or punishing the guilty.
9. The test of police efficiency is the absence of crime and disorder, not the visible evidence of police action in dealing with them.[3]

MEDIEVAL POLICE SERVICE

In the Anglo-Saxon England of a thousand years ago, every able-bodied freeman was a police officer. As Peel later asserted, "The police are the public and the public are the police." Every male from fifteen to sixty maintained such arms as he could afford. When the hue and cry was raised, every man within earshot dropped whatever he was doing and joined in the pursuit of the transgressor. Not to do so was serious neglect of duty.

Later, the constable became the chief peace officer, but the job was still unpaid and was rotated among many. Then came the justice of the peace, who was both judge and police officer, discharging certain police duties even in modern times, especially in the suppression of riots.[4] This was the beginning of judicial surveillance over the police. As towns developed, watchmen were employed for full-time work, but ordinary citizens retained a solemn duty to perform police functions.

By the seventeenth century, many abuses had appeared in this medieval police system. Unpaid constables sought to avoid duty. Some persons maneuvered their police responsibilities to serve their private interests. As towns grew into cities, this watch-and-ward system was severely strained. Thugs became the terror of the community. Finally, in the early eighteenth century, Sir John Fielding organized the Bow Street Runners, a small corps of paid police officers whose rapidly acquired reputation for success in apprehending hoodlums undoubtedly helped to persuade Parliament of the wisdom of Peel's proposals. Anxiety regarding the possible abuse of treasured English civil liberties by overzealous, paid police officers gradually dissolved in the face of accumulating evidence to the contrary.

So it is that the English declare to this day that a police officer is someone who is paid to do what it is a citizen's duty to do without pay. Consider, for example, the law of arrest. In a seventeenth-century treatise, *The Country Justice* by Michael Dalton, there appears this sentence: "The Sherife, Bailifes, Constables and other of the King's Officers may arrest and imprison offenders in all cases where a private person may." This use of every citizen's right to arrest as the standard by which the right of officers to arrest is measured is significant when compared with modern treatises.[5]

It was not until 1827 that the rule differentiating the legal powers of lay persons from those of peace officers was established in England. It is also interesting that numerous private police agencies existed in England and Europe as far back as the eleventh century—for example, associations of merchants such as the Hanseatic League, and of property owners banding together as self-appointed "thief catchers," anxious to protect their special interests. The Peel reforms incorporated into the new Metropolitan Police many private police agencies that had been organized for what we today would refer to as security purposes.

THE AMERICAN EXPERIENCE

In the United States, Peel's plan of police organization was copied in New York by 1844, and during the ensuing ten years similar organizational patterns appeared in Chicago, Philadelphia, and Boston. By 1870, the main features of the London Metropolitan Police were firmly established in this country.[6] The idea of lay people participating in police work was certainly evident in the early history of the western states. Public tribunals, councils, and vigilante activities were common, just as many private protective and security organizations exist today in business and industry.[7]

Every society recognizes that the police function is essential to its survival. The question is one of the means necessary to maintain that function. In democratic societies, order is not an end in itself; rather, it is a means to the end of justice and the sanctity of individual liberty. Three additional points are notable:

1. In their attitudes and values, not surprisingly, police officers tend to mirror the socioeconomic, cultural, ethnic, occupational, and educational characteristics of the strata of society in which they are reared. Thus, if a high proportion of officers come from lower-middle- or upper-lower-class backgrounds, having had blue-collar working parents, Indo-European ethnic traits, and the like, it follows that what they say and do as officers will reflect the attitudes and values of that background.[8] (We will examine this point more thoroughly in a later chapter.)

2. In a democratic society, unlike totalitarian systems, the police function depends on a considerable amount of self-policing by every citizen. The system is rooted in personal responsibility. Law observance is the most vital part of law enforcement. Paid police officers, even under conditions of intensive specialization and extensive training, cannot possibly perform their duties effectively without abundant self-policing by the citizen. This custom is not merely a matter of cooperation or good relations between police and community. Ideally, it is a matter of *organic union,* with the police *as part of,* rather than *apart from,* the community they serve.

3. In a democratic society the police are a living expression, an embodiment, an implementing arm of democratic law. If such a principle as due process, for example, is to have practical meaning, the nature of police behavior is important. What the police officer does and how he does it is one weighty measure of the integrity of the entire legal system for each person with whom he comes in contact. For many people, police are the only contact that they may ever have with the legal system. If democratic law is to be credible and ethical to ordinary citizens, with standards of fairness, reasonableness, and human decency, it will be so to the extent that police behavior reflects such qualities.

The importance of the police officer in our system of democratic legal process and institutions is stressed in this line of reasoning, and the overall importance of police-community relations is evident. To view the police as "pigs" or as "dirty workers" carries with it an implied indictment of the system far more fundamental and far more serious than the momentary titillation of "bugging the fuzz." This does not mean that the system should be spared from criticism. But criticism should be grounded in an understanding of the meaning of police service in a democratic society. Only through genuine police-community partnership can a police force strengthen the democratic way of life and maintain the stability of the community.

Certainly antisocial conduct must be controlled. But order must be maintained in ways that preserve and extend the values of democratic society—in short, by police methods that preserve human dignity, not by uncontrolled force. Associate Supreme Court Justice Louis Brandeis once said:

> Those who won our independence . . . recognized the risks to which all human institutions are subject. But they knew that order cannot be secured merely through fear of punishment for its infraction; that it is hazardous to discourage thought, hope, imagination; that fear breeds repression; that repression breeds hate; that hate menaces stable government; that the path of safety lies in the opportunity to discuss freely supposed grievances and proposed remedies; and that the fitting remedy for evil counsels is good ones. Believing in the power of reason as applied through public discussion, they eschewed silence coerced by law—the argument of force in its worst form.[9]

POLICE AND SOCIAL CHANGE

Seemingly, the police today are more in the public eye than ever. Why so? The general reason lies in the shift from a predominantly agricultural society to a predominantly urban one. It includes the effect of social change upon social control. It is related to the concentration of the population in big cities, and to the unprecedented physical mobility of people. Twenty percent of our population is estimated to have changed residence in each year since 1956, with approximately half of that percentage moving across state and regional lines. Some 70 percent of the population occupies only 5 percent of the land area.[10]

These are social conditions in which the police are likely to be prominently in public view. Order is more apt to be disrupted, crime more likely to be committed (in part because there are many more laws to break), a variety of social services more needed, and civil rights and civil liberties more often championed and contested. Instantaneous news coverage of social conflict situations guarantees abundant public exposure for the police. The basic, dynamic tension between collective security and individual liberty, the ancient teeter-totter of government, is severely tested. The entire apparatus of government has lately come under close public scrutiny, including the police and criminal justice processes. As taxes spiral upward, disgruntled taxpayers hold public servants increasingly accountable. As the number of automobiles on public roads increases, more demanding rules of driving increase the odds that more citizens will experience contact with the police. Many of these contacts will not be joyful for the citizen, nor will they leave either citizen or police officer ecstatic over their partnership. In the same vein, many people will blame the police for a rising crime rate, for riots and disorders, and for general social bankruptcy. As a result, some police officers may occasionally feel sorry for themselves.

POLICE RESPONSE TO SOCIAL CHANGE

The police have responded to being in the limelight to some extent negatively, as would be expected, with self-pity, with defensiveness, with attempts to shift public attention elsewhere, with occasional—and unavoidable—

apologizing, and generally with a retreat into their own subculture, isolating themselves, sometimes rather bitterly, from the community. Alas, as Gilbert and Sullivan observed, the police officer's lot is not a happy one. Typical expressions of negative reaction include remarks such as the following:

- "Being a cop is a no-win deal."
- "They expect us to solve all the problems in town."
- "I don't go for these freaks spitting on me."
- "We spend so much time these days doing social work that we haven't got time to do real police work."
- "People just don't care anymore."

However, there has also been a positive police response. During the past twenty to thirty years, this response has been made through professional development. Professional development (which will be dealt with in a later chapter) includes such things as elevation of recruitment standards, strengthening against submission to the demands of politicians, and development of a greater variety of training and educational facilities and resources for the police. In addition, there are more sophisticated activities of professional organizations in the law enforcement field; at least a beginning in crystallizing a systematic theory of criminal justice administration; and the gradual emergence of police leadership in community relations. The last of these is of special interest here.

EARLY PROGRAMS FOR POLICE TRAINING

Programs usually grow out of problem identification, when enough people are affected by a problem to care about trying to solve it. So far as can be determined, the first systematic programs in the field known today as police-community relations date back to the 1940s. These were special training courses for the police.

In 1931, the National Commission on Law Observance and Law Enforcement—popularly known, after its chairman, as the Wickersham Commission—presented its voluminous report to President Herbert Hoover. It recommended many reforms in dealing with crime and order problems—for example, putting the police in civil service and giving them better training. The slogan, "Take the police out of politics," was bandied about widely, and the idea of training for the police began to assume respectability. The 1920s had witnessed crime in dramatic headlines, and the assumption was that properly trained police could do something about it. It was not yet recognized that the police alone, no matter how well trained, can do little to prevent or control crime.

Years earlier, several American law enforcement leaders, among them August Vollmer, had begun talking about the necessity of police training. But now training began to be accepted and some police officers began to take seriously the idea of going to school. Ten years later, as this country became involved in World War II, a sociological "happening" was of decisive influence in shaping a new type of specialized police training.

The first large migratory wave of American blacks, generally from the South to the North, had occurred during World War I. It had helped substantially in breaking the worker bottleneck in war production industries. As European immigration diminished, blacks constituted a ready, unskilled labor supply, especially since the cotton industry, as the cornerstone of economy in the South, was declining. This internal black mobility was greatly accelerated with World War II, when the nonwhite population of many metropolitan areas doubled within a few years.

The social frictions, potential and actual, from these shifts in population became a matter of increasing concern to the police in many cities. Consequently, during the war years, police training courses in human relations were initiated under such titles as "The Police and Minority Groups." One such course, offered in the Chicago Park District Police Training School, was developed by Joseph D. Lohman, a lecturer in sociology at the University of Chicago, who began teaching it in 1942. This course became something of a model for other such courses. The text, mimeographed at first for Lohman's own classes but later printed for general classroom use, stated the case for this type of police training as follows:

> All of us have our jobs to do and unless we can do them with a minimum of friction and conflict, the very fabric of society will be so rent and torn as to be beyond repair. Indeed, it is questionable whether a democracy can even continue to exist unless it develops a means for peacefully mediating these differences. . . . Not only individuals but also nationality and racial groups are in competition with one another as they strive . . . to improve their economic and social status. It is almost inevitable that such competition for jobs, a place to live, access to higher social position, and the struggle for a generally higher plane of living will bring about some measure of conflict; and each in our separate ways will seek to retain whatever superior advantages we may already possess. . . . There are two essentials in the encouragement of the (police) professional attitude as it affects race and minority group problems: First, there must be brought into clearer relief the nature of the race and minority group tensions with which a police officer may be confronted. . . . Second, the individual police officer must possess the most accurate and authenticated information on the nature of racial, nationality and religious differences. He must understand the reasons for discrimination and bigotry. In addition, he must possess the best knowledge available regarding ways in which the police officer can function when incidents occur and in situations of great tension.[11]

Lohman's course included sessions on these topics:
- Worldwide and neighborhood aspects of human relations
- Background of racial, nationality, and religious tensions
- The facts about race
- The social situations in which tensions arise
- The role of the police officer in dealing with tensions
- The law and administrative controls as they affect human relations

The course devoted considerable attention (by the use of spot maps) to ecological factors in social disorganization, consistent with the approach of Robert

Park and his colleagues in sociology on the Midway campus in the 1920s and 1930s.

Harvard Professor Gordon W. Allport took more of a sociopsychological route in a similar course he developed for the Boston Police Academy in 1942. In 1944, the International City Managers' Association (now the International City Management Association) reported that more than twenty metropolitan police departments initiated human relations training during the war years.[12]

These early police training programs in human relations had certain common characteristics:

1. They focused exclusively on racial, religious, and ethnic conflict.
2. They introduced police officers to the nature and causes of these sociological problems and their relationship to crime.
3. They stimulated the police to think about crime and social disorders in *preventive* terms.
4. They often used especially trained police officers as instructors.
5. They mostly disregarded concerns of broad community relations and did not involve community leaders and ordinary citizens.

PROGRAM DEVELOPMENT: 1946–1955

Following World War II, interest in police training programs in human relations waned for a time. A few publications with relevant content appeared,[13] along with many general books dealing with race relations, prejudice, and the like. Milwaukee Chief of Police Joseph T. Kluchesky made news when he addressed the 1945 annual meeting of the International Association of Chiefs of Police on the topic, "Police Action on Minority Problems."[14] It was a speech that would be as appropriate today as it was then. President Truman's Committee on Civil Rights (1947), in its report *To Secure These Rights,* called attention to difficulties encountered by some Americans in the areas of law enforcement and judicial processes, as well as in other institutional facets of the society.

Summer workshops in human relations for teachers and other community leaders were pioneered by the National Conference of Christians and Jews and other organizations dedicated to reducing tensions between elements of the community. A few police officers enrolled in these workshops as early as 1947, seeking help in understanding human relations problems or in setting up departmental training programs on the subject.[15]

The Southern Police Institute, established at the University of Louisville in 1950, scheduled twenty-six hours of instruction in human behavior and human relations in its thirteen-week curriculum. This instruction followed immediately upon the initiation of a Lohman-designed training program, *Principles of Police Work with Minority Relations,* in the Louisville Division of Police. In 1952, the Los Angeles County Conference on Community Relations reported on police departments in more than thirty major cities that had some sort of specialized training in human relations, race relations, the police and minority groups, and similar problems.[16] In the summer of 1952 at the University of Chicago, Lohman conducted the first national seminar on the subject, "The Police and Racial Tensions." This three-week-long seminar was attended by twenty-nine police officers from approximately twenty municipalities.

Philadelphia was the site in February, 1954 of a two-day conference jointly sponsored by the International Association of Chiefs of Police and the National Association of Intergroup Relations Officials and attended by top police executives and intergroup relations professionals from approximately thirty cities. The agenda anticipated the decision of the Supreme Court in the school desegregation cases, which came a few months later, in that the conference participants discussed gaining local cooperation to achieve orderly and just communities.

COMMUNITY PROGRAMS: 1955–1967

The Philadelphia conference set in motion a process of thought and a series of steps by the National Conference of Christians and Jews (NCCJ) that led to the establishment in 1955 of the National Institute on Police and Community Relations at Michigan State University as a cooperative venture of NCCJ and the MSU School of Police Administration and Public Safety. Only a few highlights from a more detailed source need be noted here.[17]

The institute, a five-day conference, proved so useful that it was repeated each May until 1970. It brought together teams of police officers and other community leaders to discuss common problems and to develop leadership for similar programs at the local or state levels. In certain years, more than four hundred participants came from as many as one hundred sixty-five communities in thirty states and several foreign countries, and only seven states were never represented. As a result of the institute, such programs proliferated rapidly across the nation. Programs of this type are discussed further in a later chapter.

The stated purposes of the many programs initiated during this period tended to follow those of the national institute, expressed as follows:

1. To encourage police-citizen partnership in the cause of crime prevention

2. To foster and improve communication and mutual understanding between the police and the total community

3. To promote interprofessional approaches to the solution of community problems and to stress the principle that the administration of justice is a total community responsibility

4. To enhance cooperation among the police, prosecution, the courts, and corrections

5. To assist police and other community leaders to achieve an understanding of the nature and causes of complex problems in people-to-people relations and especially to improve police-minority group relationships

6. To strengthen implementation of equal protection under the law for all persons

In addition, certain basic assumptions supported these programs:

> That the law enforcement officer occupies a crucially important position in the maintenance of order in the community. Yet it is vital that the police recognize that order in itself is not the ultimate end of government in the free society.
>
> That, therefore, the principle of equal protection of the law for ALL citizens, and respect for their rights *as persons*, are absolutely fundamental under our system of government.
>
> That police interested in police-community relations are committed to their own professional development. At a minimum this means fair and impartial law enforcement regardless of personal opinions or prejudices.
>
> That today's community, which the police officer is endeavoring to serve, is vastly different in community relations from the community of yesteryear. This implies a need for new concepts in police education and police training, especially as to social and behavioral science.
>
> That police-community relations programs should involve a genuine educational process, the cultivation of dialogue across lines of diversity, and real effort to make communication more effective and mutual understanding a practical objective.
>
> That each of us has something to learn from others regarding complex community problems, in their definition, diagnosis, and remedies. The police officer has something to learn from people who are not police officers, and the converse.
>
> That police education in community relations does not add *new* burdens for law enforcement officers. That because police are in a unique position for dealing with social problems, they need help so that they may do so more effectively, particularly since conflict management has become the *main* task of the police in today's urban localities.
>
> That current problems in race relations and civil rights represent extremely important subject matter in any police-community relations institute. Yet basic issues affect the police-community relationship that have little or nothing to do with race.
>
> That there is also much more to the field of police-community relations than the traditional (and important!) matter of public relations.
>
> That the improvement of the police-community relationship should not be an end in itself. The relationship is improved as the dialogue matures, in the process of working together in interprofessional approaches to the solution of community problems. Thus, a good police-community relations program may very well be, chiefly, a program in crime prevention . . . or one focusing on the attitudes of youth toward law and authority . . . or an action project in traffic safety. Any of the great issues in the administration of justice today may conceivably be the focus or pivot for police-community relations programs or projects.[18]

The National Conference of Christians and Jews—the mainspring of so many programs in this field since 1955—was founded in 1928 against the background of the religious bigotry that characterized the presidential election campaign of that year. It was conceived as a civic organization of religiously motivated individuals seeking, through education, to promote cooperation and mutual understanding among individuals of diverse religious, racial, and ethnic backgrounds without the compromise of any particular creed or faith. Through the years, this organization has fostered a great variety of programs by means of its regional offices across the country. These programs have been directed mainly toward leaders in the social institutional "trunklines" of society, which strongly influence the formation of attitudes: religious, educational, familial, political, and community organizations; the mass media of public information; and labor and management groups. Sponsorship of Brotherhood Week annually has been an NCCJ enterprise. Religious News Service is another of NCCJ's creations. The organization became interested in police-community relations because of its commitment to orderly and just interaction among all citizens.

Generally, the programs that emerged during the 1955–1967 period accomplished the following objectives:

1. They developed what has come to be called a *concept* of police-community relations (with which chapter 2 will deal). Scholarly interest in the "sociology of the police" was stimulated.

2. They widely encouraged a teamwork or interprofessional approach to problems of police-community relations, by using a kind of laboratory method that brought together citizens of widely diversified community interests and the police and other criminal justice people to discuss problems of common interest. The essential question was, how can we work together to build a better community for all citizens?

3. They promoted the idea of police-community relations program development on a national scale.

In 1961, on a grant of funds from the Field Foundation, the School of Police Administration and Public Safety at Michigan State University conducted a national survey of 168 law enforcement agencies. The results of this survey strongly documented a case for the establishment of a National Center on Police and Community Relations. This center, with year-round services available, was activated August 1, 1965, at Michigan State, with the further help of a substantial enabling grant from the Field Foundation. The center's functions included the following:

1. Undertaking action-related research projects

2. Preparing, publishing, and circulating literature in the field of its interest

3. Developing, and sometimes conducting, educational and training programs

4. Providing direct consultative service to interested police and community organizations

5. Training young professionals for work in the field of police and community relations

The center was the recipient of several federal grants, including one with which it conducted a national survey of police-community relations for the 1966 President's Commission on Law Enforcement and Administration of Justice (also referred to as the President's Crime Commission), completed in January of 1967. As of August 1, 1973, this center was merged into the more comprehensive Criminal Justice Systems Center under a substantial federal grant, the purposes of which were primarily geared to research and manpower development, as an arm of MSU's School of Criminal Justice (renamed such in 1970).

Another study, jointly undertaken in 1964 by the International Association of Chiefs of Police and the U.S. Conference of Mayors, surveyed police-community relations in cities with a population of thirty thousand plus, with these findings:

1. Less than a third of the police departments studied had continuing, formalized community relations programs.

2. Two-thirds of the departments studied had, or were developing, plans to cope with racial demonstrations and disturbances.

3. In cities with more than a 5 percent nonwhite population, 70 percent of the departments reported that they were experiencing difficulties in recruiting nonwhite officers.

4. While more than 60 percent of the reporting departments indicated that they offered some training in police-minority group relations, there was wide diversity in the type and quality of training involved.

5. In only two regions did the responding departments report that they restricted the power of arrest of nonwhite officers—10 percent of those in the South Atlantic and 14 percent of those in the West South Central. Assignment of officers either on a nonracial basis or to racially mixed teams was becoming increasingly general.

6. More than half of the departments studied were being charged by racial groups with police brutality or differential treatment, or both. Roughly two out of ten departments reported that such complaints were increasing; about the same number reported them to be decreasing.[19]

Several federal government agencies substantially encouraged programs in police-community relations in the 1960s. One was the United States Commission on Civil Rights, whose 1961 report devoted one of five volumes to the subject of *justice.* It was a thorough job of laying bare existing deficiencies in achieving equal justice for all in criminal justice processes.

The Community Relations Service, initially in the Department of Commerce and later shifted to the Department of Justice, still provides consultant and programmatic services for many police departments and community organizations concerned about problems of police-community relations. Numerous state and local public agencies for intergroup relations also help in this cause, as do several of the better-known private organizations, such as the Anti-Defamation League of B'nai B'rith, the National Association for the Advancement of Colored People, the Urban League, the American Jewish Committee, the Southern Regional Council, and Jewish Community Relations Councils in many cities. Many private educational consultant agencies have also become interested in police-community relations projects.

Beginning in 1965, the Office of Law Enforcement Assistance of the U.S. Department of Justice (now known as the Law Enforcement Assistance Administration, LEAA) took a special interest in police-community relations programs at the local level and has since funded many diversified projects. One of its most significant contributions was the work of President Lyndon Johnson's Commission on Law Enforcement and Administration of Justice (1966–1967), whose studies were financed entirely by the Office of Law Enforcement Assistance. Many of these studies dealt with police-community relations. Consider this passage from *Task Force Report: The Police,* the commission report, for example:

The need for strengthening police relationships with the communities they serve is critical today in the Nation's large cities and in many small cities and towns as well. The Negro, Puerto Rican, Mexican-American, and other minority groups are taking action to acquire rights and services which have been historically denied them. As the most visible representative of the society from which these groups are demanding fair treatment and equal opportunity, law enforcement agencies are faced with unprecedented situations on the street which require that they develop policies and practices governing their actions when dealing with minority groups and other citizens.

Even if fairer treatment of minority groups were the sole consideration, police departments would have an obligation to attempt to achieve and maintain good police-community relations. In fact, however, much more is at stake. Police-community relationships have a direct bearing on the character of life in our cities, and on the community's ability to maintain stability and to solve its problems. At the same time, the police department's capacity to deal with crime depends to a large extent upon its relationship with the citizenry. Indeed, no lasting improvement in law enforcement is likely in this country unless police-community relations are substantially improved.[20]

COMMUNITY PROGRAMS SINCE 1967

The riots and violent upheavals that occurred in various cities during the summer of 1967, and thereafter, marked a turning point in programs on police-community relations. Suddenly, the nation was jolted into a realization of intense and profound divisions among its people, both racial and social. The assumptions of goodwill and commitment to the brotherhood of man that had more or less motivated programs in police-community relations during the 1955–1967 period were abruptly called into question. The possibilities of developing dialogue to build communication bridges across the chasms of intergroup differences were brought into instant doubt. Traditional patterns of community organization (block committees, precinct councils, and so on) were evidently not doing the job; many police officers and others began to express skepticism about whether it was "worth the effort" and to ask, "What have we done wrong?" There was widespread bewilderment. Some simply withdrew from further efforts; many adopted a "get tough" philosophy. Another presidential commission, the National Advisory Commission on Civil Disorders (popularly known as the Kerner Commission, after its chairman), proclaimed in its report that "our Nation is moving toward two societies, one black, one white—separate and unequal," and, as for police-community relations:

> The police are not merely a "spark" factor. To some Negroes police have come to symbolize white power, white racism, and white repression. And the fact is that many police do reflect and express these white attitudes. The atmosphere of hostility and cynicism is reinforced by a widespread belief among Negroes in the existence of police brutality and in a "double standard" of justice and protection—one for Negroes and one for whites.[21]

For those across the country who had been active in police-community relations programs of one kind or another during the 1955–1967 period, there may have been some tendency to overreact to the catastrophes of 1967 in our cities. Perhaps it should not have been so great a shock to discover that police-community relations programs were indeed not doing the job. There were legitimate questions to be raised about the quality of these programs, without suggesting that the programs had no merit at all. Actually, there had been little effort to evaluate these programs carefully and scientifically. In fact, there was even some resistance to such research by eager program developers who preferred not to be reminded that the attitudes of many people were not being changed and that many people were not being reached. It was also true that there had been little or no progress in solving basic societal problems that vitally affect police-community relations.

In the period 1967–1973, more police-community relations programs than ever were initiated, often grandly portrayed as guaranteed riot insurance. Many such programs amounted to pure public relations. A few LEAA-funded programs had truly innovative features, but people were still reluctant to evaluate the quality of their results.

The Urban Coalition, a private action-research organization headquartered in Washington, D.C., issued a report in 1969 indicating that the nation had made little progress in coping with the problems identified a year earlier by the Kerner Commission. Another presidential commission was activated in the wake of the assassinations of Dr. Martin Luther King and Senator Robert F. Kennedy—the National Commission on the Causes and Prevention of Violence, headed by Dr. Milton Eisenhower. This commission presented sweeping recommendations relative to violent crime—for example, that cities should undertake "increased police-community relations activity in slum ghetto areas in order to secure greater understanding of ghetto residents by police, and of police by ghetto residents." This commission has also made recommendations pertaining to group violence, firearms, television programs, and campus disorders.

The National Institute on Police and Community Relations at Michigan State University was discontinued at the end of 1969. Its demise was a commentary on the evolution of issues and social forces pertinent to the field. The purposes, assumptions, and institute design of past years may have been relevant in their time. But it became imperative now to think about police-community relations programs in different terms, with more precise purposes that could be better measured as to results, and with somewhat fewer overgeneralized assumptions. In Michigan, a newly designed continuing statewide Institute on Community Relations in the Administration of Justice was initiated to test some new ideas in program techniques with built-in evaluation aspects. This project has continued to the present, concentrating in recent years on the activities of precinct police-community relations councils in Detroit, fostered by the Detroit Round Table of NCCJ.

In early 1973, the six reports of the National Advisory Commission on Criminal Justice Standards and Goals appeared. The main interest of this commission, an LEAA-created body, was in crime reduction and prevention at the state and local levels. It was headed by former Delaware governor, Russell W. Peterson. Many of the recommendations of this commission echoed those made earlier by the 1966 President's Crime Commission, but some recommendations were more sharply drawn, some reflected clear advances in earlier thinking, and some went beyond what the preceding commission had advocated. Two theses of the more recent commission stand out vividly: its stress on developing cooperation among all elements of the criminal justice system and its stress on the need for citizen participation in criminal justice decision-making processes. [22]

Perhaps, partly as a result of the work of this commission, police-community relations programs and projects since the mid-1970s have been more apt to be identified as community-based crime prevention efforts. LEAA has strongly supported this trend, thereby stressing a primary goal of earlier police-community relations endeavors that had been subordinated in the 1963–1973 period by the challenge of preserving urban order. In the 1970s, the tide of public concern shifted to predatory crime, with acknowledgment of the necessity for police-community cooperation to achieve anything significant in preventing crime. In the 1960s, the emphasis was on preventing civil disorder, which also required acknowledging the necessity for police-community cooperation to achieve anything significant.

Although police-community relations have improved generally compared with what they were one or two decades ago, any realistic hope of further improving police relations with the community depends largely upon reforming the criminal justice system and society as a whole. Tensions in police-citizen relations are inevitably linked with social, economic, and political stresses, with the hopelessness and despair of powerless people, with racism, slums, poverty, substandard housing, unemployment and unemployability, educational discrimination, and other social malignancies. There is much more to good police-community relations than merely romanticizing the police. These interrelated social problems demand a correspondingly systematic solution.

SUMMING UP

This chapter provides background information for the study of police and community relations. The central point is that the citizen role and responsibility in police work has always been basic, going back a thousand years to the Anglo-Saxon origins of American policing. Sir Robert Peel gave the point special emphasis in his principles for a metropolitan police force.

The latter part of the chapter reviews the historical development of police-community relations programs in this country, dating back to World War II. The assumptions and purposes of these programs are cited, as well as their origins in the growing apprehension of the citizenry following the civil rights convulsions of the 1960s.

NOTES

1. W. L. Melville Lee, *A History of Police in England* (London: Methuen, 1901), chap. 12.

2. Charles Reith, *British Police and the Democratic Ideal* (London: Oxford University Press, 1943), p. 28.

3. Lee, *History of Police in England*, chap. 12.

4. Ibid., chap. 12.

5. This discussion relies heavily upon a series of three papers by Professor Jerome Hall of the Indiana University Law School, "Police and Law in Democratic Society," *Indiana Law Journal* 28, no. 2 (1953): 133 ff.

6. Raymond Fosdick, *American Police Systems* (New York: Century, 1920), chap. 2.

7. For a further discussion of lay participation in law enforcement, see Jerome Hall, *Theft, Law and Society*, 2nd ed. (Indianapolis, Ind.: Bobbs-Merrill, 1952).

8. For an elaboration of this point, see Geoffrey Gorer, "Modification of National Character: The Role of the Police in England," *Journal of Social Issues* 11, no. 2 (1955).

9. In a concurring opinion in *Whitney* v. *California*, 274 U.S. 357, 375 (1927).

10. Paul J. Mundy, "The Implications of Population Trends for Urban Communities," in A. F. Brandstatter and Louis A. Radelet, eds., *Police and Community Relations* (Beverly Hills, Calif.: Glencoe, 1968), p. 66.

11. Joseph D. Lohman, *The Police and Minority Groups* (Chicago: Chicago Park Police, 1947), pp. 3–8.

12. J. E. Weckler and Theo E. Hall, *The Police and Minority Groups* (Chicago: International City Managers' Association, 1944).

13. For example, Alfred McClung Lee and Norman D. Humphrey, *Race Riot: Detroit, 1943* (New York: Octagon, 1968), a study of the 1943 Detroit riot. Also see Davis McEntire and Robert B. Powers, *Guide to Community Relations for Peace Officers* (Sacramento, Calif.: Office of the Attorney General, State of California, 1958).

14. Joseph T. Kluchesky, *Police Action on Minority Problems* (New York: Freedom House, 1946).

15. As an example, see the description of Detroit Officer Irwin Lawler's training syllabus in Louis A. Radelet and Hoyt Coe Reed, *The Police and the Community: Studies* (Beverly Hills, Calif.: Glencoe, 1973), pp. 3–9.

16. Milton Senn, *A Study of Police Training Programs in Minority Relations* (Los Angeles: Law Enforcement Committee of the Los Angeles County Conference on Community Relations, 1952).

17. See the Introduction to Brandstatter and Radelet, eds., *Police and Community Relations* (Beverly Hills, Calif.: Glencoe, 1973).

18. Ibid. Reprinted by permission.

19. *Police-Community Relations Policies and Practices* (Washington, D.C.: International Association of Chiefs of Police and U.S. Conference of Mayors, 1964). Reprinted by permission.

20. U.S., President's Commission on Law Enforcement and Administration of Justice, *Task Force Report: The Police* (Washington, D.C.: U.S. Government Printing Office, 1967), chap. 6, p. 144.

21. U.S., National Advisory Commission on Civil Disorders, *Report of the National Advisory Commission on Civil Disorders* (Kerner Report) (Washington, D.C.: U.S. Government Printing Office, 1968), pp. 1, 5.

22. U.S., National Advisory Commission on Criminal Justice Standards and Goals, *A National Strategy to Reduce Crime* (Washington, D.C.: U.S. Government Printing Office, 1973).

2

THE CONCEPT
OF POLICE-COMMUNITY
RELATIONS

A basic difficulty in understanding police-community relations is defining the concept. There appear to be as many interpretations of what it means as there are individuals disposed to offer definitions. Police officers themselves have different conceptions of it, not to mention the often conflicting views held by various factions of the community. To some, police-community relations simply means public relations—that is, activities directed at creating and maintaining favorable impressions of a product, a firm, or an institution—in Madison Avenue terms, building an image. The emphasis is on *looking good*, not necessarily on *being* good, although public relations experts themselves insist that the best public relations is a quality product. For a police department, this means good community service.[1]

DIFFERING VIEWS OF POLICE-COMMUNITY RELATIONS

The fact is that what a police department views as good for the department may not necessarily be good for the community; or it may be good only for that part of the community to whom the police are particularly responsive and not for other parts. Frequently, some parts of the community are not adequately consulted in matters that ultimately affect all members of the community. Public relations communications have a tendency to be one-way.

Good public relations are important for any police agency. This area has been neglected in the past, apparently on the grounds that it is something of a luxury for a tax-supported service. Also, some police agencies may have preferred privacy. Some apparently still do. In any event, public relations and community relations, though often used interchangeably, are not identical. The President's 1966 Crime Commission, in *The Challenge of Crime in a Free Society*, made the distinction:

> A community relations program is not a public relations program "to sell the police image" to the people. It is not a set of expedients whose purpose is to tranquilize for a time an angry neighborhood by, for example, suddenly promoting a few Negro officers in the wake of a racial disturbance. It is a long-range, full-scale effort to acquaint the police and the community with each other's problems and to stimulate action aimed at solving those problems.[2]

This statement suggests police-community teamwork as a methodological and community action concept, a way to approach complex problem solving.

Another View of the Relationship

Another popular way of viewing police-community relations is as concerned primarily with racial and ethnic relationships, with civil rights and minority groups, with parrying charges of "police brutality," and with clamor for establishing civilian review boards. Closely akin to this is the notion that police-community relations means the control of riots, demonstrations, civil disturbances, and so forth. This latter view gained momentum following the 1967 disorders, proposed especially by those believing that forceful suppression of political dissent and social deviance improves police-community relations. Thus, more and better equipment ("hardware") for police tactics in civil disorder situations was seen as the answer. Hence, the slogan, "Law and order must prevail; support your local police!"

The rather spectacular development of police-community relations programs in the 1960s may be explained largely in terms of the tumult in race relations and civil rights happening then in this country. But again, police relations with blacks or Hispanics, important though they surely are, do not constitute the whole story of police-community relations. As with public relations, while one is an aspect of the other, the substance of one is not wholly the substance of the other. There are problematic aspects of the police relationship with the community that have little or nothing to do with racial or ethnic considerations.

The Difficulty of Definition

Perhaps the first hurdle in trying to define police-community relations is agreeing on a concept of "community." By and large, intergroup relationship problems are most acute in metropolitan areas. It is there that what Maurice Stein called "the eclipse of community" (in his book of the same title) has occurred most dramatically. In fact, it may be argued that it is precisely because "community" in the functional sense has ceased to exist—or, more accurately, because the community is less *functional* than it once was—that relationship problems begin. A definition of the functional community has interpersonal and intergroup relations as its essence. Closely knit social relations are its very heartbeat. When a community becomes dysfunctional, the chief aim of remedial programs is the restoration of social cohesiveness—to build unity where there is fragmentation. [3]

In the same line of reasoning, when we refer to "police-community" relations, we are associating entities that are quite dissimilar sociologically, and at the same time suggesting a false split. If in fact the police are part of the community, then why the hyphen? Moreover, "police" suggests a fairly unitary, compassable, intellectually manageable occupational grouping. The "community" on the other hand is an amorphous, elusive, quicksilverish concept, especially when it is applied to the modern metropolis. To speak of the police relationship with the community is therefore misleading. Which community? A metropolis has many communities—clusters of people congregated by social class and education, by ethnicity and race, by religion, by age, by sex, by occupation or profession, and by other variables. So the police and other criminal justice agencies must relate to many communities, just as must all public service institutions.

To complicate the matter further, we will be saying, for instance, that the police function as a part of several social systems—the criminal justice system, for one. On the one hand, community relations for the *police* must be seen more comprehensively than in most discussions. On the other hand, *society's* attitude toward the police is, in some measure, society's attitude toward the entire criminal justice system, and toward government as a whole. As previously indicated, correlative matters require correlative approaches.

General Definition

Having pointed out some of the pitfalls in the formidable task of defining terms, we may proceed. A general definition of police-community relations might say simply that it refers to the reciprocal attitudes of police and civilians. We are interested in the sum total of activities by which it may be emphasized that police are an important part of—not apart from—the communities they serve. We are also interested in the factors that contradict this positive principle. Properly understood, the principle is one for *total orientation* of a police organization. It is an attitude and an emphasis for all phases of police work, not merely for a specialized unit in the department. It is a way for a police officer to view his work in dealing with citizens. For citizens, it is a way of viewing the police officer: what he does and how he does it. Ideally, it is a matter of striving to achieve mutual understanding and trust, as with any human relationship. Every problem in police work today is in some sense a problem of police-community relations. Its solution depends, to some extent, upon police and community cooperation.

As the President's Crime Commission put it:

> Improving community relations involves not only instituting programs and changing procedures and practices, but re-examining fundamental attitudes. The police will have to learn to listen patiently and understandingly to people who are openly critical of them or hostile to them, since those people are precisely the ones with whom relations need to be improved . . . police-citizen relationships on the street [must] become person-to-person encounters rather than the black-versus-white, oppressed-versus-oppressor confrontations they too often are.[4]

Thus conceived, the police-and-community relation has a *preventive* charac-ter. Its thrust is in working together in the community to anticipate and to *prevent* problems, to do something constructive about problems *before crisis occurs*. It entails planning to avert crises. Police-community relations pro-grams should operate on the premise that the best way to control a riot is to prevent it; the best way to control a crime is to prevent it. When the police are in the streets armed with shotguns, volleying tear gas, and crouched behind protective shields, it is too late for police-community relations. In a word, police-community relations, properly understood, is *proactive* policing, as contrasted with *reactive*.

There are other general approaches to the definition, each of which has some merit. One is an attitudinal approach: police-community relations has to do with the *attitudes* of the police toward themselves and toward segments of the community, and the attitudes of segments of the community toward themselves and the police. Another approach having a political orientation focuses on the ways in which police use and misuse the power delegated to them. A sociological approach, with much to commend it, holds that police-community relations involves dealing with problems created by the changing relationship between social change and social control. A definition emphasizing the necessity of impartiality, fairness, and equality in the manner in which the police treat the policed is implied in some others we have noted. The key terms in all this are *accountability* and *responsiveness*, and the police are not alone among public servants currently under public scrutiny in these particulars.

THREE ASPECTS OF COMMUNITY RELATIONS

Community relations may be more specifically defined. It may be viewed as a kind of tripod,[5] based on three equal components: public relations, community service, and community participation. One leg of the tripod, *public relations*, has already been defined. For a police department, an example of *community service* would be a youth program comprising a variety of activities for children—recreation, sports, skill games, camping, music, and so forth. Community service is good public relations, but with the plus factor of providing some beneficial service to the community.

The third leg of the tripod, *community participation*, stresses interprofessional or teamwork approaches to solving community problems. It is the widely used social-work concept of community organization, with particular attention to the participation of the police and other criminal justice agencies.

The idea of community participation may be clarified by an illustration. Take the crime problem. Clearly, the police are concerned about it. So are the courts and other criminal justice institutions. So are the schools, religious bodies, social-work agencies, various community organizations, labor unions and business management, and the mass media. The crime problem is extremely complicated. No single community force, not even the police, has the total answer. Police officers have a certain experience with the problem. It is not the same experience that, say, school principals have. Thus, the police have something to contribute, out of their experience, to the definition, diagnosis, and solution of the crime problem. So do school people. And so on, with other community entities.

The art of devising programs, therefore, is that of bringing together all these forces in some sort of cooperative, coordinated venture, to cope with problems too complex for any single force to solve alone. It is in this sense that police-community relations activity assumes a problem-solving character, with crime as the problem. The program that emerges might be, primarily, one of comprehensive crime prevention. Or it might focus on some other problem—

any problem involving a sense of common social consequence and shared responsibility. A focus on crime would probably be specific to certain types of crime, such as burglary or assault, since there is, in reality, no single "crime problem."

THE RELATIONSHIPS OF TEAMWORK

But what is the point of such an indirect approach to improving police and community relations? To respond to this question in a somewhat roundabout way, we refer to a study (known as the Robbers' Cave Experiment) conducted by psychologists Muzafer and Carolyn Sherif and their colleagues at the University of Oklahoma more than two decades ago.[6] This study demonstrated that within a period of a few weeks two contrasting patterns of behavior could be produced in a group of normal children. First, the experimenters could bring the group to a state of intense hostility, and then they could completely reverse the process by inducing a spirit of friendship and cooperation.

The Sherifs showed that mere interaction—pleasant social contact between antagonists—was not sufficient to reduce hostility. The critical element for achieving harmony in human relations, according to the Sherifs, is joint activity in behalf of a *superordinate goal*. Hostility gives way when groups pull together to achieve overriding goals that are real and compelling for all concerned. The Sherif team accomplished this by certain stratagems, such as interrupting the water supply to the camp where two groups of youngsters had been turned against each other bitterly by a series of conflict-inducing incidents. The boys volunteered to search the water line for trouble; they located it and worked together harmoniously to correct the difficulty.

To translate the principle into police-community relations terms, another illustration may be helpful. Bruce J. Terris, a member of the staff of the 1966 President's Crime Commission, described the idea in the following way, with crime control and community stability as the superordinate goals:

> The problem of violent crime must be met in our ghettos where it principally occurs. Yet the state of police-community relations in these areas now makes it almost impossible for the police to deal with crime there. At the same time, both the prevalence of violent crime and the threat of disorders compound the already serious problems in our cities. Consequently, relations between the police and minority groups must be drastically and immediately improved if our cities are to reduce crime and to have the reasonable degree of stability necessary to solve their other problems.[7]

Maintaining good relationships with all elements of the population of a community should be regarded by police officials as a goal of the greatest importance on its own merits. Herman Goldstein, of the University of Wisconsin Law School, puts it in perspective:

> Any improvement in citizen contact obviously serves in a very direct manner to improve the cooperation which the police can expect from the public in combatting crime. This is a consideration of the utmost importance when one reflects upon the degree to which the police depend upon the public for assistance in reporting crimes and suspicious circumstances and in serving as witnesses and complainants in the

prosecution of criminal cases. But if lasting improvements are to be made in that aspect of police functioning that is unrelated to crime, they must be justified on their merits rather than be rationalized on the basis of the relationship such improvements will have to those police efforts that more directly relate to crime.[8]

To make our point clear, the prevention and control of crime is a superordinate goal, in which all elements of the community have an important stake. Predatory crime destroys the quality of life in a neighborhood or community. Doing something constructive about it requires organized police and community cooperation. In this process, relationships are likely to be improved.

Distinguishing Activities

It is not always easy, nor probably is it in practical terms too important, to distinguish among public relations, community service, and community participation. The activities associated with each of these three areas are listed in Table 2–1. While the activities have been categorized on the basis of their primary purpose, some of them may overlap or be appropriate to more than one area.

TABLE 2–1
Police Activities Fostering Favorable Public Response

Public Relations	Personal cleanliness and good grooming
	General politeness, courtesy, and good manners
	Telephone etiquette
	Vehicle maintenance (cleanliness)
	Modifications in the military-type uniform (redesigned blazers, jackets, etc.; inconspicuous carrying of weapons)
	Speaker's bureau activities, skill demonstrations, equipment exhibits, and so forth
	Open houses at police stations
	Dog shows, water safety shows, and so forth
	Displays on bumper stickers, car cards, billboards
	Awards and citations for outstanding police officers and citizens
	Liaison for press personnel and facilities
	Cooperation between the chief and media executives
	Tidiness and good order in administrative facilities
	American flag insignia worn
Community Service	Informational or interpretive newspaper or magazine features, newsletters and door knob hangers, radio and television presentations (for example, education on drugs, auto safety, auto theft, and home burglaries)
	Safety instruction for operating autos, bicycles, and other vehicles
	Youth programs (for example, the Police Athletic League, summer camping, and others)
	Storefront centers in neighborhoods
	Annual or periodic reports, *if* designed for public understanding
	Complaint procedure
	Public fund-raising solicitation for tuition to help improve the education of police officers (by a citizens' organization)

Ride-in-a-patrol-car programs
Sponsorship of scouting units (for example, Explorers)
Police junior band or drum-and-bugle corps
Law enforcement career clinics in high schools
Policeman Bill and *Officer Friendly* types of programs in elementary schools
Police aid and advice for parades, demonstrations, and other public activities
Emergency facilities for demonstrations
Police assignments to job opportunity centers
Assistance to crisis intervention agencies
Crime prevention literature
Helping Hand programs
Distribution of information to new residents
Tire changing assistance
Checks on vacationers' residences
Ambulance and paramedic service
Lost-and-found auctions
School counseling assistance
Social service referrals

Community Participation	Councils of social agencies, United Fund, and Community Chest Family and Neighborhood Stabilization Councils Coordinating Council on Community Relations XYZ Council on Police-Community Relations Precinct or District Police-Citizens Committees or Workshops ABC Council on Crime and Delinquency 77th Street Interdenominational Clergy-Police Council Police-Community Relations seminars (potentially) Edison Park–Hamilton Community (neighborhood) Council Citizens United for a Safer City (not vigilante groups) Neighborhood Watch or Neighborhood Alert

Some Implications of Relationships

The approach to police and community relations stressing problem solving through community participation has some implications that should be noted. It suggests, for instance, that it is not the goal of programs to persuade everyone to fall in love with the police. If, as a by-product of programs, some people learn to appreciate police officers more—even to the point of seeing them as "human," as neighbors and fellow citizens, and possibly even as friendly and personable "good guys"—this may be credited as a nice dividend. But the *primary* purposes in the community participation approach should be to solve hard problems, to improve the quality of police services, and to elevate the level of public respect for the police officer and for the system of government by law that he represents. Of course, respect must be earned, and the attitude and behavior of the police officer himself is the most important factor in this process. But citizens, also, should recognize their responsibilities in what a police officer may expect from them.

Full police participation in community problem-solving efforts assumes that police will be encouraged and motivated to rise to the highest level of their professional potential. In effect, this means the emergence of the police as authentic *community leaders*. The English social anthropologist Michael Banton refers to the policeman as "a professional citizen," no doubt mindful of the Anglo-Saxon background referred to in the preceding chapter.[9] However, the idea of the police officer as a community leader comes on even stronger in other statements, for example, this by University of Illinois sociologist David Bordua:

> We are, in short, asking the police to lead the community in race relations. For them merely to reflect the community would be a disaster. . . . It is . . . no help to have the police closely linked into the local community if that community's main concern is the suppression of Negroes. . . . The modern police cannot function simply as representatives of community culture—assuming it is coherent enough to be represented. They must stand aside from the culture to a large degree and function as community managers.[10]

This view of the police poses some difficulty. It would be rejected outright by those who claim that the police have no business acting as agents of social change. Moreover, there is a practical political consideration in the question of how far apart or ahead of their community the police can take a position on a controversial social issue. Bordua would allow for this while countering with the argument that, if the police are serious in their claims for professionalism, there are leadership responsibilities that go with it.

Bordua's target is the traditional *status quo* posture of the police. To some extent, the dysfunctionality of police service—and other aspects of criminal justice process—is deliberate, calculated, self-serving, and extremely difficult to eliminate because it is protected by organizations with some political clout, and by a phantom system of reciprocal favors and mutual back-scratching. Often in such circumstances, the public is led to believe that changes in established ways are dangerous, too expensive, unrealistic, or otherwise undesirable. Reformers should keep in mind that whenever innovative changes are contemplated, a certain amount of resistance is almost always encountered. The good faith and goodwill of all the actors in police-community relations dramas cannot be taken for granted. Reform in criminal justice processes is not as wild a dream as those who profit by preventing it may pretend.

REAL AND IMAGINARY PROBLEMS

In defining police-community relations and the problems associated with it, a question frequently arises whether a distinction should be drawn between what really *is* a problem and what people *think* is a problem. The positions taken by various segments of the population are clearly based upon differing perceptions. Individuals believe something because they see it as being so. Both police malpractice and community misunderstanding bear upon the relationship between police and community. While police officers sometimes behave unprofessionally, it is just as accurate to say that citizens sometimes misunderstand police officers, misinterpret police behavior, or behave abominably in their contacts with officers. As in any other area of human relations, some attitudes are based on fact and some on assumption, and some assumptions are incorrect. Eleanor Harlow of the National Council on Crime and Delinquency makes the point:

> Where there is anonymity of individual officers, there is generalization and stereotyping by citizens; where there is racial hatred and distrust, there is misinterpretation of police actions; and where there is lack of communication with and confidence in the police, there is also a tendency on the part of citizens to believe the worst. Thus, the actions of those police who do behave unprofessionally reflect not only upon the entire department but on police in general, and whenever questionable tactics are employed against minority groups anywhere, hostility to police everywhere is increased. . . . One important fact to consider is that whether or not police brutality exists, if significant numbers of people believe that it does, it then becomes a serious and very real problem. For example, a widespread belief that police are unjust or brutal results in loss of respect for and cooperation with any police officer. When people do not accept police authority at every point of contact, the police feel the need to assert personal authority by force in order "to handle the situation" in the absence of respect for the badge and uniform. Thus the belief that police are brutal often becomes a self-fulfilling expectation.[11]

Harvard political scientist James Q. Wilson adds a telling point:

> The fact that the police can no longer take for granted that noncriminal citizens are also non-hostile citizens may be the most important problem which even the technically proficient department must face.[12]

The evaluation of police-community relations at a given place and time is an offshoot of the perceptions the police have of the community and the community has of the police. These perceptions are commonly divergent. Public perceptions of the police represent a complex side of the matter; police perceptions of various "publics" also affect the relationship, and are equally complex. Reciprocal attitudes are rooted in these reciprocal perceptions. The police, for instance, often resent not being able to take action before violence occurs, and sometimes claim that minority groups receive preferential treatment by the courts.[13] On the other hand, community groups are extremely sensitive to any police behavior that conjures up the image of a "police state."

The main thought that we are suggesting is that police-community relations problems are defined at a given time and place by diverse, often conflicting and ambiguous perceptions and attitudes of police officers on the one hand and of individual citizens and community groups on the other. This is hardly a startling revelation; the author has dealt with it more extensively in "Attitudes Involved in Relating Community and Police";[14] and later chapters in this book will analyze it further.

The matter of defining the police-community relations concept may be summarized with this statement by the author, writing in the *Christian Science Monitor,* in 1968:

> Police-community relations is not merely a number of schemes and machines, or greater technical efficiency, or more socio-psychological training for police officers, or recruiting more Negro policemen, or a store-front operation in a ghetto, or a truly

open system for handling citizen complaints, or the activities of a specialized unit in the department. Good police-citizen relations is, ideally, a TOTAL ORIENTATION in the attitudes and behavior of a police department, bearing upon everything it does, every facet and level of the organization. If it is less than this, then police-community relations may be simply gamesmanship, a kind of insult and mockery, and a particularly ignominious species of self-serving social placation. If it is this, it makes absurd the hope for police professionalization.[15]

SUMMING UP

The *concept* of police-community relations, as it has crystallized in the past several decades in the United States, is examined in this chapter. It is a concept that has been as variously defined as the concept of crime, and its definition has depended much upon the vantage point of the definer. So we have seen sociological, psychological, political, anthropological, racial, public relations, social work, and even psychiatric approaches to the idea, each with some merit, but none as comprehensive as the definition the scope of the subject requires. Indeed, it is suggested that getting the concept properly defined has been not the least of the problems involved in building better relations between police and community.

NOTES

1. A broad overview of the field of police-community relations at the time was provided in Louis A. Radelet, "Public Information and Community Relations," a chapter of *Municipal Police Administration* (Washington, D.C.: International City Management Association, 1969).

2. U.S., President's Commission on Law Enforcement and Administration of Justice, *The Challenge of Crime in a Free Society* (Washington, D.C.: U.S. Government Printing Office, 1967), p. 100.

3. Maurice Stein, *The Eclipse of Community: An Interpretation of American Studies* (Princeton, N.J.: Princeton University Press, 1960). Also see Louis A. Radelet, "The Idea of Community," in A. F. Brandstatter and Louis A. Radelet, eds., *Police and Community Relations* (Beverly Hills, Calif.: Glencoe, 1968), pp. 80–84.

4. President's Commission on Law Enforcement, *Challenge of Crime*, p. 100.

5. This three-way analysis of community relations relies on Murray G. Ross, *Community Organization: Theory and Principle*, rev. ed. (New York: Harper & Brothers, 1955), pp. 23–26.

6. Muzafer Sherif and Carolyn Sherif, *An Outline of Social Psychology*, rev. ed. (New York: Harper & Brothers, 1948), pp. 301–331.

7. Bruce J. Terris, "The Role of the Police," *Annals of the American Academy of Political and Social Science* 374 (November 1967): 60. Reprinted by permission.

8. Herman Goldstein, "Police Response to Urban Crises," *Public Administration Review* 28, no. 5 (1968): 417–423. Reprinted by permission. Professor Goldstein adds this note: "Otherwise, continuing opposition is likely because of suspicion as to the true motives of the police." Some years ago, a so-called Model Precinct program in police-community relations in Washington, D.C. was opposed by militant civil rights groups who viewed it as an effort by the police to develop a network of informants.

9. "Social Integration and Police," *Police Chief,* April 1963, pp. 9–10.

10. "Comments on Police-Community Relations," *Law Enforcement Science and Technology II* (Chicago: Illinois Institute of Technology Research Center, 1968), pp. 115–125.

11. "Problems in Police-Community Relations: A Review of the Literature," *Information Review on Crime and Delinquency* 1, no. 5 (February 1969): 4. Reprinted by permission of the National Council on Crime and Delinquency.

12. "Police Morale, Reform and Citizen Respect: The Chicago Case," in David J. Bordua, ed., *The Police: Six Sociological Essays* (New York: John Wiley & Sons, 1967), p. 158. Reprinted by permission of John Wiley & Sons.

13. Nelson A. Watson, *Police-Community Relations* (Gaithersburg, Md.: International Association of Chiefs of Police, 1966), pp. 35–36.

14. Louis A. Radelet, "Attitudes Involved in Relating Community and Police," *Proceedings of the Institute on Police-Community Relations* (Los Angeles: University of Southern California, 1969).

15. Louis A. Radelet, "Who's in Charge of 'Law and Order'?" *Christian Science Monitor,* December 9, 1968.

3

THE ROLE OF THE POLICE
IN TODAY'S SOCIETY

BACKGROUND AND EXPECTATIONS

Let us consider the central, most fundamental issue affecting the relationship between police and the community: the role predicament. In 1968, the National Advisory Commission on Civil Disorders (Kerner Commission) clearly touched on this question:

> The policeman in the ghetto is a symbol of increasingly bitter social debate over law enforcement. One side, disturbed and perplexed by sharp rises in crime and urban violence, exerts extreme pressure on police for tougher law enforcement. Another group, inflamed against police as agents of repression, tends toward defiance of what it regards as order maintained at the expense of justice.
>
> . . . police responsibilities in the ghetto are even greater than elsewhere in the community since the other institutions of social control have so little authority: the schools, because so many are segregated, old and inferior; religion, which has become irrelevant to those who have lost faith as they lost hope; career aspirations, which for many young Negroes are totally lacking; the family, because its bonds are often snapped. It is the policeman who must deal with the consequences of this institutional vacuum and is then resented for the presence and the measures this effort demands.[1]

Our discussion in the preceding chapter of the concept of police-community relations had implications for the role of the police. For example, if the idea of the police as community leaders—or *managers*, to use David Bordua's term—is to be taken seriously, it has certain implications for role concept and role expectations. Part of the shock in considering this seemingly rash idea is in its role implications, so vastly different from the popular image that is a holdover from a past era of American police work. It is a far cry from the "strong back, weak mind" image of the police. If, on the other hand, one claims that police-community relations is simply another term for public relations, and the police are seen not as community leaders but as followers, the role implications are quite different.

Conflicting Police Role Expectations

Police and community relations depend on what the police expect from the community and what the community expects from the police. *What* the police

31

do, then, and *how* they do it are vitally important considerations in the status of the relationship. As suggested earlier, divergent perceptions and attitudes are involved in this relationship. Some scholars even describe the problems of police-community relations as essentially a matter of conflicting role perceptions and expectations, which cause what educator and sociologist Joseph D. Lohman called "dissonance" between the community and the police.

Conflicting role perceptions are not, of course, unique to police and community relations. Problems of school and community relations are created by conflicting perceptions of what teachers should do and how they should do it. School teachers themselves do not agree on this question, any more than do various factions of the community. Nor does everyone agree on what the clergy or mayors or welfare workers or college presidents should do and how they should do it.

Such conflicting views of social institutional roles and functions are inevitable and perhaps even socially beneficial. But they make relationship problems inevitable and pose the challenge of achieving the minimal working consensus necessary for the survival of the free society and its institutions. In police and community relations, moreover, a special consideration makes the role question particularly vexing, as well as particularly important: the police hold society's greatest power, that of discretion in the use of force and the authority, under certain conditions, to initiate legal process against citizens. Performance of the role necessarily involves the overt exercise of power delegated to control human behavior. The mandate comes from those to be controlled. The political implications of this point explain why police-community relations are of extraordinary interest. A social role with such repressive or punitive dimensions is bound to be the object of unusual public (and scholarly) interest and apprehension.

Law Officers versus Peace Officers. It is instructive to study the police role question in historical perspective. Recall, for instance, that Peel referred to "the basic mission for which the police exist—to prevent crime and disorder as an alternative to the repression of crime and disorder by military force and severity of legal punishment." This is a description of the police role that has dominated British policing since Peel's time and looms large in a comparative study of American and British police-community relations. The English social anthropologist Michael Banton, for example, refers to the difference between *law officers* and *peace officers:* the public contacts of law officers tend to be of a punitive or inquisitory character; whereas the public contacts of the peace officers are more in the nature of assisting citizens. In *The Policeman in the Community*, Banton distinguishes between a police *force* and a police *service.*[2]

The Anglo-American system of civilian policing has brought together a variety of both explicit and implicit functions. Since 1829, in the United Kingdom, the primary functions have been the preservation of the Queen's peace and the prevention of crime, as suggested by Peel's first principle. Other functions have been regarded as ancillary. While it is generally assumed that civilian policing in the United States has followed the British model, the similarity has actually been more theoretical than real. For in this country, the functions of peace keeping and crime prevention have not had the priority in police attention that they have had in Great Britain.

In analyzing the difference, the distinguished American social historian Oscar Handlin has cited "the exceptional diffusion of violence in our society." He points out that ours has been, from the beginning, a much more violent society than that of most European countries. Carrying arms and rounding up a posse were aspects of American history that are still glamorized in today's movies and television. Handlin also says that early American police forces had "undifferentiated functions." The police were public servants with duties pertaining to public health, clean streets, and all sorts of other odds and ends. Thus, it was easy to make scapegoats of the police for every problem. Until after 1900, the most important aspects of police work as we see it today were not performed by the police. Various private agencies took care of apprehending crooks, while the police busied themselves with menial chores, thereby cultivating the public impression that a police officer was a rather backward character, a more or less friendly simpleton.[3]

The literature dealing with British policing emphasizes the prevention of crime and the maintenance of peace as the two most important functions of the civilian police. On the other hand, American writers tend to emphasize the protection of security and the enforcement of law as the two primary functions. This difference is much more than a semantic incidental. It has a direct, practical application in the manner in which police agencies have been organized, the standards regarded as germane in recruiting, the kind of training that a police officer receives, and in beliefs and values considered important in the craft. Every police recruit inherits the ambiguities pertaining to role—what he or she is expected to do and what the priorities are.[4]

The widespread confusion and lack of consistency or consensus among police officers on the question of their role has been pointed out by many observers. One difficulty is the number of persons and groups professing some right to speak about what police officers do and how they do it. Police administrators and supervisors, police officers themselves (through their professional and fraternal organizations, and recently their unions), legislative bodies, the courts, governmental executives, assorted bureaucrats, and of course "the people"—many different factions of the population, with different perceptions of and expectations from the police—all of these forces and others rightfully demand a voice and vote in the question of what the police should do and how they should do it. Thus, the police agency is in the position of attempting to accomplish the impossible—that is, to discern some consensus among the many disparate points of view and to develop an operating mode that is acceptable to most of the people most of the time.

To see the role predicament as basically political, and to see the key to its satisfactory resolution as correspondingly political, is to recognize that all public administration in democratic society faces and must settle the constant consensus questions via the same processes, if they are settled at all. In this respect, the administration of police and criminal justice agencies is no different from that of other entities. In totalitarian systems, if any question arises about the role of the police, it is much more expeditiously settled: the political processes eschew ambiguity.

Fighting Crime versus Interacting with Citizens.   In a recent article, George Kelling of the Police Foundation has commented on how deeply engrained in our society is the myth of the police as "primarily a crime fighting, deterring, and investigating agency."[5] This view is reinforced by the media, and by police administrators in their efforts to win financial and moral support. Research conducted since 1950 indicates, as suggested earlier, that this image of police work is quite inaccurate. Kelling, Herman Goldstein, and many other analysts are pleading that a more realistic conception of what the police actually do carries with it significant implications for recruitment, training, organization, promotional standards, community relations, and patrol activities. Kelling's summary of the matter is striking:

> Research into the police function, police activities—preventive patrol, rapid response to calls for service, team policing, and investigations—and technology suggests that the emphasis on crime-related activities has failed to achieve crime reduction goals and may have exacerbated problems of police-citizen alienation and citizen fear of crime. Even at best, the police can have only a limited effect on crime. In the future, police must abandon strategies which prevent extensive contact with citizens. They must direct their attention to improving the quality of police-citizen interaction and to developing approaches to policing that reduce citizen fear.[6]

Enforcing Law versus Maintaining Order.   The President's Crime Commission (1966), the Kerner Commission (1968), and the National Commission on the Causes and Prevention of Violence (1969–70) all pointed out that the vast majority of the situations in which the police intervene are not crime situations calling for arrests. Another presidential commission, headed by former Pennsylvania Governor William Scranton, studied student unrest and college campus disorders in the aftermath of the Kent State University and Jackson State College tragedies of the spring of 1970. This commission also stressed the peace-keeping responsibilities of the police.

More recently, the National Advisory Commission on Criminal Justice Standards and Goals has added its voice to the debate on police role. Its report on the police begins with consideration of the role question, tying it directly to community relations. This commission emphasized the importance for every police agency of developing both short- and long-range goals and objectives, and of securing maximum input in this process from within the agency and from all community elements.

Harvard political scientist James Q. Wilson's summary of the police role dilemma is classic:

> The simultaneous emergence of a popular concern for both crime and order does put in focus the choices that will have to be made in the next generation of police reforms. In effect, municipal police departments are two organizations in one, serving two related but not identical functions. The strategy appropriate for strengthening their ability to serve one role tends to weaken their ability to serve the other. Crime deterrence and law enforcement require, or are facilitated by, speciali-

zation, strong hierarchical authority, improved mobility and communications, clarity in legal codes and arrest procedures, close surveillance of the community, high standards of integrity, and the avoidance of entangling alliances with politicians. The maintenance of order, on the other hand, is aided by departmental procedures that include decentralization, neighborhood involvement, foot patrol, wide discretion, the provision of services, an absence of arrest quotas, and some tolerance for minor forms of favoritism and even corruption. . . .

There is no magic formula—no prepackaged "reform"—that can tell a community or a police chief how to organize a force to serve, with appropriate balance, these competing objectives. Just as slogans demanding "taking the police out of politics" or "putting the police in cars" have proved inadequate guides to action in the past, so also slogans demanding "foot patrolmen" or "community control" are likely to prove inadequate in the future. One would like to think that since both points of view now have ardent advocates, the debate has at last been joined. But I suspect that the two sides are talking at, or past, each other, and not *to* each other, and thus the issue, far from being joined, is still lost in rhetoric.[7]

It is crucial, of course, in discussing the role question, to recognize that the debate is not over whether the police should be relieved of either of their principal functions. The argument is not one of law enforcement versus order maintenance. It is recognized that police work includes both functions. The debate has to do, rather, with *emphasis.* If, for example, the police spend most of their time in keeping peace (often called *conflict management*), why should a police agency be organized as if this were not so? And why should police officers be trained as if most of their time were spent catching crooks, when most of their time is not spent catching crooks? What then is the desirable relationship between the major functions of the police, granting that these functions are not mutually exclusive? Sometimes making an arrest helps to preserve civic peace; sometimes it can set off a riot. Is crime to be suppressed at any price? Such questions highlight the gist of the issue.

A general response is that any police agency should develop its role concept (goals and objectives) in accord with consensus requirements of the community it serves. There is no single formula that can apply everywhere. As communities (neighborhoods, precincts, or divisions in big cities) differ in their cultural, ethnic, racial, socioeconomic, educational, occupational, and demographic features, so will their police service needs and requirements differ. The order of priorities among the jobs to be performed by the police should be set accordingly.

There is nothing really new or revolutionary about this principle in police work. It is the element of seeking input from the community that is frequently aborted or "railroaded." How adequate, how representative is this input? Too often, police agencies play political and administrative games, pretending sincere interest in what poor and powerless segments of the community have to say while having no desire to serve their needs. Various excuses surface—for example, that "these people" were given an opportunity to speak their piece, but failed to appear. All of this contributes to the conclusion, long since reached by the powerless, that the police are first and foremost the police of the rich and the powerful. Indeed, the "apathy" of the poor and powerless is, more often than not, a sign that they have been completely "turned off" by the insincerity of public administrators. This often explains why they fail to appear or to speak up.

In his fascinating study of the management of law and order in eight communities, *Varieties of Police Behavior,* Wilson describes three styles of policing—the watchman, the legalistic, and the service—and relates each to local politics. He explains why the question of the role of the police is of special interest. A big-city police department is a special kind of complex, bureaucratic organization, with perplexing pressures for the patrolman "to do the right thing." As a public agency, such a police department affects the lives of many people. Wilson also points out that "the ability of the police to do their job well may determine our ability to manage social conflict, especially that which involves Negroes and other minority groups, and our prospects for maintaining a proper balance between liberty and order."[8]

Some students of police role speak of four major police functions: order maintenance (conflict management or peace keeping); law enforcement (or "crook catching"); crime prevention; and social services. Wilson reduces these to two: order maintenance and law enforcement. He dismisses social services from consideration, on the ground that such services "are intended to please the client and no one else. There is no reason in principle why these services could not be priced and sold on the market. It is only a matter of historical accident and community convenience that they are provided by the police." Wilson's special concern is with police activities, "the quality of which the client cannot be allowed to judge for himself: in short, with police efforts to enforce laws and maintain order."[9]

In an article in *Public Administration Review,* Wilson describes *order maintenance* as the handling of disputes, or behavior that threatens to produce disputes, among persons who disagree over what ought to be right or seemly conduct, or over the assignment of blame for what is agreed to be wrong or unseemly conduct.[10] Examples of this would be a family quarrel, a noisy drunk, a tavern brawl, a street disturbance by teenagers, or idle young men congregating on a street corner. Although a law may be broken in these examples of conduct, the police do not see their responsibility as simply the comparing of particular behavior to a clear legal standard and making an arrest if the standard has been violated. In many order-maintenance situations, the legal rule is ambiguous. Blame may be more important to the participants than guilt.

To illustrate the ambiguity, by what standard is "peace" defined in peace-keeping activities? University of California sociologist Jerome Skolnick notes that some communities may appear disorderly to observers (for example, a bohemian neighborhood) while maintaining a substantial degree of legality. The converse may also occur: order may be maintained amid questionable legality. More often than not in peace-keeping situations, the officer will not make an arrest, because most such infractions are misdemeanors, and in most states an arrest cannot be made unless the illegal act is committed in the officer's presence or unless the victim is willing to sign a complaint.

Law enforcement, on the other hand, is defined by Wilson as the application of legal sanctions, usually by means of an arrest, to persons who injure or deprive innocent victims; for example, burglary, purse snatching, mugging, robbery, or auto theft. Once guilt is established, there is no question of blame. The officer is expected either to make an arrest or to act to prevent the violation from occurring in the first place. The task is to apprehend or to deter the criminal. But in most instances involving crime, the officer lacks the resources to do so. Therefore, few cases are "cleared by arrest." Moreover, current studies reflect that a high proportion of crimes go unreported. Nobody knows how many crimes the police prevent, but the number is not thought to be large. And certain police tactics in so-called high-crime areas that might have the effect of preventing certain types of crime may also place the police in conflict with some elements of the community.[11] Wilson believes that whatever the police do for crime prevention, they do as part of their regular law enforcement activities. Therefore, he does not consider crime prevention separately.

Wilson asserts, with Skolnick, that the police are frequently criticized for behavior that is, to a considerable extent, integral to "the system," or "the way things work." Reform movements often concentrate on what should be done to improve police officers, rather than on what fundamental changes should be contemplated in the system itself. Wilson observes that police departments are often charged with such things as hiring unqualified personnel, manipulating crime statistics, condoning improper procedures on the street, and using patrol tactics that irritate people and heighten tensions. Community groups volunteer solutions for these matters. Because their diagnosis is often that the problems are caused by incompetent, stupid, rude, brutal, and prejudiced police officers, the remedies they suggest usually include elevated recruitment standards, more and better education for police officers, tougher internal discipline, exterior review of police behavior, and other measures focusing on police officers.

But suppose, Wilson argues, that "better" men and women officers—that is, more college-educated police officers, more black officers, more police participants in the best "sensitivity training," and even more neighborhood control of the police—should suddenly become a reality. Under such conditions, deemed ideal by many critics of the police, the crime rate might well go up rather than down, at least temporarily, and such measures would not necessarily resolve the conflict in the community between those who want less police surveillance and those who want more. Formal education might make police officers more civil, yet more impersonal in their dealings with people. A college degree for a police officer is not a guarantee that he would be any more sensitive to the feelings and needs of poor, young blacks in a ghetto. The college degree might even be a handicap in such situations, in terms of communication and rapport. In short, the ingredients that are often identified by community groups as important in creating better police-community relations must be carefully delineated and qualified.

These observations are no argument against better men and women in police work. They do suggest, however, the complexity of police-community relations problems. Something more fundamental than cosmetics (for example, changes in dress) and better qualified personnel is required if significant change is to occur. Commitment to the need for basic restructuring of police organizations should be a primary qualification for police work. Otherwise, police-community relations will continue indefinitely on the same old treadmill, along with other aspects of our system of law and justice.

Numerous other writers share Wilson's view of the essence of the police role quandary. Gordon Misner has noted, for example, that it has become increasingly fashionable for the police in various parts of the country to refer to themselves as "law enforcement officers." The intent, Misner believes, is to convey the impression to the public that they see themselves first and foremost as "real cops," not social workers. In Misner's opinion, doing so helps these officers live with the anger, frustration, and anxiety they feel about what they think is expected of them under current conditions.

"Law and order" is often a question of law *or* order, Misner says, and "the dilemma arises from the conflicting set of instructions society has historically given to policemen." He continues, echoing both Wilson and Skolnick:

> The policeman really has two role models from which to choose: he can conceive of himself as a "rule enforcer," or as a "guardian of the peace." He is helped in the choice by the role preferred by his chief and immediate superiors. In many departments, being a rule enforcer is viewed as a necessary stage of development in the growth of a mature policeman. . . . The older policeman hopes that the young prospect will realize eventually that strict enforcement of the laws is a gigantic inconvenience, not only to the public but also to the policeman himself. It is part of police folklore that an experienced policeman knows how to "stay out of trouble," and has necessarily learned that law enforcement is simply a means and not an end in itself.[12]

Misner agrees with Wilson also in the observation that the role concept of any particular police agency largely determines how the agency is organized, the priorities prescribed for specific tasks, the kind of training police officers receive, and the system of rewards. As an example, Misner refers to the less than 30 percent proportion of patrol time and resources spent in criminal process activity in larger urban areas. He adds another point:

> There are situations when non-enforcement of certain laws or regulations may actually contribute to the peace and tranquility of the community. Enforcement, therefore, is a two-edged sword that must be used with a delicate sense of balance and timing. To suggest that "total enforcement" is a magic formula for reinstituting order in a troubled community simply lulls the public into a false sense of security. It also diverts public attention from seeking more basic, long-term solutions to social problems.[13]

Crime Reduction Through Public Cooperation.   Herman Goldstein, one-time administrative assistant to the late Chicago police superintendent, O. W. Wilson, now professor of law at the Univeristy of Wisconsin, is another widely respected analyst who has also written about the role predicament of the police. His position is substantially the same as that of Misner, Kelling, and James Q. Wilson. Writing in *Public Administration Review* (1968), he argued that the police must become more, not less, involved in noncriminal activities, if they are to be effective in dealing with civil disorder and civil disobedience:

The police function in two worlds. They play an integral part, along with the prosecutor, the courts, and correctional agencies, in the operation of the criminal justice system. As the first agency in the system, their primary responsibility is to initiate a criminal action against those who violate the law. This is a highly structured role, defined by statutes and court decisions and subjected to strict controls.

The second world is less easily defined. It comprises all aspects of police functioning that are unrelated to the processing of an accused person through the criminal system. Within this world, a police department seeks to prevent crimes, abates nuisances, resolves disputes, controls traffic and crowds, furnished information, and provides a wide range of other miscellaneous services to the citizenry. In carrying out these functions, officers frequently make use of the authority which is theirs by virtue of their role in the criminal process. . . . Police spend most of their time functioning in the second of these two worlds. . . . Despite this distribution of activity, police agencies are geared primarily to deal with crime.[14]

Goldstein and his colleague at the University of Wisconsin, Frank J. Remington, were responsible for a chapter of *Task Force Report: The Police* (the report of the President's 1966 Crime Commission), the chapter dealing with the role of the police. The following is indicative of their central emphasis:

There are two alternative ways in which police can respond to the difficult problems currently confronting them:

1. The first is to continue, as has been true in the past, with police making important decisions, but doing so by a process which can fairly be described as "unarticulated improvisation." This is a comfortable approach, requiring neither the police nor the community to face squarely the difficult social issues which are involved, at least until a crisis—like the current "social revolution"—necessitates drastic change.

2. The second alternative is to recognize the importance of the administrative policy-making function of police and to take appropriate steps to make this a process which is systematic, intelligent, articulate, and responsive to external controls appropriate in a democratic society; a process which anticipates social problems and adapts to meet them before a crisis situation arises.

Of the two, the latter is not only preferable; it is essential if major progress in policing is to be made, particularly in the large, congested urban areas.[15]

The National Advisory Commission on Criminal Justice Standards and Goals leaves little doubt of its position on where the emphasis in police work should be placed. Its *Report on Police* begins with a chapter on police role, all of it turning on the centrality of police-community relations. The police are viewed as "the instrument of the people," the ultimate goal being greater public trust in the police and a resulting reduction in crime through public cooperation.

Order versus The Rule of Law.   The view of Jerome Skolnick on the police role question has already been suggested. In his writings he emphasizes the distinction between law and order and, more specifically, the conflict between two goals that might guide police behavior. One is adherence to the rule of law: police attitudes and actions that give high priority to the rights of citizens and to legal restraints upon government officials. The other is managerial efficiency: the goal of maintaining order with an efficient, technically sophisticated police organization. Skolnick feels that police in the United States tend to emphasize order as their goal, at the expense of legality. For Skolnick, maintaining order means controlling criminal behavior. His use of these terms differs from Wilson's. In *Professional Police in a Free Society*, Skolnick states his position this way:

> The common juxtaposition of "law and order" is an oversimplification. Law is not merely an instrument of order, but may frequently be its adversary. . . . The phrase "law and order" is misleading because it draws attention away from the substantial incompatibilities existing between the two ideas. Order under law is not concerned merely with achieving regularized social activity, but with the means used to come by peaceable behavior—certainly with procedure but also with the law itself. . . . In short, "law" and "order" are frequently found to be in opposition precisely because law implies rational restraint upon the rules and procedures utilized to achieve order. Order under law, therefore, subordinates the ideal of conformity to the ideal of legality.[16]

There are some implications for police professionalism in what Skolnick says, which are discussed in the next chapter. His concern for the rule of law and the importance he attaches to the police officer's role in it is shared by other observers, for instance, Jerome Hall, in the *Indiana Law Journal*:

> In sum, the policeman who conforms to law is the living embodiment of the law, he is its microcosm on the level of its most specific incidence. He is literally law in action, for in action law must be specific. He is the concrete distillation of the entire mighty, historic *corpus juris*, representing all of it, including the constitution itself.[17]

Crook-catching versus Peace-keeping. Another writer, California criminal justice Professor A. C. Germann, stresses that what the police do and how they do it, in today's urban "noncommunity," is best understood in terms of political power. In effect, police administrators count votes; their definition of police role, their interpretation of relative emphasis upon crook-catching and peace-keeping, is finely attuned to the wishes of the community's dominant political elements. If the dominant demand is for expanding the coercive role of the police, as it has seemed to be nationally since the summer of 1967, the police will act accordingly. He concludes: "anyone who would seek to blame the American police service for current orientation and attitudes would be well advised to study the majority community in terms of orientations and attitudes."[18]

Bruce Terris's view of the role question is consistent with that of others quoted:

> Improved police-minority relations require a radical change in the conception, of both the police and the community, of what police work is all about. . . . The situations in which police officers most frequently find themselves do not require the expert aim of a marksman, the cunningness of a private eye, or the toughness of a stereotyped Irish policeman. Instead, they demand knowledge of human beings and the personal,

as opposed to official, authority to influence people without the use or even the threat of force. These characteristics are not commonly found in police officers because police departments do not consider these values as paramount. As a result, persons with these abilities are not attracted to police work nor rewarded by promotion or incentive if they happen to enter a department.[19]

Views from Other Countries. In Canada, a Task Force on Policing in Ontario filed a report with the Solicitor General in February 1974 reflecting the results of its comprehensive study and making some 170 recommendations. Among them were these:

> Objectives within each police force be defined in terms of that community's requirements for crime control, protection of life and property, and maintenance of peace and order.
>
> The reality of police judgment in the application of law be squarely faced in each police force, and that deliberate and continuing steps be taken to ensure that each police officer has the ability to exercise his judgment so as to support the objectives and priorities of the force.[20]

European views on police role are described by George Berkley in *The Democratic Policeman.*[21] Significant changes have occurred in recent years in the approach of various European police forces to their work. Berkley points to developments in police education, social service activities, and the use of civilians in police work that appear to be reducing the traditional isolation of the police from the community.

The British Royal Commission on the Police had some relevant things to say in its *Final Report:*

> Efficiency is not the sole end of a good and wise administration of the police, and that the apparently confused police system which this country has inherited reflects not merely the British habit of adapting old institutions to meet new needs, but the interplay of conflicting principles of great constitutional importance which human minds have always found, and still find, the utmost difficulty in reconciling.[22]

Her Majesty's Chief Inspector of Constabulary for Scotland, David Gray, has often referred to the future of police service. Some police officers think, he says, that the police should become a highly specialized instrument of crime detection and law enforcement. Others wish to see a service combining scientific and operational efficiency with a policy of police involvement in the community designed to cultivate public confidence. The Police Advisory Board for Scotland has endorsed the latter line of development. Acting on this principle, Gray has established community involvement branches in Scottish police forces.[23] The primary aim is crime prevention. To prevent crime, as Michael Banton puts it, "the police officer needs to know and be at the service of all sections of society."[24] If his role is defined in this way, it helps to resolve a major problem in the police approach to community relations.

In effect, the point is the difference between the police as a *force* and as a *service.* Banton states it in the distinction he draws between a *law* officer and a *peace* officer:

> A division is becoming apparent between specialist departments within police forces (detectives, traffic officers, vice and fraud squads, etc.) and the ordinary patrolman.

> The former are "law officers" whose contacts with the public tend to be of a punitive or inquisitory character, whereas the patrolmen . . . are principally "peace officers" operating within the moral consensus of the community. Whereas the former have occasion to speak chiefly to offenders or to persons who can supply information about an offense, the patrolmen interact with all sorts of people and more of their contacts center upon assisting citizens than upon offenses.[25]

Banton maintains, first, that the enforcement of social regulations is central to the nature of the British police; second, that to reduce "real crime," close attention must be paid to social regulations; and third, that if the rising level of crime in England is to be held in check, "we should not divert inquisitions to administrative tribunals but should make maximum use of the public aspects of our criminal procedures in order to educate people in what is entailed." Banton accepts Skolnick's argument that social control must deal not only with the maintenance of order (in Skolnick's terms, deterring crime), but with the *quality* of the order that a given system is capable of sustaining and the procedures appropriate to the achievement of such order. In short, law enforcement policy should not be to maintain the status quo, but to improve the quality of life in the community.

T. A. Critchley, head of the Community Programmes Department of the British Home Office and author of the definitive *A History of the Police in England and Wales: 1900–1966*, made the following point:

> If ever, unhappily, confidence in the police were to be withdrawn on any significant scale, it will be evident . . . that the nation might have to accept a tougher, more authoritarian institution, in which the traditional concept of "service" gradually gave way to that of "force." The unique mildness of the British system would then be a thing of the past, and liberties that have been cherished for centuries would be set at risk. Responsibility for avoiding such an outcome rests squarely on the public as well as on the police.[26]

There is a conflicting view of the police role question, dominant among police practitioners. This is the position of Lord Devlin in England, who insists that the police should concentrate on criminal matters—that enforcing social regulations is foreign to the nature of the police (he sees drunken driving, for example, as a breach of social regulations rather than a real crime)—and that such matters should be dealt with by administrative tribunals, not by the police.

Lord Devlin's view is well articulated in this country by Director Richard Myren of American University's Center for the Administration of Justice.[27] In a paper written for the 1966 President's Crime Commission, Myren saw police functions in three categories: the performance of miscellaneous social services; the enforcement of nuisance (or convenience) norms—what Devlin and Banton call "social regulations"; and the enforcement of the criminal code. Myren considered the alleged advantages and disadvantages of police performance of each of these functions and concluded that only the enforcement of the criminal code was an appropriate police role. He argued that police performance of the other two types of function indefinitely postponed the transfer of these tasks to other, more appropriate agencies—either existing or needing to be created for a particular purpose. Furthermore, Myren held that police performance of what he deemed inappropriate duties was a serious handicap to genuine professional development of the police. And he believed that, for the police to regulate traffic, deal with drunks, and perform other "nuisance norm" enforcement, only invited corruption, whether actual or fancied. He contended that police-community relations, based upon a desirable mutual respect, could not be improved unless and until the role of the police was narrowed to no more than the enforcement of the criminal code.

Obviously, this conception of police role is popular with officers who see the job primarily and ideally as that of crime deterrence and criminal apprehension. It removes all the "social work baggage" from the work. Community expectations are neatly rearranged simply by shifting the responsibility for social services elsewhere.

Variations in Police Role Expectations

Consider the differing role expectations expressed by telling a police officer, "All persons driving more than 10 mph over the posted speed limit as checked by radar are to be ticketed"; or "Use your judgment in arresting those exceeding the posted speed limit"; or "Cars transporting suspicious-looking persons should be stopped and investigated."

Clearly, various audiences hold varying expectations of police behavior. There is much inconsistency and ambivalence in these expectations. The age, educational level, race, sex, religion, ethnic and cultural values, and socioeconomic status of the members of a community appear to be significant variables affecting their expectations from the police. A community is, in fact, many diversified population clusters with differing and often conflicting ideas about police performance. Additional variables include the location and type of police agency, departmental policies, supervisory practices, specific police assignments, departmental morale, legislative actions, and executive and judicial decisions.

Fortunately, we are beginning to see research dealing with these matters. A few such studies, including that by Jack Preiss and Howard Ehrlich, have been cited in the notes to this chapter. To these should be added some of the studies set in motion by the 1966 President's Crime Commission, important because of their pioneer nature. For instance, *Field Surveys I* and *II* pertained to the victims of crime. What attitudes exist, among those victimized by crime, toward the police and other parts of the criminal justice system? If the victim is black and poor, will these attitudes be different from what they would be if the victim were white and wealthy? These surveys marked the beginning of the crime victimology research that has since gained such momentum.[28]

Changing Views of Order and Justice

Role conflict is further complicated by varying expectations (and tolerances) in the community as to the means that the police should use, either in maintaining order or in enforcing law. It is not only *what* the police do but *how* they do it that commands police-community relations interest. James Q. Wilson refers to the ancient riddle of freedom and order when he states that some people believe that crime should be suppressed even at some cost in civil liberties; others believe that civil liberties must be protected even at some cost in crime. Again, this is the ancient riddle of freedom and order. In the culturally homogeneous community of yesteryear, there was general agreement on the norms of behavior for both police officer and citizen, and the meaning of order and justice. Today's community has no common normative guide, another way of suggesting the degree to which community has evaporated.

THE POLICE OFFICER'S ROLE

Applications of Role Theory

Sociologists devoted to role theory are not satisfied with the generalizations in which we have so far indulged. A few have found the police role question of special research interest. They have their own terminology for dealing with the question, for example, *role, role reciprocal, role set, role concept, role expectations, role performance, reference group, role model, generalized other, role conflict, isomorphism,* and so on. An example of the possibilities in the application of sociological role theory to the police is Martin Miller's "Systemic Model of Police Morale."[29] James Sterling of the staff of the International Association of Chiefs of Police has conducted an interesting study in this vein.[30]

A systematic empirical study of the police applying sociological role theory was done more than a decade ago by Jack Preiss and Howard Ehrlich.[31] Their study of a state police organization testified to the complexity of the question. They found that there is, indeed, a great deal of confusion and ambiguity in role perceptions by police officers themselves. Trial-and-error learning (occupational socialization) and "playing it by ear" are intrinsic elements of police role behavior. Preiss and Ehrlich agreed that certain dilemmas faced by policemen are part of the structure of police organization itself. They found little consensus in role perception among police officers at the same or at different levels of the organization. In turn, there was little consensus in how police officers perceived what others ("audience expectations," "significant others," etc.) required of them in role performance. Often this left the police officer (the actor) choosing from among behavioral roles without adequate guidelines.

An example of what occurs under such circumstances would be a police department that lacks clearly defined organizational goals. The result is a paucity of well-delineated departmental policy and procedures, and a correlative lack of effective supervision. As a result, the patrol officer is perplexed in attempting to determine his or her responsibilities. Unsure of requirements or of subsequent reactions, such police officers tend to be guided by informal communication among peers and are inclined to apply personal values and interests, as well as "situational opportunism," as criteria for decision making. If police officers are unsure of the standards being used to evaluate their performance, they are left to decide for themselves whether it is better to be technically proficient or decently sensitive to people. This kind of decision bears on the nebulous nature of personnel evaluation processes in police organizations.

Preiss and Ehrlich make a telling point:

> Since many of the policeman's audiences were not in agreement about their perceptions and expectations of him, they also varied in their evaluative criteria and their judgments of his performance. This variability could have lessened the impact that a precise and uniform evaluation procedure would have had on the role performance of a policeman by providing him with options and alternatives rather than one highly constraining set of role prescriptions. Perhaps . . . the existence of an acceptable range of permissible behaviors in a group provides the very flexibility which makes group survival possible.[32]

Relationship of Police Role to Values and Beliefs

Occupational role perception is always a reflection of occupational values and beliefs. While this topic is discussed more thoroughly in later chapters, some attention to it here is in order.

John Pfiffner, professor emeritus of public administration at the University of Southern California, has devoted considerable study to this matter. Pfiffner reminisces that in American society at the close of the last century, people knew their neighbors, though they may not always have liked what they saw. He refers to Jane Jacobs's commentary on the police function in such a society, "folk policing through constant surveillance by one's neighbors."[33] This folk society had ample room for people with lower skills and potentiality. Today, many such people are regarded as social problems.

About one-fourth of our families in the United States today have inadequate incomes. Many of them live in large cities. Among them are a large number of people with mental, educational, or vocational handicaps. As Pfiffner puts it, "substandard human beings are multiplying into succeeding generations of public charges."[34] People who are economically, mentally, vocationally, educationally, socially, and genetically handicapped represent a large proportion of "police problems." There has long been controversy as to "how these people got that way." Is it nature or nurture?

Depending upon where one stands in this debate, Pfiffner observes, one decides how the police should deal with antisocial behavior. Those who say that individuals should be held morally and legally responsible for what they do tend to take a punishment approach to the treatment of antisocial behavior. Those who feel that environment should be blamed tend to take a rehabilitative approach.

Pfiffner allows for individuals in any vocation who entertain beliefs that vary from the mode, but asserts that law enforcement officials generally subscribe to the classical theory of criminology. They tend to see the violator as a wrongdoer, morally responsible for his conduct, and therefore liable for the consequences. This school of thought maintains that the fear of punishment is a powerful deterrent to law transgression. Those who commit crime should be treated as enemies of society; "soft" treatment is regarded as a waste.

We will reserve for later discussion the implications of Pfiffner's theory for relationships among the various components of the criminal justice system. For the moment, it is the implications of his ideas for the question of police role that are intriguing. He contends that there is fundamental conflict between the two schools of thought he identifies. One is oriented to force and intimidation, the other, to kindness and "loving sensitivity." Of course, this is an over-simplification, as Pfiffner concedes, but he says it is nonetheless a handy theoretical construction. The question he poses is whether it may not be timely to redefine these roles. He asks: Does the welfare-therapeutic-bureaucratic society require a new concept of the police function? If so, will it be one in which the police participate more widely in the whole process of dealing with the problems of handicapped humanity? Will more of a team approach be demanded for these problems, in which the police role will be but one phase of society's cooperative effort to deal with the problems of personal and social disorganization?

These questions bring us back to our description of police-community relations as "an interprofessional approach to community problem solving," with the police (and other criminal justice agencies) as vital members of the community team, so to speak. Pfiffner's conclusion is provocative:

> Society will soon redefine the police role to include ideas, perceptions and insights which will bring the police into the area of dealing with social pathology on a scale larger than the present holding and containing operation. That role has not yet been spelled out, and is not even dimly perceived by many police administrators; indeed, perhaps most would feelingly deny it to be within the police purview.[35]

For Pfiffner, then, the role choice is this: Should the police deal with criminals only as deserving of punishment, or should the police be called upon to take part in some aspects of criminal rehabilitation? This question also comes to mind when one considers the police role championed by Myren and likeminded scholars.

CAN THE POLICE ROLE DILEMMA BE RESOLVED?

Can the police role dilemma be resolved? A beginning, as a matter of principle, is the recognition that no single formula will settle the question for all communities. It is a question to be dealt with community by community, and—in big cities—neighborhood by neighborhood. In simple terms, the style of policing should reflect the style of the community. This is the situation that has been rather haphazardly arrived at in many urban communities today. In reality, as James Q. Wilson found in his field studies, police departments use varying blends of the three styles of policing he identified.

This general principle seems simple enough. But there are problems with its current application, because it is haphazard rather than the result of calculated administrative study and consensus seeking. Also, police administrators often deny publicly that variations exist. They deny it because they feel that frank admission that police style does, indeed, vary from area to area or precinct to precinct will be interpreted as unequal protection and discriminatory enforcement. Their attitude is an example of the old belief that, in police matters, the public cannot be trusted. Because of this attitude, the police reap in return a bountiful harvest of citizen distrust. Reciprocal distrust is the heart of the police-community relations problem, which is at its worst in a society that increasingly believes that trust is naive.[36]

Another point worth noting is the fact that relatively few police agencies undertake a deliberate process of establishing organization goals, while honestly seeking and obtaining community input. Nor as a general rule is organization policy so deliberately and skillfully set. Successful business organizations are much less "instinctive" in administrative practices.

How exceedingly difficult it is to bring about massive and radical change in a large, urban police agency was demonstrated recently by the Police Foundation's six-year project in the Dallas Police Department. The expressed goal of the project was the identification of the basic needs of the Dallas community and the structuring of a police role conforming to these needs. The project failed, according to a foundation report, because as executed, it could not achieve this goal. Among other difficulties was the 1973 resignation of the police chief and his key staff and advisers, in the midst of pressure, upheaval, and dissension. The plan was said to be visionary, but there was little change in the attitudes and performance of police officers. Yet it was generally acknowledged that much could be learned from the mistakes made in this project.[37]

Toward Further Clarification

Perhaps a few concrete examples will help to illustrate the complexity of the role question in practical terms. With respect to certain judicial decisions, including some from time to time by the U.S. Supreme Court, many police officers ask why they are criticized for performing their duty of enforcing the law. Why are they denied vital tools of law enforcement when the crime rate is increasing? How can they be expected to cope with the increased demands made by the courts on understaffed and underfinanced departments? These are frustrating questions for many police officers, who are not beyond blaming the courts for making the police job tougher.[38]

Another case in point pertains to the problem of dealing with resistance to arrest. Law generally defines in broad terms the degree of force that police officers may use in carrying out their duties; however, department regulations, policies, procedures, and traditions sometimes define the *specific* types of force that may be used in typical situations. Sometimes department prescriptions and local mores are not in harmony with existing, applicable statutes, and the result—in what a particular police officer does under particular circumstances—can be disastrous. As Lohman and his associates pointed out:

> The obedient policeman performs, to the best of his own ability, up to the expectations which are set for him. If the department has not taken measures to restrict the officer's use of force, it, rather than the officer, may be to blame.[39]

We have noted that, in the nineteenth century, law enforcement in the United States was not a duty of the "watchmen" police. As Roger Lane describes it in *Policing the City*, the Boston Police Department was organized mainly as a night watch, to keep peace in the streets.[40] Even after detectives began to appear on police forces, they served private interests. They recovered loot, for a percentage; the best detectives knew the haunts and methods of thieves.

It was the increasing incidence of civil disorder—not mounting crime rates—that brought the municipal police force to fruition. The Boston police were not fully armed at public expense until 1884. And the growth of formally organized police departments did not lead initially to changes in function. James Q. Wilson points out that the maintenance of order remained the principal objective:

> What did lead to a change was twofold: the bureaucratization of the detectives (putting them on salary and ending the fee system), and the use of the police to enforce unpopular laws governing the sale and use of liquor. The former change led to the beginning of the popular confusion as to what the police do. The detective became the hero of the dime novel and the cynosure of the public's romantic imagination; he, and not his patrolman colleague, was the "real" police officer doing "real" police work.[41]

Because the public was sharply divided in opinion regarding liquor laws and such questions as Sunday closing of saloons—situations in which the police could initiate prosecutions on their own authority, rather than on citizen complaint—disastrous police-community relations problems were averted when the police simply chose to do no more than was absolutely necessary. Their motto was: better to do too little than too much. Wilson explains that the police began to provide various services to citizens who seemed likely to become instigators of public disorder. Thus, in the 1850s, the police in Boston, Philadelphia, and New York were heavily engaged in overnight lodging service, and in supplying coal for poor families, soup kitchens for the hungry, and jobs as domestics for women they thought might thereby be lured away from prostitution. Such social services by the police helped to soften their public image, whereas liquor law enforcement hardened it. Eventually, however, the organized charities opposed the rendering of such social services, apparently because they thought it inappropriate for the police to render such services, but more likely because it reflected unfavorably on them.

At the turn of the century, the maintenance of order was still the paramount function of the American police. But two early twentieth-century influences shifted emphasis away from maintaining order to that of enforcing law. One was Prohibition, which put police in the position "of choosing between corruption and making a nuisance of themselves," as Wilson phrases it; and the other was the Great Depression of the 1930s, which focused public attention "on the escapades of bank robbers and other desperadoes." Wilson observes:

> Police venality and rising crime rates coincided in the public mind, though in fact they had somewhat different causes. The watchman function of the police was lost sight of; their law enforcement function, and their apparent failure to exercise it, were emphasized.[42]

It was at this time that President Hoover appointed the Wickersham Commission. The commission considered both police and politicians as principally blameworthy, and reform became the slogan. The argument was that, since the police *can* prevent crime, intolerable crime rates meant that the police were not doing their job because of political influence. Wilson analyzed the consequences:

> If the job of the police is to catch crooks, then the police have a technical, ministerial responsibility in which discretion plays little part. Since no one is likely to disagree on the value of the objective, then there is little reason to expose the police to the decision-making processes of city government. *Ergo,* take the police "out of politics."[43]

All "superfluous" police services were questioned. These were not "real police work." The police were portrayed mainly as "crook catchers"; both the police view of themselves and the public's view of them were adjusted accordingly over a period of several ensuing decades.

Yet as Wilson says, it was a view of police work that really did not correspond with reality. The patrolman knew that he was still handling family fights and troublesome teenagers. The police also knew that they alone could not prevent crime. So they turned to manipulating crime records, to make things look better from the standpoint of public expectations. The "good pinch" and the "G Man" became symbols of "real police work." Rewards and incentives in the department—for example, promotion to detective—were geared to the crook-catching function. And the *means* of apprehending criminals were not always open to public scrutiny.

Jerome Skolnick discusses an implication of this point in *Justice Without Trial:*

> It is not surprising that the solution to "the police problem" in America has been frequently conceived as changing the quality of people, rather than the philosophies of policing. . . . Police reform means finding a new source of police, and police control is a matter of having the "right" sort of people in control. "Reform" of police means increasing the efficiency of police personnel. It is rarely recognized that the conduct of police may be related in a fundamental way to the character and goals of the institution itself—the duties police are called upon to perform, associated with the assumptions of the system of legal justice—and that it may not be men who are good or bad, so much as the premises and design of the system in which they find themselves.[44]

SUMMING UP

We have said that there is a relationship between one's position on the police role question and how one organizes a police department—how it is administered and supervised, what kind of training its personnel receive, and other such matters. Most urban police agencies in this country are organized to emphasize the law enforcement function; a few now seem to be shifting to conflict management. Wilson indicates that various combinations of the three styles of policing he describes exist among police agencies across the country. There are some indications currently of increasing interest in crime prevention and crime coping responsibilities, with heavy reliance on community cooperation. The Law Enforcement Assistance Administration has been encouraging this interest, but it is a long way from being a trend. Evidence is lacking that it has as yet seriously affected the core elements of typical big-city police organization. There are only a few exceptions to this in the United States. In the larger cities of western Canada, the shift in emphasis is much more dramatic.

We should repeat that police officers themselves reflect a wide range of views on the role question. A good way to start an argument in any police group is to quiz them about priorities in police work. Which specific tasks are most important? Which tasks are inappropriate for the police and ought to be handled by some other agency? Is it proper for a police department to operate, say, a rehabilitative facility for "drying out" chronic alcoholics? Should officers be assigned to the staff of job opportunity centers? Should they function as guidance counselors in high schools? These matters (along with the discretionary use of police power) that depend so much on the definition of police role will be our concern in the next two chapters.

NOTES

1. U.S., National Advisory Commission on Civil Disorders, *Report of the National Advisory Commission on Civil Disorders* (Kerner Report) (Washington, D.C.: U.S. Government Printing Office, 1968), p. 157.

2. Michael Banton, *The Policeman in the Community* (New York: Basic Books, 1964), pp. 6–7.

3. Oscar Handlin, "Community Organization as a Solution to Police-Community Problems," *Police Chief* 32, no. 3 (March 1965): pp. 18–19.

4. For a more detailed discussion of this point, see U.S., President's Commission on Law Enforcement and Administration of Justice, *Field Surveys IV* (Washington, D.C.: U.S. Government Printing Office, 1967), vol. 1, pp. 25–28.

5. George L. Kelling, "Police Field Services and Crime," *Crime and Delinquency* 24, no. 2 (April 1978): 173–184.

6. Ibid. See also Herman Goldstein, *Policing A Free Society* (Cambridge, Mass.: Ballinger, 1977); Peter K. Manning, *Police Work: The Social Organization of Policing* (Cambridge, Mass.: MIT Press, 1977); Arthur Niederhoffer and Abraham S. Blumberg, eds., *The Ambivalent Force: Perspectives on the Police*, 2nd ed. (New York: Dryden Press, 1976); Hans Toch, J. Douglass Grant, Raymond T. Galvin, *Agents of Change: A Study in Police Reform* (New York: John Wiley & Sons, 1975); Paul M. Whisenand, James L. Cline, George T. Felkenes, eds., *Police-Community Relations* (New York: Lippincott, 1976); and Robert Shellow and Morton Bard, *Issues in Law Enforcement* (Reston, Va.: Reston, 1976).

7. James Q. Wilson, "What Makes a Better Policeman?" *Atlantic Monthly* 223, no. 3 (March 1969): 135.

8. James Q. Wilson, *Varieties of Police Behavior: The Management of Law and Order in Eight Communities* (Cambridge: Harvard University Press, 1968), p. 3.

9. Ibid., pp. 4–6.

10. James Q. Wilson, "Dilemmas of Police Administration," *Public Administration Review* 28, no. 5: 407.

11. Ibid., p. 408.

12. Gordon E. Misner, "Enforcement: Illusion of Security," *Nation* 208, no. 16 (April 21, 1969): 488. Reprinted by permission.

13. Ibid., p. 489.

14. Herman Goldstein, "Police Response to Urban Crises," *Public Administration Review* 28, no. 5: 417–418. Reprinted by permission.

15. U.S., President's Commission on Law Enforcement and Administration of Justice, *Task Force Report: The Police* (Washington, D.C.: U.S. Government Printing Office, 1967), p. 18.

16. Jerome H. Skolnick, *Professional Police in a Free Society* (New York: National Conference of Christians and Jews, 1967), pp. 10–11. Reprinted by permission of the National Conference of Christians and Jews.

17. Jerome Hall, "Police and Law in a Democratic Society," *Indiana Law Journal* 28, no. 2 (Winter 1953): 133. Reprinted by permission.

18. A. C. Germann, "The Police: A Mission and Role," *Police Chief* (January 1970), p.17. Quoted by permission of the International Association of Chiefs of Police, Gaithersburg, Maryland. For an analysis of how societies condition social control, see Allan Silver, "The Demand for Order in Civil Society: A Review of Some Themes in the History of Urban Crime, Police and Riot," in David J. Bordua, ed., *The Police: Six Sociological Essays* (New York: John Wiley & Sons, 1967).

19. Bruce J. Terris, "The Role of the Police," *Annals of the American Academy of Political and Social Science* 374 (November 1967): 67. Reprinted by permission.

20. Task Force on Policing in Ontario, *The Public Are the Police: The Police Are the Public*, Report to the Solicitor-General of Ontario (Ottawa: Office of the Solicitor-General of Canada, 1974).

21. George E. Berkley, *The Democratic Policeman* (Boston: Beacon Press, 1969).

22. Great Britain, British Royal Commission on the Police, *Final Report* (London: Her Majesty's Stationery Office, 1962).

23. Quoted by Michael Banton in "The Definition of the Police Role," *New Community* 3, no. 3 (Summer 1974): 164–171.

24. Ibid., p. 171.

25. Banton, *Policeman in the Community*, pp. 6–7. Copyright © 1964 by Michael Banton. Reprinted by permission of Basic Books, Inc., Publishers, New York.

26. T. A. Critchley, "The Idea of Policing in Britain," *New Community* 3, no. 3 (1974): 156–163.

27. Richard A. Myren, *The Role of the Police* (Washington, D.C.: U.S Government Printing Office, 1967).

28. Several studies in parts 1 and 2 of Radelet and Reed, *Studies*, have been developed on the basis of these data. For information on crime victims, see U.S., Department of Justice, National Criminal Justice Information and Statistics Service, *Criminal Victimization in the U.S., January–June, 1973*, A National Panel Survey Report, vol. 1 (Washington, D.C.: U.S. Department of Justice, 1974). Also see Israel Drapkin and Emilio Viano, eds., *Victimology: A New Focus—Theoretical Issues* (New York: Lexington Books, 1974).

29. Martin Miller, "Systemic Model of Police Morale," in *The Police and the Community: Studies*, by Louis A. Radelet and Hoyt Coe Reed (Beverly Hills, Calif.: Glencoe, 1973), pp. 49–55.

30. James W. Sterling, *Changes in Role Concepts of Police Officers During Recruit Training* (Washington, D.C.: International Association of Chiefs of Police, 1972). This is a report of an IACP research project with a grant from the National Institutes of Health, U.S. Department of Health, Education and Welfare. The research was conducted in the police departments of Baltimore; Cincinnati; Columbus, Ohio; and Indianapolis. A modest sampling of data from this study may be found in Radelet and Reed, *Studies*, pp. 33–37.

31. Jack J. Preiss and Howard J. Ehrlich, *An Examination of Role Theory: The Case of the State Police* (Lincoln: University of Nebraska Press, 1966).

32. Ibid., p. 92. This point has also been suggested by S. A. Stouffer in "An Analysis of Conflicting Social Norms," *American Sociological Review* 14 (1949): 707–717.

33. Jane Jacobs, *The Death and Life of Great American Cities* (New York: Random House, 1961), p. 264.

34. John M. Pfiffner, "The Function of Police in a Democratic Society," *Occasional Papers: Center for Training and Career Development* (Los Angeles: School of Public Administration, University of Southern California, 1967). Reprinted by permission. Pfiffner's earlier work is reflected in his *The Supervision of Personnel*, 2nd ed. (Englewood Cliffs, N.J.: Prentice-Hall, 1958).

35. Ibid.

36. Richard H. Ward has a helpful diagram on the variables bearing on police role concept in his "The Police Role: A Case of Diversity," *The Journal of Criminal Law, Criminology and Police Science* 61, no. 4: 580–586. Copyright © 1972 by the Northwestern University School of Law.

37. Mary Ann Wycoff and George L. Kelling, *The Dallas Experience: Human Resource Development*, vol. 1 (Washington, D.C.: The Police Foundation, Inc., 1978).

38. U.S., President's Commission on Law Enforcement and Administration of Justice, *Field Surveys V*, p. 23.

39. U.S., President's Commission on Law Enforcement and Administration of Justice, *Field Surveys IV*, vol. 1, p. 28.

40. Roger Lane, *Policing the City: Boston, 1822–1885* (Cambridge: Harvard University Press, 1967), pp. 3–13.

41. James Q. Wilson, "What Makes A Better Policeman?" *Atlantic* 223, no. 3 (March 1969): 131. Copyright © 1969 by the Atlantic Monthly Company. Reprinted by permission.

42. Ibid., p. 133.

43. Ibid.

44. Jerome H. Skolnick, *Justice Without Trial: Law Enforcement in Democratic Society* (New York: John Wiley & Sons, 1966), pp. 4–5. Reprinted by permission of John Wiley & Sons.

4

POLICE PROFESSIONALISM

Logically, our idea of what it means to be a professional police officer is governed by our notion of the police officer's role in society. If we emphasize the law enforcement function, professionalism means attributes conducive to this function, for example, courage, respect for superiors, reliability, and obedience. If, instead, we emphasize the peace-keeping side of policing, then professionalism means attributes such as intelligence, common sense, friendliness, courtesy, and patience.

There also appear to be both law enforcement and peace-keeping orientations for police-citizen interaction. A law enforcement orientation emphasizes what the community should do to assist the police in such activities as containing crime, catching crooks, and providing information about "suspicious persons." This has lately been popularly referred to as "romancing the police." A peace-keeping orientation for police and community relations is more likely to emphasize what the police and community can do together as partners. *Preventing* crime as well as disorder is seen as an important objective of this partnership. In this conception, receiving information and interpreting it are two-way processes.

For the police, a law enforcement orientation for police-citizen interaction tends to emphasize public relations, while a peace-keeping orientation emphasizes community participation. The essence of the peace-keeping orientation is mutual trust, so that citizens may regard helping the police as, in effect, helping themselves to create a better community.

THE POLICE OFFICER'S ROLE

As generalized abstractions, these distinctions may be important only to theoreticians. In practice, a given police agency will probably have some of both orientations evident in its organization and activities. Inevitably, therefore, discussions of professionalism are predictably argumentative, as are discussions of role emphasis.

One of the marks of a profession is that its constituency has arrived at some consensus regarding the "product" of the profession. Thus, it may be said that policing will be recognized as truly professional when greater consensus is reached on the question of the police officer's role.

Because professional recognition depends upon public attitudes toward the police, consensus on role or product must involve both police and community. To influence public attitude favorably will require unprecedented police leadership, another mark of true professionalism. For example, public education in matters of health is carried on under the leadership of medical professionals. Instructive campaigns influence and shape public attitudes, at the same time helping to convince the public that the promoters are truly professional. Medical professionals do not follow in the wake of community opinions in health matters. They secure factual data through research from which the public is informed and educated as to what its attitudes and expectations should be. There is no great problem of consensus about the role or product in the medical profession.

As with any analogy, the comparison of medicine or public health with policing has some limitations. Yet it suggests a simple point: true professionals *lead* the community in their area of competence. While they listen carefully to community opinion in identifying community needs, they do not wait for the community in decisions and actions directed toward meeting these needs. In matters of law enforcement and crime, the police do significantly influence public attitudes. But in matters of peace-keeping, they are apt to say that they can't act "until the community is ready." Racial discrimination is a case in point.

The Definition of Professionalism

We begin to see that our definition of professionalism, or of a professional, will depend considerably upon what we regard as important in a particular field—what priorities we feel ought to be emphasized by workers in that field.

The dictionary defines a *profession* as "a calling requiring specialized knowledge and often long and intensive academic preparation, used by way either of instructing, guiding or advising others, or of serving them in some art." Special knowledge and proficiency are among the marks of a profession. Service to others, with a clearly defined purpose, is another; so is a technical terminology. Still another is the assumption that financial return is not the primary object in rendering service. A profession has a certain ethic, certain guiding moral principles, for which a self-policing provision is maintained within the profession. Members are associated in organizations for the purpose of regulating and improving the service they render. It is in this connection that professional organizations are concerned with such matters as licensing, accreditation of schools, establishment of training standards, separation of the qualified from the unqualified, and the like.[1]

The Importance of Attitude. Sometimes in discussion of professionalism, reference is made to what is called *attitude:* for example, in the aphorism "attitude makes the professional." Attitude, although elusive and difficult to define in a concrete way, becomes somewhat more manageable when it is applied to the relationship between a professional and a client. The late Alexander Woolcott had attitude in mind when he defined a professional as "someone who does his best job when he feels worst."

Professionalism versus Bureaucracy. In our society, professionalism and bureaucracy have become increasingly confused. *Bureaucracy* is a system of administration characterized by specialization of functions, by adherence to fixed rules, and by a hierarchy of authority. The question of whether bureaucracy and professionalism are compatible has been widely argued. The professional and bureaucratic models clearly clash at certain points.

Several years ago, sociologist Harold Wilensky claimed that the distinctive standards of a profession are its *technical* basis (systematic knowledge or doctrine acquired only through long prescribed training), and its adherence to *professional norms* (ethic, attitude, client relations, etc.). He emphasized *autonomous expertise* and the service ideal. Bureaucracy enfeebles the service ideal more than it threatens autonomy, Wilensky asserted, and he concluded that very few occupations will achieve the authority of the established professions. If we call everything a profession, he said, we obscure its meaning and make it less a prize to be earned only by meeting demanding requirements.[2]

Before his retirement as Washington, D.C., police chief, Jerry V. Wilson struck a sobering note. "Somehow," he wrote, "in the transition from individualized to institutionalized professions, we have come to suppose that no one but 'professionals' performs important, worthwhile tasks. The truth is that more often than not, it is the 'non-professionals' of any given work unit who perform most of the productive work."[3]

The Effects of Social Change. The emergence of many new occupations in an increasingly technocratic society has created a surge for professional recognition. This raises interesting questions about the differences between doctors and plumbers, between clergymen and computer technicians, between lawyers and trade union members. Social change has radically altered the traditional professional categories. By and large, the qualifications for being accepted in the new professional groupings that have surfaced in recent years are more demanding than in the relatively few professions of the past. The professional requirements of medicine and law are more rigorous today than they were years ago, if for no other reason than that these fields now require more knowledge.

Judged by the recognized marks of a profession, any claims that police work has achieved such status simply amount to wishful thinking. Remember, however, that professionalism has a relativistic character. Police work is relatively more professionalized today than it was years ago. Police Department *A* may be relatively more professionalized than Police Department *B*. Police Officer Smith may be relatively more professionalized than Police Officer Jones. Police *departments* tend to be relatively more professionalized than police *officers*. Of course, all such judgments involve criteria about which there is sharp disagreement.

How important is professional recognition in police work? The preponderance of opinion strongly favors such recognition. Still, professionalization may be a mixed blessing — depending, again, on how it is defined. Perhaps some insight along this line can be gained by considering some specific aspects of police professional development.

Various Views.   In 1959, James Slavin — then chief of the Kalamazoo (Michigan) Police Department, later the chief in Denver and until his recent retirement, director of the Traffic Institute at Northwestern University — told the Fifth National Institute on Police and Community Relations at Michigan State University of a number of obstacles to the professional development of American police. One was the hesitancy to carry out vigilant internal monitoring of police practices. Another was his impression that some so-called professional police organizations and associations were indistinguishable from labor and craft unions. Slavin hastened to add, on this point, that he was not critical of labor and craft unions; he was merely calling attention to the difference that is generally believed to exist between a union and a professional association.

Continuing his provocative commentary, Slavin pointed to "almost imperceptible progress in establishing documented standards for selection of police personnel from our citizenry." He said that little information was available describing what qualifications were necessary to predict a successful police career. Another shortcoming, according to Slavin, was the inadequacy of training for supervisory responsibility in police agencies. He advocated wider uses of training methods similar to those of business and industry. Slavin concluded: "The thing we fail to emphasize in our writings and discussions is that it is the characteristics that mark a profession that are worthwhile, rather than talking frequently as though what we want most of all is to be identified as a professional occupation."[4]

Slavin's is a disquieting approach to the subject of police professionalism, one to which some police officers responded rather caustically. Slavin might well make the same observation today, as not much has changed.

A commentary more popular among police officers was exemplified by a 1964 Quinn Tamm editorial in the *Police Chief* in which the retired executive director of the International Association of Chiefs of Police wrote:

> I know of no period in recent history when the police have been the subject of so many unjustified charges of brutality, harassment and ineptness. It almost seems that the better we do our job enforcing the law, the more we are attacked. The more professional we become, the more effective we become and the more effective we are, the more we impinge upon the misbehavior of society.
>
> But for this we should offer no apology. A police force is established, among other things, for the purpose of enforcing existing laws. In this respect, we are dutybound. Those who damn our actions in this regard must be made to understand that the police do not make the laws, that laws are the direct product of public desires, and if the public does not like those laws or believe them to be fair, then the public should change the laws rather than criticize the police. . . . We can no longer afford to answer unjust criticism with thinly veiled innuendoes and pusillanimous generalities. If we are right, let's say so.[5]

But the well-known authority on police management, V. A. Leonard, had earlier expressed his view of the matter:

> A system of legal justice based upon the thesis of punishment has exerted a tremendously negative effect on the professionalization of police service. As a corollary, the low quality of personnel required to exercise the police power under these conditions was not conducive to good public relations, with the result that a negative public opinion had been created. The withdrawal of public interest and support, together with public apathy and indifference, has further served to retard

the advance toward professionalization. No less important has been the fact that a substandard personnel became easy prey for corrupt political figures and others in the community who profit when the risks associated with vice operations are reduced.[6]

Yet another police analyst, one-time Kansas City Police Chief Bernard Brannon, stressed the importance of *attitude* in his discussion of professionalism in police work. He believes that being a professional police officer begins with seeing oneself as a professional. He alluded to the effort and sacrifice necessary to become a professional, emphasizing that there are responsibilities of such status accompanying the privileges. He spoke of self-discipline, dedication to the public service ideal, the importance of individual words and deeds, constant emphasis upon study and learning, and the importance of participation in community affairs. He favored the establishment of an accrediting agency for police professional education, and the enforcement of uniform standards and examinations in each state.[7]

The meaning of "professional attitude" is difficult to pin down. In the pages of the *Saturday Review,* editor Norman Cousins dealt with it, speaking of medicine:

> Finally, the good doctor is not only a scientist but a philosopher. He knows that the facts of medicine will continue to change and that, therefore, his professional training can never be an absolute guide to good practice. It is his philosophy of medicine that has to serve as the solid base of his practice. The doctor's respect for life, his special qualities of compassion and tenderness — even under the most devilish of circumstances — these are the vital ingredients of his art. To such a doctor, the most exotic diagnostic machines are not more important than the simple act of sitting at the bedside of a patient. In this sense, the ultimate art of the good doctor is to make good patients. He does this by making the patient a full partner in his recovery. Such a doctor is worth all the recognition and reward a society is capable of offering.[8]

The applicability of this statement to police and community relations is readily apparent.

The Desirability of Professionalism

So the question of the desirability of professionalism for the police is germane. James Q. Wilson states flatly that the patrolman is neither a bureaucrat nor a professional, but a member of a *craft*. As with other crafts, there is in the police field no generalized, written body of special knowledge. Learning is imparted by apprenticeship, largely on the job; the primary reference group is composed of colleagues on the job; and the members think of themselves as set apart from society because they have a special task to perform. Unlike other crafts, however, police work produces no product that can be easily judged, and it is carried on often in an apprehensive or hostile atmosphere. Wilson concludes that efforts to change policing, which he equates with maintaining order, into a profession will be largely ignored, simply because professionalization of the line officer is irrelevant.[9]

Robert Shellow and Morton Bard have raised some provocative questions about the professionalizing of the police. For example, does professionalization mean less service to the community because of more time spent by police for training and educational purposes? Who educates the policy makers so they will view policing as truly a profession? If a professionalized police are elitist, in the manner of other professionals, will this not damage community relations?[10]

Professionalism in police work is a desirable goal only when it is recognized that

1. not everyone who works in the police station needs to be a professional; and

2. police officer professionalism pivots in the *human* dimensions of police work—in such things as attitude, ethic, service and sensitivity to people of all kinds (client relations), and manifold activities directed toward earning public trust and respect.

The Outlook for Professionalism

It seems quite apparent that the confusion surrounding police professionalism is the result of disagreements about police role. And it is because of these disagreements about role that discussions of police professionalsim are so often frustrating and that the idea of professionalism is so difficult to define in generally acceptable terms. As we have seen, there is even an argument about whether police professionalism is desirable. Indeed, the question of whether a college education is necessary for effective police work continues to be debated. As Wilson points out, there is no clear evidence that middle-class, college-educated people make better inner-city police officers. Moreover, it is highly unlikely that many such people will find a police career in a large city attractive. The implications of professionalism for police and community relations turn on just such contested questions.

There are many related questions for which definitive answers are not known. For example, in community-relations terms, what factors of personality, attitude, background, education, values, and beliefs are most important for the effective police officer? How should a police organization cultivate these qualities? How are good community-relations qualities to be reconciled with good law-enforcement qualities in the same individual? Do certain personality types gravitate to police careers? What will be the community-relations and law-enforcement effects of more women police officers doing general duty?

We are only beginning to see some creditable research on questions of this nature.[11] There are few researchable subjects in the social psychology of policing more inviting (and more elusive) than the personality traits of police officers. We say more about research of this type in connection with the self-image of the police.

The outlook for police professionalism in the police departments of big American cities is rather glum, in the opinion of such observers as James Q. Wilson, Herman Goldstein, Gordon Misner, and Jerome Skolnick. Wilson, for one, does not regard this as necessarily disastrous. As a political scientist, he is inclined to emphasize the pragmatic. He says, for instance, that police and city administrators will have to work with the human material they now have, or something close to it.[12] Under such circumstances, they will tend to rely heavily on organizational and legal "prodding" to persuade the policeman "to do his duty": in short, bureaucracy. This has frequently meant "the tight ship," doing things "by the book" — what Wilson labels the *legalistic* style of policing. In effect, this approach reduces the amount of discretion officers can exercise. It makes them technicians, sometimes specialists, but *not* professionals. It gives the appearance of efficiency, oriented to the law-enforcement function rather than to peace keeping. Albert Reiss's position is similar to Wilson's, but there are also some differences. Reiss seems more hopeful than Wilson for eventual professionalization of the line officer. Wilson simply says that it may be irrelevant.

Another school of thought (loosely combining Wilson's *service* and *watchman* styles) wants police officers to be professionals stressing their community service functions. In this view, the emphasis should be on good community relations. The police officer should be trained to take a broad view of his role, with maximum initiative and discretion. Perhaps, Wilson speculates, the answer is that "the police should be bureaucratized for some purposes, professionalized for others, and left alone for still others."[13] As we have said, not everyone in the police station needs to be a professional. In this vein, the issue in not so simple as a choice of emphasis between law enforcement and order maintenance. Where there is agreement that the order maintenance role is central and primary, there is sometimes disagreement on how best to maintain order. Wilson concludes:

> In sum, the police can cope with their problems but they cannot solve them. If they were expected to do less, they might not be so frustrated by their inability to do much of anything. . . . The "problems of the police" are long standing and inherent in the nature of their function, but our definition of those problems has changed and, by changing, has misled or unsettled us.[14]

PROFESSIONALISM AND POLICE-COMMUNITY RELATIONS

An abundance of literature deals with police professionalism in general terms. It is a required subject in every standard text in police administration, with each author advancing his particular pitch on what constitutes professionalism. Most of these positions on the subject have merit from one standpoint or another. A central problem of police professionalism—closely related to the question of police role—is the problem of consensus. This means simply that police professionalization is essentially a police-community transaction. Community attitudes toward the police are crucial, because professionalism implies public certification of professional competence, with the commensurate status, privileges, and responsibilities.

There is, therefore, special significance to professionalizing police service from a police-community standpoint. This author once wrote an article on this topic, a few sentences of which are appropriate here:

> Now I would maintain that a profession serves *needs*, not *wants*. I don't particularly care about being a pal with my doctor, but I do want to respect him for his

competence, his skill and his attitude as a professional. I don't think he should go out of his way to be a pal to me either. When I need his help, I want something more from him than soothing assertions that he'll never let me down. . . . May I suggest [then] what I regard as the first implication of the professional concept [in law enforcement] for police-community relations: to woo the client's respect, not his favor—in short, to reassert authority as a necessary corollary to responsibility.[15]

A similar point was made by Jack Grossman and William Kohnke in an article on the attitudinal approach to police professionalism. They concluded that a professional law enforcement officer should have the following traits:

1. Be problem oriented rather than task oriented.
2. Have concern for people rather than self.
3. Prevent the citizen from setting the ground rules.
4. Recognize personal limitations.
5. Respect people served.
6. Take pride in self and the profession.[16]

Robert Shellow and Morton Bard discuss police professionalism in a manner similar to ours, elaborating a bit more on such key points as ethics, a clearly defined body of knowledge, on-going education, uniform minimum standards of excellence for selection, education, and performance, and an unequivocal service orientation. They conclude:

Police professionalism could help close the gap between the police and the communities they serve. Backed by better education, better in-service training, and by research aimed at discovering and answering community needs, police professionals could, perhaps once again, humanly respond to people.[17]

We observe that the police *are* indeed professionalizing—in terms of education and training, improved tools and hardware, better communication systems, and the like. Yet, as Quinn Tamm suggested, a more professionalized police force—as measured by some yardsticks—will not necessarily be more respected by the public. This is frustrating to officers and administrators who want very much to be recognized as professionals. In a matter such as civilian review, for example, the frustration mounts, as Eleanor Harlow has pointed out: "Those who argue that civilian review of police is wrong because as a 'professional' organization, the police department should be subject only to its own surveillance are basing their conclusion on a faulty comparison. If civilian review is inappropriate, as it well may be, it is for other reasons."[18]

The fact is that professionalism, as applied to the police, tends to be rather elastically defined. Efficiency in suppressing crime is widely equated with professionalization. It would be easier to evaluate these twin goals if they were kept distinct. Skolnick explains:

The problem of police in a democratic society is not merely a matter of obtaining new police cars or more sophisticated equipment, or communication systems, or of recruiting men who have to their credit more years of education. What is necessary is a significant alteration in the philosophy of police, so that police "professionalization" rests upon the values of a democratic legal polity, rather than merely on the notion of technical proficiency to serve the public order of the state.[19]

In sum, when Tamm says, "the more professional we become," he is talking about management and criminal investigation efficiency, about hardware, about training and educational expansion. Why, then, he asks, are some elements of the public still so critical of the police? The answer must be that these citizens believe that there is more to professionalism than efficiency and hardware—or perhaps it is that police professionalism *without a human dimension* is not a very significant goal, just as Shellow and Bard have indicated.

The professional growth of the police in the United States in the past thirty or so years has been uneven and erratic. In keeping with the prevailing role emphasis in police work, professional advancement has been mainly in technology and managerial efficiency, matched only recently by corresponding attention to client relations, attitudes, responsiveness to the community, and accountability. Police work is not, of course, the only sector of public affairs where this is true.

The Human Dimension in Police Work

Police work in a democratic society cannot escape from its human dimension. Its public service aspects need reemphasis, and a military-technological orientation tends to obscure its fundamental concern for relating to people and for what Jerome Hall stressed in his discussion of the democratic ethic. The Michigan State study for the 1966 President's Crime Commission recommended

> that the police place greater emphasis upon the concept of public service as a legitimate goal of their organizations. For the police, professionalism has been viewed in too narrow a focus. True professionalism is rooted in broad-based public service which commands popular respect for the police officer and the system of government by law which he represents. Increased efficiency in police work is laudable, but as a means to an end, not as an end in itself. When efficiency is coupled with a goal of crime suppression at any cost, the community is often faced with a police agency which is not responsive to community needs. Certain elements in the community do not see it as their police department.[20]

Eleanor Harlow makes a further useful distinction:

> The term professionalization is used by those who wish to free the police from community "interference" to support their contention that a professional organization is responsible for regulating and supervising its own members, free from the control of outsiders, who lack the knowledge and experience to make appropriate judgments. It is used—simultaneously but with different meaning—by those who believe that the community should "police the police" to insist that only the establishment of specific standards and procedures (presumably based on dictates from the community power structure) will insure "professional" police operations.[21]

There are difficulties with either of these interpretations of police professionalization. In our society, with the police ultimately accountable to the people and consequently subject to political process, it is evident that police work cannot be professionalized by conceding autonomy to the point of complete isolation from the community. On the contrary, we maintain that the police are integral to the community—*part of*, not *apart from*. Both community relations and justice are jeopardized, however, if the police allow themselves to become the marionettes of this or that politically dominant group in the community.

There is also some difficulty with the second interpretation of professionalization, suggested by Harlow:

> Those who use the term professionalization to mean the establishment of standards for police operation advocate the provision to police of specific instructions for handling those situations not clearly defined by law. This is an admirable goal and one which would probably please everybody; certainly the police would be relieved to know what, precisely, is expected of them. However, such procedural standards often cannot be made specific enough to apply to any given situation. Ultimately, the individual officer must be sufficiently trained and educated to use his discretion when the standard procedure is inapplicable.[22]

We deal with the implication of this point in the next chapter.

Professionalism and the Line Officer—The Service Ideal

Albert Reiss has observed that our larger American police departments have become major bureaucratic organizations. Many of their problems are, therefore, peculiar to bureaucracy. Reiss contends that most attempts to professionalize police work have led to a professionalization of the police department, to a lesser extent to the professionalization of those in staff positions, and only to a relatively minor extent to professionalization of the rank-and-file officer in the line. He states that the nature of changes within police departments has tended to work against the professionalization of the line officer. The department has been professionalized, says Reiss, through bureaucratization, and the line officer accordingly becomes no more than a technician who takes orders. Reiss also maintains that broader societal changes work against professionalization of the line officer, primarily through redefinition of the police role. He argues that the nature of police work "coerces discretionary decision-making in social situations, and both the end and the means valued by our society require that in the long run at least part of the line must be 'professional.' "[23]

Reiss is particularly interested in the relationship of the professional with clients. He characterizes this relationship as technical, in the sense of specialized knowledge to be applied in practice. The client relationship, moreover, is moral and ethical. But its central feature, Reiss asserts, is a decision about the client in which the professional decides something relating to the future of the client. This feature of the professional-client relationship is especially critical when the client has little choice about whether to abide by the decision of the professional.

To support his view that the professionalization of police departments through bureaucratization has worked against the professionalization of the line officer, Reiss points to three factors:

1. The increasing centralization of decision making in departments. A bureaucratic system where decision making is decentralized to the line would be more consistent with professionalization of the line.

2. The tendency of specialization in police organizations to be more technical than professional. It has been more "professionalization of the organizational system" than it has been professional role specialization. Writing tickets in traffic enforcement, for example, is a work assignment, a technical job specialty. It does not involve professional decision making by the line officer.

3. The making of decisions at the staff rather than the operating level of police departments, and the bringing in of professional specialists at the staff rather than the operating level. As an illustration, "human relations" in many departments is largely a staff function. It is handled through central orders, leaving little room for "professional treatment of clients" by the line officer.

Reiss's summarizing statement is helpful in our discussion at this point:

> Despite dissatisfaction with the "new" role emerging for the police officer, it seems clear that the changes underway involve a reinterpretation of client role and behavior in terms of a more "professional" ideology and practice. The dilemma for the police is to somehow balance traditional moral and quasi-legal concerns with enforcing the law and catching criminals who are to be "punished," with the emerging concerns for civil rights and legal requirements on police methods. "Professionalization" of police work appears to be one "legitimate" way to deal with the dilemma.[24]

Analysts of professionalism, in any field, emphasize the service ideal and the client relationship. These considerations are closely akin to what we mean by *attitude*. Harold Wilensky discusses the idea:

> The criterion of "technical" is not enough however. The craftsman typically goes to a trade school, has an apprenticeship, forms an occupational association to regulate entry to the trade, and gets legal sanction for his practice. But the success of the claim to professional status is governed also by the degree to which the practitioners conform to a set of moral norms that characterize the established professions. These norms dictate not only that the practitioner do technically competent, high-quality work, but that he adhere to a service ideal—devotion to the client's interests more than personal or commercial profit should guide decisions when the two are in conflict.[25]

Wilensky goes on to state that the professional norm of selflessness is more than mere lip service: "The service ideal is the pivot around which the moral claim to professional status revolves." It would be difficult to express more eloquently a major implication of police professionalism for police and community relations.

The *ethic* of professionalism is closely akin to the service ideal. There are, of course, corrupt doctors and corrupt lawyers. They insult the service ideal; one might say that they "unprofessionalize" the profession. From this point of view, corruption in police circles may be seen as the gross social cancer that it is.

Indeed, any dicussion of police professionalism tends to raise larger questions than we can consider here. The question of conflict between professionalism and a military-modeled bureaucracy is one. Another question pertains to the relationship between police professionalism and higher education. Until recently, it had long been assumed that more formal education for police officers automatically meant better, more professional police service. But a decade of rapid expansion of police education has pinpointed some puzzling problems for which a National Advisory Commission on Higher Education, created by the Police Foundation in 1976, is seeking solutions. The problems include:

1. There is no consensus about the *purpose* of higher education for police officers.

2. There is no consensus on the kind of *curriculum* that students aiming at police careers should be offered.

3. There is considerable question about whether the "right" kind of people are being educated for police work. For example, preservice education is resisted by police unions, and some police administrators are not sold on it. The question is better phrased by asking whether a college degree is really necessary for entry-level police jobs? Again, there is no consensus.

4. The *faculty* teaching in police-oriented college programs are too often underqualified, judged by prevailing standards.

5. Police agency *personnel policies*, in too many instances, fail to encourage college education.

Only a few attempts have been made, none very satisfactory, to measure police performance and relate it to officer educational level. It is, obviously, an extremely difficult research problem. Yet there are several current efforts, one in particular by David Geary of the University of South Florida, that appear promising. It need hardly be added that the difficulties in such research, as well as in the problems listed above, are traceable to the basic role dilemma of the police.

The Police as Community Managers

An earlier quotation reflected David Bordua's view of the police as "community managers" and "monitors of social change." Bordua suggested that, after a transitional period of professionalizing police *departments*, it will be necessary to professionalize police *officers*. If the police are to be community managers, they will have to participate actively in the policy-setting functions of government, as recommended in *Task Force Report: The Police* of the 1966 President's Crime Commission,[26] more recently restated by the National Advisory Commission on Criminal Justice Standards and Goals. This participation will mean a legitimate political role for the police unlike "political policing" in the past. Reforms in police work cannot occur without intelligent political role playing by police administrators. This does not imply a police state. As Bordua said, "If they [the police] are to avoid being politically maneuvered into being hired oppressors by reactionary whites or manipulated targets by extremist Negro leaders, they will have to present themselves as detached and principled specialists in community order."[27]

Some may think this notion a lofty ideal, or sheer fantasy. But the police response to current social challenges in many places already reflects this ideal in some measure.

As Herman Goldstein has observed:

> Efforts to communicate with the public more effectively are in sharp contrast with the commitment to secrecy, isolation, and aloofness that has marked the "professional" approach in the past. The willingness to accept criticism and the acknowledgement of existing inadequacies represent a substantial modification of the customary police commitment to maintaining an all-powerful image of invulnerability. Involvement in social services reflects a recognition of these tasks as appropriate police responsibilities. [28]

Yet, as various writers have told us, some of the more progressive police administrators in our large cities are confronted by a difficult dilemma. At a time when the need for new and enlightened approaches to policing is so vital, they are forced by weight of public opinion and by political "gamesmanship" to retain traditional methods. Some of the pressure to maintain the status quo comes from within departments and is wielded by police officers' associations whose members feel threatened by change. This results in a kind of tug-of-war for administrative control of the department. Even visionary and able administrators do not always win this kind of battle. Also, in smaller departments, especially those with fewer than twenty-five members, professionalism has little meaning. The fragmentation of police agencies discourages serious attention to professional goals and attributes, and is also undesirable by cost-effectiveness standards. But "home-rule" policing is as fiercely defended as the so-called neighborhood school—no matter what the cost.

Police Authority and Police Power

Michael Banton makes much of the point that police officers function most effectively (professionally?) when what they do is supported by the moral consensus of the community. Officers possess both authority and power. Authority is rightful power; it has a moral element. Banton declares that public resentment against police is usually directed against their power, not their authority, because the latter is conferred upon police officers by the community. Therefore, officers who wield moral authority act in a predictable fashion, that is, in a manner that is socially approved. Police officers whose responses are uncertain, Banton suggests, are those who rely on their individual powers, unconcerned with whether the subjects feel they are exercising them rightfully. The public will lack confidence in officers of this type, because their behavior is unpredictable. [29]

Banton's point has implications for both police role and police professionalism. Earlier in this chapter, we spoke of the hypothetical police department that lacks clearly defined goals, with corresponding inadequacies in administrative policy and supervision that leave individual policemen unsure of departmental requirements. We said that police officers in such situations tend to be guided by informal communication among peers, by their personal values and interests, and by their own interpretations of what the community expects of them. These are the conditions that produce the unpredictable behavior to which Banton refers.

At the other extreme, there is the concept of a professional police department suggested by the description "a tight ship." It is one that attempts to have a policy or rule applicable to every conceivable situation in which police officers might find themselves. It is so oriented toward efficiency that it strives for guidelines in every police activity and thus becomes a "by the book" operation. Police officers on the street are stringently limited in their exercise of discretion; as Reiss describes it, decisions are made for them "up the line" or "downtown." Idle conversation with residents of the community is discouraged as a waste of time. Instead, officers are expected to engage in "aggressive patrol" and be on the lookout for suspicious persons, especially in high crime areas. They are directed to treat citizens civilly, but never to show sympathy or other emotion toward a "mere civilian."

Bruce Terris declares that a police department can be so "professional" that it destroys community relations. He observes that "there is no inherent reason why professional police departments must . . . adopt procedures which interfere with improved police-minority relations."[30] He believes that true police professionalism can be a functional combination of management efficiency and good community relations. In fact, he says that efficiency is meaningless if it is secured at the cost of further isolating the police from the community, especially in high crime areas where police-community relations tend to be poor. It will be recalled that policing in democratic society rests on the assumption that a cooperative public is, to a large extent, a self-policing public.

PROFESSIONALISM AND LAW VERSUS ORDER

What Jerome Skolnick has to say about police professionalism is an extension of the distinction he draws between law and order:

> If the police are ever to develop a conception of legal as opposed to managerial professionalism, two conditions must be met: First, the police must accustom themselves to the seemingly paradoxical yet fundamental idea of the rule of law, namely, that the observance of legal restraints may indeed make their task more difficult. That's how it is in a free society. Second, the civic community must support compliance with the rule of law by rewarding police for observing constitutional guarantees, instead of looking to the police as merely an institution responsible for controlling criminality. In practice, regrettably, the reverse has been true. The police function in a milieu tending to support, normatively and substantively, the idea of administrative efficiency as an index of police professionalism. Steps must be taken to reverse this trend. The observance of the principles of legality will indeed be the hallmark of professional police in a free society.[31]

Skolnick's position was anticipated in the language of the *Final Report* of the British Royal Commission on the Police:

> The police systems in England, Scotland and Wales are the products of a series of compromises between conflicting principles or ideas. Consequently, in contrast to other public services such as health and education, the rationale of the police service does not rest upon any single and definite concept of the public good. Thus, it is to the public good that the police should be strong and effective in preserving law and order and preventing crime; but it is equally to the public good that police power should be

controlled and confined so as not to interfere arbitrarily with personal freedom. The result is compromise. The police should be powerful but not oppressive; they should be efficient but not officious; they should form an impartial force in the body politic, and yet be subject to a degree of control by persons who are not required to be impartial and who are themselves liable to police supervision. [32]

One clear implication is that police professionals should have autonomy, but not too much.

THE ISOLATION SYNDROME AND PROFESSIONALISM

Lofty principles are tested in the crucible of reality, a reality in which practical politics plays a decisive part. What this means in practical terms for many big city police officers has been well described by William Brown, a retired New York City police inspector, now professor of criminal justice at the State University of New York in Albany. [33] He feels that the new isolation of the police is a recoil from pressures exerted by human relations specialists, by some college professors in the police field, by other "activist academics," and by the courts. Many police officers feel, Brown believes, that these pressure groups generally propose that more restrictions be placed on the police, rather than provide support for the police by devising workable solutions to difficult problems.

So it is, Brown continues, that the police have turned "to their own councils." Leadership has developed from police fraternal organizations, which are "for the policeman." As Brown puts it, "They are his unquestioning champions and today's policeman needs a champion." Thus it is that the police respond to current pressures "by withdrawing from the professional arena to the blue-collar world." With this goes apathy, "the classic reaction of a group to what it sees as a hopeless situation." [34]

In developing basically the same thought, John Pfiffner refers to the "isolation syndrome" of the police, and his diagnosis of the pressures that explain it is similar to Brown's. As a result, Pfiffner says, the police turn to what he calls "guild protectionism," born out of self-pity and the failure to make personal adjustment to extreme vocational tensions. [35]

Police Responses to the Isolation Syndrome

James Q. Wilson has analyzed the phenomenon of police misconduct and corruption in big city departments in the same terms, but more intensively. [36] He considers two general responses of police forces to the isolation syndrome. Each response provides a different definition of "a good cop." Wilson calls one response (or code of police behavior), the system; he calls the other, professionalism. By the system, he means "the institutionalized rules and norms which express the policeman's position as a member of a group which feels keenly its *pariah* status." By professionalism, he means "an institutionalization of rules and norms expressing, not feelings of group separateness, but an external body of 'expert' knowledge about 'correct' police work."

The code of the system is internal and, in sociological terms, is *particularistic:* its value standards are derived from the significance to a particular person of his relations with particular others. The code of the professional is external, *universalistic;* its values are derived from general, impersonal, and presumably valid rules binding upon all persons possessing certain qualifications. Wilson makes this pertinent point:

> Professionalism is a term that must be understood in a special sense when applying it to policemen. Generally speaking, a profession provides a service (such as medical aid or legal advice) the quality of which the client is not in a position to judge for himself; therefore, a professional body and a professional code must be established to protect both the client from his ignorance and the profession from the client who supposes that he is not ignorant. The policeman differs from the doctor or lawyer, however, in important respects: first, his role is not to cure or advise but to restrain; and second, whereas health and counsel are welcomed by the recipients, restraint is not. If this is true, then professionalism among policemen will differ from professionalism in other occupations in that the primary function of the professional code will be to protect the practitioner from the client rather than the client from the practitioner.[37]

Wilson proceeds to consider the difference between the codes of the system and of professionalism in certain specific issues in police work: recruitment, law enforcement, informers, graft, authority, secrecy, violence, and public relations. His conclusions are interesting:

1. The prospects for a high level of professionalism in the police forces of many, if not most, large American cities seem dim.
2. The elimination of wholesale corruption of police forces by gamblers and syndicate hoodlums may be a necessary condition for the growth of police professionalism, but it is not a sufficient one.
3. Police professionalism is part of a "package"; it is possible that the benefits of police professionalism may be outweighed by the costs of other, necessarily related institutions. It is even possible that a professionalized police force is not always superior to its alternative.

The Police and Their Social Systems

Wilson makes the point that police professionalism is part of a "package." This may be interpreted several ways. One way is to observe that the police operate in the context of several interlocking social systems, each of which has an influence upon police role interpretation and all its ramifications, including the possibilities of professionalism—indeed, even how professionalism is defined. In short, *systemic perspective* is essential if one is to understand police problems. What does this mean?

A *social system* may be defined as an ordered arrangement of interrelated roles. While there is some question whether our legal or criminal justice system is truly a social system, to the extent that it is a system, the police are one of its important components. It is ordinarily the police who initiate the process of the system with prosecutor, judiciary, and corrections as other important components. It is a more or less ordered arrangement of interrelated roles, at least theoretically. Actually, there are many problems in the system pertaining to its interrelationships, which are examined in a later chapter.

In any event, this so-called criminal justice system is one of the "packages" that significantly affect what the police do and how they do it. By the same token, it may be said that the professionalization of the police, whatever this may mean, will inevitably proceed more or less apace of the professionalization of the other components in this system. It is "a package deal." The problems of police and community relations also tend to be systemic problems. To be sure, there *are* unique and specific problems of police and community relations. But, beyond this there are broader, systemic problems of community relations in the administration of justice.

The police and other parts of the criminal justice system are, in fact, part of several social systems, and these systems overlap and conflict at certain points. Police are part of a political and governmental social system, and operate in interrelated roles with legislative, executive, and judicial branches of government. Within this system, as suggested earlier, the police are influenced in what they do and how they do it by federal, state, and local law-making bodies, by city managers and mayors, by corporation counsels and city planners, and by the courts. As an illustration of conflicts between interrelated social systems, what a state legislature may decide about some aspect of the treatment of offenders may not coincide with the judgment of professional corrections personnel.

Another broad social system comprises the social institutions of society — the familial, educational, political, religious, and economic institutions and the mass media. Clearly, what the police do and how they do it is influenced by this network of social institutions.

The subject of social systems is usually explored at length in introductory sociology texts, so we will not expand on it here. But there is one further aspect of this subject that bears upon the individual police officer. He or she is the product of a particular background, or social environment. This includes certain experiences and certain social-institutional influences — family, social class, nationality, ethnic and cultural factors, race, religion, education, parental occupations, political views, and the like. The combination of these influences has produced certain attitudes, beliefs, and values in the individual police officer, as it does in any other person. How the officer sees and does things will be influenced to some extent by these background variables. One important yardstick for an effective, professional police officer in today's society will be the extent to which the officer comes to recognize that the world of which he or she is a product, and therefore the world as he or she perceives it, is not the only world there is.

SUMMING UP

We have suggested the several social system contexts of the police that bear directly on the questions of police role and police professionalism. We have also reviewed the complex question of police professionalism, integral as it is to the equally complex role question. If this discussion seems to have reflected confusion, ambiguity, and lack of consensus, it accurately mirrors the state of the art. The next chapter, dealing with the discretionary use of police power—as a correlative of role and professional concept—may identify the main issues more clearly.

NOTES

1. For further discussion of these benchmarks of a profession, see Bernard C. Brannon, "Professional Development of Law Enforcement Personnel," in A. F. Brandstatter and Louis A Radelet, eds., *Police and Community Relations: A Sourcebook* (Beverly Hills, Calif.: Glencoe, 1968), pp. 302–316.

2. Harold Wilensky, "The Professionalization of Everyone," *American Journal of Sociology* 70, no. 2 (September 1964): 137–158.

3. *Washington Post*, March 1975.

4. James M. Slavin, "How Can Policing Become a Profession?" *Proceedings of the Fifth National Institute on Police and Community Relations* (East Lansing, Mich.: Michigan State University, 1959). The discussion preceding the quote is based upon this same lecture.

5. Quinn Tamm, "Police Professionalism and Civil Rights," *Police Chief*, September 1964, p. 30. Reprinted by permission of the International Association of Chiefs of Police, Gaithersburg, Maryland.

6. V. A. Leonard, *Police Organization and Management* (Brooklyn, N.Y.: Foundation Press, 1951), p. 6.

7. Bernard C. Brannon, "Professional Development of Law Enforcement Personnel," in *Police and Community Relations: A Sourcebook*, A. F. Brandstatter and Louis A. Radelet, eds. (Beverly Hills, Calif.: Glencoe, 1968), pp. 403–408. Brannon presented these ideas in 1960; since then, much progress has been made in many states in establishing minimum training requirements for police officers.

8. Norman Cousins, *Saturday Review*, August 22, 1970, p. 32. Reprinted by permission.

9. James Q. Wilson, "Dilemmas of Police Administration," *Public Administration Review* 28, no. 5 (1968): 414.

10. Robert Shellow and Morton Bard, *Issues in Law Enforcement: Essays and Case Studies* (Reston, Va.: Reston, 1976), pp. 24–25.

11. See, for example, Melanie E. Baehr, John E. Furcon, and Ernest C. Froemel, *Psychological Assessment of Patrolman's Qualification in Relation to Field Performance* (Washington, D.C.: U.S. Government Printing Office, 1968); Elinor Ostrom, Roger B. Parks, and Gordon Whitaker, *Patterns of Metropolitan Policing* (Cambridge, Mass.: Ballinger, 1978); Leonard Territo, C. R. Swanson, Jr., and Neil C. Chamelin, *The Police Personnel Selection Process* (Indianapolis, Ind.: Bobbs-Merrill, 1977); California Commission on Peace Officer Standards and Training, *Project STAR: Impact of Social Trends on Crime and Criminal Justice* (Santa Cruz, Calif.: Davis, 1976); U.S. Department of Justice, LEAA, National Institute of Law Enforcement and Criminal Justice, *Police Educational Characteristics and Curricula*, Monograph Series (Washington, D.C.: U.S. Government Printing Office, 1975).

12. James Q. Wilson, *Varieties of Police Behavior: The Management of Law and Order in Eight Communities* (Cambridge: Harvard University Press, 1968), p. 281.

13. Ibid, p. 283.

14. James Q. Wilson, "Police and Their Problems: A Theory," in *Public Policy*, Yearbook of the Harvard University School of Public Administration (Cambridge, 1963), p. 74.

15. Louis A. Radelet, "Implications of Professionalism in Law Enforcement for Police-Community Relations," *Police*, July–August 1966, p. 82. Reprinted by permission of Charles C Thomas, Publisher.

16. Jack H. Grossman and William Kohnke, "Police Professionalism: An Attitudinal Approach," *Police Chief*, November 1976, p. 46.

17. Shellow and Bard, *Issues in Law Enforcement*, pp. 26–27.

18. Eleanor Harlow, "Problems in Police-Community Relations: A Review of the Literature," *Information Review on Crime and Delinquency* 1, no. 5 (February 1969): 13 National Council on Crime and Delinquency.

19. Jerome H. Skolnick, "The Police and the Urban Ghetto," *Research Contributions of the American Bar Foundation*, no. 3 (1968), p. 11.

20. U.S., President's Commission on Law Enforcement and Administration of Justice, *Field Surveys V* (Washington, D.C.: U.S. Government Printing Office, 1967), pp. 377–378.

21. Eleanor Harlow, "Problems in Police-Community Relations," p. 14. Reprinted by permission of the National Council on Crime and Delinquency.

22. Ibid., p. 15.

23. Albert J. Reiss, Jr., "Professionalization of the Police," in Brandstatter and Radelet, eds., *Police and Community Relations*, p. 216. The discussion of Reiss's ideas is based on this same article.

24. Ibid., p. 227. Reprinted by permission. For a similar analysis, see David J. Bordua and Albert J. Reiss, Jr., "Command, Control, and Charisma: Reflections on Police Bureaucracy," *American Journal of Sociology* 72 (July 1966.)

25. Wilensky, "The Professionalization of Everyone," p. 140.

26. U.S., President's Commission on Law Enforcement and Administration of Justice, *Task Force Report: The Police*, chap. 2.

27. David J. Bordua, "Comments on Police-Community Relations," *Law Enforcement Science and Technology*, Vol. 2 (Chicago: Illinois Institute of Technology Research Center, 1968).

28. Herman Goldstein, "Police Response to Urban Crises," *Public Administration Review* 28, no. 5 (1968): 422. Reprinted by permission.

29. This discussion is based on Michael Banton, "Social Integration and Police," *Police Chief* (April 1963): 8–20.

30. Bruce J. Terris, "The Role of the Police," *Annals of the American Academy of Political and Social Science* 374 (November 1967): 64

31. Jerome Skolnick, "The Police and the Urban Ghetto," *Research Contributions of the American Bar Foundation*, no. 3 (1968): 12.

32. Great Britain, Royal Commission on the Police, *Final Report* (London: Her Majesty's Stationery Office, 1962), p. 9.

33. William P. Brown, "Mirrors of Prejudice," *Nation* 208, no. 16 (April 21, 1969): 498–500.

34. Ibid, p. 499. Reprinted by permission.

35. John M. Pfiffner, "The Function of the Police in a Democratic Society," *Occasional Papers: Center for Training and Career Development* (Los Angeles: School of Public Administration, University of Southern California, 1967).

36. James Q. Wilson, "The Police and Their Problems," pp. 189–216. Reprinted by permission.

37. Ibid., pp. 200–211. Wilson relies here on a differentiation developed by Everett C. Hughes in *Men and Their Work* (Glencoe, Ill.: Free Press, 1958), pp. 140–141.

5

DISCRETIONARY USE
OF POLICE POWER

From policing to corrections, a common characteristic of criminal justice processes is the decisions or judgments made by designated status persons that affect the lives and destiny of other persons. Generally, these are weighty judgments, involving a well-recognized element of power to carry out enforcement and sanctions. As with all human judgments, however, there is latitude that invites argument, especially in a political climate that allows and, indeed, encourages such argument. Alternate judgments may be identified and their merits discussed. Small wonder that discretionary use of police power is perhaps the most sensitive, constant, and universal issue in police and community relations.

It is said that ours is a government by law, not a government by men. This means, of course, that those empowered by the people, from whom their authority is derived, are not free to exercise that power by whim or caprice. They are held accountable to the people to discharge their responsibilities within the limits of established law. A police officer, for example, might describe his or her job (however naively) by saying that it is his or her duty to enforce the law equally for all, no more and no less.

Would that it were so simple! If it were, there would probably be much less concern for police and community relations. But the fact is that the law is not really so impersonal, not so detached from what people do with it, from how they interpret it, and from how police enforce it. Moreover, the law does not cover every situation in which police officers may find themselves. Sometimes where there appears to be applicable law, police officers may be well advised to conduct themselves as though ignorant of the law, for to attempt to enforce it might invite Armageddon.

THE HUMAN SIDE OF THE LAW

The law is not an end in itself. Properly understood, it is a means to higher ends in human affairs, such as good order, justice, and individual liberty. In complex societies, law is an indispensable instrument of social control. It comes to life through what people make of it and what they do with it. In a totalitarian social system, law is a mechanism of tyranny, dedicated to order as an end in itself, coldly efficient because it is little concerned with the means used to maintain peaceable, conformist behavior. In a democratic society, however, there is (or should be) as much attention to procedural law as there is to substantive law. As Jerome Skolnick puts it, "The procedures of the criminal law . . . stress the protection of individual liberties *within* a system of social order."[1] Thus, we are reminded again of Jerome Hall's depiction of the police officer as "the living embodiment of democratic law."[2]

We said earlier that police work and police-community relations are of extraordinary importance in our society because police officers are authorized by the community they serve to exercise extraordinary power under certain circumstances. Both Albert Reiss and James Q. Wilson refer, in their analyses of the police-client relationship, to decisions by police officers that seriously affect the client's future, concerning which the client has little or no choice. The police officer's disposition of a case is, then, a *professional* judgment, a *discretionary* decision. As such, it presumes some latitude in choosing from among alternative possible actions, and there is responsibility for whatever determination is made.[3]

These views bring to mind Michael Banton's distinction between police authority and police power.[4] For in some decisions that the police officer must make, he cannot be sure that he has the moral support of the community. In such situations, when he acts with power but not necessarily with authority, the validity of his judgment in decision making is especially tested. An example would be enforcing gambling laws when the weight of opinion in the community prefers that such laws be ignored. In Wilson's terms, "the system" would suggest "discretion"; "professionalism" would suggest making arrests, including perhaps even one or two "city fathers." Either way, the effects on police-community relations are interesting to contemplate.

DISCRETION AND POLICE-COMMUNITY RELATIONS

The sensitivity of the question of police discretion is evident. It is heightened by the police power to restrain. Add to this the ambiguity of police role and the odds are good that police officers will be losers no matter what their decisions, because they are asked to do the impossible, that is, to leave everybody satisfied.

Because ours is a government by law, vast effort has been made to minimize the opportunities for the system to be manipulated to the advantage of the tyrant. *Officially*, therefore, police officers are allowed little room for discretion, or, one might say, little professional autonomy. It is ticklish, indeed, for police officials to speak publicly of discretionary use of police power—often called *selective enforcement*. One reason is that frank admission that police departments function with the discretionary use of police power as a basic assumption might be interpreted by the public as fundamentally undermining government by law.

By law and in theory, the police are expected to enforce all laws, to arrest everyone they see committing an offense. Clearly, this is absurd. Everybody knows that expecting the police to enforce all laws to the letter is absurd, police officers perhaps most of all; but up until the recent past, this absurdity has been kept a secret. Now, at last, police leaders are beginning to acknowledge that officers cannot function without considerable latitude in the exercise of personal discretion. Departmental policies and regulations have tended to ignore this elementary fact. Prosecutors and judges have reprimanded officers for exercising discretion, even as they wink at their own more extensive use of the same prerogative.

In short, police discretion is inevitable partly because the police cannot do everything, partly because many laws require interpretation before they can be applied, and partly because the community will not tolerate full enforcement of all laws all the time. Wilson adds a striking thought:

> In almost every public organization, discretion is exercised—indeed, from the client's viewpoint, the problem arises out of how and whether it is exercised—but the police department has the special property (shared with a few other organizations) that within it discretion increases as one moves *down* the hierarchy. In many, if not most, large organizations, the lowest ranking members perform the most routinized tasks and discretion over how those tasks are to be performed increases with rank. . . . [But in police organizations] the lowest ranking police officer—the patrolman—has the greatest discretion, and thus, his behavior is of greatest concern to the police administrator.[5]

DISCRETION AND THE POLICE ROLE

We have noted that autonomy in decision making is one of the marks of the professional. Wilson indicates that the line officer has the greatest autonomy, at least theoretically. Reiss focuses on police-officer autonomy in client relations and in coerced decisions relating to the future of clients. The key question from the client's viewpoint is correctly identified by Wilson as that of *how* and *whether* autonomy (discretion) is exercised.

Herman Goldstein points out that the law enforcement function of the police officer is relatively structured, that is, defined by statutes and court decisions. Therefore, it is somewhat controlled. Policy and supervision in the department may tighten these controls further. Even so, the patrol officer is left with considerable discretion in his law enforcement function. The use of discretion is simply a *sine qua non* of the job, however much it may be denied officially. When one considers the police officer's order maintenance function, one sees even more room for the exercise of discretion. We earlier noted Goldstein's point that, in carrying out his non-law-enforcement duties, the policeman frequently uses the authority he has by virtue of his role in the criminal process. Goldstein adds:

> Thus, the ability of a police officer to resolve a dispute and to eliminate a nuisance stems, in large measure, from widespread recognition of the fact that he has the authority to initiate criminal prosecutions. Indeed, in some situations, a police officer may actually exercise his authority—for example, by arresting an intoxicated person for safe keeping—even though he has no intention to initiate a criminal prosecution.[6]

Now the issue begins to get more complicated. If, as more and more observers insist, the order-maintenance and social-service functions of the police occupy the greater portion of patrol time, it develops that the city patrol officers spend most of their time in the least defined, least controlled aspects of their work. Here, the nature of responses is left largely to the discretion of the individual. He or she has, in effect, the decision-making responsibility of a highly trained professional, but too often is ill-prepared to handle that responsibility professionally. Hence, the community calls for a tighter rein on police-officer conduct, by one means or another, including civilian review boards and neighborhood control.

It may be, as some have speculated, that police departments insist on making their case for professionalism by stressing efficiency in law enforcement (a lesser part of their activity) partly because they sense a credibility gap if they base their case on their performance in the order-maintenance work that takes most of their time. Yet it is clearly in this part of their work that their cherished professionalism is most frequently and most critically tested. Law enforcement can ordinarily be handled by technician-specialists; it probably does not require professionals on the line, depending on how "professional" is defined. But order maintenance and peace keeping in our urban areas today call for officers possessing the autonomy and the ability of true professionals.

The demand by some community groups for tighter controls on police-officer behavior springs from what they perceive to be police abuses of delegated power. In effect, it means lack of public confidence in the professional competence of officers, and these challenges frequently relate to the performance of non-law-enforcement duties. The point is this: the more professionally competent the officers, in what they spend their patrol time doing, the less likely it is that there will be public demands for tight and rigid controls. Police organizations can best reduce public pressure for the establishment of citizen review boards and other external control mechanisms by improving the professional performance of their personnel.

SETTING GUIDELINES FOR PATROL OFFICERS

Our emphasis in this discussion is on the patrol officer who, as Wilson observes, "is almost solely in charge of enforcing those laws that are the least precise, or most ambiguous (those dealing with disorderly conduct, for example); or whose application is most sensitive to the availability of scarce resources and the policies of the administrator (those governing traffic offenses, for example."[7] Wilson goes on to mention that detectives, on the other hand, are mainly concerned with more precisely defined and serious crimes—after the crime has been committed. The patrol officer is more apt (except for vice squad detectives) to deal with offenses about which there are sharp differences in public opinion. Detectives are not much concerned with peace keeping, nor (except in juvenile work) with crime prevention.

It is seldom possible to specify in advance adequate guidelines for patrol officers' intervention, or how they should handle a given situation, especially when maintaining order. They may be told what *not* to do, but it is much more difficult to specify what they *should* do. At roll call, sergeants or lieutenants may exhort "going by the book," but experienced patrol officers know that "you can't always go by what the book says," and that there are many situations about which "the book" has nothing to say.[8]

It is therefore apparent that even in cities where police departments are enthusiastic about going by the book, much of the police work on the street is performed at the discretion of the line officer. And this can be the basis for considerable police-community tension and conflict. What is considered disorderly conduct or disturbing the peace, for example, varies widely by community and by neighborhood. In the absence of a complaint by a citizen, the police officer determines what is disturbing or disorderly.

There are two ancillary considerations. One is that many people believe in the myth that the police are the impartial enforcers of all the laws for all persons. It is when a police officer is thought to have substituted too much discretion for the letter of the law that a demand arises for more controls. "In reality," Eleanor Harlow says,

> while no doubt clear-cut violation of the law by police does occur, in many cases personal discretion is unavoidable and the problem becomes not one of eliminating discretion (an impossible goal) but of improving the ability of those men exercising it to do so in accord with community norms and values.[9]

One difficulty is that the community has many internal differences of opinion about norms and values. Another consideration is that the police officer believes that he has been endowed with special authority to guard the community against immorality, impropriety, and sundry affronts (as he sees them) to public decency. Here we may recall our initial point: problems pertaining to discretionary use of police power revert in some measure to the ambiguity of the police role. Any attempt to change the way in which patrol officers exercise personal discretion must consider the extent to which they may be persuaded to act in accordance with rules set down in advance. And this, in turn, depends upon how their job is defined.[10]

Although there still are plenty of spokesmen for the idea that police discretion does not or should not exist, the main thrust of the discussion in recent years has moved toward acceptance of the fact that it does exist and pervades all aspects of police work. So the real question is how to control or structure it. Relying to some extent on two excellent books on the subject by Kenneth Culp Davis,[11] Herman Goldstein has developed a thorough exploration of structuring police decision making. He summarizes:

> If discretion is to be exercised in an equitable manner, it must be structured; discretionary areas must be defined; policies must be developed and articulated; the official responsible for setting policies must be designated; opportunities must be afforded for citizens to react to policies before they are promulgated; systems of accountability must be established; forms of control must be instituted; and ample provisions must be made to enable persons affected by discretionary decisions to review the basis on which they were made.[12]

DISCRETION VERSUS DISCRIMINATION

Another extremely sensitive aspect of the discretionary use of police power comes to mind. If a patrol officer relies on personal judgment in dealing with people-related situations, it follows that his decisions are subject to his own personal prejudices, hang-ups, and predilections. In specific instances, it is a question of which of his decisions are legitimately discretionary or understandably "differential," and which of his decisions are patently unjust and discriminatory.

To be more concrete, Wilson states that "the patrolman believes, with considerable justification, that teenagers, Negroes, and lower income persons commit a disproportionate share of all reported crimes." Simply to be in one of these population categories makes one, statistically, more suspect than another. If, in addition, a person identified with one of these categories behaves unconventionally, the tab of "suspicious person" is promptly applied. The police would regard it as dereliction of their duty if they did not treat such persons with suspicion (to be suspicious is an important quality of the police subculture, as we shall see later), routinely question them on the street (stop and frisk), and detain them for further interrogation if a crime has occurred in the area.[13] This example illustrates the manner in which "group think"—actually, sterotypical—permeates police operations, many would say inevitably. Moreover, it also explains why some police administrators are stubborn about their concession that discretion should and must exist. As one chief phrased it, "When some people advocate the philosophy that a police officer has discretion in the field to arrest an individual or to take him home, they are talking about discriminatory law enforcement, which is police corruption."[14]

George Edwards, now a judge of the U.S. Court of Appeals and formerly Detroit police commissioner and justice of the Michigan Supreme Court, has pointed to abuses of the situation in terms of what is commonly referred to as "curbstone justice" or "alley court." Such police activity is unprofessional and frequently inhuman. It alienates citizens whose cooperation and support are essential if the police are to have any chance of coping with crime or preventing disorder.

THE DANGERS OF OVERSIMPLIFICATION

In this matter of discretion versus discrimination, however, it is easy to blame police officers and to overlook the factors that make their behavior more understandable, if not more acceptable. For example, the class composition of the particular community influences police behavior. Wilson has pointed out that, because relatively little public disorder occurs in middle-class suburban communities, it is rarely necessary for the police to intervene in situations of intense conflict in these areas.[15]

Wilson holds that harsh and unjust police treatment of blacks is as much a problem of social class as it is problem of prejudiced police officers. He does not question that many police officers are racially prejudiced. But, according to Wilson, even if all police officers were free of prejudice, blacks would still regard their treatment by the police as unjust. The reason is that a high proportion of violent crime is basically a lower-class phenomenon.[16] Blacks (and some other minority groups) are disproportionately lower class; therefore, a greater probability exists that blackness (or other visible signs of minority group status) will trigger the suspicion of police officers. As we have noted, this is a stereotypic reaction, but important in understanding police behavior in stressful circumstances. Skolnick has said that the "disposition to stereotype is an integral part of the policeman's world."[17] It is also typical bureaucratic behavior, by no means confined to the police: *When you've met one, you've met them all!*

Actually, the behavior we are discussing involves something more complex than one-way stereotyping. There are also, for example, counter-stereotypes held by members of minority groups toward police officers.

> The policeman . . . claims freedom from racial prejudice. He is, according to his own standards, not "biased," but merely truthful. Thus, the policeman would object . . . to the term racial bias as a portrayal of his attitude on two grounds: it is not descriptive, but accusatory; and it singles out the policeman when in fact he represents a wider body of opinion. His most important objection, however, would be to the ambiguity of the term when applied to the issue of how he does his job. Whatever his personal preferences, and indeed their influence upon his work, the policeman sees himself as a man who extends justice evenhandedly, a factor which in itself exerts some control over his behavior.[18]

DISCRETION AND THE PERTINENT VARIABLES

We have suggested that the exercise of police discretion depends upon a number of variables, one of which is the character and disposition of the community. Another, of course, is administrative policy and the pattern of supervision in the particular department. Still another is the officer's personal assessment of gain or loss that he or she can anticipate from intervention — for the suspect, the community, and the officer.[19]

It is a somewhat startling thought, but as the 1966 President's Crime Commission stated in *Challenge of Crime*, law enforcement policy is actually made by the patrol officer on the street. The commission referred to the criminal code, in practice, not as a set of specific instructions for police officers, but as "a more or less rough map of the territory in which policemen work. How an individual policeman moves around that territory depends largely on his personal discretion." The commission said that a police officer is "an arbiter of social values."[20] Our point regarding the officer's assessment of probable gains and losses as he or she determines the manner of intervention in a particular situation is stated by the commission in practical terms: the legal strength of the available evidence, the willingness of victims to press charges and of witnesses to testify, the temper of the community, and the time and information at the police officer's disposal.

The reference to the temper of the community needs a brief comment. In a quite basic sense, no matter what the criminal code, the particular community or neighborhood largely governs the level and pattern of policing that will be tolerated.[21] Banton implies this in his distinction between police authority and police power. He goes on to say that police officers are assisted in developing "good judgment" ("a good expression of the consensus of responsible opinion") by the courts, and by the influence of their own private life wherein they become aware of what other citizens think of them.

Communities and neighborhoods vary considerably in what they expect of the police. In effect, modern social conditions prescribe significant differences in both law enforcement and order maintenance, depending upon where one looks. In practical police terms, this means that a metropolitan police department works at its job with a different style in different precincts or divisions. This is hardly a novel organizational pattern, but little is said about it by administrators, for fear it will be interpreted as unequal protection or differential treatment. The distinctions that need to be made on questions of this kind are finely ground, and public administrators prefer to avoid them if possible. It should be understood that, in sound police administration, a policy of different styles of policing for different areas should *not* mean that some areas will get poorer service than others. These ideas obviously suggest the question of neighborhood or community control of the police, which is discussed in chapter 12.

THE QUESTION OF POLICY

The President's Crime Commission thought it "curious" that police administrators have seldom attempted to develop and articulate policies aimed at guiding the way police officers exercise their discretion on the street. There are policies and rules that deal extensively with many things, but, the commission said in *Challenge of Crime*, many choices are not covered:

> What such manuals almost never discuss are the hard choices policemen must make every day: whether or not to break up a sidewalk gathering, whether or not to intervene in a domestic dispute, whether or not to silence a street-corner speaker, whether or not to stop and frisk, whether or not to arrest. Yet these decisions are the heart of police work. How they are made determines to a large degree the safety of the community, the attitude of the public toward the police and the substance of court rulings on police procedures.[22]

The commission recognized the difficulty of designing such policies. But it insisted that the job can and should be done departmentally. The alternative is that the line officer will make policy—an administrative decision—by what he or she does or fails to do on the street. Adequate policy guidelines should still leave ample room for "professional autonomy." In like manner, surgeons are governed to some extent by necessary hospital rules and regulations. Their autonomy is certainly not absolute, but it is sufficient for their responsibility and commensurate with their professional attitude and competence. The rules and regulations protect the interests and rights of others, including the patient. The same should apply to police officers. Departmental policies and guidelines can help to make officers' conduct more predictable, and formulating and executing policy can help to make the police more conscious of neighborhood problems — more "culturally sensitive," as the Crime Commission phrased it.

> Police departments should develop and enunciate policies that give police personnel specific guidance for the common situations requiring exercise of police discretion. Policies should cover such matters, among others, as the issuance of orders to citizens regarding their movements or activities, the handling of minor disputes, the safeguarding of the rights of free speech and assembly, the selection and use of investigative methods, and the decision whether or not to arrest in specific situations involving specific crimes.[23]

POLICE ACCOUNTABILITY

Again, the theme of the Crime Commission's recommendation is the need to *control* police discretion through legitimate authority, not to pretend to eliminate it. The courts exercise control, to be sure, and—rather reluctantly—legislative bodies occasionally do it too. But there seems to be substantial support for the principle that it is best done mainly by police departments themselves. If controls are not satisfactorily handled internally by the departments, then they will be handled in one form or another by civil review. Reiss succinctly summarizes the issue:

> The issue of professionalization of the police is one of whether civic accountability will take the form of an inquiry into an individual's work within an organization, whether it will take the form of accountability of an occupational organization of police, or whether accountability rests with a local police organizational system headed by a chief as the "accountable officer."[24]

Reiss suggests that the central question is whether decision making by patrol officers is of a kind that is "open to professionalization." He asserts, as have others, that the tendency has been to professionalize police organization rather than police practice — the department rather than the individual. Thus, the key question for Reiss is whether the patrol officer's work requires truly professional abilities. If it does, then the patrol officer should have the professional autonomy corresponding with these abilities and responsibilities.

Reiss concludes that the evidence is mixed. He thinks that, in the long run, some aspects of police patrol work will require professionals, while other aspects of this work can be adequately handled by technicians. He insists that such differentiation in occupational specialties is necessary if we are to cope realistically with the problem of police professionalism.

Goldstein devotes an entire chapter to police accountability, so important does he believe it to be. He cites what he calls "one of the major paradoxes in policing in this country":

> We have insisted on maintaining the police as a responsibility of local government in order to assure accountability and an opportunity for local influence over so potentially powerful a government activity. Yet at the same time we have constructed various devices which, in attempting to protect the police from pernicious influences at the local level, effectively shield the police from the communities they serve. The net result of these conflicting aims is that considerable ambiguity exists as to who in fact is responsible for the many decisions that are made in the running of a police agency, and there is a great deal of uncertainty over how the public is supposed to control police operations.[25]

THE MATTER OF TRAFFIC LAW ENFORCEMENT

The exercise of police officer discretion in traffic law enforcement is interesting to consider. A study by John Gardiner concluded that traffic ticket writing is a bureaucratic, technical specialization.[26] It is a specialization in *work assignment*, not one of professionalism. Such decision making is technical, and subject to strict bureaucratic rules and review. Traffic enforcement officers themselves do not feel that they have autonomy; they see themselves simply as specialists. It is a job, not a profession.

Other branches of police work constitute a better case for professionalism, with correspondingly greater latitude assumed in decision making. Preiss and Ehrlich analyzed the similarities and differences in the way traffic enforcement officers in a state police agency on the one side, and the public on the other side, viewed activities such as enforcing the speed limit and using unmarked cars, semimarked cars, and radar. They found that both the officers and the public agreed on the goal: discreet enforcement. The problem was disagreement on the interpretation of *discreet*. Thus, the police-public relationship here was predicated on conflict:

> With high consensus on their goals, they clash not so much on the means to be employed but on how and by whom control is to be maintained over these means. The respective interests of both were mirrored openly not only in the claims they made for discretionary law enforcement but also in the *policeman's* concern for an uncontestable arrest and the *public's* appeal for consideration of intent.[27]

Police officers writing traffic tickets. They do not enjoy the public resentment and hostility that traffic law enforcement engenders. This is one reason the so-called quota system was invented. Traffic patrol duty may be identified as adding to the social isolation of the police from the community. So may the automated processing of traffic tickets, which allows for no discretion.[28]

AUTHORIZED AND UNAUTHORIZED DISCRETION

The police-community interest in police discretion is broader, however, than traffic law enforcement. Skolnick believes that the issue of police discretion is the epitome of the problem of order and legality. The basic issue is whether there should be, in his language, "a loosening or a tightening of restraints on the decisional latitude of the police."[29] An important distinction should be made, he argues, between *authorized* and *unauthorized* discretion; most of the problems revolve around lack of clarity on what discretion is authorized — how much, under what circumstances, and so on. Again, this confusion suggests the importance of control by policy guidelines and other means.

Even when the useful distinction between authorized and unauthorized discretion is applied, however, some difficulties remain. Complexities in decision making are still present even when discretion is clearly authorized; and they are compounded when discretion is unauthorized. Unauthorized discretion appears especially to be the issue in tense encounters where police officers exercise discretion and citizens contest their authority to do so. This exemplifies Banton's distinction between authority and power. The issue is reflected in the term *arbitrary police behavior*. For street police officers, however, the uniform constitutes authority and, as Skolnick says, they are "usually willing to back up a challenge" with all the force they can command, particularly if they perceive themselves to be in danger. At such a time, rules are no help.

The element of perceived danger is generally believed to be an important conditioner of police behavior. Banton discusses this point at some length, and

Skolnick observed that, when street police officers feel they are in control of the situation, their behavior is apt to be more tempered. When they encounter hostility, they are tempted to make strong claims of authority, sometimes with frail, if any, legal justification.[30] Another influence upon their behavior is the history of prior relations with a particular type of suspect, the perceptual shorthand that identifies what Skolnick calls the "symbolic assailant," that is, the person who uses gesture, language, and attire that officers have come to associate with violence and danger. The point is this: street police officers are influenced in their discretionary determinations, subtly but firmly, by perceived threats to their survival. Whether or not they have been delegated authority, hence legal grounds, for a particular judgment seems to be of lesser importance.

Some of the problem has to do with the training of police officers. Prevailing training methods and content do not contribute much toward inculcating qualities of good judgment, prudence, and common sense in police recruits. What *is* taught along this line is often culture-bound. These are matters mainly of training techniques and methods. To illustrate the point, if the educational objective is to develop good judgment, then case analysis and various projective instructional techniques, such as role playing, with considerable small group discussion, surpass straight lecture and tidy notebook keeping. Training method (or content) is not, of course, a panacea for patrol officers' problems in the street, where instant decisions are routinely required. But some approaches to training are surely more relevant to the real world than others.

LEGAL GROUNDS FOR POLICE DISCRETION

The law, under our system, unquestionably allows and indeed encourages discretionary evaluation and judgment throughout the criminal justice process, by the police officer, the prosecutor, the courts, and the correctional authorities. A cardinal principle is that each offender should be dealt with as an individual. The misuse or usurpation of delegated power in the system is not uniquely a police problem; judges and prosecutors have been known to stretch their discretion to unconscionable extremes of either leniency or severity.

Judges and prosecutors enjoy the luxury of time in their deliberations. The street police officer frequently has no such advantage. For this reason, legal scholars have become increasingly concerned about what Skolnick terms "introducing arrangements to heighten the visibility of police discretion to permit its control by higher authority."[31] Wayne LaFave is one of these legal analysts. He is the author of *Arrest*, one work in a series dealing with the range of the criminal justice system. He states his primary premise as follows:

> From the point of view of either the individual suspect or the community as a whole, the issue is not so much whether police are efficient, or whether the corrections process is effective, but whether the system of criminal justice administration in its entirety is sensible, fair, and consistent with the concepts of a democratic society.[32]

LaFave joins those who contend that there has been a traditional failure to recognize the existence and importance of police discretion. His discussion of the reasons for this attitude includes such factors as overly strict interpretation of substantive criminal law, the assumption that only legislative and judicial bodies should decide what conduct is criminal, concern and uncertainty whether the rule of law is adequately safeguarded by police exercise of discretion, and the assumption that prosecutors are more competent to exercise discretion than are the police.

LaFave observes that the question of police discretion has not received careful legislative attention. There is considerable evidence that legislative bodies either specifically deny police discretion, or consciously ignore it. Generally, appellate courts have not recognized the propriety of police discretion either. LaFave writes that where discretion is recognized as proper, courts have not indicated what standards ought to control the exercise of such discretion:

> The exercise of discretion by the police, which seems inevitable in current criminal justice administration, continues unrecognized. In practice, policies to guide the individual officer in deciding whether to make an arrest are not formally developed within the police agency, and no sustained effort is made to subject existing practices to reevaluation.[33]

Along lines similar to Goldstein, LaFave has analyzed the measures that might be established to acknowledge the need for police discretion while coping effectively with the hazards involved—what Goldstein refers to as "structuring" discretion. These measures include wider public understanding of the issue (with correspondingly greater likelihood that the public will support the principle of necessary, though regulated, police discretion); the elevation of the level of police professional competence; improved intradepartmental review and control of discretion through administrative policy, supervision, and discipline; more use of criminal action against officers who abuse their discretionary power; and more use by defendants of their constitutional right to equal protection—which would provoke challenges of the criteria used by the police in invoking criminal process.

As we have noted, the issue of discretion exercised by an individual police officer on the street in dealing with an individual citizen incorporates the question of dealing differently with various groups of citizens—for example, because of racial or cultural considerations, or social-class differentials—and of dealing differently with various neighborhoods or areas in a city. The policy questions involved are extremely complex, one reason they are seldom discussed. As LaFave says:

> Notwithstanding the great importance and significance of these and other instances of discretionary enforcement, the police have failed to evaluate carefully such enforcement policies or even to acknowledge that such practices exist. Rather, most departments attempt to maintain the existing stereotype of the police as ministerial officers who enforce all of the laws, while they actually engage in a broad range of discretionary enforcements.[34]

"It is understandable," LaFave continues,

> that a police administrator may be willing to have the myth of full enforcement continue. Full enforcement is consistent with impartiality, while acknowledged discretionary enforcement may be challenged as unfair, inconsistent, or arbitrary. The

image of full enforcement raises less of a public relations problem than does the image of the police agency as a formulator of enforcement policy. Finally, police training is an easier task in a department committed to the facade of full enforcement than in one in which it is assumed that police officers must share some responsibility for making decisions with important social implications.[35]

Jerome Hall and Joseph Goldstein (of the Yale Law School; not related to Herman Goldstein) are among those who have taken a somewhat more conservative stance on the subject of police discretion. Hall subscribed to the thesis that there must be a sharp demarcation between police and judicial functions, and that therefore the police should be strictly confined to so-called ministerial duties. It is not the police officer's job, he insisted, to decide whether a person under arrest is guilty of a crime; the police arrest only "on reasonable ground." Nor is it the police job, he continued, to define or declare any general rules of law. And finally, he said, "whatever the police in our system may think the rules of law mean, their interpretations are not authoritive."[36]

However, most of those who have studied the issue of police discretion would probably agree with LaFave:

> There are ways of recognizing police discretion and of controlling its exercise. Legislatures can give explicit attention to police discretion and prescribe criteria to guide the exercise of that discretion. This is the trend at the sentencing and correctional stages of the criminal process, and there is no reason to believe that this sort of legislation would be less appropriate at the arrest stage. Courts can subject police discretion to the kind of review which sometimes occurs in regard to economic regulatory agencies.
>
> The development of an "administrative law" in the enforcement field is as important as it is in the field of economic regulation, but while the one has been given sustained attention, the other has been completely neglected. Greater legislative and judicial recognition of the importance of police discretion might in turn encourage police administrators to acknowledge its importance and attempt to devise methods of meaningful evaluation of existing policies.
>
> The obvious complexity of the task of dealing adequately with police discretion at the arrest stage makes it all the more important that a start be made immediately.[37]

THE GRAVITY OF THE ISSUE

Taken collectively, the questions that arise in connection with the exercise of discretion by police officers constitute a major issue, perhaps *the* major issue, in police and community relations. Human judgments about the use of such extraordinary delegated power are bound to attract critics, some righteous, some malevolent. The genius of checks and balances within the democratic system is again sharply underscored. In the case of the police, the issue of discretion is always touchy and explosive. Stephen Wildstrom, former managing editor (1968–69) of the *Michigan Daily* at the University of Michigan, expressed a view indicative of this in an article in the *Nation:*

> American society will never be peaceful so long as significant portions of that society are systematically terrorized by the police. There will be no peace because, as blacks have learned and students are learning, the cops are above the law, and the only satisfying way to respond to their violence is with violence of one's own. And no

matter what kind of pronouncements come down from the police brass, the terror will continue as long as individual cops are immune from attempts by citizens to make them responsible for their acts. Despite the assertions of commissioners, chiefs and mayors, police departments have proved themselves to be at best unable, and at worst unwilling, to discipline their own.[38]

Such a view of the police, not uncommon today in our big cities, reveals how wide and deep some observers believe the chasm between police and community to be. Many police officers, not surprisingly, find such a view very difficult to digest, and indeed threatening. Skolnick has raised the question of the conditions under which the police, as authority figures, may feel threatened. William Westley was one of the first to deal with this question in his study of the conditions under which the police turn to violence.[39] We earlier mentioned the so-called symbolic assailant, the individual the police officer responds to as embodying disrespect for and attacks on his authority. Violent response to such individuals is justified as "handling the situation," saving face, "not taking any crap," and so on.

As Westley said, given the working-class family backgrounds of many police officers, when physical force *is* used, it is often justified by officers as a way of dealing with disrespect. As police officers perceive more and more situations as challenges to their authority, they tend to close ranks, to shore up their own internal solidarity, and to defend themselves against outside influences with what Pfiffner calls guild protectionism.

Both Westley and William Kephart found in their research that a negative attitude toward blacks was common among white police officers. Kephart observed that the higher the actual rate of black arrests in a district, the higher was the degree of overestimation of that rate by white policemen in that district.[40] The point here is one Skolnick makes:

> The Negro population is no longer so cowed as it once was, unfortunately for the patrol police. . . . When a policeman pushes a man who knows his rights, he receives an understandably hostile response. In an earlier period (as Westley found), the police used outright violence to maintain respect. It is now more difficult for them . . . to maintain control through these techniques. . . . But it is not color that is necessarily the determining factor. . . . When a citizen [read: *any* citizen] makes a policeman sweat to take him into custody, he has created the situation most apt to lead to police indignation and anger.[41]

Arthur Niederhofer, a retired New York City police officer, vividly portrays the police officer's approach to a situation in terms of the vital importance of "handling his beat."[42] We referred earlier to police officers' pleading that "you can't always go by the book." Showing "who is boss" appears to be very high on the list of values that street police officers hold sacred. As such, it is a weighty consideration in understanding what the police officer calls the *practicalities* of his job, with particular relevance in understanding his exercise of discretion.

SUMMING UP

Our discussion has moved inevitably into the intriguing matter of the self-image of the police officer, because self-image is closely related to questions of police role, police professionalism (it is said that a professional police officer is first of all an officer who *sees himself* as a professional), and into the difficult question of discretionary use of police power. The self-image of the police officer will be our focus as we begin part 2.

How to conclude on the matter of discretion? We may say that the street patrol officer necessarily exercises discretion, both in keeping order and in suppressing crime. In managing conflict, the patrol officer's task is to maintain civic peace amid circumstances in which various parties often disagree on what constitutes a fair settlement. In these circumstances, the officer is frequently aware of hostility toward him, of challenges to his authority as represented by disrespect, and of the ever-present danger of violence in which his own survival may be at stake. He is strongly motivated to control the situation by whatever means he deems necessary, often without too much attention to its by-the-book legality.

In suppressing crime, the officer is likely to base judgments about persons on their appearance, their attitude, the possible history of past relations, and stereotypic images of symbolic assailants and suspicious persons. Often such judgments are based upon doubtful authority (for instance, authority to question or to search suspects), and thus create an ambiguous and often controversial basis for his actions, especially since there is often no departmental policy on such matters, and the law is nondirective.

Herman Goldstein provides an appropriate sequel:

> The police have sought professional status. But professional status does not normally accrue to individuals performing ministerial functions. One of the marks of a true profession is the inherent need for making value judgments and for exercising discretion based upon professional competence. To deny that discretion is exercised gives support to those citizens who maintain that the job of a police officer is a simple one, that it is not worthy of professional status. By acknowledging the discretionary role the police do fulfill, the drive toward a higher degree of respect and recognition for law enforcement personnel is given impetus.[43]

NOTES

1. Jerome H. Skolnick, *Professional Police in a Free Society*, (New York: National Conference of Christians and Jews, 1967)

2. Jerome Hall, "Police and Law in a Democratic Society," *Indiana Law Journal* 28, no. 2 (Winter 1953).

3. Albert J. Reiss, Jr., "Professionalization of the Police," in A. F. Brandstatter and Louis A. Radelet, eds., *Police and Community Relations*, (Beverly Hills, Calif.: Glencoe, 1968) p. 216.

4. Michael Banton, "Social Integration and Police," *Police Chief*, April 1963, pp. 8–20.

5. James Q. Wilson, *Varieties of Police Behavior*, p. 7. Reprinted by permission.

6. Herman Goldstein, "Police Response to Urban Crises," *Public Administration Review* 28, no. 5 (1968): 417. Reprinted by permission.

7. James Q. Wilson, *Varieties of Police Behavior: The Management of Law and Order in Eight Communities* (Cambridge: Harvard University Press, 1968), p. 8. Reprinted by permission.

8. Ibid., p. 66.

9. Eleanor Harlow, "Problems in Police-Community Relations: A Review of the Literature, *Information Review on Crime and Delinquency* 1, no. 5 (February 1969): 16. Reprinted by permission of the National Council on Crime and Delinquency.

10. Wilson, *Police Behavior*, p. 11.

11. Kenneth Culp Davis, *Discretionary Justice* (Baton Rouge, La.: Louisiana State University Press, 1979); and by the same author, *Police Discretion* (St. Paul, Minn.: West, 1975).

12. Herman Goldstein, *Policing A Free Society* (Cambridge, Mass., Ballinger, 1977), p. 100.

13. Wilson, *Police Behavior*, p. 40.

14. A. O. Archuleta, "Police Discretion v. Plea Bargaining," *Police Chief*, April 1974, p. 78.

15. James Q. Wilson, "Dilemmas of Police Administration," *Public Administration Review* 28, no. 5 (1968): 411. Reprinted by permission.

16. For documentation of this point see, for example, U.S., President's Commission on Law Enforcement and Administration of Justice, *Crimes of Violence*, prepared by Marvin E. Wolfgang (Washington, D.C.: U.S. Government Printing Office, 1967), pp. 166–169.

17. Jerome H. Skolnick, *Justice Without Trial: Law Enforcement in Democratic Society* (New York: John Wiley & Sons, 1967), p. 83.

18. Ibid, p. 104. Reprinted by permission of John Wiley & Sons.

19. James Q. Wilson has devised a helpful chart reflecting significant variables related to police exercise of discretion. The chart appears in James Q. Wilson, *Varieties of Police Behavior*, p. 85.

20. U.S., President's Commission on Law Enforcement and Administration of Justice, *The Challenge of Crime in a Free Society* (Washington, D.C.: U.S. Government Printing Office, 1967), p. 10.

21. For an interesting case study of the adaption of a metropolitan police department to community mores and temper, see Howard S. Becker and Irving Louis Horowitz, "The Culture of Civility: Deviance and Democracy in the City," *Transaction* 7, no. 6 (April 1970): 10–19. See also Egon Bittner, "The Police on Skid-Row: A Study of Peace-keeping," *American Sociological Review* 32 (October 1967): 699–715; and by the same author, "Police Discretion in Emergency Apprehension of Mentally Ill Persons," *Social Problems* 14 (Winter 1967), published by the Society for the Study of Social Problems.

22. U.S., President's Commission on Law Enforcement and Administration of Justice, *Challenge of Crime in a Free Society* (Washington, D.C.: U.S. Government Printing Office, 1967), p. 103.

23. Ibid., p. 104.

24. Albert J. Reiss, "Professionalization of the Police," p. 222. Reprinted by permission.

25. Goldstein, *Policing a Free Society*, p. 132.

26. John A. Bardiner, "Police Discretion: The Case of Traffic Law Enforcement" (Ph.D. dissertation, Harvard University, 1966).

27. Jack J. Preiss and Howard J. Ehrlich, *An Examination of Role Theory: The Case of the State Police* (Lincoln: University of Nebraska Press, 1966), p. 153.

28. Jerome H. Skolnick, *Justice Without Trial*, pp. 55–56, 73–80.

29. Ibid., p. 71.

30. Ibid., p. 90.

31. Ibid., p. 71.

32. Wayne R. LaFave, in the Foreword to *Arrest: The Decision to Take a Suspect Into Custody* (Boston: Little, Brown, 1965). Reprinted by permission. See also: Sanford H. Kadish, "Legal Norm and Discretion in the Police and Sentencing Processes," *Harvard Law Review* 75 (1962): 904–931; Joseph Goldstein, "Police Discretion Not to Invoke the Criminal Process: Low-Visibility Decisions in the Administration of Justice," *Yale Law Journal* 60 (1960): 543–594.

33. LaFave, *Arrest*, pp. 81–82.

34. Ibid., p. 494.

35. Ibid., pp. 494–495.

36. Hall, "Police and Law."

37. LaFave, *Arrest*, pp. 494–495.

38. Stephen H. Wildstrom, "Mugged by the Sheriffs: An Anecdote,"*Nation* 208, no. 16 (April 21, 1969): 496–497. Reprinted by permission.

39. William A. Westely, "Violence and the Police," *American Journal of Sociology* 59 (July 1953): 34–41.

40. William M. Kephart, *Racial Factors and Urban Law Enforcement* (Philadelphia: University of Pennsylvania Press, 1957), pp. 94–95.

41. Skolnick, *Justice Without Trial*, p. 88.

42. Arthur Niederhoffer, *Behind the Shield* (Garden City, N.Y.: Doubleday, Anchor Books, 1969), p. 60.

43. Herman Goldstein, "Police Discretion: The Ideal Versus the Real," *Public Administration Review* 23, no. 3 (September 1963).

SUMMARY OF PART 1

Our main objective in part 1 has been to lay a foundation for the study of police-community relations. We began by reviewing the historical background. We next discussed its scope through various concepts. Then we analyzed three interrelated, fundamental issues that must be considered in order to gain an understanding of current problems of police-community relations:

1. The question of police role.
2. The question of police professionalism
3. The question of discretionary use of police power

The Anglo-Saxon background of English and American policing was based on the principle of self-policing, with every citizen expected to do police work. The people were the police, and the police were the people. When the idea of an organized metropolitan police force appeared in the early nineteenth century, British parliament was forthrightly opposed to it on the ground that it threatened liberty. But the so-called Peelers came into being, and their influence soon became evident even in the United States. Gradually, however, the important principle of self-policing—of widespread participation by private citizens in police work—faded. In the recent past, the isolation of the police from the community reached a serious stage in the United States.

In democratic society, the conduct of the police officer is ideally the living expression of the rule of law, with all its values and potentialities. Democratic law is *ethical* law, and this must be stressed in the training of all police officers. If the police officer's behavior conforms with the values of this system, he becomes the most important official in its hierarchy.

The police officer of today seems to be more in the public eye than in the past. Social change, particularly its effect on people-to-people relations, is the cause of this phenomenon, to which the police have responded both negatively and positively. Among the evidences of positive response has been the development during the past thirty years of police leadership in community relations.

Specialized police training in community relations dates back to the 1940s. Institutes on police and community relations were initiated in the 1950s, and many varied projects and programs were undertaken throughout the country in the ensuing years. Dramatization of the deficiencies of these programs in the later 1960s produced greater concern for the effects of such programs on the attitudes and behavior of both police and nonpolice participants.

The idea of police community relations has been defined many different ways. A sound conception views it as a combination of public relations, community service, and community participation. The community participation aspect uses interprofessional or teamwork approaches to solving community problems: for example, crime prevention through combined efforts of police and community. The appropriate emphasis in police-community relations programs is preventing both crime and civic disorder. The concept is also increasingly systemic in its scope, recognizing that the community relations problems of the police are, in large part, problems of the entire criminal justice system. Thus, it follows that police problems must be studied in systemic perspective.

Assuming that there is, theoretically at least, a certain ideal relationship between police and community, it would clearly depend upon mutual expectations: What should the community expect from the police? What should the police expect from the community? The question of the role of the police in today's society is, therefore, a central consideration in effecting an ideal relationship between police and community.

In broad terms, the police have two primary and complementary functions: (1) law enforcement, and (2) order maintenance and social service. In the early years of organized American policing, the emphasis was placed upon the second function, coinciding with the British model. Twentieth-century American policing, however, has moved toward emphasizing law enforcement and crime suppression. With the two main roles clearly interrelated, and every police department expected to fulfill both, the present predicament regarding the role of the police is basically a question of *emphasis:* Which function ought to be paramount? The two roles place demands upon the police that are conflicting and literally impossible for them to fulfill, because they require conflicting responses. In the terms of sociological role theory, it is a classic case of role conflict and role ambiguity.

The essence of the role hang-up lies in the absence of general agreement between police and socially heterogeneous communities on what should be stressed in police work, and how it should be carried out. Techniques that may conceivably result in suppressing crime are also sometimes techniques that may conceivably cause civic tension and turmoil. Some people want crime suppressed even at some cost in civil liberties; others want civil liberties protected even at some cost in crime.

Where a police administrator stands on this issue will strongly influence such matters as departmental organization, operational strategies and tactics, recruitment standards for officers, training methods for police recruits, and every other significant facet of agency policy. Both traditionalist and progressive positions appear on the role question, in and out of police departments, and the dispute is currently lost in rhetoric. Hence, we see one more example of contemporary political and social groups drawing away from each other instead of seeking to reconcile their views through reasoned communication. There is, in effect, a combative encounter of opposing political and occupational value systems.

Questions hinging directly on the definition of police role concern the meaning of police professionalism, how desirable a goal professionalism is, and how it may be achieved. If, for example, the primary duty of the police is to suppress crime through organization for law enforcement, the model professional police agency will stress managerial and operational efficiency. If, on the other hand, the primary police responsibility is peace keeping and conflict management, the model professional police agency will stress humanistic values. The problems of police professionalism and police-community relations will remain unresolved until the question of police role is resolved. This is so because the key to police professionalism lies in client relationships with the police, and in public attitudes toward and expectations of the police.

This point is well illustrated in the matter of discretionary use of police power. The desirable relationship of order and freedom, of authority and liberty, is routinely tested in the decisions of the patrol officer. This is a crucially important extension of the role-professionalism dilemma into the realm of practical police work. So intense is this philosophical conflict that the police refrain from publicly acknowledging that they exercise discretion— indeed, that it is impossible to conceive of their work without it—for fear of negative public reaction to the discretionary principle, for fear, in fact, that they might even be accused of undermining the system.

The issue is complex, but comes down to this: modern police work makes discretion in the exercise of police power inevitable and, in fact, desirable. This idea harmonizes with the assertion that street patrol duty in our cities requires genuine professional competence, and that professionals must have a certain amount of professional autonomy within a structure of departmental guidelines and controls. But the difficulty is that, because most patrol officers today lack this professional competence, their appropriate authority is too often improperly used.

In the recent move to shift police work to a professional level, more attention has been devoted to professionalizing police organizations than to professionalizing police practices. Discretion and discrimination are frequently confused. Police power is commonly imposed arbitrarily, especially where the police officer feels that his authority is challenged or that his life is endangered by "suspicious persons" or symbolic assailants.

Some guidelines are essential, therefore, in controlling police behavior, even when the patrol officer is assumed to be a full-fledged professional. Legislatures and courts have some responsibility in providing such controls, but most of it should be provided by departmental policies, supervision, and discipline. The growing concern that it is already too late for this action has been reflected in agitation for establishment of various forms of external control. One way or another, the police must be held accountable to the community for what they do and how they do it. This means to *all* the community, for the police must be the police of all the people.

PART 2

Psychological Considerations

6

THE SELF-IMAGE
OF THE POLICE OFFICER

We have noted that the police have attracted unprecedented public and scholarly attention in recent years. Concern about civil disorders and about rampant crime has caused citizens and scholars to take a hard look at law enforcement capabilities and practices. The police have been accused of not being able
to handle either of these situations, and sometimes of contributing to both. To
be a police officer in these times requires a certain hardiness. Many people
wonder why a person would want to be a police officer, all things considered.
Recruitment has been and still is a problem in some places, despite improved
financial incentives, and not many officers choose to remain in the service
beyond retirement age when circumstances permit a choice. The morale of the
police is also a matter of unusual scholarly interest.

THE MORALE PROBLEM

The situation commonly referred to as the "morale problem" of the police is as
variously defined as is police professionalism, with a tendency to settle for
rather superficial explanations; for example, that the police morale problem is
largely a matter of money. Accordingly, improved police salaries and pension
benefits are seen as the answer. There is certainly no opposition here to improvement of the financial security of police officers, but the problem is not that
simple.

To explore the morale problem requires some analysis of the psychological
dynamics of police work, with special attention to the individual police officer.
Morale pertains to the attitude, mental and emotional, that an individual has
about the tasks he or she is expected to perform. What is called *good* morale is
a state of well-being that stems from a sense of purpose and confidence in the
future. It depends on role conception, role performance, and role satisfaction.
Morale is intimately related to self-respect which, in turn, contributes to a
positive self-image.

Simply defining morale in these terms provides a clue to the particular
problem of the police officer. If morale is related to role, and if police work is a
classic example of role conflict and role ambiguity, it follows that police officers
must have a special kind of self-image problem. Our purpose in this chapter is
to discuss this hypothesis.

THE QUESTION OF PERSONAL IDENTITY

How does a person learn who he is? Psychologists tell us that an individual discovers a large part of the answer to this question in the feedback he gets from others. To illustrate this point, we may say that people harbor certain attitudes regarding what a person does—his job or calling. This is what is meant by *ascribed status*. Some jobs have high status, others, low status, depending upon such attitudes. The status of a person's job or occupation is an important factor in the satisfaction he gets from it, but it is, of course, not the only factor.

What a person does for a living is one basis of feedback for his self-image, for learning who he is and how he rates in the status hierarchy of a given society. The feedback process means simply that each of us governs his actions according to the estimate he believes others are making of him. This may be tabbed the *social self*. An individual discovers who he is by seeing himself reflected in the actions of others toward him.

We have said that occupation is one source of personal identity. Possessions, where we live, what we do for recreation, and what we wear are others. However, we tend to screen or filter the information that comes to us in the feedback process, to be selective in what we perceive and accept about ourselves. We tend to see and accept what is pleasant about ourselves and provides a positive image, to reject what is negative, and often to project on others what we cannot accept in ourselves. Some psychologists say that the closer our self-image is to the image that most people hold of us, the nearer we are to good mental health. Achieving this realistic appraisal of ourselves is the process and goal of maturation.

The Socialization Process in Childhood

A brief review of elementary childhood psychology is helpful here. Socialization begins with birth. The helpless infant identifies with the adults around him for satisfaction of his basic needs. In time, the child begins to see himself through the eyes of the adults. Through their behavior toward him, he develops self-confidence and self-respect, or the opposite. His actions are strongly affected by the picture he has of himself. As Oberlin College sociologist J. Milton Yinger puts it:

> Environments that fill a child with self-doubt and even self-hatred lay the basis for later attacks on one's self, in the form of alcoholism, mental illness, or irresponsibility—or attacks on the community, in the form of crime and disregard of the interests of others.[1]

Allison Davis and Robert Havighurst, in *Father of the Man*, expressed the idea as follows:

> If a child is to develop an effective conscience, two conditions should be met. First, the child should receive complete *love* from his parents, or from his parent-substitutes; second, he should receive socially appropriate *prohibitions* from them.

The love-relationship seems to be necessary as a basis for the best type of identification. The prohibitions are necessary in order that the child may take into himself a
warning and punishing voice. Thus, parents who never punish their children (either
by corporal punishment or by withdrawing affection from them) would not be able to
instill a warning, punishing conscience in them. On the other hand, parents who
never show affection to their children would not instill a conscience in them either, *no
matter how much they punished them*, because their children would not love them
enough to want to be good.[2]

Wayne State University educational psychologist Mildred Peters adds this
point:

It is a well known fact that children and adults who find it hard to relate to others, or
who are unwilling to show respect for the rights of others, are people who have
either been denied love returns for giving up instinctual demands, or they are people
who have never been helped to bear frustration.[3]

Conscience and self-respect, then, are basic requirements in sound personality development. Needless to say, many children grow up without either.
Clear, consistent standards of behavior and supportive affection are not provided by parents or by significant others. If a child is to be a successful adult,
he needs models of successful adults with whom to identify. This is expressed,
for example, in the collecting of baseball cards. Boys need adult male models to
teach them what it is to be a man. When such models are not available, crude
and inadequate definitions of manhood are created, which may result in painful
answers to the question, who am I? And as Yinger points out, there is a
self-perpetuating quality to this kind of pattern: children who have had a
problem of identity become the parents of another generation for whom they
cannot supply the proper balance of affection and discipline.

The most difficult task in growing up is in coming to terms with one's self, of
learning who one is, what one can do, and how one stands in relation to others.
For those in seriously disadvantaged environments, this task is especially
difficult. Deeply insecure, self-hating, and frustrated, they often invent a cultural world of their own, a world in which they can be dominant and set the
standards. John Rohrer and Munro Edmonson refer to the world of the gang,
which is not necessarily a criminal group, but one in which youngsters try to
salvage some sense of dignity and control. They search for the feeling that they
are "somebody," at least to each other. The behavior is described in this way:

The gang demands aggressive independence, a touchy and exaggerated virility, and
a deep, protective secrecy. Acceptance by the gang provides almost the only source
of security for its members, but such acceptance is conditional upon continual proof
that it is merited, and this proof can only be furnished through physical aggressiveness, a restless demonstration of sexual prowess, and a symbolic execution of those
illegal deeds that a "sissy" would not perform.[4]

The "us kids" groups of little boys may become the gangs of older boys, a
seemingly tough and masculine answer to the question, what is a man? and the
related question, who am I? The exaggerated assertions of manliness are often
a camouflage for doubts.

Multiple Roles, Multiple Selves

All of us belong to many groups, and each group judges us by different standards. The average adult plays a number of social roles in the course of a day, each involving a pattern of conduct that a person occupying a specific position in society is expected to follow. Being a parent, for example, is a social role. A person may be a male, a husband, a father, a police officer, a student or teacher, a PTA officer, and a scoutmaster, and be active in sundry religious or civic organizations. Each involves a social role. Each implies a certain pattern of socially prescribed behavior. As we have seen, role behavior may involve conflict or ambiguity when standards are not clear or consistent. One prime example is the discretionary use of police power.

Multiple social roles mean, in effect, multiple selves. Thus, from adolescence onward, a person faces the problem of integrating the several different selves required by different and sometimes conflicting roles. Our perceptions of self depend on the context, varying somewhat with what has gone before and with whom we have been dealing, as well as the immediate situation. Another point worth noting is that we encounter and relate to different people in the various social roles we play. Some people see us exclusively in one role, others, in another. Therefore, it is possible that the feedback will vary, so that a person may receive more favorable feedback in one role than he does in another. In short, he may be viewed as a more successful husband or father than he is a police officer or a teacher, or vice versa.

In the complex of the many selves of the individual, each one may be far from simple. A rapid shift in roles requires quick changes in habits, because roles standardize behavior, and often in attitudes and values as well. Adjustments to the requirements of changed roles are often difficult. Role changes frequently involve frustrations—for example, those experienced by civilians becoming soldiers or soldiers becoming civilians. Or how about the issues of equal rights for women? What are the implications in terms of traditional roles of men and women?

THE POLICE OFFICER'S SELF-IMAGE

With the above as a cursory review of some relevant general considerations pertaining to the self-image, our specific interest is in the self-image of the police officer. In a 1969 survey conducted by the International Association of Chiefs of Police (IACP), police officers from many departments, ranging in rank from patrol officer to inspector, were asked a series of questions as to how they saw themselves and their job.[5] Following are some of the questions and responses:

It should be added that 90 percent of the same officers answered yes to the question, "Do you plan to make law enforcement your life career?" and 66 percent said that the dangerous aspects of police work seldom worried them. Two out of three believed that punishment was effective in crime control. Four out of five thought that punishment for crime ought to be more severe. Seven out of ten thought that the police did not have enough authority. Only 55 percent believed that the police should be concerned with social problems, such

	PERCENT ANSWERING "YES"
Do you feel tense and "under pressure" during duty hours?	47
Do you find your home life made difficult by annoyances, irritations, and aggravations which are a "hangover" from your job?	41
Is your physical condition suffering or deteriorating from duty requirements?	32
Is the police "image" favorable in your community as far as you can determine?	40
Do you feel that officers in your department are just "cogs in a big machine"?	60

as education, jobs, and housing discrimination. But 90 percent asserted that the police should be involved in recreation programs for youth.

In their written comments on the same questionnaires, about one out of three officers complained about one aspect or another of their work, some with marked bitterness and defensiveness. Yet only a few admitted occasional shame at being a police officer. Many revealed characteristics of a persecuted minority: hypersensitivity, the feeling that everyone was against them, cynical despair, displaced aggression, and the like. When asked why they continued as police officers, the main reasons given were:

- The position offers good fringe benefits other than salary.
- It is an interesting job.
- It's steady work; I don't have to worry about layoffs, strikes, plant shutdowns, etc.
- I'm trapped. I'd quit if I didn't have so much time invested; I have to go on now until I retire.

On the whole, these officers seemed to value their job for its security, but many did not think that it rated very highly in conferring social status.

Reasons for Becoming a Police Officer

Why does one become a police officer in the first place? The IACP survey showed that 46 percent of white policemen, 52 percent of black policemen, and 54 percent of policewomen came into police work almost by accident: they had tried several jobs and finally settled on police work. A substantial majority stated that the job turned out to be different from what they anticipated. An even larger proportion (approximately 80 percent) had given little or no thought to leaving police service; however, the higher the educational level of the respondents, the larger was the percentage who had thought about leaving.

The same survey revealed that police officers considered "too much paper work" and "not enough chance for advancement" as their two main job-related problems, followed by such things as "ineffective supervision," "many officers don't know what they are doing," and "not enough freedom of judgment." As to personal problems, 57 percent said "not enough pay"; 16 percent said "little respect shown by others for my profession"; and 11 percent cited "inability to relax at home; can't leave the job behind." Other responses showed 47 percent of the officers citing the manpower shortage as the most pressing problem facing their department. Only 14 percent thought the most pressing problem was lack of understanding and support by citizens.

For an article that appeared in the *Atlantic*, Patricia Lynden asked a number of New York City police officers why they joined the force. Their responses are illuminating, as suggested by the following selections:

> A year ago, I was a cop-hater. I decided to try to find out. I was a beatnik when I came on. It's a noble profession. I'd rather have it in my hands than someone else's.

> I always wanted to become a cop. It was a matter of getting up some Saturday morning and taking the test. . . . I came to the police force because I felt I could better myself here monetarily and social-wise.

> I really don't know why I came on. I used to work for Chase-Manhattan, and I was about to become head teller. The money was better here. I never was a cop-hater.

> I have no desire to be other than what I am. . . . I was a pro baseball player. Then I went into the Marine Corps. I was out in California. I never had any bad or super-stitious attitudes toward the police. They weren't the bogeyman to me. [The police in California] have an *esprit de corps.* On being discharged [from the Marines], we got a recruitment lecture from the Los Angeles Police Department. I was impressed.

> Why did I become a cop? I don't actually know. I used to take all the city tests as a hobby. I was a butcher by trade. In 1957 I had taken the test for policeman, and I got called in November, 1958. I didn't really want to become a policeman, but I was working all hours as a butcher. I thought that every city job was a form of retire-ment. When I went on, I had every intention of taking it easy. I found out my first day at the academy that it wasn't an easy job, but I like it. . . . I think it's the greatest work a person could go into. . . . I get a lot of personal satisfaction from it.[6]

How representative these views may be of police officers in general is a question. But they do provide some insight into the range of motivations for entering police service, from "I always wanted to be a police officer," to "I really don't know why I came on."

Actually, the reasons some men and women join the force are somewhat more complicated. In 1960–61, James Q. Wilson surveyed all the sergeants of one large American police department to secure data on why police careers are of continuing importance to second-generation Irish.[7] He found several reasons. One was the possibility that the Irish patrol officer was the beneficiary of a promotional system that had been biased in his favor. At least the non-Irish respondents saw it that way. However, there was no evidence that such a bias actually existed in the promotional system.

Another factor disclosed in the study was that the second-generation Irish sergeant was more likely than the non-Irish sergeant to come from a police family, to associate mainly with other police officers, and to have a police officer as his closest friend. In short, the son of an Irish immigrant was more likely than the son of a European immigrant or native American to have a family background and a set of attitudes predisposing him toward a police career. Incidentally, over 75 percent of all sergeants felt that financial security was the principal incentive *for other officers* to have joined the force; when asked what the chief incentive was *for themselves*, the proportion mentioning security was much lower.

In his study of black police officers, *Black in Blue*, Nicholas Alex considered the questions of why blacks enter police work and why they stay in it once they join. His findings indicated that most black police officers in New York City applied for police work only as one possibility among other, similar civil service jobs. As Alex put it, "Their goal was not police work as such but the benefits of a civil service job." He continued:

> For those Negroes whose aims are to enter the mainstream of American society and to move up from predominantly lower-class positions, civil service is a crucially important path . . . to gain economic mobility, they selected a relatively low prestige job that had little intrinsic meaning for them. . . . Police work was actually considered an occupational area to avoid because it was thought of as a routine job, menial and onerous, limited in scope for the individual with talent and imagination, and the "butt of everybody's problems."[8]

We should note that, in several studies, both white and black police officers responded to the question of why they joined the police force in ways that suggested that their choice contributed to self-hatred because they had selected an unsatisfying job when there was no available alternative. This implicit incongruency of goals between officer and department, and the resultant inevitable frustrations, has an obvious bearing on the question of morale. In the case of black officers, this problem may be especially complicated. Where the civil rights movement has made a claim on their consciences as blacks who happen to be police officers, there is additional stress between their occupational role and pressures to join the rebellion against the Man. As Alex observed, the problem is one of double marginality, in classic sociological terms.

While most of the black police interviewed in Alex's study signed up for the reasons given, it should be noted that approximately 30 percent chose the police occupation specifically, and not merely for economic reasons. They *wanted* to be police officers, because they thought police work promised more prestige than other jobs they had had, and because it "offered the potential of satisfying their personal interests in youth, community work, and law." They felt that police work had brought them status and mobility, and they identified strongly with its high ideals. For the *civil-service-oriented* black police officer, staying in police work was largely a matter of finding no alternative that paid as well. For the *police-oriented* black police officer on the other hand, police work was a kind of calling, with a sense of mission.[9]

Securing Qualified Personnel for Police Work

As noted earlier, there are those who say that nothing is to be gained by securing "qualified personnel" (whatever that may mean) for police work, because after a few years of experience in the field, "they become like all the rest of them." This is to say, the role shapes the self, as opposed to the position that a relatively immutable self shapes the role. Those taking the latter position would argue that personnel who are initially selected for high quality would substantially improve police service.

James Sterling gave some attention to this conflict of views in his study *Changes in Role Concepts of Police Officers During Recruit Training.* His research suggested that experienced police officers expected that police experience would bring about some change in police recruits as persons. As Sterling observed, "Where the expectation for change is widely perceived, conditions are favorable for change." His hypothesis was that "subjects who did not feel that others held the expectation that police experience will change them will themselves show less change over time."[10] This is significant for those interested in the occupational socialization of the police, since its primary outcome—for the police recruit—is to develop awareness of the expectations of role-related reference groups. In Sterling's terms:

> Socialization for the police recruit includes both the adoption of normative modes of police behavior and the extinction of certain other behaviors which were appropriate for his previous civilian roles. In learning the new role, the police recruit undertakes a complex process of learning which includes more than just knowledge and skills. He will also learn a system of attitudes, beliefs, perceptions and values. The most important learning related to perception concerns the identification of role relevant reference groups and a sensitivity to their expectations and evaluations.[11]

John McNamara explored similar questions in his oft-quoted study of the backgrounds and training of New York City police department recruits. He described the orientation of many police training programs and the strong influence these programs may have on individuals. Following are some of his summarizing conclusions:

> In attempting to develop an *esprit de corps*, the academy seems not to have been successful in immunizing patrolmen against experiencing a strong feeling that their work is one that rates quite low in prestige in the eyes of the public. At the same time, the emphasis on police professionalization in recruit training probably increases the patrolman's perception of the discrepancy between the socioeconomic status that officers should have and the status they actually have.[12]

Pertinent to certain of our considerations in preceding chapters, McNamara continued:

> Perhaps our most significant inference . . . is that a training program for police recruits faces two major dilemmas in preparing recruits for their later duties in the field. The first involves the question of whether to emphasize training strategies aimed at the development of self-directed and autonomous personnel, or to emphasize strategies aimed at developing personnel over whom the organization can easily exercise control. It appears that the second strategy is the one most often emphasized.
>
> The second dilemma is that involving the inconsistencies between what the academy considers ideal practices in police work and what the majority of men in the field consider to be the customary and perhaps more practical procedures in the field. The training program appears to emphasize the former approach.[13]

Seeing Oneself as a Professional

Bruce Olson found, in his study, "The City Policeman: Inner- or Other-Directed?" conducted in one midwestern police department, that respondents in each of five police ranks rated *other-directed* traits as more important than *inner-directed* traits (using David Reisman's categories) in job success for patrol officers. This would be surprising to those expecting emphasis on such inner-directed qualities as forcefulness, imagination, independence, self-confidence, and decisiveness, as compared with other-directed qualities of cooperation, adaptability, caution, agreeableness, and tact. But the results of Olson's research were not easy to reconcile. For example, the higher ranking officers rated imagination nearly twice as high as the lower ranking officers, but the same higher ranking respondents rated independence very low.[14]

So it appears that obtaining "qualified" people is not guaranteed to produce professionalism. Moreover, "good" people may become absorbed—swallowed by the values and pressures of what is—and forget their original commitment to basic structural, functional, and systemic change. Some would phrase this differently, suggesting that the young and inexperienced simply come to recognize that the old ways are best. The compromising of goals often results from the delicate interplay between the desire to make changes and the need to keep a job.

Police leadership must be concerned with the job survival of young careerists entering the field with a commitment to change. Conditions *ought* to be such that they are retained in the system long enough for their influence to be felt. But the fact is that *any* system tends to protect itself against change. The result is that young careerists with inspiration and competence to be agents of change are discouraged from entering the system initially, or become frustrated and drop out at some later point, or survive only to the extent that they compromise their commitment to change. Thus the system remains self-insulated and self-perpetuating, a haven only for those conforming to its standpat values.

A glimmer of hope for the change-minded comes from the possibility that the community served by the organization will demand change and insist upon the creation of conditions conducive to it. Where police work is concerned, this has happened far too rarely in the past. Sophisticated police-community partnership could bring it about more widely in the future. It is a healthy and dynamic state of organizational affairs for administrators to be pressured into periodic reexamination of goals, policies, practices, structures, and priorities. An old way *may* be better than a new way, in some instances. But to have to show empirical evidence to demonstrate it either way—that is the stuff of professionalism and better service to the community. And this, in turn, will have a bearing on problems of morale.

While more than attitude is required to make a professional, believing that one is a professional and striving to behave in a manner consistent with a professional model are surely important in making an earnest effort toward that objective. In his study, James Leo Walsh discovered some interesting things about police attitudes.[15] Walsh observed police officers in four midwestern departments and concluded that officers who see policing as a profession have attitudes toward their work considerably different from those who see what they do as just a job. This contrast extends to attitudes toward minorities and to the use of force, as well as to other matters. Walsh found, for example, that the "professionals" were much more concerned about public approbation, respect, and support than were the "jobbers." The latter were more apt than the professionals to say that riots and the poor constitute the number one police problem today. Nearly half of the jobbers felt that the use of force in police work actually helped their standing in the community, while 60 percent of the professionals said that the use of force, although sometimes necessary, was detrimental to their efforts to achieve professional status.

The professionals were inclined to attach much more importance than the jobbers to public service in police work. The jobbers tended to stress physical size and strength as desirable qualifications for police work. Walsh also discovered some political differences: the jobbers were more likely than the professionals to have voted for far-right candidates in the 1968 election. Thus, occupational self-conception appears to be related to voting behavior. The Walsh study also suggested that generalization regarding the values and beliefs of police as a group are hazardous.

David Bayley and Harold Mendelsohn, in their study of Denver police officers, observed that "very little credence is given by policemen to charges that policemen treat minority people unfairly or improperly."[16] This has also been indicated by Skolnick, as earlier noted. Walsh found that the jobbers were much more likely than the professionals to claim that unequal treatment was the fault of minorities themselves. Some 62 percent of the jobbers felt that the poor and minority groups actually get better treatment than do the middle class and the rest of us. Another 23 percent of the jobbers felt that the poor and minority groups have problems because they are "too lazy" to improve their lot in life. Only a small percentage of the professionals subscribed to these notions.

Walsh described a central hypothesis of his study as follows:

> To be proud of one's occupation and to view it as a profession enjoying positive standing in the community should lead to attitudes toward the work done by members of the profession different from those one would expect from other practitioners whose view of the occupation is that it is simply a job—something one does because he can't find anything else, or because it is the most secure position available, or something that anyone could handle with little or no training.[17]

Cynicism Resulting from Conflicting Roles

There is still the question of why many police officers, especially in our big cities, are not proud of their occupation. Why are so many of them so cynical about their professional prospects? Why the continuing evidences of corruption and other signs of low morale?

James Q. Wilson examined this phenomenon some years ago.[18] He recognized that there is no single explanation for police morale problems. For the individual police officer in a big city, the main concern, Wilson asserted, is finding some consistent, satisfying basis for his self-conception: to be able to live with himself in reasonable tranquility. The gravity of this concern, of course, varies with individual officers and departments. Wilson contends that the problem of morale results from two aspects of the police officers' role. First, they often deal with their clients as adversaries. Second, they are frequently under pressure to serve incompatible ends. We have already noted the latter point in relation to the functions of law enforcement and order maintenance: the public cannot make up its mind what it wants from the police.

To alleviate the police morale problem, therefore, some consensus must be reached as to what is expected of the police, community by community. It is basically the role question again. Police and community must move together toward clearer directional signals than presently exist as to the police exercise of discretion. This is, in effect, a matter of political process in a democracy, involving coalitions, compromise, and consensus. On the police side, the reality of the heterogeneity of the community must be recognized and dignified— another way of saying that the police must become the police of *all* the people.

Wilson's description of the police officer's difficulty is best conveyed in his language:

> The awareness that he is viewed with hostility and judged in terms of inconsistent standards can, unless other factors intervene, lead a policeman to believe that he has chosen an occupation which sets him apart from others. Even during off-duty hours, he is rarely allowed to forget that he is a policeman—even if by nothing more than the joking remarks of his friends. To live with himself and with others, he must develop some acceptable and consistent standards by which to evaluate himself. In the extreme case of which we are here speaking, such standards cannot be found in the expectations of others. In adapting to this situation, the policeman comes to be governed by norms different from, and sometimes in conflict with, those which govern the persons with whom he comes in contact.[19]

Wilson goes on to pinpoint a disparity between the importance attached by the public to the role performed by the police, and the status of the police in public eyes:

> To the extent that the policeman feels the need to develop a police "sub-culture" or "code" different from that of civilians, he can be said to be "alienated." . . . The two major causes of the morale problem for policemen seem analogous to two of the many meanings of alienation. First, the "pariah feeling" implies not only that the individual (or his occupation) is given low esteem, but more particularly that the esteem accorded is much lower than the ostensible importance of the goals he is to serve. The individual (in this case, the policeman) is obliged to perform a social function of the highest importance but is told that he will not be given an appropriately high status even if he is successful. Second, the problem of serving incompatible ends implies that society has so defined the policeman's situation that he can never act in accord with that definition. Stated another way, the inconsistent expectations of society imply that the policeman will be called upon either to use socially unapproved behavior to attain socially approved goals, or vice versa.[20]

Wilson's analysis suggests the subtlety of what may be involved in an indeterminate number of situations where a police morale problem exists. His explanation cuts deeper than most. But there are often additional complications, such as incredibly poor administrative leadership and supervision, bureaucratic inertia and the failure of a department to use personnel effectively, and the feelings of police officers that they are ill-prepared, in training and education, for what is expected of them. These and other considerations of this type have an important bearing upon morale. For example, the IACP survey of police officer opinions indicated that 60 percent of the respondents felt that they were just cogs in a big machine.

PSYCHOLOGICAL STRESS

Psychological stress connected with the job is another facet of police morale. There has been increasing attention to this in recent years. By its nature, police work feeds feelings of frustration, aggression, and bitterness. This theme is transmitted in such expressions as "a policeman's lot is not happy," "the police deal with the seamy side of life," and "the police are dirtyworkers (or community garbage men)." Police officers have a collective way of putting it: "A cop has to put up with a lot of crap!" And then they add, "and cops are human too!" In psychological terms, the frustration-aggression complex is acute in the world of the police officer. Some officers worry about the possibility that they may work off their feelings on their families. Arthur and Elaine Niederhoffer have done significant research on the families of police officers, described in their book, *The Police Family.*[21]

Until recently, we could say that not much was being done regarding psychological stress in police officers. More than one wag had remarked that "there ought to be a heavy punching bag in every police station." Niederhoffer had early delineated the cynicism syndrome in the New York City Police Department and elsewhere, asking, "Why is the police system with all its concentrated effort incapable, in so many cases, of dissipating that cynicism or encouraging the potent idealism?"[22] He distinguished between police cynicism directed against life, the world, and people in general, and cynicism aimed at the police system itself.[23]

Significant insights regarding the psychological pitfalls of police work are provided in the fiction-based-on-fact works of such authors as Joseph Wambaugh[24] and Richard Dougherty.[25] A more clinical diagnosis is found in the articles of several psychiatrists, for instance, Dr. Martin Symonds, consulting psychiatrist to the New York City Police Department.[26] Hans Toch proposed more than a decade ago that "the police role itself, as defined and practiced today, is conducive to social tensions and therefore self-defeating."[27] From this basic premise, Toch deduces a theory of psychological stress for police officers not unlike a more recently conceived explanation by the experienced police executive, Bernard L. Garmire. Today's police officers, Garmire writes, suffer from conflicts between professed and practiced values; between how they want to be valued and how they are valued; and between the role they most value but least perform.[28]

Closely related to all this are questions that are today being studied seriously for the first time—questions pertaining to alcoholism and drug addiction among police officers, divorce, suicide, and mental disorders.[29] These are questions in which the community obviously has a stake and probably much greater responsibility than has been recognized in the past.

THE SUBCULTURE OF THE POLICE

Occupational socialization creates occupational subcultures. For our purpose, *subculture* may be defined as the meanings, values, and behavior patterns that are unique to a particular group in society. In chapter 4, we alluded to the various social systems that affect what the police do and how they do it: the criminal justice system, the governmental-political system, and various social-institutional systems. We referred also to the familial and social backgrounds of police officers. All of these variables are pertinent to police subculture.

Most communities seem to be unaware that they expect their police to perform impossible tasks. The police, quite naturally, are defensive in their reactions to community expectations that they cannot fulfill. They are too often reminded of their failures by people who do not understand the problems of the police. Because police officers are, by occupational prescription, inclined to be suspicious, they tend to isolate themselves from an unsympathetic, critical, untrustworthy, and uncomprehending community, and to form their own in-group alliances with fellow officers. This supplies needed emotional and ideological support—what Wilson calls "a code"—with elements of secrecy and ritual, even a special language and other subgroup trappings.

Dean Victor Strecher of Sam Houston State University's Criminal Justice Center has described police subculture by utilizing a theoretical paradigm comparing the police with medical students. He borrows from H. S. Becker and his associates for the medical part of the chart.[30]

Medical	*Police*
The concept of medical responsibility pictures a world in which patients may be in danger of losing their lives and identifies the true work of the physician as saving these endangered lives. Further, where the physician's work does not afford (at least in some symbolic sense) the possibility of saving a life or restoring health through skillful practice . . . the physician himself lacks some of the essence of physicianhood	The concept of police responsibility pictures a world in which the acts and intended acts of criminals threaten the lives or well-being of victims, and the security of their property. The true work of the police officer is the protection of life and property by intervention in, and solution of, criminal acts. Further, where the policeman's work does not afford (at least in some symbolic sense) the possibility of protecting life or property by intervening in criminal acts, the police officer himself lacks some of the essence of police identity.
Those patients who can be cured are better than those who cannot.	Those cases that can be solved are better than those that cannot.
"Crocks" . . . are not physically ill and . . . are not regarded as worthwhile patients because nothing can be done for them. (*Note:* To a medic, a "crock" is a hypochondriac.)	Chronic neighborhood complainants are not worth taking seriously because there is no substance to their complaints, and nothing can be done for them.

Medical	*Police*
Students worry about the dangers to their own health involved in seeing a steady stream of unscreened patients, some of whom may have communicable diseases.	Policemen worry about dangers to their own safety involved in approaching a steady stream of unknown persons, some of whom may have serious behavioral problems and intentions of causing them injury or even death, because of circumstances unknown to the policemen.
Perhaps the most difficult scenes come about when patients have no respect for the doctor's authority. Physicians resent this immensely.	When a citizen makes a policeman sweat to take him into custody, he has created the situation most apt to lead to police indignation and anger.[31]

Beyond childhood and adolescent socialization, the police officer, Strecher asserts, undergoes a process of occupational socialization through which he becomes identified as a police officer and begins to share all the perspectives relevant to the police role. There is substantial coherence and consistency among these perspectives. Moreover, because all police officers occupy the same social-institutional position, they tend to face the same kinds of problems arising out of the nature of the position. Therefore, the demands and inhibitions of the *police role*, as we have suggested, are decisive in shaping the kaleidoscopic perspectives of the police officer.

Strecher holds that police officers do not simply apply the perspectives they carry over from previous experience or backgrounds. He believes that background may have indirect influence in many ways, but goes on to say:

> The problems of the police officer are so pressing and the policeman's initial perspectives so similar that the perspectives developed are much more apt to reflect the pressures of the immediate *law enforcement* situation than of ideas associated with prior roles and experiences.[32]

To Strecher, therefore, police subculture is a shorthand term for "the organized sum of *police perspectives* relevant to the *police role.*" Other researchers might argue with Strecher on the question of how important prepolice background is in explaining officer attitudes. "Background" is an all-encompassing term that covers a great deal of territory. Jerome Skolnick is interested in the sociology of occupations and devotes considerable attention to what he calls "the working personality" of the police officer—an analysis of the effects of the occupation on the personality of the officer—some features of which we noted earlier. The literature dealing with the effects of one's work on world outlook is extensive.[33] Skolnick suggests that

> the police, as a result of combined features of their social situation, tend to develop ways of looking at the world distinctive to themselves, cognitive lenses through which to see situations and events. The strength of the lenses may be weaker or stronger depending on certain conditions, but they are ground on a similar axis.[34]

In another publication, Skolnick observes that the police officer's attitude toward his work is much like that of the combat soldier. For the working officer, life is "combat." People are either good or bad, the situation is safe or unsafe—the "we-versus-they attitude." Like the soldier, the police officer is irritated by minor organizational rules, what he calls "legal technicalities," and long-winded, sociological explanations. Quoting Skolnick again:

> Additionally, as one observes police, one notices their employment of two predominant models of discourse. One of these models, which might be termed "office language" or "working language," is frequently profane, loud, and good-humored. Transported into the cold light of print, the words might have a shocking effect upon delicate sensibilities. But such discourse would ring familiar to a steelworker or longshoreman, a ball-player or a soldier. . . .
>
> Off the street, police frequently resort to an alternative model—"officialese"—out of fear that "working language" might spill out and offend officialdom. An outstanding example of police officialese is the substitution of the word "altercation" for "fight." . . . So the policeman is often not a graceful or moderate speaker or writer, and his inability or perhaps unwillingness to conceal true feelings gets him into trouble.[35]

To relate these insights of Strecher and Skolnick to our initial point, we note the variables that influence personality: childhood development, the experiences one has had before taking a certain job, and the job itself. Each of these factors comes into play for an individual's developing self-image; the degree to which one factor or another may predominate depends on the individual and his situation. It appears to Strecher and Skolnick that in a police situation the occupational influence upon attitudes and the self-image is especially strong. But, as we shall see in a moment, this view is not entirely accepted by other analysts.

Personality Traits of Police Officers

As we have indicated, the questions of why a person would want to be a police officer and what type of personality tends to gravitate to police work are of interest to researchers. The stereotypic assumptions of yesteryear, such as that of a "police type," are being carefully scrutinized, and in considerable measure, decimated. Even a decade or so ago, when the first studies of this kind were attempted, such scholars as Ruth Levy were cautious and conservative about their research objectives. Levy proposed that certain personality traits established early in life were clues to whether a person would be able to stand the pressures of a police career. She said:

> We find that the appointees most likely to remain in law enforcement are probably those who are more unresponsive to the environmental stresses introduced when they become officers of the law than are their fellow-appointees. These stresses include becoming a member of a "minority" (occupationally speaking) group, need to adhere to semi-military regimen, community expectation of incongruous roles and the assumption of a position of authority complete with the trappings of uniform, badge, holster and gun, and all these imply. The officers who remain in law enforcement may well be the sons of fathers who imposed a rigid code of behavior to which their children learned to adhere, and who do not feel a strong need to defy or rebel against authority.[36]

In our discussion of the police role in chapter 3, we referred to John Pfiffner's analysis of the occupational belief system of the police, the very essence of the subculture. Pfiffner held that the police subculture consisted of a set of values, standards, and job goals "more appropriate to the days of public hangings than to a society which is making some progress toward ameliorating the lot of those who for one reason or another have not adjusted to the demands of society."[37]

Pfiffner asked some provocative questions about the police subculture—and ventured his own tentative responses:

> How strong is the right-wing orientation of those engaged in the police vocation? . . . One senses that it may be more prevalant than in the general population. . . .
>
> Do the police tend to think didactically? . . . The police may regard themselves as the custodians of a public conscience to which society gives only lip service. . . .
>
> Are the police anti–social science? . . . The investigators are in a sense natural enemies because of their opposite values . . . [thus] it is little wonder that the police should adopt a certain skepticism or aloofness toward social science research. . . .
>
> How prevalent is the anti-social-work bias among law enforcement people? . . . This implication [that police work is social work] is distasteful to some policemen who regard the rehabilitation apparatus as foreign territory. . . .
>
> Is "authoritarian" leadership a product of the police sub-culture, or does police work attract men with natural tendencies in that direction? . . . If this is authentically an ingredient of the police sub-culture, certain other questions present themselves. . . .
>
> To what extent does the police operation resist administrative coordination? . . . There may have been at one time and among certain officers a feeling that because police receive their powers from the state, they are therefore immune from general administrative supervision. . . .
>
> Is there an equitation complex among the police, using that term as symbolic of the survival of outmoded procedures? . . . Equitation thinking is resistance to change. . . . Are they [the police] now hung in their Maginot Line of technical effectiveness in meeting traditional police problems?[38]

All of this was in the context of a discussion in which Pfiffner alluded to the "guild protectionism" of the police, earlier mentioned, growing out of what he labeled as their "isolation syndrome." His description of this is pertinent:

> Some police administrators prefer to deny, or at any rate overlook, the statement that the police feel isolated from the opinion-making elements in the community, but one cannot probe their intimate thoughts without becoming aware of the existence of an isolation syndrome. There is quite definitely this feeling of being at cross-purposes with the social scientists and social workers. . . . In a very generalized sort of way, it may also be said that the intellectual community has an anti-authority complex which in a vague manner is transferred to the police. The police also harbor a feeling that they have been deserted by that portion of the legal profession which sits on the judicial bench, and the civil libertarians.[39]

Pfiffner's vantage point in his view of the police was that of public administration. Numerous psychologists have also been interested in the matter of police personality, some quite critically, for example, Hans Toch, speaking of the police as a kind of minority group:

The police inhabit a ghetto of their own, and they are doomed to segregation. They have little hope of man-to-man conversation with civilians, who—even if favorably disposed to law enforcement—tend to be nervous and self-conscious in encounters with officers. The average person finds it difficult to feel open and at ease with a man who sports a conspicuous firearm, who is entitled to question, search and arrest him.[40]

Toch contends that police officers sense these attitudes on the part of civilians, and their defensive reaction is typical of minority groups: they become self-righteous. They seek the exclusive company of one another, and "regale one another with their own virtues, sometimes enhancing these to superman proportions. Self-regard and pride slide into chauvinism, especially . . . built on a foundation of persistent self-doubt."[41] Thus, Toch explains the underlying psychological dynamics of police militancy, generally known as "blue power." Incidentally, Toch points out the limitations in referring to the police as a minority group, if an analogy to blacks is implied.

The Pariah Feeling

For William Westley, in his early study of violence and the police, the term for isolation syndrome was *pariah*—an outcast, a person despised by society. James Q. Wilson and Michael Banton have used the same term; for example, Banton writes:

Couple this experience of the public with the policeman's feelings that in his social life he is a pariah, scorned by citizens who are more respectable but no more honest, and it need surprise no one that the patrolman's loyalties to his department and his colleagues are often stronger than those to the wider society.[42]

James Sterling questions the validity of the emphasis placed on police clannishness, in comparison with certain other occupations. He thinks the point is a weak one; what is not considered is the fact that clannishness is a characteristic of all occupations where shift work is practiced.[43]

The central thesis in Skolnick's description of the working personality of the police was that certain features of the police officer's environment, such as danger, authority, and efficiency, interact with the paramilitary character of police organizations to produce distinctive ways of perceiving and responding, that is, the working personality.[44] Westley was interested in the manner in which secrecy is endemic to policing. His data suggested that the norm of secrecy emerged from common occupational needs, was collectively supported, and was considered of such importance that police officers would break the law to support it.[45]

The manner and degree to which the police subculture is shaped and governed by organizational phenomena has been competently analyzed by Peter K. Manning in a number of articles and books in recent years.[46] Manning shows how the police mandate (role) has been gradually shifted from simple protection of citizens and their property from the "dangerous classes" to the paramilitary "crime fighting" of today. The myths and rituals surrounding police work, both within and beyond the police organization, are described by Manning as basic to what he calls the inherent contradictions of police-community relations. He contends that the police are not really in the crime-control business. What they spend most of their time doing, he says—and do badly because they do not consider it "real" police work—is supplying human services. As long as the police encourage the public to think of them as "crime fighters," Manning asserts—which in today's society they cannot be—and refuse to develop new modes of crime control and service delivery, they will be caught in the middle of public and political controversy.[47]

In Manning's language, the role dilemma of the police is this:

> They have charted a course of claiming responsibility for the maintenance of public order and the prevention of crime, yet their resources in the sense of public consensus and the level of cooperation that facilitates effective action are diminishing. They are the targets for ever-increasing public demand for a level of public order and crime prevention they cannot possibly fulfill. They, like any other reasonable organizations faced with an uncontrollable environment, an indifferent audience seldom moved to cooperative action, and massive discrepancies between their claims and their accomplishments, have resorted to the dramatic management of the appearance of effectiveness.[48]

PERSONALITY PATTERNS FOR SUCCESS IN POLICE WORK

Predicting and measuring successful police-officer performance is currently of extraordinary interest to researchers. The accumulating data and information on this and related topics would make a sizable book. We can only point to a few examples and highlights, doing so because the police subculture, as we have defined it, is feeling the effects of such research.

We have cited Ruth Levy's early study. The University of Chicago work by Baehr, Furcon, and Froemel was an expansion of Levy's effort.[49] The researchers developed a battery of psychological tests that they claimed would accurately predict future performance of patrol officers, determine specific patterns of successful and unsuccessful performance, and identify subgroups exhibiting these patterns among the officers tested. The patterns could be used for purposes of selection, placement, duty assignment, and promotion.

The tests showed that, apart from an average level of intelligence, the most important personal attributes of successful patrol officers were all related to *stability*. These attributes included personal self-confidence and the control of emotional impulses, maintenance of cooperative rather than hostile or competitive attitudes, resistance to stress, and a realistic rather than a subjective approach to life. Officers displaying this stability had a background of early assumption of family responsibilities and involvement in family activities. All the desirable attributes were measured by the tests, and patrol officers who scored high in these attributes were, in general, those who were independently given high ratings for performances by their supervisors. The study focused on Chicago officers in the Patrol Division who had at least one year of service and who were currently assigned to uniformed street patrol. The same research team repeated the project in Detroit, using a similar design, and variations of it have since been attempted in other cities.[50]

Both the Chicago research and that by Levy point to the importance of stability, or what may be called "stress resistance," in successful police careers. Levy observed that young police officers do not find conformity to the system stressful. Conformism is a phychological trait related to security. The conformist, as stated by Watson and Sterling, receives approbation from the wielders of power and at the same time rids himself of the uncertainty of decision making in matters covered by the rules.[51]

When one shares the values of the larger society, as Banton says police officers do, one's behavior tends to harmonize with society's expectations. Accordingly, many police officers as well as others who hold strongly to established values, are inclined to react strongly against those who wish to change these values. Student rebels and black or white extremists are regarded as threats to stability. The larger society actually encourages the police to exercise their discretion in handling such threats in ways that would probably not be tolerated with "more respectable" adversaries. For their part, the police are committed by their oath to maintaining the status quo. Moreover, if Levy and others are correct, they are also so committed by psychological disposition, hence "do not find it distasteful"—as Watson and Sterling put it—"to function in this manner."[52] This point carries implications for agents of change within police organizations.

Conservatism and Class Origins of Police

No one should be startled by the observation that political conservatism and police work go together. A decade ago, political sociologist Seymour Martin Lipset pointed to the increasing body of evidence "which suggests an affinity between police work and support for radical-right politics, particularly when linked to racial unrest." Lipset contended that this was because police were recruited largely from the undereducated, typically conservative working class, and because their job inevitably stressed toughness, authority, and "a skeptical view of human behavior." Skolnick alluded to conservatism as the dominant political and emotional persuasion of the police. The late Los Angeles chief of police, William H. Parker, asserted that the majority of the nation's peace officers were "conservative, ultraconservative, and very right wing."[53] It appeared to many observers in the 1960s that the John Birch Society was popular in police circles.

Research of the type we have mentioned, dealing with background characteristics of those aspiring to police work, provides some information as to the generally conservative orientation of the police establishment. Lipset thought that this was the result of a combination of social background and occupational role factors. For example, he cited Niederhoffer's observation that between 1954 and 1969, a period of relative economic prosperity, the bulk of New York City police candidates were upper lower class with a sprinkling of lower middle class, and 95 percent had no college training.[54] Lipset quoted McNamara's findings to substantiate other aspects of his thesis, of which this is an expression:

In general, the policeman's job requires him to be suspicious of people, to prefer conventional behavior, to value toughness. A policeman must be suspicious and cynical about human behavior. As Niederhoffer points out, "he needs the intuitive ability to sense plots and conspiracies on the basis of embryonic evidence." The political counterpart of such an outlook is a monistic theory which simplifies political conflict into a black-and-white fight, and which is ready to accept a conspiratorial view of the sources of evil, terms which basically describe the outlook of extremist groups, whether of the left or right. [55]

It will be recalled that James Q. Wilson referred to the working-class backgrounds of police offers in many communities and their preoccupation with working-class values: maintaining self-respect, proving one's masculinity, "not taking any crap," and not being "taken in."[56] The literature is rich with similar references. Westley early alluded to the working-class origins of most police officers. Even earlier, Gunnar Myrdal described the American police officer as economically and socially insecure and always on the defensive, "creating the impression that he is crude and hard-boiled.[57] In the same vein, Sam Blum wrote in *Redbook:*

> The police therefore have been forced to write off the better-educated as a source of recruits. In addition, no one can say precisely what type of person (if there is any one specific type) can function most successfully as a policeman. In large cities it is a virtual certainty, however, that police recruits will be drawn from the less-well-educated and the lower income groups. According to Milton Rector, "There is a high correlation between violence and the lower cultural-economic levels. If you recruit from these levels, you run the risk of obtaining people who have built-in violent reactions when they run into problems, as the police do. Before you recruit from these levels, you have to assess carefully their attitudes and stability."[58]

A. L. Cornelius said essentially the same thing a half century ago:

> Policemen as a class are usually not well educated, skilled mechanically or industrially. They are men above average in physical strength and appearance who have lacked sufficient persistence to acquire an education or learn a trade.[59]

Watson and Sterling provided a contradicting analysis of various ramifications of social class factors and the police, based on their national opinion sampling. They raised questions regarding the assumptions prevailing in the views quoted above:

> [Data show] that today's police officers have come from the families of craftsmen and foremen, and service workers (including police) in larger proportion than is true for the general adult work force. Conversely, the data show that proportionately fewer police officers than other adults are the children of professional, technical and managerial workers; clerical and sales workers; operatives; farmers; and laborers. By and large, . . .the data cast doubt on the accuracy of the view that "most policemen are products of lower-middle-class environments."[60]

Watson and Sterling concluded that differences in *educational attainment* among police were more significant than any other variable in explaining the contrasting opinions expressed by officers they sampled regarding many issues affecting police work. One might argue that educational attainment is class oriented and, therefore, that social class is actually the most important variable. Implicit in the entire discussion is, of course, the assumption that persons from class levels other than lower-middle or working class would make better police officers, by some definition of "better." Banton may have the key point:

> To do his job properly, the policeman, like the minister of religion, has to be to some extent a "classless" figure. He has to deal with subjects of different class and his relationships with them must be determined by his office, not by his class position. [61]

To which Watson and Sterling append, "we would hasten to add that the policeman should be an *educated* classless figure." [62]

The discussion of whether there is a personality model for police work will undoubtedly continue indefinitely. Some social scientists, exemplified by Manning, will emphasize the important influence of organizational factors in shaping police behavior. [63]

The Value Gap Between Police and Policed

Studies dealing with contrasts among occupational value systems are fairly common in contemporary literature. One of this kind was done at Michigan State University by Milton Rokeach, Martin Miller, and John Snyder, probing the question of whether there were noteworthy differences between the values of police officers and those of representative samples of other black and white Americans. [64] They discovered a somewhat larger value gap, on the whole, between police and blacks than between police and whites, but the gap was considerable in both cases. The police officers tested ranked high such values as *a sense of accomplishment, capable, intellectual,* and *logical.* They devalued such modes of behavior as being *broadminded, forgiving, helpful,* and *cheerful.* They ranked *equality* significantly lower than a national sampling of whites and far lower than a national sampling of blacks. This ranking of equality was interpreted as an indicator of conservatism.

The Michigan State researchers regarded this discrepancy in the importance of equality as the most significant component of the value gap between police and policed. Their findings supported Lipset's contention that police derive their conservatism from their working-class backgrounds, with the added consideration that police work appeals primarily to those of working-class background "whose personalities have been shaped in such a way that they value subservience to authority and an 'escape from freedom' [Eric Fromm's term]." [65] In effect this suggests what Bayley and Mendelsohn and others have concluded: that the background and prepolice personality of police recruits are more important in shaping their value patterns than is the occupational socialization process after they enter police work. There appears to be some dissent on this point from Sterling, Strecher, and Walsh.

The Uniform as a Symbol

Lipset cited the various analysts (Westley, James Q. Wilson, Skolnick, and others) who have underlined the importance that police officers attach to respect for law and authority, and more specifically to respect for the individual police officer. Several studies indicate that police officers feel that lack of respect for the police is America's primary law enforcement problem. We mentioned this in our discussion of discretionary use of police power. We noted the symbolic importance ascribed by the officer to his uniform, especially in situations where he perceives that his authority is being challenged. He expects deference to be shown; as Skolnick points out, for a citizen to make an officer sweat to take him into custody—for instance, by going limp—is to create a situation calculated to elicit the officer's anger and indignation.

Walsh looked into the question of the meaning of the uniform to the police officer, as did David Bayley and Harold Mendelsohn.[66] Walsh asked the question of the officers he interviewed: "Some have suggested that police work could improve its image if it were to encourage officers to wear suits, not uniforms, while on duty. Do you agree?" Almost 90 percent of the respondents disagreed. Among these, the importance of the uniform as a "symbol of our identity or mark of distinction" went up as professional striving went up; the "professionals" were stronger in their disagreement with the question than the "jobbers." The latter saw the uniform as important, but mainly as a deterrent to those who might break the law.

Effects of Elements of Danger and Suspicion

Significant factors in the attitudes and behavior of police officers are the elements of danger and suspicion. Both Skolnick and Banton analyzed these factors so thoroughly in their descriptions of the police subculture that there is no need here to do more than invite attention to their work.

Other researchers have been concerned with the reactions of military personnel in stressful situations. Samuel Stouffer said, in *The American Soldier: Combat and Its Aftermath*, that the fear reaction to a dangerous situation is "apt to interfere so seriously that the men are unable to exercise good judgment or to carry out skillfully an action which they had been trained to perform."[67]

Sterling explored this matter in his study of police recruits. He observed, as Westley had earlier, that the prospect of danger in the work has little meaning for the police recruit. It is only incidentally covered in training; it is learned through the occupational socialization process. According to Sterling, perception of danger is related to length of experience as a police officer.[68]

To begin with, the recruit may have some vague notion, as he begins training, that policing is more hazardous than barbering. Then he comes to recognize that the element of danger is, to some extent, predictable by specialization; a bomb specialist, for example, faces more danger than a training director. He also learns that danger for the patrol officer is largely *unpredictable*. This is the point where "the message" begins to take hold. About this, James Q. Wilson says:

> Statistically, the risk of injury or death to the patrolman may not be great in order maintenance situations, but it exists, and worse, it is unpredictable, occurring . . . "when you least expect it. . . . " I would add that the risk of danger in order maintenance patrol work . . . has a disproportionate effect on the officer partly

because its unexpected nature makes him more apprehensive and partly because he tends to communicate his apprehension to the citizen.[69]

Sterling indicated that danger may also be considered in its spatial and positional characteristics (the "ecology" of danger?); for example, so-called high crime areas, office work as against street patrol, and so on. Still another consideration is the danger potential associated with the appearance and conduct of people. This is where Skolnick's observation regarding the police stereotype of "suspicious persons" and the "symbolic assailant" are relevant. The perceptions involved and the related emotions are learned through experience. Carl Werthman and Irving Piliavin described this learning process:

> Policemen develop indicators of suspicion by a method of pragmatic induction. Past experience has, in large part, led them to conclude that . . . Negroes are more likely to cause public disturbances than whites, and that adolescents in certain areas are a greater source of trouble than other categories of the citizenry. On the basis of these conclusions, the police divide the population . . . into a variety of categories and make some initial assumptions about the moral character of people.[70]

Finally, danger may also be considered in relation to situations. This aspect usually does get some attention in police training. For example, the recruit is told that disturbance calls are often dangerous. Westley alluded to the high danger level associated with family disputes, because the parties have a tendency to direct their hostility toward the officer. It may be noted in this regard that, speaking of the soldier, Stouffer said, "Fear reactions in combat may be due, in part, to an attitudinal factor, the feeling that one has not had sufficient training."[71]

SUMMING UP

We have had a panoramic and somewhat rudimentary look at a number of interesting facets of the self-image of the police. In some respects, this is the most fundamental aspect of the study of police and community relations. Surely it is one of the most important considerations if one is to understand the social-psychological dynamics of police-citizen interaction.

Our analysis began with the question of police morale. Do the police have some special kind of self-image problem? To find an answer to this question, we briefly reviewed what is known of the socialization process in infants and children: how each of us learns who he is. We noted the importance of the feedback we get from how other people behave toward us. The relationship between our multiple social roles and our multiple selves was our next consideration.

Then we focused on the police officer. Most police, we learned, think that what they do is an important job, but they are also conscious of their low social status. Why people want to join the police force, and why they stay with it once they join, are therefore good questions for study. These are especially good questions with black (and other minority group) officers.

How police officers see themselves depends on various influences, one of which is early-life socialization, another of which is occupational socialization after one has entered police service. Researchers disagree as to which is more important; probably no generalized principle is valid. Securing qualified personnel reflects one approach, but qualified men and women may be socialized by the police subculture to a point where the status quo is left undisturbed.

Some research suggests that the attitudes and behavior of police officers are strongly influenced by whether they see their work as a profession or merely as a job. This underscores the importance of self-attitude. But why are so many police so cynical—why the morale problem? It appears that the problem relates to society's ambivalent, inconsistent, and impossible expectations. This is the principal explanation for the so-called police subculture, which is essentially a defensive reaction rooted in the need of the police to find some acceptable and consistent standards by which to evaluate themselves.

In terms of personality, what traits are significant in successful police careers? Why is it said that police hate liberals, and vice versa? What is known about the value and belief patterns of the police as compared with those of men and women in other occupations? How important is the police officer's uniform as a symbol of his authority? How important are the elements of suspicion and perceived danger in understanding the attitudes and behavior of police under stress?

These were the questions discussed in the concluding sections of this chapter. The subject of police self-image has broad implications. It is often regarded as marshy, swampy ground for the student, because so much about it remains inconclusive. But recent research is concentrating on this area and promises the harder dividends of scholarship. We are left, however, with the impression that we have dealt with only one side of the coin. If the self-image is so largely governed by what we think others think of us, then it follows that the self-image of the police officer depends heavily upon the public image of the police officer—the other side of the coin. This is our subject in the next chapter.

NOTES

1. J. Milton Yinger, "Who Are We?" (Speech delivered to a Northern Ohio Institute on Police and Community Relations at Cleveland, Ohio, November 21, 1964). Reprinted by permission.

2. Allison Davis and Robert J. Havighurst, *Father of the Man* (Boston: Houghton Mifflin, 1947), pp. 177–178.

3. Mildred Peters, "A Look at Ourselves: Elements of Misunderstanding," in A. F. Brandstatter and Louis Radelet, eds., *Police and Community Relations* (Beverly Hills, Calif.: Glencoe, 1968), p. 55. Reprinted by permission.

4. John H. Rohrer and Munro S. Edmonson, *Eighth Generation* (New York: Harper & Brothers, 1960), p. 160. Reprinted by permission of Harper & Row, Publishers, Inc.

5. Nelson A. Watson and James W. Sterling, *Police and Their Opinions* (Washington, D.C.: International Association of Chiefs of Police, 1969). Reprinted by permission.

6. Patricia Lynden, "Why I'm a Cop: Interviews from a Reporter's Notebook," *Atlantic* 223, no. 3 (March 1969), pp. 104–108. Copyright © 1969 by the Atlantic Monthly Company. Reprinted by permission. See also, Arthur Niederhoffer, *Behind the Shield:*

The Police in Urban Society (Garden City, N.Y.: Doubleday, 1967), pp. 140–142; and Alan F. Arcuri, "Police Pride and Self-Esteem: Indications of Future Occupational Changes," *Journal of Police Science and Administration* 4, no. 4: 436–444. Copyright © 1976 by the Northwestern University School of Law.

7. James Q. Wilson, "Generational and Ethnic Differences Among Career Police Officers" (paper delivered at the Fifty-eighth Annual Meeting of the American Sociological society, Los Angeles, August 1963).

8. Nicholas Alex, *Black in Blue: A Study of the Negro Policeman* (New York: Appleton-Century-Crofts, 1969), pp. 34–35.

9. Ibid., p. 52.

10. James W. Sterling, *Changes in Role Concepts of Police Officers During Recruit Training* (Washington, D.C.: International Association of Chiefs of Police, 1969), pp. 21, 76.

11. Ibid., p. 155. Reprinted by permission.

12. John H. McNamara, "Uncertainties in Police Work: The Relevance of Police Recruits' Background and Training," in David J. Bordua, ed., *The Police: Six Sociological Essays* (New York: John Wiley & Sons, 1967), p. 250. Reprinted by permission of John Wiley & Sons.

13. Ibid., p. 251.

14. Bruce Olson, "The City Policeman: Inner- or Other-Directed?" *Public Personnel Review*, April 1970, pp. 102–107.

15. James Leo Walsh, "The Professional Cop" (Paper presented at the Sixty-fourth Annual Meeting of the American Sociological Association, September 1969).

16. David H. Bayley and Harold Mendelsohn, *Minorities and the Police: Confrontation in America* (New York: Free Press, 1969), p. 148.

17. Walsh, "Professional Cop," p.1.

18. James Q. Wilson, "The Police and Their Problems: A Theory," *Public Policy*. Yearbook of the Harvard University Graduate School of Public Administration (Cambridge, 1963), pp. 189–216.

19. Ibid., p. 192. Reprinted by permission.

20. Ibid., pp. 192–193.

21. Arthur and Elaine Niederhoffer, *The Police Family* (Lexington, Mass.: Lexington Books, 1975).

22. Arthur Niederhoffer, *Behind the Shield* (Garden City, N.Y.: Anchor Books, Doubleday, 1969).

23. See John P. Clark, "Isolation of the Police: A Comparison of the British and American Situations," *Journal of Criminal Law, Criminology and Police Science* 56 (September 1965): 313. See also R. M. Regoli, *Police in America* (Washington, D.C.: University Press of America, 1977). This is a report of a recent study extending Niederhoffer's hypotheses regarding police cynicism.

24. Joseph Wambaugh, *The New Centurions*, 1970; *The Blue Knight*, 1972; *The Onion Field*, 1973; *The Choirboys*, 1975; *The Black Marble*, 1978 (New York: Dell Books).

25. Richard Dougherty, *The Commissioner* (Garden City: Doubleday, 1962).

26. Martin Symonds, M.D., "Emotional Hazards of Police Work" (paper presented

before the Academy of Police Science, New York City, February 26, 1969). In Niederhoffer and Blumberg, *The Ambivalent Force: Perspectives on the Police* (Waltham, Mass.: Ginn, 1970), pp. 58–64.

27. Hans H. Toch, "Psychological Consequences of the Police Role," *Police* (Springfield, Ill.: C. C. Thomas) 10, September–October 1965): 22–25.

28. B. L. Garmire, "Value Shock," parts 1 and 2, *Texas Police Journal* 22, no. 12 (January 1975): 17–21; and 23, no. 1 (February 1975): 12–16.

29. The entire issue of *The Police Chief* (International Association of Chiefs of Police) for April 1978, and articles in the May 1978 issue, pp. 42 and 73, are relevant. Also see John Blackmore, "Are Police Allowed to Have Problems of Their Own?" in *Police* (New York: Criminal Justice Publications), pp. 47–55.

30. Victor G. Strecher, "When Subcultures Meet: Police-Negro Relations," in Sheldon Yefsky, ed., *Science and Technology in Law Enforcement* (Chicago: Thompson, 1967). The study of medical students referred to is H. S. Becker et al., *Boys in White* (Chicago: University of Chicago Press, 1961).

31. The last statement on the police side of this paradigm is Skolnick's.

32. Strecher, "When Subcultures Meet," pp. 703–704.

33. For example, see: Everett C. Hughes, *Men and Their Work* (Glencoe, Ill.: Free Press, 1958); Henry Borow, ed., *Man in a World at Work* (Boston: Houghton Mifflin, 1964).

34. Jerome H. Skolnick, *Justice Without Trial: Law Enforcement in Democratic Society* (New York: John Wiley & Sons, 1966), p. 42. Reprinted by permission of John Wiley & Sons.

35. Ibid., p. 42.

36. Ruth J. Levy, "Predicting Police Failures," *Journal of Criminal Law, Criminology, and Police Science* 58, no. 2 (1967): 275.

37. John H. Pfiffner, "The Function of Police in a Democratic Society," *Occasional Papers: Center for Training and Career Development* (Los Angeles: School of Public Administration, University of Southern California, 1967).

38. Ibid. Reprinted by permission.

39. Ibid. Also see "The Asshole" and other pertinent essays in Peter K. Manning and John Van Maanen, eds., *Policing—A View From the Street* (Santa Monica, Calif.: Goodyear, 1978).

40. Hans Toch, "Cops and Blacks: Warring Minorities," *Nation* 208, no. 16 (April, 21 1969): 491. Reprinted by permission.

41. Ibid.

42. Michael Banton, *The Policeman in the Community* (New York: Basic Books, 1964), p. 170. Copyright © 1964 by Michael Banton. Reprinted by permission of Basic Books, Inc., Publishers, New York.

43. Sterling, *Changes in Role Concepts During Recruit Training.*

44. Jerome H. Skolnick, "A Sketch of the Policeman's Working Personality," a chapter in *Justice Without Trial.*

45. William A. Westley, "Secrecy and the Police," *Social Forces* 34 (1956).

46. Peter K. Manning, *Police Work: The Social Organization of Policing* (Cambridge, Mass.: MIT Press, 1977).

47. Ibid., dust jacket.

48. Ibid., pp. 19–20.

49. U.S. Department of Justice, LEAA, *Psychological Assessment of Patrolman's Qualifications in Relation to Field Performance* (Washington, D.C.: U.S. Government Printing Office, 1968).

50. John Furcon is currently the director of the Law Enforcement Human Resources Division, Industrial Relations Center, University of Chicago. He is the principal investigator in the LEAA-funded National Police Officer Selection Project. See also Clifton Rhead, Arnold Abrams, Harry Trosman, and Philip Margolis, "The Psychological Assessment of Police Candidates," *American Journal of Psychiatry* 124, 11 (May 1968): 1575–1580. Copyright © The American Psychiatric Association.

51. Watson and Sterling, *Police and Their Opinions*, p. 4.

52. Ibid.

53. Seymour Martin Lipset, "Why Cops Hate Liberals—and Vice Versa, *Atlantic* 223, no. 3 (March 1969): 76; William H. Parker was quoted by Lipset, ibid. Copyright © 1969 by the Atlantic Monthly Company. Reprinted by permission.

54. A profile of police subculture based on Niederhoffer's study appears in Louis A. Radelet and Hoyt Coe Reed, *The Police and the Community: Studies* (Beverly Hills, Calif.: Glencoe, 1973), pp. 56–68.

55. Lipset, "Why Cops Hate Liberals," p. 78.

56. James Q. Wilson, *Varieties of Police Behavior: The Management of Law and Order in Eight Communities* (Cambridge: Harvard University Press, 1968), pp. 33–34.

57. Gunnar Myrdal, *An American Dilemma* (New York: Harper & Brothers, 1944), p. 540.

58. Sam Blum, "The Police," *Redbook*, February 1967, p. 121.

59. A. L. Cornelius, *Cross Examination* (Indianapolis, Ind.: Bobbs, 1929).

60. Watson and Sterling, *Police and Their Opinions*, p. 119. Reprinted by permission.

61. Banton, *Policeman in the Community*, p. 181.

62. Watson and Sterling, *Police and Their Opinions*, p. 124.

63. An excellent, panoramic review is provided by Robert W. Balch in "The Police Personality: Fact or Fiction?" *Journal of Criminology, Criminal Law and Police Science*, March 1972, pp. 106–119.

64. Milton Rokeach, Martin G. Miller, and John A. Snyder, "The Value Gap Between Police and Policed," *Journal of Social Issues* 27, no. 2 (1971): 155–171. See also Jacob Chwast, "Value Conflicts in Law Enforcement," *Crime and Delinquency* 11 (April 1965): 151–161.

65. Op. cit., Rokeach et al., p. 168.

66. Walsh, "Professional Cop"; Bayley and Mendelsohn, *Minorities and the Police: Confrontation in America* (New York: Free Press, 1969), pp. 50–51.

67. Samuel A. Stouffer et al., *The American Soldier: Combat and Its Aftermath* (Princeton, N.J.: Princeton University Press, 1949), p. 223. For an example of other research in this area, see R. R. Grinker and S. P. Speigal, *Men Under Stress* (Philadelphia: University of Pennsylvania Press, 1945).

68. Sterling, *Changes in Role Concepts During Recruit Training.*

69. James Q. Wilson, "The Patrolman's Dilemma," *New York,* September 1968, pp. 19–20. Copyright © 1968 by The New York Times Company. Reprinted by permission.

70. Carl Werthman and Irving Piliavin, "Gang Members and the Police," in Bordua, ed., *The Police: Six Sociological Essays,* p. 75.

71. Stouffer et. al., *American Soldier,* p. 227.

7

THE PUBLIC IMAGE
OF THE POLICE

"If you don't get a haircut, what will people think of you . . . (and of us, your parents)?"

"Why do you insist on looking like a creep by letting your beard grow?"

"We must keep our house and yard tidy so the neighbors will think well of us."

"Mind your manners so people will think you're a nice girl."

"Just remember this: the customer is always right."

These are commonplace expressions of the importance we attach to what others think of us. The unspoken implication is that what others think of us is an omnipotent value. Successful politicians and business firms give a lot of attention to their "image." But what does it mean to be thought of as "nice"? What standards determine who looks "like a creep"? What must one have, or be, in order to qualify as "well thought of"? Not everyone answers these questions in the same way.

We are taught that respect for others begins with respect for self. And self-respect is built on what we think others think of us. Thus, an interaction between individual human beings takes place. Divested of all its complexity, the human equation depends upon how well we understand ourselves and others.

As we have noted in the preceding chapter, the process of building self-respect begins in childhood. If parents say to a child, "You are a fine child; we are glad you are ours; you are honest and generous," the child comes to see himself in these terms. His public image is good; the feedback he is getting from people who matter to him is favorable. His self-confidence and self-respect, or lack thereof, are not innate, but develop out of these basic early experiences. It is not, of course, simply the words of parents and others that count. Yinger explains that their actions speak even louder:

> Parents may say to a child that he is a fine boy even while their treatment of him says plainly that they think he is ignorant (why can't you learn?), bad (you naughty, naughty child!) and a thorough-going nuisance. Having no other source of attitudes towards himself than the people around him, the child begins to see himself in the same way they do.[1]

125

THE PREOCCUPATION WITH IMAGERY

The self-image and the "other-image" (or public image) are two sides of the same coin. Our society is obsessed with imagery. Business and industry thrive on building a good image for their product. An apparently infinite number and variety of businesses are dependent upon imagery in some sense. Consider what one of the media, television, has done with this phenomenon. Not only is imagery the heartbeat of many of our economic institutions, it is intricately woven into our political, religious, and educational institutions.

Most people are concerned about what other people think of them and their "product." In business, a good self-image is measured largely by sales and profits. This is a relatively concrete index of one's public image. If the product sells, we feel good about ourselves—as a business, that is. And if the product doesn't sell, the image must be improved.

Simple enough. But suppose that the product is a public service, such as that of the police department, and the operation is supported by taxes? The measures of the public image in such a case are not as concrete as in hard-product business firms. It is much more difficult to tell whether the customer is satisfied. In fact, in police work, as we have seen, it is sometimes very difficult to tell what he expects, and he tends to change his mind, sometimes rapidly, to suit the circumstances. The customer also tends to want one kind of service for other people and another for himself. And there are many different kinds of customers to be served, often with conflicting expectations.

It is possible to ascertain the types of police services that particular types of customers may want, but the more heterogeneous the community, the more likely it is that there will be differing expectations of the police. While the police product is community services, which are clearly not as tangible a commodity as toothpaste, there is nonetheless a feedback process, as with all governmental services in a democratic society. The customer can and sometimes does say when the product fails to meet his expectations. If he is unhappy, he has recourse to certain remedial actions. The taxpayer controls, indirectly, but more or less effectively, the dollar input to the police department. If he is dissatisfied with police services, he can insist that the time has come to fire the chief, call for civilian review of police conduct, or even demand that he "run the department" in his neighborhood.

If a businessman who sells yachts discovers that his product does not enjoy a good public image among black families with annual income of less than $3,000, he does not worry much about it. He shrugs it off as unfortunate but irrelevant. However, the police are in a somewhat different position. They are expected to be the police for *all* the people. Therefore, it should not be too comforting to be told by public opinion pollsters that most of the people approve of the police most of the time. The more heterogeneous the community served by a police department, the less likely it is that such soothing assurances will be forthcoming.

CONSENSUS AND THE IMAGE OF THE POLICE

We are hardly the first to discover that the main problem of democratic government (or of any social system) is that of achieving noncoerced consensus.

We noted earlier how consensus applies to interpretations of police role and its related questions and asserted that this is the fundamental problem of police and community relations. In a way, the problem of the public image of the police (and of their self-image, too) is simply a repetition, in only slightly different terms, of the identical problem: sufficient *consensus* to make political processes reasonably functional in maintaining order with justice for the common good.

Approximately 70 percent of our people reside in big cities. The population of these cities is disparate from every conceivable standpoint. In such circumstances, what is the value of talking about the public image of the police department? So long as it is a *generalized* image, it has very little meaning. The important question is, on what issues regarding the police can so diversified a population achieve minimal consensus? There may even be some difference of opinion about superficial issues such as how important it is to keep patrol cars washed. On issues that are more important, however, informed opinion is difficult to come by. This lack is the legacy of a past in which it was widely agreed that "police business should be left to the police."

The range of questions that arise is wide: What kind of uniform should police officers wear? How should they carry their equipment? What about weapons? How about one-person patrol cars? Should the police provide social services? If so, how extensively and what types of services? Should the police sponsor drag-strip activities for teenagers? Should the police operate a rehabilitation facility for chronic alcoholics? What should a police officer be paid?

Such questions can divide a community, or perhaps the community is already divided, and questions concerning police work merely sharpen and deepen the cleavages. In any event, how is minimal consensus to be achieved? How can the many conflicting public images of the police be at least minimally and workably reconciled? This process is precisely the art of governing in a democracy, "the art of the possible" in politics and public administration, applied to building good police-community relations.

How the General Public Views the Police

In any sizable jurisdiction, various polls and public opinion surveys may be cited to show that the general public image of the police is good. The National Opinion Research Center reported to the President's Crime Commission in 1966 that only 8 percent of the people polled thought that the police do a poor job of enforcing the law; only 9 percent felt that the police were deficient in protecting people in their neighborhood. Gallup and Louis Harris surveys have produced similar results. So have a myriad of localized opinionaires. What the public thinks of the police has commonly been regarded as a hot topic for the survey-minded, despite wide acknowledgment that the information secured is unreliable and ephemeral.

The public generally believes that the police do not engage in serious misconduct. A Gallup poll in 1965 showed that only 9 percent of the public believed that there was any police brutality in their area. A Harris poll in 1966 found that only 4 percent of the public believed that many law enforcement officers in their community took bribes. Several studies reflect that most people believe that police and community relations are good. There has been a resultant tendency in some quarters to dismiss the concern for community relations as hogwash. As the 1966 Crime Commission states, "if the persons showing greatest skepticism toward the police were evenly distributed through all kinds of communities and neighborhoods, one might conclude that there was no serious police image problem."[2]

In such a conglomerate society, it is the image of the police held by specific segments of the public, rather than by the general public, that is of greatest consequence in the study of police and community relations. It is not simply a matter of majority rule. Because the police have everywhere traditionally acquiesced to the wishes of those with political and economic clout, it should not be surprising that popularity polls reflect predominantly favorable public opinion.

While localized, general public-opinion polls regarding the police remain popular, the national polls have in recent years tended to concentrate on more specific questions. For example:

Louis Harris Poll:

December, 1978—The country has been too slow to find ways to control violent crime.

November, 1978—School teachers, firemen, and police officers should be denied the right to strike, but sanitation and garbage collectors may strike.

September, 1978—Inflation is America's Number 1 domestic problem; crime control ranks fifth.

August, 1978—80 percent of the public supports gun control, a record high percentage.

Gallup Poll:

February, 1977—Parents see a link between television violence and crime.

December, 1977—The public is becoming less concerned with crime.

April, 1978—Sixty-two percent of the public favors the death penalty for murder, but not for other crimes.

There is little doubt that the police today are under much closer public scrutiny than in the past. Public pressure has increased for more effective service and for higher professional standards in matters involving the treatment of offenders, racial and sexual bias, corruption, and the use of deadly force. The police are retaliating by unionizing, using collective bargaining to secure improved financial benefits, and striking as the ultimate action. All of this is happening during a period of tightening budgets. Police "productivity" is a big subject. A recent federally financed Rand Corporation study of twenty-five police departments raised serious questions about the effectiveness of detectives. A 1974 study of 17,000 arrests made in Washington, D.C. (by the Institute for Law and Social Research) discovered that more than 70 percent of the arrests did not result in convictions. The failure of the police to find witnesses and evidence was cited as the main reason.[3]

The view that the police have no serious image problem appears to be substantiated by criminal victimization surveys in thirteen big cities, completed in 1975. The percentage of those questioned who believed that police performance was "good" or "average" increased from 79 to 81 percent between 1972 and 1975.[4]

Yet the United States Commission on Civil Rights reported that in 1977 it received an increasing number of complaints regarding police misconduct. In the same year, the United States Department of Justice logged some 12,000 complaints about police officers' use of excessive force. On the other hand, the FBI reported that 111 law enforcement officers were killed and that there were nearly 50,000 incidents of assault on police officers during 1976.[5]

Tables 7-1 through 7-7 provide information about the public's attitude toward the police, based on the 1975 National Crime Survey.[6] These tables include information about the public's attitude towards the way the police respond to crime.

Table 7–1

Evaluations of police performance in the 1972/73 and in the 1975 surveys of the eight Impact Cities and the Nation's five largest cities

	Evaluation of police performance					
	Good	Average	Poor	Don't know	No answer	Estimated number[a]
1972/73 Surveys	42%	37%	13%	7%	0%	(14,621,640)
1975 Surveys	40%	41%	12%	7%	0%	(15,386,335)

[a] Unless otherwise noted, in this and subsequent tables, estimated numbers refer to the population estimates of the cities derived from samples taken in the NCS. The estimates refer only to persons 16 years old or older, except when age is included as a variable in the table.

Table 7–2

Perceived need for improvement of local police in the 1972/73 and 1975 surveys of the eight Impact Cities and the Nation's five largest cities

	1972/73	1975
Estimated number[a]	(13,489,638)	(14,259,389)
No improvement needed	16%	15%
Improvement needed	67%	68%
Don't know	13%	15%
No answer	4%	2%
Most important suggested improvement (1975):[b]		
Hire more policemen		24%
Concentrate on more important duties, serious crime, etc.		11%
Be more prompt, responsive, alert		15%
Improve training, raise qualifications or pay, recruitment policies		4%
Be more courteous, improve attitude, community relations		9%
Don't discriminate		2%
Need more traffic control		1%
Need more policemen of certain type (foot, car) in certain areas or at certain times		27%
Other		7%
Estimated number[c]		(9,697,652)

[a] Excludes respondents who did not express an opinion on the evaluation of police performance question (item 14a in Appendix A).
[b] Response categories used in 1972/73 and 1975 surveys were not fully comparable.
[c] Only respondents who indicated that improvement was needed.

TABLE 7–3

Rating of police by two indicators of respondent fear of crime; 1975 NCS city surveys

	Rating of police[a]				
	(Positive)		(Negative)		
	1	2	3	4	Estimated number
Neighborhood safety at night:[b]					
Very safe	16%[c]	39%	33%	12%	(1,898,696)
	18%[d]	16%	10%	12%	
Reasonably safe	12%	33%	44%	10%	(5,729,744)
	40%	40%	43%	32%	
Somewhat unsafe	11%	31%	45%	13%	(3,455,194)
	22%	23%	26%	24%	
Very unsafe	11%	32%	39%	19%	(3,128,564)
	20%	21%	20%	32%	
Estimated number	(1,745,571)	(4,693,707)	(5,937,325)	(1,835,596)	(14,212,199)
Comparative neighborhood danger:[e]					
Much more dangerous	7%	23%	35%	35%	(149,101)
	1%	1%	1%	3%	
More dangerous	9%	26%	40%	26%	(791,585)
	4%	4%	5%	11%	
Average	10%	28%	48%	15%	(6,067,640)
	34%	36%	49%	50%	
Less dangerous	14%	37%	39%	10%	(5,591,913)
	45%	45%	37%	30%	
Much less dangerous	19%	43%	31%	8%	(1,517,164)
	16%	14%	8%	6%	
Estimated number	(1,730,224)	(4,655,109)	(5,907,603)	(1,824,468)	(14,117,404)

[a] Respondents who did not express an opinion on the evaluation of police performance question (item 14a in Appendix A) were not given a scale score.
[b] Excludes respondents who gave no answer. For exact wording, see item 11a in Appendix A.
[c] Row percentages.
[d] Column percentages.
[e] Excludes respondents who gave no answer. For exact wording, see item 12 in Appendix A.

TABLE 7-4

Most important suggested improvements for local police by reasons for not reporting personal victimizations to the police; 1975 NCS city surveys

Reasons for not reporting	Most important suggested improvements[a]									Estimated number[b]
	Hire more policemen	Concentrate on more important duties, etc.	Be more prompt, etc.	Improve training, etc.	Be more courteous, etc.	Don't discriminate	Need more traffic control	Need more policemen of certain type, etc.	Other	
Nothing could be done; lack of proof	20%	13%	15%	3%	13%	2%	1%	28%	6%	(151,861)
Did not think it important enough	18%	14%	12%	4%	16%	2%	2%	25%	8%	(104,368)
Police wouldn't want to be bothered	21%	17%	17%	5%	12%	3%	0%	17%	7%	(32,862)
Did not want to take time; too inconvenient	16%	18%	9%	4%	9%	3%	0%	29%	11%	(24,182)
Private or personal matter	10%	15%	15%	5%	13%	3%	3%	24%	11%	(49,203)
Did not want to get involved	20%	10%	19%	3%	6%	2%	0%	21%	18%	(12,817)
Afraid of reprisal	25%	14%	14%	4%	13%	3%	0%	20%	7%	(18,102)
Reported to someone else	17%	9%	14%	5%	11%	2%	1%	30%	10%	(22,272)
Other	16%	15%	10%	7%	11%	1%	0%	25%	15%	(45,045)

[a] See item 14b in Appendix A for exact wording of category labels.
[b] Indicates number of unreported victimizations in which the victim cited the reason for not reporting shown. Numbers sum to more than the total number of unreported victimizations because some victims cited more than one reason for not reporting.

TABLE 7–5

Evaluation of police performance by selected respondent characteristics; 1975 NCS city surveys

	Evaluation of police performance					
	Good	Average	Poor	Don't know	No answer	Estimated number
Age:						
16-29	29%	48%	16%	6%	0%	(4,971,233)
30-49	38%	42%	13%	6%	0%	(4,627,084)
50 or older	50%	33%	8%	9%	0%	(5,788,018)
Race:						
White	47%	37%	9%	7%	0%	(10,872,109)
Black/other	24%	50%	19%	7%	0%	(4,514,226)
Sex:						
Male	40%	41%	13%	5%	0%	(6,882,142)
Female	40%	40%	11%	8%	0%	(8,504,193)
Family income:						
Less than $5,000	40%	36%	14%	9%	0%	(2,898,064)
$5,000-11,999	38%	42%	13%	6%	0%	(5,173,635)
$12,000 or more	42%	42%	10%	5%	0%	(5,654,310)
Not ascertained	36%	40%	13%	11%	1%	(1,660,690)

TABLE 7–6

Evaluation of police performance by race and age of respondent; 1975 NCS city surveys

Race and age	Evaluation of police performance					
	Good	Average	Poor	Don't know	No answer	Estimated number
White:						
16-29	36%	45%	12%	6%	0%	(3,304,181)
30-49	46%	37%	10%	6%	0%	(3,060,294)
50 or older	54%	30%	7%	8%	0%	(4,507,635)
Black/other:						
16-29	16%	54%	24%	5%	1%	(1,667,053)
30-49	23%	52%	19%	6%	0%	(1,566,790)
50 or older	34%	43%	13%	10%	0%	(1,280,383)

TABLE 7–7
Rating of police by two indicators of respondent perceptions of crime trends; 1975 NCS city surveys

| | Rating of police[a] | | | | |
| | (Positive) | | (Negative) | | |
	1	2	3	4	Estimated number
Neighborhood crime trend:[b]					
Increased	9%[c]	30%	43%	17%	(6,358,179)
	41%[d]	47%	52%	65%	
Same	15%	35%	41%	9%	(5,392,291)
	53%	47%	42%	29%	
Decreased	13%	34%	39%	14%	(723,266)
	6%	6%	5%	6%	
Estimated number	(1,490,657)	(4,057,886)	(5,269,849)	(1,655,345)	(12,473,737)
Changes in chances of being attacked or robbed: [e]					
Up	10%	32%	43%	14%	(9,115,143)
	57%	64%	68%	71%	
Same	15%	35%	40%	11%	(4,023,007)
	36%	31%	27%	24%	
Down	16%	33%	39%	12%	(712,268)
	7%	5%	5%	5%	
Estimated number	(1,674,418)	(4,555,285)	(5,822,046)	(1,798,669)	(13,850,418)

[a] Respondents who did not express an opinion on the evaluation of police performance question (item 14a in Appendix A) were not given a scale score.
[b] Excludes respondents who had not lived in the neighborhood long enough to estimate crime trends, who said they didn't know, or who gave no answer. For exact wording, see item 9a in Appendix A.
[c] Row percentages.
[d] Column percentages.
[e] Excludes respondents who had no opinion or who gave no answer. For exact wording, see item 15a in Appendix A.

General public opinion surveys regarding the police present difficult methodological problems in social science research. The prevailing current view among experts in these matters is that such survey data are not reliable, especially when utilized as a basis for police policy decisions. To illustrate the criticism:

> . . . the overwhelmingly favorable picture of police-community relations reported by some may be a function of misinterpretation of items as well as a function of the level of specificity of the items utilized in the research. . . . on general items the

public reports a favorable image of the police reflecting their support for the institutional foundation of this criminal justice agency. While on more specific items the favorable image decreases tremendously, reflecting a rather negative evaluation of specific police officeholders and practices. . . . most of the empirical literature assessing the mood of the public toward criminal justice agencies is not useful for informing policy decisions.[7]

The earliest attempts to survey public opinion regarding the police were made in the 1950s. It is instructive to describe the technique. G. Douglas Gourley, then a Los Angeles police officer studying public administration at the University of Southern California, undertook a survey of public attitudes toward the police in Los Angeles for his master's dissertation. A similar study was conducted in Houston in 1959 by a University of Houston Law School class in police-community relations, under the direction of the late Larry W. Fultz, at the time an inspector in the Houston police department.[8]

The basic premise of these early studies was the recognition that, no matter how well a police department is organized, or how efficient and honest its administration, it is judged by individual citizens and, consequently, by the nature of its public contacts. Both studies concluded that actual contacts with the police are the single most important determinant of the public image of the police.

The basic survey instrument in these studies was a multiple-choice questionnaire. Random sampling was done by contacting respondents in groups carefully chosen to contain a variety of ages, economic levels, occupations, political viewpoints, education levels, and cultures. All the multiple-choice answers pertained to the attitudes and beliefs of the general public toward police officers, on the premise that what people *believed* was important, even when not supported by facts. Following are some examples of choices and the percent of responses in each set, using the Houston study as an example:

Influence of Politics

1. Apprehend criminals indiscriminately without regard for pressure brought by influential persons. (26.9%)
2. Occasionally show favoritism to politicians. (48.7%)
3. Lose jobs by refusing to obey orders of political bosses. (6.2%)
4. Do not know. (18.2%)

Influence of Social Position

1. Not influenced by social position of violators. (25.5%)
2. Occasionally influenced by social position of violators. (45.0%)
3. Often influenced by social position of violators. (15.2%)
4. Do not know. (14.3%)

Treatment of Suspects

1. Never engage in brutality toward suspects. (15.5%)
2. Seldom engage in brutality toward suspects. (40.5%)

3. Often engage in brutality toward suspects. (22.9%)
4. Do not know. (21.1%)

Minority Groups

1. Usually fair in dealing with minority groups. (37.9%)
2. Sometimes unfriendly in dealing with minority groups. (31.6%)
3. Definitely prejudiced against minority groups. (10.4%)
4. Do not know. (20.1%)

Overall Evaluation

1. One of the very best Police Departments in the country. (14.7%)
2. About on an average with other large Police Departments. (55.3%)
3. Definitely below standard in comparison with other large Police Departments. (17.0%)
4. Do not know. (13.0%)

The Houston survey results, as reflected in the random sample (very similar to the Los Angeles results), are more interesting when broken down to comparative responses from specific publics. For example, taking the age differential, among respondents under 18 years, 39.9 percent felt that the police were usually fair in dealing with minority groups, and 6.9 percent thought the police were definitely prejudiced. However, in the age group over 50 years, 51.9 percent thought that the police were usually fair in their treatment of minority groups, while only 5.4 percent thought the police were definitely prejudiced.

As another example, on the question asking for overall evaluation of the department, 16.2 percent of the male respondents checked the most favorable category compared with 12.5 percent of the female respondents; 57.3 percent of the males checked the second most favorable category to 52.6 percent of the females; 16.5 percent of the males checked the third category to 17.8 percent of the females; and 10 percent of the male respondents checked "do not know" to 17.1 percent of the female respondents. In terms of occupation, only 9.0 percent of housewives had a high opinion of the police department, as compared with 19.9 percent of transportation workers and 30.0 percent of public servants. Only 11.5 percent of black respondents expressed the belief that Houston had one of the best police departments in the country, whereas 24.1 percent of the Mexican Americans and 14.5 percent of the remaining respondents felt that way. At the other extreme, 32.6 percent of the blacks, 14.6 percent of the Mexican Americans, and 15.0 percent of the remaining respondents stated that the department was below standard in comparison with other large departments. Black females were more favorable in their opinion of the department than black males, and Mexican-American females rated it higher than Mexican-American males. Curiously, females not included in either the black or Mexican-American groups were outspokenly critical of police.

Our point in discussing these early surveys of the public image of the police is to emphasize the importance of the opinion of *specific* audiences or reference groups, by age, by social class, by educational, racial, ethnic, sex, and occupational differentiations. The methodological lesson in this point was not adequately heeded by the public opinion surveyors of the 1960s.

The Importance of Contacts

That public attitudes toward the police are strongly influenced by actual contacts with the police is stressed in the observations of a number of theorists. For instance, Claudine Gibson Wirths of the University of North Carolina analyzed attitudes toward law enforcement as a specific aspect of more general attitudes toward authority and authority figures that originate in childhood, beginning with the training and protecting of an infant by the mother. As we have noted, the way this early life-and-death authority is imposed upon the child sets the pattern for how the child will view all people in authority later in life. Wirths stressed that specific attitudes toward the police reflected an interplay of society, family culture, and personality; therefore, these attitudes are complex. She concluded:

> The specific actions of family and friends are the earliest attitudinal conditioners. How a dad behaves when he gets a parking ticket or jury duty influences his son far more than parental preachings on the subject. In general, children learn a little from what they are taught, and a lot from the examples they see. Consequently, the actions and attitudes of law enforcement people themselves probably constitute the greatest single cultural influence on public attitudes toward law enforcement.[9]

Wirths mentioned Geoffrey Gorer's notable study of public attitudes toward the police in England, which showed how these attitudes were drastically changed by Peel's major overhaul of the system.[10] The important point is that effective police work tends to encourage favorable public attitudes, and this comes down to the behavior and attitudes of the individual officer. He holds a position of special psychological influence in the community. This is why a crooked or corrupt police officer is so serious a problem. A "grandstanding" officer is a related concern. The importance of one officer's example in encouraging positive public attitudes toward police can hardly be exaggerated.

Audience Expectations

As suggested by Wirths, public attitudes toward the police are psychologically complicated. While actual contacts with police officers are important, exposure to particular attitudes toward the police is also a factor. Frequently, the interaction between police and civilian is governed by sterotyped perceptions formed by the background of experiences on each side; or as the role theorists might say it, behavior is grounded in *self-fulfilling role enactment*. This involves audience expectations: beliefs and demands about what should and should not be done. Applied to the public image of the police, this means that the expectations of the public at large and of specific groups, as well as the public's evaluation of the adequacy with which these expectations are met, are potent conditioners of the occupational role performance of police officers.

We have already stressed that the public's expectations of the police are not static. Even in the law enforcement part of police work, the law and its interpretation is a constantly changing social force. Different parts of the same community, especially in big cities, have different expectations of the police, partly because of differing perceptions of the law. Therefore, if one is interested in securing information about public attitudes toward a police department, it makes a difference what one asks, of whom one asks it, and under what circumstances. The Los Angeles and Houston studies demonstrated this point.

Another strong element in attitudes toward the police in a democratic society is that the power to control police activities resides in the public, as we saw in chapter 1. This is effective power, as Jack Preiss and Howard Ehrlich point out, "because the role performance of policemen is both highly observable and easily confronted with public sanction."[11] Thus many police organizations today are trying to make their activities more visible—more subject to audit, for instance—through a maze of report forms and paper work, to the annoyance of many police officers. Police organizations tend to be hypersensitive in matters of public complaints, investigations of alleged misconduct, and internal disciplinary procedures.

In their study of the public image of a state police agency, Preiss and Ehrlich presented data in which the configuration of the variables of age, sex, occupation, education, minority-group status, and the degree and kind of contact with the police provided some interesting patterns. The most positive composite image of the police was found in a middle-aged, white, female college graduate who had had no contact with the police and whose husband was engaged in a nonexecutive capacity in a white-collar occupation. By contrast, the most negative composite image was held by a somewhat younger nonwhite male manual worker with a grade school education or less, who had had some, but not extensive, contact with the police.[12]

There is more of interest in this study. Women, for example, were twice as likely as men to view the police as primarily a service organization, rather than one primarily responsible for criminal or traffic enforcement. Women who had had some contact with the police tended to describe the police officer's demeanor as impersonal; men with experience in such contacts tended to see the officer as friendly. Somewhat surprisingly, this study found little significant effect of either education or occupation upon attitudes toward the police. A bit puzzling was the finding that persons with no contact with the police had the most favorable attitude (what is the source of their image?); persons with limited personal contact were next most favorable; while those with considerable negative contact appeared to be more favorably inclined than those with only limited negative contact. Conjecturing the possible reasons for these responses makes a stimulating discussion.

Crime victimization studies in recent years have provided some useful insights about the nature of crime. What do crime victims think of the police and of criminal justice processes generally? One study, done in Seattle by Paul Smith and Richard Hawkins, involved a random sample of the population, 72 percent of whom held positive views of the police.[13] A majority of the respondents—55 percent—reported having been criminally victimized within the preceding twelve months, although less than half of these incidents had been reported to the police by the victims. In the total sample, the only background variables (education, income, occupation, sex of respondent, etc.) that appeared to affect attitudes toward police significantly were age and race. Fear of property crime victimization did not influence views of the police. Differences in such views between victims of property crimes and crimes against the person were slight. Unsatisfactory experience with police investigating victimization had a negative effect on attitudes toward the police. Observing officers "do wrong" produced more negative feelings about the police. Some 14 percent of the sample had been arrested during the preceding year. Their attitudes toward the police were more negative than those of persons who had not been arrested. Knowing individual officers personally did not seem to influence attitudes toward the police in general.

Another recent study of this type, done by Theodore Poister and James McDavid of the Institute of Public Administration at Penn State University, centered in Harrisburg.[14] This analysis used data on members of victimized households drawn from a community survey, just as the Seattle study did. The line of questioning on victimization incidents moved from perceptions of response time and investigations to whether a suspect was arrested or convicted. Respondents were asked about their satisfaction at various stages of this process, as well as with overall police performance. Overall satisfaction varied with the type of crime and response time more than with socioeconomic characteristics. Follow-up investigations and arrests influence overall satisfaction beyond satisfaction with the initial investigation. Satisfaction with police performance decreases at later stages of the process.

THE MINORITY-GROUP IMAGE

Both studies noted above found that black respondents tended to be less satisfied with police performance (or more negative in attitudes) in the handling of victimization incidents. This finding is consistent with the disclosures of virtually all the general surveys of public opinion and the police. Blacks and other minorities perceive the police more negatively than do whites.

The Preiss and Ehrlich study included some data regarding the image held by members of minority groups. Item by item, minority-group members were significantly more likely to view the police in a relatively negative manner. The 1966 National Opinion Research Center survey for the President's Crime Commission produced similar findings. Blacks were markedly more negative than whites in evaluating police effectiveness in law enforcement. On questions pertaining to police discourtesy and misconduct, the disparity between the attitudes of blacks and whites was even greater. About two-thirds of whites, but only one-third of blacks, thought the police were "almost all honest."[15]

While the surveys indicate that blacks are substantially more hostile to police than whites, blacks also strongly feel the need for police protection. The Michigan State University study for the President's Crime Commission revealed that the primary complaint of blacks against the police was of permissive law enforcement and inadequate protection and services in areas where blacks reside. This has been confirmed in studies by the United States Civil Rights Commission and others. The Michigan State study also found that Hispanics tend to "look upon the police as enemies who protect only the white power structure." The University of California survey in Philadelphia discovered that some Hispanic leaders felt even more alienated from the police than did blacks.[16] Various surveys have shown that young people are generally more negative than older persons in their attitudes toward the police. Similarly, the poor have generally less favorable attitudes toward the police than the affluent.

The simple conclusion to draw from all of this is that positive public attitudes toward the police are associated with perceptions of fair, competent, and responsive service. Elements of the public tending to criticize the police usually do so with allegations of unfair, incompetent, and/or unresponsive treatment.

Attitudes of Hostility

A good idea of the hostility involved in some police-citizen interactions can be gained from the following statements found in various sources:

> From the front seat of a moving patrol car, street life in a typical Negro ghetto is perceived as an uninterrupted sequence of suspicious scenes. Every well-dressed man or woman standing aimlessly on the street during hours when most people are at work is carefully scrutinized for signs of an illegal source of income; every boy wearing boots, black pants, long hair, and a club jacket is viewed as potentially responsible for some item on the list of muggings, broken windows, and petty thefts that still remain to be cleared; and every hostile glance directed at the passing patrolman is read as a sign of possible guilt. The residents of these neighborhoods regard this kind of surveillance as the deepest of insults.[17]

> Then he started asking questions, identification, what were we doing and all like that. And he searched us and got our names down on the book and everything. We wasn't doing anything except what we usually do on that corner. (What's that?) Stand there bullshitting. They do anything to get our names in the book. You know. They want us to know they in charge.[18]

> If they ever pick you up and look at your records, they automatically take you in. They see where your sister been to jail, your brother, or if you ever went to jail. And they start saying, "Your whole family is rotten. Your whole family is jailbirds." . . . And this is what really makes you mad, when they tell you your mother don't know how to read.[19]

> The implacable hostility of the police toward the ghetto inmates is fundamentally a clash of widely separated social strata, one armed with authority, the other charged with despair.[20]

> Thus, to many Negroes, police have come to symbolize white power, white racism, and white repression. And the fact is that many police do reflect and express these white attitudes. The atmosphere of hostility and cynicism is reinforced by a widespread perception among Negroes of the existence of police brutality and corruption and of a "double standard" of justice and protection—one for Negroes and one for whites.[21]

> Anyone who says there is not considerable malpractice is not being realistic. There is widespread prejudice . . . and hostility. Policemen are more suspicious of

Negroes than whites, because there are such misconceptions. . . . they stop more Negroes without probable cause. . . . given these prejudices, hostility, the police-man's authoritarian personality, limited training and ignorance of the law, there has to be police malpractice.[22]

Hostile attitudes toward the police are likely to be reciprocated in hostile police attitudes toward those who "bug" them. William Westley concluded that it was a universal complaint of police officers that the public would not help them and in fact often hindered them in their duties.[23] Albert Reiss and his associates at the University of Michigan looked into several aspects of this in their study for the 1966 President's Crime Commission. Reiss indicated that there are frequent instances in which a citizen is victimized by crime and yet does not report it to the police. The reason most often given is that the victim believes it is unless or futile to do so. This may be because victims think the police regard the experience as so minor that they do not want to be bothered. Past experience may support the victim's beliefs. For example, the police in big cities occasionally respond to breaking and entering complaints in slum areas by suggesting that the citizen buy a dog or a gun, or move.

Another reason given for failure to report crimes was that the citizen felt it too troublesome to do so. But the Reiss study produced little evidence that citizens' failure to report crime was due to a belief that the police were against them. And only one percent of those interviewed said they had failed to report an incident they had witnessed that looked as though it might be a crime. Reiss concludes:

Quite clearly, citizens do not always feel the obligation to call the police to report a crime. . . . there does seem to be reason to believe that citizens do not call the police unless they regard a matter as something where they were seriously wronged or they are personally affronted, or where they have something personally to gain from it, such as gain from an insurance claim. But any gain has to be worth the effort of calling the police and "getting involved." Apart from such motivations to call the police, citizens are inclined to disengage themselves from any responsibility to call the police.[24]

Role Reference Groups and Public Image

Additional complications often increase the reciprocal hostility in a police-civilian transaction. This may be illustrated by two factors that James Sterling has identified. One is that the police are sometimes viewed as behaving too impersonally. In a demonstration situation, for example, the taunts of the demonstrators may not produce any perceptible police reaction. This can become irritating to the demonstrators, and in itself may provoke inflammatory behavior, because the police fail to act as they are expected to act; therefore, they are "inhuman," not because they overact, but because they underact.

The other factor identified by Sterling pertains to police concern for uniform application of the law. Police officers wonder how they can function on the basis of the principle of equal justice if there are different standards of community conduct, and therefore of expected police behavior, in each community or neighborhood. The conflict here is more apparent than real for those who understand the distinction between equality and equity, as most police officers are well aware.

We have seen that the occupational socialization of police recruits includes both the adoption of standard modes of police behavior and the gradual shedding of behaviors that are inappropriate for the police role. The most important aspect of this socialization is the identification of role-relevant reference groups and the development of a sensitivity to their expectations and evaluations. This process is precisely the connection between police behavior and police public image. However, the role-relevant groups that the police recruit chooses are seldom as diverse as the community he or she will serve. Sterling explains this as follows:

> There are many groups who observe and evaluate the role performance of a police patrolman. There are fewer groups who hold expectations for and evaluations of the police which the patrolman attends to. Whenever the patrolman does attend to their expectations and evaluations, they constitute an audience or reference group for him. [For the recruit in training] there are very few persons in his role related reference groups. There are other new patrolmen, trainers, personal friends who are police officers, and perhaps some role models. . . . Once he enters the new role of apprentice patrolman, [however], the number of relevant reference groups enlarges. As Skolnick said, " . . . the whole civilian world is an audience for the patrolman."[25]

Obviously, however, the individual patrol officer does not and cannot attend to the expectations and evaluations of "the whole civilian world." As Preiss and Ehrlich state, what the patrol officer does is to "develop a hierarchy of audience groups."[26] Westley said it as follows:

> Policemen seem to distinguish and define these groups on the basis of their supposed attitude toward the police, their values, . . . their politics and their relationship to the ends of the police. In their concern for public approval, they analyze these groups in terms of the degree of influence which they have over the police and the way in which they must be treated in order to obtain respect and other social goals of the police.[27]

The abstract theory of the sociologist as applied to the public image of the police could hardly be better translated into the pragmatism of the "average cop." It would appear that police officers know a great deal about the pecking order. They see it as a simple matter of occupational survival.

POLICE AND POLICED AS ADVERSARIES

Because police-citizen interaction is inherently conflictual, especially regarding the law enforcement function of the police, the public view of the police inevitably has an adversary element. There are frequent references to it in the literature. A common expression of it, by police officers, is that they are not in business to win a popularity contest. Malinowski, the great scholar of primitive law, posed the following basic question:

> Is it not contrary to human nature to accept any constraint as a matter of course, and does man, whether civilized or savage, ever carry out unpleasant, burdensome, cruel regulations and taboos without being compelled to? And compelled by some force or motive which he cannot resist?[28]

Part of the police job is suppressive and punitive. James Q. Wilson alludes to it when he asserts that the police often deal with their clients as adversaries: "The policeman in the *routine* case is often (though not always) dealing with his clientele as an *antagonist*, in that he issues summonses, makes arrests, conducts inquiries, searches homes, stops cars, testifies in court, and keeps a jail."[29]

As the Houston study put it:

> It is unlikely that any single instance of police action has ever been completely satisfactory to everyone concerned; for no matter how efficient or brilliant the example of police work may be, it is not likely to be viewed with enthusiasm by the thwarted or apprehended offender or his family or friends.[30]

The adversarial aspect of police work has implications for the delineation of the goals of police and community relations programs, as indicated in chapter 2.

Some analysts have gone on to say that the inherent conflict between police and policed is further aggravated by various other considerations. Discussions of this point have tended to fall into categories according to the particular academic or operational vantage point of the observer: sociology, psychology, politics, philosophy, anthropology, psychiatry—or civil rights, legalistic, judicial, and so on. Michael Banton's view on the subject, which is influenced by his English environment, is somewhat unique. Banton does not deny that, in dealing with certain types of criminals, or in a tough, urban neighborhood, "there may be justification for the view of policemen and public as adversaries." But in general, Banton rejects the adversary conception in three related arguments:

1. The police officer spends very little time "chasing people or locking people up." He spends most of his time helping citizens in distress.
2. It is misleading to describe a policeman's job as law enforcement. A policeman's activities "are governed much more by popular morality than they are by the letter of the law."
3. Even criminals recognize the moral authority, as opposed to the power, of the police. When people grumble at the police, they are really "trying to make their violations seem excusable to still their own consciences."[31]

Banton goes on to make a key point in comparing British with American policing: that in the "comparatively more highly integrated society that Britain is, there is greater consensus about the right way to respond to given situations" (greater *predictability* in police behavior, Banton says in another place). Then he adds, speaking as a social anthropologist:

> The moral authority of the police officer depends upon the level of social integration and moral unity of the community, and one cannot compare the work of British and American policemen without recognizing these differences in the context in which they have to operate.[32]

Quite clearly, the social and cultural environment strongly influences the degree to which citizens view the police as adversaries.

The American social historian Oscar Handlin recalls that the organized police force is a relatively recent historical phenomenon in England and the United

States. He reminds us that there were opponents of this idea who thought that freedom and democracy would be jeopardized by a paid professional police force. Handlin believes that current American public attitudes toward the police are partly rooted in residuals of the historic past in Europe and America, when police were seen as agents of tyranny and oppression, as functionaries for "keeping people down" under the aegis of czars and emperors.[33]

A Psychiatric View of the Adversary Relationship

Several psychiatrists have shown keen interest in police and community discord in recent years, Karl Menninger among them.[34] In 1960, psychiatrist Chester M. Pierce addressed a Police-Community Relations Institute in Cincinnati and presented his diagnosis of police-citizen conflict. Pierce reported that psychiatrists and psychotherapists often deal clinically with police officers. He surmised that police officers are frequently perplexed about their public image. They would like to be thought of as benevolent, sacrificing, and strong protectors, but fear that they are seen, in extreme cases, as "weak, greedy flatfoots." From this observation, Pierce drew two inferences:

1. In police-citizen interaction, there is a "lock-key" arrangement. On the one hand, the police officer finds people whose personal problems facilitate the solution, although unsatisfactorily, of the officer's own problems. On the other hand, citizens invite their own catastrophes with police officers by using the officer to solve their problems, also in an unsatisfactory manner.

2. Police-community conflict reflects an on-going modification related to the emancipation of women in our society. With the concomitant diminution in the importance of the father in the family prestige system, public attitudes toward police authority have changed, since the police officer is a father equivalent.[35]

Pierce's meaning may be clearer in the following passage:

> The policeman . . . must be conservative and sober in aims and objectives. Thus, he is timebound, and he functions in an organized setting which is authority-centered and militaristic.[36]

In a sense, Pierce opines, the police officer has the unpopular job of thwarting change. Law is, by definition, "an enlightened revision of custom," he says, and therefore demands a conservative, sober, objective approach to impartially protecting all spheres of the society. This means that a common public perception of the practical work of the police officer is that of conservative guardian of the status quo. Pierce continues:

> The citizens of a community are individually-centered and supportive of independent assertion. Their approach to problems, in contrast to the policeman, would tend to be more individually subjective, more impressionistic, more impulse-ridden.[37]

Pierce believes that, to the police officer, the greatest strain in police-citizen relations is the failure of someone to observe the status quo. To the citizen, the greatest strain is failure of the officer "to exert kindly enough treatment of an individual."[38]

Other Views of the Adversary Relationship

We have alluded to the views of various psychologists who have studied police and community relations. In effect, each has asked himself why there is a problem in the relationship between police and policed? Why is it in some sense an adversarial interaction?

Because psychologists are concerned basically with behavior, their research interest in police and community relations focuses on such questions as these:

- To what degree is police-citizen antagonism a matter of conflicting *perceptions;* for example, of the police role in today's society?

- In the sense of prepolice background, specifically in terms of attitudes, beliefs and values, what type of individual (personality) finds policing an attractive career?

- What happens to the "police personality" as a result of occupational socialization, in terms of attitudes, beliefs, and values?

- Are there significant personality differences, in the same terms, between police officers and members of other occupations?

- To what extent is the behavior of police officers the result of society's impossible expectations from them? What are the implications of this for the police self-image?

- Where do the police stand in the violence phenomenon?

These questions are illustrative of the type psychologists raise; there are numerous others. We have cited such psychologists as Hans Toch, Milton Rokeach, Ruth Levy, Melany Baehr and her University of Chicago associates, as well as the social psychology–oriented views of Jerome Skolnick, Seymour Martin Lipset, William Westley, J. Milton Yinger, Mildred Peters, James Leo Walsh, and James Sterling. Their views are indicative of psychological approaches to questions of police and community relations. Because these relations sometimes involve conflicting behavior, psychologists view the relationship as an adversary one in some respects. They are interested in discovering why this is so and in suggesting what may be done to deal constructively with the problem. Naturally, their contributions reflect their discipline, as do those of psychiatrists (Pierce),historians (Handlin), and anthropologists (Banton). Environmental psychologists see police and community relations as an aspect of their study of community mental health.

Arthur Stinchcombe, a sociologist at the University of California at Berkeley, long interested in the sociology of policing, is of the opinion that the manner in which the police exert authority is the decisive consideration in generating citizen resentment. Stinchcombe believes, as does Skolnick, that legal standards and restraints are much less important than *norms located within police organizations* in governing police behavior.[39]

Reiss and Bordua contend that, in a way, the police are their own clients, and this helps to explain their supermoralistic tendencies, as if they were engaged in a private war against crime. Even prosecutors and the courts are dubious allies, as viewed by the police, since both often reject decisions made by the police.[40]

Perhaps this helps to explain also the tendency of the police to take almost personal offense at what they see as the failure of the public to assume appropriate responsibility in coping with crime. Many officers feel that their main problem is the indifference and apathy of the public toward problems that the police feel are of major importance. There is, of course, some basis for this feeling, but public apathy is not confined to matters of interest to the police. Apathy, moreover, is an effect rather than a cause. What causes apathy and what can be done about it—this is the question.

These days, more and more people are direct victims of crimes against property and person. There is widespread concern for the victims of crime, even to state (federal program pending) compensation for damages. This can be applauded. We can also applaud the increasing number of citizen action programs, often generated by crime victims, to work with the police and other social institutions in programs to *prevent* crime. Where such programs have been initiated, the results have been dramatic.

A CLASS ANALYSIS OF POLICE–COMMUNITY ANTAGONISM

The adversary relationship between the police and the public outlined above can be traced to several diverse sources.[41] The dominant framework in police-community relations today uses a *consensus* model, in which the legal code and police enforcement of it are seen as democratically determined and equally beneficial to all segments of the community. Because the police reflect and enforce common interests and shared values, according to this model, an efficient police force should be welcomed by all members of a community. Any conflict between police and citizen groups is therefore traced to imperfections that develop within their relationship itself, rather than to basic contradictions in the mandate of the police. Thus, the friction between the police and the policed is attributed to problems of poor police performance or improper public understanding of its role, with police professionalization or community relations programs suggested as necessary and sufficient solutions. However, this approach has had only partial success, as reflected by the persistence of police-community antagonisms in areas with even the most modernized and innovative police policies. The limits of this approach can be understood only by locating the roots of the adversary feelings beyond the situational context of the police-community relationship.

An alternative approach utilizes a *conflict-repression* model, in which the legal code and its enforcement are seen as primarily reflecting the interests of the most powerful segments of the community. It views the police as basically a tool for maintaining the existing inequalities of the class structure. Through both the nature of the law and its differential enforcement, the interests of the small minority who own businesses and receive profits from the labor of others are given preference over those who must sell their labor for wages. This dominant segment of the community is roughly equivalent to the one percent of the population who, in 1972, owned 20.7 percent of all personal wealth.[42] Their clout is particularly obvious in corporate and personal tax laws, where deductions and exemptions tend to preserve and amplify economic inequalities.

Another influence of class inequalities or legal codes concerns injustices that are not legislated as illegal, so that, for example, it is legal for corporations to extract extraordinary profits on inferior services or commodities, but illegal for consumers to shoplift even the most inexpensive item. Thus, consumer and corporate behavior can be seen as governed by contradictory standards of justice when incorporated into legal codes.

Biases in legal codes are only one source of the adversary relationship between the police and the community. At least three additional characteristics of the police are seen in this perspective as supporting the interests of the dominant class: their repression of dissent, their selective enforcement of laws, and their lack of concern with the causes of crimes, which are rooted in class inequalities. The police are viewed as repressive when they intervene to prevent or to extinguish overt challenges and resistance to class domination, such as in the civil rights movement, antiwar demonstrations, union strikes, or the ghetto rebellions of the 1960s.

Selective law enforcement also parallels class lines. Edwin Sutherland and Donald Cressey point out that fraud is probably the most prevalent crime in the United States, and that approximately 90 percent of all large corporations would be considered habitual criminals if the criteria applied to individual offenders were applied to them.[43] Yet, police continue to concentrate their efforts on the poor, young, male, urban minorities. This overlooks what the Center for Research on Criminal Justice calls "crime in the suites":

> Offenses such as embezzlement, fraud, tax fraud, and forgery resulted in a loss of $1.73 billion in 1965. In the same year, robbery, burglary, auto theft, and larceny resulted in a loss of $690 million—less than half as much.[44]

Finally, insofar as most traditional criminal behavior can be conceptualized as symptomatic of alienation from an economic system that excludes and exploits certain segments of the community, the police are seen as part of a repressive criminal justice system that offers nothing to ameliorate the economic miseries and social disorganization that generate criminal activities. Because the police have little power to remove the social and economic roots of crime, their actions are seen as addressing only the symptoms of alienation and frustration, not their basic essences or causes. The police role is contradictory in that it focuses on those who are induced to pursue illegal sources of income, not the system that generates such motives for criminal activity.

In sum, this model views many functions of the police as fundamentally opposed to the interests and situation of the economically exploited groups in the community. Rather than locating the problem in the imperfections of a police-community relationship, it locates the problem in the more encompassing realm of the class relationships through which the police-community interaction is structured.

According to the conflict-repression model, the central historical function of police-community relations has been to *legitimate* the hidden repressive functions of the criminal justice system. The incorporation of such programs into the strategy of police organizations is seen as a formal effort to pacify the hostility and criticism other police activities have catalyzed, and is necessary only insofar as routine police practices generate community resentment. As such, public relations programs are seen as ideological mechanisms through which police control the community, rather than vice versa. Their central function is to overcome and bureaucratically channel resistance through sophisticated image management designed to camouflage their class bias and to encourage popular consensus and acquiescence in the "deviant" classes. These programs serve as ideological supplements to the more coercive tactics of social control used by the police, which, despite the altruism of individual officers, operate to disguise the actual interests that the police are organized to preserve and protect.

In this perspective, the problem of antagonism between citizens and police is inseparable from the more encompassing problem of class inequality and the distribution of wealth and power in the community. As those analysts who adhere to this general model have argued, the social reorganization necessary for decent police-community relations is beyond the abilities, mandate, or desires of any police organization to generate. Nevertheless, they do support vast changes in police organization itself, which, though not solving the problem, will increase the responsiveness of the police to the problems of crime and exploitation in the community. Local control of police organizations and administration is a necessary first step, with a transformation of police priorities to reflect a heightened level of responsiveness to the needs of all segments of their communities. This implies a different form of policing, not an extension of current tactics, which would be based on respect and understanding of the needs of the neighborhoods involved. Tony Platt has documented the tremendous impact of street crimes in lower-class areas, and the distrust that the police have earned, which discourages residents from requesting assistance.[45] A responsive police organization would also oppose economic exploitation of citizens of lower-class areas by businesses and employers, and assertively protect the more traditional forms of human rights which are routinely violated in hiring, housing, educational, or public welfare practices. Such changes, of course, are dismissed by most as idealistic and utopian. However, adherents of this model predict that only when the police become an asset in the class struggles of the dominated group in their communities will citizens return the respect on which satisfactory police-community relations are based.

MEASURING POLICE PERFORMANCE

We said at the beginning of this chapter that, because the police product is a public service, it is difficult to measure the customer's reactions. This suggests an additional aspect of the public image problem of the police, the question of productivity. Reiss and Bordua discussed this question in terms of how the success of a police department can be measured. If we are concerned with the self-image of the police officer, the question is one of measuring individual performance. If we are concerned with the public image of the police, the question is one of measuring agency effectiveness.

Because the department's legally defined task is to enforce the law, Reiss and Bordua observed that the typical annual report of a police department contains statistical information on crime rates, arrests, crimes cleared by arrests, convictions, value of stolen property recovered, and the like. But the police themselves largely determine the criteria by which their success is measured. There are difficulties in interpreting the data to the public so as to make an acceptable case for success.

In a market-oriented society, police administrators must try to maintain public confidence in department productivity. Sometimes this leads to the manipulation of statistics. The problem is further complicated because the police do not control the outcomes of cases they initiate in the enforcement process. Prosecutors and courts make the eventual determinations. The police officer's sense of justice is vindicated only through convictions, but he has little control over this. As Reiss and Bordua say, "while department arrest figures may define the policeman's success, acquittals in court may define his failures." They continue:

> These dilemmas in defining success are partially resolved by the development of a complex bargaining process between police and prosecutors, the shifting of departmental resources in directions of maximum payoff from a conviction point of view, the development of a set of attitudes that define the police as alone in the "war on crime," and the elaboration of success measures that do not require validation by the courts.[46]

Public impressions of "the crime problem" are generally what the police want them to be. Although questions of manpower and budget often prevail, there is a risk that the police may be considered failures if the volume of crime is too high. Because police success is measured by arrests and convictions, and police law enforcement is separated from outcome, an element of friction between the police and the judicial system (*antagonistic cooperation* it has been called) is inherent in the situation. The police want not only conviction, they want the guilty to be punished. They interpret this and this alone as vindication of their sense of justice, as appreciation for their efforts, and as upholding morality.[47]

Another complication is the fact that effective police-community teamwork in crime control may, in the short run, produce *higher* rates of reported crimes of certain types, more apprehensions, and so on. This might be interpreted in a manner unfavorable to the police. Consequently, police executives tend to be wary of community-based crime control programs. The yardsticks of success are "soft," not easily defined in computerized terms, and very difficult to interpret to city councils, the media, and the general public. In short, productivity data are not easily quantified.

RECENT RESEARCH REGARDING PRODUCTIVITY

Recent research on quality policing can be classified under several headings. First, there is the relationship between various personal characteristics and subsequent officer performance. This research relates to the problem of screening applicants. Second, there is the problem of evaluating job performance itself. Third, there is the problem of ensuring sufficient applicants with the desired characteristics.

We have already noted that the first of these categories has been a favorite research area for some years. The questions dealt with have included the racial and ethnic composition of police agencies, studied as an aspect of the search for an ethnically unbiased method for validating tests. This is motivated by the widespread legal challenges to existing methods that have arisen in the aftermath of the Supreme Court's decision in the Duke Power and Light case.[48]

Then there is the refinement of screening procedures that relate personality traits to effective police performance, as in the Chicago work described in chapter 6. Perhaps the most difficult type of research in this area is that pertaining to attitudes—for example, attempts to link job attitudes and selected background variables. Studies of the job effectiveness of women police officers are also being done.

Various indicators suggest that there are serious questions about the reliability of written tests as predictors of successful police performance. Screening procedures increasingly stress extended interviewing aimed at the identification of important personal history clues, such as occupational shifts, education, and early family history. The Detroit Police Department was among the first to go in this direction, and more recent examples are numerous. A Police Foundation project initiated it in the Dade County, Florida, Department of Public Safety, and there was also a Northern Virginia Police and Fire Validation and Test Revision Project. An evaluation technique called the Biographical Inventory Index is coming into increasing use in police selection procedures.

As this is written, the several volumes in the report of LEAA's National Manpower Study have recently appeared. It promises to have an important bearing on selection and performance standards for police personnel, as well as on training and education. An LEAA-funded police selection standards project based in Sacramento involved a series of job-analysis workshops, with the participants drawn from police agencies across the country. Such studies and projects of recent vintage have aimed at viewing the police selection process as part of an integrated personnel management system.

One especially interesting aspect of police officer selection procedures is psychological testing. Opinion is sharply divided among police administrators as to whether such testing is valuable. Several LEAA research projects have been directed to this subject, including a three-year study in the Minneapolis Police Department. So far, only a few states have implemented a statewide psychological testing requirement.

Considerable research is being done on police performance measurement, reflecting unprecedented and concerted attention to productivity, accountability, and cost effectivensss. A National Commission on Productivity was established by presidential action in 1970 to develop recommendations for programs and policies to improve the productivity of the United States economy. In its publications, this commission stated that the measurement of police activities, as with all public-service organizations, is difficult because the goals and objectives of the activity are not easily quantifiable.

A study of the police services provided to residential neighborhoods in the St. Louis metropolitan area was conducted in 1973 by the Workshop in Political Theory and Policy Analysis, Indiana University.[49] One important conclusion of this study was that a synergistic combination of indicators bearing upon the same or different facets of policing provides much deeper insight into police performance than is possible with even the most accurate single indicators.

Professor Gary T. Marx of MIT has pointed out that the performance measures now used by police tend to be internally rather than externally generated. Supervisors, rather than peers, self, or clients, set performance standards. Therefore, these measures tend to conform to bureaucratic standards only indirectly related to the actual objectives of police work. The tendency is to measure how much or how many rather than how well. Marx further observed that this kind of evaluation dwells on general qualities rather than on behavior in specific situations, and it is more concerned with law enforcement than with community service or conflict management. Furthermore, evaluation is used more to punish failure than to reward success.[50]

An experiment that attracted national attention was an incentive program in police officer performance devised by the city of Orange, California. This program relied upon a wholly quantitative evaluation, tying police salaries to reductions in the incidence of certain types of crimes (rape, robbery, burglary, and auto theft). The program was initiated in July 1973, but its results have been inconclusive. The plan has a potential for serious abuse, as John M. Greimer of the Urban Institute pointed out in an early report.[51]

The St. Louis metropolitan area study cited above examined several challenging questions, one of which was the effects of training and education on police attitudes and performance. Data were secured from both police officers and citizens to test certain hypotheses relating training and education to specific attitudes of individual officers, and other hypotheses relating aggregate departmental training and education to performance evaluation by citizens. The summary conclusion was that the direct relationship between training and attitudes is negligible to weak. The relationship between education and attitudes is only slightly stronger. The findings on the relationship between training and education and citizen evaluation of police performance were similarly discouraging for advocates of higher levels of police training and education. However, other researchers have raised serious questions about the reliability of this study.

Writers and commentators galore on the topic of police productivity suggest that it is as slippery as a wet bar of soap. The preoccupation with volume measurements should not obscure considerations of the *quality* of service rendered and the actual impact on the problems of concern to the police. As various administrators have pointed out, productivity measurement is a management art, and it is central to questions of public confidence in the police.[52]

CITIZEN PERCEPTIONS OF POLICE MISCONDUCT

We referred earlier in this chapter to various surveys dealing with public perceptions of police misconduct. This merits additional comment. The University of Michigan study for the President's Crime Commission showed that as many as 38 percent of the public think the police in their area take bribes and payoffs. Blacks were more apt to believe this than whites. Almost a third of all those interviewed reported that they had seen a police officer do something they felt was wrong, and an additional 17 percent said they were told by someone about something a police officer did that was wrong. When asked what was the most serious wrong thing they saw a policeman do, the largest proportion replied by alluding to the threat or actual use of undue physical force against a citizen. Obviously, a judgment is involved as to what constitutes "undue" force.

Only 10 percent reported actually seeing an officer solicit or accept a bribe; 2 percent reported personal knowledge of a police officer's committing a serious crime. Seventeen percent reported knowledge of minor infractions by policemen—for example, drinking on duty. A substantial majority (79 percent) agreed that the police should have the right under certain conditions to stop and ask them their name and address; 56 percent set no conditions for such stops. But considerably fewer were willing to submit to questioning going beyond identification and even fewer, to search. Almost no citizen was opposed to allowing the police the right to question them if there was reasonable indication of wrongdoing. The Reiss summarization is of interest:

> On the whole, citizens are reasonably positive in their attitudes toward the police. They nonetheless report specific attitudes that indicate they think the police in their city could be better, that they do not think of them as free from misconduct, and that they do not believe many police officers behave in a professional manner toward citizens. Negroes are less positive toward the police than are whites, but there is a substantial minority within both groups that would opt for a more professional police. . . .[53]
>
> It is doubtful that most citizens would see themselves in a pro- or anti-police position, or in a pro- or anti-civil rights position. They are concerned about the crime problem and many of their attitudes and perceptions relate more to these concerns than they do to any position vis-a-vis the law enforcement or criminal justice system.

CORRUPTION

No discussion of the public image of the police is complete without some attention to the question of corruption. So-called police scandals occur so often that a crooked cop surprises no one. The stereotype of the police officer invariably includes the graft factor. James Q. Wilson's description of American urban policing in the 1920s, as it backgrounded the Wickersham Commission and its recommendations, was summarized in chapter 3. Recall that Wilson's interest in big-city police morale problems was prompted by his curiosity about corruption. Recently, we have witnessed another spurt in public attention to the subject as a result of emphasis on accountability, the activities of the Knapp Commission in New York City, and developments in various other cities.

As we saw in chapter 6, Wilson's analysis of corruption traces it primarily to the police role dilemma. But as he indicates, this is a complicated matter, and no one-dimensional explanation suffices. One can approach it from a management-policy-supervisory standpoint, or a selection-training-performance-incentive standpoint, or from a police-community standpoint. Each of these approaches to police corruption quickly leads into the others.

Lawrence Sherman has assembled a useful anthology of monographs on the subject, in sociological perspective. His first statement in the preface to this work is telling: "The problem of police corruption is merely a slice of the larger problem of official corruption in American society." He heralds the evidence that "police administrators have begun to bring the problem out of the closet."[54] In one essay appearing in Sherman's anthology, Ellwyn R. Stoddard writes:

> The guiding hypothesis of this study is that illegal practices of police personnel are socially prescribed and patterned through the informal 'code' rather than being a function of individual aberration or personal inadequacies of the policeman himself.[55]

Such a view of the problem immediately plunges the discussion into the bottomless pit of arguments about individual versus environmental responsibility for aberrant behavior. It curiously parallels the arguments among police people and others about the relative weight of the same influences in explaining criminal behavior. Such arguments end indecisively, as they should. The same may be said for debates about whether the police or the community are more to blame for corruption. For our purpose here, it is enough to recognize that the corruption issue is a matter of *shared* responsibility, for causes as well as for solutions.

In the same anthology, John A. Gardiner reflected about the preconditions for corruption. One such precondition, he suggested, is "substantial conflict over the goals of the legal system."[56] An illustration of this is legislation that attempts to restrict what is regarded as immoral behavior. A related precondition is a substantial demand for illegal goods and services, and tolerance by the appropriate government agency of activities to satisfy these demands, in return for some kind of payoff. Other preconditions, Gardiner asserted, pertain to a number of internal variables in the governmental agency itself, and in the political system in which it operates.

Police corruption is a topic of special interest to Herman Goldstein and he has written a good deal about it in recent years. He has discussed the complexities of defining corruption, the reluctance of police to talk openly about it, its impact upon a police organization and the quality of its services, the variations in the magnitude, patterns, and causes of it. He also assesses the strengths and weaknesses of various remedial proposals. He writes:

> Corruption is endemic to policing. . . . Difficult as it has been to stamp out all corruption, it is clear that it can be reduced, and, in some specific situations, eliminated. Moreover, it is important that a view of the problem not be restricted to the failures. Many police agencies have had a great deal of success in maintaining the integrity of their personnel.[57]

In a foreword to the Goldstein work, Patrick V. Murphy writes:

> The reduction and control of police corruption can be complex. Many well-meaning police administrators have been unable to master the uses of power, unable to obtain public support and unable to control a large bureaucracy in ways sufficient to achieve substantial control of corruption. Holding top and middle management strictly accountable through the use of powerful sanctions is essential if the police adminis-

trator is to deal successfully with corruption and avoid the high risk of personal blame for its existence. Yet, the environment engendered by the civil service mentality can protect the echelons immediately beneath the chief while the chief is held accountable for the corruption. Therefore, despite civil service restraints, the chief must find ways to make his subordinates in management actively participate, and hold them strictly accountable, for a positive approach to the control of corruption.[58]

This statement clearly defines the responsibilities of the police manager. Community responsibilities also need to be clearly defined. Goldstein maintains that police corruption is, to a great extent, initiated and sustained by the community. Corruption and productivity are obviously at cross-purposes in any organization. Many feel that not much can be done about corruption. If this view is accepted, then the outlook for professional policing is bleak indeed, as is the prospect of being able to do much significantly to maintain effective police and community relations.

That something can be done is spelled out by Lawrence W. Sherman in a 1978 LEAA report of a carefully designed project in four cities where there had been major scandals over police corruption.[59] All four cities had a high level of organization in police corruption before the scandal. Three of the police departments adopted policies aimed at preventing and detecting ongoing corruption, and one adopted policies aimed only at responding to allegations of past corruption. The policies aimed at ongoing corruption, included tighter administrative control, attempts to change the aspects of the organizational environment encouraging corruption, and covert internal investigations initiated by internal policing units. Conclusions:

1. Premonitory strategies (aimed at ongoing corruption) for corruption control can reduce the level of organization of police corruption.

2. Postmonitory strategies (aimed at past corruption) for corruption control do not seem to be as effective as premonitory strategies.

3. The same strategies for corruption control can be employed in a police department of any size, although the tactics may differ.

Among big-city police departments where concerted efforts have recently been made to develop a well-designed system for detecting and dealing with police (and other city employee) misconduct are Louisville and Kansas City, Missouri.[60] Detroit is set on following suit, under a new city charter and a civilian police commission.

The issue of corruption is closely related to falsification and distortion of facts. Peter Manning finds the seeds of police corruption in the organizational environment to which we referred in the preceding chapter. He has reflected that "since the police are representatives of the moral order in everyday life, their credibility reflects upon the legitimacy of the politico-moral order." He continues:

If lying is endemic in police operations, it is not an isolated commentary on either the moral status of policemen as individuals or even of police organizations; it is a commentary on the society in which the activity is rooted. For in some areas, a society has and deserves precisely what it gets from its police.[61]

SUMMING UP

In this chapter, we have discussed the public image (more accurately, "images") of the police, which is integrally related to their self-image. We began with some general observations regarding the universal concern for how one looks in the eyes of others. The businessman's stake in the customer's reaction to his product was noted; it was acknowledged that the feedback from customers is more difficult to interpret when the product is a service, as it is in police work, and when the customer cannot make up his mind what he wants.

The problem of achieving minimal consensus as to public expectations from the police was again underlined. We described some attempts made during the 1950s to survey the public image of the police. These surveys indicated that, in general terms, this image appeared to be favorable. But in terms of certain specific publics—for example, the poor, the young, the black—the image is not so favorable. Public attitudes toward the police are influenced by contacts with the police, by the behavior and attitudes of police officers, and by expectations of particular groups and the degree to which they feel the police fulfill these expectations. One difficulty is that the expectations are frequently inconsistent or ambivalent: thus the police are left to determine on their own terms what they think they see in public attitudes.

Hostility directed toward the police produces hostile responses from the police, and vice versa. Even impersonal, overly civil police behavior is sometimes interpreted as "inhuman," and therefore hostile. The police recruit discovers quickly that the most important part of perceptive learning for him is to identify role-relevant reference groups, in and out of his department, and to interpret the sensitivities and expectations of such groups as accurately as he can. His career success is at stake in this process.

There is an inevitable adversary element in police-citizen relations, evident in the law enforcement responsibility of the police. Various historians, psychiatrists, psychologists, sociologists, and political scientists argue that this functionally inherent conflict is aggravated by other considerations in the officer's background: attitudes, values, training, occupational socialization, role ambiguity, and the like. The relations between the police and other agents of the criminal justice system also contain an adversary element. Many police officers take personal offense at what they feel is a lack of understanding and cooperation from prosecutors and the courts and from the public at large, where apathy is blamed for problems of greatest concern to the police. As a police officer might say: "It's not so much that people hate us as it is that people just don't care!"

Police administrators face a dilemma in how the public measures the success of the police. The manipulation of crime statistics is a result of this dilemma. Police corruption is a complex manifestation of a combination of variables, some internal to police organizations and subculture, and some pertaining to the societal environment in which the police operate.

Through several chapters, we have considered perceptions, attitudes, beliefs, and values as they relate to personality structure and human behavior, with particular reference to the police. In the next chapter, we shall deal more directly with these concepts.

NOTES

1. J. Milton Yinger, "Who Are We?" (speech delivered to a Northern Ohio Institute on Police and Community Relations at Cleveland, Ohio, November 21, 1964). Reprinted by permission.

2. U.S., President's Commission on Law Enforcement and Administration of Justice, *Task Force Report: The Police* (Washington, D.C.: U.S. Government Printing Office, 1967), p. 146.

3. Cited in *US News & World Report*, © 1978. April 3, 1978, p. 37.

4. National Crime Panel, *Criminal Victimization Surveys in 13 American Cities*, U.S. Dept. of Justice, LEAA, National Criminal Justice Information and Statistics Service, June, 1979—and James Garofalo, Project Coordinator, Criminal Justice Research Center, Albany, N.Y., *Public Opinion About Crime*, U.S. Department of Justice, LEAA, NCJISS, 1977.

5. Cited in *US News & World Report*, April 3, 1978, p. 45.

6. *Op. cit.*, James Garofalo, Project Coordinator, Criminal Justice Research Center, Albany, N.Y., *Public Opinion About Crime*, U.S. Department of Justice, LEAA, NCJISS, 1977.

7. Mervin F. White and Ben A. Menke, "A Critical Analysis of Surveys on Public Opinion Toward Police Agencies," *Journal of Police Science and Administration* 6, no. 2: 204–218. Copyright © International Association of Chiefs of Police, Inc.

8. G. Douglas Gourley, *Public Relations and the Police* (Springfield, Ill.: C. C. Thomas, 1953); and *Public Relations and the Police: A Survey of Public Opinion*, prepared under the direction of Larry W. Fultz (Houston, Texas: University of Houston, 1959).

9. Claudine Gibson Wirths, "The Development of Attitudes Toward Law Enforcement," *Police* 3, no. 2 (1958): 52. Reprinted by permission of Charles C Thomas, Publisher.

10. Geoffrey Gorer, "Modification of National Character: The Role of the Police in England," *Journal of Social Issues* 11, no. 2 (1955).

11. Jack J. Preiss and Howard J. Ehrlich, *An Examination of Role Theory: The Case of the State Police* (Lincoln: University of Nebraska Press, 1966), p. 124.

12. Ibid., p. 129.

13. Paul E. Smith and Richard O. Hawkins, "Victimization, Types of Citizen-Police Contacts, and Attitudes Toward the Police," *Law and Society Review* 8, no. 1 (Fall 1973): 135–152.

14. Theodore H. Poister and James C. McDavid, "Victims' Evaluations of Police Performance,"*Journal of Criminal Justice* 6, no. 2 (Summer 1978): 133–149.

15. U.S., President's Commission on Law Enforcement and Administration of Justice, *Field Surveys II, Criminal Victimization in the United States: A Report of a National Survey* (Washington, D.C.: U.S. Government Printing Office, 1967).

16. U.S., President's Commission on Law Enforcement and Administration of Justice, *Field Surveys V*, p. 30; idem, *Field Surveys IV*, vol. 1, 105 (Washington, D.C.: U.S. Government Printing Office, both 1967).

17. Carl Werthman and Irving Piliavin, "Gang Members and the Police," in David J.

Bordua, ed., *The Police: Six Sociological Essays* (New York: John Wiley & Sons, 1967), p. 56. Reprinted by permission of John Wiley & Sons.

18. Ibid., p. 62.

19. Ibid., p. 74.

20. William W. Turner, *The Police Establishment* (New York: G. P. Putnam's Sons, 1968), p. 119.

21. U.S., National Advisory Commission on Civil Disorders, *Report of the National Advisory Commission on Civil Disorders* (Kerner Report) (Washington, D.C.: U.S. Government Printing Office, 1968), p. 93.

22. *Police Power and Citizens Rights* (New York: American Civil Liberties Union, n.d.).

23. William A. Westley, "The Escalation of Violence through Legitimation," *Annals* 364 (March 1966): 126.

24. President's Commission on Law Enforcement, *Field Surveys III*, vol. 1, p. 69.

25. James W. Sterling, *Changes in Role Concepts of Police Officers During Recruit Training* (Washington, D.C.: International Association of Chiefs of Police, 1969). Reprinted by permission.

26. Preiss and Ehrlich, *An Examination of Role Theory*, p. 124.

27. William A. Westley, "The Police: A Sociological Study" (Ph.D. dissertation, University of Chicago, 1951), p. 163.

28. Bronislaw Malinowski, *Crime and Custom in Savage Society* (Cambridge, England: Routledge and Kegan Paul, 1966), p. 10.

29. James Q. Wilson, "The Police and Their Problems: A Theory," *Public Policy*, Yearbook of the Harvard University Graduate School of Public Administration (Cambridge, 1963), pp. 191–192.

30. *Public Relations and the Police* (Houston study), p. vi.

31. Michael Banton, "Social Integration and Police," *Police Chief*, April 1963, pp. 10–12. Reprinted by permission of the International Association of Chiefs of Police, Gaithersburg, Maryland.

32. Ibid., p. 12.

33. Oscar Handlin, "Community Organization as a Solution to Police-Community Problems," *Police Chief* 32, no. 3 (March 1965): 18.

34. Karl Menninger was a consultant to the President's Crime Commission in 1966 and also a consultant to the development of the Lemberg Center for the Study of Violence at Brandeis University. See his book *The Crime of Punishment* (New York: Viking Press, 1968).

35. Chester M. Pierce, "Psychiatric Aspects of Police-Community Relations," *Mental Hygiene* 46, no. 1 (January 1962), pp. 107–115.

36. Ibid., p. 111.

37. Ibid.

38. Ibid., p. 112.

39. Arthur L. Stinchcombe, "The Control of Citizen Resentment in Police Work" (n.d.); idem, "Institutions of Privacy in the Determination of Police Administrative Practice," *American Journal of Sociology* 69, no. 2 (September 1963): 150–161.

40. Albert J. Reiss, Jr., and David J. Bordua, "Environment and Organization: A Perspective on the Police," in Bordua, ed., *The Police*, p. 30.

41. This section was developed by Michael L. Radelet, Ph.D., Departments of Sociology and Psychiatry, University of Florida.

42. U.S. Bureau of the Census, *Statistical Abstract of the United States, 1977* (Washington, D.C.: U.S. Government Printing Office, 1977), table 752, p. 464.

43. Edwin H. Sutherland and Donald R. Cressey, *Criminology*, 10th ed. (Philadelphia: J. B. Lippincott, 1978), pp. 96–97.

44. Center for Research on Criminal Justice, *The Iron Fist and the Velvet Glove*, 2nd ed. (Berkeley, Calif.: Center for Research on Criminal Justice, 1977), p. 13.

45. Tony Platt, " 'Street' Crime—A View from the Left," *Crime and Social Justice* 9 (Spring–Summer 1978): 26–34. A cogent presentation of the conflict-repression model of criminal justice processes, indicative of the so-called New or Radical Criminology, is Richard Quinney's *Critique of Legal Order* (Boston: Little, Brown, 1974).

46. Reiss and Bordua, "Environment and Organization," p. 36. Reprinted by permission of John Wiley & Sons.

47. Jerome H. Skolnick treats various aspects of this matter in *Justice Without Trial: Law Enforcement in Democratic Society* (New York: John Wiley & Sons, 1966). See also Jerome H. Skolnick and J. Richard Woodworth, "Bureaucracy, Information, and Social Control: A Study of a Morals Detail," in Bordua, ed., *The Police: Six Sociological Essays* (New York: John Wiley & Sons, 1967).

48. *Griggs* v. *Duke Power Co.*, 91 S. Ct. 849.

49. Elinor E. Ostrom, R. B. Parks, and D. C. Smith, "A Multi-Strata Similar Systems Design for Measuring Police Performance" (presented at the annual meeting of the Midwest Political Science Association, May 1973).

50. Gary T. Marx, "Alternative Measures of Police Performance," in Emilio Viano, ed., *Criminal Justice Research* (Lexington, Mass.: Lexington Books, 1975), pp. 179–193.

51. John M. Greimer, "Tying City Pay to Performance," LMRS Special Report (Washington, D.C.: Urban Institute, 1974).

52. See *The Police Yearbook*, 1976 (International Association of Chiefs of Police, Papers and Proceedings of the 82nd annual conference, Denver, September 1975, Workshop on Productivity and Priority). See also National Commission on Productivity, *Opportunities for Improving Productivity in Police Services*, 1973, pp. 65–70; and Joan L. Wolfle and John F. Heaphy, *Readings on Productivity in Policing* (Washington, D.C.: The Police Foundation, 1975). Also Gary K. Tyler and Charles R. Hastorf, "PRODME: Productivity Measurement for Patrol Officers," *The Police Chief* 45, no. 6 (June 1978): 68–73.

53. President's Commission on Law Enforcement, *Field Surveys III*, vol. 1, pp. 113–114.

54. Preface to Lawrence W. Sherman, ed., *Police Corruption: A Sociological Perspective* (Garden City, N.Y.: Anchor Books, 1974), p. vii.

55. Ellwyn R. Stoddard, "The Informal Code of Police Deviancy: A Group Approach to Blue-Coat Crime," in Sherman, ed., *Police Corruption*, pp. 227–304.

56. John A. Gardiner, "Law Enforcement Corruption: Explanations and Recommendations," in Sherman, *Police Corruption*, p. 316.

57. Herman Goldstein, *Police Corruption: A Perspective on Its Nature and Control* (Washington, D.C.: Police Foundation, 1975), p. 52; and by the same author, *Policing a Free Society* (Cambridge, Mass.: Ballinger, 1977), chap. 8.

58. Patrick V. Murphy, in foreword to Goldstein, *Police Corruption*, p. i.

59. Lawrence W. Sherman, *Controlling Police Corruption: The Effects of Reform Policies* (Summary Report), U.S. Department of Justice, LEAA, National Institute of Law Enforcement and Criminal Justice, 1978. The LEAA grant for this project was to the Department of Sociology, Yale University, and Albert J. Reiss, Jr., was the Project Director.

60. Operational Policy, Internal Affairs Unit, Louisville Division of Police; and Fred M. Broadway, "Police Misconduct: Positive Alternatives," *Journal of Police Science and Administration* 2, no. 2. Copyright © 1974, Northwestern University School of Law.

61. Peter K. Manning, "Police Lying," *Urban Life and Culture* 3, no. 3 (October 1974): 301–302.

8

PERCEPTION, ATTITUDES, BELIEFS, AND VALUES

Psychology is concerned primarily with three basic behavioral processes: learning, motivation, and perception. All systems of psychology are interested in these processes, although with different emphasis. Some psychologists emphasize learning, while others emphasize perception or motivation. They have different perspectives, but all agree that these processes are closely related.

For example, if one regards learning as fundamental, one thinks of behavior as resulting from a stimulus that may be inside or outside the body; therefore, in this context, motivation is discussed largely in terms of stimulus. If one regards motivation as fundamental, one might analyze body changes and conditions that give rise to certain behavior. For our purpose, it is not necessary to discuss all the details of these complex psychological phenomena; it is enough simply to be aware of their existence and implications as reviewed in this chapter.[1]

PERCEPTION OF POLICE

Three Schools of Thought

The psychologists who study learning (often called behaviorists) stress an objective, detached, scientific approach to the study of behavior. It is essentially stimulus and response, "input" and "output," that interests them; the school of thought they represent is often associated with conditioned reflexes. It is a cause-and-effect approach to behavior; a given cause produces a given (largely predictable) result. In this theory, emotion is a conditioned response to environmental elements.

Psychologists who concentrate on motivation (often called psychoanalysts) tend to look inside the person to identify the needs, impulses, and emotions that cause his behavior, with special attention to subconscious and irrational elements. G. M. Gilbert describes this theory:

> Man gets along in society by suppressing his primitive instincts. This is a continuously frustrating experience, the theory goes, and creates a reservoir of pent-up aggression which must inevitably erupt into overt actions of hostility. . . . the best we can hope to do is to contain the aggression which is the price of civilization.[2]

Then there are those psychologists who study the process of perception (sometimes called phenomenologists). They assume the individual relates and gives meaning to the world around him. How does the individual come to understand and deal with this world? For this school of thought, behavior is a response to the world *as it is perceived*. The assumption is that man is a rational creature. One individual may see the world in terms that seem irrational to another, but once it is discovered *how* he sees it, his behavior becomes understandable.

Each of the three schools of thought has produced evidence to support its views, and each has been applied to significant problems. All three schools are represented in reputable professional psychotherapy and on university faculties.

The Perception Process

In the preceding chapters, we discussed how police officers perceive themselves and how others perceive police officers. It may be helpful to review some elementary points about perception as a behavioral process. We begin with the assumption that people—at least from their own point of view—behave in a rational, purposeful, logical manner, depending upon how they perceive the objective world. Each of us responds to the world according to the way he or she perceives it. Fortunately for human welfare and progress, we do not all see the world in the same way. Yet however we see it, each of us will behave rationally *within that framework*. The basis of our individual point of view is the nature of the self, as we have seen, and not necessarily what really happens in the world outside the self. Each of us helps to create a personal reality. And perhaps the ultimate maturity and wisdom, for each of us, is the recognition that *the world we perceive is not the only world there is*.

Hadley Cantril, a communications psychologist, has used the example of the three baseball umpires to illustrate three ways of viewing reality. One said, "Some are balls, some are strikes, I call 'em as they are." The second umpire retorted, "Some are balls, some are strikes, I call 'em as I see 'em." And the third one mused, "Some are balls, some are strikes, and *they ain't nothing until I call 'em*."

If we combine the truth in the different approaches of the umpires, we might conclude (1) that we respond to things in accordance with the physical realities out there in nature; (2) that the physical reality is perceived in accordance with some possible distortions in our subjective processes; and (3) that we enter into a transaction with the energies of nature and abstract components that we integrate with our perceptual processes to create the world within which we operate.

Essentially the same ideas may be arranged in the following sequence:

1. When we talk or write about something, what we describe is something that happens inside us as much as what happens outside.

2. What each of us can talk or write about is only a very small part of reality.

3. Many of our problems in communication arise because we forget that individual experiences are never identical.

4. Since each of us perceives the world in bits and pieces, we tend to communicate about it in bits and pieces. To a certain extent, our individual experience teaches us *what* to see and hear.

5. Communication is a human transaction. It depends upon symbols—words, gestures, etc. But the symbols do not have the same meaning for others with different experiences. Hence, what we call a "communication breakdown."[3]

Perceptions and the Self. How we perceive the world, then, is based upon the *self:* our own unique experience. Earlier we observed that each of us actually has many selves, not just one. We noted that these selves are related to our positions in the social scene, our social roles. We also indicated that our perceptions of self depend upon the context at the moment, varying with what has gone before, who or what we have been thinking of, and the immediate situation we face.

Because our roles are social, the word symbols we use to designate them often denote reciprocal human relationships (i.e., *transactions*). The associations are often implied "pairings"; for example: man–woman; boy–girl; lecturer–audience; parent–child; teacher–student; writer–reader; police officer . . . what? How one completes this pair will probably reveal his or her perception of the principal role of the police. Police officer and law breaker? Police officer and lost child? Police officer and derelict drunk?

For efficient functioning, flexibility is required of all of us, as we shift from one self to another. Thus, we should strive to be open-minded in our perceptions of others, not only to be sensitive to the role they are playing at the time, but also so we can empathize with them. We limit perception when we insist on dealing with others in terms of our own fixed ideas as to what they are.

Each of us tries to maintain a stable world in spite of evidence to the contrary. We tend to shape things according to our conceptions and our purposes. This tendency, of course, varies by individuals. Some people are relatively more rigid or dogmatic than others and take a long time to accept and adapt to reality. Some people are relatively adaptable and easily shift and adjust to changing situations. It is a question of how much stability a particular individual needs, regarding either his self-image or the outer world. Some individuals resist the forces of exterior change, inappropriately, by forcing a posture of outer stability. This repeats what we said earlier about the difficulty some individuals have in adjusting to rapid and drastic changes in social role; for example, civilian to soldier, soldier to civilian, single to married, married to divorced, and so on.

Consider again the first two umpires. So long as we think there is a real world out there, we may kid ourselves into believing that we adapt to it reasonably well: "I call 'em as they are." However, if we recognize the truth in what the third umpire said, we should recognize that our "reasonable adaptation" may reflect a greater ability to *distort* the real world than to adjust to it: "They ain't nothing until I call 'em."

Rigidity and Flexibility. Let us say that a certain professor has in class a student who the professor *knows* is cheating during examinations. The student has not been caught at it (the student being very clever), but the professor is nonetheless sure that the student is guilty. The professor knows this because of the way the student sits and looks around the room and at the ceiling during exams. The professor is certain that some day the student will blunder and be caught red-handed.

Could the professor be wrong in his judgment? "Just a hunch," he might say, "based on years of experience." He could be right. And then again, he could be wrong. Lots of people get fixed ideas about other people for which there is no factual evidence. It is a human trait to maintain our images of self and of others, to seek consistency and stability and the comfort of predictability. It requires much less effort to think stereotypically than to think in individualistic terms. "If you've seen one, you've seen them all!" Stereotyping is a form of perceptual shorthand.

This tendency is something each of us must learn to control We must stretch our perceptions to enable us to see the contrary evidence, the unfamiliar, the unexpected. True, it is difficult to do. People of different backgrounds not only see things differently; they also *fail* to see things, even though presented right before their eyes. An abundance of psychological research and numerous tests, exercises, and even party games provide convincing evidence of this fact. For example, an individual's tendency toward a closed mind (dogmatism) can be scientifically measured. Basically, it is a blocking of perception. [4]

We see the accustomed and the familiar; we see those things that are not emotionally threatening, those that agree with our special professional training, and those that support our own point of view. Contrary or conflicting reality is "filtered out" of our perceptual orbit. We cannot stand to face this about ourselves, perhaps, or about others in the world "out there." As the wag puts it, "Don't confuse me with the facts. My mind's made up!"

Perceptual Shift. Studies have shown that when people are asked to evaluate material that carries strong social and personal importance for them, they will displace the material from what should be its true scale placement. [5] The psychological term for this is *displacement;* a popular term is *perceptual shift.* Perhaps an example will best show what these terms mean.

John Q. Trustworthy considers himself a completely law-abiding citizen. He will not knowingly violate a law. He thinks that major violators are evil and minor violators are bad. He is annoyed by people who do not obey parking regulations or who ignore no-littering admonitions. John Q. is also a dog lover, and when he walks his Border Terriers, their requirements are quite important to him. In his entire life, John Q. has received but one summons from a police officer, and that for creating a public nuisance with his dogs.

John Q. does not see how his dogs' activities could possibly be construed as a nuisance. But a police officer saw it that way. As a result, John Q.'s perception of the police shifted. John Q.'s feelings about law enforcement were more than a little changed. This is displacement, and any experienced police officer would have no trouble in supplying further examples. Law-abiding citizens often tend to be in favor of strict observance of the law—when it applies to *other people.*

Perception and Role Performance

Having noted that how we see ourselves, how we see others, and how others see us are subject to the psychological dynamics of the perceptual process, we should also check the connection between perception and role theory. What is the relationship between perceived role expectations and actual role performance? We have given some attention to this question. But to underline our point, here is a formulation by Jack Preiss and Howard Ehrlich of an important aspect of the matter, drawn from the police officer's world:

> In the eyes of the *new* policeman, the whole evaluation system appeared as "a jungle with a few landmarks." The diversity of post practices and the ambiguities of policies on law enforcement made it necessary for him to "play it by ear" and to cultivate a kind of practiced opportunism with regard to matching others' expectations with appropriate behavior. In the final analysis, the payoff of high evaluation was promotion. Strategic informal contacts and skill in identifying and satisfying the expectations of superior officers were considered more important assets than formal civil service ratings and examination scores. "Getting an inside track" and "playing the game" were seen as the major techniques for achieving career success.[6]

"Playing it by ear" seems to be an intrinsic element of the police officer's role behavior. It exemplifies role performance governed by perceived audience expectations, although the actor does not necessarily conform to the expectations of any given audience. To the extent that he does not, there will probably be tension in some facet of police-community relations, caused by opposing or conflicting perceptions of role. Logically, the solution to this problem will be found in more *consensual* agreement in the role perceptions (hence, expectations) of diverse audiences.

All of this we have earlier suggested. Again, the question of consensus emerges, at this point as a question of how different people *see* things, how they are influenced by their differences in experience, culture, values, and so on. To repeat: some consensus is necessary for a social system to operate, but there must be further consensus for the system to operate efficiently.

It is not difficult to translate this into police and community relations terms. Our way of seeing a problem or situation is not the only way there is to see it. If we insist that our way of seeing it is "the whole story—as any fool should see," our rigidity impedes the prospect for consensus in transactions with others who see it differently. If we insist that problem-solving efforts be on our terms exclusively, there is no chance for success. For in effect, we are imposing our experience and our perception upon others.

In doing so, we often cite our credentials: what we consider a particularly germane kind of experience, our "professional know-how," our educational accomplishments, or merely "I knew somebody once who. . . ." To the extent that the credentials reflect actual experience of some kind in dealing with a problem, there is probably some value in the recitation, however trying it may be for others. Yet it is only a single experience, one person's perception of the situation. Complex problems in today's world, exemplified by the police-community relations field, require more than single perceptions and experiences to solve them. The diversity of perceptions and experiences complicates the problems. It is also the key to possible solutions. This is a pivotal principle in police and community relations programs. It means patiently listening to what others have to say about a problem, no one person having a monopoly of either experience or wisdom. This is a simple point but it goes to the heart of perceptual sophistication. Sometimes we call this *perspective;* sometimes we call it *insight.* Either way, it is of great benefit in problem solving.

Perceptions and Police Work. Additional illustrations of the relation between perception and role enactment may be helpful. An aspect of Sterling's research that should be mentioned again pertains to the manner in which perceptions of role attributes change. His assumption is that training and education are among the variables that affect role perceptions. If a police recruit at the start of training conceives of police work as consisting largely of physical tasks carried out in a hostile environment, he or she will logically see such role attributes as physical strength and courage as essential for the work. After training, if the recruit comes to recognize an important role for the police in performing various public service tasks and sees that people can be influenced more readily through verbal rather than physical skills, he or she will value more highly such role attributes as verbal skills, courtesy, and "people knowledge."

Niederhoffer makes some additional points that are relevant here:

1. The police are *perceived,* by members of minority groups, as a symbol of white oppression. Members of minority groups are *perceived* by the police as symbolic assailants and suspicious persons. On both sides, there are experiences to bolster the perceptions. But both perceptions are nonetheless stereotypic, and the stereotypes are mutually reinforcing, especially if there are no breakthroughs of significant contrasting experiences on either side.

2. Having more minority group police officers on the force may be one important possible breakthrough, with vital effect upon perceptions of the police department. On the other hand, the black police officer may be perceived as an "Uncle Tom," as a traitor, as demanding from his own group a standard of behavior more stringent than that expected of others.

3. Certain people in the community simply do not perceive the police as trustworthy; contrarily, the police do not perceive certain people in the community as trustworthy. The current term for this is *credibility.* Obviously, it is basically a problem of perception.[7]

Hans Toch has dealt with this in a brief article. He refers to police officers who often cite their "experience" in support of sundry opinions. But, he says, the kind of person one is (including the kind of job he holds) has much to do with what he experiences, as opposed to what anyone else might experience in the same situation. A police officer is supposed to be good at spotting trouble. Yet the ability to spot trouble does not necessarily mean that one understands the reason for it. Some might even argue that the police need not understand the causes of crime—that their job is enforcement.

If one takes this position, Toch continues, then on what basis can police officers lobby for the death penalty, or criticize probation officers, or insist that sex offenders should be kept in prison? Certainly they may express their views *as interested citizens.* But they should keep in mind that their *police* experience does not bear on these matters, by their own role definition. Toch concludes:

My point here is that the police officer's "experience" is highly specialized, and no more conducive to an *accurate* picture of people than that of other observers. It is, of course, experience that is relevant to police work . . . but even here in a rather narrow way. If the professional police officer dealt with the public courteously, fairly and effectively, his relevant experiences would be a string of courteous, fair and effective dealings with people. Unfortunately, many "experienced" officers find themselves substituting for this requirement an imposing string of tense encounters, displays of confidence, "conning" talks, transparently patronizing intimacies, bluffs that may or may not have worked, and force that did. This sort of "experience" may give the *illusion* of competence to deal with people, but the people involved have not been consulted in arriving at this illusion.[8]

Toch summarizes by saying that all of us have a capacity for arranging the world in such a way that incorrect perceptions are confirmed. We see, selectively, what we want to see, what we expect to see, and weight it with our values: good–bad, true–false, acceptable–unacceptable, and so on. Thus, we have the sorting process, separating the "good guys and the bad guys," the "white hats and the black hats," the "ins and the outs." Whatever the particular terms, it's *we* and *they.*

The self-fulfilling principle is also operative in our perceptual transactions. Because we tend to see what we expect to see—blocking out evidence that does not fit our preconceived picture—there is a tendency to see only what substantiates our predisposition. Persons thought of as suspicious therefore act suspiciously; police officers thought of as brutal act brutally.

Every stereotypic "bad" trait that we attribute generally to a group of "bad guys" stems from some impulse that all of us have. We accuse some groups of being belligerent and hostile, others of being dirty, and others of grabbing all they can get. We were taught in childhood that these are undesirable qualities; therefore, "bad" people are so characterized. We forget that the real war is between the "good guys" and the "bad guys" *within each of us,* the good self and the bad self. Both good and bad feelings are in each of us, and the crucial task is to use those that are appropriate to the reality in which we find ourselves. Refinement of our own perceptions in such a manner helps to modify the perceptions others have of us.[9]

Indeed, differing philosophies of police work and of judicial and corrections activities seem to spring from differing philosophies about the nature of man and society. A tendency to sort people into good and bad produces a point of view toward such work that contrasts with the view produced by recognizing the capacity for good and bad in each of us. There are also different views regarding the nature and source of authority in society. These are grounded in theology and metaphysics, and reflected in social anthropology. A lively and provocative discussion can be activated by intoning any particular philosophical position on these matters.

Factors in Perceptual Distortion. Because perception is a behavioral process, it is well to be aware of the sources of perceptual distortion. Some important ones are these, their relative importance varying with individuals and situations:

1. Personal rigidity or dogmatism; relative difficulty in adjusting to the forces of change.
2. Emotional "loading." Illustrated by perceptual shift (displacement) in the example of the dog lover.
3. Experiential limitations—difficult sometimes to recognize and accept realistically—but part of the human condition.
4. Cultural myopia—sometimes called "tunnel vision." Our perceptions are weighted by the attitudes, beliefs, and values we accept as part of our ethnic, racial, social class, and other similar affiliations.

Perception and Attitudes

The subject of perceptual distortion leads us directly to a consideration of the relationship between perception and attitudes, beliefs, and values. The perceptual process begins with sensation: audio, visual, olfactory, and the like. Perception is the meaningful interpretation of sensations as representative of external objects—*apparent* knowledge of reality.[10]

Sensations and perceptions are distinct. A color (sensation) differs from a specific colored object (perception). Hence, as Jozef Cohen explains:

> Combinations of sensations, by repetition, become associated with a novel external object and the "memory" retained. The perceiver unconsciously compares sensations present to sensations stored (as a modern computer processes data) and involuntarily "bets" that current sensations are evoked by equivalent external objects.[11]

Perceptions are the *sole* internal representatives of reality; they are the mind's reflection of matter. Aristotle noted, "Nothing is in the mind that does not pass through the senses," and Leonardo da Vinci declared, "All of our knowledge has its origins in perceptions." Only a few contemporary psychologists would challenge this. Most would agree that perception is an interpretation of sensations; a few would say that perceptions are "invariants" of sensations.[12]

In any event, our perceptions are the basis for our opinions on any given subject. These are ideas we may or may not have thought out; they are open to dispute and subject to relatively easy change. But some of our opinions assume a certain constancy. They take deeper root, and we are less willing to change them. They become convictions on which we are prepared to act. These convictions are *attitudes*. The basis of our attitudes is in social experiences, *as perceived*. A *belief*, in turn, is a kind of attitude. So is a *value*. To distinguish, let us say that one takes the position that people with green hair should not be permitted to live in a certain neighborhood. This is an attitude. Or simply to say, "I can't stand people with green hair." If, however, one goes on to add, "because people with green hair cannot be trusted," one thereby cites a *belief* to explain the attitude. This is the plausible *rationalization* for the attitude. The *value* is implicit: the quality of not being trustworthy is evil, wrong, undesirable. A value is a norm of behavior, an index of good and bad. Basically, a value is itself an attitude and a belief—based upon perception. And as we have observed, perception cannot always be trusted.

Attitudes develop primarily because they tie an individual to a group that he feels can aid him in attaining goals important to him. Thus, the choices a person makes, such as to affiliate with this organization rather than that, to join this party rather than that, to read this newspaper rather than that, are often decisions based on a certain set of attitudes, beliefs, and values. *We tend to prefer what coincides with what we already believe.* Our perceptions of opposing attitudes, beliefs, and values tend to support what we already believe. Therefore, our attitudes, beliefs, and values tend to be self-insulating and reinforcing, because we shut out of our perceptions any contrary or opposing evidence. The alternative creates internal *value conflict,* which can be very upsetting, because it involves the recognition that a cherished belief may need some qualification.

What we have been suggesting in closely related to prejudice, which is an attitude functioning as both a cause and an effect of perceptual distortion. It should be emphasized that our attitudes frequently have a significant emotional dimension. An attitude involves strong feelings about something or somebody. This point provides an important clue for attitude change.

THE COMMUNICATION PROBLEM

Problems of human relations are everywhere referred to as "communication" problems. There is some validity to this characterization, but the complexity of the communication problem is not always grasped. Sometimes it is suggested, for instance, that "talk sessions" will cure the problem, communication being defined simply as "talk." If the parties can be brought together in conversation, all will be well.

One implication of our discussion in this chapter is that the communication problem—for instance, in police and community relations—will not be so easily solved. This is true for several reasons, each emphasizing that mere messages do not usually produce mutual understanding. We may summarize our analysis by indicating a few of the reasons the communication problem is so formidable:

1. Any message in a communications situation may touch upon at least three levels of meaning. A message may contain seeming *fact*—a report of reality *as the communicator sees it.* A message may also contain *inference.* And it may also contain *judgment.* Thus, a message may report an event: it may include conclusions drawn about the event; and it may include a personal evaluation of it. Much argument takes place between people and groups at all three of these levels of meaning—the latter two directly and the first implicitly.

2. A second important barrier to clarity in communication may be in the *difference of values.* This is sometimes referred to as the "value gap." It pertains to differences in the conditions of life—age, education, occupation, experience, sex, social class, ethnicity, culture, race, religion, and so on—that, as we have seen, vitally influence our perceptions and, consequently, our attitudes, beliefs, and values. This is, of course, a common cause of difficulty in intergroup communication. So ingrained

and deeply rooted are our values that we seldom have occasion to identify them specifically, even to ourselves. Thus, when confronted with groups of persons who evaluate differently, we are likely to think of them as strange, primitive, stubborn, inferior, or even badly motivated. Moreover, *unstated* values lie behind stated attitudes and beliefs. Indeed sometimes the speaker or actor may not be fully aware of these values and the degree to which they influence what is said or done.

3. Difficulties in intergroup or interpersonal communication are created by our *defenses against reorientation*. One such defense is selective perception: we see what we want to see, what we expect to see. Another is selective retention: we consciously retain only a very small fraction of our perceptual input—usually that in which we have a personal interest. For example, if someone we do not like says something with which we agree, we tend to remember the statement but to forget who said it.

4. Still another communication obstacle is the tendency *to place too much emphasis on the message*. All communication systems comprise a source, a channel, a message, and a receiver. The relationship between the source and the receiver merits much more attention than it ordinarily gets. This is the essence of the so-called credibility question. In a nutshell, *we believe people whom we trust*. The place, then, to begin establishing more effective communication between police and community is not with the message to be communicated, or even the system by which it is to be communicated. The place to begin is with existing *attitudes* between source and receiver: the police and the community audiences. It is the *quality* of this relationship that will be decisive.[13]

There is more to communication than mere talk, more to understanding others than ostensibly listening to what they say. *Dialogue* is the term recently employed to convey the real meaning of interpersonal and intergroup communication. For it is apparent that discussion does not always cast light on problems. Sometimes the deaf talk to the deaf, and separation is aggravated. Why so?

The French scholar Marcel Deschoux has offered this explanation. In most discussions, each side enters the discussion "with guns loaded." Each insists that experience is all on his side. We ask others to wake up and see the truth, to "let the facts speak for themselves." The difficulty is, of course, that the facts do not speak. So we presume to speak for them. That our neighbor might possess some precious particle of the truth hardly occurs to us. We ask him only to accept our terms for a solution.

This is a combatant approach to problem solving. True dialogue has no chance. The aim is to vanquish others involved in the discussion, to disqualify them, even to embarrass and humiliate them and attack their personhood. Anything goes: smug statements, pretended indignation, mockery, shrugging of the shoulders, irony, play on words, intended ambiguity, pomposity, inflammatory gestures, and the like. We gloat over reducing to silence someone with whom we started out to have a discussion. Forceful argument becomes more force than argument. Deschoux concludes:

It is the spirit of peace that is the condition for authentic dialogue, War, attack, violence . . . have no place here. The essential thing is to accept fully the presence of someone else, and to open ourselves to his influence. What makes a dialogue is reciprocal presence and actions based on recognized equality. In both the action and the presence, there is mutual involvement. Dialogue is related to propaganda as love is to rape. For any authentic dialogue, therefore, there is work to be done first within ourselves. For it is, after all, *truth*—as Emerson insisted—that is the third party in dialogue.[14]

PREJUDICE

The author of this text once spoke to a group on the subject of prejudice. Following the talk, several listeners gathered around the speaker. One lady said: "That was a delightful speech. But we are fortunate not to have these problems in our town. We have no X, Y, or Z people here, and we probably never will have, because they know they wouldn't be welcome here!"

The lady had made a better speech than the author about the nature of prejudice. This is a subject about which a library full of books and articles has been written and countless speeches and exhortations have been delivered. The last of these is not in sight. One hesitates to be critical of high-minded evangelism, yet one may venture the observation that so much of the rhetoric about prejudice seems to deal with *other* people's prejudices rather than with one's own. Sometimes one wonders if there may not even be such a thing as prejudice against those whom one regards as prejudiced!

Definitions

Recall what we have said about the relationship between perception and attitudes. Prejudice is a kind of attitude. The word means "to prejudge." It is an attitude formulated with reference to objects, persons, groups, or values on the basis of limited information, association, or experience. Because prejudice is an attitude, it involves an *action* element (discrimination) and an *emotional* element (strong feelings about the object of prejudice). All attitudes are wholly *acquired*. We are not born with our prejudices, although various studies have indicated that prejudicial attitudes are acquired at an early age. One such study, of preschool age children in Philadelphia, revealed that these subjects had already developed some clearcut we-and-they differentiations in their play patterns.[15]

Prejudice is, in large part, irrational judgment. It springs from emotional roots in personality; it is charged with feelings. By and large, prejudice is more the result of affective than cognitive learning. Information alone will rarely cure a prejudice. A person may "know better" and still be prejudiced. In particular instances, anti-Semitism, for example, might be lessened, even markedly, by information about Judaism. The thrust of one definition of prejudice is that it is "being down on what one is not up on." However, as an epidemic social disease, prejudice—as exemplified by anti-Semitism—will not usually submit meekly to facts. Too many of what Harry and Bonaro Overstreet called "the gentle people of prejudice" do not wish to be deprived of their feelings by mere facts.[16] Anthropologists may prove in a hundred ways that there are no essential differences among the races of man. Alas, there are many people who remain at least mildly skeptical, and many more who refuse to be influenced by objective, scientific information. An occasional maverick social theorist supplies encouragement for the skeptics.

Types

There are many ways of classifying prejudice. We have already touched on the difference between prejudice and discrimination: the latter is prejudice "acted out" in behavior. This is the target in antidiscrimination legislation pertaining to employment, education, housing, public accommodations, and so on. Those who shout "you can't legislate against prejudice" find this distinction difficult. Moreover, a convincing case can be made for the contention that antidiscrimination legislation has significant *educational* effects.

Prejudice connotes a tendency to act; discrimination is overt action. The relationship may be described in this manner:

1. There can be prejudice without discrimination.
2. There can be discrimination without prejudice. (If discrimination is widely practiced—for example, in employment—individuals who may not be prejudiced come to accept the discrimination tacitly and unquestioningly.)
3. Discrimination can be among the causes of prejudice. (Some of the individuals mentioned above may come to believe that there is "something wrong" with those discriminated against.)
4. Prejudice can be among the causes of discrimination.
5. Most frequently, prejudice and discrimination are mutually reinforcing.[17]

Is there a distinction between harmless and harmful prejudice? Obviously one's preference for shrimp and refusal to so much as try rattlesnake steak is harmless. No one is hurt by this attitude, although it is culturally prescribed and may not conform to the rules of right reason. But when the object of prejudice is people, someone is usually hurt; therefore, the prejudice is harmful.

Prejudice may also be classified as favorable or unfavorable. Can one be prejudiced in favor of something or somebody, as distinct from prejudiced against? Again, there may be prejudgment involved in either case. Some say that a favorable prejudgment is bias, and an unfavorable prejudgment is prejudice. But the two terms are generally used interchangeably, without this distinction, and the dictionary does not distinguish between them in this way.

Gilbert speaks of three types of prejudice, with the categories clearly overlapping.[18] First, there is the common garden variety of prejudice: that based on our desire for social conformity. To win the approval of others whom we consider important, we will do whatever we think will please them and gain their acceptance. We tend to be steered by our perception of what a given group requires as a "membership card." Such social pressures have the effect of manipulating the values of the individual, leading him to adopt the prejudices of the group.

The second type of prejudice, in Gilbert's classification, is an extension of the first: institutionalized discrimination, legitimized by policy or legislation. In effect, it is the cultivation of prejudice by supportive public practice. It is the epitome of a tragic story: if enough people believe it, feel that they gain by it, and succeed in marshalling the votes for it, prejudice becomes a law, imposed upon those who view it as immoral. Thus, we have had restrictive immigration laws, justified for the wrong reasons; we have had miscegenation laws, similarly justified; we have had blacks counted as three-fifths of white persons; and we have had an assortment of laws and policies to restrict certain people in voting, housing, and the like. Beyond this, custom and ways of doing things have been even more restrictive.

Third, there is what Gilbert calls "pathological prejudice." This is exemplified by the fanatics, the chronic haters for whom bigotry is compulsive paranoia. Such people are seriously ill in a psychiatric sense, and they are dangerous because some of them have demagogic influence with a loose constituency. Fanatic race hatred is viewed by psychologists as an extension of intense self-hatred. It is a defensive mechanism, a type of projection or scapegoating, that compensates for one's own sense of inferiority. Adolph Hitler was a classic case. He used a group with whom he had reason to identify (he thought he might have been partly Jewish) as a scapegoat to divorce himself from them.

Social Aspects

There are those who take the position that what they think and believe is their own private business, and they resent "busybodies who stick their noses into what doesn't concern them." Perhaps a telling response to this is John Donne's seventeenth century prose, which reads:

> No man is an island, entire of itself; every man is a piece of the continent, a part of the main. If a clod be washed away by the sea, Europe is the less, as well as if a promontory were, as well as if a manor of thy friend's or of thine own were. Any man's death diminishes me, because I am involved in mankind, and therefore never send to know for whom the bell tolls; it tolls for thee. [19]

A similar theme appears in the writings of many poets and authors and in the work of many other artists.

The plain fact is that our attitudes *are* social. They are transmitted from person to person. Prejudice is *taught,* and it is also *caught,* like a cold; it is, as we suggested above, a highly contagious social malignancy. Our attitudes are not privately held possessions devoid of social significance. They are closely related to our striving for *social status.* As we have already noted, attitudes grow because they tie one to a group with which one wishes to affiliate. One accepts the values of the group, because without such acceptance, one cannot become an integrated member of that group.

However, we have also seen that group-determined values tend to restrict one's perception of, understanding of, and communication with other groups holding different values. This is particularly true if the differing group is perceived as a competitor for treasured goals: jobs, salary hikes, promotions, and such. Largely because of the absence of free, two-way communication—in the sense in which we described it earlier in this chapter—the groups become hostile and develop suspicions and hatreds that are impervious to logical, rational appeals. This is the typical dynamic of intergroup prejudice in its social sense.[20]

Why prejudice will generally not capitulate to information alone becomes increasingly clear. Information has a very difficult time getting past the selective perceptions engendered by prejudice. To say, therefore, that prejudice is simply ignorance or stupidity is acceptable, provided it is understood that the phenomenon is somewhat more complex than these terms commonly suggest. We may add: provided also that an individual is prepared to recognize that each of us is a little ignorant and a little stupid. A judgment by one person as to what constitutes prejudice in another person is in itself based on a value and is therefore a delicate and hazardous venture. We show that we realize this by telling a third person about someone else's prejudice, rather than making the accusation directly. Each of us would be well advised to look to his own prejudices, because the malady is universal in the human family.

Someone might retort that, if this is so, why worry about it? This is equivalent to asserting that, because the common cold is so common and there is no presently apparent cure for it, we might just as well simply live with it. Or to saying that ignorance is a persisting part of the human condition and we should close the schools and abandon our futile efforts to eradicate it.

Multiple Faces

Prejudice is usually thought of in racial, religious, ethnic or—currently—sexist terms. Part of the so-called generation gap is prejudice based on age. Not so common these days is the differentiation that was once made between a "city slicker" and a "hick" or "hayseed." Then there was the contrast drawn between the folks who lived "on the other side of the tracks," and those who lived "on the hill." There are "hillbillies," "Indian givers," and "skinheads." In industrial relations, there are epithets such as "union goons" and "titans." In police and community relations, it is "the fuzz," "the pigs," "the freaks," "the jocks," and worse. And in other types of intergroup relationships, there are distinctive ways by which the parties brand each other as reprehensible, barbarian products of questionable parenthood. One speculates that even "armchair psychiatrists" may be working off their hostilities on the people whom they amateurishly diagnose. Ethnic jokes are still making the rounds, with the nationality shifting according to the teller, the listeners, and the circumstances: "I don't know if you like Polish jokes, but I heard one the other day . . ."

The victims of prejudice become quite adept at recognizing behavior intended to mask prejudice. For example, there is the patronizing, condescending manner of those who begin a conversation with: "I'm not prejudiced. In fact, some of my best friends are———, but. . . ." Or another version: "*You people* really are happier by yourselves, aren't you? You don't really want all this agitation and stirring things up." Or another: "Haven't I always taken good care of *you people* and looked out for you?"

The many faces of prejudice suggest that racial differences are important chiefly because of cultural attitudes that make them important. Race is a symbol of one type of group differentiation, although anthropologists testify that scientifically it is not a very significant differentiation. In some cultures, racial differences are simply disregarded.

Tools

Stereotyping or overcategorization is one of the working tools of prejudice. It is a sweeping generalization regarding an entire group or category: Norwegians are giants, Englishmen lack a sense of humor, police officers are corrupt, and so on. Walter Lippmann referred to the stereotype as "a picture in the head," "a short-cut for thought," as "looking at all members of a group as if they were alike." Gordon Allport argued that a stereotype is not a category, but "often exists as a fixed mark of a category." "Policemen" is a category; "corrupt" is the stereotype. Allport indicated that stereotypes may or may not be based on a morsel of truth; that they aid people in simplifying categories; that they are used to justify hostility; and that sometimes they serve as "projection screens for our personal conflict." Stereotypes are often socially supported—by the mass media, novels, short stories, newspaper items, movies, stage, radio and television. [21]

Allport might well have added jokes and anecdotes of the type that would fall flat without stereotypic props. Comedians have made much of this, particularly in lampooning their own group, though it appears to be a fading practice. Richard Wright in *Black Boy* described the black elevator operator who exaggerated his accent and affected traits ascribed stereotypically to his racial group. The anti-Semitic story, or that of the "two colored boys," or of the priest, rabbi, and minister, or of Pat and Mike, or of the "two Polacks," are variations on these themes. This is still a significant mechanism for perpetuating stereotypic caricatures. Some defend it in the name of humor, terming it "laughing at ourselves," "not taking ourselves too seriously." But as Mark Twain wrote: " 'Tis said that a fish-hook doesn't hurt a fish . . . but it wasn't a fish who said it." [22]

No aspect of prejudice has been more thoroughly researched than that pertaining to stereotypes. Gilbert, for example, worked with what he called the "fading effect" of stereotypes, years ago at Princeton. Hartley asked several groups of college students to mark, on a standard social-distance scale, their attitudes toward a large number of groups. He included the names of three groups that never existed. Those who revealed the most intolerant attitudes toward groups that do exist tended to display similarly intolerant attitudes toward the nonexistent groups. One conclusion was that prejudice does not necessarily require actual contact between groups. It may be based simply on contact with attitudes about groups. [23]

Another mechanism or tool of prejudice is called *projection*—more generally known as *scapegoating*. It means that we all tend to look for the causes of our failures outside ourselves; we blame the hammer for a smashed finger. Allport defines it as "the tendency to attribute falsely to other people motives or traits that are our own, or that in some way explain or justify our own."[24] Scapegoating in itself is not an adequate theory to explain prejudice, but it is closely allied with stereotyping (for example, to hold that one did not secure a promotion because of the characteristic cunning of a certain group combines scapegoating and stereotyping).

Another tool of prejudice is rationalization: an accommodation of an attitude and an overgeneralized belief. As Allport puts it, "the belief system has a way of slithering around to justify the more permanent attitude."[25] Few people know the real reasons for their prejudicial attitudes. The reasons they invent are usually rationalizations, efforts to make the attitude seem plausible. All of us have trouble recognizing the difference between our *verbalized* reasons for behaving as we do toward others and the *real* reasons: the emotions from which the latter frequently spring may not be understood or acknowledged. Most of us are unaware of the psychological function that prejudice serves in our lives. It is a kind of crutch, to prop up our feelings of insecurity and inadequacy, and to serve as an outlet for feelings of frustration, aggression, and guilt.

Causes

Prejudice has many causes. No single theory of causation is adequate, and the causative factors are undoubtedly interactive. One school of thought regarding causation tends to emphasize *personality* factors. The focus is on the prejudiced person himself. Another theory stresses *social structure* as an explanation for prejudice. The focus is on power arrangements in society. Prejudice is seen an economic and political weapon. A third concept emphasizes the *cultural* causes of prejudice. Folkways nurture prejudice; social conformity motivates it. This is what psychologist S. H. Britt had in mind when he referred to entire lives oriented to "the ready-made acceptance of ways." This theory of causation holds that prejudice is simply accepted, without challenge, as a cultural norm.[26] Any single prejudiced individual may reflect all the causes of prejudice because of the mutually reinforcing pattern of these factors.

Having identified three broad approaches to the causes of prejudice, it may be well to touch on a few specific examples from the literature. Proponents of the personality theory of causation include some who stress that prejudice is a product of frustration. They argue that the blocking of goal-directed behavior frequently generates hostile impulses in the individual. This hostility may be directed toward self, or it may be "stored up" (repression), or it may be directed toward an innocent target (projection or displacement). Stereotyping, scapegoating, and rationalization are the tools, as we have noted. Britt identifies another: "traumatic experience," which is actually a form of rationalization. The person explains his attitude by referring to a harrowing emotional event. For example, a member of a minority group may be held responsible for the death of a loved one, as someone once told this author: "And that's how it was, when I was six years old, that my dear old granny passed away, frightened to death by that runaway horse driven by that colored boy."

Personality factors are reflected, too, in the projection of impulses that we have trouble controlling in ourselves onto the supposed behavior of an out-group; for example, feelings about sex or the use of violence.

The whole gamut of repression, guilt, and projection is exemplified in the hackneyed conversation-stopper: "Would you want your daughter to marry one of them?" Fear is at the base of it, fear that "one of them" will ask one's daughter, that the daughter might accept, or even that it might eventually be discovered that an interracial marriage is no great social castastrophe. Simpson and Yinger devote an entire chapter to a discussion of intermarriage and sexual relations of an interracial, interreligious, and interethnic character. Allport said that the intermarriage issue is not rational. He called it "a specious rationalization for prejudice." Quoting him:

> It [the marriage issue] comprises a fierce fusion of sex attraction, sex repression, guilt, status superiority, occupational advantage, and anxiety. It is because inter-marriage would symbolize the abolition of prejudice that it is so strenuously fought. [27]

The theory that personality is the cause of prejudice was given considerable impetus by *The Authoritarian Personality* studies. The central hypothesis of this research was that prejudice is often a symptom of a basic personality problem. The general finding was that prejudice is directly related to rigidity of outlook, to intolerance for ambiguity, to superstition, and to suggestibility and gullibility. Subsequent studies, for example, that by Rokeach mentioned earlier, substantiated this theory. [28]

Such research suggests that prejudiced persons look for hierarchy in society. They like definite power arrangements, something predictable. They like authority and discipline; they tend to distrust other people and to see the world as a hazardous place. [29] They are the Archie Bunkers in our midst. But again, amateur diagnosticians can cause havoc by going about gleefully pointing to these behavior patterns in others and failing to see that their own behavior in so doing may be pathogenic. Not every advocate of "law and order" is "sick," "up-tight," or "prejudiced."

The effect of prejudice—for the prejudiced, and for the victims of it—has had the attention of numerous writers. [30] It is difficult to separate the causes of prejudice from its effects. What is a gain and what is a loss are questions tied up with the values of the prejudiced, the values of the victims of prejudice, or the values of those who make a judgment, including those who write on the subject.

The preceding reference to those who prefer hierarchical, predictable, and definite power arrangements in society illustrates the point that theories of causation for prejudice blend together. So-called authoritarianism in personality pattern accommodates most easily to a highly ordered and orderly social structure. This suggests the second of the broad schools of thought regarding the causes of prejudice: the social structure emphasis. Muzafer Sherif described the theory well:

> The scale or hierarchy of prejudice in settled or stable times flows from the politically, economically, and socially strong and eminent down to lower hierarchies of the established order. . . . The most elaborate "race" superiority doctrines are products

of already existing organizations of superiority-inferiority relationships and exploitations. The superiority doctrines have been the deliberate or unconscious standardizations of the powerful and prosperous groups at the top and not the ideas of the frustrated and deprived majority at the bottom.[31]

In short, prejudice exists, according to this theory of causation, because a person is convinced, deliberately or unconsciously, that he gains by it. The doctrinaire Marxist holds that the fundamental cause of prejudice is class conflict. The doctrinaire psychoanalyst disagrees. But there is a great deal of support today for the power theory of prejudice, manifest in "black power," "brown power," and so on. In police and community relations, particularly since 1967, there appears to be an increasing tendency to believe that there can be no significant improvement, where such relationships are at their worst and most incendiary, unless and until there are basic changes in existing economic and political power arrangements. Dialogue and community organization are regarded by those of this belief as the preoccupations of "do-gooders," having little or no effect upon attitudes or behavior or upon aspects of the system that are thought to be unjust. Militancy even to the point of violence, massive voter registration drives, separatism as a strategy for identity and power—these have become identifying characteristics of the power or social structure school of thought regarding prejudice. Its proponents are little affected by pleas to contain violence and to maintain law and order. Their retort is to call attention to how little is done to deal constructively with the human misery and injustice that precipitate violent behavior.

With reference to the school of thought that holds that prejudice has its roots mainly in the perpetuation of the cultural heritage, Allport lists ten sociocultural conditions that seem to encourage prejudice:

1. Heterogeneity in the population.
2. Ease of vertical mobility, erratically distributed.
3. Rapid social change with attendant *anomie*.
4. Ignorance and barriers to communication.
5. The relative density of minority group population.
6. The existence of realistic rivalries and conflict.
7. Exploitation sustaining important interests in the community.
8. Sanctions given to aggressive scapegoating.
9. Legend and tradition that sustain hostility.
10. Unfavorable attitudes toward both assimilation and cultural pluralism.[32]

The overlapping of theories regarding the causes of prejudice is apparent in this listing.

Self-Hatred.   The rejection of self, or of one's group identification, is a fascinating aspect of the study of prejudice. In our discussion of the self-image in chapter 6, we observed how the motivations for childhood behavior become increasingly social as the child grows. Gradually, children absorb into their own behavior and attitudinal motivations the values of the people around them. They learn from others what they should want to do, what they should want to be, and what is more (and less) important in life.

One does not go very far in studying motivation in human behavior without recognizing that anticipated reward figures prominently in it. A child who is motivated to do his best in school, to show some consideration for the interests and feelings of others, to postpone immediate satisfactions for larger and later satisfactions is a child who has experienced some rewards for such behavior. But what happens when a society more or less systematically cuts off parts of its population from the opportunity to know and share in the rewards for careful preparation and responsible work? Obviously, social motives for good behavior do not flourish in such circumstances. It is therefore fruitless to say: prove yourself a responsible, well-motivated individual, and opportunities will then materialize. Responsible motivations develop only in an environment in which these opportunities are present.

This point was dramatically emphasized by Ralph Ellison:

> I can hear you say, "What a horrible, irresponsible bastard." And you're right. I leap to agree with you. I am one of the most irresponsible beings that ever lived. Irresponsibility is part of my invisibility; any way you face it, it is a denial. But to whom can I be responsible, and why should I be, when you refuse to see me?[33]

Self-rejection, then, is basically a question of identity, as we saw earlier. It bears on the answer to the query, who am I? If the answer comes back, "I am a nobody—and nobody cares," we may come to accept prejudice against ourselves as a fact of life, or prejudice against others as a way of dealing with our own sense of inadequacy. While there are many causes of prejudice—political, economic, social, and so on—*deeply prejudiced people have often had a childhood filled with threat.*[34] People who have difficulty in finding a satisfactory answer to the question, who am I? will sometimes take steps to establish who they are not. Among adolescents, this often takes the form of clannishness, of overidentification with a clique or gang. Forthwith, everything the gang does is good. The relationship to delinquency, crime, and other socially deviant behavior is evident. These are ways of lashing out or of striking back at others and at society in general, out of feelings of insecurity, frustration, hostility, bitterness, hopelessness, and ultimate despair.

Yinger summarizes the matter in this way:

> To an important degree, prejudice is a way of trying to deal with a negative picture of one's self. The world seems threatening, because of early experiences filled with unpredictability and unhappiness. Members of another racial or nationality group were not the cause of a person's problems, but if he has been taught a prejudice, he may use it to control his own feelings of threat by blaming and attacking them. Prejudiced persons are often characterized by what psychiatrists call a weak ego. They are fearful of their own impulses; their picture of themselves, which has been reflected back to them by the behavior of others toward them, is an uncomplimentary one, and they are afraid of it. They may love their parents, but because their parents have given them a negative picture of themselves, they also hate them, but they cannot admit their hate. They repress it, and transfer it to the minority group

against whom they are prejudiced. Because they are insecure, they become rigid-minded in an attempt to get some stability and predictability in life. Any suggestion that the relationship between the dominant group and the minority group might be changed is rigidly rejected. [35]

Social Conformity. We have stated that common prejudice is cultivated by our desire for social acceptance. How strong is this influence? Various research experiments have been conducted to find out. The answer has been loud and clear: stronger even than self-preservation, under certain conditions. Para-trooper trainees jump off training towers under threat of being called "chicken" if they do not. Milton Rokeach has noted the point we mentioned earlier in this chapter, that society often encourages evil by "legitimizing" it, by condoning it through norms, laws, and folkways that sanction man's inhumanity to man. [36]

A well-known experiment designed to test the respondents' reactions to authority was carried out at Yale University under the direction of Stanley Milgram. The idea was to discover the extent to which the subjects had an individual conscience, as against mechanically responding to commands from authority figures regardless of the morality of the commands. In the experiment, simulated electric shocks were administered to a subject who was really an accomplice of the experimenter. The actual subjects were third persons (taken singly) who were to administer shocks to the accomplice. Of course no electricity was actually transmitted: it was merely set up to appear so. The experimenter issued a series of commands to the accomplice. Each time the accomplice failed to comply with a command, the real subject was asked to administer a shock to the accomplice; each shock was apparently graduated in intensity, with 30 volts for the first button pushed, 60 for the second, 90 for the third—all the way to 330 volts, which was labeled: "Danger, severe shock." Each time a shock was administered, the accomplice (a gifted student of drama) screamed with increasing apparent pain. The real subject assumed that shock was actually occurring. It was startling to find that 65 percent of the real subjects, both students and adults, pushed all the buttons, obeying orders all the way. The subjects were all of middle-class background.

Evidently, many people will condone evil when it is socially legitimized. This is sometimes called "the Eichmann syndrome." It appeared to Rokeach in the 1960s that much of the social protest of the time was directed against socially legitimized evil.

None of us likes to be thought of as an oddball. If social pressures, particularly from people whom we wish to impress favorably, seem to condone a certain type of attitude or behavior, it is extremely difficult to rebel against the prevailing pattern. Indeed, there is often some reward for conforming and penalty for failure to conform. One frequently hears references to "dead heroes" or "unemployed crusaders." The pressures are often subtle, vicious, hard to prove, shrewdly and adroitly fabricated. If one speaks out in protest, he may be accused of being a lunatic or a troublemaker. One may be laughed at, or made to look ridiculous. Social heroes and heroines are often lonely, and sometimes pay a dreadful price for their heroism.

Minority Groups

Definition. Implicit in our discussion is the question of how a *minority group* is defined. A nationally known and highly respected intergroup relations consultant, the late Harold Lett, approached this question in a manner similar to that used by Allport, identifying six characteristics of a minority group:

1. Ease of identification of members of the group enables picking them out of a crowd on sight or through casual contact.
2. The out-group is defined by the slowness with which it is assimilated into the total population, i.e., how long "difference" persists in the public mind.
3. The minority group's identity is fixed by the degree to which it exists in such numerical strength in a community that it irritates just by constant presence.
4. Their numbers and their demands for recognition place them in a position of threatening the dominant group's notions of its own superior status, or prior claim to desirable jobs, or unchallenged control of political affairs.
5. The intensity of dominant group reaction to the minority group can be measured by the history of emotional contact between the groups, flowing from such things as labor strikes, teenage gang outbursts, sensationalized crimes of violence involving members of minority groups, and even carry-over from Old World conflicts.
6. The number and kind of rumors that circulate, emphasizing the criminality, sexual depravity, or diabolical plotting of the minority group.[37]

Lett's characterization of a minority group blends the various schools of thought regarding the causes of prejudice. Most observers approach the determination of a minority group in terms of power. It has little to do with numerical considerations, as in electoral processes where the majority system is operative. The vital question is, where is the source of power? Who makes the decisions that matter? In these terms, the really significant relationship is that between the *powerful* and the *powerless*.

Lett goes on to consider the typical patterns of minority group reaction to their status:

1. Adjustment, adaptation, accommodation, repression, etc.
2. Submission, with consequent sacrifice of individuality, incentive and ambition.
3. Resistance, in various ways:
   a. To excel (Show them!)
   b. To repel (Do our own thing!)
   c. To rebel (Burn, baby, burn!)[38]

What about the typical behavior patterns *of the prejudiced?* Allport offers two types of classification, the first of which focuses on how individuals act out prejudice:

1. *Antilocution.* People tend to talk about their prejudices with like-minded others. Many people never go beyond this talk stage.

2. *Avoidance.* When a prejudice is more intense, the individual will go to considerable trouble to avoid contact with the group he dislikes.

3. *Discrimination.* The prejudiced person makes detrimental distinctions of an active sort. Exclusion in employment, education, housing, etc. Segregation is an institutionalized form of discrimination, enforced legally or by common custom. Obviously, it is a form of social stratification.

4. *Physical Attack.* Under conditions of heightened emotion, prejudice may lead to violence, riots, etc.

5. *Extermination.* Lynching, pogroms, massacres, and genocide.[39]

Another Allport classification focuses on how conflict is handled:

1. *Repression.* Illustrated by the story with which this section (p. 169) began: "We have no problems here." Or by the individual who says: "Now I'm not prejudiced, but . . ."

2. *Defensive rationalization.* To marshal "evidence" seemingly supportive of the prejudice. Aided by selective perception, and by *bifurcation:* "I like Jews, but I hate kikes"; Negroes are good; niggers are bad."

3. *Compromise solutions.* Illustrated by *alternation:* turning prejudice on or off, depending on the situation. One kind of behavior in church, and another at a stag party.

4. *Integration.* True resolution. Goes beyond repression, rationalization and compromise. Wholeness; to bring into common and equal membership.[40]

The sociological term for integration is *assimilation.* It is a process of blending one culture with another. Years ago, we spoke of America as a "melting pot." However, it is now recognized that this metaphor had an unfortunate connotation. It conveyed the idea of an eventual goal of *complete* assimilation, with the consequent disappearance of unique and distinctive cultural traits of the many peoples who compose our population. Insistent Americanization of our minorities, with the implication that their ways are unacceptable, has come to be recognized as an undesirable way to define the goal. The term "cultural pluralism" is preferable: it signifies *unity in diversity.*

Intragroup Prejudice. We have been discussing *intergroup* prejudice and *intergroup* relations. What about *intragroup* prejudice and *intragroup* relations? Prejudice may be expressed by a minority group toward the dominant group, toward another minority group, or within the same minority group by some of its members toward other members. The latter is intragroup.

The prejudice of a minority group toward the dominant group is at least partly a matter of reciprocity and reaction, a *result* of dominant group prejudice and, at the same time, a reinforcing *cause* of the same. The prejudice of a minority group toward another minority group, as exemplified by Negro anti-Semitism, is in part displaced prejudice—using another minority group as a substitute target for the hostilities felt toward white gentiles—and in part a reciprocal prejudice against whites in general. Some of it may also be the result of the disenchantment of militant blacks with white liberals, in a particular sense, for instance, with white Jewish entrepreneurs who are regarded as exploiters of urgan ghetto blacks.

The prejudice of a member of a minority group toward other members of the same group (shanty Irish versus lace-curtain Irish) is usually a matter primarily of social class differentiation, although other factors may contribute to it; for example, religious and political considerations (again, Irish versus Irish) or more subtle criteria of "acceptability." Among Puerto Ricans, for instance, there is a term, *troigaño,* which is used to refer to another Puerto Rican who is perceived as an acceptable prospective friend or spouse. The term has no relation to differences in skin pigmentation, or religion, or of family wealth. Apparently, it is a general term for a composite of likable personal characteristics.

Rumor and Prejudice

Rumor and prejudice are invariably companions.[41] Rumors explain, augment, and justify prejudices and hostilities. Gordon Allport and L. Postman have said that no riot ever occurs without the aid of rumor.[42] Rumor enters into the pattern of violence at several stages:

1. Stories of the misdeeds of the hated outgroup, accusing it of conspiring, plotting, storing up guns and ammunition, preying on women and children, and so on. Rumor is a kind of barometer of community tension. A rumor in itself may be the spark that ignites the powder keg: "Some white cop beat hell out of a black kid, cut his head open and all, because the kid wouldn't tell where he lives." In short order, this may become: "Ten white cops raided this hangout where some black kids were shooting craps, and six of the kids are in the hospital." A bit later, it might be: "A bunch of cops shot up the neighborhood and killed two black kids, looking for some dudes who knocked off a liquor store."

2. General and preliminary rumors build up to "marshalling" rumors, for example, "Something is going to happen tonight in the park by the river."

3. During a riot or disorder, rumors sustain the excitement—sometimes to a point of utter hallucination.[43]

A rumor is a verbal expression of hope, of fear, or of hate. Thus, the story that a promotional list has been posted on the bulletin board at the police station may engender *hope.* The story that "usually reliable sources" are predicting an earthquake may engender *fear.* The story that Black Panthers are raping white women may engender *hate.* The story that "cops" have gunned down three Hispanic teenagers may engender both *fear* and *hate.* And so on.

The discrediting of rumors is important, therefore, in controlling tension in the community. Recognizing this, communities where intergroup tensions are rife will often establish tension control centers, the chief function of which is to provide factual information to the public in circumstances where rumors are rampant. Newspapers, radio and television stations, human relations agencies, and sometimes police departments have provided facilities and auspices for such centers. Allport asserts that the exposure of rumors, in itself, probably does not change any deep-rooted prejudices. What it does, he says, is to warn those of mild or negligible prejudice that wedge-driving rumors contribute substantially to community disruption by aggravating and sometimes triggering violence. [44]

HOSTILITY AND THREAT

Prejudice implies *hostility*—a sense of *threat*—with we-and-they differentiation at its base. "We" are better than "they" (attitude) because we got here first (belief), or because the Bible says so (at least as we interpret it), or because they are "subhuman." If one grants the premise, for example, that "they" are "subhuman," prejudice and discriminatory behavior seem justified. Thus a hierarchy of mankind is arranged to support one's perceptions, and one feels very strongly about it. So strongly, indeed, that one will not entertain even the possibility of compromise.

Just as with the self-image, in which the individual has a generalized self as well as multiple specific selves, each of us has both general and specific attitides. A person has a general attitude or outlook toward life, toward the world in general, and toward other people. Terms such as introvert and extrovert, optimist and pessimist, happy-go-lucky and gloomy Gus, refer to such generalized attitudes. A person also has specific attitudes regarding specific things. Psychologists agree that a person who is prejudiced toward one group will usually be prejudiced toward other groups: it becomes a generalized pattern of thinking. Allport said that entire lives are profoundly committed to values that take for granted, without any question, the innate inferiority of certain others. [45]

Our feelings of superiority about "our" group, as opposed to other groups, are called *ethnocentrism*. Oliver Wendell Holmes described it as the conviction that "the axis of the earth runs down the center of the Main Street of our town." [46] Around "our town," we build a high wall, so to speak, by our selective perceptions of reality. The pattern tends to be self-perpetuating: perceptual input is governed by determinations based on attitudes, beliefs, and values for which we will admit no challenge.

The hostile feelings that are the basis of prejudice tend to be most marked when directed against people who are seen to be socially nearest those harboring the prejudice. This implies the threat element. In the 150 years or so of the history of immigration to this country, there has been ample evidence of this. Philip Hauser observed, "The problem of hostility and distrust and prejudice was never the monopoly of any one group in our history. It was democratically available to everybody." Hauser continued:

> As a matter of fact, one way to tell pretty much whether a people has yet made the grade in terms of disappearing into the community has been the attitude that they have toward the *newest* newcomer. Normally in our history, the 150% Americans were those who had not yet quite made the grade themselves—they had to have someone to look down upon. After they had been here long enough, they could relax and . . . become just one hundred percenters. [47]

DEALING WITH PREJUDICE: CONSTRUCTIVE CONFLICT

The treatment of prejudice should be tailored to the particular causes in a particular situation. The literature on treatment is even more extensive than that on causes. The many civil rights and intergroup relations organizations in this country, though they work in different ways and with different philosophies, share the common purpose of combating prejudice and discrimination. Some are committed to broad educational-type programs, others to political action.

Because prejudice is so often thought of in intergroup relations terms, numerous programs foster rather far-reaching activity in community relations and community organization. National promotions, such as Brotherhood Week and Negro History Week, have sought to make the overt expression of prejudice unpopular. Generally speaking, the trend in organizationally promoted programs has been to try to cope with prejudice as a group or societal problem. To emphasize that it basically comes down to the *individual* would seem to be too threatening, as so-called sensitivity training quickly establishes. It is also less threatening, as we noted earlier, to focus on the other fellow's prejudices, rather than on one's own. "Who, me? Prejudiced? You gotta be kidding! I just gave $100 to the United Negro College Fund."

Rather than attempt to catalog the various types of programs that have been undertaken to cope with prejudice, we will footnote several pertinent references where such information may be found. [48] Robert Merton has provided a useful classification of four types of persons, for each of whom a different treatment would be appropriate:

1. The unprejudiced nondiscriminator, or all-weather liberal (Merton comments: "Beware of such liberals, 'who talk to themselves' about prejudice—[obviously, other people's]—and produce all sorts of false assumptions, e.g., that things are getting better—or worse, as the case may be. This is the fallacy of privatized solutions.")

2. The unprejudiced discriminator, or fair-weather liberal. Despite his own lack of prejudice, he will support discrimination if he sees it as profitable.

3. The prejudiced nondiscriminator, or fair-weather illiberal. This is the reluctant conformist, e.g., the bigoted businessman who profits from the trade of the minority group. To convert him, discrimination must be made costly and painful.

4. The prejudiced discriminator, or all-weather illiberal. He believes that differential treatment is not discriminatory but discriminating. He is consistent in belief and practice. He may be moved toward Type 3 by legal and administrative controls, but such movement will be reluctant. [49]

Intergroup education in schools has been an important facet of antiprejudice programs for the past four decades in the United States, with organizations such as the National Conference of Christians and Jews and the Anti-Defamation League of B'nai B'rith in the vanguard. [50] Such "old line" organizations as the National Association For the Advancement of Colored People, the National Urban League, and the American Jewish Committee go on with their programs, as they have for half a century, without any sign that the reason for their existence is any less compelling than it was initially. No one dares to say what the status of human relations in this country would be without their collective efforts.

One of the most dynamic principles to emerge from intergroup relations programs during the past half-century holds that prejudice (unless deeply rooted in the personality of the individual) may be reduced by equal-status contact between majority and minority groups, in pursuit of common goals. The effect is greatly enhanced if this contact is sanctioned by institutional supports, and if it is of a sort that leads to the perception of common interests and humanity between members of the groups.[51] This principle is, in effect, Sherif's concept of *superordinate goals*, referred to in chapter 2. An assumption of this approach is that conflict of interest is inevitable in the free, pluralistic society. This point merits further analysis.

That interpersonal and intergroup conflict can and must be directed to constructive and positive ends, if a pluralistic society is to remain free, is a thought at first somewhat startling. The idea is that conflict is both inevitable and, in some measure, indispensable. Capitalism is based on it. So are the so-called checks and balances of political power—legislative, executive, judicial. A social scientist at Brandeis University, Richard Sennett, says this about conflict:

> The image of "order" in our culture is an image of peace and harmony. . . . These images of order create a culture where people are inexperienced and terribly frightened when conflict does break out. Because people try to exclude disorder from their daily lives, it seems as though the abyss is opening up whenever a difficult conflict arises. Because people do not know much about how to act in a situation of social conflict, they can only fear the worst.
>
> This naivete about disorder leads in two directions. It leads people to believe that conflicts not easily solved must inevitably escalate to a violent level, and that in order to prevent this, the forces of law and order must use preventive violence first.[52]

Many social analysts maintain that progress in dealing with social problems comes only as a result of tension-producing conflict. By this concept, wars and riots have an eventual, socially redeeming feature. Marxism has its roots in class conflict. Utopia is often built on ashes! Community organizers subscribing to the conflict resolution philosophy of the late Saul Alinsky induce cooperation among adversaries and clearly assume that conflict is potentially of great personal and social value. This theory contends that conflict prevents stagnation, stimulates interest and curiosity, and is a medium through which problems can be aired and solutions arrived at; it is the mainspring of personal and social change.

Morton Deutsch of Columbia University observes that various psychological theories are aimed at a utopia of conflict-free existence. But fortunately, he says, none of us has to face this prospect. The question is not how to eliminate or prevent conflict, but rather how to make it productive, and how to prevent it from being destructive. Deutsch speaks of *mutual gain* and *mutual satisfaction* for the parties to the conflict, not of conflict that is productive for the winner and destructive for the loser. His interest is in what he calls "impure conflict," that is, a mixture of cooperative and competitive elements.

What, he asks, is the difference between cooperative and competitive processes in conflict resolution? Concerning perception, Deutsch avers that a *cooperative* process tends to encourage the perception of similarities and common interests, while minimizing the salience of differences. *It stimulates a convergence or conformity of beliefs and values.* A *competitive* process, on the other hand, tends to increase sensitivity to differences and threats, while minimizing the awareness of similarities.

Deutsch considers at length the conditions that give rise to either cooperative or competitive processes in conflict resolution, whether interpersonal or intergroup. Regarding the latter, of special interest in police and community relations, he suggests some general propositions:

1. Any attempt to introduce change in the existing mode of relationship between two parties is more likely to be accepted if each expects some net gain from the change than if either side expects that the other side will gain at its expense.

2. Conflict is more likely to be resolved by a competitive process when each of the parties in conflict is internally homogeneous but distinctly different from one another in such characteristics as class, race, religion, political affiliation, etc., than when each is internally heterogeneous and they have overlapping characteristics.

3. The more coincidental conflicts there are in other areas between two parties, the less likely a conflict in any given area will be resolved cooperatively; the more cooperative relationships there are in other areas, the less likely it is that they will resolve a conflict in any area by a competitive process. [*Note:* Sherif's Robbers' Cave experiment is a good illustration. See chapter 2.]

4. A competitive process of conflict resolution is less likely as the exchange of memberships between the groups increases.

5. The institutionalization and regulation of conflict increases the likelihood of a cooperative process of conflict resolution.

6. Conflict is more likely to be regulated effectively when the parties in conflict are each internally coherent and stable rather than disorganized or unstable.

7. Conflict is more likely to be regulated effectively when neither of the parties in conflict see the contest between them as a single contest in which defeat, if it occurs, would be total and irreversible with regard to a central value.

8. The anticipation of a hopeless outcome of conflict, such that nothing of value is preserved, makes the effective regulation of conflict less likely.

9. Conflict is less likely to be regulated effectively if the rules for engaging in conflict are seen to be biased, and thus themselves the subject of conflict.[53]

In intergroup conflict situations, what functions are performed by a third-party mediator? These are some that Deutsch identifies: helping to remove blocks and distortions in communication (translate and interpret); helping to reduce tension between the two sides by careful listening, blunting or narrowing the issue in conflict; reducing stereotypes; reducing the sense of threat; helping to establish norms for rational interaction; helping to determine what solutions are possible; helping to get the issue redefined so that different aspirations may be realized; helping to make a working agreement acceptable to the parties, for example, to establish conditions in which retreat is possible without loss of face; and helping to make the solution attractive and prestigeful to interested audiences.

Clearly, there is a kind of science of conflict resolution; more accurately, conflict resolution is an extremely important facet of social psychology, with great relevance for police and community relations. Deutsch's views are indicative. In recent years, some big-city police agencies have moved away from the nomenclature of police-community relations, preferring to call it conflict management or crisis intervention. There is both an organizational strategy and an academically respectable philosophy behind this change.

SUMMING UP

In this chapter, we have reviewed some aspects of basic psychology related to behavioral processes, particularly perception. So much of what we had already said pertained to attitudes that it seemed timely to discuss attitude structure in personality, with its dimensions of beliefs and values. Understanding attitude structures helps one understand the complexity of what are often called "communication problems" in human relations.

Prejudice is attitudinal, and prejudice is frequently an element in the relations of police and community. Discussions of prejudice sometimes have one reflecting, "Well, okay, I must try to be more careful about these things in my various activities." This is, of course, a commendable resolution. But it is easily forgotten when the chips are down, especially with regard to big issues.

What we have been discussing is as applicable to the affairs of the United Nations as it is to the transactions of two youngsters at play. Human transactions range in complexity and in sophistication. Take, for example, the long-haired, unmanicured types associated (stereotypically) with civic unrest. The line goes as follows: "What's the matter with them? What kind of people do things like that? Why do they do such things? Do they really think anything good can come of such antics?"

The eminent Harvard psychiatrist, Robert Coles, addressed himself to such questions, though his view is not apt to be widely popular. It invites disagreement because it is so starkly rational. Some of its flavor may be transmitted in the following quotation:

> In the distant past, but also in recent times, dissenters have been banished to prison or sent to their death (or sent to America!) for their noisy, unorthodox, unsettling, and provocative words and acts. Many of us no doubt find such out-and-out repression distasteful, but we are not beyond our own ability to call a person we oppose only thinly disguised names, to insult him and at the same time ignore the thrust of his declared purposes, his stated intentions, his deeds—which surely ought to be open for discussion on their own merits, rather than the merits of one or another person's psychiatric status. We dismiss, belittle, and run down those we disagree with *substantively* by doing them in *personally*. [54]

Saying "Okay, I must try to do better" is not enough to eliminate prejudices. A more disciplined response is necessary: "I will examine and try to recognize my prejudices. I will try to understand why I have come to be prejudiced. I will work at eliminating my prejudices because they hurt others and myself." Prejudice attacks *personhood*. Carried to its extremes, it is the Holocaust.

NOTES

1. This part of our discussion is based generally on two presentations made by Eugene L. Hartley to the National Institute on Police and Community Relations at Michigan State University in May 1961 and May 1965.

2. G. M. Gilbert, "What Makes Us Behave as People?" in A. F. Brandstatter and Louis A. Radelet, eds., *Police and Community Relations* (Beverly Hills, Calif.: Glencoe, 1968), p. 46. Reprinted by permission.

3. These ideas are effectively presented in "Communications," an issue of *Kaiser Aluminum News*, house organ of the Kaiser Aluminum Company, vol. 23, no. 3, 1965. See "Points on Perception," in Louis A. Radelet and Hoyt Coe Reed, *The Police and the Community: Studies* (Beverly Hills, Calif.: Glencoe, 1973), pp. 69–79.

4. Milton Rokeach has been prominent among psychologists researching this matter. See, for example, his study *The Open and Closed Mind: Investigations into the Nature of Belief Systems and Personality Systems* (New York: Basic Books, 1960).

5. See, for example, Carl Hovland and Muzafer Sherif, "Judgmental Phenomena and Scales of Attitude Measurement: Itme Displacement in Thurstone Scales," *Journal of Abnormal and Social Psychology* 47 (1952) 822–833; 48 (1953): 135–141.

6. Jack L. Preiss and Howard J. Ehrlich, *An Examination of Role Theory: The Case of the State Police* (Lincoln: University of Nebraska Press, 1966), p. 30. Both Niederhoffer and McNamara refer to the "rabbi" system in the New York City Police Department. In this context, "rabbi" means a person with influence in the department, who can help officers "get ahead."

7. Arthur Niederhoffer, *Behind the Shield* (Garden City, N.Y.: Anchor Books, Doubleday, 1969), pp. 182 ff.

8. Hans Toch, "A Note on Police 'Experience', " *Police* 11, no. 4 (1967): 89. Reprinted by permission of Charles C Thomas, Publisher.

9. These ideas are adapted from Mildred Peters, "A Look at Ourselves: Elements of Misunderstanding," in Brandstatter and Radelet, eds., *Police and Community Relations*, pp. 58–61.

10. Jozef Cohen, *Sensation and Perception*, Eyewitness Series in Psychology (Chicago: Rand McNally, 1969), pp. 5–6.

11. Ibid., p. 6.

12. For example, James J. Gibson contends, in his book *The Senses Considered as Perceptual Systems* (Boston: Houghton Mifflin, 1966), that sensory inputs generate sensations and also information about the exterior world. *Changeful* information is not perception; only permanent, stable, *invariant* information is perception.

13. This summary is, in part, dependent on an article by William R. Carmack, "Practical Communication Tools for Group Involvement in Police-Community Programs," *Police Chief* 32, no. 3 (March 1965): 34–36.

14. Marcel Deschoux, *L'Homme et Son Prochain*, originally a lecture presented at the Eighth Congress of the Sociétés de Philosophie de Langue Français, held in Toulouse, ca. 1960 (Presses Universitaires de France).

15. Helen G. Trager and Marian Radke Yarrow, *They Learn What They Live: Prejudice in Young Children* (New York: Harper & Brothers, 1952).

16. Harry and Bonaro Overstreet, *Where Children Come First: A Study of the PTA Idea*, 3rd ed. (Chicago: National Congress of Parents and Teachers, 1958).

17. George E. Simpson and J. Milton Yinger, *Racial and Cultural Minorities*, rev. ed. (New York: Harper & Brothers, 1953), p. 20. Reprinted by permission of Harper & Row, Publishers, Inc.

18. G. M. Gilbert, "What Makes Us Behave as People?" in A. F. Brandstatter and Louis A. Radelet, eds., *Police and Community Relations*, pp. 47–49. See also by the same author, *Nuremberg Diary* (New York: Farrar, Straus, 1950) and *The Psychology of Dictatorship* (New York: Ronald Press, 1950). Dr. Gilbert was chief psychologist for the United States government at the Nuremberg trials and also a witness at the trial of Adolph Eichmann in Israel.

19. John Donne, *Devotions Upon Emergent Occasions* (Ann Arbor: University of Michigan Press, 1959), pp. 108–109.

20. Frederick M. Berrien and Wendell H. Bash, *Human Relations: Comments and Cases*, 2nd ed. (New York: Harper & Brothers, 1957).

21. Walter Lippmann, *Public Opinion* (New York: Harcourt, Brace, 1922), pp. 59 ff; Gordon W. Allport, *The Nature of Prejudice* (New York: Addison-Wesley Publishing, 1958), p. 158.

22. Samuel L. Clemens (Mark Twain), *The Writings of Mark Twain*, Author's National Ed. (New York: Harper & Brothers, 1917).

23. G. M. Gilbert, "Stereotype Persistence and Change Among College Students," *Journal of Abnormal and Social Psychology* 46 (1951): 245–254; Eugene L. Hartley, *Problems in Prejudice* (New York: King's Crown Press, 1946), p. 26.

24. Allport, *Nature of Prejudice*, p. 360. See also by the same author, *The ABC's of Scapegoating*.

25. Ibid., p. 14.

26. Stuart H. Britt, *Social Psychology of Modern Life*, rev. ed. (New York: Rinehart, 1949). The three-way classification of the causes of prejudice used here is borrowed from Simpson and Yinger, *Racial and Cultural Minorities*.

27. Allport, *Nature of Prejudice*, p. 354. For a classic analysis of sexual factors in American race relations, see John Dollard, *Caste and Class in a Southern Town* (New Haven, Conn.: Yale University Press, 1937); for a personal account, see Claude Brown, *Manchild in the Promised Land* (New York: Macmillan, 1965).

28. T. W. Adorno et al., *The Authoritarian Personality* (New York: Harper & Brothers, 1950); Milton Rokeach, *The Open and Closed Mind: Investigations into the Nature of Belief Systems and Personality Systems* (New York: Basic Books, 1960).

29. Allport, *Nature of Prejudice*, p. 382.

30. See Simpson and Yinger, *Racial and Cultural Minorities*; Dollard, *Caste and Class*; S. A. Fineberg, *Punishment Without Crime* (New York: Doubleday, 1949); *Emotional Aspects of School Desegregation*, Report No. 37 (New York: Group for the Advancement of Psychiatry, 1967).

31. Muzafer Sherif, *An Outline of Social Psychology* (New York: Harper & Row, 1968), p. 343. Reprinted by permission.

32. Allport, *Nature of Prejudice*, p. 233.

33. Ralph Ellison, *The Invisible Man* (New York: Random House, 1952), pp. 16–17.

34. Selma Hirsh, *The Fears Men Live By* (New York: Harper & Brothers, 1955), p. 110.

35. J. Milton Yinger, "Who Are We?" (speech delivered to a Northern Ohio Institute of Police and Community Relations at Cleveland, Ohio, November 21, 1964). Reprinted by permission.

36. Milton Rokeach, "Police and Community—As Viewed by a Psychologist," in Brandstatter and Radelet, eds., *Police and Community Relations*, pp. 50–53.

37. Adapted from Harold A. Lett, "A Look at Others: Minority Groups and Police-Community Relations," in Brandstatter and Radelet, eds., *Police and Community Relations*, pp. 123–124. Reprinted by permission.

38. Ibid., pp. 125–126. See also Simpson and Yinger, "The Consequences of Prejudice: Types of Adjustment to Prejudice and Discrimination," a chapter in *Racial and Cultural Minorities*.

39. Allport, *Nature of Prejudice*, pp. 14–15.

40. Ibid., pp. 316–321.

41. See "Points on Rumor," in Louis A. Radelet and Hoyt Coe Reed, *The Police and the Community: Studies* (Beverly Hills, Calif.: Glencoe, 1973), pp. 92–98.

42. Gordon W. Allport and L. Postman, *The Psychology of Rumor* (New York: Henry Holt, 1947). See also E. T. Fitzgerald, "The Rumor Process and Its Effect on Civil Disorders," *Police Chief* 38, no. 4 (April 1971): 16–32.

43. Graphically described by Alfred McClung Lee and Norman D. Humphrey in *Race Riot* (New York, Octagon Books, 1967).

44. Allport, *Nature of Prejudice*, pp. 61–63.

45. Gordon W. Allport, *ABC's of Scapegoating*, Freedom Pamphlet (New York: Anti-Defamation League of B'nai B'rith, 1948), p. 39.

46. Oliver Wendell Holmes, *The Autocrat of the Breakfast Table* (Boston: Houghton Mifflin, 1891), p. 126.

47. Philip M. Hauser, "Implications of Population Trends for Urban Communities" (paper presented at an Institute on Metropolitan Problems, University of Wisconsin at Milwaukee, February 1, 1958).

48. See, for example, part 3 of Simpson and Yinger, *Racial and Cultural Minorities*. Also Part 8 of Allport, *Nature of Prejudice*, and periodic reports and publications of the U.S. Commission on Civil Rights.

49. Robert K. Merton, in R. M. MacIver, ed., *Discrimination and National Welfare* (New York: Harper & Row, 1949), p. 104. Reprinted by permission.

50. See, for example, various publications resulting from the Intergroup Education in Cooperating Schools project, sponsored by the American Council on Education in cooperation with the National Conference of Christians and Jews, Hilda Taba, Project Director.

51. Allport, *Nature of Prejudice*, p. 267. A similar approach to community problem solving is called the *normative sponsorship theory*, developed by Christopher Sower of Michigan State University. See his *Community Involvement* (Glencoe, Ill.: Free Press, 1957); see also Robert C. Trojanowitz and Samuel L. Dixon, *Criminal Justice and the Community* (Englewood Cliffs, N.J.: Prentice-Hall, 1974).

52. Richard Sennett, "The Cities: Fear and Hope," *New York Times*, October 20, 1970, p. 43. Copyright © 1970 by The New York Times Company. Reprinted by permission.

53. Morton Deutsch, *Conflict and Its Resolution*, Technical Report No. 1, National Science Foundation Grant No. G5-302 and Office of Naval Research Contract No. NONR-4294 (October 1965).

54. Robert Coles, "A Fashionable Kind of Slander," *Atlantic* 226, no. 5 (November 1970): 54. Copyright © 1970 by The Atlantic Monthly Company. Reprinted by permission.

SUMMARY OF PART 2

Our principal purpose in part 2 has been to provide an overview of some of the more significant psychological considerations in problems of police-community interaction.

Perhaps the pivotal psychological aspect of police and community relations is the question of the self-image of the police officer. Actually, the self-image and the public image are so intertwined as to constitute an essential whole. Because morale is so much a matter of self-respect, study of the self-image of the police officer must explore what "good" morale means for the individual officer. We started with the query: How does a person learn who he is? To deal with this, we reviewed some salient points pertaining to the childhood socialization process, for example, the formation of conscience and self-respect.

We next examined the relationship between our social selves and our social roles, a crucial facet of personality integration. What this means specifically for the police officer then became our focus. Why become a police officer? How important is it to secure qualified personnel for police work, and for what objectives? Why does cynicism so often characterize the police officer's attitude toward his job? Here we discussed the basic predicament of the big-city officer: the paradox between the importance society ascribes to his role and his relatively low social status; and the problem of incompatible ends, which implies that society has so defined the police officer's situation that he can never act in accord with that definition. These perplexing aspects of police morale and self-image lie at the heart of the police-community problem.

The subculture of the police was our next consideration. We defined it as the organized sum of police perspectives relevant to the police role. We weighed the comparative influence of background and occupational socialization in the composition of the police subculture. We posed the question: Who succeeds in police work? Some interesting research is being done on this and associated matters.

Why do the police appear to hate liberals and vice versa? We looked at this question in terms of the so-called value gap between police and some of the policed. As we considered the public image of the police, we saw that it is the expectations of specific segments of the public that are crucial—and certain of these are known to be quite negative in their assessment of police performance. Numerous surveys in recent years have found that the police have a special public-image problem with youth, with the poor, and with powerless minority groups. Hostility begets hostility; we reviewed the relevance of this hypothesis in particular police-community interactions.

This brought us to the so-called adversary concept in police-citizen relations: the position that, to some degree, this relationship is inevitably conflict-laden. We explored this idea and noted its application to the law-enforcement part of the police officer's job. Academicians of various disciplines have claimed that the adversary element is aggravated by certain other considerations of officer background, attitude, training, and behavior. We sampled some of these opinions and gave some attention to the question of how successful police work is measured.

Self-images and public images are affected by attitudes, beliefs, and values. Relationship problems in a democratic, pluralistic society arise out of conflicts in perceptions. We related perception and its possible distortion to role performance of the police officer. We noted in several different ways the axiom that the world perceived by any one person is not the only world there is. We saw how the manner in which one perceives is related to one's attitudes, beliefs, and values, and what are often called "communication problems." We concluded that the communication problem rooted in value gap is much more complex than is usually assumed.

An example of this complexity is the problem of prejudice. Prejudice is a type of attitude embodying hostility and threat, springing from emotional roots in personality, nourished by stereotyping, scapegoating, and rationalization. We reviewed typologies of prejudice and described the schools of thought regarding its causes. Strategies for coping with prejudice and discrimination were discussed, with special attention to the principle of equal-status association in efforts to achieve superordinate goals. The constructive use of interpersonal and intergroup conflict was particularly stressed. Rumor, often a companion of prejudice, was briefly considered.

Problems in police and community relations are generally referred to in terms of minority groups and the disaffected, and it is true that the problems with these groups are frequently most acute. However, it is apparent that a general problem exists in police and community relations, even before specific issues are introduced. The specific is a complication of the general: an already difficult relationship becomes more difficult when certain elements of the population are combined.

What are some of the causes of the *general* problem of police and community relations? Here are ten we have noted:

1. Social change, in the sense of changed people-to-people relationships, that has drastically altered the dynamics of social control in society and requires a restructuring of the relationship between police and policed.

2. Changing attitudes toward authority systems and toward authority figures, including the criminal justice system and the police officer. Authority viewed as arbitrarily imposed is being questioned and challenged in many spheres, worldwide.

3. Depreciation or deterioration in the United States of the Anglo-Saxon principle of self-policing as a citizen's duty, resulting in a widened gap between police and the people.

4. The fundamental role paradox of the police in today's democratic society and its manifestation in such matters as discretionary use of police power.

5. The adversary nature of the law-enforcement aspect of police work and of the larger criminal justice system.

6. Alienation of police and community resulting from the paradox of role and status for the police officer and the inconsistency and ambivalence of society's expectations from the officer.

7. Unrealistic recruitment and educational standards for the police, given the demands of modern policing in the big cities where most of our population is concentrated.

8. The effects upon police and community relations of overcriminalization on legal moralism and the military model of police organization.

9. The dynamics of the perceptual process in human behavior, with particular reference to *we-and-they* differentiations in our attitudes, beliefs, and values.

10. Prejudice and bigotry in interpersonal and intergroup relations.

PART 3

Sociological
Considerations

9

SOCIAL PROCESSES, POPULATION TRENDS, AND THE URBAN ENVIRONMENT

Crime is a kind of human behavior. As with any kind of human behavior, its causes include individual and group factors in complex configuration. In academic terms, criminal behavior is deviant behavior of special interest to psychology and sociology in a basic sense and to political science, social work, psychiatry, urbanology, and several other disciplines in a derivative sense. The study of crime is innately cross-disciplinary, whether one is concerned with causes, effects, or remedies. Because it is behavioral, it is people-related or humanistic.

GROUP RELATIONSHIPS

Psychologists and sociologists, all interested in human behavior, differ in focus. The psychologist tends to concentrate on *individual* behavior, the sociologist, on *group* behavior. Social psychology represents the blending of these disciplines. Distinctions among the behavioral and social sciences are thin, as may be illustrated by the question: Is human personality a social product? To deal with this question adequately, one would delve into sociology, psychology, anthropology, and biology. For our purpose, it is sufficient to say that, as our analysis shifts slightly, and perhaps imperceptibly, from psychological to sociological considerations, we shall focus somewhat more on *group relationships.*

Just as there are psychological processes in human behavior—perception, motivation, and learning—there are also social processes in group interaction. When two or more people meet, the ensuing interaction, if sustained to any extent, assumes some sort of pattern. This pattern of interaction is always erratic and inconsistent, but over a period of time, it can be plotted and given an identifying label. Many interpersonal or intergroup contacts do not go beyond "small talk," if indeed that far. But often enough, there is some exchange of opinions and ideas, some "sociability," and a dynamic interplay of personal and social forces is set in motion. [1]

Which pattern predominates in social interaction, cooperation or conflict? Complex systems of social theory have been built around this question, most holding that cooperation is the dominant social process, a few holding that competition and conflict are dominant. To what extent is it a "dog-eat-dog" world? If one takes an extreme position on this question, how does one explain that people do, in fact, live together in harmony, mutual aid, and trust? Civilization survives and thrives precisely because of helping and sharing and trusting.

Social relations are, of course, an extension of individual human nature: a mixture of positive and negative, love and hate, good and bad, cooperation and conflict. Historians and anthropologists tell us that there are cultures and societies that have emphasized one far more than the other. In early America, for example, there were peaceful as well as warlike Indian tribes. Cultural considerations seem to explain these differences. Our society contains many examples of limited cooperation among competitors, which exemplifies the practical admixture of the processes.

SOCIAL PROCESSES

In the sociological sense, *competition* is the struggle for what are seen as desirable but limited goods: wealth, customers or profits, prestige, jobs, promotions, parental affection, and the like. The prevailing culture establishes what is regarded as desirable. People reared in a noncompetitive culture find it difficult to adjust to highly competitive conditions. Unregulated competition easily becomes destructive and takes unfair advantage of others. Thus there develops wide recognition of the need for ethical and legal controls. If the parties to the competitive process are of unequal strength, exploitation and injustice are likely results. Again, the ancient political question is asked: How much individual freedom, how much regulation, to achieve the common good?

Competition is usually impersonal and unconscious. It may exist without personal contacts. People may not be aware that what they acquire through competition may deprive someone else. But sometimes the scarcity of the good is only a *felt* scarcity, as with parental love, when theoretically there is no actual scarcity.

When competition becomes conscious and personal, it is *conflict.* Sometimes it is difficult to distinguish one from the other. Conflict may be internal, as in the concerns of the psychologist or psychiatrist. Sometimes internal conflict is caused by external forces; for example, in the case of value conflict, as we observed in chapter 8. What sociologists call *contra-cultural conflict*, the clash between the values of differing cultures, illustrates this point: it may cause personality disorganization, as Kane and others have pointed out.[2] Then there is interpersonal conflict, for instance, in marriage or other prolonged, close associations of human beings. There are also intergroup conflicts, as when groups compete for limited goods. And there are international conflicts, nation against nation.

Cooperation is a social process in which two or more persons or groups work together in mutual helpfulness. It exemplifies "associative" social interaction: the parties are inclined to want to work with one another, to join together, to gravitate toward each other, to pool their resources. The ultimate of this social process is *love*. Interaction may, on the other hand, cause individuals or groups to draw apart, a "dissociative" tendency. The ultimate of this is *hate* (war).

Between these poles, there are varying degrees of association or dissociation. Conflict tends to be an intermittent rather than a continuous social process. As we noted in the preceding chapter, conflict can be, often is, and must be turned to constructive, positive, cooperative ends. This is just another way of saying that individual behavior is sometimes cooperative, sometimes anything but cooperative. Social equilibrium, to the degree evidenced in a conflicting, pluralistic society, is often maintained through some form of *accommodation.* This is a process of limited cooperation—cooperation under certain conditions. *Coercion,* or forcing people to act contrary to their wishes, is the lowest level of accommodation. It is outward conformity in order to escape an alternate penalty viewed as worse. Less demeaning to human dignity is *compromise,* a form of accommodation in which each of the conflicting parties agrees to give some ground and accept some losses. Conciliation, mediation, and arbitration are formalized types of compromise used in conflict situations between large groups.

Toleration is a type of accommodation in which differences cannot be compromised, but are accepted for what they are, and are subordinated to cooperation and mutual participation. *Conversion* is the settlement of a conflict situation by a shifting of a person's beliefs, loyalties, or emotional attachments. ("If you can't lick 'em, join 'em!")

The difference between conversion, as a form of accommodation, and *assimilation* is slight. The latter is a process through which persons or groups acquire the habits and values of other persons or groups and become parts of a common system. It is a blending or fusion of two or more cultures. Anthropologists use the term *acculturation* to refer to this process. The sociological concept of *marginality* refers to persons who participate partly in two different cultures. They may not be fully accepted in either. An example is the black police officer. Another example would be blacks who have "made it" by the standards of white middle-class society, but who entertain strong sentiments of loyalty and concern for other blacks who have not. Such ambivalence, when translated into behavior, makes one subject to conflicting role expectations that are not easily reconciled.

Amalgamation is a biological term for the social process whereby races or cultures are merged through intermarriage. In itself, amalgamation creates no problems. The principal barriers to it are culturally prescribed: ethnocentrism, caste, class, and the like. *Stratification* is the division of society into horizontal levels, evaluated and arranged hierarchically on the basis of such standards as learning, sex, occupation, age, effectiveness in war, social class, caste, race, and religion. The standards for stratification are many, often quite subtle, frequently pernicious and arbitrary, and are commonly imposed by law, public opinion, custom, and tradition.

In the United States, it is said that ours is an *open-class* system. This means that shifting of social class is possible for all. Many poor whites and blacks feel that the system is actually quasi-caste, which means that the chances of change are remote, indeed. Stratification in terms of social class is the point of departure for Marxism. Stratification in terms of gender is the point of departure for the women's liberation movement. Stratification in terms of age (the "generation gap") is the point of departure for gerontology and activist senior-citizen's groups such as the Gray Panthers. Some form and degree of stratification may be cause or effect of competition and conflict; in somewhat more subtle fashion, it may also be the result of accommodation. Whether it is a positive or negative social arrangement varies according to one's criteria.

SOCIAL CONTROL

Viewed as a whole, social interaction is based on the assumption that the participants will usually act rationally and predictably. It is, in this sense, "coordinated." Obviously, the survival of society depends on a considerable amount of mutual trust. The more complicated the society, the more vital the latent reliance of persons on one another. Take the automobile as a simple illustration. When we drive a car, we rely on the work of many others whom we do not know and probably will never meet. We depend on other drivers to respect the rules of the road, and they similarly rely on us even though we do not know, nor shall we ever meet, most of them. The mutual trust is impersonal, but real. It holds things together.

The automobile is but one facet of a complex social arrangement that depends utterly on such depersonalized mutual trust. This arrangement is *social integration*. It is achieved through *social control*, a variety of techniques, means, and pressures by which society brings individual members and groups into some measure of conformity. There are institutionalized or formal means of social control and noninstitutionalized, informal means. The law is an example of the former; public opinion, art, ceremony, praise, flattery, rewards, gossip, and ridicule are examples of the latter. The basic idea is to maintain behavior patterns within a certain range of acceptability, called "normality." What is acceptable or normal varies according to the culture, the circumstances, and the impact of social change. Advertising, propaganda, namecalling, pressure groups, and lobbying are further examples of common social control mechanisms. A political campaign involves all of these and many more.

Law as a means of social control is, of course, of special interest to us here. Law is the expressed will of the state and consists, in the United States, of the common law, statutory law, and court decisions. The prohibitions of law are an index of the range of behavior that the people of a democratic society will tolerate. Law is a society's ultimate weapon in controlling the conduct of its members. For law carries with it, as does any other mechanism of social control, a sanctionary element: rewards for conformity and penalties for deviance. Both the rewards and the penalties reflect shifting standards of public opinion, as evidenced in the history of penology.

Social Change and Social Control

fewer laws

Relatively few laws are needed in a culturally homogeneous society in which everyone respects the existing informal norms, especially if there is little spatial and social mobility. But in a complicated, technological, and culturally heterogeneous society such as ours has become, many laws are required. The

more laws

trend toward legal controls increases as basic institutional means of control, such as the family and religious bodies, diminish in influence. In short, social change and social control are intimately related. The study of police-community relations is the study of issues created by the effects of social change on the criminal justice aspects of social control.

We have discussed the importance attached to the principle of self-policing in the history of British and American police work. The number of people who obey the law voluntarily and who thereby assume some responsibility that might otherwise fall to the police—without ever giving a thought to the police—is striking evidence of the power of social norms. The social control exemplified by law observance is the best kind of law enforcement.

The question of whether more people abide by the law because of consideration for others, or because of fear of penalties, has sparked debate down through time. Again, the various answers to this question are grounded in differing theories as to the nature of man and society. Plato, Machiavelli, and Hobbes were preoccupied with questions of social order and control. So, too, are many modern political and sociological theorists. If crime is viewed as deviant behavior, as it universally is, then social control may be studied in terms of reactions to deviance.[3]

The prevalent view is that most people condition their behavior (and thus accept authority) in rational deference to social and moral considerations. Obviously, this means that a minority are prompted more by fear of consequences. If this seems to be another we-and-they categorization, let it be added that each of us is, on occasion, in one category, and, on other occasions, in the other. But each of us behaves more often with what might be called the positive motivation. Such is the prevailing opinion.[4]

Michael Banton provides an excellent analysis of the effect of social change on social control. Following is a series of quotations that convey his key points:

> The communities with the highest level of social control are small, homogeneous, and stable. . . . In such communities, social control is maintained to a very large extent by informal controls of public opinion, and there is little resort to formal controls such as legislation or the full-time appointment of people to law enforcement duties. . . . The small society with a simple technology can afford to have its "village idiot"; the large and complex one cannot, for many people would not recognize him and he might easily hurt himself or create havoc in the affairs of others. . . .
>
> People who live together like this are agreed in what they consider right and wrong, so it can be said that the highly integrated society is characterized by a high level of consensus, or agreement on fundamental values. . . . The policeman obtains public cooperation, and enjoys public esteem, because he enforces standards accepted by the community. . . . This gives his role considerable moral authority. . . .
>
> No social changes are without their costs, and one of the principal costs of making the social structure more flexible is the decline of social integration. An index of this is the crime rate. . . . As the problem of maintaining order becomes more severe, societies increasingly adopt formal controls, summarized by an anthropologist as "courts, codes, constables and central authority."[5]

Some police officers today imply that they have made a remarkable discovery when they say, "Being a cop today is a lot tougher than it used to be!" Yes, indeed, and the same is true for school teachers, clergymen, medical practitioners, social workers, and storekeepers. The police officer is an agent of society's system of social control. And social change, in many ways, has made the social control function infinitely more challenging than in the society of yesteryear. Among the obvious evidences are the "automobile revolution," and the resulting unprecedented mobility of people. But some of the marks of social change are less discernible, as for instance, in the matter of community relations.

The Community and Social Control

Banton's analysis suggests that social control is a function of the status of social relations in a given situation. Its level is determined by the kinds of social relationships that exist among individuals and groups who make up a society. Banton describes it in terms of relative social integration or disintegration. This is the essence of a functional definition of *community*, which we touched on in chapter 2. An ideal community is socially integrated: it encompasses a sharing of common experiences and a sense of belonging.

In another place, the author has commented on the idea of community:

> The community that is our goal is a community of COMMON UNITY. It is a community which dignifies the right to be different. It is a community in which there is no penalty or sanction exacted upon those who protest. It is a community disposed in spirit to the dialogue. It is a decent society in the sense of Jacques Maritain's emphasis, viz., a society which helps people to be *persons*, i.e., "bearers of values." . . . the root of the idea of community is *participation;* not condescension, not patronage, not rescue, but the dignity and worth that men and women on any level of life experience when they are part of what is important to their fellows.[6]

The main point here is to understand the relationship between social change and social control and to emphasize that social control and community relations are interdependent. As change occurs in people-to-people relations, in the transition from a simple to a complex society, social controls—as Banton says—are more apt to be imposed by formal mechanisms.

When someone asks, "What has happened to community?" or declares, "We must restore a sense of community," it is well to keep in mind what we are talking about. A community is not simply a place or a location. It is not necessarily a small town or a big town. Eric Fromm has said simply that "a community is love."[7] He may be accused of oversimplifying, but he has captured the gist of the idea.

Banton comments on urban community as follows:

> In contrasting village society with the big industrial nation, it is difficult not to convey a false impression. Even in the small-scale stable society, consensus is never perfect; it is only relatively high. An even greater mistake would be to imply that consensus is absent under urban conditions. Certainly in some urban situations, the moral controls are weak and the formal organization has to impose strict penalties, but there are many basic issues—such as ideas of duty to kinsfolk, work-mates, and neighbors—where popular morality remains powerful. In many urban residential

neighborhoods, there is a very real sense of community, even if informal social controls are less extensive than in the village. Policemen, being subconsciously aware of their dependence upon these mechanisms of control, prefer to work as peace officers and to see their role in these terms. [8]

Banton's observations suggest that police officers in modern urban settings often play the umpire role, even to the functions of mediation and arbitration. So we are back again to what we observed in chapter 3, to what James Q. Wilson calls order maintenance, what Banton calls work as peace officers, what others today have in mind when they refer to conflict management, preventive or proactive policing, crisis intervention, and the like.

POPULATION TRENDS

We have referred to social change in the sense of spatial and social mobility. Because this is so important with reference to the police officer's "umpire" function in social conflict, it merits further attention.

The first sociology course taught at Notre Dame University by the author of this text, as a graduate fellow in 1939, was Population Problems. The class used several standard references on the subject at that time. These sources unanimously predicted that the population of this country would reach a maximum of 165 million toward the end of the century, remain stationary for a time, and possibly decline thereafter. What has actually happened, of course, is that population passed the 165 million mark in 1955, and the 1970 census put the figures in the neighborhood of 205 million. By the mid-1970s, the figure was between 212 and 215 million. The explanation is largely in the completely unanticipated boom in marriages and births that characterized the post-1945 period. This trend has shifted rather abruptly in the past several years to approximate zero population growth.

Several demographic trends of special interest to us may be identified. One is the increasing *concentration* of population in big cities—what the Bureau of the Census calls Standard Metropolitan Statistical Areas, defined as a core city having a population of 50,000 and up, with surrounding suburban satellites in one or more counties. In the early 1900s, about one-third of our population lived in such centers. By 1950, this had become 57 percent of the population, living in what were then 168 such complexes. By the 1970s, virtually 70 percent of the population resided in about 220 metropolitan areas. Today, there are 272 such areas.

The trend toward concentration may be identified in another way. In the first half of this century, our metropolitan areas absorbed 73 percent of the total population increase of the country. This became 81 percent during the decade between 1940 and 1950 and 97 percent during the decade between 1950 and 1960. In 1960, the Chicago metropolitan area, by way of a specific example, had a population greater than that of any of 43 states. In effect, somewhat more than two-thirds of our population today is concentrated on approximately 5 percent of our toal land area. This is what is meant by "metroplexity."

A second trend relates to the *decentralization* of population within the large metropolitan areas. During the first half of the present century, the growth of suburban communities—outside central cities but within metropolitan areas—compared with the growth of central city population in a ratio of 1⅓ to 1. It was 2½ to 1 during the 1940s; it became 7 to 1 during the 1950s and was about 8 to 1 during the 1960s.

A third trend has to do with the *qualitative nature of the decentralization trend* in the metropolitan areas. The outreaches of the big cities tend to provide more desirable residential housing than the core. The dwelling units are newer, and they are functionally more efficient. Historically, as newcomers have come to the city, they have tended to settle in the inner, less desirable parts, because so many of them must start at the bottom of the socioeconomic ladder. As they have worked their way up this ladder, they have moved out to where the more desirable housing is, while newer newcomers have filled the center.

This general pattern has gone on to a point where vast sections of our inner cities have deteriorated to an ugly mix of small business establishments, old dwellings converted to dilapidated, multiple-family units, and heavy industry. As a result, our vast urban renewal programs have developed, to raze and rebuild whole neighborhoods. This imposes new ways of living on millions of relocated people and creates manifold adjustment problems for them. Our main point is, however, that the outward movement of people, from core city to suburbia, has been a highly selective phenomenon. The qualification has not been entirely socioeconomic, such as whether a family can afford an improved residential situation. It has frequently been a question of race, of language and culture, and sometimes of religion.

Industries have tended to follow the decentralization pattern, moving out to suburban industrial parks. The clustering of factory workers, predominately white, in low-cost suburban housing near their jobs foreshadows a new type of slum. Segregated living has not been the monopoly of any one people in our history. People of the same culture, language, and institutions have tended to flock together initially in the inner city, then have moved out and dispersed throughout a metropolitan area. In the beginning, each newcomer group has been viewed with suspicion, hostility, and distrust. There was contra-cultural conflict aplenty, beginning with the Indians and the early settlers.

As each group has moved away from the city's inner zone, its members have invaded middle-class, conservative neighborhoods, bringing cultural habits that often are threatening to established ways. This prompts many who have resided in such neighborhoods to move further out or to form "neighborhood protective associations." Former Detroit City Council President Mel Ravitz put the matter this way:

> How do those who are middle class and who administer and control the schools, the churches, the government, the social agencies, and all of the other organizations of the urban community learn to relate effectively with these people who have come and who are coming to these cities and who want to remain and be accepted?[9]

This problem is a continuing challenge to America's belief in cultural pluralism. It also reflects the challenge facing today's big-city police in their role as managers of social conflict.[10]

Additional demographic developments should be noted because of their effect on the social environment for intergroup relations, including police and community relations.[11] These developments are:

- Natural increase in population (the number of births over deaths) is close to zero in dozens of metropolitan centers. What this may mean when translated into housing markets, school systems, labor and employment patterns, retail business, land use, health policy, and the like has not yet been faced realistically.

- Movement of the population, outward from the core of big cities to surrounding suburban and rural areas, continues to boom. There is a net migration of 600,000 people a year to nonurban localities. Seven of the top seventeen metropolitan areas lost population between 1970 and 1975. The chief reason was out-migration. The top seventeen areas had a net loss of nearly two million people.

- American families on the move are increasingly heading South. Between 1970 and 1975, the number of people living in 16 Southern states grew by 5.3 million. This is a striking reversal of the pattern in the 1940s and 1950s when blacks and poor whites were moving North in search of jobs. Apparently, many are going back to the South.

- More people are living longer as the overall death rate continues to fall— from 841.5 per 100,000 persons in 1950 to 760.9 in 1960, to 714.3 in 1970, to 666.2 in 1974.

- The present projection is for a total U.S. population of 260 million by the year 2000.

- If present trends continue, about 17 percent of the population will be 65 or older by the year 2030, compared to 10.5 percent today. On the face of it, this carries implications for such things as schools, social security, crime rates and the nature of crime, employment, political programs and pressures, welfare, geriatrics and health care, pensions and retirement. It is being called "gray power." To illustrate, the American Association of Retired Persons today has 11 million members and a $30 million budget.

- At the moment, youth aged 14 to 24 constitute 21 percent of the population, as compared to 18 percent in 1966. A decline is not far off. Meanwhile, crime rates are affected, a problem worsened by the huge numbers of young people, especially minority youth, who cannot find jobs at a time of rapid inflation. Overcrowded prisons have several causes, but one major element currently is the post–World War II baby boom, now evident in the 20 to 29 age group.

- New immigrants have been entering the country at a legal entry rate of nearly 400,000 annually, the highest level in a half century. Along with further mixture of customs, colors, and languages, this trend increases the demand for jobs, housing, welfare and health services, schools, and the like. Ethnic pride and "consciousness" are strong, and immigrant expectations are high. Then there are illegal immigrants, estimated to number 8 million already here, plus one million more each year.

· The average American workweek has been shrinking—39.8 hours in 1950, 38.6 hours in 1960, 37.1 hours in 1970, 36.1 hours in 1975. Some big labor unions are campaigning for a 32-hour workweek, ostensibly to create more jobs by spreading the available work among more people. But experience in the steel industry over the past decade and a half does not substantiate this argument. So it remains for further study to determine what the actual effects of a shorter workweek will be.

Blacks in the Metropolis

Looking back over the past several decades, with particular reference to the relations between the police and the policed in American cities, special attention should be given to certain demographic facts regarding black citizens. For a number of historical reasons, blacks have been the newest of the newcomers in most of our metropolitan areas. There are some exceptions to this; for example, Puerto Ricans in some cities, Spanish-speaking Mexicans and Latin Americans in others, and white Appalachian migrants in still others. By and large, however, in the period from World War I until the very recent past, it is the blacks who have been the latest to arrive, and in the largest numbers.

Between 1790 and 1820, blacks made up about 20 percent of the population of the United States. By 1930, this proportion had dwindled to 10 percent of the total. Today, it is estimated to be 11 or 12 percent for the country as a whole. Just prior to the Civil War in 1860, 92 percent of all blacks in this country lived in the South. In 1910, 89 percent still lived there. The first large migratory wave of blacks from the South to the North occurred during World War I. The reasons were basically economic: the need for manpower in northern war-production industries, and the virtual end of European immigration as a source of the needed manpower.

World War II brought a similar internal migration of blacks, generally from rural to urban localities, and from the South to the North and West, although many blacks also moved to southern cities. The changing proportion of non-white to white residents of urban communities is evident in these figures: in 1940, 48 percent of the nonwhite population of the country and 57.5 percent of the white population was urban; by 1950, this had become 59 percent for each; by 1960, 70 percent of the white population was urban, as compared to 72 percent of the nonwhite population.[12]

How well prepared were black migrants for life in a metropolis? Within the span of a generation and a half, a people from a folk culture in the rural, economically depressed South were catapulted into metropolitan living. For immigrants to this country, the adjustment and adaptation process was one of assimilation, acculturation, or just plain "Americanization." But for Afro-Americans, we have had a rather peculiar situation. They have been Americans longer than most whites, but only in the past fifty years or so have they found themselves suddenly transplanted into the urban way of life. This process of adjustment has not been "Americanization" in the traditional sense, but rather one of urbanization or metropolitanization. Adapting to the demanding patterns of big-city living has been, for most blacks, a struggle against monumental disadvantages that few whites are able to comprehend.

There are those who ask, "Why can't *they* do what various immigrant groups did—lift themselves up and prove their worth by hard work and iron-willed determination?" Aside from the ethnocentric and chauvinistic implications of such a question, there are two points to keep in mind. One is that many Americans have inherited from their European cultural background a bias against people with darker skins. The other is that no other immigrant group coming to this country found itself shackled for almost 250 years by a highly institutionalized system of slavery. To be reminded of these considerations is still regarded in some quarters of our country, North and South, as highly inflammatory. But the question with which this paragraph began is equally inflammatory to black citizens.

In the matter of the urbanization problems of blacks, it is also pertinent to note that, as recently as 1950, the average schooling of blacks in the rural South was 4.8 years. This is below the level of functional literacy, the level at which a person can read a daily newspaper easily. Although this condition has been improved, it should be observed that the parents of many black teenagers in the inner cities today have this level of formal education.

Chicago as an Example

Chicago is typical of what has happened as a result of population shift. Between 1950 and 1960, about 600,000 whites left the central city and moved to suburbia. During that decade, the central city's net white population loss was 400,000, because there was an excess of 200,000 white births over deaths. The black population increased by about 350,000 in the same period, from slightly more than 500,000 to almost 850,000. The black population of Chicago was 30,000 in 1900; by 1920, it was 120,000. The nonwhite population of Chicago quadrupled between 1900 and 1920, increased by more than 28 times between 1900 and 1960, and by more than 7 times between 1920 and 1960. By 1960, blacks constituted 14 percent of the population in the six counties of northeastern Illinois and 23 percent of the population of the city of Chicago. These percentages are higher today.[13]

Many rural white migrants (and a sizable number of American Indians) have also settled in our big cities during the past fifty years. The economic and political forces underlying the spatial and social mobility of these years can hardly be ignored. We have alluded in chapter 8 to black power and brown power. Analysis of today's political scene in numerous big cities throughout the nation reveals a rapidly changing panorama. In terms of potential if not actual political power, the balance has shifted more and more to nonwhites. As in Chicago, it becomes increasingly difficult to determine the majority and the minority in racial terms.

The Plight of Our Cities

We have noted a number of population trends that affect the social environment, as we put it, of intergroup relations, including police and community relations. To this should be added some description of what is happening to our cities, on the premise that police-citizen encounters most often occur in urban settings. Some urbanologists are saying that no amount of money can possibly solve the economic woes of our cities. Following are some characteristics of this plight:[14]

- As whites have moved outward, the central city has been left increasingly to the black, the poor, and the aged. As the tax base has diminished, the need for many services and facilities that tax dollars provide has increased immensely. A Brookings Institution study, comparing 56 cities with their suburbs, found only 10 cities that compared favorably in such vital matters as employment, housing, and income. The larger the city, the heavier tends to be the per capita tax burden.

- The new black middle class is also moving outward, seeking upward mobility, fleeing crime and seeking better schools for their children. But for some, the move to predominantly white areas has not been without problems.

- Crime inside cities is far more common than outside.

- The job market is shrinking in many cities, especially in the East, North, and West—with some exceptions, such as Denver.

- Hospital and health services are deteriorating.

- When teachers in the schools are laid off, the remaining teachers are forced to take on larger classes, and shorter class days give students less education and more time to get into trouble. Vandalism of school property is enormous. Violence in school corridors sometimes reaches incredible proportions.

- With city police forces reduced, petty crimes and vice are more blatant.

- Libraries cut staff and reduce hours. Museums and galleries go begging for support.

- Industries leave the city because of taxes, wages, and prices. The construction of business edifices comes to a standstill. Conventions and conferences go where hotels flourish.

- The inner ring of older suburban cities, immediately surrounding the core of many of our largest metropolitan centers, are also sick, with no growth, and with businesses and industries dead or dying. This pattern may predict the future for suburban communities farther out.

- Wealthier suburbanities, meantime—in increasing number—appear to be buying inner-city real estate, at least partly because of what is referred to as the "rehab craze." Substantial prices are being paid for rundown row houses, with renovation as the aim. There is real promise in this development, with implications for family life, city finances, racial makeup, neighborhood facelift, and school salvation. On the other hand, this rebound movement could boomerang, creating a new army of displaced poor.

- There has been a dramatic rise in recent years in the number of one- and two-person households, predominantly in the cities. The Census Bureau reported in 1978 that nearly half of the nation's 71.1 million households were of this character. The report stated that 51 percent of the 13.9 million persons who live alone are over 65, three-fourths of them women. Roughly 49 percent of one-person households are occupied by persons under 35. Family experts regard this age segregation as having serious social consequences.

· In July 1977, New York City had a total electric power failure. The Bushwick section of Brooklyn, with a population of 137,000, provided a study in the collapse of an urban neighborhood. In a decade and a half, a thriving, well-kept area had become a wasteland of vandalism, firebugging, and barbarism. Affluent white and black residents had moved. Real estate operators had exploited Bushwick's decline. Government ignored it. Housing and schools went downhill. During the 25-hour blackout, 88 Bushwick stores were looted, 48 were burned, police arrested 150 persons, sanitation workers picked up 60 tons of debris. In this area where 80 percent of the residents are black or Hispanic, there have been 4,000 fires since 1975, according to city figures, 900 of them probably arson.

· Welfare programs in our cities constitute an administrative and bureaucratic maze that defies description. These programs, now three generations along in cumulative problems, cost American taxpayers about $40 billion a year. There are 23 million people who receive welfare benefits of one kind or another. Almost 350,000 employees are involved in the administration of programs. Obviously, reform of the system on a grand scale is long overdue. Elimination of programs, in itself, will solve nothing.

What do all of these things have to do with police and community relations? The plight of our cities, in all the particular ways in which people are caught up in problems beyond their individual capacity to manage or cope, directly affects the dynamics of what occurs in police-citizen interaction.

AGAIN, A SPECIAL LOOK AT BLACKS

It is obvious in every big city that "the people caught up in problems" are, in large number, black, or members of some other visible minority. In the next chapter, we focus on police relations with minorities.

Taking blacks again as our example, the question arises as to how they have fared since the mid-1960s? The Joint Center for Political Studies of the U.S. Department of Commerce reports that the average income of black families increased from $4,875 in 1967 to $8,779 in 1975. Comparing this with average income of white families during the same period, and allowing for inflation, the apparent gain is not all that significant. The number of black elected officials increased from 103 in 1964 to 4,309 in 1977. In 1966, 10 percent of blacks aged 18 to 24 were in college. In 1976, it was 23 percent. But the unemployment rate for nonwhites in 1967 was 7.4 percent. In 1977, 13.2 percent were jobless. The unemployment rate for black teenagers in August 1977 was 40.4 percent, almost three times as high as the rate among whites of the same age. Most of this black joblessness is concentrated in the inner cities, where 58 percent of all black Americans live. As US News & World Report put it (December 5, 1977, page 22): "Poorly educated, untrained for available jobs, often unmotivated to seek any type of gainful work, they cluster in big-city slums to form a subculture that leans heavily on welfare, crime, drugs and alcohol."

A term of European origin—underclass—has come to be applied to people "stuck at the bottom," mostly impoverished urban blacks—hostile, socially alien, intractable—described in *Time* magazine (August 29, 1977, cover story) as "victims and victimizers in the culture of the street hustle, the quick-fix, the ripoff, and not least, violent crime." The Haves versus the Have Nots is, of course, a worldwide struggle, and it is not new. But the numbers of the poor and the hungry are increasing, with 70 percent of the world's people living in more than 100 less-developed nations making up the so-called Third World, wanting more than their present 11 percent of total productive income.

POVERTY AS A SOCIAL FORCE

Poverty is everywhere endemic to minority group status. The 1960s were marked by a declaration of war on poverty at the highest executive and legislative levels in this country. It became evident, however, that the war was declared without sufficient education as to the nature of the enemy. William McKenzie of Southern Illinois University identified some of the favorite myths about poverty, which we paraphrase as follows:

> The myth that poverty is inevitable.
>
> The myth that poverty is simply a matter of being without money or other resources. This leads to the faulty conclusion that poor people are "just like us," except that they lack resources. Of course there are people who are temporarily "down on their luck." But the *culture of poverty* is much more complex. Moreover, the discount-store phenomenon operates on the assumption that the poor do have some resources. And one may question that some of the poor really want to be "like us."
>
> The myth that the poor are blacks, and that blacks are poor. This entire concept is false. Blacks belong to many classifications. Twenty-five percent of the population of this country are persistently poor, so obviously many are white. However, having said this, one may proceed to assert that there are many blacks in poverty—also Indians, Southern Appalachian migrants, Chicanos, Puerto Ricans, and even some white police officers. No one group should be used as a model for the whole.
>
> The myth that the poor are without culture. One thinks of such expressions as "the culturally deprived," "the culturally disadvantaged," etc. This is patent nonsense. The simple fact is that the poor live in a *different* culture. The Navajos of New Mexico are poor, but no one would suggest that they are "culture-poor."
>
> The myth that poverty breeds crime. Laws define crimes, and laws are made by dominant groups and provide maximum protection for those who make them. Even crime statistics are largely culturally derived. Where there is an apparent coincidence of crime and poverty, one must look beyond poverty for the cause of crime.[15]

McKenzie mentioned other, minor myths about the poor: that poverty causes family disruption; that the poor are dependent in spirit as well as in sustenance; that the poor are inarticulate.

What are some of the significant *truths* about poverty? Some have been implied above. Adapting from McKenzie, we may add:

Poverty is more of a culture or subculture than it is a social class. Identifying the poor with the lower class is similar to identifying the upper class with the rich. The difficulty is that a central middle class concern, i.e., economic resources, is taken as the measure of two groups for which it is not a central concern.

Poverty is socially invisible. It is overwhelmingly taken for granted as part of the scenery. Poor people tend to be seen as picturesque natives, living in the only way they know.

Poverty means institutional nonparticipation. The poor do not make our institutions and they do not manage them, but they are subject to them. They are expected to live by a moral code established by people with quite a different experience. To be poor is to live in someone else's world.

Poverty means immediacy. To be poor is, as it is said, "to live from hand to mouth." The poor are not much concerned with the long ago, and even less with the distant future. Thus, the values of the poor are often difficult for others to understand. If fortune smiles, the poor man buys his automobile or television—today. Tomorrow will take care of itself; it can't be any worse than yesterday. To be poor is to live continuously in the now.

To be poor is to have identity. Poverty has a place for everyone, and everyone is in his place. The feeling of lack of identity, of dislocation, of disassociation, of alienation is not a product simply of being poor. The poor know who they are; as with crime, we must look beyond poverty for the causes of disaffection.

Studying the poor in the United States by following roughly 5,000 families over a period from 1968 to the present, the University of Michigan's Institute for Social Research has reported some interesting findings, based on the official poverty definition:[16]

- Education is the single, most important factor in determining whether a family is poor.
- Disintegration of families is a major factor in the movement of people into poverty.
- Rural residents run a bigger risk of being poor than city dwellers.
- Blacks are much more likely than whites to be poor.
- Relatively few "hard core poor" stay that way year after year.

The study reveals that one of every eleven American families may be rated as poor in any one year, but only 25 percent remain poor over a five-year period. Whites benefit from schooling more than blacks. Unemployment of itself is not a major cause of the poverty problem, according to these researchers. It does, however, compound the problem. A family headed by a female is more than twice as likely to be poor, and stay poor, as one headed by a male. Besides being less educated and earning less than whites as a group, blacks more often are poverty-stricken because they tend to have more children and more families headed by women, according to the study.

SUMMING UP

In this chapter, we have briefly reviewed some basic considerations in a sociological approach to police-community relations. Our purpose has been to set the stage for the discussion in forthcoming chapters. The central message of the chapter may be summarized as follows: the relationship of people is fundamentally a matter of social interaction, the possible patterns of which are called social processes—cooperation, competition, conflict, accommodation, assimilation, amalgamation, stratification, and so on. To maintain stability, and, indeed, for a society to survive, social controls are necessary, controls by which a society secures conformity to its norms. Law is an important means to this end, but there are many social control mechanisms, formal and informal.

Social change, especially as it has affected people-to-people relations, has made social control in our society much more complicated than it once was. Population trends provide evidence of this fact. The resultant greater probability of contra-culture conflict, particularly in our big cities, has underlined the growing importance of the conflict-management role of the police officer. The urbanization problems of blacks and other minority groups during the past half century are of special interest to students of police-community relations. So, too, are problems associated with the plight of our cities, which we reviewed, and problems associated with "the culture of poverty," for the relationship between the police and poor people has frequently been bad.

Someone has said that revolution is a continuing part of the American experience. In other words, change is the only social constant. In recent years in the United States, specifically since 1954, we have been in the midst of what many people have referred to as a revolution in race relations. This movement has been in the forefront of concerns in police and community relations, to the point where many people have seen it as *the* problem. The next chapter discusses this and related problems.

NOTES

1. Any standard introductory textbook in sociology covers these matters in detail. Our aim in this chapter is to elicit principles relevant to relationships of the police and the community, in particular to the concerns of the following chapters. Some of the discussion is based on the works of the late Raymond W. Murray, C.S.C., former chairman of the Department of Sociology at Notre Dame.

2. John J. Kane, "Personal and Social Disorganization," in A. F. Brandstatter and Louis A. Radelet, eds., *Police and Community Relations: A Source Book* (Beverly Hills, Calif.: Glencoe, 1968), pp. 61–66.

3. Jack P. Gibbs, *Social Control*, Module 1 (Andover, Mass.: A Warner Modular Publication, 1972), pp. 1–17.

4. See, for example, Talcott Parsons, *The Social System* (New York: Free Press, 1951).

5. Michael Banton, *The Policeman in the Community* (New York: Basic Books, 1964), pp. 2–11. Copyright © 1964 by Michael Banton. Reprinted by permission of Basic Books, Inc., Publishers, New York.

6. Louis A. Radelet, "The Idea of Community," in Brandstatter and Radelet, eds., *Police and Community Relations*, p. 82. Reprinted by permission.

7. Erich Fromm, *The Art of Loving* (New York: Harper & Brothers, 1956), pp. 7 ff.

8. Banton, *The Policeman in the Community*, p. 7.

9. Mel Ravitz, "Contra-Cultural Conflict in the Metropolitan Community," in Brandstatter and Radelet, eds., *Police and Community Relations*, p. 75.

10. In early 1975, another population trend was of interest. The Census Bureau announced that the average size of the nation's households had dipped below the three-person level for the first time in history. A household is defined as any group of persons occupying a single housing unit. Among 69,859,000 households in the nation, 19.1 percent were one-person units in March 1974, as compared with 16.7 percent five years earlier.

11. The statistics cited in this section are in the public domain and are readily available in reports of the U.S. Bureau of the Census, the U.S. Department of Commerce, and the Bureau of Labor Statistics.

12. Paul Mundy, "The Implications of Population Trends for Urban Communities," in Brandstatter and Radelet, eds., *Police and Community Relations*, p. 67. See also "The Negro Population of the United States," in Louis A. Radelet and Hoyt Coe Reed; *The Police and the Community: Studies* (Beverly Hills, Calif.: Glencoe, 1973), pp. 101–108. It may be further added that a report published jointly in February 1969 by Urban America, Inc., and the Urban Coalition showed that whites had sharply accelerated their movement from the central cities in the aftermath of 1967 racial disturbances in many large urban centers. At the same time, blacks had even more dramatically slowed migration into them. Inner-city ghettos had spread in area, and slums had begun to emerge in the suburbs.

13. Ibid., Paul Mundy, p. 68.

14. Some points made in this section are based upon Associated Press stories in the daily press, and upon articles appearing in *Time* magazine and *U.S. News & World Report*.

15. William R. McKenzie, "The Face of the Enemy: A Brief Introduction to the Theory and Practice of Poverty" (paper presented at the Midwest Philosophy of Education Society meeting held in Chicago, December 4, 1965). See also U.S., Department of Health, Education and Welfare, *About the Poor: Some Facts and Fictions*, by Elizabeth Herzog, Children's Bureau Publication No. 451–1967 (Washington, D.C.: U.S. Government Printing Office, 1968).

16. As reported in *U.S. News & World Report*, November 8, 1976, pp. 57–58.

10

THE POLICE AND
MINORITY GROUPS

During the past thirty years, every social institution of our society has felt the effects of the civil rights movement. In the political arena, the movement has focused on changing the balance of power and the status quo, restructuring the establishment, increasing voter registration and exercise of the vote, and the like. Black businesses and industries attest to the effects of the movement upon economic institutions, and so does the emergence of tougher fair employment practices laws and affirmative action programs.

With religious institutions, the effects have been spotty and erratic. Some religious bodies have earnestly endeavored to take a position in the vanguard of social change, while others have continued to debate the relative merits of admitting nonwhite members, or have hidden behind a facade of ostensible openness in policy while actually discouraging the participation of "certain people." Suburban churches have been especially adept at playing this game.

Educational institutions have been interested in intercultural or intergroup matters since the early 1940s, when the first specialized human relations workshops for teachers were held, coinciding with the earliest police training programs with a similar focus. Schools and colleges have been in the vortex of the civil rights movement during the past thirty years. Their involvement has ranged from the enactment of fair educational practices legislation to power battles regarding administrative control, curriculum matters, and busing.

Certainly the media of public information have been caught up in the civil rights movement: many would say, not always constructively as "monitors of social change," if this is a fair way of describing one important role that the media might play. (We will discuss the media further in chapter 16.) Music and the arts, organized sports and recreation, and other leisure-time institutions also have had an uneven record relative to civil rights, with some of these demonstrating exemplary leadership for change while others are still engaged in fierce conflict or are striving to duck the issue. Voluntarily joined civic-social organizations also have had a checkered record regarding civil rights questions: many of them skirt and dodge such matters at all costs. Lively arguments still take place as to whether one should or should not join a club or society where one can be "among one's friends" and "with people of similar interests." The "black ball" and so-called "gentlemen's agreements" still carry special connotations. Perhaps most pernicious of all these days, in questions of racial justice, is the tendency to deny racial or ethnic connotations to positions taken on such issues as busing, affirmative action, and so-called red-lining in housing. Closely akin to this is the position that Senator Daniel Patrick Moynihan has called "benign neglect": simply ignoring problems and, indeed, referring to those not inclined to share this posture as "troublemakers," "dewy-eyed liberals," and the like.

POLICE RESPONSE TO THE CIVIL RIGHTS MOVEMENT

Police work and other aspects of the administration of justice have also been vitally affected by what has been happening in civil rights and race relations. Some would contend that the police have been particularly hard hit, but this conclusion may be the result of measuring the effects in terms of street encounters and risk of life and limb. To argue the point of "who has suffered most" is an idle rhetorical exercise. It is enough for our purpose to observe that the civil rights movement has undoubtedly contributed substantially to widening the opportunities for police officers to demonstrate creditable professional behavior—or its opposite.

The first thing to be noted regarding police response to the civil rights movement has already been indicated, that is, the development of specialized training programs to cope with new dimensions of the police task.[1] Police generally feel that they are not responsible for the conditions that fomented the crisis in civil rights, yet they feel that they have been expected to supply most of the solutions. They see themselves as easily available targets of abuse and criticism and as convenient scapegoats for all manner of social problems. In our big cities, which have become so heavily populated by blacks and other minority groups, the police have more continuous contact with them than has any other predominantly white organization. Numerous police officers have daily face-to-face transactions with black citizens, involving—as Robert Mills of the University of Cincinnati has pointed out—adjudicating family disputes, personal counseling, making arrests, setting ground rules for future behavior, or simply passing the time of day.[2]

For most blacks, the white world remains rather remote and inaccessible, but the white police officer has made his presence felt in neighborhoods where all or most of the residents are black. He is visible and he is *there*, and he is perceived as the custodian of "Whitey's law" and "Uncle Charley's system," indeed as the *personification* of that system. Therefore, the police officer—even if he is black (in which case he may be perceived as a "fink" or an "Uncle Tom")—takes the brunt of the frustrations, the anger, the hostility and bitterness vented by blacks. He is seen as a symbolic agent of injustice, never to be trusted under any circumstances. James Baldwin's description of this phenomenon is classic:

> The only way to police a ghetto is to be oppressive. None of the Police Commissioner's men, even with the best will in the world, have any way of understanding the lives led by the people they swagger about in twos and threes controlling. Their very presence is an insult, and it would be, even if they spent their entire day feeding gumdrops to children. They represent the force of the white world, and that world's criminal profit and ease, to keep the black man corralled up here, in his place. The

badge, the gun in the holster, and the swinging club make vivid what will happen should his rebellion become overt. . . .

It is hard, on the other hand, to blame the policeman—blank, good-natured, thoughtless, and insuperably innocent—for being such a perfect representative of the people he serves. He, too, believes in good intentions and is astounded and offended when they are not taken for the deed. . . . He is facing, daily and nightly, people who would gladly see him dead, and he knows it. . . . There are few things under heaven more unnerving than the silent, accumulating contempt and hatred of a people. He moves through Harlem, therefore, like an occupying soldier in a bitterly hostile country; which is precisely what and where he is, and is the reason he walks in twos and threes.[3]

This is, of course, a stereotypic view of the police. Evidences (and there are actually many) of compassionate, humanistic policing tend to be dismissed as rare exceptions. The apparent preoccupation of civil rights organizations with police conduct stems from the frequency of intimate contact between the police and the minority groups. There is an underlying implication that, if the police and the criminal justice system cannot adhere to the equal protection principle, it is fruitless to expect it in employment, education, housing, and so on.

In short, the police officer is a convenient object of the displaced hostility of the minority group, however stereotypic the image may be. Much of the criticism directed against the police by minorities is really intended for the larger white power structure, but it is *displaced* to a more readily available, identifiable target. This explains the sometimes irrational elements that appear in minority complaints against the police. As with any stereotype, there are fragments of truth and, often enough, actual experiences to bolster it. There *are* some crooked, brutal, inhuman police, and there *are* memories (or stories that are believed) of harrowing experiences with such officers.

The police, on the other hand, do not enjoy being drafted for front-line duty in the civil rights struggle. They often say that, once again, they are in the middle. However, a factor that tends to warp many big-city police officers' outlook on questions of black civil rights is the difficult and dangerous job of trying to contain what is erroneously referred to as "Negro crime." There is, of course, no such thing, any more than there is Jewish crime or Belgian crime or freckled-faced crime. There are crime-breeding social conditions that happen to predominate in areas where blacks and other minorities live in great numbers. The elimination of these social cesspools is, as Mills observes, one way of explaining what the civil rights movement is all about.

The racial theory of crime causation has long since been discounted and rejected by criminologists. But the police officer on a ghetto beat has his own ways of identifying those who give him a bad time. If most of the people living in the neighborhood are black, it follows that most of those who are troublesome to the officer will be black. In due course, blackness itself becomes a reason for troublesomeness in the reflex thinking of a harried officer. As an agent of a bureaucratic organization that tends, as with all bureaucracies, to deal with people and situations stereotypically, the officer comes to associate "cussedness" with skin color. The remarkable aspect of it is the number of white officers who work the black slums and somehow manage to develop excellent rapport and understanding with the residents.

DUAL STEREOTYPING

The police officer's perception of the people of the ghetto is often as stereotyped as their perception of the police officer. The mutually reinforcing character of this dual stereotyping is central to understanding police and minority-group relations, particularly in big-city ghetto situations. It is reinforced by the fact that the police officer himself seldom resides in the area he polices. Police officer and civilian have little opportunity to get to know each other on a person-to-person basis. In fact, the very impersonality of the joint stereotyping is appalling: "Naw, I don't know his name, but he's a cop, and I hate cops!" And the reverse of this: "To me, he's just another nigger!"

Further, these stereotypes are typically self-fulfilling. If some blacks are viewed as "bastards," any police officer is seen as such. On either side, attitudes are justified on the ground that "you can't afford to take a chance. It's better to be wrong a hundred times than dead once." Communication deteriorates to name calling and obscenities. On the one side, there may be a move for establishment of a civilian review board or for neighborhood control of the police. On the other side, there is often an exceedingly defensive police reaction, partly rooted in long experience as society's favorite fall guy for social and moral problems.

THE ISSUE OF BRUTALITY

The most emotion-packed complaint directed against the police is that of brutality, but little thought is given to what the term means. The assumption is that everyone knows what it means and that everyone attaches the same meaning to it.

One meaning of brutality is its literal interpretation: the use of undue or unreasonable physical force in some aspect of police action. Ordinarily, the police react to the charge of brutality at this level of definition. Usually they will respond by conducting an investigation and, more often than not, reporting that there is no basis for the charge. Then they are dismayed when the matter does not end there. They insist that brutality charges are exaggerated, that they are the "straight men" in a political game.

Another level of definition for police brutality is verbal or psychological brutality. The accusation is that an officer has insulted someone by using derogatory language. This is demeaning, therefore brutalizing. Police officers are often nonplussed by such criticism and will sometimes reply that they meant nothing by it. But words and language do betray our stereotypes.

A third level of definition for brutality may be the most significant. It pertains to the police officer as a symbol of the establishment, the white power structure. The minority-group member feels that he is a victim of systematic brutalization by this system, which attacks his very personhood. Thus, the police officer—as symbol of the system—is brutal because the system brutalizes.

In situations where brutality charges are leveled against the police, there is frequently a communication problem created by definition differences. These situations are further complicated by emotional outbursts on both sides, by charges and countercharges, and by media stories that often accentuate the negative. It is difficult to bring reason to bear on the matter and to get at the question of exactly what is being contested. Police officers sometimes make the point that the public is quick to accuse an officer of brutality, but not so concerned when the officer is attacked, assaulted, insulted, spit upon, stoned, or killed.

The ticklish brutality question is a symptom that something is seriously wrong in police-citizen transactions. Being philosophical about it is not very helpful in the heat of the situation. After all, it is not very comforting to a hospitalized police officer, or to a hospitalized victim of an officer's wrath, to be told that there was really nothing personal intended, that it was merely symbolic warfare, springing from dual stereotyping. Such an explanation does not pay medical bills.

There is no question that there are police officers for whom beating up or defaming people are grim means of job satisfaction. With some such officers, this may be why they joined the force; with others, it is more a result of what happens to them after they join. With some, it is plain fear in the face of what may be termed "statistical danger," a perception and interpretation of what seems necessary for survival. And it is true that the abuse and provocation absorbed by police in line of duty is little known and far from appreciated. The mendacity, defiance of law, family abuse, impulsive and immoral conduct, alcoholic and drug-addicted behavior, and other socially destructive acts that police officers witness are more than a little discouraging to the maintenance of a balanced and constructive perspective about their jobs and about the people with whom they most frequently come in contact. The warped and cynical attitude often evident in police officers who have long worked in depressed areas is a great obstacle to their understanding of civil rights problems and sympathy for the goals of social justice.

The real solution to the brutality problem is long-range, for it will be solved only when oppression and second-class citizenship have been abolished. But there are many constructive steps that can be taken in building good police and community relations, which will diminish the intensity of the emotional charges and countercharges. Heightened mutual trust between police and community can do much to reduce the number of instances where brutality insinuations are made. A first step is understanding what brutality charges really mean.

CHIEF COMPLAINT OF MINORITIES

It is commonly assumed that brutality is the principal complaint of minorities against the police. Several studies, including the Michigan State University survey for the President's Crime Commission in 1966, debunk this assumption.[4] The chief grievance is inadequate police protection and services in inner-city neighborhoods. It is regarded by minorities as the worst form of discrimination.

The "expectation of unfair treatment by the police" ranks next highest among minority group complaints. Harassment and verbal brutality come next. Differential treatment in field interrogations, in such things as "stop and frisk" and "failure to move on," follows. Physical brutality rates next. Finally, there is resentment over what minority groups view as discrimination in police personnel practices—in hiring, promotions, and so on. The point here is not that most police departments today do not want more minority group officers, but rather that existing policies and practices have long been weighted against the minority-group applicant. These procedures are often defended as "fair for everybody; after all, the majority have rights too!"

Reflecting on crime and police service in the ghetto, Kenneth Clark has written:

> In a disturbing sense, there remains the possibility that homicide in the ghetto is consistently high because it is not controlled, if not encouraged, as an aspect of the total network of the human exploitation of the ghetto. The unstated and sometimes stated acceptance of crime and violence as normal for a ghetto community is associated with a lowering of police vigilance and efficiency when the victims are also lower-status people. This is another example of the denial of a governmental service—the right of adequate protection—which is endured by the powerless ghetto.[5]

COUNTERCOMPLAINTS OF THE POLICE

The police also have their favorite complaints, directed against the minority community. The Michigan State University study found them to be the following:

1. Many police feel that the public is apathetic to their problems, and they have been abandoned in the war against crime, particularly in the ghetto.

2. The police feel that most of the charges made against them by "vocal minorities" are patently unfair.

3. Many police officers strongly resent what they regard as the overemphasis on the rights of the individual at the expense of the rights of society.

4. The police are torn by uncertainty as to their role in today's society. Why, they ask, should there be cries for more civilian control of the police when the police are better trained, better educated, and more efficient than ever?[6]

5. Many police officers express great concern over what they perceive as the moral decay of society. Their view of life places them on a collision course with segments of the population who see the system that the police represent as an anachronism.[7]

In sum, most police officers tend to see themselves as "trying to do good," fighting sin, lawlessness, and evil. They feel hurt by the storm of criticism that breaks around them and by what they consider a "nobody cares" public attitude. In the ghetto, where social conditions are the worst and where beleaguered minorities are most visible, a police officer may tend to see "these people" as the personification of all that frustrates and disturbs him. Both the police and the people feel powerless to change the conditions that basically make the police-community relationship so hostile, so sterile. They blame each other for their many problems and thereby freeze communication further.

This tendency to find someone to blame for problems too overwhelming to sort out is not unique to any particular place, period, or person. Writing in the *New York Times*, Russell Baker recalled the America of the 1930s when President Herbert Hoover was blamed for all trouble. In the 1940s, it was Germany and Japan that were blamed. In the 1950s, it was Communism. Nowadays, Baker thinks, the paranoia has metastasized: "Everybody and everything is the cause of all the trouble."[8] And indeed, the list of contemporary scapegoats is long: dewy-eyed liberals, hard-nosed conservatives, black (or brown or any other color) militants, hippies, faggots, Doctor Spock, unwashed kooks, the establishment, government bureaucracy, the military-industrial complex, the Eastern media, the FBI or the CIA, the courts, Ronald Reagan, inflation, the New York Yankees, the unions, the conglomerates, and lots more. The truth is, as Pogo put it: "We have met the enemy—and he is us."

THE POLICE AS DIRTY-WORKERS

Some years ago, sociologist Lee Rainwater wrote a provocative article in which he referred to American police officers as "dirty-workers."[9] Borrowing from fellow sociologist Everett Hughes, he pointed to the Nazi S.S. in Germany as a cadre that had carried out the dirty work of anti-Semitism while Germans in general were silent about what was going on in the concentration camps. Rainwater wondered whether something similar to this might not be happening in America. Many white Americans feel that ghetto blacks and other minorities must be controlled and confined. These same Americans are ashamed and uncertain as to how this should be done, and they prefer to conceal from themselves much of the detail of how the doers of this dirty work—the police, the teachers, the welfare workers—actually go about their assigned tasks. Rainwater wrote:

> As the ghettos in this country grow, a new dimension is added, a dimension of silence and ignorance about exactly what these functionaries are expected to do, and how in fact they do carry out society's covert orders to control and cull out those who must be excluded from ordinary society. If the teachers, social workers and cops were ever to spell out in detail what their duties are in order to justify their wage demands, they would threaten the delicate balance preserved by silence about their dirty work—no one wants to learn that they [sic] are striking for "combat pay."
>
> The dirty-workers are increasingly caught between the silent middle-class, which wants them to do the dirty work and keep quiet about it, and the objects of that dirty work, who refuse to continue to take it lying down. Individual revolts confront the teachers with the problems of the "blackboard jungle," the police with the problem of "disrespect for law and order," and the welfare workers with the problem of their charges' feigned stupidity and real deception. These civilian colonial armies find their right to respect from their charges challenged at every turn, and often they must carry out their daily duties with fear for their physical safety.[10]

Some might feel that Rainwater's is an overly harsh view of the situation. But there are harsher descriptions, for example, this sarcastic one by W. H. Ferry:

> Let me show why we must have a police state. It is because we have run out of other remedies. . . . We simply do not know what to do about 25 million black Americans. It is only a little less true that we do not know what to do with our agitating children and hippies and other self-evictees of respectable white society. . . . As middle-class America looks across the tracks to blacktown, it does not understand what it sees there. But it is clear enough . . . that middle-class America does not see other human beings like themselves. . . . Blacks are never sufficiently grateful for the kindnesses and favors done them by whitetown.[11]

A retired police inspector, Professor William Brown, wrote this in the late 1960s:

> To the police, one of the most unsettling features in the police-black relationship is that the prescriptions which they were only recently given for establishing "community relations" are hopelessly inadequate for understanding, let alone dealing with, the problems created by the black activists. The police official who has determined (somewhat late and somewhat under pressure) to be fair and impartial is now willing to accept rational discussion of objectives, the setting of boundaries and all the other devices for the control of noncriminal civilian groups which seemed to be the answer to meeting the black protest movement only a few years ago. Having accepted the model of fairness, the police seem particularly disturbed by what they regard as the unfairness of the blacks. "What do they want?" "Why do they provoke, taunt, refuse to agree to reasonable regulations?"[12]

Former Detroit police commissioner George Edwards, now a Federal Court of Appeals judge, has observed that, in the past, the police have rarely sought civilian assistance in any systematic way and least of all in those areas where the forces of law enforcement have been hardest pressed.[13] Judge Edwards believes that three factors have particularly complicated police and minority group relations on the urban frontier: (1) The civil rights movement has decreased the blacks' tolerance of indignities inflicted by the police and greatly intensified the demand for equal law enforcement; (2) demonstrations, no matter how peaceful, require considerable police manpower to handle, with an acute sense of risk involved as police officers see it; and (3) every time illegal violence is employed, either by demonstrators or by the police, it increases the mutual animosity.

Recalling the Michigan State study described in chapter 6, in the matter of values of importance to various occupational groups, it is pertinent here to repeat that the police ranked *equality* markedly lower in value priority than did a national sample of whites and far lower than a national sample of blacks. The MSU researchers rate this the most significant aspect of the value gap between police and policed, and in their words:

> Given the especially large discrepancy in value for *equality* between police and blacks, it is hardly surprising that black residents of the ghetto will view policemen

as enemies who are there to preserve "law and order," i.e., to preserve the conservative value pattern of a white power structure.[14]

THE THEORY OF COGNITIVE DISSONANCE

The theory of *cognitive dissonance*, first proposed in 1957 by Leon Festinger and elaborated in 1962 by Brehm and Cohen, is based on "the notion that the human organism tries to establish internal harmony, consistency, or congruity among his opinions, attitudes, knowledge, and values. There is, in short, a drive toward consonance among cognitions."[15] Festinger explains further that the relation between pairs of cognitive elements can be incongruent, that is, they do not support each other and are therefore *dissonant;* or the relation can be congruent and therefore *consonant,* that is, one element supports the other. Thus, dissonance refers to the strain or tension between two items of knowledge, two attitudes, opinions, or values.

Contra-cultural conflict is a collective form of cognitive dissonance. Festinger identified five general conditions under which cognitive dissonance occurs:

1. Dissonance almost always exists after a decision has been made between two or more alternatives.
2. Dissonance almost always exists after an attempt has been made, by offer-ing rewards or threatening punishment, to elicit overt behavior that is at variance with private opinion.
3. Forced or accidental exposure to new information may create cognitive elements that are dissonant with existing cognition.
4. The open expression of disagreement in a group leads to the existence of cognitive dissonance in the members.
5. Identical dissonance in a large number of people may be created when an event occurs which is so compelling as to produce a uniform reaction in everyone.[16]

The magnitude of post-decision dissonance varies with the importance of the decision, the relative attractiveness of alternatives not chosen, and the similarity of both chosen and unchosen alternatives. Festinger puts it this way:

> The magnitude of the dissonance resulting from an attempt to elicit forced compliance is greatest if the promised reward or punishment is either *just sufficient* to elicit the overt behavior or is *just barely not* sufficient to elicit it.[17]

The central hypothesis of the theory of cognitive dissonance is that "the presence of dissonance gives rise to pressures to reduce that dissonance,"[18] and that the pressure to reduce dissonance depends on the magnitude of the dissonance. Reducing dissonance calls for changing one of the dissonant elements of knowledge, opinion, attitude, or value; adding new, consonant elements to support the decision taken; or decreasing the importance of the dissonant elements.

What does this have to do with police relations with blacks? Victor Strecher has analyzed its relevance.[19] He defines the concept of "culture shock," which has become familiar in training personnel for such overseas programs as the Peace Corps. In *An American Dilemma*, Gunnar Myrdal described four stages in the culture shock syndrome:

1. A kind of "honeymoon" period, during which the individual is fascinated by the novelty of a strange culture. He is polite, friendly, etc.

2. The individual settles down to a long-run confrontation with the conditions of life in the strange culture and the need for him to function effectively there. He becomes hostile and aggressive toward the culture and its people. He attributes his difficulties to trouble-making on their part. He develops elaborate, stereotypic caricatures of the local people.

3. Here the individual (if he has survived Stage 2) is beginning to open a way into the new cultural environment. He may take a superior attitude but he will joke about local behavior rather than criticize it. He is on the way to recovery from shock.

4. The individual's adjustment is as complete as it can be. He accepts the other's customs as just another way of living and doing things.[20]

Strecher's analysis traces the pattern in the urban experience of lower-class blacks. First, there was the exodus of millions of blacks from the rural South and their migration to the metropolitan areas of the North and West. The social adaptation process, which might be called "survival techniques," produced black behavior patterns clearly *dissonant* with the conventional norms of the larger society, patterns that formed a distinctive black, urban subculture. Cognitive dissonance exists in the lower-class black's simultaneous awareness of the conventional norms and the substituted norms by which he actually lives. He also realizes that his way of life does not work out nearly as well as those not living it say it does. So he rejects the conventional goals and legitimate ("responsible") ways of achieving them, and allies himself with other goals and means that bring his behavior and norms into consonance in his "world."

Of the police officer's side of the picture, Strecher says:

> Enter the policeman, who has problems of his own. He is recruited from the middle and working classes, and as a result of historical racial segregation patterns knows almost nothing of the Negro poverty subculture. His occupational socialization produces a self-conception centered upon crime-fighting and life-protection, and a set of subcultural perspectives which tend to reject all roles dissonant with his self-conception. . . . [In addition], the policeman who is assigned to work in predominantly lower-class Negro neighborhoods . . . experiences a culture shock reaction to social strangeness, loss of familiar cues and symbols, and his inability to interact spontaneously with the Negro residents. . . . It is natural for him to react to this uncomfortable experience aggressively. . . .
>
> Lower-class Negro behavior is dissonant with the police view of social order, morality and propriety; the implicitly moralistic evaluation of lower-class Negro lifestyle by policemen reactivates for the Negro dissonance between behavior and conventional ideals, up to then reduced by his subcultural solution.[21]

Two comments may be appended to Strecher's analysis. First, if his linkage of concepts is valid, it has clear implications for programs to improve police and minority-group relations. If Strecher is right, it is no wonder that so many such programs miss the mark. Second, although his theory focuses particularly on police relations with lower-class blacks, it is also relevant (with some adjustments) for police interaction with other disaffected groups.

THE EXTENT OF DISSONANCE

How serious is the dissonance between the police and lower-class blacks? Gary Marx reported in his 1967 study of the attitudes of blacks toward the police in four cities that 64 percent of adult blacks in Chicago thought the police treated blacks "very well" or "fairly well," as compared with 56 percent who said this in New York City, 53 percent in Atlanta, and 31 percent in Birmingham.[22] Hans Toch has this to say:

> In general, police and blacks are obsessed with the need to instill respect in each other. For both, the demand for respect is for recognition on the basis of group membership rather than for a positive reaction to personal qualities. . . . For each group, the other symbolizes threats that lurk on every corner of the ghetto. The young black does not know how to react to police incursions, and the young officer feels helpless in dealing with difficulties posed by his tense encounters with hostile blacks. Each man comes to feel that he must rely on his group identification—badge or color—as a substitute for answers he cannot find in himself. . . . Neither party need conclude that it has to make the delicate judgments implicit in personal encounters: the matter is prejudged; two men approach each other, not as human beings but as uniformed members of military forces engaged in a doomed truce in a no-man's land.[23]

For perspective on the question of how great the dissonance, it is useful to dwell for a moment on comparative opposites: black militancy and white militancy. Black militancy in the United States began to crystallize in the late 1950s, climaxing in the 1960s as reflected in dissatisfaction with basic social institutions: the schools, political parties and government, the police, and the criminal justice system. The old, unquestioned values have been questioned and rejected by militant blacks, as well as militant members of other minorities.

Militancy in the 1960s was especially pronounced among black youth, who tended to view the more militant leaders—for example, Malcolm X—as heroic figures. Their central position was that change would not occur substantially enough nor fast enough within existing systems. They said that power is never relinquished voluntarily; that it has to be taken.

Kenneth Clark conveyed something of the flavor of the black militant attitude in such interviews as these:

> Man, age about 33:
> The white cops, they have a damn sadistic nature. They are really a sadistic type of people and we, I mean me, myself, we don't need them here in Harlem. We don't need them! They don't do the neighborhood any good. They deteriorate the neighborhood. They start more violence than any other people start.

Man, about 35:
I think we should all get together—everybody—all get together and every time one draws back his stick to do something to us, or hits one of us on the head, take the stick and hit *him* on *his* head, so he'll know how it feels to be hit on the head, or kill him, if necessary. Yes, kill him, if necessary. That's how I feel. There is no other way to deal with this man. The only way you can deal with him is the way he has been dealing with us.

Man, age 21:
Everything is a big laugh in this dump unless you kill a cop. Then they don't laugh.[24]

In the American historical tradition, white militancy is aroused when white factions rise up to defend home, family, or country against forces considered alien or threatening. Militancy of this kind has often assumed the form of direct vigilante action, in which racism and nativism join forces in intermittent reigns of terror against minorities and those considered "un-American." As so many writers have said, violence is embedded in our history, although most people today repudiate it. But white militancy of the recent past, directed against advances in black civil rights, was not simply the preoccupation of a relative handful of extremists. It was a basic element in the separating force in our cities: increasingly militant blacks (and other minorities) versus increasingly militant white resistance.[25]

In this situation, the police officer—overworked, undertrained, underpaid, undereducated, and underappreciated—has been caught between conflicting community pressures that make it next to impossible to function in his expected role. Discord in police-community relations is a symptom of more fundamental problems: poverty, discrimination, and society's inability to handle legitimate and socially healthy dissent. Little wonder, then, that the police and other "dirty-workers" have voiced their protest by such tactics as slowdowns, "blue flu," unionization, lobbying, and other moves toward political power. The politicization of the police is quite understandable, if not altogether desirable. We shall devote more attention to this subject in chapter 17, for it has become a critical question in police and community relations today.

Seymour Lipset has said that police "rebellion" of the 1960s was a response to the "confrontation tactics" of students and black radical militants, whose strategy was to enrage the police and provoke overreaction.[26] Such overreaction obviously can be exploited to the advantage of those intent upon disrupting, embarrassing, or overturning the existing political institutions. Minority militance views killing a police officer not as murder, but as a legitimate act of self-defense, under any circumstances. "A cop is *the enemy*, and the enemy must be liquidated." This is clearly the typical reasoning of so-called political crime, in some of the forms it takes.

Lipset believes that the tensions between the police and New Left student and black nationalist radicals were probably the most extreme examples of deliberate provocation that American police have ever faced. He observes:

Police understand as normal the problems of dealing with crime or vice. They may resent violence stemming from minority ghettos, but this, too, is understandable and part of police work. But to take provocative behavior from youths who are socially and economically much better off than they and their children is more than the average policeman can tolerate.[27]

POLICE PREJUDICE AND POLICE BEHAVIOR

It is timely to recall James Q. Wilson's point that race is not the decisive factor in inner-city police-citizen embattlement. No doubt, he says, race makes the potentiality for dissonance greater, but in the late 1960s, Wilson observed:

> If all Negroes were turned white tomorrow, this hostility—only slightly abated—would continue. Throughout history the urban poor have disliked and distrusted the police, and the feeling has been reciprocated; the situation will not change until the poor become middle-class, or at least working class, or until society decides to abandon the effort to maintain a common legal code and a level of public order acceptable to middle-class persons. . . .
>
> One reason for the increasing complaints of "police harassment" may be that, in large cities, Negroes are being brought under a single standard of justice; one reason for the complaints of discrimination may be that this process is proceeding unevenly and imperfectly. As the populations of our large cities become, through continued migration, more heavily Negro, more heavily lower income, and more youthful, we can expect these complaints to increase in number and frequency, especially if, as seems likely, organizations competing for leadership in the central cities continue to seek out such issues in order to attract followers.[28]

The high visibility of the *black* poor exaggerates the police officer's distorted view. But Wilson's emphasis upon social class should not, of course, be interpreted as absolving police officers from accusations of racial bias. Having touched upon this question in chapter 5, we will repeat only a few pertinent comments. David Bayley and Harold Mendelsohn reported in their Denver study that little credence is given by police to charges that police treat minority people unfairly or improperly. William Walsh found that police officers who viewed their work as only a job were far more likely than those who viewed themselves as professionals to claim that unequal treatment was the fault of the minorities themselves. Some 85 percent of the "jobbers" thought this, of whom 62 percent believed that minorities actually enjoy more privileged treatment than they deserve. Yet 40 percent of the officers who viewed themselves as professionals were willing to admit that the problems of police-minority relations were caused, at least in part, by police officers.[29]

William Westley, William Kephart, and Jerome Skolnick found evidence of considerable racial prejudice among the police they studied.[30] But Skolnick observes—as we noted in chapter 5—that from the point of view of the police officer, the term "racial bias" is not an accurate description of his attitude toward blacks. In private conversation, many white police express strong negative feelings toward blacks. But they do not admit to being racially prejudiced, (1) because one may hate somebody without being *biased* against him, and (2) because if a police officer admits to racial bias, it tends to make a scapegoat of him. He feels that he is no more prejudiced than his fellow citizens who are isolated from contact with blacks.

Thus, by his own standards, the police officer is not biased: he simply tells the truth. And he concludes that while he is not more nor less prejudiced than others, it is irrelevant anyhow, because it is his job to extend justice evenhandedly, no matter what his personal feelings. As a "professional," he sees his behavior as not necessarily governed by his personal attitudes. He has a job to do, and he must do it. In a predominantly black residential neighborhood, the officer sees his job as *combat*. From the vantage point, therefore, of both police officer and community, their relationship is warfare—enemy to enemy. But the officer would insist that racial prejudice has nothing to do with it.

It is a curious jumble of human attitudes. Police behavior that is seen as bigoted by ghetto blacks is shrugged off by the officer as "just doing my job"—not bigotry, even though privately the policeman admits to racial prejudice. In effect, the officer is saying, "I may be prejudiced, but when I'm on duty, I'm fair. I treat 'em all alike, no matter what color they are." In like manner, a so-called crackdown by the police in a high-crime area where the population is largely black may be viewed by residents as racially discriminatory. The opposite of this, what is viewed by residents as "lousy service," is also seen as discriminatory, as we noted earlier. But the police explain that these matters have nothing to do with race but depend more on manpower deployment in the department, the decisions of dispatchers in sorting out priorities, contrasting crime rates from precinct to precinct, and so on.

What is the problem, basically? The problem is a complex of reciprocal images, of mutually reinforcing stereotypes, of communication, and of environmental circumstances. Skolnick summarizes it well:

> To the extent that police are bigoted and manifest prejudices in the daily performance of their duties, to the extent that they employ different standards, to the extent that they insult black people living in the ghetto, they receive the hostility and hatred of the black man in the ghetto. This hostility and hatred in turn, reinforces the policeman's bigotry, the policeman's hatred, the policeman's fear, and the social isolation of the policeman from those black citizens with whom he must come in daily contact. . . . Thus, as social conditions prod the black man into increasingly hostile responses, the police are on the receiving end and are themselves tempted to respond with renewed hostility.[31]

RACISM

Racism in police and other criminal justice processes mirrors that of the larger society in its degree, nature, and level. The dynamics of racism in our society today are not generally as brazen and direct as in the past. Contemporary racism, in and out of criminal justice, tends to be more subtle, more indirect, and more deviously expressed. As an illustration, consider the difficulty of distinguishing legitimate discretion from not-so-legitimate discrimination in police patrol activity. Racism also works deviously to affect perception and other psychological processes, as we saw in chapter 8. The racist often pretends innocence: "All I asked was how many Lithuanians there are on the Supreme Court."

There are those who say that racism in the United States is dead. They point to progress here and there. There has been some progress, but the amount is comparable to a rise in Arctic temperature from 75 degrees below zero to 50 below. In Detroit, a black off-duty police officer was beaten to the ground by two dozen white off-duty police officers during a demonstration protesting police layoffs. In Boston, three thousand delegates from eight states attended a convention of ROAR (Restore Our Alienated Rights), ostensibly organized to protest school busing. We have mentioned the current unemployment rate for black, urban youth. The nation's educators have come to recognize that mixing black and white students in the same classrooms does not produce racial integration, especially in junior and senior high schools. One astute observer asserted that, when the last public meeting on busing has taken place, it will then be time to ask if racism is really dead. Until then, racism will remain a serious national issue, and a serious issue in police-community relations.

A few police departments sometimes get national notoriety for situations that might easily be matched in other places. In 1977–78, the Houston Police Department was limelighted because of the case of Joe Campos Torres, Jr., a Mexican-American laborer who was drowned in Buffalo Bayou while in police custody. The subsequent legal battle, which resulted in the sentencing of several police officers, was marked by bitter controversy. One aspect of the publicity focused on the fact that, while 26 percent of Houston's population was black and 14 percent Mexican American, only about 4 percent of the city's police officers were black, and 5 percent Mexican American.[32]

In a report published in February 1978, the U.S. Commission on Civil Rights had this to say:

> Allegations of police abuse, brutality, and harassment of citizens, particularly minorities, have for too many years constituted an unresolved and galling public problem in America. Instances of police misconduct, beatings, shootings, and intimidation of citizens undermine public safety, trust, and confidence in law enforcement. In 1977 the Commission on Civil Rights received an increasing number of citizen complaints and reports indicating that police misconduct remains a widespread phenomenon that has, in some cities, become so pervasive as to appear to be officially sanctioned.[33]

But the problem is broader than merely police treatment of minorities, and its history goes back much farther than the past several decades. "The extension of the protections of the law," Judge Lois Forer of Philadelphia Common Pleas Court writes, "—to women, children, nonwhites, the elderly, laborers, migrant workers, the poor, the mentally ill, and the convict—has been achieved through bitter and often bloody struggles as well as through a continuing series of legal battles fought in the legislatures and in the courts."[34] Yet, as Judge Forer observes, there remains a long way to go. It is no accident that our prisons are so largely populated by the poor, the minorities, and the young.[35]

RACE AND CRIME

Several aspects of the relationship between race and crime call for analysis. One is the question of the validity of racially delineated crime statistics, which is part of the difficult general problem of criminal statistics. Police tend to view racial and ethnic delineation of such data as an aid in the investigation of crime and the apprehension of suspects. The dangers that social scientists see in this practice grow out of correlating race with criminal behavior, as suggested by the notion of "Negro crime." A widely accepted myth is no less a potent factor in distorted communication simply because it is a myth.[36]

Not only is there overwhelming scientific evidence that race as such is not a cause of crime, but there is considerable data to substantiate that criminal acts are predominantly *intragroup* and *intraracial*. Marvin Wolfgang and Bernard Cohen have brought together information on this matter, and they point out that "when crime and color converge, the person is in double jeopardy." They say further that:

> To the visible badge of color is added the label of criminal, reinforcing attitudes of prejudice and compounding acts of discrimination. . . . What is most regrettable is that many people—partly from exaggeration of a few facts, partly from a readiness to believe—strongly associate the two factors of color and crime. . . . The private citizen, clinging to a false premise, is soon beset by a host of false fears and driven to hasty reprisals that damage society's efforts to integrate community life.[37]

This is the danger of perpetuating the "crime in the streets" specter. It is not that street crime may not actually be increasing; it is rather the implied association of race and crime in stereotypic terms. To paraphrase Robert Mills, something much more sophisticated than the shotgun collection of statistics by race is needed to pinpoint the social cancers that produce crime and related problems.

Demonstrating how pernicious the direct association of race and crime is, Kephart's 1952 study of a thousand white police officers in Philadelphia found that these officers overestimated the percentage of arrests of blacks in their districts. The higher the real arrest rate of blacks, the greater was the overestimation. Actually, about 70 percent of all persons arrested were blacks, but estimates by white officers averaged over 95 percent.[38]

Another illustration of the point is the police saturation of some predominantly black neighborhoods. This may well produce a larger number of arrests of blacks. But it is not so much the behavior of blacks that produces the higher crime rate as it is the increased police activity that results in more arrests. Corresponding results might occur in circumstances where all the variables remained the same except for the color of those residing in the area.

Yet there is an undeniable paradox in this matter. Although the practice of employing racial designations in crime records poses problems, it is defended in another sense by Wolfgang and Cohen:

> As long as segregation and discrimination persist, and the struggle for more partici- pation in society continues, there may be some utility in the statistical designation of race, simply to keep an accounting of social problems and to measure the progress of change in the economic and political status of minority groups.[39]

This point has wide application, far beyond the specific question of race and crime. The key consideration is the proper and discreet use of such information. However, there are three additional considerations that have important bearing on this practice:

1. There is a great need to reevaluate the methods of crime data collection and presentation, a need that is now rather generally recognized by criminologists.

2. Police administrators should realize that certain types of statistics that are administratively, operationally, or analytically useful need not necessarily be made a matter of public reporting.

3. The average police officer is not an anthropologist. Even if he were, could he be sure of his judgments as to who is Chinese or Japanese, Indian or black, Puerto Rican or Mexican? What anthropologist would support this lumping together of race and nationality? What about blacks who have passed as white—by the thousands? How black is black, how white is white? If a person is mulatto, is his crime to be recorded as half white and half black? The absurdities multiply as analysis of the question deepens.

POLICE PROTECTION AND CRIME STATISTICS

We asserted above that criminal acts are known to be predominantly *intra-group* and *intraracial*. This reflects well-known information regarding the victims of crime, substantiated by President Johnson's 1966 Crime Commission, the Kerner Commission, and more recent victimization studies. The problem of violent crime is, in large part, a problem of crimes committed by blacks against other blacks in the ghetto. The President's Commission on Crime in the District of Columbia found that 85 percent of the murders, 79 percent of the rapes, and 84 percent of the serious assaults in Washington were perpetrated by blacks against blacks.[40]

As Bruce Terris pointed out, the crimes reflected in these statistics occur in areas where police and community relations are poorest. And as we have said, the chief complaint of minority people against the police in big cities is "lousy service in our neighborhood." These factors merge into a pattern. There must be some constructive breakthrough, not only if there is to be improvement in police and community relations, but also if there is to be any significant progress in coping with crime where it is statistically at its worst. Indeed, the improvement of police and minority relations is the only route that offers any hope of ameliorating some of the more visible aspects of crime.

In too many places, crimes committed by blacks, with other blacks as victims, are considered less serious than crimes committed by whites against whites or by blacks against whites. Crimes committed by whites with blacks as victims also tend to be considered less serious. As John Dollard declared more than thirty years ago:

> The formal machinery of the law takes care of the Negroes' grievances much less adequately than that of the whites, and to a much higher degree the Negro is compelled to make and enforce his own law with other Negroes. . . . The result is that the individual Negro is, to a considerable degree, outside the protection of the

white law, and must shift for himself. This leads to the frontier psychology. . . . [Such] condoning of Negro violence . . . may be indulgent in the case of any given Negro, but its effect on the Negro group as a whole is dangerous and destructive. . . . So long as the law does not take over the protection of the Negro person, he will have to do it himself by violent means.[41]

To do something about serious crime in predominantly black neighborhoods where blacks are the victims looms as a logical goal of constructive efforts in police and community relations. Crime prevention and crime control for neighborhood and community stability should be the main objective; the improvement of police-citizen relations may well be a dividend of such efforts. When he was executive director of the National Association for the Advancement of Colored People (NAACP), Roy Wilkins said that at least part of the black community was ready "to blow the whistle" on the robbers, muggers, and knife-wielders. He added that crime control becomes a real possibility as soon as law-abiding blacks, always in the vast majority, take an active role against crime and criminals.[42]

In discussing this situation, Robert Pearman, a reporter for the Kansas City, Missouri, *Star*, observed that the cries of moderate black leaders for better police protection were tempered by ambivalence. They want stronger police protection, but they also want more humane police treatment. Pearman quoted the former Kansas City police chief and FBI director, Clarence Kelley, as doubting there is any conscious lessening of effort on the part of the police officers because of race or economic status. Kelley reportedly conceded that what may have an effect is a feeling among officers of "what's the use, this can only cause trouble. . . . there is always the threat that the victim either won't prosecute or that the officer himself will be charged with misconduct." Pearman described Kelley as deeply disappointed that black businessmen and moderate leaders, themselves often victims of crime, had not "stepped forward with a plea for good law enforcement."[43]

Wolfgang and Cohen conclude their analysis of race and crime with a poignant paragraph:

> Thrust any child, white or colored, from the womb to a world that offers the rewards of status and success. With a moat of discrimination, cut him off from the mainland so that there are few or no opportunities to achieve those rewards. Let him continue to wish for the same things the mainlanders desire, but make him move around much more, lose a father to death or desertion, and a mother to work and dependency. Give him less knowledge to absorb, less money than the mainlander receives for the same tasks. Surround him with examples of unlawful achievers, and make him fight to protect the mainland without fully participating in the rules to govern it. Shorten his length of life, expose him to disease, treat him as if he were biologically inferior and call him nasty names to convince him of it. Even if the mainlanders value the service he gives them and the feeling of importance his contrast offers, he is lost.[44]

SOCIAL CHANGE AND CRIME

In a discussion of social change and the association of race and crime, Frank Remington of the University of Wisconsin Law School faculty begins with this statement:

In a period of rapid social change, it is important to ask how an officer can steer a course of neutrality if he cannot rely upon the principle of full enforcement of the law against all citizens, regardless of social or racial status. The difficulty of the task makes it tempting for police to pretend that the problem does not exist, or that the responsibility is not theirs, a common and understandable public attitude of many police officials today.[45]

Remington turns to a consideration of assaultive conduct. He says that race is a very convenient way to classify the statistical incidence of assaultive behavior, even though it is apparent that social and cultural factors are causal, not race. But statistics for the real causes are said to be "not workable." Remington believes that the police should assume the initiative in setting a law enforcement policy that distinguishes between serious and nonserious assault on the basis of factors other than race. It will be difficult, he admits, but "trying is certainly better for the community and, in the long run, for the police than is falling back on the easy alternative of claiming full enforcement, and administratively relying upon race as a simple, readily available indication of behavioral differences."[46]

Remington cites the use of aggressive, preventive patrol as an example. It is, as we have noted, a police practice usually confined to high-crime areas, commonly districts where the majority of residents are members of minority groups. It is acknowledged that the easiest and most practical classification of such areas is geographical-racial. To devise an alternative policy is difficult. But aggressive, preventive patrol raises serious questions about the validity of police actions; for example, it relies heavily on street searches, which are frequently illegal. Remington views such procedures as self-defeating for the police.

These are surely not simple questions. But Remington offers some possible guidelines:

1. Police insistence that police illegality is essential for adequate law enforcement is self-defeating; inevitably, it places police in conflict with minority groups, and it perpetuates the common belief that police authority should be drastically limited because they will abuse whatever authority they are given.

2. Police insistence that their responsibility is to fully enforce the law perpetuates a myth that is impossible of achievement, and undesirable if it could be achieved.

3. In the development of law enforcement policy, race ought, wherever possible, to be rejected as a basis of classification. The factors which cause crime are nonracial.[47]

POLICE LEADERSHIP

Remington is not alone in his plea for more police leadership and responsibility in social and civic policy. David Bordua developed the same thesis in a paper prepared for the National Advisory Commission on Civil Disorders. Bordua observed that the problem of race relations in the United States is only secondarily a police problem and only secondarily a problem that can be dealt with by improving this or that aspect of public administration. The problem, Bordua contended, is basically political in the larger sense, and its long-run solution will require political action to provide equal opportunities for blacks and to improve the competitive abilities of disadvantaged blacks.[48]

The full entrance of blacks into civil society means, Bordua continued, that they become legitimate claimants to protection *by* the police as well as protection *from* the police. The balance between these is hard to strike, but Bordua thought that this went to the heart of the issue in police relations with blacks. Until recently, in many American cities—not all of them in the South—a priority mission of the police was control of the black community. Police maintained good relations with the white community by being tough on blacks. But now, as blacks become more politically significant, they demand that they be heard and that they be seen as part of a community to which the police are responsible. Actually, Bordua contended, there is some evidence that blacks sometimes have a better relationship with the police than they do with other segments of society. In many places, it is possible for a black to receive decent treatment in a station house while not being allowed to join the country club.

As we noted in chapter 4, Bordua called for the police to be "out in front, showing the way" in race relations, in effect, to join the civil rights movement. He thought this would be truly professional demeanor requiring "principled norms of conduct," as against being guided by subgroup prejudice. Bordua joined Remington in acknowledging that doing so would not be easy. Indeed, there are many police leaders in England and the United States who hold to the position that the police should *not* be leaders of social change. Bordua suggested some possible guidelines for police recruitment and training and for departmental policies and procedures:

1. As community managers and monitors of social change, the police should enforce the law as vigorously as possible, but short of the point where vigorous enforcement produces more strain than the system can stand. (This means that the police ought to be as much concerned about the social and civic state of the ghetto as they are about the crime rate therein.)

2. The vulnerability of the police as the symbolic repressive agents of society must be decreased, one way being for the police to exert pressure on other agencies that now shrink from the "dirty work" of exerting authority. Bordua asserts that American society has a long history of abandoning the police and, in effect, segregating them from the rest of the social order.

3. Communication *to* police about the ghetto should be improved, as should communication *between* police and ghetto residents.

4. Police should increase the amount of supportive service that they perform.[49]

MINORITY POLICE OFFICERS

The black minority and other minority groups have been seriously underrepresented in the personnel of virtually all police organizations in the country. There has been wide concern about this among police administrators and civil rights agencies, who have tried to cope with the situation by using imposed formulas or public relations gimmicks that have often produced disappointing results.

Equal opportunity legislation and affirmative action programs have made inroads on this problem in the past few years, but the eventual solution will be long-range and largely dependent on social change in a far broader context than police administration.

Police departments today are, of course, generally required by law to operate on the basis of a merit system in employment and personnel practices. However, the general complaint of police administrators with respect to minority-group applicants has been that not nearly enough are qualified. On the face of it, this is a plausible and defensible administrative posture, widely assumed in various facets of public affairs and usually crowned with the statement, "and we certainly can't *lower* our standards." Getting qualified applicants of any background for police work today is something of a challenge, and the difficulty is much more acute in the case of the black or the Hispanic applicant. What is the problem?

It is astonishing that there should be so much apparent difficulty in understanding what the problem is. The factors explaining it are fairly obvious. Yet various recruitment campaigns and promotions are mounted in a manner to suggest that the instigators really believe that such things as television and radio spots and billboard posters will get the job done. There is consternation when these ploys simply do not work.

As with any other problem, solutions must be meshed with causes. What, then, are the causes of the problem of underrepresentation of minority people in police agencies? Following is an outline of some of the more important considerations:

1. In the past, minority-group applicants have not been particularly sought by police agencies.

2. Minority-group young people have not viewed police work as an attractive or inviting career because they see police organizations as predominantly white, English speaking, and so on, and also because what they have seen of police in so-called high-crime neighborhoods hardly elevates their estimate of the occupation.

3. In the minority-group community, especially in low-income areas, to aspire to be a police officer is frequently to be regarded by one's peers as a traitor. One pays a high price for such aspiration.

4. The above point suggests the difficult problem of marginality—for example, for the black police officer.[50]

5. The complex question of qualifications for police work is currently undergoing reexamination and reevaluation. What should it take to qualify? The qualities that are most useful in today's police function may not be measurable in such terms as years of formal education, or how tall an applicant is, or what he or she weighs, or how sharp his or her eyesight. The important question is: What are the *relevant* qualifications? We too easily succumb to doing it the easy way: for example, requiring more formal education, which we equate with "elevating standards." Assumptions of this type urgently need rethinking, to reveal the superficiality of the administrative stance: "We can't get enough qualified applicants";

"We can't lower our standards." White, middle-class bias taints much that is said and done about this.

6. Many minority-group people have reason to doubt that they are really wanted in police agencies, because they have reason to know that there is considerable racial prejudice and discrimination therein.[51]

7. As a result of past educational discrimination and present civil-service-type "merit examinations" for police service, minority people are in fact at a disadvantage in the educational requirements. Also, because many such testing instruments are tilted by culture and social class and weighted with paper-and-pencil and reading skills, minority people are further handicapped. Across the country, numerous suits involving the development of nondiscriminatory tests of "merit" have been in litigation. Who decides the criteria for "merit"? This is a key question.

8. For *social* rather than racial reasons, numerous young blacks—again as an example of the typical minority-group situation—have a criminal record, making them technically ineligible for police service. This, too, calls for reevaluation, with careful attention to the individual applicant and the particular nature of the crime, rather than reliance on broad, no-exceptions, bureaucratic classifications.

9. Attitudes within police organizations toward minority-group personnel often create problems internally, a significant factor in the difficulty of *retaining* such personnel even when initially secured. One indication of this is the development of "defense" organizations to protect the interests and rights of minority-group police officers, for instance, the Guardians, the National Society of Afro-American Policemen, the Council of Police Societies, and Officers for Justice. Their purposes are more serious than fraternity and fellowship. There is one theory that some of the negativism among police rank-and-file directed against actual or prospective minority-group colleagues is grounded in the self-image problems of some officers. They fear, for example, that police work will increasingly come to be regarded as what they call "nigger work." It should also be noted that, historically, there has been an attitude sometimes evident in the white community (and occasionally in the black community) that "a black cop is not a real cop."

10. Many educationally better-qualified blacks have taken positions in business, industry, and the professions rather than in public service, simply because salary and other incentives are far better.

While some of these factors are gradually fading, the change is far from swift. There is no question that the minority-group police officer is a very important figure in police and community relations. This recently acquired importance is a telling symptom of the gravity of police and minority group polarization. It is probably true that there is a resultant "counter-momentum," a tendency for police departments to expect too much from the minority-group officer, almost to a point of suggesting that, if only there were enough black police officers, all problems of police-black relations would evaporate. Some black police may be able to do certain things better than some white police in a predominantly black neighborhood, but the same thing is also true in a predominantly white neighborhood. In the long run, it may be recognized that blackness or whiteness is not a very important determinant of an effective police officer. It comes down to individual traits of personality, sensitivity, attitude, knowledge, and the like. Some black officers do not know the culture of certain black neighborhoods. Some black police officers are rougher in black neighborhoods and are despised more by the residents than are white officers. At present, the importance of the black police officer on the police and community relations scene is mainly symbolic. This in no way detracts, however, from the fact of his importance. On the contrary, it underscores again the opportunity for police and criminal justice agencies to lead the way in race relations.

As a result of wholesale revamping of personnel practices and procedures pertaining to the recruitment of police personnel in recent years, many big-city departments—Detroit is an outstanding example—have made great strides in improving their minority representation.[52] The dramatic advances have tended to be in large police agencies serving cities with large minority populations—black, Hispanic, or Oriental. Detroit's aim is 45 percent black by 1980. In 1963, only 3.8 percent of the personnel of the Detroit Police Department were black; in early 1973 18.9 percent were black.[53]

AFFIRMATIVE ACTION

As with other facets of public service, criminal justice has been involved in the continuing recent debate regarding the merits and demerits of affirmative action. As mentioned earlier, police departments in many places have been targeted in legal suits to test personnel policies and practices, first by various minority defense organizations, and more recently by police unions and line fraternal groups. The Bakke and Weber cases were as closely watched in police circles as in colleges and businesses. There is little question that affirmative action and equal opportunity programs, persuasively mandated by the Law Enforcement Assistance Administration (LEAA) in its grants, have had something to do with the improvements that have occurred in minority representation in criminal justice staffing.

The Supreme Court's 5–4 decision in both the Bakke and Weber cases was indicative of the political climate bearing on the issue. This rather accurately reflected the dilemma of the basic issue itself and clearly predicted an extended future of continuing litigation. Can preferential treatment on racial grounds ever be benign? Is the problem of discrimination best dealt with by compensatory treatment *after it occurs*, or ought we as a society to be asking more fundamental questions about the distribution of *all* opportunity?[54]

These are ways of stating the central question about which the debate revolves. We cannot answer it here and now. Sometimes it is a mark of vital social and moral progress for a society simply to reach the point where the essential questions can be asked.

RIOT CITIES: TEN YEARS AFTER

The summer of 1967 saw some 164 civil outbreaks in this country, with an estimated damage of $200 to $500 million.[55] In the relative calm of ten years later, what has been happening? Some of the riot areas still look much as they did then. But a solid black middle class has emerged, with higher school and college enrollments and many more black elected officials. Yet black unemployment is up, especially among youth, as noted earlier. Neighborhood restoration has been slow. A larger proportion of blacks living in poverty is a trend side by side with a larger proportion with annual income above $15,000. The summary story is that there is significant progress in some respects, but in other respects, the flashpoints remain. The youthful black unemployment rate is a case in point.

The so-called civil rights movement is still alive to the present, but inclined to stress different strategies, particularly political action in one form or another. A major cause of concern is the manner in which school busing and affirmative action have tended to split the membership of civil rights organizations. In the 1960s, for example, the NAACP had a 25 percent white membership, but it more recently appears to be increasingly all-black.

While the news that the Mormon Church now permits black priests and that Americans are more tolerant of interracial marriages than they were a decade ago is applauded by civil rights proponents, some problems temper their enthusiasm, several of which have been cited. A few more examples are:

- In places where a high proportion of poor people are white, such as Boston, the antagonism generated against blacks in the rivalries for jobs and housing is incendiary.

- There is apprehension about a possible rift between upward-bound blacks and poor blacks. Blacks who have "made it" find it difficult to maintain their former relationships. The less fortunate feel they they have been abandoned.[56]

- In the first decade of its existence (1964 to 1974), the Federal Equal Employment Opportunity Commission had ten different chairpersons, and as many staff directors. At the end of 1976, the commission had a backlog of 122,000 cases.[57] Many workers who file complaints wait years to learn whether their charges have merit.

- There are signs that the traditional coping capacity of extended black families is breaking down. Welfare policies and unemployment seem to be contributing factors. Jobs, homes, and education are the stabilizing elements, with black or white families.

Again, what bearing do these considerations have on police-minority relations? Are the police expected to solve the problems of minorities? The answer to the first question is implicit in the nature of the problems. The answer to the second question is that no single social institution can solve the problems, alone. But if every social institution of our society denies a part of the responsibility, what hope is there for mankind?

OTHER MINORITIES

We have focused on blacks as our example of a minority group. There are defensible reasons for this. It should be emphasized, however, that much of what we have said applies as well to other groups. Yet the difficulty with such a statement is that it is too general; it conveys an impression of uniformity, of alikeness, when in fact we mean *similarity* allowing for some *uniqueness.*

Take, for example, Spanish-speaking Americans. Puerto Rican citizens of varying skin pigmentation are one subgroup. But not all Puerto Ricans can be lumped together, either. And then there are the Spanish-surname people of the Southwest and other places throughout the nation, some of them migrant agricultural workers, others not. In their study of police and minority relations in Denver, Bayley and Mendelsohn say that people of Mexican-American (Chicano) heritage have in common the Spanish language, a historical tradition, and a sense of cultural uniqueness.[58] The authors go on to observe that blacks participate to a greater extent than the Spanish-named in the culture of America. Blacks generally do not, for example, speak a different language; it is their distinctive physical appearance that sets them apart. To complicate things further, there are, of course, many Spanish-speaking blacks of Latin-American background.

The Denver study reflects differences in the experiences of blacks and the Spanish-named in many facets of police and community relations. For example, the Spanish-named were twice as critical as blacks of the job done by the police in their respective neighborhoods. Over twice as many Spanish-named claimed that they or someone in their family had been badly treated by the police. A study by the U.S. Commission on Civil Rights cites many serious problems in the treatment of Mexican Americans in the Southwest by the police and other justice agencies.[59] It should be noted that location and culture affect these matters: Denver may be one thing, Los Angeles or Santa Fe another.

The point is that minority groups are not all alike in every respect, and one should flatly reject the notion that "if you've seen one, you've seen them all." There are, of course, certain problems that are common to minority groups, as earlier indicated when we defined the concept, for instance, sociopolitical powerlessness. Our centering upon blacks assumes that there are some common attributes in police and minority-group relations, *not* that there are no important distinctions. Swastikas in Skokie in 1978 bring to mind one kind of fear and hatred. A March on Washington by hundreds of Indians, or a demonstration in the same place only a week earlier by 40,000 advocates of the Equal Rights Amendment, expose another of the faces of prejudice and discrimination. Then there was the Poor People's March of 1968 and the "Tractorcade" of 1977. The police and the courts are involved whenever and wherever people parade in protest.

Another minority that has recently been added to civil rights jurisdictions is the handicapped. In Michigan, race still constitutes the basis of the most complaints filed with the State Civil Rights Department—about 45 percent. Sex ranks second at 15 percent, with handicaps at 10 to 12 percent, and complaints of discrimination based on age at 4 percent.[60]

Confrontation tactics have brought the police into direct conflict with militant members of many minority groups. The core issue in all instances is the threat to entrenched power, as represented by the police. The tactics of confrontation garner a heavy toll for both winners and losers, and it is often difficult to tell which is which. Perhaps this is why ultimate recourse is increasingly to conventional, orderly processes to settle disputes and to effect rights peaceably. The essential lesson seems to be that survival requires that we have rules of some kind to control our relationships. And rules assume some measure of mutual accommodation.

Certain white minorities are also struggling for acceptance in this country. As Paul Mundy has said, "The third generation remembers what the second generation would like to forget, namely, his ethnic identity." Various ethnic groups in major cities are demanding a voice on boards and commissions to influence such matters as curriculum content and choice of history books in schools. Italian Americans are acting to eliminate the stereotypes they find offensive. Many police officers come from ethnic white minority group backgrounds, and ethnically based clubs and societies of police are common in our larger cities. There are still a few places, too, where religious cleavages are strong within police organizations. The Knights of Columbus and the Shriners are still prominent in police circles and have considerable influence in some quarters.

Another kind of minority in our society is represented by homosexuals and transvestites. In recent years, Gay Liberation has been taking cues from other minorities, and the police are a favorite target. Allegations of mistreatment are frequently made. The case for fair police treatment of transsexuals has been promoted by Louisiana's Erickson Educational Foundation, publishers of a periodic newsletter on the subject. The fact that police audiences are often amused by references to these individuals and groups suggests that there may be cause for concern. Some sign of social maturity may be indicated in the fact that a few years ago these matters were never mentioned in police training programs, while today many training programs devote frank attention to them.

OTHER CRIMINAL JUSTICE COMPONENTS

We have discussed some of the implications for the police of the civil rights movement. What about other parts of the criminal justice system? A more thorough consideration of this appears in part 4, but as to the specific question raised above, the courts may be taken as an example. How the judicial apparatus acts in time of civil crisis is an important test of a society's capacity to uphold democratic values and protect civil liberties. During urban disturbances in the late 1960s and early 1970s, defendants were deprived of adequate representation, subjected to the abuses of overcrowded facilities, and held in custody by the imposition of high bail. These measures, taken under the duress of mass arrests and ostensibly for the prevention of further disorders, amounted to preventive detention and the suspension of due process.[61]

Skolnick points out that the inability of the courts to cope with civil emergencies results in a decline in public respect for legal authority. Demonstrators and militants have come to believe that legal institutions serve only the powerful and are incapable of redressing social and political grievances. Skolnick attributes the crisis in the courts to three factors:

1. The quality of justice in the lower criminal courts during routine operations is quite low.

2. In response to community and political pressure for immediate restoration of order, the courts tend to adopt a police perspective of "riot control," becoming in effect an instrument of social control relatively unrestrained by conditions of legality.

3. The courts are not suited to the task of resolving the political conflicts which occasion civil crisis and mass arrests.[62]

Skolnick is especially concerned that the trend toward devising "emergency measures" does not become routinized as the main social response to crises that go deeper than the need to restore order.

SUMMING UP

So much has been said and written in the past few years about urban crisis, and indeed specifically regarding police relationships with minority groups, that any overview is necessarily limited to a selection of points and issues. We have not touched all the bases in this chapter, surely, but we have mentioned some of the more important considerations, with the hope of stimulating thought and discussion.

There remain several matters, however, that merit more extensive analysis: collective behavior and civil disobedience, police-youth relations, and citizen complaints. These will be dealt with in the next three chapters.

A final point with reference to the police and minority groups is stated well by Bayley and Mendelsohn:

> The police are important for minority people not just because of what they do but because of what they are. Minority people recognize that other problems must be solved if substantial improvements are to be made in the quality of their lives. Yet what they experience at the hands of the police is of enormous emotional significance. It symbolizes for them the backhanded treatment they receive from society as a whole. The police are the ubiquitous, public, authority-laden symbols of their own second-class citizenship. Upon them is vented the accumulated frustrations of lifetimes of inequality and subservience. . . . In sum, the position the police occupy in the minority world is only partly a result of what police do in that world; more importantly, their position is a function of fundamental emotional judgments made by people subjected to pervasive deprivation and inequality. This being the case, substantial improvements in police-minority relations cannot be expected solely as the result of changes in police policy and behavior. It will be necessary to change their symbolic status as well, and that is a function of a total system of majority-minority relationships.[63]

NOTES

1. An informative historical reference in this regard is: California, Attorney General's Office, *Guide to Community Relations for Peace Officers*, by Davis McEntire and Robert B. Powers (Sacramento, 1958).

2. Robert B. Mills, "Police-Community Relations: A Psychologist's Viewpoint" (paper presented at an Institute on Police-Community Relations at Xavier University, June 8, 1964).

3. James Baldwin, *Nobody Knows My Name* (New York: Dial Press, 1961.)

4. U.S., President's Commission on Law Enforcement and Administration of Justice, *Field Surveys V: A National Survey of Police and Community Relations* (prepared for the commission by the National Center on Police and Community Relations, Michigan State University School of Police Administration and Public Safety, 1967), pp. 14 ff.

5. Kenneth B. Clark, *Dark Ghetto: Dilemmas of Social Power* (New York: Harper & Row, 1965), p. 86. Reprinted by permission.

6. Writing in the July–August 1978 (vol. 5, no. 2, pp. 60–63) issue of the *Civil Liberties Review*, William Preston, chairman of the history department at John Jay College of Criminal Justice in New York City, suggests that improvement in the professional skills and attitudes of the police has moved them away from the community and from due process. As police autonomy has increased, popular, democratic control of the police has waned. One result is lessened accountability. There are those who point to the FBI, the CIA, and in Canada, to the RCMP, as examples.

7. President's Commission on Law Enforcement, *Field Surveys V*, pp. 21 ff.

8. *New York Times*, May 11, 1971.

9. Lee Rainwater, "The Revolt of the Dirty-Workers," *Transaction*, November 1967, p. 2.

10. Ibid.

11. W. H. Ferry, "The Police State, American Mode" (Starr King Commencement Speech, Unitarian Church of Berkeley, California, October 10, 1969).

12. William P. Brown, "Mirrors of Prejudice," *Nation* 208, no. 16 (April 21, 1969): 498. Reprinted by permission.

13. George Edwards, *The Police on the Urban Frontier: A Guide to Community Understanding* (New York: Institute of Human Relations Press, 1968), pp. 17 ff., 77.

14. Milton Rokeach, Martin G. Miller, and John A. Snyder, "The Value Gap Between Police and Policed," *Journal of Social Issues* 27, no. 2 (1971): 162.

15. Leon Festinger, *A Theory of Cognitive Dissonance* (Palo Alto, Calif.: Stanford University Press, 1957), p. 260.

16. Ibid.

17. Ibid., p. 263.

18. Ibid. Compare Festinger's theory with that of Morton Deutsch regarding conflict resolution, discussed in chapter 8.

19. Victor G. Strecher, "When Subcultures Meet: Police-Negro Relations," in Sheldon Yefsky, ed., *Science and Technology in Law Enforcement* (Chicago: Thompson, 1967).

20. Gunnar Myrdal, *An American Dilemma: The Negro Population in the U.S.* (New York: Harper & Brothers, 1944), pp. 50–64. Reprinted by permission of Harper & Row, Publishers, Inc.

21. Strecher, "When Subcultures Meet," p. 706.

22. Gary Marx, *Protest and Prejudice: A Study of Belief in the Black Community* (New York: Harper & Row, 1967), p. 36.

23. Hans Toch, "Cops and Blacks: Warring Minorities," *Nation* 208, no. 16 (April 1969): 492. Reprinted by permission.

24. Kenneth B. Clark, *Dark Ghetto*, pp. 4 ff.

25. For discussion of this issue, see U.S., National Commission on Causes and Prevention of Violence, *The Politics of Protest* (Washington, D.C.: U.S. Government Printing Office, 1969). Note especially chapters 4–7. See also *The Iron Fist and the Velvet Glove: An Analysis of the U.S. Police*, by the Center for Research on Criminal Justice (Berkeley, Calif.: 1975).

26. Seymour Martin Lipset, "Why Cops Hate Liberals—and Vice Versa," *Atlantic* 223, no. 3 (March 1969): 82. Copyright © 1969 by The Atlantic Monthly Company. Reprinted by permission.

27. Ibid.

28. James Q. Wilson, *Varieties of Police Behavior: The Management of Law and Order in Eight Communities* (Cambridge, Mass.: Harvard University Press, 1968), pp. 297–299. Reprinted by permission.

29. David H. Bayley and Harold Mendelsohn, *Minorities and the Police: Confrontation in America* (New York: Free Press, 1969), p. 148; James Leo Walsh, "The Professional Cop" (paper presented at the Sixty-fourth Annual Meeting of the American Sociological Association, September 1968).

30. William A. Westley, "Violence and the Police," *American Journal of Sociology* 59 (July 1953): 34–41; William M. Kephart, *Racial Factors and Urban Law Enforcement* (Philadelphia: University of Pennsylvania Press, 1957); Jerome H. Skolnick, *Justice Without Trial: Law Enforcement in Democratic Society*, 2nd ed. (New York: John Wiley & Sons, 1975).

31. Jerome H. Skolnick, "The Police and the Urban Ghetto," *Research Contributions of the American Bar Foundation*, 1968, no. 3, p. 9.

32. Bruce Cory, "Police on Trial in Houston," *Police* 1, no. 3 (July 1978): 33–40.

33. *The State of Civil Rights: 1977*, a Report of the U.S. Commission on Civil Rights, February 1978 (Washington, D.C.: U.S. Government Printing Office). Also, another report of the same commission, *Social Indicators of Equality for Minorities and Women*, August 1978.

34. Lois G. Forer, "The Law: Excessive Promise and Inadequate Fulfillment," *Crime and Delinquency* 24, no. 2 (April 1978): 197–206.

35. Research and references in the literature dealing with racial factors in police and criminal justice are plentiful. Indicative of this are several articles on the attitudes of black and white police officers in the *Journal of Social Issues* 31, no. 1 (1975); and several articles on the police and minority groups in *Police-Community Relations: Selected Readings*, Paul F. Cromwell, Jr., and George Keefer, eds. (St. Paul, Minn.: West, 1978).

36. See Gilbert Geis, "Statistics Concerning Race and Crime," *Crime and Delin-*

quency 2, no. 2 (1965): 143; President's Commission on Law Enforcement, *Field Surveys V*, chap. 7.

37. Marvin E. Wolfgang and Bernard Cohen, *Crime and Race*, rev. ed. (New York: Institute of Human Relations Press, 1970), p. 3.

38. William H. Kephart, *Racial Factors and Urban Law Enforcement* (Philadelphia: University of Pennsylvania Press, 1957).

39. Wolfgang and Cohen, *Crime and Race*, p. 9.

40. U.S., President's Commission on Crime in the District of Columbia, *Report of the President's Commission on Crime in the District of Columbia* (Washington, D.C.: U.S. Government Printing Office, 1966), pp. 42, 44, 54, 78.

41. John Dollard, *Caste and Class in a Southern Town* (New Haven, Conn.: Yale University Press, 1937), pp. 274–281.

42. Quoted by Edwards, *The Police on the Urban Frontier*, pp. 77 ff.

43. Clarence Kelley, as quoted by Robert Pearman in "Black Crime, Black Victims," *Nation* 208, no. 16 (April 21, 1969): 500–503.

44. Wolfgang and Cohen, *Crime and Race*, pp. 101–102.

45. Frank Remington, "Social Change, the Law and the Common Good," in A. F. Brandstatter and Louis A. Radelet, eds., *Police and Community Relations: A Sourcebook* (Beverly Hills, Calif.: Glencoe, 1968), p. 236. Reprinted by permission.

46. Ibid., p. 238.

47. Ibid., p. 240.

48. Remington and his colleague at the University of Wisconsin Law School, Herman Goldstein, presented their case in the draft of chapter 2 of U.S., President's Commission on Law Enforcement and Administration of Justice, *Task Force Report: The Police* (Washington, D.C.: U.S. Government Printing Office, 1967); David J. Bordua, "Comments on Police-Community Relations," *Law Enforcement and Technology II* (Chicago: Illinois Institute of Technology Research Center, 1968), pp. 115–125.

49. Bordua, "Comments on Police-Community Relations," pp. 122–123.

50. Effectively analyzed by Nicholas Alex in *Black in Blue: A Study of the Negro Policeman* (New York: Appleton-Century-Crofts, 1969). As he says, black police officers experience *double* marginality: they cannot escape their racial identity while serving their official roles, nor can they escape their identity as a "cop" in the black community.

51. See President's Commission on Law Enforcement, *Task Force Report: The Police*, pp. 167–175; also the same commission's *Field Surveys V*, pp. 19–20. See also National Advisory Commission on Civil Disorders, *Report*, pp. 165–166. Some police departments have tried cadet and precadet programs for minority youth as young as 14 or 15 years of age in an attempt to overcome long-standing suspicions regarding police work.

52. See Thomas G. Ferrebee, "Black Recruiting in Detroit," in J. Leonard Steinberg and Donald W. McEvoy, eds., *The Police and the Behavioral Sciences* (Springfield, Ill.: C. C. Thomas, 1974), pp. 124 ff.

53. As reported by the Associated Press, February 1973.

54. "Affirmative Action: Confronting the Dilemmas," *Phi Kappa Phi Journal*, Winter 1978, Stephen W. White, editor (Richmond, Va.: William Byrd Press).

55. *U.S. News & World Report*, August 29, 1977, p. 50.

56. *U.S. News & World Report*, June 5, 1978, p. 51.

57. *U.S. News & World Report*, Dec. 13, 1976, p. 35.

58. Bayley and Mendelsohn, *Minorities and the Police*, p. v.

59. U.S., Commission on Civil Rights, *Mexican Americans and the Administration of Justice in the Southwest* (Washington, D.C.: U.S. Government Printing Office, 1970). See also Louis A. Radelet and Hoyt Coe Reed, *The Police and the Community: Studies* (Beverly Hills, Calif.: Glencoe, 1973), pp. 127–132.

60. As reported in the *Lansing State Journal*, February 21, 1978.

61. Substantiated by both the National Advisory Commission on Civil Disorders and the National Commission on Causes and Prevention of Violence.

62. Jerome Skolnick, *Politics of Protest* (New York: Simon & Schuster, 1969). Reprinted by permission.

63. Bayley and Mendelsohn, *Minorities and the Police*, pp. 141–142.

11

COLLECTIVE BEHAVIOR, TERRORISM, AND CIVIL DISOBEDIENCE

Collective behavior is defined by sociologists as relatively unstructured social behavior that is not fully controlled by cultural norms—such as that occurring in crowds, riots, revivals, and even sometimes with rumor and fads. It brings into play emotions and unpredictable personal interaction.[1] For obvious reasons, collective behavior is of major concern to the police.

CASUAL SOCIETAL GROUPS

There are many different classifications of societal groups. Some groups are established, some are casual. Examples of the former are vertical and horizontal groupings, ingroups and outgroups, primary and secondary groups. Casual groups include crowds, mobs, and assemblages. Then there are related types of group behavior, such as social movements, social epidemics, fashions, fads, and crazes.

A *crowd* is a temporary gathering of people engaged in some type of collective behavior, ranging from casual strolling to a riot. It differs from an *aggregation*, which is simply an assemblage of individuals in spatial proximity. In a crowd, the individuals are also in psychological contiguity. Crowds often begin as aggregations, evolving through an interactive process known as *circular stimulation*. This means the reciprocal stimulation of individual emotions, causing behavior responses that are less deliberative and less critical than would normally be expected. As a result, members of a crowd are apt to act under the influence of commonly felt emotion.

An *audience* is a type of crowd responding primarily to a single source of stimuli while engaging in only minimum social interaction. Thus, in an audience, there is little circular stimulation. Attention tends to be focused on a performance rather than on other crowd members. A *mob*, on the other hand, is a crowd with a purpose, often contrary to law, often highly emotional, that confers a sense of anonymity on its members. A mob is sometimes characterized as an *acting crowd*, with considerable circular stimulation and an aggressive attitude toward a common object. It feels bound to no conventions and acts solely on the basis of aroused feelings. Collective excitement submerges critical thought and deliberate conduct even more than in a crowd.

The element of <u>psychological suggestibility</u> present in a mob easily leads to violence. There is even a tendency, as in lynch mobs, to hold violence justifiable, so intense is the feeling about righting a supposed wrong. Cowards feel brave in a mob. A *riot* is mob behavior that erupts into public violence, tumult, and disorder. In their study of the 1943 race riot in Detroit, Alfred Lee and Norman Humphrey said:

> Riots are the products of thousands upon thousands of little events that have affected the habits and emotions of thousands upon thousands of people, both future rioters and future innocent bystanders.[2]

William E. Dowling, Wayne County prosecutor at the time, described that riot in the *Detroit Times:*

> The Sunday night of the riot, a gang of colored boys and girls ranging from 13 to 20 years went to Belle Isle with the expressed purpose of driving the white people from the island. They started out, knowing that 85 percent of the approximately 100,000 people on the island were colored, and beat up a white boy.
>
> Next, they attacked a man and his wife who were eating a picnic lunch. They went on around to the bridge and one of the colored girls was pushed into a white girl who was accompanied by a sailor. A fight followed and it spread across the bridge
>
> One of the colored boys raced downtown to a club and had it announced over the public address system that a Negro woman and her baby had been thrown into the river.
>
> Then it started. By 4 A.M., 400 stores owned by whites in the colored district had been wrecked, looted, pillaged and destroyed. A street car had been stopped and 50 white factory workers were taken out and beaten. It was 5 A.M. before the whites started to retaliate.[3]

Many would quarrel with this version of what happened, on the grounds that it is biased. But in a mob and riot situation, there are no completely trustworthy observers. Objectivity is lost in the stampede. Power and righteousness are felt to abide in the surge of the impassioned mob.

The art of crowd control is important to the police. Typical tactics include directing attention away from the common objective, efforts to divide members of the crowd physically and psychologically, and attempts to divert the leaders so as to dilute their integrating influence. The primary aim is to relieve the emotional tension caused by circular stimulation.[4]

Related Group Behavior

A *social movement* is a collective attempt to bring about a change in existing practices or institutions. The women's liberation movement is an example. It implies dissatisfaction with some phase of existing social organization.

A *fashion* is a movement characterized by vertical ascent or descent through social classes. It is imitation throughout a social structure of a particular "elite," in clothing, manners, art, or ideas. Distinction, novel experience, and conformity are among the motivating forces.

Fads, crazes, and *social epidemics* are types of fashion movements. They are usually more eccentric than fashion, more localized and of shorter duration, and pertain to frivolous things not of great importance to the total culture.

Herbert Blumer pointed out long ago that the members of a social movement often have high morale, dependent on belief in the absolute rightness of their purpose and in the possibility of ultimate attainment of their goal. It takes on the character of a sacred mission. Often the members of a social movement see all opposing forces as evil.[5] "If you're not for us, you're against us!" The objective is so right and necessary that it cannot possibly fail. Parades, rallies, and "pep meetings" provide ceremony and ritual and help enhance the feeling of being a select group with a "manifest destiny." A feeling of personal expansion comes from association with others (rapport) in the movement. Sometimes special uniforms, slogans, hymns, and gestures help "turn people on."

The Police and Collective Behavior

We tend to think of police action in collective behavior situations in terms of protecting society against disorder, pandemonium, violence, and unlawful activity. Just as important, however, are the activities of groups engaged in nonviolent demonstrations which are not illegal, but which nonetheless require police action to protect the demonstrators in the exercise of their rights to assemble and speak freely.

Police, of course, are sympathetic with the philosophy that the best way to deal with a riot is to prevent it. Therefore, the "triggering incident" receives considerable attention in police training. It is recognized that the triggering incident is the culmination of what is usually a long series of events, occurring in an inflammable social situation. But the incident that sets off the conflagration may be quite innocent and may have no direct connection with the real issue. Many police departments have had to confess: "We looked for something to happen here, and instead of that, it happened way over there, where we least expected it!"

William Brown has emphasized that a major disorder is almost always the culmination of a building-up process. Planning for control of disorder, he says, is based on a combination of conventional police mobilization tactics and *an understanding of the community*.[6] Tension control centers, where established in the 1960s, carried out such functions as:

1. Receiving and evaluating reports of tension.
2. Getting background; fact finding; area surveys.
3. Diagnosing the problem (identifying causes).
4. Setting up programs to relieve tension, stressing *communication* and *interpretation*, two basic processes in tension control.

The prevention of riots is not the responsibility of the police alone. A just social order for all is the ultimate answer, and achieving this goal is the most important responsibility of the entire society. Law is based on the behavior of individuals, not groups. A police officer arrests only individuals who violate the law. This is one reason group behavior is difficult for the police to handle. The late Nelson Watson put it this way:

Police cannot take into court a whole group and present evidence against them en masse. If the police are unable to identify and arrest individual violators and present evidence of the specific violation, case by individual case, all they can do is suppress the violence. It is inevitable that in large-scale disorder many violations of the law will go unpunished. This makes it doubly important to devise preventive programs involving all interested segments of the community.[7]

Watson further pointed out that police methods in dealing with collective behavior situations will vary according to circumstances, time, geography, area in a given community, the socioeconomic and cultural variations among people, and other such conditions. He emphasized the importance of flexibility in police policies and operational procedures in heterogeneous, social-conflict-laden communities. He pinpointed some special problems of poor communities as follows:

> Since many lower-class persons are unskilled and are poorly equipped educationally, the most important fact of life for them is the means of obtaining the necessities. For many, existence is a series of crises or emergencies in which food and shelter are principal concerns. The net result is that satisfying their basic needs for the moment demands such a large proportion of their physical and psychological resources that they are unable to devote adequate time to the development of the symbolic skills so important in today's complex society. Their survival problems are much closer to them than those of the more affluent in our society.[8]

Watson concludes that police approaches to the control of crime, violence, and disorder must be designed to match the varying psychological and sociological circumstances of the people involved. This is the principle that we enunciated earlier: that dealing with people in their individuality does not easily submit to mass-oriented, bureaucratically processed classifications and "no-exception" practices. A school system, a university, or a police department cannot be administered in this way in today's American society without encountering turbulence. The evidence of this is widespread. No one should make his case for democracy on the basis that it is necessarily efficient or tidy.

Symbols and Symbolic Behavior

Crowds, mobs, and social movements often employ various types of symbols and symbolic behavior. Mentioned earlier were parades, rallies, uniforms, slogans, hymns, and gestures. Terms such as "soul brother" and "soul sister" were part of a special language that developed in the civil rights and youth "counter-cultures" of the 1960s.

To pursue one interesting avenue of this a bit further, there is the constitutional question as to whether the First Amendment places a limitation on the power of school administrators to control student behavior exhibited as a symbolic expression of belief. A series of relatively recent court decisions has dealt with this issue, in questions regarding the wearing of armbands, headbands, buttons, and the like.[9] Harry Mallios of the University of Miami at Coral Gables has summarized the matter as follows:

> . . . individuals may desire to wear a particular type of symbol or insignia, and the courts have interpreted this as behavior constituting communication of an idea which is subject to protection of the Constitution. Nevertheless, explicitly implied is that

the rights of students not sharing the expression exhibited should not be abused and, therefore, they are equally protected. When the expression exhibited produces a disturbance or disruption to the school or violates the legal rights of other students, restrictions by school authorities prohibiting this expression have been upheld.[10]

Symbols and symbolic behavior are endemic to collective behavior. They represent an effort to structure disorganized situations in some small degree, a way for participants in social movements to communicate with each other in a rapport-building manner and to impart a sense of common cause. The same thing occurs, for basically the same reason, in all subcultures, including that of the police. Incidentally, rumor serves something of the same purpose: to share a "hot tip" is a way of enhancing fraternal feeling, although it may backfire.

The symbols used in collective behavior usually carry strong emotional undertones that can quickly arouse people to irrational responses, particularly in group settings. Demagogues play on these feelings and manipulate gatherings in support of their particular purposes, which are sometimes socially questionable.

Symbols are often based on group stereotypes. Whether positive or negative, the symbol tends to perpetuate and lend credence to the stereotype. Take police-black relations in the ghetto. So much of what passes for communication here is symbolic: language, gestures, namecalling, insignia or dress, and the like. A term such as "the system" is illustrative. So are "hippie," "freak," "pig," "Amerika," "Mr. Charley," and various obscene expressions that might be cited. This is symbolic language, all of it stereotypic. As with any stereotype, it shortcuts thought and rationality. It has a rationale without being entirely rational.

So it is that symbols tend to be dysfunctional in genuine human relationships because they encourage categorization of people and events. Their utility in collective behavior situations is ephemeral. However, symbolism is a necessary and inevitable part of human communication, and there are unquestionably *good* (or, in any event, harmless) symbols.

Social Response to Collective Behavior

Studies of collective behavior and its implications for the police have been done on a massive scale in recent years. Some of these study reports are public property, easily accessible to those who ask what causes such behavior and what can be done to prevent it from getting out of hand. One example was the study done in 1967–68 by the National Advisory Commission on Civil Disorders, whose report is prefaced by this statement from President Lyndon Johnson:

> The only genuine, long-range solution for what has happened lies in an attack—mounted at every level—upon the conditions that breed despair and violence. All of us know what those conditions are: ignorance, discrimination, slums, poverty, disease, not enough jobs. We should attack these conditions—not because we are frightened by conflict, but because we are fired by conscience. We should attack them because there is simply no other way to achieve a decent and orderly society in America.[11]

The president might well have added that this is the only ultimate solution for problems of police and community relations.

Another study of collective behavior in America was conducted in 1968–69 by the National Commission on the Causes and Prevention of Violence. This commission declared:

> In our judgment, the time is upon us for a reordering of national priorities and for a greater investment of resources in the fulfillment of two basic purposes of our Constitution—to "establish justice" and to "insure domestic tranquility."[12]

Still another study of collective behavior was made in 1970 by the President's Commission on Campus Unrest, which asserted:

> Too many Americans have begun to justify violence as a means of effecting change or safeguarding traditions. We believe it urgent that Americans of all convictions draw back from the brink. . . . Students who bomb and burn are criminals. Police and National Guardsmen who needlessly shoot or assault students are criminals. All who applaud these criminal acts share in their evil. We must declare a national cease-fire.[13]

In an analysis written for the National Commission on the Causes and Prevention of Violence, Jerome Skolnick stated that collective behavior has come to mean the behavior of outsiders, the disadvantaged and disaffected. "Panicky" and "crazy" are terms usually reserved, he wrote, for social movements and insurrections. Skolnick questioned typical governmental responses to civil disorders, which—he claimed—have historically combined long-term recommendations for social change with short-term calls for better strategy and technology to contain disruption. He offered five reasons for so questioning:

1. As the Kerner Commission stressed, American society urgently requires fundamental social and political change, not more firepower in official hands.
2. We must set realistic priorities. We must carefully distinguish between increased firepower and enlightened law enforcement.
3. Police, soldiers and other agents of social control have been implicated in triggering and intensifying violence in riots and other forms of protest. A nonlethal weapon is still a weapon, and it does not solve social problems.
4. Riots are not merely pathological behavior engaged in by riff-raff. Neither are they "carnivals." They are spontaneous political acts expressing enormous frustration and genuine grievance. Forceful control techniques may channel grievances into organized revolutionary and guerrilla patterns.
5. In measuring the consequences of domestic military escalation, we must add the political and social dangers of depending on espionage as an instrument of social control, including its potential for eroding constitutional guarantees of political freedom.[14]

Skolnick further observed:

> If American society concentrates on the development of sophisticated control techniques, it will move itself into the destructive and self-defeating position of meeting a

political problem with armed force, which will eventually threaten domestic freedom. The combination of long-range reform and short-range order sounds plausible, but we fear that the strategy of force will continue to prevail. In the long run this nation cannot have it both ways: either it will carry through a firm commitment to massive and widespread political and social reform, or it will become a society of garrison cities where order is enforced with less and less concern for due process of law and the consent of the governed.[15]

Police action is unquestionably an important aspect of social response to collective behavior. Jerome Hall recalled that the posse is historic in our culture, but he reminded us that a critical situation provides an excellent opportunity to actualize the ideal of self-policing. He pointed out that several hundred citizens were deputized as peace officers in the 1919 Harlem riots, and voluntary service by socially minded white and black citizens has frequently emerged in civil disorder situations.[16]

The gravity of mob disorder is reflected in the prohibition under criminal penalty of two less serious situations that tend to culminate in riot: unlawful assembly and rout. While it is generally true that preparation to commit a crime is not a crime, this is not true with unlawful assembly or rout, in which the incipient stages of riot are recognized and prohibited. As Hall pointed out:

> The police are familiar with arrest for assault and battery and for disorderly conduct, but they have ignored other available controls and legal measures which can be taken before crimes are committed or before serious aggressions occur. First among these is the peace bond, used in family disputes and in rural areas, but ignored as a control of incipient symptoms of serious disorder. . . . There are other noteworthy legal controls which were designed to check criminal conduct in its incipient stages. At common law, a threat, privately made, was not criminal unless it amounted to extortion. But under many statutes a threat uttered publicly in conditions tending toward a breach of the peace is "disorderly conduct," as is insulting, profane language in public. More serious is the common law crime of solicitation or incitement to commit a crime, and incitement to riot is one form of that offense. Conspiracy extends incipient criminal behavior to the conduct of two or more persons; there are reported cases where convictions of conspiracy to commit a breach of the peace were upheld.[17]

The police should, of course, be familiar with these and other possible legal controls, but the greater wisdom is knowing when and how to apply them. A well-intentioned police action to maintain or to restore order has been known to result in volcanic violence and disorder.

TERRORISM

Terrorism is a kind of ultimate political weapon, with a long history and many different forms. It involves the use of fear and violence to intimidate or subjugate people. In our time, terrorism has become an international phenomenon. Its different forms include train and airplane hijackings; the massacre of Olympic athletes; the kidnapping for high ransom (and sometimes the assassination) of key political and industrial figures; the intimidation of school administrators, teachers, and students; the holding of hostages; embassy attacks; bombings; kneecapping; and the like. Given the rapidly growing literature on this intriguing and complex subject, a general text should touch only briefly on one or two points.[18]

Is terrorism an appropriate topic to discuss when studying police-community relations? Emphatically, yes. Why so? For two major reasons:

1. Terrorism tests the basic political values, structures, and processes of liberal democracies, as well as the balance between security and liberty.[19]

2. In a more focused sense, terrorism tests criminal justice processes—police, courts, and corrections—in their social-control reactions to deviance.

Years ago, terrorism was usually directed against the wealthy or influential. Not so in recent years; terrorist incidents nowadays are much more likely to involve innocent people as victims.[20] In 1968, the CIA reported only 37 international terrorist incidents: in 1976, there were 239.[21] Some of this increase (perhaps 15 percent) could be explained in terms of conflict in the Middle East, specifically as the result of an increasing number of terrorist acts perpetrated by Palestinians or others sympathetic to the Palestinian cause. But the CIA's analysis of the situation pointed to broader causes:

1. Technological advances provided terrorists with new mobility, new weaponry, and worldwide publicity.

2. The growth of global and regional ties provided terrorists with a host of new targets for attack, including centers of transportation, communication, and commerce.

3. A "revolutionary" turn occurred in the overall political environment.[22]

Some observers, such as Sean MacBride (a member of the Irish Republican Army in the 1920s and 1930s, and a 1974 Nobel Peace Prize winner), attributed the recent upsurge in terrorism to a general escalation of violence and cruelty in the world. Particularly puzzling has been the outburst of political violence by youthful terrorists in Western Europe. Since 1968, citizens and property of the United States have been increasingly caught up in more than 1150 incidents, including kidnappings, murders, and bombings.[23] There are several identifiable trouble spots where terrorism has come to be regarded almost as part of the way of life: the Middle East, Italy, Ireland, Japan, and West Germany.

Modern terrorism is a complex subject. Its pattern varies from country to country. Take West Germany as an example: how explain terrorism here? The country's political situation is stable and democratic, its wealth is reasonably well distributed, its society is open and moderate. History haunts the Germans, and they are very sensitive about their world image. West Germany's dilemma is like that of other democratic systems in their efforts to deal with terrorism: what measures should be taken to be tough enough, without going to extremes? As Lance Morrow wrote in *Time*, "In fact, the terrorist activity is a lefthanded tribute to democratic institutions. A repressive society would not have tolerated the intellectual dissent that led to terrorism."[24]

But the primary point here (without going into the intricacies of the German diagnosis) is that understanding German terrorism does not mean you will understand terrorism in Ireland or Iran or Japan or Italy. There are common patterns in terrorist behavior, but little that is common in the combination of causes behind it from place to place, other than the generalizations suggested by the CIA. Some distinctions are, of course, useful. For instance, there is nationalist-separatist terrorism, practiced in Northern Ireland and Palestine and by Basque terrorists in Spain. Then there is "internal" terrorism, as Professor Walter Laqueur of the Center for Strategic and International Studies in Washington calls it, such as the Weathermen in this country, the Baader-Meinhof gang in West Germany, and the Red Brigades in Italy.[25] The relative absence of terrorism in Communist countries is explained by Professor Laqueur as due to the fact that a certain amount of freedom must exist in a society before terrorist activities can occur. There is an old political maxim that "one man's terrorist is another man's freedom fighter."

Captain Frank Bolz, terrorism specialist of the New York City Police Department, estimates that there are 140 clearly defined terrorist organizations active in the world today.[26] There is the possibility of some sort of loosely knit global linkage or confederation, perhaps even under a single leader—although there is no evidence of this at the moment. The CIA has identified at least a dozen foreign governments which deliberately foster the spread of terrorism.[27] Congress and the White House are increasingly apprehensive. Many American corporations have taken firm steps to protect their employees and plants from terrorist violence. The terminology of these efforts is interesting for students of police-community relations, for "crisis management" teams have been formed, specially trained, and backed up by intricate security systems. The FBI is intensifying antiterrorist training at its national academy, which in turn results in more SWAT (Special Weapons and Tactics) squads in local and state police departments.[28]

Proactive preparedness for coping with terrorism emphasizes improved intelligence, better physical defenses, and well drilled crisis management teams,[29] including not only the police but also Army specialists. Some of the same techniques the military uses in playing war games are involved in the training of these antiterrorist squads. The worldwide "get tough" trend in coping with terrorism appears to be making it more difficult and dangerous. But the modern terrorist seems to be as ready to die as to kill. Moreover, terrorists invariably get the massive publicity they seek.

Another important point influencing the police's ability to deal with terrorists is that police intelligence efforts directed towards terrorist groups have been sharply restricted in this country in recent years. Many intelligence files have been destroyed as the result of growing public concern to preserve personal privacy. It must be acknowledged that these restrictions on intelligence activities represent a reaction to past police abuses of civil liberties. The solution appears to be the refinement of police intelligence tactics under strict guidelines, as the 1973 National Advisory Committee on Criminal Justice Standards and Goals recommended.

In response to the gravity and complexity of contemporary terrorism, an interdisciplinary quarterly called *Terrorism: An International Journal* was initiated in 1977, with Jonah Alexander as editor-in-chief. Its aim is intellectual dialogue on terrorism, focusing on such key questions as these: What acts constitute terrorism? What are the underlying causes? How can and should we deal with it? Hans J. Morgenthau is the chairman of the editorial advisory board of this publication.[30]

The role of the media in the coverage of terrorist incidents is a matter of considerable debate. Many analysts, Walter Laqueur among them, contend that press and television have contributed to the growth of terrorism. LEAA's Task Force on Disorders and Terrorism, in a 1976 report, found that "often, after the use of novel and seemingly successful terrorist techniques has been widely publicized, they have been imitated and embellished by other terrorists."[31] The question of the relationship between media coverage and terrorism is similar to the question of the relationship between television and violence. At present, there is no definitive answer to either question. Although there are more than 20,000 homicides committed annually in the United States, there is more to an understanding of this phenomenon than the fact that most homicides get media attention. Yet this is not a valid analogy, because terrorists *do* seek publicity for their cause as a primary aim. Suppose there were little or no publicity given to acts of terrorism?

Hostage taking is often a terrorist tactic. It is not difficult to understand why. As Irving Goldhaber puts it:

> The political terrorist who is willing to risk his own life while he capitalizes upon our cultural reverence for his hostage's life, and hence our commitment to do everything possible to bring the hostage out unharmed from his clutches, has discovered a cost-effective method of creating public awareness of conceivably public acceptance for his cause.[32]

Goldhaber goes on to say that the police have two capabilities in dealing with hostage taking: negotiation and assault. He recommends negotiation so long as the next move of the hostage taker can be predicted with certainty. Assault action begins at the point where negotiation is exhausted.

In discussing terrorism from the viewpoint of police-community relations, the following are relevant questions:

1. What are the causes of various types of terrorism?
2. What are some of the typical strategies and tactics of terrorism?
3. Is terrorism ever morally justified? If so, under what conditions?
4. What counterstrategies and tactics are open to governments and security forces?
5. What are the dangers of underreaction and overreaction?
6. What countermeasures might be taken locally, nationally, and internationally?
7. What standards should guide the media in news coverage of terrorist incidents?

CIVIL DISOBEDIENCE

Collective behavior often reflects noncompliance with generally accepted norms. One of its methods or strategies may be civil disobedience: the deliberate violation of a law, or of a regulation having the force and effect of law, believed to be immoral or unjust. It is a deliberate challenge of civil authority, with the expectation of incurring sanctions, by persons whose values compel their loyalty to what they see as a higher order of authority. It is not anarchy—not utter rejection of all authority—but a choice of authority priority.

Authentic acts of civil disobedience are engaged in by relatively few people, a small minority raising its voice against a prevailing and generally accepted norm or practice. Civil disobedience challenges what the majority deems acceptable, and puts social conscience to a test. Little wonder, then, that acts of civil disobedience are repugnant to many people. The police are especially disturbed by civil disobedience, one reason being that it puts them squarely in the middle between conflicting moral positions on what is usually an emotionally charged issue. The national poll of police opinions conducted by the International Association of Chiefs of Police in 1969 showed that nine out of ten police officers disagreed with the proposition that a person has a right to deliberately disobey a law that he believes to be immoral or unjust. About the same proportion believed that persons who deliberately violate the law to attract attention to their "cause" should be arrested, searched, and booked in the same manner as other violators.[33]

Discussion of the topic of civil disobedience in conferences on police and community relations has been known to become so dominated by feelings as to produce a recommendation that all civil disobedience should be prohibited by law. As Nelson Watson observed, this is equivalent to insisting that it is illegal to do anything illegal. To alleviate some of the tension, some important distinctions should be made in any discussion of civil disobedience. To begin with, it is not always a question of deliberate violation of a law. It may also be a way of protesting a court order. It may be more a matter of taking issue with the way a law is enforced than with the substance of the law itself.

Other distinctions are in the domain of logic. Is civil disobedience illegal? Obviously it is, most of the time. (It could be a protest against a policy, rather than a law.) Is civil violence illegal? Yes. But civil disobedience is not necessarily civil violence, and the latter is not necessarily civil disobedience. Not all illegal acts involve violence, nor is all violence illegal. It is surprising how frequently discussions of civil disobedience bog down in exactly such seeming minutiae, which, on closer examination, are seen to be important distinctions.

Another distinction was advanced by the late John Morsell of the NAACP, who stated in 1964 that a restaurant sit-in or a freedom ride was *not* an act of civil disobedience. He argued that these actions were based on the premise that exclusion from a licensed public facility on the ground of race was a violation of constitutional right. If these acts violated local laws, it was the local laws, not the freedom rides or sit-ins, that defied the law of the land. A school boycott, on the other hand, is civil disobedience. But the boycott of a business firm accused of discriminatory hiring practices is not civil disobedience, for there is no law requiring anyone to buy in that store.[34]

Watson described the relationship between civil disobedience and collective behavior as "disorderly fallout." To illustrate, reactionaries against civil disobedience may form a mob, and a riot is possible. Watson pointed out that most law enforcement is done by the people, not by the police. It is a matter of law observance by most of the people, most of the time. In connection with civil disobedience, however, even when the plan and intentions of the participants are peaceful, nonparticipants may become involved with participants emotionally, and then physically. Suddenly and spontaneously, there is disorder and violence. The police must move in to protect property and persons of whatever persuasion, participants and nonparticipants alike.[35]

Many law enforcement officials feel that a tragic result of civil disobedience is that it encourages young people to adopt an attitude of general disrespect for the law and all public authority. Yet this is largely speculative, and as Watson said, evidence is lacking to prove that there actually is such a transfer. In fact, there is a counterargument that acts of solemn and considered civil disobedience actually cultivate greater respect for *just* law.

Watson added a further point:

> The object of civil disobedience is to call attention to a condition which the participants want to have changed. Naturally, the more widely and dramatically the acts are publicized, the better for the purpose. Unfortunately, this publicity often makes the police look bad, especially if violence breaks out. And not only that, it also gives the officers a lot of hard and unpleasant work to do. And not only that, the cases are often dismissed and the officers then feel that their work was all for naught. So I think we can conclude undeniably that civil disobedience is quite unpopular with the police.[36]

Philosophy: Thoreau and Gandhi

It is evident that civil disobedience is a complicated subject and requires study going beyond superficialities. Some further probing of it seems appropriate.

Henry David Thoreau and Mahatma Gandhi are generally thought of as leading philosophers of civil disobedience. Gandhi tested and changed his ideas on the subject time after time in the course of a lifetime of experiences; Thoreau spent one night in jail and telescoped his thinking into one great essay, *On the Duty of Civil Disobedience*. The following is an attempt to chart a sampling of the main ideas of the two.[37]

Two Philosophies of Civil Disobedience

Thoreau	Gandhi
We should be men first, and subjects afterward. Undue respect for law is dangerous.	The citizen's obligation to the authority of the State depends upon the extent to which the laws of a State are just and its acts nonrepressive. Submission to the State is a price paid for an individual's personal liberty, but it is always a conditional price.
I do not wish to be the agent, through the State, of an injustice to another, or to pursue a neutral life that lends support to the State in some sense.	

Thoreau

There are times when the injustice is so great that a calculus of consequences of civil disobedience is not required—no possible consequences out-weigh the obligation to resist the injustice.

The State has no real utility. In fact, I pity it because it does not know friend from foe. The State does not have a decent, civilized purpose. To go to jail is a way of withdrawing from it. Jail is the only proper place for the just man.

Civil disobedience is a form of political action. Going to jail is a means of communication, with some hope for its public effectiveness.

Gandhi

The very notion of authority implies that the individual is an author and is morally autonomous in some sense; otherwise authority cannot be distinguished from force or power.

The validity of one's appeal to one's conscience is wholly independent of social recognition.

Non-cooperation and passive resistance are distinct from civil disobedience; the latter is a last resort by a select few—a deliberate breach of immoral statutory enactments where one invokes the sanctions of the law and invites penalties and imprisonment.

Civil disobedience presupposes the habit of willing obedience; if a man is not respected generally as law-abiding, his act of disobedience is less authentic.

Civil disobedience is despicable if it is a mere camouflage for some other goal or end, such as a cover for concealed violence.

The civil resister is not an anarchist; he wishes to convert, not to destroy. True civil disobedience is reluctant, it is defensive, and very rare in the well-ordered State.

Mass civil disobedience in the pure sense must be spontaneous, not organized, not manipulative.

The prerequisites for civil disobedience include concern for the justice of the cause; strict non-violence in thought, speech and deed; the capacity and willingness to suffer; moral discipline; humility; and above all, self-purification by good works among the people on behalf of whom one offers resistance.

It is evident that Thoreau's arguments were not analytically strong, but Gandhi recognized—as University of Chicago law professor Harry Kalven has pointed out—"that the power of civil disobedience was that it did not use entirely rational persuasion but a symbolic behavior, because there is a more immediate means of moving a person than simple rational argument."[38]

A Question of Law

Consider what is most often challenged by an act of civil disobedience: the law. The standard definition of law is familiar: it is a rule of reason directed to the common good and promulgated by proper authority. There are questions inherent in each part of this definition. Is a given statute truly *a rule of reason?* Who determines this? By what special insights? By whose reason? Is a given statute truly *directed to the common good?* Again, who determines this? By what standards? And so on. Is a given statute truly *promulgated by proper authority?* From whence does this authority spring?

Scott Buchanan, a former resident scholar of the Center for the Study of Democratic Institutions, reminds us that there are those who take seriously the theory that lawmakers *discover* rather than make law, finding that genuine law is what the people *ought to want.*[39] This means that such things as justice, peace, freedom, and order are *discovered* as products of continuing dialogue among people of diversified background, interests, and perceptions—and this is what "the consent of the governed" in democratic, pluralistic nations should ideally mean.

Buchanan borrows from the theology of the late Martin Buber, who set out to show how the Old Testament—the Torah—could be interpreted as a continuous dialogue between the people and God. It was through this dialogue that the Jews became the chosen people, "the people of the law." The law was not imposed by a tyrannical God, for the people talked back to Him. Buchanan concludes that the Torah is "the demonstration in dramatic form of the doctrine that law is a teacher." The law, therefore, is not dogma; it is "a question to be pursued."[40]

Such a conception of law has implications for civil disobedience. This is not to suggest that *any* act of protest, purportedly for "good cause," is ipso facto justifiable. As Buchanan observes:

> In grammatical terms, laws are obviously imperative sentences; they are, in positivistic terms, commands issued by an authority to be obeyed by subjects on pain of punishment. But if the subjects are free persons who can object, talk back, and disobey, there is at least a moment when the law is a question. . . . If the moment is extended, there will be an argument with many more questions, questions about the jurisdiction of the law, about the meanings of killings, stealing, lying, and adultery, about the purpose of the law and the common good. These are familiar questions in the courts and *mutatis mutandis,* for the legislature and the executive. In fact, whenever the law is in operation, it is itself a question and is up for questioning.[41]

This is not a new doctrine, nor was it invented by Buber. It is cited in the works of Plato, and Gandhi lived it out. Our First Amendment freedoms of speech, press, assembly, and petition are important as individual rights, but under this concept of the law, these freedoms become the apparatus of the continuing dialogue through which—as Buchanan says—laws "become imprinted in the habits and hearts of the citizenry. *They are the means by which the laws are continually improved and adjusted to change.*"[42] Clarence Darrow, the famous criminal lawyer of the 1920s, felt that laws should, like clothes, be made to fit the people they are meant to serve.

This perspective on law certainly makes it no easier for a police officer to deal with a limp civil disobedient. However, there is a certain social and moral drama in what the officer does under such circumstances, and how he does it, for in effect *we are learning law by acting out justice or injustice in the streets.*

The authority of the law in a democratic society is the consent of the governed, freely given, and their willing compliance. However, dialogue and questioning as to what the law should be, and how it should be interpreted and implemented, constitute the essential dynamic of participatory democracy. This is what sociologists refer to as a *consensual* concept of authority in society, of particular importance in comparison with autocratic societies.

Rationale

Challenges to government, law, or policy are inherently threatening and invariably produce questions as to the authenticity, sincerity, or morality of a given action. How can "the real thing" be tested or evaluated? What are the conditions that distinguish ordinary infractions of the law from civil disobedience? "If everyone were to disobey the law, the results would be disastrous; consequently, nobody has that right." True or false?

Such a question goes to the heart of the concept of civil disobedience. To repeat a point made earlier, there are many popular misconceptions of civil disobedience. It should be recognized that many protest actions are not civil disobedience. Some, in fact, are civil *obedience*—for example, distributing literature, parading with a permit, voter registration programs, teach-ins, and picketing with a permit. Another point: civil disobedience is not antilaw; it is in the democratic tradition, and, in the sense of the law as a question, perfectly compatible with the dignity of law.

From the point of view of simple morality, the question of testing a civilly disobedient action may be approached in a manner similar to the question of deciding if a war is just. Some of the queries in such an approach would be:

- Is the issue truly a grave matter? (One does not commit an act of war or an act of civil disobedience frivolously.)
- Have all other reasonable, feasible, possible, conceivable means of resolving the issue been explored?
- Is the act merely an excuse for violence—as Gandhi put it, "a camouflage" for some other purpose? (Does the act have an ordinary criminal intent?)
- Is the act a chosen course, not accidental?
- How clear is the purpose? (To call public attention to injustice, to bring about a change, etc.) Is there a reasonable chance for success in achieving the purpose?
- Is one prepared to accept the consequences of the action? (One should not be surprised if one is arrested and jailed.) What harm may come to other parties as a result?

It is interesting to set these questions beside the conditions delineated by Sidney Hook (compare also with Gandhi) under which individuals—on ethical grounds—may refuse to obey a certain law:

1. It must be nonviolent, peaceful not only in form but in actuality.
2. Resort to civil disobedience is never morally legitimate where other methods of remedying the evil complained of are available.
3. Those who resort to civil disobedience are duty-bound to accept the legal sanctions and punishments imposed by the laws.
4. Civil disobedience is unjustified if a major moral issue is not clearly at stake.
5. Where intelligent men of good will and character differ on large and complex moral issues, discussion and agitation are more appropriate than civilly disobedient action.
6. Where civil disobedience is undertaken, there must be some rhyme and reason in the time, place, and targets selected.
7. There is such a thing as historical timing. Will the cumulative consequences of the action, in the current climate of opinion, undermine the peace and order on which other human rights depend?[43]

Martin Luther King, in the *Letter from Birmingham Jail*, wrote pertinently in this passage:

You may well ask, "Why direct action? Why sit-ins, marches, etc.? Isn't negotiation a better path?" You are exactly right in your call for negotiation. Indeed, this is the purpose of direct action. Nonviolent direct action seeks to create such a crisis and establish such creative tension that a community that has constantly refused to negotiate is forced to confront the issue. It seeks so to dramatize the issue that it can no longer be ignored. . . . I have earnestly worked and preached against violent tension, but there is a type of constructive non-violent tension that is necessary for growth. Just as Socrates felt that it was necessary to create a tension in the mind so that individuals could rise from the bondage of myths and half-truths to the unfettered realm of creative analysis and objective appraisal, we must see the need of having non-violent gadflies to create the kind of tension in society that will help men rise from the dark depths of prejudice and racism to the majestic heights of understanding and brotherhood. So the purpose of the direct action is to create a situation so crisis-packed that it will inevitably open the door to negotiation.[44]

In the same vein, J. L. LeGrande has listed the following tenets:

1. Governmental laws and societal practices may be evil.
2. Every individual has the right and duty to evaluate laws and practices in order to establish their moral propriety.
3. After determining that laws or practices are evil or unjust, an individual is morally obligated to resist their imposition.
4. When the traditional legal remedies have been exhausted or are ineffective, the individual must employ disobedient behavior to dramatize the injustice before society.
5. The violation or disobedience must be public and nonviolent.
6. The individual must be willing to accept the legal penalties or social criticisms that follow as consequences of his acts.[45]

Harrop Freeman of the Cornell University Law School makes the following points:

1. Civil disobedience is a recognized *procedure* for challenging law or policy and obtaining court determination of the validity thereof.

2. Theories of *jurisprudence* recognize the propriety of nonviolent challenge to law or policy.

3. The *obligation to obey the law* is not absolute but relative, and allows for some forms of nonviolent challenge.

4. Protests and civil disobedience should receive *protection under the First Amendment.*

5. Even if the act of protest or disobedience is found to be a technical violation of law, the purpose of the disobedience should in some instances *cause the punishment to be nominal.*[46]

Freeman adds some interesting comments. He says that if civil disobedience were never justified, it would deaden moral and democratic sensitivity and prevent legal change. He points out that many laws are disobeyed in that they are simply ignored, without any active concern by the state. As to the argument that it would be disastrous if everyone disobeyed the law, Freeman calls this an illogical deduction from the specific to the general. The civil disobedient does not urge disobedience of all laws. He does not argue that one disobedience justifies all disobedience.

On this point, Richard Lichtman offers the following observation:

> The civil disobedient can meet the argument that general civil disobedience would produce undesirable consequences only with the counter-argument that this prospective evil is less compelling than the gross brutality or injustice against which the act of disobedience protests. And so, in fact, all such dissenters have contended, from Socrates to Gandhi, that in view of the malignancy of the world, their act of defiance is a necessary course.[47]

Freeman poses the key question: How far is a society willing to go in the latitude it permits for dissent? The minimum level is tolerance, or forbearance without approval. A somewhat greater indulgence would be at the level of peaceful coexistence, as in Immanuel Kant: "Every action is right which, or according to the maxim of which, the freedom of will of each can coexist with the freedom of everyone according to a general law." A third level identified by Freeman is that of simple charity: to love a person, even if one disapproves of his folly or errors—and try to convert him, as in Wordsworth: "By discipline of time made wise, we learn to tolerate the infirmities and faults of others." At a fourth level, according to Freeman, a society might say that the individual has a *right* of dissent (and of civil disobedience) because of the advantages to society of free and open discussion.[48]

Other Interpretations

Other views of the conditions or prerequisites for civil disobedience are instructive. Bayard Rustin, who has worked in civil disobedience movements on every continent, asks these questions of the civil disobedient:

1. Are you attempting to break a law or are you attempting, rather, to adhere conscientiously to a higher principle in the hope that the law you break will be changed and that new law will emerge on the basis of that higher principle?

2. Have you engaged in the democratic process and exercised the constitutional means that are available before engaging in the breaking of law? (Is what you perceive so monstrous that you do not believe there is time for dealing with it by constitutional means?)

3. Have I removed ego as much as it is possible to do so? (Or do I just want to get my picture in the paper?)

4. Do the people whom I ask to rebel feel there is a grievous wrong involved?

5. Am I prepared cheerfully to accept the consequences of my acts?

6. Am I attempting to bring about a new social order by my rebellion, or a new law that is better than the one that now exists?[49]

Rustin says that a seventh question springs from Kant's categorical imperative: Would the world be a better place if everybody, not just in my country and not just those who are black, but everyone in the world did likewise? (What happens to war if *everyone* burns his draft card?)

Rustin's six-point rationale for civil disobedience is also of interest:

1. Civil disobedience in a democratic society is sometimes the only instrument left to dramatize the injustice that has been hidden and to bring it to the surface.

2. Civil disobedience insures religious and civil liberty as nothing else can.

3. Civil disobedience can create and establish just law when legislatures are not necessarily prepared to do it.

4. Civil disobedience forces the implementation of law that is on the books, but which, for a number of reasons, is ignored.

5. No society is safe which does not attempt to curtail civil disobedience but in which there are not individuals who will engage in it.

6. Civil disobedience often affects and directs court decisions.[50]

Another approach is taken by Richard Wasserstrom, formerly of the Stanford Law School, later dean of arts and sciences at Tuskegee Institute. He contends that an act of civil disobedience, as differentiated from other acts of protest, must involve *disobedience of the law*, with no fudging. If an act is performed under a claim of ultimate constitutional right, it is not civil disobedience. On this point, Wasserstrom disagrees with Freeman.[51]

Second, Wasserstrom stresses that the act must be one of *civil* disobedience. This means that it requires nonviolence. Force may sometimes be necessary to overcome oppression, but this is not civil disobedience. Third, an act of civil disobedience must be a public rather than a private act, because its primary function is educative. Willingness to suffer legal punishment as a consequence of the illegal conduct is implied. Also implied is the necessity for prudent choice of technique and integrity of purpose. Civil disobedience involves strategy as well as moral conviction. Sincere belief alone does not justify the employment of this particular pedagogical device.

It is evident that there are some common denominators in the thinking of all whom we have quoted. However, as Wasserstrom indicates, there is no set of mechanical rules by which to determine when disobedience to the law, and particularly civil disobedience, is justified. Neither is there in any other sphere of morality.

SUMMING UP

Joseph Sax, professor of law at the University of Michigan, has addressed himself to what he calls "the miracle of prosecutorial discretion," which produces or ignores criminality virtually at will. The law, he contends, is so vast in its technical coverage and so open-ended in its possibilities for interpretation by police officers, prosecutors, and judges that "it becomes almost meaningless to talk about civil disobedience as if there were conduct which 'the law'—as some external force—declared illegal." It is no easy task, Sax continues, "to make lawyers peek out from behind that supposedly value-free facade, 'the law,' and begin to talk about unjust laws and unjust administration of the law; but out they must come and face the reality of prosecutorial and judicial discretion."[52] Sax wryly observed:

> Nobody is opposed to civil disobedience; people simply want the laws that they deem important to be vigorously enforced and those they consider unfair to be ignored. Most motorists consider the idea of a speedtrap outrageous, but rarely complain when policemen conceal themselves in public washrooms to ferret out homosexuals. The annual antics of American Legion conventioneers are viewed as harmless enough fun, but let political protestors go out in the streets and all the rigors of the law relating to trespass, obstruction of traffic, and disturbing the peace are suddenly remembered, whereupon we are solemnly told that acquiescence in illegality is the first step on the road to anarchy.[53]

There may be those who would say that we have slanted our discussion of civil disobedience. While we would argue this point—our sources agree on some aspects of civil disobedience and disagree on others—there is an obligation of fairness to all sides on a subject so charged with feelings and so open to question.

Following, then, is a series of excerpts from an article by Chicago attorney Morris I. Leibman, whose position may be summarized thus: the crowning achievement of the American constitutional system has been the development of the "law society." But this society has, in recent years, been threatened by organized and deliberate civil disobedience justified by concepts that are semantic traps. The only enduring method of realizing the goals of those who engage in civil disobedience is the use of society's means for orderly change. In Leibman's words:

> No society can give its citizens the "right" to break the law. There can be no law to which obedience is optional, no command to which the state attaches an "if you don't mind."

No individual or group at any time, for any reason, has a right to exact self-determined retribution. All too often retaliation injures the innocent at random and provokes counter-retaliation against those equally innocent. . . . The only solution is the free and open-law society.

. . . Those who reject our legal methods and choose terror, force, violence, hate and bigotry only play into the hands of the international Communist conspiracy. I wish it were possible to have the ideals of justice and freedom in all their perfect form at this moment. But the cry for immediacy is the cry for impossibility. What is possible is to continue patiently to build the structures that permit the development of better justice.

We must be for equality under the rule of law. We can only be for freedom under law, not for freedom against the law. We must avoid unreal questions, e.g., is justice more important than order, or vice versa? Order is the *sine qua non* of the constitutional system.

I cannot accept the right to disobey when the law is not static, and effective channels for change are constantly available. Our legislatures have met the changing times and changing needs of our society, and our courts need not apologize for their continued dedication to the liberty of all men. Our law is not only a guardian of freedom, but the affirmative agent for freedom.

Civil disobedience is an *ad hoc* device at best, and *ad hoc* measures in a law society are dangerous. It is at best deplorable and at worst destructive.[54]

Concluding our discussion of this important topic, we repeat the observation that no comprehensive, general formulas are going to resolve the infinitely varied questions that arise in connection with dissent, protest, and civil disobedience. As we have said, distinctions must be made in the kinds of actions that fall into these categories. The central question is that of the justice with which the law is enforced. Sax argues that the public is responsible for just enforcement:

A public less bedazzled by the mystique of "the law" and more willing to look through to the question of *justness* will inevitably be strengthened in its ability to impose upon public officials pressure to be less (or as the case may be, more) vigorous in seeking to attribute criminality to particular kinds of conduct. . . . To abdicate that responsibility is only to begin the march in law-abiding lockstep toward moral oblivion.[55]

What we have seen of street demonstrations in the recent past leaves many observers questioning the relevance of theoretical-ethical considerations of civil disobedience. The fine-line distinctions of scholarly analysis seem far-fetched to a police officer facing an unruly mob bent on blocking a street. The officer might suggest that these circumstances are hardly conducive to philosophical contemplation. And one would be inclined to sympathize with the officer's position. But somewhat parallel circumstances have failed to discourage inquiry into the ethics of war. Scholarly perspective requires, after all, stubborn and persistent endeavor to deal rationally with behavior, especially in circumstances where action or reaction may be regarded by some as irrational. To this end, theory and philosophy are essential, even when somewhat provocative. Where grave moral questions are at stake, prodence suggests calm deliberation.

NOTES

1. Definitions used in this section are from William J. Goode, *Vocabulary for Sociology* (Flushing, N.Y.: Data-Guide Distributing Corp., 1959). Deviant behavior is defined as action that violates a group norm or rule.

2. Alfred McClung Lee and Norman D. Humphrey, *Race Riot* (New York: Octagon Books, 1967), p. 5.

3. *Detroit Times*, July 17, 1943.

4. Raymond M. Momboisse, "Demonstrations and Civil Disobedience," *Police* 12, no. 2 (1967): 76–82.

5. Herbert Blumer, "Collective Behavior," in Alfred McClung Lee, ed., *New Outline of the Principles of Sociology* (New York: Barnes & Noble, 1946), pp. 203–211.

6. William P. Brown, "The Police and Community Conflict," in A. F. Brandstatter and Louis A. Radelet, eds., *Police and Community Relations: A Source Book* (Beverly Hills, Calif.: Glencoe, 1968), pp. 322–334.

7. Nelson A. Watson, "Group Behavior and Civil Disobedience," in Brandstatter and Radelet, eds., *Police and Community Relations*, p. 108. Reprinted by permission.

8. Ibid., p. 109.

9. *Tinker* v. *Des Moines Independent Community School District*, 393 U.S. 503 (1969); *Hernandez* v. *School District No. 1, Denver, Colo.*, 315 F. Supp. 289 (D. Colo. 1970); *Aquirre* v. *Tahoka Independent School District*, 311 F. Supp. 664 (N.D. Texas 1970).

10. Harry C. Mallios, "Symbolic Expression: The New Battle Facing School Administrators," *Intellect* (Society for the Advancement of Education, New York, N.Y.) 101, no. 2344 (November 1972): 118.

11. U.S., National Advisory Commission on Civil Disorders, prologue to *Report* (from an address to the nation on June 27, 1967).

12. U.S., National Commission on the Causes and Prevention of Violence, preface to *The Politics of Protest: Violent Aspects of Protest and Confrontation* (staff report written by Jerome H. Skolnick) (Washington, D.C.: U.S. Government Printing Office, 1969).

13. U.S., President's Commission on Campus Unrest, *Report: Campus Unrest* (Washington, D.C.: U.S. Government Printing Office, 1970), p. 1.

14. Jerome H. Skolnick, *Politics of Protest*. Reprinted by permission.

15. Ibid.

16. Jerome Hall, "Police and Law in a Democratic Society," *Indiana Law Journal* 28, no. 2 (1953): 133 ff.

17. Ibid. Reprinted by permission.

18. W. P. Lineberry, *Struggle Against Terrorism* (New York: H. W. Wilson, 1977); Albert Parry, *Terrorism: From Robespierre to Arafat* (New York: Vanguard, 1977).

19. P. Wilkenson, *Terrorism and the Liberal State* (Somerset, N.J.: John Wiley and Sons, 1977). See also Sandra Stencel, "International Terrorism," in *Crime and Justice* (Washington, D.C.: Congressional Quarterly, Inc., 1978), pp. 21–44.

20. Michael Waltzer, "The New Terrorists," *The New Republic*, August 30, 1975, p. 13.

21. Central Intelligence Agency, "International Terrorism in 1976" (Washington, D.C.: U.S. Government Printing Office, 1977), p. 15.

22. Central Intelligence Agency, "International and Transnational Terrorism: Diagnosis and Prognosis" (Washington, D.C.: U.S. Government Printing Office, 1976), p. 2.

23. *U.S. News & World Report*, May 22, 1978, p. 31.

24. Lance Morrow, "Terrorism: Why West Germany?" *Time*, December 19, 1977, p. 37.

25. *U.S. News & World Report*, May 22, 1978, pp. 35–36.

26. *Time*, October 31, 1977, p. 45.

27. Jack Anderson, *The Lansing State Journal*, July 7, 1978.

28. There are numerous pertinent articles on terrorism and hostage taking in *The Police Chief* 46, no. 6 (June, 1979). See also Richard W. Kobetz and H. H. A. Cooper, *Target Terrorism* (Gaithersburg, Md.: International Association of Chiefs of Police, 1979).

29. Interview with Dr. Robert H. Kupperman of the U.S. Arms Control and Disarmament Agency, Copyright © *U.S. News & World Report*, March 6, 1978, pp. 66–68.

30. Published by Crane, Russack & Co., Inc., 347 Madison Ave., New York, N.Y. 10017. A biweekly newsletter called *Intersearch* is published by the International Terrorist Research Center, P.O. Box 26804, El Paso, Texas 79926.

31. LEAA Task Force on Disorders and Terrorism, "Report on Disorders and Terrorism" (Washington, D.C.: U.S. Government Printing Office, 1976), p. 9.

32. Irving Goldhaber, "A Typology of Hostage-Takers," *The Police Chief* 46, no. 6 (June, 1979), p. 21.

33. Nelson A. Watson and James W. Sterling, *Police and Their Opinions* (Washington, D.C.: International Association of Chiefs of Police, 1969), p. 59.

34. John A. Morsell, "A Rationale for Racial Demonstrations," in Brandstatter and Radelet, eds., *Police and Community Relations*, p. 148.

35. Watson, "Group Behavior," p. 112.

36. Ibid., p. 113.

37. Adapted from Raghavan N. Iyer, "Gandhi," and Harry Kalven, Jr., "Thoreau," in *Civil Disobedience* (Santa Barbara, Calif.: Center for the Study of Democratic Institutions, 1966). Reprinted by permission.

38. Kalven, "Thoreau," p. 28.

39. Scott Buchanan, "Martin Buber," in *Civil Disobedience*, pp. 29–32.

40. Ibid., p. 29.

41. Ibid., p. 30.

42. Ibid.

43. Sidney Hook, "Social Protest and Civil Disobedience," *Humanist*, Fall 1967.

44. Martin Luther King, Jr., *Letter from Birmingham Jail* (Philadelphia: American Friends Service Committee, 1963).

45. J. L. LeGrande, "Nonviolent Civil Disobedience and Police Enforcement Policy," *Journal of Criminal Law, Criminology and Police Science*, September 1967. Reprinted by permission.

46. Harrop A. Freeman, in *Civil Disobedience*, pp. 5–10.

47. Richard Lichtman, in *Civil Disobedience*, p. 16.

48. Immanuel Kant and William Wordsworth quoted by Freeman, in *Civil Disobedience*, p. 10.

49. Bayard Rustin, in *Civil Disobedience*, p. 11.

50. Ibid., p. 12.

51. Richard Wasserstrom, in *Civil Disobedience*, pp. 18–19.

52. Joseph I. Sax. "Civil Disobedience: The Law Is Never Blind," *Saturday Review*, September 26, 1968, p. 24.

53. Ibid., p. 22. Reprinted by permission. See also Abe Fortas, *Concerning Dissent and Civil Disobedience* (New York: New American Library, 1968).

54. Morris I. Leibman, "Civil Disobedience: A Threat to Our Law Society," *American Bar Association Journal* 51 (1965): 645–647. For those who may regard this as an extremist position, attention is invited to another article: Earl F. Morris, "American Society and the Rebirth of Civil Disobedience," *American Bar Association Journal* 54 (1966): 653–657.

55. Sax, "Law Is Never Blind," p. 56.

12

YOUTH, WOMEN, AND THE ELDERLY

Some readers might protest our referring to youth, women, and the elderly as "minorities." Suppose, then, that we simply avoid an argument and settle for the observation that police-youth relationships are quite often problematic, further that the subject of women in police and criminal justice work merits special attention, and finally that the same may be said for the subject of crime and the elderly. These three matters constitute our agenda in this chapter.

BASIC CONSIDERATIONS OF POLICE–YOUTH RELATIONSHIPS

In an earlier chapter, we reviewed police-minority group relations. Some of our observations apply as well to police-youth relations. With youth who are poor and black, poor and Puerto Rican or Chicano or Native American, police relations are frequently at their worst. Under these circumstances, the often-tense interaction between the police and youth generally becomes even more hostile.

To analyze this phenomenon, we are especially concerned with youthful attitudes in their crucial period of "jelling," although we will give some attention to both younger and older youth. The junior high school age (11 to 15, approximately) seems to be especially interesting in the matter of attitudes toward all authority systems. Youthful attitudes toward the police are a specific example of more generalized attitudes toward authority systems and figures. An assumption, not yet adequately tested by research, is that youthful attitudes toward the police may vary according to the age and probably the sex, socioeconomic status, and racial-ethnic background of particular youth. It may be, too, that police attitudes toward youth also vary according to the situation and tend to interlock reciprocally with youthful attitudes toward the police.

Many would hold that reciprocation in the attitudes of youth and the police is one of the key elements in police and community relations. Better police-community relations in the future depend heavily on today's work in police-youth interactions. This work is too often interpreted to mean merely the prevention of juvenile delinquency, or police handling of the delinquent, or the functions of a special juvenile unit in a police agency. It is not our intention to turn our discussion in the direction of another analysis of delinquency and what the police should do about it. There is, however, a systemic aspect to our subject, in the sense suggested in chapter 4, that relates to *attitudes*. Consequently, we are interested here in the social institutional (systemic) influences that bear on attitudes: family, school, religion, and the like.

ATTITUDES TOWARD AUTHORITY

Recall what we said in earlier chapters about the development of attitudes toward authority. We discussed the process of *socialization* and its effects on self-image and identity. We said that the manner in which authority is imposed upon the child early in life sets a pattern for how the child will view people in authority later in life. Without getting into the relative merits of "discipline" and "permissiveness" in rearing children, we are interested at this point in some underlying reasons for the changing attitudes toward authority and social controls and the changing role and functions of social institutions. Their relevance to the present subject requires repetition of several points made earlier.

In a simple, homogeneous, folkway society, where primary group restraints are strong, attitudes toward authority are simple and efficient because there is a single, dominant code or norm of behavior. Nonconformity in such a society is rare, and when it appears, the sanctions for it are immediate and often quite harsh. On the other hand, in a complex, heterogeneous society, there are many dissonant attitudes toward authority, and social controls are correspondingly numerous and intricate. In such a society, there are numerous competing and conflicting codes or norms of behavior.

Plainly, the appropriate relationship between liberty and security is much more difficult to achieve (because consensus is more difficult to achieve) in the urban, bureaucratic society than it is in the rural, folk society. Also, today, more people insist upon having something to say about questions of liberty and authority. Kenneth Boulding has observed that, as the powers to control men have increased (big government, big business, etc.), the *authority* to do so has come under increasingly severe challenge.

What about change in the social institutions that have such a vital influence on attitudes and behavior—including, of course, attitudes toward authority? Consider, for example, the family of yesteryear in just one respect: it was multifunctional as to social, economic, religious, and educational requirements, as compared with the family of today. Or take what a man did for a living. Once, work in our society was a moral calling, a way of life and an important means of self-identity. Today, one specializes, works as a cog in a bureaucracy, or loses his identity on a production line. Yesterday, government was a local affair centering in the town meeting, and the citizen felt that he had voice and vote in decision making. Today, decisions are made remotely, by "experts." Further, education beyond the early grades was once regarded as the privilege of a few rather than the expectation of most young people. And so on.

What then, in the kind of society ours has become, is the "proper" attitude toward authority and authority figures? Who decides this and how, and on the basis of what standards? Who is really to say that today's youthful attitudes toward authority are worse—or better—than yesterday's? If one contends that today's youth have less respect for law and authority than yesterday's— and that this is bad—it may reveal more about the values of the contender than it does about the values of youth.

PROBING DEEPER INTO YOUTH ATTITUDES

An eminent child psychologist, Cornell University's Urie Bronfenbrenner, writes that children *used to be* brought up by their parents. He asserts that de facto responsibility for upbringing has shifted away from the family to other settings in society where the task is not always recognized or accepted. As Bronfenbrenner states it:

> While the family still has the primary moral and legal responsibility for developing character in children, the power or opportunity to do the job is often lacking in the home, primarily because parents and children no longer spend enough time together in those situations in which such training is possible. This is not because parents don't want to spend time with their children. It is simply that conditions of life have changed.[1]

Professor Herbert Wright and his associates at the University of Kansas have systematically compared the daily life of children growing up in a small town with the lives of children living in a modern city or suburb. The differences are significant. Bronfenbrenner points to how little we know about the influence of the peer group—or of television, for that matter—on the lives of young children. As for adolescents, James Coleman's studies have been helpful. Some of his conclusions were:

> The aspirations and actions of American adolescents are primarily determined by the "leading crowd" in the school society. For boys in this leading crowd, the hallmark of success was glory in athletics; for girls, it was the popular date.
>
> Intellectual achievement was a secondary value. The most intellectually able students were not getting the best grades. The classroom wasn't where the action was.
>
> Home background was the most important element in determining how well a child did at school. This was especially true for Northern whites, applied to a lesser degree to Southern whites and Northern Negroes, and was actually reversed for Southern Negroes, for whom the characteristics of the school were more important than those of the home.
>
> Such items as per pupil expenditure, number of children per class, laboratory space, number of volumes in the school library, and the presence or absence of ability grouping contributed little to the child's intellectual achievement. Teacher qualifications were more important. But the most important factor was the pattern of characteristics of other children attending the same school. If a lower-class child had schoolmates coming from more advantaged homes, he did reasonably well; if all the other children came from deprived homes, he did poorly. But the performance of advantaged children remained unaffected. Good home background appeared to be the difference.[2]

It may be added that a number of studies show that peer pressure to engage in aggressive behavior is very difficult for teenagers to resist in American society.

The general conclusion to be drawn from such references is that "school culture" and "peer culture" (and probably "television culture") have become exceedingly important influences on youthful behavior and attitudes—probably more important, by and large, than "family culture" or "religious culture." What are the implications of this for youthful attitudes toward the police? In the schools, we find what is called "citizenship training," concerned with the preparation of youthful citizens for participation in democratic society, what social scientists call the *political socialization process*. There are numerous indications that this process, which is actually lifelong, is not being managed very well in our society. Witness, for example, the proportion of people who do not vote in general elections. Witness the ignorance of the public in police and governmental matters. Witness what Fred Inbau calls "the philosophy of irresponsibility and unaccountability."[3]

Generally speaking, there is widespread indication of rather adverse youthful attitudes toward the law, law enforcement, and law enforcement officers. Studies bear this out, subject to variations by specific age (the attitudes of grade schoolers are generally more favorable than the attitudes of high schoolers), race, socioeconomic status, and so on. Police officer attitudes toward youth are also interesting to analyze; for example, Reiss reported in his study for President Johnson's Crime Commission that eight out of ten police officers interviewed in Boston, Chicago, and Washington, D.C., saw juveniles as harder to deal with currently than when they started their careers as officers.[4] These officers saw juveniles as changing mainly in that they are more aggressive, defiant, and rebellious, show less respect for law and authority, and are more aware of the restrictions on police conduct. There was some evidence that officers sometimes exacerbate their relations with juveniles by treating them with less civility than they would use with adults.

David Bayley and Harold Mendelsohn reported in their Denver study that police officers immediately think of two groups in which they feel there has been a noticeable decrease in respect for the police in recent years: teenagers and minorities. Some 14.5 percent of the officers interviewed in that study thought that teenagers had a *particularly* unfavorable view of the police. These officers felt that children under twelve were the most favorably disposed; teenagers not in college, the least well disposed; and college students, somewhere in between.[5]

POLITICAL SOCIALIZATION

We have said that youthful attitudes toward the police are part of a larger context of attitudes toward authority and political institutions. So-called citizenship training in schools is directed toward political socialization based on the assumption that attitudes can be stabilized so that authority is obeyed because citizens learn to accept political institutions and leaders (including police) as possessing legal and rightful power. Laurence Kohlberg speaks of the person's *internalizing* the values of the society in a sequential development.[6] From their intensive political socialization study of a large sample of public school children, David Easton and Robert Hess concluded:

> Every piece of evidence indicates that the child's political world begins to take shape well before he even enters elementary school and it undergoes the most rapid change during these years. . . . The truly formative years of the maturing member of a political system would seem to be those years between the ages of three and thirteen.[7]

Until the recent past, much citizenship instruction in the primary grades in this country was in the form of patriotic rituals and rather superficial civic instruction.[8] Relatively few experimental programs at this level departed from the usual pattern. In Los Angeles, an exception was the Patrolman Bill program, which reinforced civics lessons on safety, responsibility, law, and law enforcement. Robert Derbyshire studied this program, with some interesting results.[9]

Derbyshire hypothesized a greater degree of antipathy toward police on the part of pupils of low socioeconomic backgrounds, and a positive change in perception of the police on the part of those low socioeconomic status pupils who took part in the Patrolman Bill program. Third-grade public school pupils from three divergent ethnic and social-class categories were asked to draw pictures of the police officer at work, as an art class assignment. One low socioeconomic status group from Watts was asked to draw the pictures two weeks prior to Patrolman Bill's visit and on the third day following the visit. Each picture was then evaluated by four independent raters on a seven-point scale for the degree of aggressiveness, authoritarianism, hostility, kindness, goodness, strength, or anger expressed in the picture. An additional rater, working separately, performed an item analysis of police task performance on the basis of the picture's content. Comparison of ratings yielded no significant difference between the item analysis and the evaluation by the four raters on the entire field of the picture.

From the results, the image held of police behavior fell into four categories:

- *Aggressive:* fighting, chasing, shooting
- *Assistance* (with negative overtones): unloading a paddy wagon, searching a building, in a car with prisoners, giving traffic tickets
- *Neutral:* walking, riding in a patrol car, directing traffic
- *Assistance* (with positive overtones): talking with children, giving directions

In the pre- and posttest group, there was a significant shift of responses from neutral or negative to positive assistance, which tended to verify the hypothesis that "personal contact with policemen under informal, nonthreatening conditions significantly reduces children's antipathy." Significant differences also appeared between the three highly diverse groups tested: one predominantly black and of low socioeconomic status; one predominantly Spanish-speaking and of low socioeconomic status; and one suburban, middleclass white. The group from Watts expressed less antipathy toward the police after the Patrolman Bill program than was originally expressed by the most positive (white, middle-class) group. Whether similar gains would hold with children of other ethnic or socioeconomic backgrounds is uncertain. Just how permanent is the attitude change resulting from the program is another question: Derbyshire cautioned that "experience of others who have researched attitudes and attitude changes suggests that changes of this nature last only until further negative experiences."[10]

A program similar to Patrolman Bill called Officer Friendly was initiated in Chicago elementary schools (along with a companion program called Our

Firefighter) in 1966, financed largely by the Sears Roebuck Foundation. This program was subsequently launched in a number of other school systems throughout the country. The stated goals of the Officer Friendly program are:

1. Providing the opportunity to develop understanding of the rights, responsibilities and obligations of living in the modern urban environment.
2. Developing rapport between the child and the uniformed officer.
3. Developing a wholesome image of the police department (and other public service agencies) in the mind of the child.
4. Reinforcing basic rules and regulations which govern experiences and activities within the child's environment.
5. Promoting interest in establishing goals and seeking positive and immediate ways of building toward their attainment.[11]

The Officer Friendly program consists of three phases, encompassing an entire school year. The first phase is orientation, where pupils and teacher become acquainted with the program by meeting Officer Friendly and by reviewing materials that lay the groundwork for phase two. The second phase is an instructional period in which Officer Friendly, the teacher, and the pupils participate in a structured teaching-learning experience in keeping with the purposes of the program. Phase three is a reinforcement lesson and includes a merit award presentation conducted by Officer Friendly. At the conclusion of this final phase, all materials go home to be shared with family and friends, to acquaint those around the child with the program. The program is not an isolated unit but a resource unit to supplement the regular social studies curriculum. Unfortunately, the Officer Friendly program has not been evaluated in a manner comparable to the Derbyshire study in Los Angeles.

OTHER PERTINENT STUDIES OF POLITICAL SOCIALIZATION

With various associates, Robert Hess inquired into early political socialization in a study of over 12,000 grade-school children in four regions of the United States. Hess and Easton found that the phenomenon in the realm of politics most apparent to most children is the existence of an authority outside the family and school; this external authority is specifically represented in the Presidency and the police officer. The child becomes increasingly aware of other institutions of authority, such as courts, Congress, and local elected officials, as he grows older. Emotional rather than rational processes explain these cognitions of external authority; favorable feelings are developed, for instance toward the Presidency, long before concrete knowledge of it materializes.

Hess and Torney theorize that reciprocal role relationships are the key to political socialization, that the child learns to see his own behavior in relation to that of some other person or institution, and that role expectations are *learned*. The child learns the rights and duties of the individual in relation to the rights and duties of the system. As Hess and Torney see it, early political socialization begins with an attachment to the nation, which is stable, basic, and exceedingly resistant to change. Authority figures and institutions are perceived by the child as powerful, competent, benign, infallible, and to be trusted. Laws are just and unchangeable, with punishment inevitable for wrongdoing.[12]

The child's points of contact with the system are persons—the president and the police officer. These later become institutions, abstractions, and the *roles* occupied by the persons. The points of contact—the president and the police officer—are also the visible authority figures, and compliance with authority and law is mediated through these figures. Hess and Torney point out that the family can also strongly influence attitudes toward authority, roles, and compliance. While the family and strong authority figures influence *attitudes*, the school appears to be the primary source for content, information, and concepts. For children of low socioeconomic class status, it may be the *only* such source. The Hess-Torney study indicated that the school is a "central and dominant force in the political socialization of the young child," and that the period between grades three and five is especially important in acquiring political information.

Where and how, then, do significant attitude changes occur? First, Hess and Torney point out, there is a fund of positive feeling for the government, especially for the president, that extends to include law, as we have noted. Second, the child's socialization occurs through a "core" of respect for power wielded by authority figures, especially police. But some strain in this image gradually develops. While the school presents a positive image of the police, the child discovers early that the police have the duty, not only to capture lawbreakers, but also to *punish* lawbreakers. This discovery leads to mixed feelings about the police, a beginning of what we earlier identified as the adversary concept. There follows, third, experience in compliant roles at home and school, and finally, normative belief that all systems of rules are fair.

David Easton and Jack Dennis did some extensive work with political socialization data, especially as they relate to the police officer.[13] Perhaps borrowing from Derbyshire, a free-drawing exercise was utilized as an exploratory instrument in which more than 600 elementary school children drew pictures of various authority figures. Evaluation of the pictures was done on the basis of content; for example, whether the police officer was seen as performing a protective, prohibitive, or punitive activity. Over 50 percent of the resultant drawings emphasized prohibitive or punitive activity, which suggested that the officer's capacity to direct and punish emerged as salient to the child. The police officer also appeared in the drawings as physically dominant, being drawn several times larger than such comparison objects as an automobile or other people. The officer was also portrayed as physically and verbally active. Crime detection and prevention activities seldom appeared in the drawings, which suggested that the children were not aware that the police played such roles.

On a questionnaire rating, 78 percent of the second graders and 68 percent of the third graders thought the police officer "can make many people do what he wants." Of the fourth graders tested, 66 percent thought the police officer "can punish many people." Easton and Dennis concluded that "the child is impressed with the presence of a power over and beyond that of father or mother and one that even parents, as potent as they may appear to the child, cannot escape."

Police are seen as the "seed out of which a sense of the legitimacy of the authority structure springs." Through the police, the child "is encouraged in the belief that external authority should and must be accepted," which reinforces a similar posture he is earlier encouraged to adopt toward the president and the government.

Lending further legitimacy to the police officer in the child's eyes is the affective impression of benevolence and dependability. However, these feelings were highly ambivalent, as indicated by the way the children rated the police officer on the questionnaire. For example, while 71 percent of second graders thought the police "would always want to help me if I needed it," and another 14 percent said "almost always," they rated the police officer very low in such statements as "I like him" and "is my favorite."

The conflict here, according to Easton and Dennis, is between the punitive cognitive image and the affective impression of benevolence and dependability. Nonetheless, they concluded that the children in general had a fairly high level of respect for the police officer.

MORAL DEVELOPMENT

Laurence Kohlberg characterizes society as a system of defined complementary roles, in a manner similar to that of Hess and Torney.[14] In becoming socialized into the system, the child must implicitly take the role of others toward himself and toward others in the group. Kohlberg theorizes that these *role-taking* tendencies, representing various patterns of shared or complementary expectations, form the basis of all social institutions.

In the Kohlberg study, the moral development (attitudes and values concerning right and wrong, good and bad) of 75 boys was observed at three-year intervals over a twelve-year period. In addition, cross-cultural studies were carried out in several foreign countries. Kohlberg concluded that moral development is an invariant sequence of six stages, coming one at a time and always in the same order. This sequential nature of moral development did not vary by countries, therefore does not appear to be culture bound. Only the *rate* of development varied.

The six stages may be classified at three levels: preconventional (stages one and two), conventional (stages three and four), and postconventional (stages five and six). At the preconventional level (ages 4 to 10, with significant growth from age 8), "good" and "bad" are interpreted in terms of physical consequences regardless of human meaning or value, or in terms of the physical power of those who enunciate the rules and the labels of good and bad. Toward the end of this period, reciprocity develops as the child enters stage two, but on a pragmatic quid pro quo basis. At stage three (conventional level), "good" is what pleases or helps others and is approved by them; the child conforms to stereotypical images of what is majority or "natural" behavior.

Maintenance of the status quo is perceived as valuable in its own right at stage four. The postconventional level is characterized by a major thrust toward autonomous moral principles with validity and application apart from the authority of groups or persons who hold them, and apart from the individual's identification with these persons or groups. Stage five is the "official" morality of American government as embodied in the Constitution, with a "social contract" orientation defining "right" actions in terms of standards critically examined and agreed upon by the whole society. Stage six is oriented toward decisions of conscience and toward "self-chosen ethical principles appealing to logical comprehensiveness, universality and consistency," principles such as justice, the reciprocity and equality of human rights, and respect for the dignity of human beings as individual persons.

The development of attitudes and values appears to be related to cognitive development, with increasing differentiation and increasing integration at the various stages. Kohlberg theorizes that the reason for the invariant developmental sequence, regardless of culture, is that "each step is a better cognitive organization than the one before it." Each stage takes account of everything present in the previous stage, but the child makes new distinctions and organizes into a "more comprehensive or more equilibrated structure."[15]

As an afterthought regarding programs of the Patrolman Bill and Officer Friendly type, it may be noted that we do not know enough about the role played by the socializers—teachers, police, and parents—and the extent to which such programs affect *their* attitudes. This would appear to be a *probable* correlative of the effects upon the attitudes of the children. It is surprising how much such programs often teach the socializers about political institutions; also, teacher and parent attitudes toward police, and police-officer attitudes toward teachers and parents, are worthy of study, particularly as they might influence children's attitudes.

William Dienstein's work might be mentioned in this regard. He found something of the same conflict as Pfiffner did in the relationships among police, social workers, educators, and probation officers. Dienstein's primary interest was in the causes of delinquency, and he concluded:

> While each agency is dealing with delinquency, and each may handle the same violator, their approaches to the same problem tend to take on polar aspects—control and punishment on the one hand, and treatment on the other—and they find no route to mutual understanding, communication, or cooperation. Working thus, at cross purposes, they cannot hope to succeed.[16]

If these conflicting patterns and goals of behavior (in Pfiffner's terms, the police-rehab conflict) are based on significantly different interpretations of the needs and characteristics of youngsters themselves, the socialization process may be correspondingly unsuccessful. In short, it is possible that some of the ambivalence that develops in the attitudes of children toward the police and other authority figures may be due to divergent and conflicting values of the several occupations working with youth.

Other significant studies bearing on youthful attitudes toward the police give plentiful evidence that adults and youth are not in meaningful contact and that adults admit their inability to understand certain youthful behavior. Various analysts have identified a distinctive adolescent subculture, Franklin Patterson and James Coleman among them.[17] We have already mentioned some of Coleman's thinking, to which may be added:

> With his fellows, he (the adolescent) comes to constitute a small society, one that has most of its important interactions within itself, and maintains only a few threads of connection with the outside adult society.[18]

John Clark and Eugene Wenninger's findings regarding the attitudes of juveniles toward legal institutions support the notion of a general antiauthority syndrome on the part of juveniles and a common rejection and hostility toward certain juveniles on the part of parents, school teachers, and representatives of legal institutions.[19] Clark and Wenninger found that socioeconomic class was not closely related to the attitudes of youth toward legal institutions. But there were notable differences in such attitudes in different communities that they studied.

A Detroit study by William Wattenberg and Noel Bufé concluded that time spent by a police officer with a youth is highly influential in favorably affecting the attitudes of youth toward the police and legal institutions.[20] Other studies—for instance, of the Youth Service Corps project of the Detroit Police Department, and of the Positive Actions for Youth project in Flint, Michigan—reached the same conclusion. But in the Detroit program, a significant percentage of the youths maintained a negative attitude toward police, including 10 percent who did not believe that police are necessary in society, and 12 percent who felt that police do more harm than good. David Krebs found a group of delinquency-prone youths who were not amenable to positive change because of a lack of relational ability in their personality background.[21]

Many empirical studies have dealt with intergenerational conflict. For example, Gerald Pearson attributes the problem to the emerging ego of the adolescent in interaction with the older generation, which manifests stubborn resistance to the development of a personal identity and the assumption of adult roles by the adolescent. Robert Amos and Reginald Washington discuss the differences between teachers and pupils in identifying student problems. In this study, teachers identified fewer problems as characteristic of students than did the students themselves and appeared especially unaware of the extent of student problems with money, work, the future, and health and physical development.[22]

JUNIOR HIGH SCHOOL YOUTH

It mentioned earlier that the junior high school or middle school age group (11 to 15) is widely regarded as especially relevant in the study of changing youthful attitudes toward the police and authority in general. Several notable studies with this focus have been undertaken. Robert Portune studied 1,000 Cincinnati junior high school students in a pioneer study;[23] he and his associates have continued to plow new ground in subsequent projects. His investigations provide evidence that the beat patrol officer lacks clear understanding of adolescent behavior and, correspondingly, that adolescents appear to have little understanding of the police officer and his role. Portune writes:

> The obligation to develop favorable attitudes toward law enforcement is especially pressing in the junior high school. Junior high school students are in a transition period, breaking away from the opinions of mom and pop, trying to fit society to their own personalities and egos, developing their own attitudes toward the world around them. I think we have to catch them at this age. School people are more and more coming to the realization that early adolescence is a key period in life, especially with respect to attitude formation. Thus, with the school's growing responsibility for attitude formation and the junior high school youngster's growing importance, our target group seems well chosen. . . .
>
> Perhaps there are isolated social studies programs in isolated school districts that concentrate on the particular institutions of law enforcement—perhaps there are programs designed to build favorable attitudes through attitude research that we hope to achieve our objectives.[24]

Portune found inconclusive evidence as to the effect of socioeconomic level on attitudes of youth toward police. This coincides with the Clark and Wenninger finding. However, Donald Bouma and his associates found—in studying junior high school youth in several Michigan cities—an inverse relationship between social class and antagonistic attitudes toward police among adolescents.[25]

Relying considerably on Portune's work, Martin Miller and associates at the National Center on Police and Community Relations at Michigan State University conducted a study of Lansing junior high school youth in 1968. They developed a design for evaluation, in terms of attitude change among pupils, of a unit of instruction in citizenship education placed in the curriculum of four Lansing junior high schools during the school year 1967–68. The actual instruction was handled by police-teacher teams over a period of four weeks. The evaluation design was a test-retest, longitudinal pattern with a control group provision. The instruments used included a general information sheet, the Short-Nye Self-Reporting Delinquency Scale (1958), the Portune Attitude-Toward-Police Scale (1966), the Clark Attitudes-Toward-Legal-Institutions Scale (1964), the Rokeach Value Survey (1967), and a sentence completion technique tailored for the project by the research team.[26]

An indication of one aspect of the results of this study has been provided in earlier references to the values of police officers.[27] Beyond this, the MSU study found that the values of teachers and police officers who work with children come across loud and clear to the children and are reflected in children's attitudes toward what the study calls "compliance systems." The research also disclosed slightly positive changes in children's attitudes toward police as a result of the instruction and suggested that the socioeconomic background of the children did not appear to be a significant factor in these attitudes, although the MSU researchers agreed with Portune that the evidence was inconclusive.

These early efforts to study teenagers' attitudes toward the police are interesting for their method as well as findings. More recent studies have not been significantly different.

GANG ATTITUDES

Gang culture and its indigenous attitudes toward police and legal institutions has been a matter for special attention in the consideration of police-youth relations. We have suggested some of the flavor of this in various places in this text.[28]

One aspect of the matter appears to be of singular importance. The point is one analyzed by James Q. Wilson, Jerome Skolnick, and others. It pertains to the patrol officer's "signals" of *danger* and *impropriety* in confronting a citizen. As Wilson puts it:

> The patrolman believes with considerable justification that *teenagers* [italics ours], Negroes, and lower-income persons commit a disproportionate share of all reported crimes; being in those population categories at all makes one, statistically, more suspect than other persons; but to be in those categories *and* to behave unconventionally is to make one a prime suspect.[29]

This attitude affects the officer's handling of situations on the street. As Wilson observes, from the standpoint of those who are "handled," it appears as license for the police officer "to speak harshly or discourteously, to search without cause, and to behave in a patronizing manner." In the extreme, it means actually to be manhandled physically. Resentment about this kind of treatment is likely to be keen among young men on the street, especially when they are associated in gangs.

Alvin Echols has pointed to a related aspect of this matter:

> Young people are rebelling against the hypocrisy of a society that sets certain values and then lives up to their opposite. Young black offenders can find few good examples inside or outside their community, while the conditions which make delinquent acts an attractive choice are created and maintained by the entire society. The strategy set up by the society to contain black juvenile delinquency has three elements: the deadline—keeping blacks in black neighborhoods; vengeance—a judicial and confinement system that punishes and does not rehabilitate; and tribute—programs to buy off trouble temporarily. This strategy has worked only in the sense of making poor blacks the most frequent victims of black juvenile crime. The blame for the strategy's failure to reduce crime has been placed on the black culture rather than the society that devised the strategy and carries it out.[30]

DISAFFECTED YOUTH

This brings us to the matter of disaffected youth, particularly in relation to the civil rights movement of the 1960s. Youthful disaffection with the establishment is, of course, not a new phenomenon, nor is it something uniquely American. But it did assume an unprecedented character in this country during the past decade. This disaffection has troubled many people, not least of all the police, who are invariably involved whenever *what is* comes under serious challenge by significant numbers of the population bent upon change to what they believe *ought to be.*

Recent years have seen an impressive assortment of studies, analyses, dissertations, and "pundit-ry" pertaining to the youth problem. Again, as with race relations, we seem to understand pretty well what the problem is. At least there is an abundance of plausible diagnostic theory. The difficulty, as with race, ecology, and poverty, is that we seek to solve the problem without seriously disturbing anyone or without changing the things that need changing. As Echols says, we mount programs to buy off trouble temporarily—programs that deal with symptoms rather than with causes—programs of the "too little and too late" variety.

When we speak of "the youth problem," what are we talking about exactly, and what has it to do with police and community relations? By and large, it appears that youth today—and we have in mind particularly youth of high-school and college age—are better educated, more morally and politically sophisticated than past generations. Any such generalization will be questioned by some who may ask, for instance, "What do you mean by 'morally and politically sophisticated'?" We mean, as an example, the idealism of youth, as it has been reflected in participation in the civil rights movement, in antiwar protest, in ecological-environmental and Peace Corps programs, and in sundry activities that have prodded universities and other institutions to do some long overdue thinking, evaluating, and changing. We think this is moral and political sophistication, however erratic and amateurish.

As Skolnick has said, such direct action by youth—with the disaffection of student activists, their pessimism over the possibility of genuine reform, and frequent resort to tactics of confrontation—cannot be explained away as high jinks, or as a matter simply of personality maladjustment, or of youthful intransigence, or simply as delinquency.[31] The ideology of youthful protest and activism has focused on several identifiable areas. One is civil rights and race relations. Another is war—war in general in the case of pacifists, the war in Southeast Asia more particularly with youth who were not necessarily pacifists—Selective Service, ROTC, the military-industrial complex, the Pentagon, and so on.

Still another focus has been environment and ecological problems. Women's liberation has attracted some youthful activists; a few have gravitated to organizations such as FREE (Fight Repression of Erotic Expression). Villification of the police has been common ideological ground for all youthful activists. The campus encounters of a few years ago between the police and demonstrators were frequently vitriolic, sometimes intensely violent, and tended to aggravate tensions and make even minimal communication unthinkable. In such circumstances, the "generation gap" becomes a horrendous abyss. We quoted Seymour Lipset earlier in his characterization of these confrontations as "the most extreme example of deliberate provocation which the police have ever faced." Writing in 1969, Lipset elaborated:

> It is doubtful that the American New Left students will ever come to see the police in a sympathetic light, as exploited, insecure, alienated members of the under-privileged classes. As members of the first leftist youth movement which is unaffiliated with any adult party, they are unconcerned with the consequences of their actions on the political strength of the larger left-wing movement. To a large extent, their provocative efforts reflect the biases of the educated upper middle class. Lacking a theory of society and any concern for the complexities of the "road to power"

which have characterized the revolutionary Marxist movement, they are prepared to alienate the police, as well as conventional working-class opinion, in order to provoke police brutality, which in turn will validate their total rejection of all social institutions. Hence, we may expect a continuation of the vicious circle of confrontation and police terror tactics.[32]

CAMPUS UNREST

The Kerner Commission (National Advisory Commission on Civil Disorders) underlined the youthful thrust of the civil rights movement in the 1960s. According to this commission, it was college student sit-ins in the South during the winter and spring of 1960 that marked a decisive break with the past. Even though student demonstrations in the South ended in what seemed to be failure in many instances, the participating youth "had captured the imagination of the Negro community and to a remarkable extent the whole nation." The commission went on to say:

> The Southern college students shook the power structure of the Negro community, made direct action temporarily preeminent as a civil rights tactic, speeded up the process of social change in race relations, and ultimately turned the Negro protest organizations toward a deeper concern with the economic and social problems of the masses.
> Involved in this was a gradual shift in both tactics and goals: from legal to direct action, from middle and upper class to mass action, from attempts to guarantee the Negro's constitutional rights to efforts to secure economic policies giving him equality of opportunity, from appeals to the sense of fair play of white Americans to demands based upon power in the black ghetto.[33]

The point is that the civil rights movement of the 1960s was largely a *youth* movement. Studies of serious riot and disorder situations in 1967–68 pointed out the high proportion of youth and young people participating. The student movement in civil rights revolutionized the existing structure of black civil rights organizations. For instance, the organizing meeting of the Student Nonviolent Coordinating Committee (SNCC), at Raleigh, North Carolina, in April 1960, was convened by Martin Luther King, but within a year this group considered King too conservative and broke with him.

The President's Commission on Campus Unrest, in the aftermath of the tragedies in the spring of 1970 at Kent State University and at Jackson State and the attendant student strikes and class boycotts on many campuses, listened to witness after witness attribute the main causes of student demonstrations and disorders to problems of the larger society: the war in Vietnam, racial discrimination, poverty, pollution of the environment, and so on.[34] This commission carried on its work under difficult conditions: a combination of the intense emotionalism aroused by, and the complex nature of, the problem it was charged to study, plus the coincidence of its investigations with an off-year national political campaign. Chairman William W. Scranton warned that "playing politics with the problems is to guarantee further alienation and radicalization of young people."[35] He may have had in mind the words of President John

F. Kennedy, spoken to the Organization of American States ten years earlier: "Those who make peaceful revolution impossible make violent revolution inevitable."

The general theme of the commission's report on campus unrest was that there is blame enough for all, and it appealed to all sectors to join urgently in national reconciliation. As usual, there was an inordinate preoccupation, in the wake of publication of the commission's report, with ascribing blame for the problem: the president, the administration, "permissive" parents, university administrators and faculty, the students, the police, the National Guard, an apathetic public. Again, "to pin it on somebody" seemed to be more important than to understand the problem and take steps to deal with it. In this way, existing divisions are aggravated.

The commission recommended that police and National Guard forces be better trained to deal with campus disturbances in a firm but nonlethal manner. It also called for greater coordination among local, state, and college security forces and clearer guidelines for action in campus disorder situations. It held that those who commit criminal acts should be sternly prosecuted. It asked universities to spell out specific codes of permissible conduct and pleaded for more effective self-policing by faculty, students, and administrators. It urged more federal support for higher education, particularly for black colleges. The nation's slow response to the issues of war and race, the commission said, had contributed to the escalation of student disorder. Moral leadership from the president was cited as essential to prevent violence and create understanding.

Clearly, the Commission on Campus Unrest repeated and emphasized points that had been made earlier by other bodies and sources. The conflict in cultures between the young and the old had been identified in many quarters. The racist character of American society had been rather thoroughly analyzed by the Kerner Commission. President Johnson's Crime Commission had been concerned about such things as the need for greater coordination and better training of police operations and personnel. The violence phenomenon had been the focal concern of another presidential commission. All of these commissions had, in one way or another, pointed to the signs of corrosion in America's social institutions. In 1968, the Carnegie Commission on Higher Education had recommended increased federal aid to colleges and universities with emphasis on equal opportunity for low income students, easing problems of minority students, and spreading the community college movement to all the states.

Indeed, in July 1970—several months before issuance of the report of the Commission on Campus Unrest—presidential advisers Alexander Heard and James Cheek had called for greater awareness of student attitudes and more student participation in the formulation of foreign and domestic governmental policies. Their memorandum described the deep moral commitment underlying student revolt, its seriousness of purpose, and its sincere intent to eliminate what students believed to be weaknesses in American society. In effect, the Heard-Cheek message was this: our youth are trying desperately to tell us something of great importance; let us listen to them, and let us be guided by their counsel "as full-fledged constituents of government."[36]

The Heard-Cheek memorandum also spoke of four basic causes of "the communication problem" with college youth:[37]

1. The President uses words that mean one thing to him and something different to many students.
2. What the President regards as successes, students often regard very differently.
3. To some students, the President appears not to understand the nature of the crisis that has come over the country.
4. The President and some students proceed from vastly different assumptions.

It should be borne in mind that Heard and Cheek were special presidential advisers; their recommendations focused on what they saw as a need for presidential initiative in various facets of the situation.

In a survey conducted for the President's Commission on Campus Unrest by the Urban Institute, a Washington research organization, it was disclosed that:

- Campus disturbances had occurred most often at large, eastern, liberal arts colleges with high admission standards and ROTC programs.
- The three reasons most frequently cited by college administrators, faculty and students for campus disturbances were the war in Indochina, lack of internal campus communication, and the perceived unresponsiveness of the Federal government to domestic problems.
- Only 22 percent of the smallest colleges reported incidents of any kind, compared with 60 percent of the largest colleges.
- Violent incidents and incidents of all types occurred about twice as often in liberal arts cilleges and those with relatively high spending per student, compared with other categories.[38]

Few observers analyzed the situation as astutely as Terry Sanford, president of Duke University and former governor of North Carolina:

This college generation needs no apologist. These students are more closely allied than we might realize with that remarkable group of men who rethought all prior concepts and precepts of government, and then produced our Constitution nearly two hundred years ago. Their instincts are humanitarian. They are convinced that the individual is the denominator that counts. They take their freedoms very seriously, although sometimes a little too self-consciously. In the students' rethinking of our institutions and society, we may all be the beneficiaries.[39]

THE CAMPUS TODAY

The campus unrest between 1967 and 1971 shook our colleges and universities, our high schools, the police, and many other social institutions. Notre Dame's president, Father Theodore M. Hesburgh, made this point:

Maybe the university is the only place on earth where we can bridge the generation gap by common moral concern on the part of young and old, faculty and students. Granting that students are often naive in their concern for instant solutions to very complicated problems, granting their addiction to absolute black and white judgments in matters that are often very gray, granting their lack of a sense of history,

their rupture with tradition, and their inability to appreciate experience and competence, they still are concerned and are unafflicted by the anomie that is the cancer of
so many of their elders.[40]

Worthy of note, also, was a report released in 1970 of a study of the attitudes
of almost 7,000 junior and senior high-school students in Greater New York and
Philadelphia by the sponsor, the Center for Research and Education in American Liberties, Teachers College, Columbia University. This study, done with a
grant from the U.S. Office of Education, found that most student unrest *at the
high-school level* was not basically over racial and national political issues. This
marked a difference between high-school and college unrest. More than 50
percent of the high-school students surveyed stressed issues of school governance and individual rights as sources of conflict. These high-school students
reported that 68 percent of their hang-ups were with persons in authority, and
only 20 percent with their peers. The Columbia University researchers concluded:

> In all schools, in the urban ghetto and suburbs, the incidents of conflict reported by
> students involve school governance. Of all American institutions, it is particularly
> ironical that the one institution charged with the mission of teaching democracy is
> usually perceived by the student as one that leaves him powerless.[41]

Climaxed by the tragedies of Kent State and Jackson State, a total of 524
educational institutions experienced disruptive protests during the 1969-70
school year, resulting in fourteen deaths and more than $9 million in property
damage. By the fall of 1970, many college students began to wonder whether
they had been manipulated by radicals. The radicals seemed to be quarreling
among themselves, and their motives began to look more like commotion than
reform. Important changes had been instituted in many colleges, however
belatedly, to meet legitimate student complaints and to improve communication. College administrators were dealing more sensibly with student grievances. Campus security forces were learning to react more sensitively to
student antics. Faculty members remembered that academic freedom and intellectual pursuit require a peaceful, noncoercive environment. And during the
summer of 1970, no fewer than thirty-two state legislatures passed punitive
laws pertaining to campus unrest.

A report of a special task force of the National Education Association
summed things up pretty well:

> A revolution in rights has begun throughout our society during the last decade.
> Those who claim rights are being required to recognize the rights of others. A man's
> right to control other men is being challenged. A man's right to make his own
> decisions and act on them is being recognized and exercised. . . . Out of the struggle,
> a more balanced concept of rights is emerging.[42]

Unquestionably, another notable event was the extension of the vote to
eighteen-year-olds, and a corresponding adjustment in the tactics of politicians.[43] The radical gap left by the demise of Students for a Democratic Society
was filled, to some extent, by the communes, collectives, and cadres. There
seemed to be as much or more attention to self-rehabilitation as there was to
the cause of peace or to "bagging" ROTC. A survey during the summer of 1970

of fifty colleges and universities by the League for Industrial Democracy found that what was once a more or less unified movement with uniform goals, following a widely accepted leadership, had become a melange of grouplets, projects, and styles "with no shared sense of direction, and very often with profound and even bitter internal differences."[44] There were many bomb threats in and around schools and colleges during the fall of 1970, and a few actual explosions—the most serious occurring in August at the University of Wisconsin. By and large, however, the threats seemed to be far more a matter of harassment by pranksters and practical jokers than they were inspired by radical student elements. (It is easier, of course, to say this in retrospect than it is at the point of administrative decision whether or not to order a school closed in the case of a bomb threat.)

In late November 1970, an assemblage of students, street people, revolutionaries, faculty members, and assorted curiosity-seekers took place at the State University of New York in Buffalo. The week-long activities included poetry readings, films, talks, puppet shows, and "spontaneous outbursts"; it was called "The New Nation Celebration." While its advertised purpose was to "help fuse together all aspects of revolutionary culture—spiritual, political and social," only about a dozen hands went up when the throng was asked how many were "really politically active." Allen Ginsberg appeared more as an entertainer than as a guru of the college generation.[45]

In the aftermath of the election in November 1970, James Reston wrote in the *New York Times:*

> Somehow, the students seem more interested in the personalities rather than the problems of American politics. They seldom express any allegiance to either major political party, have very little to say about any of the Democratic party's Presidential candidates, but say a great deal about President Nixon and Vice President Agnew, most of it critical and some of it unpublishable.
>
> In short, for the moment, a lot of them seem to be saying that national politics is not very relevant to their lives, but they are muttering about it rather than shaking their fists and spoiling for physical confrontations, as they were last spring.[46]

Clearly, the American campus is a dynamic environment where attitudes and behavior patterns are extremely fluid. In the 1970–71 academic year, things "quieted down," and so it has generally remained. But every professor, every administrator, and every student was influenced by the period of unrest. Old ways were recast. There was a brief flare-up in June 1972 over the mining of Haiphong harbor, but the memory of campus events of two years earlier prompted many peace demonstrators to wonder whether anyone was listening—or really cared.

Grades and careers have again become major concerns of college students. Suitable jobs upon graduation are much harder to locate, and hard-pressed parents cannot indefinitely sustain financial support. Thus, the demands of making ends meet—"getting it together"—get top billing these days in the priorities of college students, and this has a sobering effect on campus cause-related, ideological activities. There is a prevailing cynicism about social problem solving, nurtured by Watergate and related public disclosures.

Time magazine has referred to this as the "self-centered generation." As one student put it: "Students still care but not with the old passion. There's no unpopular war going on now."[47] If you call a riot, nobody comes. Eating regularly has to take precedence over street demonstrations and protest, so studying and working one's way through school are the important concerns.

To soften the blow, beer and toga parties are "in." Marijuana may have slipped a little in popularity, but it is still commonplace and $5 fines for possession are largely ignored. Hard drugs are comparatively rare, although cocaine has come on in recent years. Student consumption of alcohol is a matter of increasing concern. Cheating is not much discussed, so it is difficult to determine whether there is more or less of it. The things that arouse student interest are tuition increases, housing shortages and landlord gouging, parking spaces, and various aspects of impersonalized academic bureaucracy.

DRUGS AND YOUTH

Drug addiction is not, of course, a problem exclusively or necessarily of youth. It is not our intention here to canvass this vast and complex subject and all that has been written about it in the growing anxiety of recent years. However, certain aspects of drug culture are of deep concern in police and community relations. The basic problem for the police is how to deal with clashing moral positions in the community, corresponding to divisions of opinion as to what the criminal code should say about drugs, and with more "nice families" in the community with "hooked" members. For the police, it is the old story of trying to find community consensus where there is none. It becomes a question, to use Banton's terms, of police authority as against police power. The problem is further complicated by the connection with organized crime through illegal suppliers of drugs. The plain fact is that doing something about street crime in our cities today means, most of all, doing something about hard drugs.

A good beginning is to try to understand what is happening and why, and there is a monumental literature to refer to for help in this. Taking drugs is a species of "cop-out," a form of social escapism, like alcoholism. For some addicts, it is a kind of ultimate rebellion that supplies boldness for acts that are, as the saying goes, "pretty far out."[48] Yet, we should be wary of single-track explanations. People take drugs for all sorts of personal reasons, and in this sense there is no such thing as *the* drug problem. As Horace Sutton puts it:

> Not merely a youthful frivolity to be equated with the roarings of the Twenties, not just the trappings of a new world order, not only the enlightened way of life of an untethered generation, the drug epidemic may be the shadow of an end-of-the-century plague. It may also be only one part—the more visible part—of a larger set of socio-medical problems: suicides and alcoholism as well as narcotism, in which few medical advances have been made. Society is reacting strongly against drugs (which in New York accounts for only one-sixth as many deaths as alcoholism) because it afflicts the young and the innocent and breeds crime.[49]

Substance abuse is a complex subject. There is no point in trying to reduce it to a few paragraphs here. Public attitudes toward drugs are highly emotional, sharply divided and therefore controversial, and, in this country, extremely unstable. The result is that attempts to deal with the matter through the criminal code—once sadly attempted in the case of the Eighteenth Amendment—have not worked out very satisfactorily. This has meant that relations between the police and the policed are often strained when the issue at hand is the enforcement of such laws. Moreover, drugs are frequently connected with organized crime, widely perceived as sinister and bewildering. This mystique tends to discourage community initiative in coping with drug problems, many citizens feeling that it's a job for professionals, or that nothing can be done.

COMMUNITY CONCERN AND RIGHTS OF YOUTH

Every community (and every police agency) worries a lot about its young people. Adults spend considerable time and money on programs aimed at helping youth, "keeping them out of trouble." Each adult generation feels sure that "our kids ain't what they used to be." One can agree or disagree with such a statement without knowing what it really means, because there is no way to check it.

Contemporary alarm about the problems of youth, therefore, may be the same old generational cycle merely repeating itself. On the other hand, there may be something really special this time around. No one can be sure. While avoiding any such judgment, the following are examples of the kind of events that cause the current widespread concern:

- More young people are being arrested for serious crimes, state by state. But public funds to finance juvenile programs are being reduced. In 1974, Congress passed a Juvenile Justice and Delinquency Prevention Act. However, the implementation of the act has lagged in various ways, including appropriations.
- Violence in urban schools has soared in the past decade, and it has been spreading to suburban and rural areas.
- Cheating on the college campus is a constant concern.
- Some 26 million Americans have tried marijuana, with use among youngsters of school age alarming many people. In Michigan, the state Office of Substance Abuse Services estimates that the social costs of alcohol abuse in that state are $1.5 billion, and for miscellaneous drug abuse, $420 million.
- Derelicts on urban skid rows are younger, on the average, than they were years ago. More and more are in their twenties; without skills or even a high-school diploma, many are unemployable. Alcohol is the pervasive problem.
- Runaway and "throwaway" youngsters are roaming the country in numbers hitherto unthinkable. (A throwaway, or "push out," is an unwanted child who is encouraged by parents to leave home.) Tight economic conditions are a factor; so are increases in divorce and in emotional instability of the type reflected in child abuse.

- The hydralike problems of youth include several curious paradoxes. For example, there is the matter of schooling. On the one hand, it is estimated that there are two million American children who want to go to school but are forced out by school officials and policies. If a child is truant, the penalty is often suspension. Some cannot attend because of conditions related to poverty. Others seem to be out because they are black, or Spanish-speaking, or in some other way different from the majority. Some are adjudged retarded without having been tested. At the higher levels of education, there are frequent reminders that discrimination has by no means disappeared. A major national commitment made during the 1960s to increase the number of blacks attending college seems to have been forgotten; black college enrollment has been going down for the past few years.

- To complete the paradox, there is the kind of dropout who is out of school because he or she doesn't want to go. This side of the problem is also of grave concern.

On the more positive side, some progress has been made in questions of children's rights. For example, Public Laws 93-380 and 94-142 provide for "an individualized, appropriate, free public education in the least restrictive environment."

Yet much remains to be done in the area of children's rights, including the question of the procedural rights of children under the law. In Michigan, seventeen is referred to as "the witching age" for youth in trouble: there are no programs, no funds, and no facilities to help the youth who is neither child nor adult; therefore, the courts are looked to for assistance, prompting fresh interest in the juvenile code.

In numerous states, Michigan included, children under eighteen can be punished for so-called status offenses, crimes that would not be crimes if committed by an adult. Truancy and running away are examples, along with smoking, drinking, curfew violations, ungovernability, waywardness, and others. The National Council on Crime and Delinquency sees status offenses as unfair on the grounds of denial of due process. There is movement in various states to revise the juvenile justice code to eliminate status offenses in a way supportive of children's rights. In the view of those backing such change, the essential issue is equal protection. The movement for children's rights has precipitated lively debate, at base an argument over the concept of parental authority.

However, children's rights is not a new issue. In 1967, the U.S. Supreme Court, in a single decision (*in re* Gault), brought about a reexamination of the entire relationship between children and the state. The result has been accommodation of constitutional due-process standards in juvenile proceedings, making such proceedings more adversary in the manner of legal machinery for adults. Some see these developments as undermining parental responsibility for the behavior of minor children. The question of whether teenagers should be able to secure medical services where sex is concerned, without involving their parents, is causing wide controversy.

More recent Supreme Court decisions (typically by five-to-four margins) herald the end of schools' unquestioned control over students. One such decision, in 1969, argued that students "don't shed their constitutional rights at the schoolhouse gate."[50] Another, in early 1975, held that students have a constitutional right to prompt notice and hearing for punishment even in a case as minor as a single day's suspension. Public education was judged a property interest protected by the due-process clause of the Fourteenth Amendment. In still another case, a month later, the Supreme Court made it easier for students to sue school board officials who deprive them of due-process rights. Many educators have said that these decisions still do not go far enough. Others retort that an increasingly adversary relationship is being engendered among students, teachers, administrators, and parents.

On the surface, these questions seem to bear little relevance to police and community issues. Yet closer examination reveals that there is little difference in substance, where the rights of youth are concerned, between the schoolhouse door and the jailhouse door. In this sense, the treatment of children by teachers and by police officers has much in common.

WOMEN'S RIGHTS

The matter of the rights of women in our society has been at least as newsworthy in recent years as the matter of the rights of children and youth. Again, this is not the appropriate place to cover this labyrinthian subject. There is, however, an aspect of it that requires our attention, suggested by our earlier discussion of affirmative action, more specifically as it pertains to women in criminal justice.

Why discuss this in a text preoccupied with police and community issues? There are several reasons, beginning with the general observation that prevailing assumptions about feminism in a society affect every facet of public services, surely including police and criminal justice activity. Lucy Komisar, former vice-president of the National Organization for Women, writes:

> The definition of manhood that judges masculinity on a scale of power, dominance, toughness, violence, and aggression is anathema to feminists, partly because women have been its chief victims. Rather than insist that women, too, ought to feel free to express these traits, feminists assert that males and females ought to develop a new human ethos based on an end to hierarchies, dominance and force.[51]

Another generalized but pertinent point is the fact that racism and sexism interlock in several ways—in the dynamics of prejudice and discrimination, in victim blaming and stereotyping, and most significantly, in the elements of power.[52]

In a narrower sense, there is no unanimity even among women who gravitate toward law enforcement careers as to their desired role. Indeed, there are signs of considerable ambiguity in discussions of the subject. On the one hand are the demands for full and equal participation in all police functions, including patrol work on the streets. This *generalist* position on the role question contrasts, on the other hand, with the *specialist* position, along the line that has been traditional for policewomen since Alice Stebbins Wells was appointed to the Los Angeles Police Department in 1910. The specialist role concept is oriented to social work, with assignments to the missing persons' bureau, to the vice squad, or to the juvenile and women's unit. Many of these specialists would consider an assignment to patrol duty as a demotion. Clarice Feinman, a teacher of criminal justice at Trenton State College, asks why it is not possible for policewomen to be both generalists and specialists.[53]

The Police Foundation Study in Washington, D.C., of policewomen on patrol addressed three decisive questions:[54]

1. Is it appropriate, from a performance standpoint, to hire women for patrol assignments on the same basis as men?
2. What advantages or disadvantages arise from hiring women on an equal basis for patrol work?
3. What effect would the use of a substantial number of policewomen have on the nature of police operations?

Among the major findings were these:

Assignment

- New women were assigned to regular uniformed patrol less frequently than comparison men.
- The type of patrol units to which new women and comparison men were assigned was frequently different. In particular, men were less often assigned to station duty and more often assigned to one-officer cars.

Performance

- Comparison men handled somewhat more patrol incidents per tour, primarily because they initiated more traffic incidents (usually, issuance of written citations).
- New women patrolling alone tended to handle more service calls assigned by police dispatchers than did men patrolling alone.
- New women and comparison men responded to similar types of calls while on patrol and saw similar proportions of citizens who were dangerous, angry, upset, drunk, or violent.
- New women obtained results similar to those of comparison men in handling angry or violent citizens.
- Arrests made by new women and comparison men were equally likely to result in convictions.
- New women and comparison men worked well with their partners in two-officer units. The partners shared the driving about equally, took charge with about the same frequency, and were about equal in giving instructions to the other.
- New women and comparison men received the same amount of backup, or assistance, from other police units.
- New women and comparison men showed similar levels of respect and general attitude toward citizens.
- New women and comparison men received similar performance ratings from the police department in its standard review of police officers after the first year of performance.

- Police officials in an anonymous special survey gave new women lower ratings than comparison men on ability to handle domestic fights and street violence, and on general competence. Women were rated equal to men in handling upset or injured persons.
- Captains and lieutenants gave new women higher performance ratings on a special survey in 1973 than they had in 1972. Their 1973 ratings gave new women and comparison men similar scores on general competence.
- There was no difference between new women and comparison men in the number of sick days used.
- There was no difference between new women and comparison men in the number of injuries sustained or the number of days absent from work due to injuries.
- There was no difference between new women and comparison men in the number of driving accidents in which they had been involved since joining the police force.
- Comparison men were more likely than new women to have been charged with serious unbecoming conduct.
- Citizens showed similar levels of respect and similar general attitudes toward new women and comparison men.
- Citizens interviewed about police response to their calls for assistance expressed a high degree of satisfaction with both male and female officers.
- Citizens who had observed policewomen in action said they had become somewhat more favorably inclined toward policewomen.

Attitudes

Citizen Attitudes

- Citizens of the District of Columbia, regardless of their race or sex, were more likely to support the concept of policewomen on patrol than to oppose it.
- Citizens believed that men and women were equally capable of handling most patrol situations, but they were moderately skeptical about the ability of women to handle violent situations.
- The police department was highly rated by citizens in 1972, and this rating has not been affected by the introduction of women into the patrol force.

Police Attitudes

- Patrolmen doubted that patrolwomen were the equal of men in most patrol skills.
- Patrolwomen felt that their patrol skills were as good as patrolmen's in most cases.
- Patrolmen, patrolwomen, and police officials agreed that men were better at handling disorderly males, that women were better at questioning rape victims, and that there was no difference between men and women in skill at arresting prostitutes.

- Police officials agreed with patrolmen that patrolwomen were not as likely to be as satisfactory as men in several types of violent situations.
- Patrolmen had a definite preference for patrolling with a male partner. Patrolwomen had a slight preference for patrolling with a male partner.
- Patrolwomen felt they received a greater degree of cooperation from the public than patrolmen did.
- Patrolwomen felt that police supervisors were more critical of patrolwomen than of men. Patrolmen felt there was no difference.
- Black police officials and black policemen were somewhat less unfavorable toward policewomen than white male officials and policemen.
- Male patrol officers who said that women "should not be a regular part of the patrol force" had less formal education and were more likely to believe in arrests as a performance measurement than other patrolmen.
- Police officials were somewhat more positive toward policewomen in 1973 than they had been during the initial months of the experiment in 1972.
- There was little change in the attitudes of patrolmen toward policewomen between the start and the conclusion of the experiment.

The National Council on Crime and Delinquency has adopted a strong policy statement, urging all criminal justice agencies "to implement procedures aimed at removing all restrictions to equal opportunity" for women, including management positions.[55] The 1966 President's Crime Commission and the 1973 Commission on Criminal Justice Standards and Goals sounded the same theme. Lewis J. Sherman has identified a number of significant benefits that accrue from assigning women a broader police role:

1. A probable reduction in the incidence of violence between police officers and citizens when women are assigned to patrol.
2. A probable improvement in an agency's crime-fighting capability, since women have demonstrated proficiency in certain facets of investigative work.
3. Women in the patrol function will probably better police and community relations, as the public will see the police more as public servants.
4. An overall improvement in patrol work will probably result from more emphasis on social services.
5. Police agencies hiring women for patrol duty are likely to be more responsive to the community because their personnel will be more representative of the population.
6. By introducing women into jobs that have been held exclusively by men, departments will likely be forced to rethink and reevaluate other traditional policies and "conventional wisdom."
7. Hiring women on the basis of equal opportunity is in accord with the law, therefore of particular importance in law enforcement agencies in terms of public attitudes.[56]

Not all analysts agree with Sherman's positive evaluation.[57] The most controversial question regarding women in policing is whether or not it makes a difference in the quality of police patrol performance. The emerging research seems to indicate that there are differences. What remains to be determined is whether the plus factors outweigh the minus factors, judged by performance standards not as yet reflecting anywhere near consensus.

DOMESTIC VIOLENCE

Two issues of special concern to women have come to loom large in public attention lately, and something should be said here about both. One is the problem of battered women; the other is child abuse. Some states have initiated innovative programs (shelters, halfway houses, specifically trained police units, legal assistance) to assist battered women. The majority of states, however, do not provide such services or protection.

Wife beating has always been a troublesome challenge for the police. Lacking specialized training in crisis intervention and mindful of the perils of life and limb often involved in "domestics," many officers reflect hostility or indifference in such situations. Feminist groups are concerned about this attitude, pointing out that, because of it, many women simply refuse to call for help. There are, of course, other reasons for this, also. One result is that accurate statistics on the extent of the problem are hard to come by. Relatively few police departments offer special training for coping with wife abuse. Usually the training that does exist stresses the importance of avoiding arrests, because battered wives seldom file complaints and because such arrests might leave an officer vulnerable to lawsuits.[58]

George E. Berkley cites figures released by the National Institute of Mental Health indicating that between 1½ and 2 million children are kicked, punched, or bitten every year by their own parents. Nearly 50,000 youngsters are actually attacked by parents wielding, and often using, knives or guns.[59] As Berkley asserts, the police are frequently able to spot a child abuse situation. They can usually conduct an investigation easier than can social workers. Often the police can act more expeditiously to do something about the problem, granting that this requires careful coordination with other agencies as to who will do what. Some police people resist such involvement on the grounds that they already have too much to do, forgetting perhaps that an abused child can grow into a serious police problem. Berkley concludes that police action in this area calls for a two-pronged educational effort: externally, with other social agencies, and internally, with reluctant police personnel. A few police agencies have initiated child abuse units, and the outlook is for more in the near future.[60]

Numerous police departments around the country have instituted programs for spouses of police officers, mainly of a counseling and educational nature. The need is reflected in the high rate of police divorce, heart attacks, suicide, alcoholism, and on-the-job deaths. As earlier noted, the psychological stress connected with police work is immense; the personal and family disasters are many.[61]

CRIME AND THE ELDERLY

Persons 65 and older comprise the largest part of the nation's live-alone population, and this proportion is growing steadily. Often these older people are trapped in shoddy hotel rooms, fearful of venturing out. The prevailing problems of the aged are many, and need not be detailed here. The over-65 group has nearly 1 in 6 persons living in poverty, compared with 1 in 10 of those under 65. Nearly 60 percent are women.

Elderly persons are frequently the victims of serious crimes. More often than not, they are *helpless* victims. Their circumstances and problems call for special study and understanding by the police as well as by other public and private services. Fortunately, many programs for the aged have been developing in cities across the country, ranging from reduced public transportation fares to so-called outreach centers to assist elderly persons with their problems. Interest in their predicament is growing, but there still remains a long way to go in local, state, and federal action.

LEAA has funded Criminal Justice and the Elderly, a national research and resource center, which publishes a quarterly newsletter and has seven affiliated demonstration projects:

1. The Senior Citizen Anti-Crime Network in New York City.
2. The Elderly Victimization Prevention and Assistance Program in New Orleans.
3. The Model Antivictimization Project in Washington, D.C.
4. The Senior Citizens Crime Assistance and Prevention Program in New York City.
5. Security Assistance for the Elderly (SENIOR SAFE) in Los Angeles.
6. The Senior Citizens' Community Safety Program in Chicago.
7. The Crime Prevention-Victim Assistance Project for Senior Citizens in Milwaukee.

The talents, wisdom, and experience in a wide range of career fields of many senior citizens are potential resources that police agencies would be well advised not to overlook. Budgets as they are, administrators should consider older persons for volunteer duties in crime prevention, communications, records, and crime analysis.[62]

SUMMING UP

This chapter has reviewed the particular challenge of police relationships with youth, the participation of women in criminal justice work, and the special problem of the elderly with respect to violent crime. These topics are adjuncts to the discussion of the police and minorities—an area requiring specific analysis and specific police and criminal justice strategies.

We have had a lot to say about *responsibility*, in this chapter and others— community responsibility, police responsibility, the responsibilities of minority groups, youth, and so on. One is led to wonder about the meaning of responsibility, and how it is taught or caught or somehow acquired. The dictionary says that responsibility is the quality or state of being responsible, as in moral, legal, or mental accountability, reliability, trustworthiness. It appears, then, that responsible action involves decision making, often regarding moral questions. This implies that deliberate choices must be made from among alternatives.

For example, a police officer must decide on what constitutes "probable cause" or a "reasonable search" or "undue force."

How is "responsible" behavior acquired? The answer is that it is acquired by *practice*, by *training* in decision making, and *by being expected to live with the consequences of the decisions one makes*. The latter is the hard part, especially where youth are concerned—in their relationship, for instance, with parents—and admittedly there must be some limit to how far the consequences should be carried. All we are saying is what has been said better by many others: children learn responsible behavior by participating in the process of reaching decisions that affect them, as nearly as possible (depending upon age, maturity, etc.) with full voice and vote.

Archibald MacLeish is one of those who makes the point better:

> Only when freedom is as human as humanity is free can a nation of men exist. Only when the balance between society and self is both harmonious and whole can there truly *be* a self, or truly a society.[63]

NOTES

1. Urie Bronfenbrenner, "The Split-Level American Family," *Saturday Review*, October 7, 1967, p. 60. Reprinted by permission.

2. James S. Coleman, *The Adolescent Society* (New York: Free Press, 1971).

3. Fred E. Inbau, "Lawlessness Galore," *Vital Speeches* 32 (November 15, 1965): 96.

4. U.S., President's Commission on Law Enforcement and Administration of Justice, *Field Surveys III* (Washington, D.C.: U.S. Government Printing Office, 1967), vol. 1, sec. 2, p. 83.

5. David H. Bayley and Harold Mendelsohn, *Minorities and the Police: Confrontation in America* (New York: Free Press, 1969), pp. 45–46.

6. "Moral Development and Identification in Child Psychology," *Yearbook of the National Society for Studies in Education* 62 (1963), part 1.

7. David Easton and Robert Hess, "The Child's Political World," *Midwest Journal of Political Science* 6 (1962): 229–246.

8. See Fred I. Greenstein, *Children and Politics* (New Haven, Conn.: Yale University Press, 1965).

9. Robert L. Derbyshire, "Children's Perceptions of the Police: A Comparative Study of Attitudes and Attitude Change," *Journal of Criminal Law, Criminology and Police Science* 59 (1968): 183–190.

10. Ibid., p. 188.

11. *Officer Friendly* Resource Unit, available from the Sears Roebuck Foundation, Skokie, Ill.

12. U.S., Department of Health, Education and Welfare, Office of Education, *The Development of Basic Attitudes and Values Toward Government and Citizenship During the Elementary School Years*, part 1, CRP1078, prepared for the Bureau of Research by Robert Hess and Judith V. Torney (Washington, D.C.: U.S. Government Printing Office, 1965).

13. U.S., Department of Health, Education and Welfare, Office of Education, *Development of Attitudes Toward Government*, Final Report CRP1078, prepared for the

Bureau of Research by David Easton and Jack Dennis (Washington, D.C.: U.S. Government Printing Office, 1968).

14. Laurence Kohlberg, "Moral Development and Identification in Child Psychology," *Yearbook of the National Society for Studies in Education* 57 (1963). See also by the same author, "The Child as Moral Philosopher," *Psychology Today* 2 (September 1968): 12–15.

15. Kohlberg, "Moral Development," pp. 313–325.

16. William Dienstein, "Conflict of Beliefs About Causes of Delinquency," *Crime and Delinquency* 6, no. 3 (1960): 293. Reprinted by permission of the National Council on Crime and Delinquency.

17. Coleman, *The Adolescent Society;* and Franklin K. Patterson, ed., *The Adolescent Citizen* (Glencoe, Ill.: Free Press, 1960).

18. Coleman, *The Adolescent Society*, p. 3.

19. John P. Clark and Eugene P. Wenninger, "The Attitude of Juveniles Toward the Legal Institutions," *Journal of Criminal Law, Criminology and Police Science* 55, no. 4 (1964): 482–489.

20. William W. Wattenberg and Noel Bufé, "The Effectiveness of Police Youth Bureau Officers," *Journal of Criminal Law, Criminology and Police Science* 54, no. 4 (1963): 470–475.

21. David G. Krebs, "Perceptual Defense in the Delinquent Child," *Dissertation Abstracts* 25, no. 9 (1964): 53–84. See also Brendan Maher and Ellen Stein, "The Delinquent's Perception of the Law and Community," in Stanton Wheeler, ed., *Controlling Delinquents* (New York: John Wiley & Sons, 1968).

22. Gerald H. J. Pearson, *Adolescence and Conflict of Generations* (New York: W. W. Norton, 1958); Robert T. Amos and Reginald M. Washington, "A Comparison of Pupil and Teacher Perceptions of Pupil Problems," *Journal of Educational Psychology* 51, no. 5 (1960): 255–258.

23. Robert G. Portune, *Changing Adolescent Attitudes Toward Police* (Cincinnati, Ohio: W. H. Anderson, 1971).

24. Ibid., preface.

25. Donald Bouma, *Kids and Cops* (Grands Rapids, Mich.: Eerdmans, 1969).

26. Martin G. Miller, "Socialization and the Compliance System: An Attitudinal Study of Adolescents, Their Teachers, and Police Officers" (Ph.D. dissertation, Michigan State University, College of Social Science, 1971).

27. See Milton Rokeach, Martin G. Miller, and John A. Snyder, "The Value Gap Between Police and Policed," *Journal of Social Issues* 27, no. 2 (1971): 155–171.

28. See Carl Werthman and Irving Piliavin, "Gang Members and the Police," in David J. Bordua, ed., *The Police: Six Sociological Essays* (New York: John Wiley & Sons, 1967).

29. James Q. Wilson, *Varieties of Police Behavior. The Management of Law and Order in Eight Communities* (Cambridge, Mass.: Harvard University Press, 1968), pp. 40–41. Reprinted by permission.

30. Alvin E. Echols, Jr., "Deadline, Vengeance, and Tribute: A Prescription for Black Juvenile Delinquency," *Crime and Delinquency* 16, no. 4 (October 1970): 357.

31. U.S., National Commission on the Causes and Prevention of Violence, *The Politics of Protest* (Washington, D.C.: U.S. Government Printing Office), chap. 3.

32. Seymour Martin Lipset, "Why Cops Hate Liberals—and Vice Versa," *Atlantic* 223, no. 3 (March 1969): 83. Copyright © 1969 by The Atlantic Monthly Company. Reprinted by permission. For an extreme view of the gravity of the polarization described by Lipset, see Jerry Rubin, *Do It!* (New York: Simon & Schuster, 1970). Also see Mitchell Cohen and Dennis Hale, *The New Student Left* (Boston: Beacon Press, 1967).

33. U.S., National Advisory Commission on Civil Disorders, *Report* (Washington, D.C.: U.S. Government Printing Office, 1969), p. 107.

34. The commission's report, *Campus Unrest* (Washington, D.C.: U.S. Government Printing Office, 1970), includes special reports on Kent State University and Jackson State College, together with an extensive bibliography.

35. *New York Times*, September 24, 1970, p. 28.

36. *Time*, August 3, 1970, p. 9.

37. Adapted from the July 6 memorandum.

38. *New York Times*, November 5, 1970. Copyright © 1970 by The New York Times Company. Reprinted by permission.

39. *New York Times*, November 17, 1970, p. 43. Copyright © 1970 by The New York Times Company. Reprinted by permission.

40. *New York Times*, October 17, 1970, p. 29. Copyright © 1970 by The New York Times Company. Reprinted by permission. For analysis of the causes of campus unrest, see Kenneth Keniston and Michael Lerner, "The Unholy Alliance Against the Campus," *New York Times Magazine*, November 8, 1970, pp. 28–86. See also Kenneth Keniston, *The Uncommitted: Alienated Youth in American Society* (New York: Harcourt, Brace & World, 1965), and by the same author, *Young Radicals* (New York: Harcourt, Brace & World, 1968).

41. *New York Times*, September 22, 1970, p. 29. Copyright © 1970 by The New York Times Company. Reprinted by permission.

42. As reported by Fred M. Hechinger, *New York Times*, July 12, 1970. Copyright © 1970 by The New York Times Company. Reprinted by permission.

43. The Twenty-sixth Amendment granting eighteen-year-olds the vote was approved by the required number of states in July 1971.

44. *New York Times*, August 26, 1970, p. 22.

45. *New York Times*, November 22, 1970, p. 51. Copyright © 1970 by The New York Times Company. Reprinted by permission.

46. "Student Involvement or Detachment?" *New York Times*, November 25, 1970, p. 37.

47. *U.S. News & World Report*, January 13, 1975, pp. 34–37.

48. Horace Sutton, "Drugs: Ten Years to Doomsday?" *Saturday Review*, November 14, 1970, pp. 18–21, 59–61.

49. Ibid., p. 18. Reprinted by permission.

50. *Tinker* v. *Des Moines Independent School District et al.*, 393 U.S. 503 (1969).

51. Lucy Komisar, "Where Feminism Will Lead," *Civil Rights Digest* (U.S. Commission on Civil Rights) 6, no. 3 (Spring 1974), p. 6.

52. Robert Terry, "The White Male Club," *Civil Rights Digest* 6, no. 3 (Spring 1974), pp. 69 ff. See also U.S. Commission on Civil Rights, *Social Indicators of Equality for Minorities and Women* (Washington, D.C.: U.S. Government Printing Office, 1978).

53. Clarice Feinman, "Policewomen: The Crisis in Identity," *Criminal Justice Columns* (Allyn and Bacon/Holbrook Press), vol. 2, no. 3, p. 3.

54. Peter B. Bloch and Deborah Anderson (of the Urban Institute), "Policewomen on Patrol: Final Report" (Washington, D.C.: The Police Foundation, Inc., 1974). See also Catherine Milton, *Women in Policing* (Washington, D.C.: The Police Foundation, Inc., 1972).

55. Board of Directors, National Council on Crime and Delinquency, *Crime and Delinquency*, January 1976, pp. 1–2.

56. Lewis J. Sherman, "A Psychological View of Women in Policing," *Journal of Police Science and Administration* 1, no. 4: 383–394. Copyright © 1973 by the Northwestern University School of Law. See also Bernard L. Garmire, "Female Officers in the Department," *FBI Law Enforcement Bulletin*, June 1974; Glen Craig, "California Highway Patrol Women Officers," *The Police Chief*, January 1977; Peggy E. Triplett, "Women in Policing," *The Police Chief*, December 1976; and William O. Weldy, "Women in Policing: A Positive Step Toward Increased Police Enthusiasm," *The Police Chief*, January 1976.

57. For example, see Anthony Vastola, "Women in Policing: An Alternative Ideology," *The Police Chief*, January 1977.

58. Joan Potter, "Police and the Battered Wife: The Search for Understanding," *Police* 1, no. 4 (September 1978), pp. 40 ff. Copyright © 1978 by Criminal Justice Publications, Inc. See also M. Borland, ed., *Violence in the Family* (Atlantic Highlands, N.J.: Humanities Press, 1976); and Betsy Warrior, ed., *Working on Wife Abuse*, 6th rev. ed. (Cambridge, Mass.: Betsy Warrior, Publisher, 1978).

59. George E. Berkley, "Child Abuse: A Police Problem?" *Criminal Justice Columns* (Allyn and Bacon/Holbrook Press), vol. 2, no. 2, p. 2.

60. Richard Steen, "Child Abuse Units in Law Enforcement," *The Police Chief*, May 1978, pp. 38–39. See also R. Kalmar, *Child Abuse—Perspectives on Diagnosis, Treatment and Prevention* (Dubuque, Iowa: Kendall Hunt, 1977).

61. Joan Potter, "The Liberation of the Police Wife," *Police* 1, no. 2 (May 1978): 39. Copyright © 1978 by Criminal Justice Publications, Inc. See also Martin Reiser, "The Problems of Police Officers' Wives," *The Police Chief*, April 1978, pp. 38 ff.

62. See Gerald J. Dadich, "Crime, the Elderly and Community Relations," *The Police Chief*, February 1977; George Sunderland, "The Older American: Police Problem or Police Asset?" *FBI Law Enforcement Bulletin*, August 1976; Ordway P. Burden, "Enlisting Senior Citizens to Stretch Police Budgets," *Law Enforcement News*, September 11, 1978. The newsletter mentioned is called *Criminal Justice and the Elderly* and is sponsored by the National Council of Senior Citizens' Legal Research and Services for the Elderly, under grants from LEAA and the Ford Foundation. Editorial offices are at 1511 K Street N.W., Suite 540, Washington, D.C. 20005.

63. Archibald MacLeish, "Trustee of the Culture," *Saturday Review*, December 19, 1970, pp. 18–19. Reprinted by permission.

13

COMPLAINTS AND THE POLICE

When Sir Robert Peel said that the police are the public and the public are the police, he was saying something important about police accountability for police actions. We have noted that policing in democratic society is a public, political function. The police are ultimately and clearly answerable to the public for their every move. Because the source of police authority is the community, the responsibility for controlling police behavior also lodges in the community. Police administrators are expected to see to it as an important part of their delegated prerogatives. Should they fail to do it, to community satisfaction, there are predictable rumblings. Thus, how a police agency deals with complaints about officer behavior is a critical police and community relations consideration.

The police are seldom questioned when they operate in a manner clearly supported by community consensus; their *authority* is recognized and generally accepted. But when they operate, as they sometimes must, in a manner involving their *legal power*, and where community consensus is questionable, there may well be citizen complaints. As Michael Banton puts it, power is not necessarily morally rightful. Authority, on the other hand, includes a moral element. If someone has power over someone else, he can force a certain action; if someone has authority, his commands will tend to be obeyed voluntarily.[1]

Under social circumstances, therefore, in which authority systems and authority figures are challenged—and questioned especially as to the arbitrary exercise of power—it is predictable that police conduct will come under closer scrutiny by the public. This is what has occurred in recent years. Logically, police behavior will tend to be particularly scrutinized by elements of the population (generally speaking, the powerless) who are insisting more and more emphatically that they be counted as part of the community to whom the police are accountable. For the police are expected to serve *all* the people, as with any public institution. The matter of citizen complaints against the police has been heatedly debated in recent years, and it calls for careful analysis.

A BASIC PHILOSOPHY

One's opinion on questions pertaining to complaints against the police will, first of all, probably be governed by a certain philosophy. We have already stated our belief, for instance, that the police should be held accountable to the public for their behavior, with no equivocation. We have asserted that this should mean *all* of the public, the powerless as well as the powerful. We have implied that we believe, with Banton, that police activity should be based, insofar as possible, on the moral authority of the office, rather than solely on its legal power. We have earlier acknowledged the difficulty in today's American society of securing the minimal community consensus without which the moral authority of the police may be repeatedly questioned.

So much, then, as the beginning of a philosophy regarding citizen complaints. Now to add to it.[2] Traditionally, the administrator of a police organization has the responsibility for supervision and discipline of personnel. This administrative prerogative is conditioned, to some degree, by public opinion—in a vague, general way. It is somewhat more specifically and directly influenced, at the municipal level, by city councils, commissions or other legislative bodies, by mayors, city managers or other executives, and by police or public safety boards, commissions, civil service bodies, and so on. It is a general working principle to keep interference with *proper* administration at a minimum. Questions are sometimes raised as to what "proper" may mean. Efficient administration is not necessarily effective administration from the point of view of community relations. Efficiency may become an end in itself, which dehumanizes administration and creates serious internal or external problems. Police *effectiveness* in social control is closely linked with their moral authority; it is dependent in large degree on community support. A key question is how to channel grievances constructively, inside and outside the department.

In this context, by a "complaint" we mean a grievance. In police vocabulary, there is some semantic difficulty with the term. When a citizen calls to charge that his neighbor is disturbing the peace, the police practice is to record the call as a complaint. The complaint is against the neighbor, not against the police. This is not our meaning in this chapter. We mean a grievance of (1) a citizen against the department; (2) a citizen against one or more police officers; (3) a departmental employee against the department; or (4) a departmental employee against another employee. Hence, (1) and (2) are *external* complaints, while (3) and (4) are *internal*.

We believe that there is a direct relationship between the number and type of external complaints and the level of public confidence in a police organization. As a general rule, in a community where there are numerous complaints against the police and accompanying clamor for establishment of a civilian review board or some other external mechanism for control of police behavior, there are police-community relations problems and usually other problems of a serious nature. The demand for civilian review is typically a telling symptom. And the likelihood is that the mechanism proposed for dealing with complaints against the police will strike more at the symptoms than at the roots of problems. We will elaborate on this point shortly.

THE POLICE AND COMPLAINTS

As a beginning in guidelines for dealing with complaints, the following points are recommended:

1. A starting point in any police agency sincerely intent upon dealing constructively with public complaints is to recognize that some citizens

truly believe that some officers do sometimes mistreat some citizens. Incidents happen often enough to make the belief plausible. To respond to this with a heated "It's a damn lie" is worse than no response at all. The belief that it does occur is real to some people, and the mistreatment itself may be. So how are mutual trust and confidence to be developed? This is the decisive question. Certainly it cannot be done through reciprocal excoriation.

2. Columbia Law School Professor Walter Gellhorn has posed these basic questions: *Should* the police control police? *Can* the police control police? If the answer to the first question is yes, then it is clear where the burden of proof lies with respect to the second question.[3]

3. Initiative for improvement of complaint procedures should come from police administrators, ideally in circumstances where it is not likely to be interpreted publicly as defensive or reactionary, or as "crisis oriented," or as an opportunistic gimmick to relieve political pressure.

4. If persons who believe they have been treated unjustly have no forum that they trust to explore their claims, their attitude of distrust is never dispelled.

5. There is an inconsistency between police lamenting, on the one hand, the apathy of the public regarding problems that loom large for the police, and on the other hand resisting the right and obligation of citizens to complain about what they perceive as improper police conduct. However negative a citizen complaint may be initially, it is a way by which the citizen has his say about governmental service and *participates* in democratic political process. With a *positive* police philosophy regarding complaints, the matter can often be turned to positive good for police service and for police and community relations. Some complainants may eventually become staunch allies of the police and valuable contributors to worthwhile programs and projects, as experience shows.

This last point is one on which Gellhorn elaborates:

If the police authorities are to earn the public's approval of their stewardship, they must themselves be willing to do the job they are unwilling to allow others to do in their stead. This does not mean upholding every charge against a subordinate; accusations are easily made, not easily proved. It does mean that the authorities must be wholeheartedly interested in exploring complaints—just as interested, indeed, as are the complainants in having exploration made. The suspicion of whitewash, of unwillingness to expose wrongdoing because of a misguided sense of loyalty, will not die speedily. It rests on too much disillusioning experience in days past. If, however, the police begin to make frank disclosure of how they have acted on each complaint and what they have found; if they are willing to allow the complainant to comment and make further suggestions should he care to do so; if they are prepared to subject their completed work to examination by an external critic; if, in sum, they cease thinking of themselves as a brotherly band beleaguered by citizens (and, of course, other hostile forces) and start thinking of themselves as public servants within a specialized law administration organization, the gap between them and the community they serve should begin to close.[4]

In this passage, Gellhorn presents a philosophy for dealing with complaints that is in keeping with truly professional public service. There is more to it than mere machinery for handling complaints. There are implications for administrative policies, for organizational planning, for public information and interpretation, and for the training of police personnel. Indeed, there are implications for governmental administration in a broader context than the police department. It is hard to see how a police organization can operate with one philosophy in this matter, while the larger governmental system of which it is a part operates with an opposing philosophy.

THE OMBUDSMAN

Gellhorn recognizes this larger context of complaint philosophy. He has become well known in this country as a leading proponent of the "ombudsman" plan for dealing with citizen grievances against any branch of governmental service, including the police. Gellhorn thinks that an official with authority to examine the entire range of municipal administration "holds more hope for the future than does a special tribunal for trying citizens' complaints against individual policemen." The ombudsman approach does not single out the police department for special treatment. Gellhorn further observes:

> It does not remove from police hands the power to direct, judge, and discipline the staff members whose actions have been challenged, but—as in the case of other departments—leaves to the professionals the job of appraising fellow professionals. . . . Far from opposing this concept, policemen should find in it much to welcome. The Scandinavian countries and New Zealand have already put it into practice with good results.[5]

The ombudsman is a highly placed functionary authorized to inquire into the merits of any citizen's grievance about official actions or failures to act. He then recommends, but may not command, whatever action he thinks is suitable in the light of his investigation. The ombudsman is, in effect, an appellate office. It is by no means a substitute for complaint procedure within, for example, a police department, to deal with internal or external grievances. Experience with the plan in other countries shows that it has done much, as Gellhorn states, "to reinforce citizens' confidence in public administrators by showing the flimsiness of accusations that had at first seemed grave." While the ombudsman plan has been tried in numerous places in the United States in the recent past, it has not as yet had sufficient testing to establish its feasibility and merits. Some American universities are experimenting with it as a means of bolstering due process in handling complaints of students, occasionally of faculty members, and conceivably even the complaints of administrators.

THE CONTROL OF DELEGATED POWER

The ombudsman procedure is based on realization of a question of government that has been of concern from the beginning: How is the use of delegated power to be controlled? Because the police have a particularly sensitive delegated power, the problem with them is especially touchy. Control of their behavior most frequently becomes a matter of public contention under circumstances in which confidence in them is shaky. Monrad Paulsen, one-time colleague of Gellhorn's on the faculty of the Columbia University Law School and presently Dean of the Law School at the University of Virginia, refers to the "anarchistic strain in all of us." He observes that Americans like to "manipulate law and legal roles," and cites as supporting evidence the fact that old movies about police and law enforcement often contain "wink situations." Paulsen says that "our habit of following the rules only when a policeman is looking over our shoulder has contributed to mistrust of authority and mistrust of legal process."[6]

This attitude, Paulsen believes, is further embellished by stereotypic perceptions of the police officer as a "tough bully-boy," and by the fact that "we have given the police a job to do, but we haven't told them what the rules are." As an illustration, the Supreme Court upsets convictions because the police work is held to be unconstitutional and thus places the police in a bad light. The police are, in effect, held accountable on a Monday for violation of a rule established on Sunday that—it is decreed—should have guided their conduct the previous Saturday. This is the type of thing that is sometimes apparent in citizen complaints against the police, and it is the type of thing that at least partly explains why so many police are defensive about complaints. Keep in mind, however, that few of us, indeed, bear up well in the face of complaints about our behavior!

How is the use of power to be controlled? *Quis ipsos custodes custodiet?* Who will watch the watchers? The late Stanford University Law Professor Herbert Packer analyzed this basic question, asserting that "the trouble that the police and the rest of us are now in is largely the result of our improvident reliance on the criminal sanction to perform a lot of messy social tasks for which it is not especially suited." Packer asked what business the Supreme Court has trying to educate or discipline the police. He suggested that this is happening because no one else is doing it. Who else could? The police themselves might do it, but they often have not. Most of the professional progress in police work in recent years, Packer felt, has been in reducing corruption and in increasing efficiency. While these are certainly worthwhile achievements, "the revolution in rising expectations among urban minority groups and the due process revolution in the courts will not be satisfied with efficiency."[7]

Who else might police the police? Legislatures might do it and Packer contended that such bodies are best suited for it—far more so than the courts—and he indicated why he believed this. But the fact is, he continued, that legislatures have utterly abdicated this responsibility. Packer thought that the Supreme Court's performance in the criminal procedure area had been increasingly unsatisfactory as its constitutional interpretations had become more legislative in tone. Along with Paulsen, he questioned whether the familiar sanction against the police represented by the exclusionary rule of evidence is adequate. Incidentally, Paulsen defies anyone to try to explain that rule to a European, "lest he be committed as a lunatic." In this country, the exclusionary rule seeks to discourage police misconduct in the handling of suspects by court refusals to convict persons who have been victims of such misconduct, for example, in obtaining evidence. It also frees the malefactor so he may again victimize some innocent person. It does not compensate the victim of police misconduct. In short, it has little to commend it, Paulsen argues, though conceding that it has probably had some small impact on police procedures.

Both Packer and Paulsen think that the question of sanctions is basic, and they have similar notions as to what "the stick" might be. Packer suggested that one possibility might be the right to file suit against the governmental unit that employs the police officer, accompanied by provisions for recovery of minimum or fixed damages, counsel fees, and the like. The strategy would be "to build respect for due process into the policeman's model of efficiency. The policeman who persistently violates the norms costs his employers money and is therefore seen as inefficient."

THE CIVILIAN COMPLAINT REVIEW BOARD

Another possibility considered by Packer, Paulsen, and Gellhorn is some kind of administrative complaint and review structure aimed at making the internal process of police discipline more responsive to values other than efficiency. The so-called civilian review board is what Packer called "a crude model" of what might be designed. However, none of these three analysts is enthusiastic about the civilian review board. Paulsen refers to endless public debates and bitter political infighting, such as that in New York City in the mid-1960s, which focused on the question of whether there should be civilian domination of a complaint review board.[8] Paulsen and Gellhorn object to such review boards, even with civilian participation, and favor the ombudsman plan, for similar reasons:

1. Experiments with review boards in Philadelphia, Pennsylvania; Rochester, New York; and a number of other cities have not been very successful. There were problems of publicity, of staffing, of budget, and of limited powers. In Philadelphia, the police department conducted investigations, raising doubts as to the independence of the board. In Rochester, the board was confined to dealing only with complaints of brutality. In both places, litigation by police officers' organizations brought injunctions, keeping the board from functioning.

2. Review boards bring no lasting relief. Stronger medicine is needed to cure community ills. Mere palliatives cannot contend with discrimination and poverty.

3. The review board symbolizes and assumes conflict between the poor and public authority. Moreover, it singles out the police for special blame and overlooks the existence of closely allied official activities.

4. The review board system presupposes a polarization, the complainant on one side and the accused police officer on the other. This makes for burdensome procedures, simply because of the adversary nature of the proceedings, and tends to discourage the expression of grievances, or

turns the proceedings into acrimonious exchanges when grievances are processed. It leaves complainants wondering if the ordeal is worth the effort.

5. The problems brought to light by a review board may be such as to require upper level administrative action in a police agency. A review board (as contrasted with an ombudsman) will probably not have sufficient clout to persuade administrators to effect such changes. Moreover, the desirable administrative changes may well pertain to a larger context of public service than merely the police department.

William Brown was among those in the 1960s who argued that review boards for the police did not go far enough.[9] Such a view, by a retired New York City Police Inspector, was news at the time Brown expressed it—in the aftermath of the controversy over the review board question in New York City during the summer of 1965. Brown stated that a bureaucracy in a democracy should be responsive to the needs of even the poorest and least vocal of those it serves. Therefore, he continued, not only conscience, but also sound administration called for the establishment of some mechanism that would assure any person aggrieved by official action a chance to be heard, and to know that his complaint would be listened to with respect and by a power able to correct wrongful administrative actions or positions. Brown delineated some important requirements for an adequate review system: honest and competent administration, concern for due process, provision for appeals, a positive philosophy to correct rough spots in a system, and clearly stated functions of the review process.

Brown contended that the civilian complaint review board did not meet these requirements. It was too much a symbol of the antagonism between police and minority groups. It tended to widen the communication gap rather than to narrow it. It diverted attention away from more fundamental and broader issues. Something more was needed, Brown concluded. He advocated serious consideration of the ombudsman system.[10]

The ombudsman system, it should be repeated, is not a substitute for resolute police administration that is intolerant of offensive conduct by police officers. As Gellhorn puts it:

> The behavior of policemen is not a great force of nature beyond human control. If superiors from the top of the chain of command to the bottom are determined to correct subordinates, if they themselves are held accountable for inexcusable failures to detect and discipline offenders, they can eliminate much of the behavior that now brings police establishments into disrepute. . . . The police *can* control the police. . . .
>
> What is needed at this point is not a further institutionalizing, through a civilian board, of the notion that a complaint signalizes a dispute between two individuals alone. What is needed, rather, is acceptance of the view that a citizen's complaint about a policeman, just like a citizen's complaint about any other public servant, deserves the attention of superior administrators who are intent upon reducing irritations and improving services. If anyone believes that the responsible superiors have not given the desired degree of attention, an outsider's inquiry becomes desira-

ble. The issue then presented is not the guilt or innocence of a particular public servant, but the probity, efficiency, and policies of those who have weighed citizens' allegations about shortcomings or misdeeds. These are to be judged by a review of what the superiors did, not by a trial of what the subordinates are accused of having done. Persons who wish to protest about police operations should indeed be able to bring their protests before a competent authority wholly outside the Police Department. But this should not operate to supplant the Police Department as the primary investigator and decider of charges against its members.[11]

To this, Packer added his main point, one which Jerome Skolnick, Wayne LaFave, Frank Remington, and others have also stressed:

The aggressively interventionist character of much of our criminal law thrusts the police into the role of snoopers and harassers. There is simply no way for the police to provide so much as a semblance of enforcement of laws against prostitution, sexual deviance, gambling, narcotics, and the like without widespread and visible intrusion into what people regard as their private lives. Ideally, the police should be seen as the people who keep the law of the jungle from taking over. . . . It is only when the police are seen, as they are in our society, as the guardians of conventional morality and ideological purity that such a slogan ["Support your local police"] could become as emotive and divisive as that one has.[12]

In short, the best procedures for handling citizen complaints against the police will still leave the more basic task of evaluating a criminal code that insists upon putting police in indefensible positions where citizen complaints are inevitable. On the other hand, what has happened too often in recent years is that police unions have fought tenaciously against the idea of civilian complaint review boards—sometimes even using selected quotations from Packer, Paulsen, Goldstein and others—but have carefully neglected to study and include accompanying passages from the same authors. The result has been pure propaganda calculated to influence the public, bereft of educational integrity. Sadly, one observes that in this respect the behavior of police unions is no better than that of certain professional associations.

Accountability and responsiveness. These are the key ideas for administrative policy and practices in dealing with complaints. The Police Foundation has made a substantial investment in the development of a "model" in Louisville, geared to the primary goal of improving police service to the community. The slogan is: *Quality Service and Conduct—Help Us Serve You Better.* The Internal Affairs Unit of the Louisville Division of Police solicits citizen cooperation in reporting three forms of officer misconduct:

- Misconduct—Official Duties
  Example: Use of excessive force in making an arrest.
- Criminal Misconduct.
  Example: An off-duty law violation by an officer.
- Criminal Official Misconduct
  Example: An officer accepts a bribe in return for special treatment.

Actually, the program extends to all city employees, not only to police officers. It was strongly resisted by the Fraternal Order of Police. Literature describing the program refers to "the history of dealing with police misconduct

[as] a history of avoiding the problem." The emphasis in the Louisville approach is on management rather than investigative methods. The policy manual for the program is very detailed and covers a wide variety of areas.[13]

RECOMMENDATIONS OF PRESIDENTIAL COMMISSIONS

Several special presidential commissions in recent years have considered the matter of citizen complaints against the police. In its general report, *The Challenge of Crime in a Free Society*, President Johnson's Commission on Law Enforcement and Administration of Justice recommended that every jurisdiction should provide *adequate* procedures for full and fair processing of all citizen grievances and complaints about the conduct of any public officer or employee.[14] The *Task Force Report: The Police* of the same commission discussed in some detail internal procedures within a police organization, including internal investigations, citizen complaints, external review, court appeals, civil remedies, civilian review boards, and the ombudsman system.[15]

A more specific analysis of the functioning of the grievance systems in the San Diego and Philadelphia police departments was provided in *Field Surveys IV* of the same commission. This included a thorough description and evaluation of the Philadelphia Police Advisory Board, originally called the Philadelphia Police Review Board, created in 1958.[16]

The National Advisory Commission on Civil Disorders (Kerner Commission) expressed particular concern in its 1968 report for opening channels of communication between government and urban ghetto residents. It recommended establishment of joint government-community neighborhood action task forces and formal mechanisms for the processing of grievances relating to the performance of city administrators. The commission did not specify the form of such mechanisms, but did identify certain criteria of adequacy:

- The grievance agency should be separate from operating municipal agencies.
- The grievance agency must have adequate staff and funding to discharge its responsibilities.
- The grievance agency should have comprehensive jurisdiction, bringing all public agencies under scrutiny.
- The grievance agency should have power to receive complaints, hold hearings, subpoena witnesses, make public recommendations for remedial actions, and in cases involving law violation, bring suit.
- The grievance agency should be readily and easily accessible to all citizens.
- Grievants should be given full opportunity to take part in all proceedings and to be represented by counsel. Results of investigations should be reported to grievants and made public. Expanded legal services should be made available to ghetto residents in various types of legal-aid-to-the-poor programs.[17]

The same commission emphasized that making a complaint should be easy and convenient. The procedure should have a built-in conciliation process to attempt to resolve complaints without the need for full investigation and processing. Excessive formality should be avoided. Because many citizen complaints pertain to departmental policies rather than to individual conduct, information concerning complaints of this sort should be forwarded to the departmental unit that formulates or reviews policy and procedures. Information concerning all complaints should be forwarded to appropriate training units so that any deficiencies correctable by training can be eliminated.

The National Commission on the Causes and Prevention of Violence stated emphatically that aggrieved groups must be permitted to exercise their constitutional rights of protest and public presentation of grievances. To enable the less affluent to obtain effective and peaceful redress of grievances, this commission recommended additional steps to meet their needs for legal assistance and encouraged state and local jurisdictions to experiment with the establishment of grievance agencies to serve all citizens.[18]

The President's Commission on Campus Unrest said in its 1970 report that the most urgent task for government must be to restore faith of Americans in their government, in their fellow citizens, and in their capacity to live together in harmony and progress.[19] This commission recommended reforms in the governance of institutions of higher education to include special attention to such things as:

· Increased participation of students, faculty, and staff in the formulation of policies.

· Procedures for dealing with grievances, to insure that such are promptly heard, fairly considered, and—if necessary—acted upon.

This commission went on to declare that many grievances are legitimate and correctable, but even when they are not—even when they are but a pretext for disruption—they often arouse emotions that are more than ephemeral. Within the limits of practicality, every complaint should be investigated and answered by as informal a process as may be appropriate in particular instances. Unwarranted charges should be repudiated, policies misunderstood should be explained, unfounded rumors should be dispelled, and facts should be provided.

The same commission observed that campus grievance committees generally have not worked very well. Problems with such committees have been the polarization of their members, a tendency to handle grievances on the basis of policies rather than merit, and slowness of response. Variations on the ombudsman system have been tried on some campuses. To be successful in such circumstances, the ombudsman must have both great autonomy and the support of top university administration. He or she must not be penalized by the administration if findings and recommendations embarrass university leaders. Some institutions have appointed special student affairs administrators or advisory bodies to act as liaison between students and administration.

The 1973 National Advisory Commission on Criminal Justice Standards and Goals, in their *Report on Police*, joined the chorus calling for immediate implementation in every police agency of procedures to facilitate complaints alleging employee misconduct, whether the complaint is initiated internally or externally. The commission spelled out some of the principles that should apply, for example, that making a complaint should not be accompanied by fear of reprisal or harassment, that all complaints should be promptly and thoroughly investigated, and that a police agency should keep the public well informed of its complaint procedures.[20] In all citizen grievance procedures, the rights of individual police officers should be carefully protected.

How much police misconduct actually takes place? In 1977, the U.S. Commission on Civil Rights reported that police misconduct was still widespread and "in some cities had become so pervasive as to appear to be officially sanctioned."[21] Citizen complaints in numerous big cities during that year alleged verbal and physical abuse by police of persons stopped for minor violations, as well as beatings and violations of constitutional rights during lengthy interrogations. However, the Police Foundation noted "a clear national trend among police agencies toward establishing restraint in the use of firearms."[22] Nevertheless, the foundation study indicated that local police still need clear directives and sanctions regarding the use of deadly force.

DEFINITION OF COMPLAINTS

Early in this chapter, we proposed a four-dimensional definition of complaints. Some aspects of it have been neglected in our discussion to this point. In complaints of departmental employees against the department, it is usually "unfair practices" that are involved. The belief is growing that a police department has an obligation to provide suitable channels through which all employees may offer criticisms and recommend changes, without peril. Much more attention must be devoted to this than in the past. Police unionization is gaining in strength and in political power, indicating the need for administration to be genuinely concerned for the welfare of all personnel. We shall have more to say shortly about internal control mechanisms. Even the military services are currently devoting unprecedented attention to internal grievance procedures.

The second type of complaint that we identified—that of a departmental employee against another departmental employee—includes complaints made by a superior officer against a subordinate, those of a subordinate against a superior, and those of an employee against another employee of equal rank. The Michigan State University study for the President's Crime Commission indicated that, while police departments respect the right of superiors to voice complaints against subordinates, there is rarely any established procedure for complaints of subordinates against superiors, or of employees against employees of the same rank.[23] The importance of providing suitable machinery for these types of complaints cannot be overstressed. So-called police scandals frequently occur in circumstances where subordinates fear reprisals if they attempt to complain formally about superiors. Military-type organization has fostered this atmosphere. Formalized complaints of employees against other employees of equal rank often result also in subtle (and sometimes not so subtle) recrimination against the complainant.

In the third category of complaints—that of a citizen against the department—are such charges as unfair, discriminatory, improper, or inefficient practices on the part of the police organization. Sometimes departmental policies are questioned, and reevaluation is the prudent response. An applicable administrative principle is the recognition that policies in a police organization are not solely the possession and private domain of police administrators. The very nature of this type of complaint calls for public airing.

The fourth classification of complaints is the most common—that of a civilian against a police officer. Usually the allegation is that an individual officer or group of officers has, by committing or omitting some act, violated either the law or departmental policy. The most frequent complaint of this type, studies show, is discourtesy. The use of unnecessary force is second in frequency, and mishandling a traffic ticket is third. Contrary to popular impressions, blacks are not disproportionately represented among complainants. But a high proportion of complainants are of lower socioeconomic class background.

External complaints are obviously important in terms of community relations; however, this in no way minimizes the need for establishing sound procedures for handling internal complaints. Any complaint can, at a given time and place, create serious administrative problems. The community often displays a fickle attitude in the way it views complaints. It may focus on alleged discrimination in police hiring or promotions today and on alleged corruption or abusive tactics or some form of favoritism in personnel assignments tomorrow. What a given administrator considers unimportant may suddenly emerge in public attention as a matter of great importance, or vice versa. The wise administrator will not ignore or belittle what any element of the community thinks is important. At the same time, he must try to persuade the community not to ignore or belittle what may well be more important, long-run considerations.

THE SPECIAL CASE OF BRUTALITY

In chapter 10, we devoted some attention to police brutality. We were particularly interested, at that point, in the various definitions of the term and the inherent communication difficulties. It should be stated again that police brutality is the most explosive and most disputed claim made by minority groups against police officers.

Generally speaking, the police definition of what constitutes brutality is narrower than the definition of those community elements who are most likely to make such charges. All agree, however, that the use of unnecessary or unreasonable physical force constitutes brutality. The argument on this point tends to focus on what constitutes unnecessary or unreasonable force. As to so-called verbal brutality, some police officers have trouble understanding why calling a black man "boy" should be regarded as brutal. Police officers are inclined to doubt that unaffected citizens in the community would consider this brutality. But studies show that this police assumption is largely erroneous.[24] Less than a third of the police officials canvassed in one national survey felt that such things as sarcasm, ridicule, curtness, and disrespect should be considered brutality. But more than half of the Caucasian community leaders and almost three-fourths of the black community leaders thought so.

James Walsh devotes attention to the tendency of police officers to label some persons "animals." This concept covers a variety of persons but centers especially on those with whom, as Walsh puts it, "very little likelihood of a positive outcome faces the officer as he sets out to handle a family dispute, to face a mentally disturbed person, a belligerent drunk, a neighborhood quarrel in which the police must play 'umpire,' or the known cop-fighter."[25]

The heart of the police officer's trouble with what are called "animals" is the "can't win" nature of the encounter. If the officer physically abuses a citizen, he or she faces criticism and possible counterattack, probable insolence, and the chance of enhancing the standing of the "animal" in the eyes of the latter's peers. If, on the other hand, the officer avoids forceful and aggressive tactics, he or she is subject to the insults of the "animal," possible jeers and taunts of bystanders, and loss of respect on all sides, including that of other officers.

Walsh found that a high proportion (80 percent) of the police officers who strive to be professional felt that physical force was most apt to be used by an officer when dealing with an "animal." Adding to the officer's resentment was the expectation that the "animal," if arrested, would soon be released by the courts and returned to the street to give the officer further trouble.[26] This is dirty work that the police wish they could escape but know they cannot, and it becomes a contributing factor in their cynicism.

There has been a tendency for police officials to assert that brutality charges are seriously exaggerated. They point to statistics compiled by the FBI that record a very small number of convictions. But the U.S. Commission on Civil Rights has cited the inadequacy of the salient federal statute for handling flagrant cases of brutality.[27] J. Edgar Hoover admitted the ineffectiveness of existing procedure for dealing with charges under this statute. Incidentally, there is nothing in the statute that can be construed as covering *verbal* brutality.

In any event, the important consideration is whether significant numbers of people *believe* that police brutality, however it is defined, really occurs. There is abundant evidence that such a belief is fairly widespread, especially among the poor and minority groups. It is an aspect of their generally unfavorable attitude toward the police. Moreover, there is evidence of sufficient actual incidence of police brutality, physical and verbal, to lend credence to the belief and fuel the conclusion that brutality is more common than it really is. Such is the stuff that nurtures distrust of the police and, reciprocally, prompts many police officers to distrust "troublemakers" in the community. The police officer says, "They're just out to get us, that's all." The poor black says, "Those fink bastards lie in their teeth." Apparently, it never occurs to those who speak of the police in this manner that officers are often the *victims* of both physical and verbal affronts.

It appears that disrespect and verbal abuse constitute the type of police brutality that requires the greatest attention today. Physical beatings have not disappeared, but they are rarer than they were some years ago. Verbal attacks, on the other hand, are rampant in police-citizen encounters, almost always two-way to be sure, but verbal affronts are especially offensive when employed by "professional" peacekeepers who personify the majesty of the law. Frequently, "communication" between police officer and citizen is in the rhetoric of racism or profanity. And verbal abuse can quickly become physical abuse, as we noted in our discussion of collective behavior.

Verbal brutality involves questions of policy and supervision. Superiors in a department will say that they do not condone such behavior by a subordinate officer. Too often, sanction stops there. If questioned about this, the superior may cautiously refer to the police union, suggesting that disciplinary action for such a minor offense might bring down the wrath of the union. This response begs the question as to who should exert discipline. Thus an administrative-supervisory position develops that is extremely vulnerable from several standpoints, including the possibility that the union might *support* appropriate disciplinary action in clear-cut cases.

Many departments have little statistical data related to brutality charges. In regard to the use of excessive physical force, the Michigan State University study for the President's Crime Commission had access to records in five major cities, which—if accurate—revealed odds that an officer would be convicted of using excessive force once in every 18 years in city A, once in every 30 years in city B, once in every 19 years in city C, once in every 23 years in city D, and once in every 29 years in city E. There was some evidence that citizen complaints increase as public confidence in the police increases, at least in the short run.[28] This is the kind of thing that makes the criteria of *good* police-community relations difficult to define.

Internal investigations in police agencies often arouse public suspicion, as mentioned earlier. The charge of "whitewash" grows out of a low percentage of sustained charges, a correspondingly small proportion resulting in disciplinary action, and a general tendency to "sweep it under the rug" when there is evidence to support the complaint. Sometimes a local newspaper will exert pressure in such circumstances, at the risk of straining police-press relations and inviting an accusation of sensationalism. The newspaper is not always well informed in such situations, to put it mildly; but sometimes it might be, as experience in several cities illustrates.

In any event, the statistical and records-keeping variances, discrepancies, and inadequacies in many departments highlight the general problem of sloppy handling of citizen complaints. The orientation of too many police agencies toward complaints is negative rather than positive. They see complaints as threatening, as something that must be "headed off at the pass" at all costs. Sometimes this attitude seems to prevail even in otherwise relatively progressive police organizations. This stance is, of course, understandable in an elementary human sense. But it is also, in part, a carry-over of a past when it was considered administratively useful to perpetuate a certain mystique about the daily happenings in a police station.

Such an attitude toward citizen complaints clearly boomerangs in lessened trust and confidence in the police, reflected in movements to establish some form of strong exterior control over their behavior. Thus, if police officials insist that the police *should* control police conduct, it must be clearly demonstrated, to the satisfaction of all community audiences, that the police *can* control police conduct. To the extent that this can be achieved with a *positive* orientation where citizens feel that their complaints are contributions to better police service for all, the rancor associated with the matter of complaints can be alleviated.

A CRITIQUE OF EXISTING CONTROL METHODS

It may be helpful to enumerate some of the main criticisms that have been leveled against existing ways of dealing with citizen complaints against the police. These are necessarily generalizations with no particular place or police department in mind; the criticism may not be valid in specific cases, but it holds often enough to justify its inclusion here:

1. Insufficient training of police officers, both preservice and inservice, in human relations.
2. Ineffective administrative policies and supervision relative to police misconduct.
3. Serious credibility questions regarding internal discipline and investigative procedures.
4. Inadequate statistics, data retrieval systems, and record keeping relative to citizen complaints.
5. Deficiencies in public information and interpretation regarding complaint procedures. Closely allied with this is an attitude toward complaints that makes the procedure overly formal, unduly difficult, inconvenient, embarrassing, or even legally foreboding for the complainant, for example, the use of lie detectors.
6. Numerous police agencies have no established pattern of complaint procedure, handling same in a haphazard manner, for example, the chief of police deals with all complaints personally, or he assigns an officer to investigate when he thinks the charges warrant.
7. Too often, the complainant is not advised of the disposition of the case.
8. Few departments provide for systematic, periodic evaluation of their complaint procedures, with or without provision for public participation in such evaluation.

Having listed some of the principal criticisms of existing complaint procedures, it is well also to list some recent positive developments:

1. Many police departments see it as the duty of any and every police officer to be a complaint hearer, either by way of supplementing the activity of a special unit or in some cases as a "better system" than that represented by a special unit. (The latter is open to argument.)
2. Commendable due process provisions applying both to the complainant and to the accused, in hearings conducted as part of investigations into serious charges, are increasingly evident.
3. Provision in complaint procedure for appeals to a next higher level, if desired, is no longer rare.

4. Some form of external *advisory* group for internal investigative units exists in many departments. Admittedly, there is considerable variation in the actual influence of such advisory forums, and some question as to whom they represent.

5. The secretive climate that has tended to surround complaint and investigative procedures in the past is slowly evaporating.

6. Many departments are moving away from complicated procedures that scare away complainants. The widespread use of standard, simple, mail-in complaint forms (pioneered by the Oakland, California, police department) is indicative of this trend. It should be noted, however, that efforts to assure a dispassionate inquiry into a complaint, and at the same time to safeguard the rights of an official whose occupational future may be at stake, may have the unintended effect of discouraging the expression of grievances.

It should be added on the positive side that an increasing number of police agencies are taking steps to remove the basis for each of the eight criticisms earlier listed.

EVALUATING COMPLAINT PROCEDURES

External Complaints

We have mentioned the need for systematic, periodic evaluation of complaint machinery. What guidelines or checkpoints may be suggested for this purpose? Depending on local community and departmental variances, the following questions may be helpful:

1. Is there policy or law requiring that all complaints reported be recorded at a central point to insure proper data retrieval?

2. Is there policy or law that prohibits employees from attempting to discourage any civilian from making a complaint?

3. Does the department make conscious efforts to cause complainants a minimum of inconvenience and embarrassment?

4. Is the machinery for hearing and processing complaints fair, impartial, and objective?

5. Is the machinery adequately publicized and interpreted so that all citizens know of it and can get further assistance if they need it?

6. Are all complaints adequately investigated?

7. Are there reports to the party making the complaint so that he is aware of developments from the time he makes the complaint until the time of disposition?

8. Does the department have a reputation for integrity with the entire community? (Do all members of the community consider it *their* police department?)

9. Is there an avenue for formalized appeal of police decisions or findings?[29]

With some input from randomly selected citizens on some of these checkpoints, the police administrator will acquire a fairly reliable gauge as to the adequacy of complaint procedures. The ninth question, of course, takes procedure outside the department—to a police or safety commission, to the city council, to the city's community relations commission, to an ombudsman, to the prosecuting attorney, or to the courts.[30]

Internal Complaints

The aforementioned checkpoints pertain to the external complaint—those of a citizen, directed against the police department or against a police officer. For internal complaints—those of an employee against the department, those of a superior officer against a subordinate, of a subordinate against a superior, or of an employee against another employee of equal rank—some checkpoints may also be suggested, again subject to local variances:

1. All employees must be held strictly accountable for their behavior.

2. Supervision is the crucial function relative to internal (and external) complaints. The supervisor must have authority commensurate with responsibility. But if supervisors abuse this authority, they should be held strictly accountable. Guidelines are useful in prescribing and proscribing supervisory responsibilities.

3. Administrative directives should clearly delineate the rights and responsibilities of employees at every level in the department. Such policies should also clearly indicate available grievance and appropriate disciplinary procedures. Top administrators in the department should not be handling minor rule infractions while line supervisors are handling more serious matters.

4. Administrators also should have authority commensurate with their responsibilities. As a general rule, this includes discipline to the point of terminating an officer's service, subject only to the limitation of advisory consultation with the chief executive of the particular governmental jurisdiction, and the right of appeal by the officer to a civil service or other board of review. The latter should *not* have the power to overrule the police administrator, but only to review the administrative action and to make their findings public.

5. Members of the organization at all levels should know that they can call attention to the improper conduct of other employees without incurring organizational penalties. Indeed, this should be made clear in departmental regulations.

6. Some method or system of staff inspections should be routine, with reports made directly to the chief administrator.

7. Some sort of internal staff unit for the investigation of charges of employee misconduct is desirable in departments of sufficient size to justify it. The Michigan State University study report suggests the duties of such a unit.[31]

8. Departmental trial boards can be administratively advantageous in departments of appreciable size. Important features of such boards are suggested in the same study report.[32]

The importance of carefully defined, widely disseminated, and adequately interpreted employee grievance procedures should be emphasized again. Due process provisions of such procedures should be loud and clear. It bears repeating that problems of *internal* relations in an organization inevitably are projected in *external* relations. The Michigan Department of Civil Service has recently established an ombudsman position, to investigate and to mediate objectively the grievances that may be filed by any of 66,000 state workers. The Michigan Department of Corrections has an ombudsman to assist prisoners with their problems.

Some Additional Observations

There are a few points to be added on this extremely important matter. One is the observation that a patrol officer on the street is something of a neighborhood ombudsman. Unless there is reason for an individual officer to be avoided, people will tend to look to him for information, direction, assistance when in trouble, a helping hand in rain or snow, a listening ear in frustration, some friendly counsel, or referral to the agency or persons appropriate to a particular need. If the officer turns them off or turns them away, many people have no idea where they may find assistance. Police officers on street duty are accustomed to hearing complaints about many things. Most of the time, they are able to offer something: a suggestion, a word of advice, a cautionary note, a bracing thought, an encouraging idea. The best of police-community relations is not done through big projects, committees, and programs. It comes down to the one-to-one contacts of a police officer and a citizen.

In our discussion of discretionary use of police power in chapter 5, we referred to the central question of police accountability. We quoted Albert Reiss in his delineation of the possible options in this regard. He acknowledges that a system of external review creates problems, especially when there is review of an individual's performance within an organization. This form of accountability, he points out, interferes with both institutionalized forms of professional control of practice and with organizational forms of control to protect its boundaries. Public-school teachers in this country, when faced with the same kind of question, formed professional organizations that have resisted school board review "on professional grounds." The police have lacked extralocal, line, professional organization, although there is currently a beginning of movement in that direction.

Regarding the ombudsman system, Reiss has this to say:

Without doubt, attempts to institutionalize the role of ombudsman in American society would encounter considerable resistance, particularly from lawyers and judges, who perhaps have been most exempt from public scrutiny among the professionals in the United States (unless it be physicians). Quite clearly also, their resistance would be stipulated on "professional" grounds of competence to control practice. Since police in the United States are inextricably linked to the system of criminal justice, they are inclined to regard with cynicism a civic accountability system of their organization that exempts the office of public prosecutor and jurist. But they are more vulnerable to client claims. Unlike the lawyers and social workers in the criminal justice system, their claim is based primarily on local police organizational control of police malpractice, rather than on professional association control of malpractice.[33]

Reiss's comments suggest an important question about professional fields, reminiscent of our discussion in an earlier chapter of the perils of professionalism. An often-accepted protocol of professionalism is the development of considerable insulation from other professions, cultivated by jargon, journals, certification and accreditation of schools, and the like. Interprofessional cooperation is always welcome, so long as *our* profession prescribes the terms. Police professionals need to remember that the nature of the business makes a wide range of knowledge imperative, involving many disciplines and fields. This is the crucial case for police education, in the broadest sense.

THE QUESTION OF NEIGHBORHOOD CONTROL

In tune with Reiss, James Q. Wilson maintains that:

> Though the [civilian review board] issue is passionately debated, it is not clear that, however it is resolved, it will have much effect on the *substantive* police policies that are in effect—partly because some are not "policies" at all but styles created by general organizational arrangements and departmental attitudes, and partly because grievance procedures deal with specific complaints about unique circumstances, not with general practices of the officers.[34]

The question of control of the police tends to revolve around what has happened, under duress of social change, to the idea of *local* government. In the big, heterogeneous, impersonal, bureaucratic, insensitive city, "local" is a euphemism. The question of who's in charge of the police, under such circumstances, may become a matter of long-range skirmishing with distant, remote, forbidding, somewhat mysterious forces "downtown." If one is poor and powerless and resides in a ghetto, it is like trying to deal with a foreign power via diplomatic gibberish. Under such circumstances, one might wish that there could be a truly local, neighborhood police, close enough to be held fully accountable to residents of the neighborhood for all activities and services. Precinct stations might serve this purpose, were it not for a tendency to handle complaints at that level by saying, "We're sorry we can't help. We take our orders from headquarters."

As we have seen, the issue of control is complicated by the conditions that make the management of conflict the police officer's most important task. It is a task that is more difficult in places where conflicting behavior norms and values are most evident and where attitudes and behavior deviate the most from the standards of the middle class. This describes a social milieu in which the bases of political power are apt to be shifting, with social groups splitting, coalescing on new issues, and polarizing in a struggle for power. Eleanor Harlow describes the situation as follows:

> Because what the police should do and how they should do it cannot be standardized for every situation, they are required to decide for themselves, often instantly and in

a hostile environment, not merely what is "legal" or illegal, but what is right and wrong, what is "order" and when does order become "disorder," what is an "antisocial" act within a given context, and what behavior can be considered "disturbing" to society. These are issues which social scientists and lawyers might be hard put to answer and over which different groups and individuals certainly would disagree. The police cry that no matter what they do they are criticized is valid, and probably necessarily so. In a situation of competing and conflicting values and norms, someone is going to feel that police interference was unnecessary, morally wrong, inadequate, illegal, discriminatory, badly undertaken, or unjust.[35]

One Side of the Argument

Those who have advocated steps to impose community or neighborhood control on the police obviously begin with the assumption that the police in the American metropolis are no longer under civilian control; that is, democratic public control. For them, it is a question of how to make the police more responsive to the needs of all groups in the community. Their feeling is that the police increasingly control themselves, in a manner irrelevant to community needs and wishes. In this sense, the police are seen as having become "too damn independent," and with the rise of police unions, the speculation is that they are likely to become even more so. The argument is that such things as psychological screening of police recruits, human relations training, and "all the talk about police professionalization" have not worked to restore civilian control of the police—that, in fact, the gap between police and civilians is greater than ever.

What to do? Arthur Waskow of the Institute for Policy Studies in Washington has identified three possible directions:

1. Formal restructuring of metropolitan police departments into federations of neighborhood police forces, with control of each neighborhood force in the hands of neighborhood people through elected commissions.

2. Creation of countervailing organizations (in effect, "trade unions" *of those policed*), responsible to a real political base, able to hear grievances and force change.

3. Transformation of the police "profession" and role so as to end the isolation of policemen from the rest of the community, thus to establish *de facto* community control by chiefly informal means.[36]

The first of these alternatives, Waskow explains, would be institutionalized by the election of neighborhood or precinct police commissions which would (1) appoint high-level precinct officers (perhaps with the approval of metropolitan headquarters, the mayor, or a civil service commission); (2) approve the assignment in the precinct of new police officers and be able to require transfers out; (3) discipline officers, perhaps with the concurrence of a citywide appeal board; and (4) set basic policy on law enforcement priorities in the neighborhood.

Those fostering such an arrangement feel that it would respond to the allegation that no great metropolis can be democratically governed from City Hall. Second, they feel that it responds to the concentration of blacks (and other minorities) in certain neighborhoods and allows for police service fitting the needs of particular parts of the city, just as presently exists in suburbia. Police might even be required to live in the neighborhood where they work, although this could be difficult to enforce.

To those who object to this proposal on the grounds of "hot pursuit" considerations, it is said that such difficulties already exist across police jurisdictional boundaries. Similar practical solutions can be worked out. Moreover, it may even be possible to visualize a single metropolitan police organization of diverse and largely autonomous neighborhood forces: a confederation of sorts, organized, perhaps, in the pattern of the national police system of England. And it is added, there is really nothing new about the idea of different styles of policing from neighborhood to neighborhood: it already exists in metropolitan areas, *defined by the police rather than by the public.*

Certain aspects of police organization would, under this proposal, continue to be handled at central headquarters: records, fingerprinting, radio communications, certain specialized squads, training, planning and research, crime in the business district, and the like.

As to the second proposal—the control of the police through countervailing power—a few experiments have been attempted. The Community Alert Patrols in Watts (and counterparts elsewhere) and the Community Review Board established by the Mexican-American community in Denver are examples. So-called citizen observer teams also come to mind. These are to be carefully distinguished from civilian review boards, in that they attempt to mount independent political power to confront that of police forces, without utilizing a quasi-judicial model. Political pressure comes, rather, through appeals to public opinion.

One advantage of the countervailing power approach, Waskow points out, is that it can be undertaken without the agreement of those in power. Another is that it is not necessarily anchored in a neighborhood. A third point is that, it is easier to organize the powerless to *oppose* police power than it is to organize them to *grasp* it, a point just as true in other spheres of social change. Moreover, "the enemy" is seen as not only the formal police command and its ties with the metropolitan power structure, but also the informal police subculture, with its "blue curtain" political power through unions and fraternal associations.

The third option identified by Waskow—transformation of the police role—would require, he believes, radically *deprofessionalizing* some police roles, particularly on-the-street, peace-keeping functions. Waskow foresees much of this type of police work being performed by nonsworn personnel, not carrying arms, and dressed in an unmilitary style uniform. Such personnel would live in the neighborhood where they work. Waskow's description of these peace-keepers is similar to that of the community service officers, sometimes called paraprofessionals, depicted by the 1966 President's Crime Commission. The main point, for Waskow, is that such personnel would be the most visible police officers and would be perceived by residents in any neighborhood as "our police," thereby establishing informal control. This plan also splits police work into distinct roles, which Waskow feels is one of its strengths.

We may suggest parenthetically, however—reflecting our opinion—that Waskow seems to underestimate what is involved in on-the-street order maintenance. He says that this role is not a highly technical or specialized one, but depends rather on a "fairly widespread and certainly nonprofessional skill in conciliatory human relations."[37] We think this point would draw an argument from many police, including even some who heartily dislike "calming people down." One line of the argument would probably be: "How do you educate an escaping armed robber so he will refrain from shooting the peace-keeping officer, not knowing that the officer isn't a *real* police officer?" There has been an instance or two in which black community service officers of a police department were shot to death by snipers in a predominantly black neighborhood. This is certainly not an argument against the judicious use of paraprofessionals. But, to draw a parallel with the use of teacher's aides in urban public schools, the aide is most effective when paired with a knowledgeable, experienced teacher.

Waskow's sympathy for neighborhood control is representative of a significant feeling in numerous large cities about both schools and police. The central issue is political power, and conflict is inevitable no matter which option (or combination of options) materializes. Waskow concludes, with reference to the police:

> It is hard to see how democratic civilian control over a staff of armed men who are widely believed to hold a monopoly over legitimate violence and who are well organized in a separate subculture and a strong political force can be reestablished without intense political conflict.[38]

The experience with decentralized neighborhood school boards in New York City, in Detroit, and in other metropolitan areas has been instructive. Measured by the standard of improving the quality of education, the experiments have fallen considerably short of the expectations of the most avid proponents.

In policing, where responsiveness and accountability are so much the labels for maintaining public control of delegated power, neighborhood (or precinct or divisional) police-community relations councils have exercised such control, in varying degree. So have police advisory groups of one kind or another. So does a team policing approach (democratic model) to patrol operations. The key question is: How much decentralized control seems necessary in a given setting?[39] It should be added that some studies do indicate a consistent pattern of higher levels of police performance by small police forces under local community control, as compared with large, city-controlled operations.[40]

Another Side of the Argument

James Q. Wilson has presented another side of the question.[41] What is involved, he says, is two competing models of how best to maintain order. One model—held by police officers generally—is what may be called *institutional*. In this view, law must be strictly enforced and with special vigor in those areas where community and familial norms appear weakest. Furthermore, according to this model, high-crime or high-disorder areas offer too many temptations for corruption to police officers, which are best controlled by centrally directed police activity. Moreover, ensuring due process of law requires administrative regularity, strongly enforced departmental rules, and central authority.

Opposed to this is what Wilson labels the *communal* model. This position begins with the observation that most police work is concerned, not with serious crime, but with regulating public conduct. Wilson refers to this model as, in effect, *suburbanizing* the central city; that is, permitting each neighborhood (usually defined along lines of class and race) to determine its own style of police service by a system of participatory democracy.

Wilson sympathizes with the objectives of the communal model but questions the means, for these reasons:

1. A central city cannot be fully suburbanized because it is, by definition, *central*—a place where many competing life styles come into frequent contact. It is here that the deepest social cleavages exist.

2. Therefore, giving central city neighborhoods control of the police risks making the police power an instrument for interneighborhood conflict. It might well put the police "at the mercy of the rawest emotions, the most demagogic spokesmen, and the most provincial concerns." The possibility of a small, self-serving minority seizing control of the police (or the schools) would become "very great indeed."[42]

Wilson points out that these are arguments against plans *to disperse the authority* that governs the police, not against ways to *decentralize the functions* of the police. The latter tends to strengthen local units; the dispersal of authority, in contrast, tends to weaken them. As Wilson phrases it: "Precinct commanders in a *decentralized* department would have greater freedom of action and more control over their patrolmen; precinct commanders in a *dispersed* department would surrender that control to whatever constellation of political forces the neighborhood might produce."[43]

Wilson opts in favor of what is, in effect, Waskow's third alternative: an approach to the patrol officer's role definition that emphasizes order-maintenance functions, which would have the effect of bringing the officer closer to the people in a neighborhood, even to the possible requirement that the officer live in the neighborhood. But Wilson does not seem to share Waskow's view that the patrol officer's function in this respect is less than professional. Wilson further observes that "a community concerned about lowering its crime rates would be well advised to devote its attention and resources to those parts of the criminal justice system, especially the courts and correctional agencies, which—unlike the police—spend most of their time processing (often in the most perfunctory and ineffective manner) persons who repeatedly perpetrate these crimes."[44]

To those who defend the communal model for police control on the grounds that it avoids the middle-class bias of the legal code and of moral order, Wilson retorts that if this means a concern for the security of persons and property and a desire to avoid intrusions into one's privacy and disturbances of one's peace, it is not clear why this is a bad thing. If on the other hand it means a dislike for eccentric dress or manners, the term "bias" is aptly chosen.

Another objection Wilson has to the communal model is that it fails to provide for social-class differences within a given neighborhood. For example, middle-class blacks now often live close to lower-class blacks. How can one style of policing in such a neighborhood be satisfactory for both? There are presently complaints about "a single standard of justice" on a communitywide basis; why would it be more acceptable on a neighborhood basis?

SUMMING UP

This chapter focuses upon *accountability* in public service. The assumption is that police power is not a private right, but rather that it is a public loan. A proper philosophy and procedure for handling both external and internal complaints are therefore imperative for any police agency. Yet there remains considerable resistance to this rather obvious point, evident in miscellaneous shenanigans that appear directed toward hoodwinking the public and, in effect, often making complaints a very trying process indeed for citizens.

It is apparent that the issue of community control of the police revolves largely around the question—again—of role definition. If the major function of the police in big cities is conflict management, as most analysts claim, there will be inevitable disagreement (therefore complaints) as to what should be done, how, and to whom. Until the poor become middle class, as Wilson puts it, the question of control of the police (and of the schools) will continue to be a hotly contested political issue.

However, much can be done to remedy the situation short of turning to a plan for control that may succeed only in aggravating tensions because it copies, on a smaller logistic scale, what is presently wrong with the system on a larger scale. The principal objective is to develop conditions in which the police are truly responsive to the needs of people residing in particular neighborhoods, so as to encourage perceptions of the police as "our police." As the needs and life styles of people differ from community to community and neighborhood to neighborhood, so the style of policing should differ. There appears to be no reason this objective cannot be achieved under centralized, imaginative, truly professionalized administration—and all that this implies for policies, supervision, planning, recruitment standards, and training of personnel.

Community control, of course, poses drastic challenges to the political status quo. In the case of public schools in many large cities, the idea is vigorously opposed by many professional educators and politicians who see it, quite naturally, as a threat to their "turf." Advisory councils, on the other hand, are not threatening because no shift in authority is involved. One way or another, community involvement is the name of the game—with schools or police—and controversy on this issue has become an urban commonplace.

NOTES

1. Michael Banton, "Social Integration and Police," *Police Chief*, April 1963, p. 12.

2. Parts of this chapter rely on chapter 4, "Police Conduct and the Public," of U.S., President's Commission on Law Enforcement and Administration of Justice, *Field*

Surveys V: A National Survey of Police and Community Relations (prepared for the commission by the National Center on Police and Community Relations, Michigan State University, School of Police Administration and Public Safety) (Washington, D.C.: U.S. Government Printing Office, 1967), pp. 128–257. That chapter was written by John E. Angell.

3. Walter Gellhorn, "Police Review Boards: Hoax or Hope?" Reprinted by permission from *Columbia Forum* 9, no. 3 (Summer 1966), p. 10. Copyright © 1966 by The Trustees of Columbia University in the City of New York. All rights reserved.

4. Ibid.

5. Ibid. See also the following works by Gellhorn: "Administrative Procedure Reform: Hardy Perennial," *American Bar Association Journal* 48 (1962): 243–251; *Ombudsmen and Others: Citizens' Protectors in Nine Countries* (Cambridge, Mass.: Harvard University Press, 1966).

6. Monrad G. Paulsen, "Police Conduct and the Public," in A. F. Brandstatter and Louis A. Radelet, eds., *Police and Community Relations: A Sourcebook* (Beverly Hills, Calif.: Glencoe, 1968), p. 267.

7. Herbert L. Packer, "Who Can Police the Police?" *New York Review*, September 8, 1966. See also by the same author, *The Limits of the Criminal Sanction* (Stanford, Calif.: Stanford University Press, 1968); also see Herman Goldstein, "Administrative Problems in Controlling the Exercise of Police Authority," *Journal of Criminal Law, Criminology and Police Science* 58, no. 2 (1967): 160–172.

8. See Algernon D. Black, *The People and the Police* (New York: McGraw-Hill, 1968). Also see Dan W. Dodson, "Police and Community Relations as a Political Issue," in Brandstatter and Radelet, eds., *Police and Community Relations*, pp. 259–266.

9. William P. Brown, "The Review Board Proposals Do Not Go Far Enough" (paper presented at the Seventy-first National Conference of Government, held in New York, November 17, 1965).

10. See also Donald C. Rowat, ed., *The Ombudsman: Citizen's Defender* (Toronto: University of Toronto Press, 1965).

11. Gellhorn, "Police Review Boards," p. 20.

12. Packer, *The Limits of the Criminal Sanction*, p. 283.

13. Allen R. Bryan and Lt. Mike Duffy, *Operational Policy*, Internal Affairs Unit, Division of Police, City of Louisville, mimeographed, n.d.; and City of Louisville, "Reporting and Investigating Problems of Conduct Among Government Employees" (brochure published by the City of Louisville, n.d.).

14. U.S., President's Commission on Law Enforcement and Administration of Justice, *The Challenge of Crime in a Free Society* (Washington, D.C.: U.S. Government Printing Office, 1967), p. 103.

15. U.S., President's Commission on Law Enforcement and Administration of Justice, *Task Force Report: The Police* (Washington, D.C.: U.S. Government Printing Office, 1967), pp. 193–204.

16. U.S., President's Commission on Law Enforcement and Administration of Justice, *Field Surveys IV*, vol. 1, pp. 167–175; vol. 2, pp. 195–284.

17. U.S., National Advisory Commission on Civil Disorders, *Report of the National Advisory Commission on Civil Disorders* (Kerner Report) (Washington, D.C.: U.S. Government Printing Office, 1969), pp. 151–152.

18. U.S., National Commission on the Causes and Prevention of Violence, *To Establish Justice, To Insure Domestic Tranquility* (Washington, D.C.: U.S. Government Printing Office, 1969), p. 10.

19. *Report: Campus Unrest* (Washington, D.C.: U.S. Government Printing Office, 1970), pp. 215, 202–206.

20. National Advisory Commission on Criminal Justice Standards and Goals, *Report on Police* (Washington, D.C.: U.S. Government Printing Office, 1973), pp. 480–494.

21. U.S. Commission on Civil Rights, *The State of Civil Rights: 1977* (Washington, D.C.: U.S. Government Printing Office, 1978), pp. 27–28.

22. Police Foundation, *Police Use of Deadly Force* (Washington, D.C.: The Police Foundation Inc., 1977), p. 11.

23. President's Commission on Law Enforcement, *Field Surveys V.*

24. Ibid., p. 151.

25. James Leo Walsh, "The Professional Cop" (paper presented at the Sixty-fourth Annual Meeting of the American Sociological Association, September 1968).

26. A similar conclusion is reached by Albert J. Reiss, Jr., and David J. Bordua, "Environment and Organization: A Perspective on the Police," in David J. Bordua, ed., *The Police: Six Sociological Essays* (New York: John Wiley & Sons, 1967), pp. 33–37.

27. *United States Criminal Code* (Title 18), Section 242.

28. President's Commission on Law Enforcement, *Field Surveys V*, p. 168.

29. Ibid., pp. 228–229.

30. One possibility regarding such appeals is described in "A Model for Handling Citizen Complaints," in Louis A. Radelet and Hoyt Coe Reed, *The Police and the Community: Studies* (Beverly Hills, Calif.: Glencoe, 1973), pp. 145–150.

31. President's Commission on Law Enforcement, *Field Surveys V*, pp. 235–242.

32. Ibid., pp. 243–245.

33. Albert J. Reiss, Jr., "Professionalization of the Police," in Brandstatter and Radelet, eds., *Police and Community Relations*, p. 223. Reprinted by permission. For a study of the grand jury in California as ombudsman, see Bruce T. Olson, "Ombudsman on the West Coast: An Analysis and Evaluation of the Watchdog Function of the California Grand Jury," *Police* 12, no. 2 (1967): 12–20. See also William H. Hewitt, "New York's Civilian Complaint Review Board Struggle: Its History, Analysis and Some Notes," *Police* 11, nos. 5 and 6, and 12, no. 1.

34. James Q. Wilson, *Varieties of Police Behavior: The Management of Law and Order in Eight Communities* (Cambridge, Mass.: Harvard University Press, 1968), pp. 229–230.

35. Eleanor Harlow, "Problems in Police-Community Relations: A Review of the Literature," *Information Review on Crime and Delinquency* 1, no. 5 (February 1969): 19. Reprinted by permission of the National Council on Crime and Delinquency.

36. Arthur I. Waskow, "Community Control of the Police," *Transaction*, December 1969, p. 40.

37. Ibid., p. 5.

38. Ibid., p. 7.

39. See Richard A. Myren, "Decentralization and Citizen Participation in Criminal Justice Systems," *Public Administration Review 32* (October 1972): 718–732; Gary T.

Marx and Dane Archer, "Citizen Involvement in the Law Enforcement Process," *American Behavioral Scientist* 15, no. 1 (September–October, 1971); Joseph F. Zimmerman, "Neighborhood Governments and Service Provision" (paper prepared for a caucus of a New Political Science panel, annual meeting of the American Political Science Association, Chicago, August 29–September 2, 1974); Milton Kotler, "The Ethics of Neighborhood Government" (paper prepared for American Political Science Association caucus mentioned above); and Alan A. Altshuler, *Community Control* (New York: Pegasus, 1970).

40. Elinor Ostrom and Gordon Whitaker, "Does Local Community Control of Police Make a Difference? Some Preliminary Findings" (based on a paper presented at the Western Political Science Association meeting, Albuquerque, New Mexico, April 8–10, 1971), *American Journal of Sociology*, 1973, pp. 43–76.

41. James Q. Wilson, "Controlling the Police," *Harvard Today*, Autumn 1968. Reprinted by permission. The same argument also appears in James Q. Wilson, *Varieties of Police Behavior*, pp. 284–299.

42. Ibid.

43. Ibid.

44. Ibid. Myren discusses the decentralization of all criminal justice processes in "Decentralization and Citizen Participation in Criminal Justice Systems."

SUMMARY OF PART 3

Our general purpose in part 3 has been to consider some of the sociological aspects of contemporary problems of police and community relations. We began by alluding briefly to the standard sociological classification of the various patterns of group interaction called *social processes:* cooperation, competition, conflict, acculturation, and others. We were especially interested in the measures by which a society brings its individual members and subgroups into sufficient conformity to permit the survival of the society. These measures are referred to by the collective term *social control,* and law is its most obvious form. Therefore, the vital functions of law observance and law enforcement are universally recognized.

Social change, however—especially in its effects upon group interaction in modern society—has radically transformed social control. One way of explaining current problems in police and community relations is by discussing the relationship between social change and social control. To ask what has happened to *community* is another way of suggesting the same thing. Unquestionably, social control has become infinitely complicated. We illustrated this by describing current population trends in the United States: the increasing concentration of our people in big cities; the movement of people outward, from central city to suburbs; and the qualitative nature (in the human relations sense) of the suburban movement. We analyzed in particular how the latter trend has affected black people in the metropolis, caught up for the past two and one-half generations in adjustment to urbanization. We devoted special attention to the so-called culture of poverty and to contemporary problems of urban localities. These are crucial matters in police and community relations, given what is known about the reciprocal attitudes of police and minority groups, and of police and the poor.

Against the background of the civil rights movement in the United States of the 1960s, we next considered the critical subject of police and minority-group relations. Many people tend to equate police-minority relations with police-community relations. We earlier noted a distinction, saying among other things that one is an important aspect of the other. So we devoted a chapter to analyzing the relationship of the police with minority groups specifically. We saw the base of the problem as one of power: the police as symbolic agents of the *powerful* elements, legally required to serve *all* the people, interacting with the *powerless,* many of whom are black or of other minority groups, and many of whom, white or black, are poor. The dual stereotyping and displaced hostility in this interaction were pointedly emphasized. Many would hold that efforts to improve police and minority-group relations in the 1960s amounted only to a "holding action," with little effect on the real problem.

"Brutality" is the emotion-packed charge often directed against the police by the powerless. It is not usually defined with great care; we characterized three levels of definition for the term by way of suggesting one of the communication obstacles. We delineated some of the most frequent complaints and counter-complaints of the police and of minority groups. Has society at large made "dirty-workers" of the police, with their main task that of controlling those who do not share equitably in society's largesse?

The black and police subcultures were next analyzed by the effects of the sociopsychological concept of *cognitive dissonance*. The dissonance is great indeed. But it was observed that race itself is much less the decisive friction factor than is social class. The association of race and crime lends itself to facile statistical classification, bolstered by perpetuated stereotypes. It is easier to refer to "Negro crime" than it is to develop classifications reflecting the fact that the causes of crime are nonracial.

We then posed a startling question: Can the police lead the community in race relations? Can they be monitors of social change in their main job of social-conflict management? By any contemporary barometer, the police officer of minority-group background will be of great strategic importance. But such officers have been difficult to recruit. We reviewed ten reasons for this. We concluded the chapter with a brief consideration of police relationships with minority groups other than blacks and of the manner in which the civil rights movement has affected other components of the criminal justice system.

Social upheaval in urban America in the 1960s was manifest in various forms and degrees of collective behavior: crowds, mobs, social movements, riots, and so on. We referred briefly to such phenomena, noting their special importance to the police, and we touched on social responses to the collective behavior associated with the civil rights movement. We devoted a section to the currently fearsome matter of terrorism. Next, we considered the intriguing subject of civil disobedience. We distinguished what it is from what it is not, compared the ideas of Thoreau and Gandhi on the subject, explored the meaning of law, and reviewed the approach of various writers to the conditions for moral justification of civil disobedience.

The civil rights movement in the 1960s was, in considerable degree, a *youth* movement. The reciprocal attitudes of youth and police are of special interest in the study of police and community relations. The roots of youthful attitudes toward authority systems and authority figures (e.g., the police officer) are established, as we saw in an earlier chapter, in the political socialization processes experienced by individual children. We referred to a number of studies dealing with this subject, including several focusing on the junior high school age level, which is thought to be a particularly important age group in attitude research of this type.

We alluded to the special nuances of police-youth attitudes in the context of teenage gangs and "disaffected" youth. The college scene was our next consideration; we moved from this to a passing comment regarding drugs. We moved on to the matter of women in police work and criminal justice, noting recent developments in this regard and assessing this trend in police and community relations terms. The chapter ended with a brief look at the increasingly important questions of crime and the elderly.

The issue of citizen control of the police was our central concern in the final chapter of part 3. We analyzed several questions that arise in the matter of complaints, internally within a police agency, and externally when a citizen lodges a complaint against the department or against one or more of its personnel. We recommended a positive philosophy for dealing with complaints of all kinds. We applied this philosophy to a critique of existing complaint procedures in police agencies, one conclusion being that so-called civilian review boards are not generally the answer. We suggested that the Scandinavian ombudsman system merits more testing in this country, for it appears to have much to recommend it. We identified criteria for evaluating the adequacy of both external and internal complaint mechanisms. Finally, we discussed the pros and cons of community control of the police at the neighborhood level—a topic of lively contemporary interest in big-city school administration, also.

What are some of the "benchmarks" of the *specific* problems of police and community relations in relation to minority groups, the poor, the disaffected, and the powerless? The following may be suggested, to be placed side-by-side with the more generalized points enumerated in the summary for part 2.

1. The stereotype held by minority groups of the police officer as a symbolic agent and representative of the powerful, therefore "the enemy"—a matter of displaced hostility.

2. The counterstereotype in the police officer's image of the minority group; for example, the idea that crime is racially caused.

3. The problem of value gap and cognitive dissonance indicated in a comparison of police subculture and that of poor blacks, and the accompanying communication chasm.

4. The underrepresentation of minority groups in the personnel of police agencies.

5. The inadequacies of citizen complaint procedures in the matter of public control of police behavior.

6. Special problems for the police in dealing with civil disobedience.

7. Problems for the police associated with youthful attitudes toward authority.

8. The "dirty-worker" public image of the police.

9. Deficiencies in police recruitment standards and in police training, especially pertaining to the conflict management aspects of police work that have become so important.

10. Police administrative and supervisory traditionalism in failing to see police and community relations as basically a *management* concept.

To set the stage for part 4, we may say that there are five subjects in the purview of this text that merit more attention than we have devoted to them up to this point, though all have been mentioned. These are:

1. Relationships within the criminal justice system between the police, prosecution, and the courts.

2. The special problems of community relations for corrections agencies.
3. Police-press relations—in the broader sense, relations between the criminal justice system and the media of public information.
4. The police and their political-governmental relationships.
5. Community-based crime prevention.

Part 4 includes chapters on each of these five subjects.

PART **4**

Other Important
Considerations

14

THE CRIMINAL JUSTICE SYSTEM: POLICE, PROSECUTION, AND THE COURTS

We have referred more than once to the fact that the police are part of several overlapping social systems, one of which is called the *criminal justice system*. We defined a *social system* as a pattern of continuing social relations among individuals or groups. A social system, then, is a presumably harmonious arrangement intended to bring order out of confusion, an interacting or interdependent group of factors and functions forming a unified whole. This definition clearly contains an idealistic element: that a social system integrates through predominantly positive relations among its components, else it may not function well as a system. No serious relationship problems should be present within an authentic, properly functional social system, speaking idealistically.

But social systems are, after all, human inventions relating people in various parts of a process. A given social system is more or less functional depending upon the quality of these relationships, in exactly the same way as a community or a large police department (both complicated and multiple social systems in and of themselves) are more or less functional as measured against their purposes. Hence, the relationships within the criminal justice system— between police and prosecutor, between police and the courts, between prosecutor and the courts, between police and corrections, between the courts and corrections—are highly important aspects of what we mean by *community relations* in the major theme of this book. Indeed, the difficulties in *external* relations of any single criminal justice component, we believe, are frequently the projection of difficulties in *internal* relations.

Difficulties may be caused by dissimilarities in role or function, giving rise to differences in attitude, style, priority, and philosophy. These differences may be within a particular subsystem, between two or more subsystems, or between the entire complex of criminal justice and other professions or disciplines (such as psychology or sociology), or between the justice complex and society in general.

Take only one example: to the police officer, society—in the person of the victim—is the client. To a corrections counselor, the offender may be the client. That difference would be between the police and corrections subsystems. But it is also a difference between the philosophies of custody and treatment within

337

corrections itself. Further projected upon a larger screen, the conflict could be between the public and the criminal justice complex as fear and indignation demand strict enforcement and mandatory sentences.

Because the criminal justice system in the United States is vast and extremely complex, our discussion,of it requires some limitations. We will look at part of the system in this chapter, and part in the next. An avalanche of literature deals with the system—descriptively, analytically, and, in the recent past, more and more critically. We will not attempt to recapitulate much of it here; however, we will stress that a considerable part of what is dysfunctional in the criminal justice system has to do with relationships among its components, and between each of these components and the larger community. Therefore, in discussing the internal and external relationships of the criminal justice system, we will be considering matters at the core of its deficiencies. In short, we contend simply that the paramount problems of the criminal justice system are largely and fundamentally *relationship* problems. Consequently, their solution requires improved relations, both as means and as end. This is the central thesis of this and the following chapter.

CRIMINAL JUSTICE AS A SYSTEM

In the first National Institute on Police and Community Relations at Michigan State University in 1955, we implied that a social system is more or less functional, therefore more or less truly a system depending upon the quality of relationships (coordination) observable. We stated the point as follows:

> The administration of criminal justice, viewed as a totality, may seem to be a continuous and coordinated process. However, when examined at close hand, serious gaps and barriers become apparent. Inconsistencies inhibit cooperation; chasms cut communications. The process of criminal justice becomes a series of segments, separated from each other by differences in philosophy, purpose, and practice. Moreover, the segments themselves are often characterized by internal conflicts and confusion. The blanket of the administration of justice, when seen at close range, becomes a patchwork quilt.[1]

As we have observed, it is more like a system in search of systematizing.

Identifying the Problems of the System

What are the main problems? We identify them as follows:

1. Problems of the age of the offender. These include questions of procedure, questions of due process, and questions of custody or treatment.
2. Problems of the so-called youthful offender, lying athwart the fields of juvenile delinquency and adult crime, thus of the dual processes of juvenile and adult justice.
3. Problems of judicial process in the disposition of felonies and misdemeanors. A particularly thorny problem is the county jail, where treatment programs are rare, where secure storage is regarded as more important than treatment, and where many persons are confined for

long periods before they have been found guilty of any crime. In short, there is no coherent system of justice for the adult offender; rather there is one system for the misdemeanant and another for the felon.

4. Problems of different and, to some extent, opposing philosophies within the system, particularly in functions and goals (i.e., court decisions upholding due process that restrict police powers); punishment versus rehabilitation (or custody versus treatment) of offenders; conflicts arising from overspecialized functions and poorly defined roles.

5. Problems of conflicting theories in the causes of and responsibility for crime. One theory emphasizes societal and environmental factors; another, individual choice; and there are other, in-between theories.

6. Problems of professional education in the criminal justice field. This reflects the basic questions just suggested: goals, roles, functions, specialization, theories of crime causation, and so on. Teachers tend to perpetuate their insular interests and approaches. Truly systemic perspective that is *problem centered*, rather than agency bound or too narrowly professional, is difficult to come by. Stereotyping, defensiveness, and scapegoating abound within the system. Ties to community agencies, such as education and welfare, are often not effectively established or coordinated. In short, our approaches to crime and delinquency prevention and treatment frequently fail because they tend to deal with the problem in fragments, compartments, pieces. The critical test of a criminal justice system is the degree to which it succeeds in coping with the crime phenomenon as a *totality*.[2]

This is a good beginning in pinpointing the relationship problems of the system. Elmer H. Johnson of the Center for the Study of Crime, Delinquency and Corrections at Southern Illinois University has examined the dilemmas in contemporary law enforcement and concludes that they are traceable to relationship problems among law enforcement programs. Johnson begins his analysis with the police role question, observing that to deal with criminals depends largely on suppression and control measures oriented to viewing the offender as an enemy. But most of the patrol officer's time is spent at tasks of social-behavioral and political matters that do not lend themselves to suppressive measures. Therapeutic and preventive ideologies are favored in these latter tasks (shades of Pfiffner's terms again). Johnson states that "the tasks of greatest quantitative importance involve the officer in problems for which he is inadequately equipped to deal and which involve the police agency in ideological conflicts."[3]

Johnson points out that one response to this problem—as we have seen—is the view that the police should be limited to dealing with "real" crime.[4] Johnson refers to this as a "cops-and-robbers" model of law enforcement, conducive to a "barracks" mentality among police officers. (Pfiffner calls it an *equitation complex*.) It is based upon the adversary concept of police-citizen relations. It "assumes falsely that sharp delimitation of function will free law enforcement from the dilemma of being compelled to frame policies while overtly denying that police executives have the obligation to assume policy-making responsibilities."[5]

Johnson argues further that limiting police responsibility to dealing with "real" crime "ignores the fundamental fact that law enforcement operates within a larger social sphere requiring coordination of police actions with the working of the other social institutions of the community."[6] This point is crucial, for in effect Johnson is declaring that a narrow definition of police role as "crook catcher" has tended to isolate the police from the community and its social and political structure. It therefore exemplifies the fragmented, compartmentalized approach to crime and order mentioned earlier. Only in the past few years, largely as a result of Law Enforcement Assistance Administration (LEAA) influence and funding, have police agencies begun to see community cooperation and assistance as absolutely essential to their crime-coping function. The long-latent central message of police and community relations is slowly penetrating, although today it is identified by different labels.

Interrelated Efforts of the System

Johnson sees the interrelation of various efforts to deal with crime as necessary, for the following reasons:

1. The various aspects of the work of a typical police agency should form a cohesive whole. This requires considerable managerial skill in a large agency. The misuse of specialization can, for instance, jeopardize the sense of interdependence that binds the employees of the agency into a common effort.

2. Historically, police agencies in this country have been tied to local governments. The fragmentation of government has created a fragmentation of law enforcement agencies and of law enforcement perspective. But crime is not structured in such a manner. The fragmentation of crime control agencies makes coordination on a metropolitan, regional, or national scale difficult. (This was a major emphasis of the President's Crime Commission in 1966 and has more recently been stressed by the Law Enforcement Assistance Administration and by the 1973 National Advisory Commission on Criminal Justice Standards and Goals.)

3. Police work is but one phase of the overall social control system of a society or community. Various social institutions share this responsibility. The quality of interrelatedness among these agencies and institutions is therefore of vital importance.

Johnson refers to the police agency as a social institution in these terms:

The ultimate purpose of criminal law and law enforcement is to lend support to the network of social institutions which maintain order and regularity in the human relationships within the community. Each social institution consists of a number of culturally defined behavior patterns, closely related to each other, which are transmitted through the generations to afford a set of expectations whereby the behavior of individuals is made consistent with the particular social purposes served by the particular institution.[7]

A police department obviously depends upon and must cooperate with other social institutions. Police work cannot be a thing apart. But some forces and factors team with organizational and professional chauvinism to work against cooperation and coordination. Johnson identifies some of these influences. One is the tendency to view police officers as specialists in law enforcement, thus implying that the average citizen and other social institutions are free of the obligation, held earlier in history, to participate actively in police work. Another influence is the organization of police bureaucracy along semimilitary lines, favoring the development of organizational loyalty surpassing loyalty to the larger community. This type of organization encourages the formation of a distinct police subculture that, as with any subculture, tends to separate police from the larger community. (As we noted earlier, police organizational *propaganda* takes precedence over community *education* in these circumstances.) Another divisive influence is officer resistance to activities that might be interpreted as social work. Building and maintaining cooperation with other agencies and institutions is often interpreted in this way.

In addition to the factors mentioned above, the criminal justice system has been placed under increasing pressure as the focus of recent demands for social institutional reforms. Thus, while the police are a favorite target and scapegoat for general social and moral default, they are also expected to control the unrest and disorder that frequently mark demands for change. This places the police in the peculiar position of being at once the agents of a holding action on behalf of the status quo, and, at the same time, the symbols of what the reform-minded want changed. This position is not conducive to cooperative relationships between the police and the community.

Furthermore, the interrelationship of the police and other social institutions causes the imperfections of these institutions to spread to police agencies. Take, for example, the relationship between the police and the courts. The separation of powers is a source of potential conflict on such issues as admissibility of evidence, methods of interrogation, status of confessions, and use of force. Tension also develops because the courts determine the disposition of cases, thereby creating a test of the success of police work which the police cannot control. As Johnson says: "Critics of the courts charge that police are being handcuffed. Critics of the police contend court control is required to prevent police lawlessness. While the debate rages, the failure to establish effective policies leaves an institutional vacuum."[8]

One final source of conflict between the police and other social institutions is the fact that the police—unlike other agencies—are organized for street work. Therefore, they are more likely than social service agencies to contact the "hard-to-reach." Thus, as Johnson phrases it, "they deal with the problems of the poor and ignorant which other agencies are not anxious to serve."[9] To quote Johnson again:

> In urban ghettos, the flight of "respectable" people to the suburbs, and the erosion of social institutions, have left the police the major representative of middle-class values among a population of socially and economically underprivileged people. This pattern is consistent with the tradition of assigning the police those tasks disgusting to others.
>
> The police are handicapped in serving these needs because of the lack of an effective functional division of labor among the social service agencies for specialized

emergency services. The lack of an integrated system forces the police to provide services, although the social service agencies do not regard their work as legitimate.[10]

To spell it out plainly, what happens is that social agencies, including the police, the courts, and corrections, feel themselves under pressure to show success in their work. Therefore, the most difficult cases—those seen as least promising by the usual standards of success—are batted around from agency to agency, each claiming lack of responsibility, resources, or competence. So it is that the toughest, most demanding, most needful cases become nobody's responsibility, and success is measured quantitatively by what is done for the less challenging cases. Thus, failure, as measured by popular but not very reliable yardsticks, is always someone else's fault.

THE POLICE CONCEPT OF RELATIONS

Given these considerations, it becomes clear why the police often adopt a concept of relations that means, in effect, "help us do our job, *as we see it.*" This concept is intended, as Johnson points out, to preserve the status quo for the police department while other agencies and institutions do all the changing. It is not conducive to cooperative problem solving in the community. It is, rather, a concept in which ballyhoo, press agentry, propaganda, and whitewashing are apt to be featured. The police are cast in these activities as the father who knows best, trying to deal (alone) with wayward children. This paternalistic attitude is particularly aggravating to minority groups, because it is patronizing and counter to the sense of identity inculcated by current movements.

To repeat a point that bears repeating, the police have no monopoly on this inner-directed pattern of thought regarding relationships. It is matched, for instance, by the attitude of many public school professionals: "Yes, cooperation with other community agencies is good and necessary. But it must be on our terms. After all, we are professionals, and we know best." Organizational, institutional, and professional chauvinism has many faces; that the criminal justice system has its fair share is hardly headline news. Yet in times of unusual social instability, stubborn conformity to old ways hardly contributes to enlightened community services, nor to the development of coordinated, cooperative efforts to deal with problems that can be dealt with in no other way. Johnson's conclusion is a crisp summary:

> The dilemmas faced by the police executive stem from the interrelatedness of social institutions, all of which are undergoing a crisis. Because the ultimate significance of police work is its contribution to the social order, law enforcement is affected by any condition affecting the social order. The final solution of the dilemmas of the police awaits resolution of the institutional crises encountered by the community as a whole.
>
> Because law enforcement is largely a local matter, the reform of inadequacies of local government is a vital prerequisite. Because of the inherent linkages between law enforcement and the judiciary, the possibilities of revision of police procedures will depend on the outcome of changes in the procedures of courts. The place and function of the police must be determined clearly with an integrated system of social

service appropriate to the needs of the particular community. Because the adversary role characteristic of the contemporary policeman does not lend itself to social service functions, a new role is likely to emerge in the case manager model wherein the police agency provides emergency services and acts as a referral agent within a more specifically articulated system of social service agencies.[11]

Initiative is needed for change. When police problems are said to be aspects of broader systemic and social institutional pathology, the police may conclude that nothing can be done about their problems until something happens elsewhere. So why do anything?

While ultimate responsibility for the police and the broader criminal justice system lies in the community, leadership and initiative must come—if it is to come at all—from the police and other professionals in the system. The community must be educated and stirred to understand what needs to be changed. The police, at the same time, should demonstrate the type of leadership for change that is sensitively tuned to community needs. In other words, the educational process is a two-way street. Leadership is an abstract and malleable concept sometimes interpreted to mean maintaining the status quo, continuing to do the wrong things, more efficiently. As we have said before, police leadership in these times includes educating the community in what it *ought to want*. In this fashion, communication may be encouraged that will legitimize the need for change in the system, although not solely on the terms of the police, nor of any other one party, special interest, or faction.

Students of criminal justice processes, when asked to draw a diagram of how the system ideally flows, would be likely to respond with something like this:

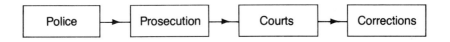

The trouble with the system, in practical terms, is that each of its components habitually visualizes itself as central in the system, as suggested by this sunburst concept depicted by a Detroit judge.

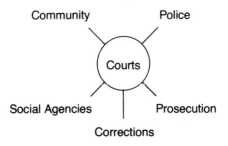

POLICE DISCRETION, AGAIN

The fact that prosecutors and judges exercise wide discretion in the disposition of offenders has not been surprising to the community. There has not been any particular effort to conceal it. To judge, after all, means literally to make discretionary decisions. However, in police discretion, there has been—as we have seen in an earlier chapter—a history of pretending to do only what the law mandates. The police thereby respond to their understanding of what is expected of them by legislatures and by a substantial segment of the general public. Behind this facade, in subrosa fashion and with an air of illegitimacy and impropriety, the police have necessarily functioned with broad discretion in carrying out their multiple responsibilities. Herman Goldstein has written to this point:

> This business of formally subscribing to one concept while operating on the basis of a conflicting one has had a profoundly negative effect upon police services. It has, as one commentator put it, stunted the healthy growth of police organizations. It has placed a curb on forthrightness in dealing with the public and has forced the police to violate the law in order to do their jobs.[12]

This same point regarding police discretion has had a marked effect on relationships within the criminal justice system. For one thing, it has contributed to the police sense of being "outprofessionalized" by other justice entities. This feeling is accentuated when the courts chastise the police for particular discretionary decisions, and on occasion seem even to criticize the police for taking the law into their own hands.

A symptom of latent attitudes is in the observation that guidelines for the exercise of discretion by the *police* are nowadays frequently prescribed, indeed are almost as frequently spelled out in specific recommendations. Rarely, however, do we find guidelines spelled out for the exercise of discretion by prosecutors or judges. In a question such as the appropriateness of prosecution, one looks in vain for standards. The same point holds for decisions bearing on diversion, a variant of screening. Plea bargaining goes on constantly without reference to consistent standards or guidelines, a fact well known to police officers who are seldom so much as consulted. One further example: career criminal projects stress the prosecutor's role in prompt identification of such individuals and the assignment of an assistant prosecutor to follow through on the case, all the way to verdict. There is a great deal of discretionary "elbow room" inherent in such programs. More about this shortly.

THE NEED FOR REFORM

The maelstrom presently gripping criminal justice comprises many conflicts and strange alliances. Change in one part of the system activates change in another. Of late, these changes have been rather abrupt and tempestuous. The Free Speech movement, civil rights turmoil, and antiwar protests, the rights rebellion of youth and women, expansion of due process to all aspects of justice, changing sexual ethics, Watergate, the deterioration of cities, terrorism and violent crime becoming commonplace, inflation, taxes, unstable international relations—all of these happenings and more have contributed to public uneasiness, apprehension, frustration, resentment, sometimes even despair. There is a prevailing negativism about finding answers and an accompanying narcissism, with a me-first disposition emphasizing the agenda of factions and special interests at the expense of the general welfare. It is not a good time for consensus, coalition, and compromise.

In such an attitudinal environment, discussion of what to do about crime and criminals tends to become gloomy. Some patterns of development are distinguishable:

1. The so-called medical model for dealing with offenders is undergoing reexamination. Rehabilitation and the treatment ideal are no longer confidently advocated as "the answer." Robert Martinson has become identified as the chief spokesman for the "nothing works" school of thought, though unfairly because what he has actually said is that nothing works *for every offender*.[13] If nothing works, there seems to be little need for the indeterminate sentence and only a limited function for a parole board.

2. On the brighter side—although there are those who do not see it in this light—is what has been happening with due process. Visibility and accountability have been the keystones. The Kent and Gault cases gave juveniles rights that had been lost in benevolent informality. In police work, guidelines for discretion are hardening, as noted earlier. In corrections, inmates have been provided with law libraries and counsels. The essentials of due process are required in dealing with parole violations *(Morrisey* v. *Brewer)*. Prison grievance and ombudsman procedures have been initiated. Standards for adequate health care in correctional institutions have been implemented. The county jail has been showcased to some extent, and some of its worst inadequacies have been reduced in some places.

3. Extending what we have said about prosecutorial discretion:

   In the American system of criminal justice, power over punishment is allocated primarily among four types of governmental decision-makers: legislatures, prosecutors' offices, courts, and correctional agencies (including, most notably, parole boards). The thrust of many recent proposals for sentencing reform has been to reduce or eliminate the discretion of both courts and correctional agencies and to increase the extent to which legislatures specify criminal penalties in advance. In fixed sentencing schemes, statutes specify the exact penalty for each offense; in presumptive sentencing, statutes specify a 'normal' sentence for each offense but permit limited departures from the norm in atypical cases. Although prosecutors' offices have in practice probably had a greater influence on sentencing than any other agencies (not excluding state legislatures), the call for sentencing reform has largely ignored this prosecutorial power.[14]

4. Moving along another step in the criminal justice continuum and still on the theme of discretion, we come to judicial discretion in sentencing. The limitations that are placed on police discretion and, to a far lesser extent, on prosecutorial discretion are based upon a combination of the

application of due process and the spirit of even-handed justice that is the shining but sometimes elusive goal of Anglo-Saxon justice. But nowhere should justice become more clear and effective than in the judicial function where, having been applied in the arrest, prosecution, and trial, it must be continued in sentencing. Seldom is discretion so broad as at the trial's conclusion where, within the limits set by the community through the legislature, the court proceeds to impose a penalty.

The same principles of uniformity, equity, and due process apply, of course, to the parole board. The role of discretion in the parole process will be considered in the next chapter.

But once the rehabilitative theory comes into question, its close companion, the indeterminate sentence, is "up for grabs." This is precisely where "we're at" today in the matter of judicial discretion in sentencing. As a consequence, the models of determinate, mandatory, or presumptive sentencing are being generally scrutinized and cautiously applied in several selected jurisdictions.[15]

Norval Morris, former dean of the University of Chicago Law School, speaks of current sentencing explorations as drawing together strange bedfellows and refers to a discussion on sentencing which took place in the Illinois legislature. He found that several "sensible proposals" on sentencing were "enthusiastically supported by those mindless members of the legislature who were interested only in the prolongation of terms of imprisonment and were moved by the simple but silly belief that the crime problem will be substantially solved by a draconic [that is, Draconian] restructuring of sentencing."[16]

5. Plea bargaining is everywhere justified on the grounds of expediency. The difficulty with it is not so much acceptance of its pragmatic inevitability as it is the unprincipled manner in which it operates. Much could be done to make it more principled and more just if, as Norval Morris argues, "the proper interests, including those of the victim, are represented at pretrial dispositional hearings."[17]

6. The principle of *just desert* in sentencing was intoned by C. S. Lewis several decades ago.[18] Norval Morris, having earlier replied to the Lewis article,[19] has subsequently stressed the need for:

   a. *Parsimony:* the least restrictive (punitive) sanction necessary to achieve defined social purposes should be imposed.

   b. *Dangerousness:* prediction of *future* [emphasis ours] criminality should be rejected as a base for determining that the convicted criminal should be imprisoned.

   c. *Desert:* no sanction should be imposed greater than that which is "deserved" by the last crime, or series of crimes, for which the offender is being sentenced.[20]

This latter point brings us to what is referred to as the doctrine of *inequality of uniformity*. Individuals who violate identical criminal laws can differ markedly in criminal history and the circumstances which led to the offense, as well as the manner in which the crime was committed. The same could be said of co-defendants. One example should suffice (the names are fictitious and details have been altered sufficiently to protect identities):

> Herbert Smith and William Jones kidnapped Mary White at gunpoint, took her to an isolated area and raped her. Both men were identified, tried, found guilty, and sentenced.
>
> Both men were black. Smith was older and had an extensive record of serious assaults. Jones was young and inexperienced. Smith raped the girl brutally and callously while Jones held the gun. In turn, Jones raped the girl, but gently and apologetically. "Now," said Smith to Jones, who was holding the gun, "finish her off." Instead Jones turned the gun on Smith and said, "I'm taking her out of here and you're staying."
>
> But the car stuck in the sand. Down the road Jones and the girl walked. Soon Jones handed the girl the gun to show her she had nothing to fear from him. Later the lights of a car approached from behind them. Thinking it was Smith, she handed the gun back to Jones on her own volition. The car passed without stopping. It was not Smith. So Jones walked Miss White home.
>
> Both men were given identical sentences of thirty to fifty years.
>
> The parole board later asked the sentencing judge for special consideration for Jones (a prerequisite for parole prior to the minimum). The request was refused. The judge's successor later gave his consent.
>
> The facts given here are from the presentence report, verified by Mary White's statement. You be the judge.

A variety of measures have been proposed for making sentences more consistent and avoiding disparity. In Michigan, for example, this occurred through appelate review. Previously, no appeal could lie where the minimum sentence was less than the maximum set by law, even though the difference was only *one* day. Finally, the Michigan Supreme Court held that such a sentence, in effect, nullified parole and was therefore unlawful. The court held that a minimum sentence should not exceed two-thirds of the maximum.

Federal courts have experimented with sentencing councils. In World War II a joint Army and Air Force Sentence Review Board was established to ensure uniform sentence procedures and reduce disparity. Sentencing standards could well be considered and a basis for case law on sentences developed as a result.

VOICES FOR REFORM

The voices for overhaul of the criminal justice system are legion. That substantial change must be wrought appears to be a virtually unanimous verdict; exactly *what* changes, and *how* they are to be made are continually contested questions.

A few years ago, former Attorney General Ramsey Clark wrote a widely read book in which he blasted slums, poverty, racism, overpopulation, unemployment, ignorance, ill health, bad housing, unreliable crime statistics, organized crime, drugs, guns, undertrained and underpaid prosecutors, imprudently picked judges, court delays, antiquated and overcrowded jails and prisons, seriously deficient rehabilitation facilities and procedures, and insufficient recourse to science in crime detection and the study of criminal behavior.[21] Clark was also critical of capital punishment and the suppression of dissent. He said he believed in local law enforcement and closer ties between police and community. He stood against preventive detention but for the indeterminate sentence.

In reviewing Clark's work, Isadore Silver concluded:

> The crucial questions are whether a modern society can depend upon a criminal justice system—even a perfect one—to maintain a viable Social and Moral Order, whether the very concept of "criminal justice" (and how that term grates upon the ear) is meaningful, and whether we have the knowledge and means to find creative alternatives to *any* criminal justice system. Would Clark's estimable—and often courageous, though traditional—reforms really "create a wholesome environment" and eliminate or significantly reduce what we choose to call "crime"? Do all societies need a concept of "crime" to define themselves, and can modern societies afford such a concept? We—and I include myself as well as Mr. Clark—being good Americans, do not often choose to face those questions. We, liberal and conservative alike, cannot be but losers because of such failure.[22]

Irving Reichert, who has been associated with the Continuing Education of the Bar program at the University of California and is currently the director of the San Francisco Bar Association, contends that the center of our criminal justice problems is philosophical.[23] Argument rests, he says, on whether it is better that some guilty men go free to endanger the community, than it is to have all men live in fear of the state. The founding fathers of our country opted in favor of freedom. But this did not settle the debate, a debate that becomes particularly sharp in times of increasing lawlessness. Reichert pointed out that the present period is certainly not the first in our history when this argument has been especially fierce. One constitutional lawyer has asked, when *wasn't* there a crime crisis? But this point is hardly reassuring, and surely not intended to engender complacency. Yet, in perspective, neither should the Bill of Rights be repealed.

Former President Richard M. Nixon maintained that ways must be found to clear the courts of an endless stream of so-called victimless crimes, such as minor traffic offenses, loitering, and drunkenness cases. He advocated other steps to expedite criminal process, for example, a requirement already copied by several states from the British system: that accused persons be brought to trial within sixty days. Former President Gerald Ford called for reform of the chaotic system of federal laws, along with other steps to make our legal system a means of ensuring domestic tranquility and making America safe for decent, law-abiding citizens. He supported more mandatory sentences and more programs to compensate crime victims, but he did not support federal registration of guns or gun owners. Many of his proposals were contained in proposed legislation designed to revise the federal criminal code.

Chief Justice Warren Burger has called for the establishment of a national clearinghouse for states to pool their ideas on reforming the court system. He has said that the American system of criminal justice "in every way . . . is suffering from a severe case of deferred maintenance."[24] The American Bar Association and various associations of police, prosecutors, and judges have been saying similar things for years. A National Center on State Courts was established in June 1971. The American Bar Association picked up the Burger theme for upgrading legal education and for regulating lawyers' conduct. Congress moved more slowly on the suggestion of the chief justice that a judiciary council be created. His dissenting opinion in a 1971 case had brought the so-called exclusionary rule into question. "For more than 55 years," he wrote, "this court has enforced a rule under which evidence of undoubted reliability and . . . value has been suppressed and excluded from criminal cases whenever it was obtained in violation of a defendant's Constitutional rights." This rule does not deter improper conduct by police officers, contended the chief justice, nor does it serve the cause of justice.[25]

President Johnson's Crime Commission accomplished the most thorough and comprehensive analysis to date of all aspects of the criminal justice system. This was its essential task. Its recommendations were numerous, more or less innovative regarding specifics, and to the present time still largely ignored. There is no scarcity of information about what is wrong with the system.

The American Law Institute has given impetus to the reform of criminal codes through its Model Penal Code, produced after a decade of sustained labor. In numerous states, movement toward reform of the criminal code has frequently bogged down in legislative debate over controversial features.

The Advisory Commission on Inter-governmental Relations (ACIR), comprising twenty-six governors, mayors, judges, and city and county executives, presided over by Chairman Robert M. Merriam, adopted at its meetings of September 1970 and January 1971 an extended series of recommendations dealing with state-local relations in the criminal justice system. Still timely today, the commission's comprehensive recommendations included:

1. *The Courts*

- That each state establish a simplified and unified court system, abolish or overhaul justice of the peace courts, compensate judges by salary rather than by fees, and require judges to be licensed to practice law.

- That all courts in each state be subject to administrative supervision and direction by the supreme court or chief justice in that state, toward the end of uniform rules of practice and procedure.

- That all states provide an administrative office of the state courts.

- That state and local governments adopt a merit plan of selecting judges, and that judges so appointed be required to submit themselves to voter approval at an election at the end of each term.

- That states require judges to retire at seventy, and that all judges devote full-time to their judicial duties.

2. *The Prosecution*

- That states strengthen state responsibility for prosecution, by enhancing the attorney general's authority to oversee the work of local prosecutors, and empower the supreme court of the particular state to remove a prosecuting attorney pursuant to prescribed procedures and safeguards.

- That states centralize the local prosecution function in a single office responsible for all criminal prosecution.
- That states require prosecuting attorneys to be full-time officials and that their jurisdictions be redrawn so that each is large enough to require full-time attention of such an official and provide financial resources to support this office.
- That states pay at least 50 percent of the costs of local prosecuting attorney's offices.
- That states enact legislation authorizing prosecutors to bring indictments through either grand jury or information procedures. Grand juries should be used primarily in cases of alleged official corruption or extraordinary public concern.

3. The Defense Counsel for the Indigent

- That each state establish and finance a statewide system for defense of the indigent, making either a public defender or coordinated assigned counsel service readily available to every area of the state.

4. The Police

- That all local governments in metropolitan areas assure the provision of full-time patrol and preliminary investigative services to their residents. County governments should assume this responsibility where necessary, charging costs to local governments. Where the county does not assume these services, the state should mandate consolidation of police services in metropolitan jurisdictions that do not provide basic police services directly or through interlocal agreements.
- That counties be empowered and encouraged to perform specialized, supportive (staff and auxiliary) police services for constituent localities in single county metropolitan areas, for example, records, communications, crime laboratory, etc. In multicounty or interstate metropolitan areas, states should encourage appropriate area-wide agencies to perform such services, for example, regional criminal justice planning agencies, councils of government, and so on.
- That states authorize or encourage the creation of specialized police task forces to operate throughout multicounty and interstate metropolitan areas, to deal with extralocal and organized crime.
- That states enter into interstate compacts giving carefully circumscribed extraterritorial police powers relating to "close pursuit" of felonious criminal offenders and to geographically extended powers of criminal arrest.
- That state governments improve the capabilities of rural police systems.
- The states consider granting the appropriate state law enforcement agency a full range of statewide law enforcement powers and removing geographic limitations on the operation of such an agency. Further, that an appropriate state agency be encouraged to provide centralized records and crime laboratory services to all local agencies within a state, that a uniform intrastate and interstate crime reporting system be established

and that all local agencies be required, on a periodic basis, to report all felony arrest and identification records to the state agency.

- That where needed the office of sheriff be placed on a statutory rather than on a constitutional basis.
- That states give metropolitan counties the option of assigning basic responsibility for countywide police services to an "independent" county police force under the control of the county chief executive or county board of commissioners.
- That states abolish the office of constable and transfer its duties to appropriate lower court systems.
- That states abolish the office of coroner, with the duties accruing to an appointed local medical examiner and to the local prosecuting attorney.
- That states create Councils on Police Standards to develop and maintain minimum standards for police selection and basic training.
- That state legislatures revise their criminal code to better define the scope of discretionary police activities—particularly as to arrest powers, search procedures, and interrogation practices. States should also enact legislation providing comprehensive tort liability to protect state and local police from tort action arising out of legitimate use of discretionary powers.
- That states modify existing laws which restrict local chief executives from appointing local police chiefs from the ranks of any qualified applicants and which restrict local police chiefs from appointing division heads and assistants reporting directly to them. States should also modify veterans' preferences and state civil service regulations that unduly limit or otherwise restrict the selection, appointment, and promotion of qualified local police officers.

5. *The Agencies*

- That local criminal justice coordinating councils be established in jurisdictions having substantial administrative responsibility for at least [two] of the major components of the criminal justice system. The work of such councils should be coordinated with the Law Enforcement Assistance Administration regional criminal justice planning agencies.
- That state and regional criminal justice planning agencies and local criminal justice coordinating councils take primary responsibility for improving interfunctional cooperation in the state-local criminal justice system.
- That because a workable partnership between police and community residents is necessary to effectively prevent crime, local governments should substantially increase their efforts to involve citizens in the law enforcement and criminal justice process through the establishment of police-community relations machinery and programs.

Quite clearly, the principle of *systemic interrelatedness* is an underlying theme of these recommendations.

Some progress has been made in the establishment of local and regional criminal justice coordinating councils. The 1966 President's Crime Commission encouraged such organizations in its recommendations. Both the National Advisory Commission on Civil Disorders and the National Commission on the Causes and Prevention of Violence spoke in the same vein, and the Omnibus Crime Act of 1968 and Safe Streets Act of 1970 stimulated national, state, and metropolitan organization in such a pattern. An example was the establishment of the New York City Criminal Justice Coordinating Council.

The 1973 National Advisory Commission on Criminal Justice Standards and Goals, in its *Report on the Criminal Justice System*, acknowledged that criminal justice processes were failing more frequently than in the past in the objective of reducing crime. This commission recommended standards for what it called the "crossroads," the point at which the various components of criminal justice merge: criminal justice planning, information systems, criminal justice education, and criminal code revision.

PILOT PROGRAMS FOR REFORM

Such sweeping recommendations for reform centering on the interdependence of the components of the criminal justice system are plainly important in setting goals. The system so desperately needs reform that only those who are reform-minded should be encouraged to begin careers in any phase of it. But progress toward reform is so slow as to discourage all but the extraordinarily persevering. The LEAA has aroused hope, and some progress has certainly been made under its impetus, despite the turbulence of the political waters that sometimes threaten to engulf it.

One organization that has earned wide respect in the criminal justice field in recent years is the Vera Institute of Justice in New York City. This institution has conducted a number of pilot projects carefully assessing the strengths and weaknesses of specific experiments for changing parts of the system. It was established in 1961 as a private institution financed mainly by foundation grants and some government funds, and has concentrated especially on the relationship of criminal justice administration and the poor, primarily in New York City.[26]

The Vera Institute has identified particular problem areas and has designed experimental programs aimed at benefiting both the defendant and the relevant criminal justice agency. Its first project was bail reform; the second, a police summons project. The Vera approach to bail reform was a departure from the traditional system in which a defendant was required to remain in jail awaiting trial if he could not make bail. The costs to the defendant, his family, and New York City were substantial. From 1961 to 1964, with the cooperation of the courts and other agencies, Vera experimented with a different approach that incorporated interviewing and gathering information about the defendant, his job, his family situation, and such. Vera then recommended release without bail of certain defendants. Under the experiment, 3,505 persons were released, and only 56 willfully failed to return to court. In the fall of 1964, the city Office of Probation took over the program for the entire city. Later, similar bail programs were initiated in numerous other cities, and the project was also influential in the drafting of the Federal Bail Reform Act of 1966. Vera moved on to an experiment with release at an earlier stage in criminal process by providing for a police summons at the time of arrest, in the case of certain misdemeanors. This also turned out to be a successful experiment, widely emulated.

Jameson Doig of Princeton University has identified the main features of the Vera approach:

- Sufficiently extended involvement in the project to provide a reasonable test
- Manpower to conduct the project, at Institute expense
- Acceptance of responsibility for possible failure
- Careful evaluation of what occurs
- Building support for an idea in the face of hostile or lukewarm reception
- Working in close cooperation with operating agencies and securing the full support of top city administrators
- An unusually able staff, building on the prestige of past successes.[27]

Vera has moved on to such projects as testing alternatives to arresting skidrow alcoholics, experimenting with ways of handling juvenile offenders, and assigning a Community Service Patrol Corps in Harlem. With continuing assistance from the Ford Foundation and other sources, the Vera Institute is also interested in

- continued development of techniques for eliminating unnecessary court appearances by police officers and civilian witnesses.
- development of a pilot program to provide employment opportunities for offenders (including drug users) who have not been able to hold regular jobs.
- organization of programs in high-crime neighborhoods to train and use local residents to perform quasi-police, quasi-probationary, and quasi-adjudicatory services.
- development of methods for evaluating judicial prediction of a defendant's dangerousness and for increasing the accuracy of such judgments.

The Vera approach is not, of course, a panacea for all problems in the criminal justice system. But it does show ways in which change can be introduced, not painlessly, perhaps, but with minimum political risk to those for whom such considerations are vital. State criminal justice planning agencies might well consider the Vera plan and strategy, as LEAA's National Institute of Law Enforcement and Criminal Justice seems to have done.

Another organization with considerable influence in the field is the National Council on Crime and Delinquency (NCCD), a nonprofit citizen organization supported by contributions from United Funds, foundations, business corporations, and interested individuals. The NCCD was founded in 1907 and has a membership of approximately 60,000; its chief interest is the rehabilitation of juvenile and adult offenders. On a community, state, and national level, NCCD works to develop effective juvenile, family, and criminal courts; to improve probation, parole, and institutional services and facilities; and to stimulate community programs for the prevention, treatment, and control of delinquency and crime. The council

- offers direct consultation and makes studies of correctional services as practical guides to action.
- develops professional standards and guide materials for use by judges, correctional workers, and laymen.
- drafts model legislation and gives legal advisory service to legislative committees, courts, bar associations, correctional agencies, and citizen groups.
- conducts an annual national conference on crime and delinquency, organizes training institutes, stimulates professional training for career service in probation and parole, and assists in conducting merit examinations for the selection of professional personnel.
- publishes literature and serves as a clearinghouse for information about correctional work, maintains an extensive library, stimulates research, and provides technical data to public information media.

RELATIONSHIPS WITHIN THE SYSTEM

In an earlier chapter, we referred to several factors that tend to engender relationship problems within the criminal justice system among the police, prosecution, the courts, and corrections. For example, some recent decisions of criminal and appellate courts defining the limits of interrogation, search of the person and property and the seizure of evidence, and of the use of force have been seen by both the police and the courts as limiting discretionary latitude. The clear implication of such court rulings is that the police must be subject to the authority of law, the prosecutor, and the courts, or to the authority of some type of civil procedure for external review.

As Albert Reiss, David Bordua, and others have pointed out, this comes down to a jurisdictional dispute, within the system. It is at times, as we have earlier suggested, a matter of professionals (lawyers and judges, presumably) seeking to restrict the powers of "would-be professionals" (the police), as Reiss puts it; and conflict is therefore inevitable. Through arrest, the police introduce suspects into the system, but the power of assessing outcome of arrest as well as police procedure resides with the prosecutor and the courts. Reiss summarizes the problem:

> Whenever a number of roles are involved in making decisions about the *same* case, problems of overlapping jurisdiction and rights to make the decision arise. Where professionals are involved, there will be competing claims to professional competence to make the decision. The role of the patrol officer, occurring as it does at the lowest rank order in the decision-making system, makes his role most vulnerable to counterclaims to competence, and least defensible. Paradoxically, however, it is the officer's original decision that controls whether law enforcement and criminal justice agents can process the decision at all. He has the broadest possible range of discretion and jurisdiction, and therefore of possibilities for the exercise of "professional"

judgment, but the most vulnerable position in the system of law enforcement and criminal justice for restricting his jurisdiction.[28]

Curiously, Reiss observes, what the police want to have clearly defined, the courts want to leave open for interpretation. And what the courts want clearly defined, the police want to leave open for interpretation. A result of this dilemma is described by Reiss and Bordua:

> Dilemmas in defining success are partially resolved by the development of a complex bargaining process between police and prosecutors, the shifting of departmental resources in directions of maximum payoff from a conviction point of view, the development of a set of attitudes that define the police as alone in the "war on crime," and the elaboration of success measures that do not require validation by the courts.[29]

Reiss and Bordua nicely summarize the pertinent points to which we earlier alluded: the police are hedged in by officials whose formal discretion is greater than theirs. Although the prosecutor and the judge are traditional figures, the system has come to include probation officers and juvenile court people, with whom the police must also bargain. And in this bargaining, the police are dealing with role incumbents who are potentially hostile to the police. Thus, "in the system of maintaining law and order, other people have the law and the police get stuck with the order."[30]

THE CASE FOR PLURALISTIC PLANNING

Perspective is important in viewing relationships within any social system. It is a matter of seeing the particular in the context of the general, and vice versa. How does a part affect the whole, how is one part affected by another part, and how does the whole affect each part? Carl Hamm, a retired Milwaukee police captain, later on the staff of the International Association of Chiefs of Police and of LEAA, has considered the matter as follows:

> The criminal justice system within the United States is essentially an aggregate of bureaucracies which, collectively, are alleged to serve the needs of the community and the "client" (traffic violator, misdemeanant, or criminal) in a society with a mixed bag of values, morals, laws, and regulations and a conglomerate of standards for their application. Pluralistic planning, or advocacy, is the combination of opposition, confrontation, approval, and modification of official planning or action in accordance with the wishes of the ward, neighborhood, block group, or participant within or affected by the plan, regardless of whether involvement is through choice or circumstance.[31]

Hamm explains that pluralistic planning provides

> for the complainant to be not only heard, but heeded, and further, to receive a response. A glimpse of pluralistic participation may be seen in the traditional administration of the English village by a triumvirate composed of the clergymen [sic], the constable, and the physician. Its modern counterpart is apparent in many boroughs within the Greater London Council: still a triumvirate, it consists of the police station, health clinic, and social services. . . . Thus, one of the largest cities in the world has neighborhood soccer fields, borough events, local health and social services, and its own police station, whose staff reside within that precinct or borough.[32]

Hamm concludes with the point that community participation and pluralistic planning (systemic planning) require an open line of communication between citizens and public officials. This is what we mean by systemic perspective.

SYSTEMS ANALYSIS

How can pluralistic planning be made to work in the world of social reality? To reply to this question with a concrete illustration, we refer to what is called *systems analysis, systems research, operations research,* or *systems engineering.* The concepts involved are not new, but in recent years this functional emphasis has been applied to military operations, transportation, education, economics, and other social systems, stimulated and facilitated enormously by computer science and technology. Alfred Blumstein has explained that systems analysis focuses on:

1. A particular *system*—a collection of people, devices, and procedures intended to perform some function.
2. The *function* of the system—the job it is supposed to perform.
3. *Measures of effectiveness*—the measure of calculation of how well alternative system designs perform the function.
4. *Alternative* system designs—the comparison of designs.
5. A *mathematical model*—a means of calculating the measures of effectiveness associated with each alternative system design.[33]

Impressed with the possibilities of such an approach to the police department of a large city, or to the criminal justice system more generally, some police departments are well along in applying it to crime control. But police departments and the criminal justice system have other functions that raise different issues. Blumstein believes that the mathematical model is the most useful contribution of systems analysis:

> In its pure form, systems analysis is supposed to provide quantitative comparisons of the consequences of alternative decisions, in terms of both cost and effectiveness. These comparisons, however, are rarely sufficient for making most decisions, since the qualitative value considerations are usually at least as important as those that can be quantified. But by putting numbers on the measurable aspects of a question, the debate no longer need center on those questions, as it now so often does. Then the public debate and the administrative decisions can focus on the critical questions involved in the weighing of conflicting social values.[34]

Perspective, then, is a basic tenet of systems analysis that places important but narrow questions in a broader systems context, ordinarily difficult to do because of the complexity of a given system. Looking beyond the limited question brings considerations previously ignored ("It's their problem, not ours"), or tranquilly accepted ("We do only what we are told") into focus. For example, Blumstein asks:

· What is the impact of higher arrest rates on the corrections process and on future crimes?

- What is the impact of community-based corrections on both the near- and long-range crime rates?
- What is the impact of non-bail release on the rate of guilty pleas and on court work load?
- Would it be more economical to add court resources to cut the court backlog and reduce the cost of detention while awaiting trial?
- What will be the effect on correctional work loads of providing free counsel more widely?[35]

Questions of this type call for interactions among all parts of the criminal justice system, between it and other social systems, and between it and various community groups. Such questions require *wholeness* of perspective, the combined views of all concerned groups. Ideally, such interactions will force an assessment of goals, roles, values, alternatives, and other elements upon which improvement depends. For example, with crime control as the focus, how can the system reduce crime? Crime might be reduced by intense policing. But at some point, intense policing is socially objectionable. Too much crime control may be oppressive; too little may be anarchy. At what point is it too much or too little? Judged by what criteria? And so on. Other examples: What effect have longer prison sentences on crime control? Who can be rehabilitated and by what kind of correctional treatment? *Who* are the people deterred from committing *what* crimes by *which* procedures of the criminal justice system?

Systems analysis can provide data to make the discussion of such questions more productive. Systems thinking has created new ways of understanding complex situations. Guesswork is reduced, and the interplay of many variables can be depicted in constructing decision models. The clashes in differing values will still persist, and working consensus will still be hard to secure. But dialogue and transactions enlightened by factual information on *quantitative* questions are much more likely to result in breakthroughs on *qualitative* questions. Data obtained via systems analysis can be of great help in getting problems more adequately defined, in ways that many diverse audiences can accept. Problem-solving efforts in community relations frequently bog down at this first step. Systems analysis can be a strong ally of pluralistic planning in solving problems, both in and out of the criminal justice system.

THE ISSUE OF OVERCRIMINALIZATION

It is often said that one of the main problems in criminal justice processes is case overload. The discussion of this point logically leads to the question of *overcriminalization,* sometimes called *legal moralism.* Is the criminal sanction being employed too widely in matters where it is ineffective or inappropriate, thus debasing its effectiveness in matters where it might be more applicable? This is one of the briar patches of conflicting values in goals, roles, and so on. We will not settle this argument here, but some consideration of the issue is in order.

Many states and the federal government have been critically reviewing, and in some cases revising, their substantive and procedural criminal codes. We have mentioned the American Law Institute's Model Penal Code. A National Commission on Reform of the Federal Criminal Code has completed a 336-page report containing a proposed new Federal Criminal Code, some sections of which are considered radical in some quarters. For instance, the commission recommended the abolition of capital punishment, an easing of curbs on marijuana possession, and outlawing private ownership of handguns. No revised criminal code with such provisions gets through a legislative body without reverberations sometimes approximating an earthquake.

President Johnson's 1966 Crime Commission observed that most of the cases in the criminal courts consist of what are essentially violations of moral norms or instances of annoying behavior rather than of dangerous crime. Almost half of all arrests were said to be on charges of drunkenness, disorderly conduct, vagrancy, gambling, and minor sexual violations. The commission said that such behavior is generally regarded as too serious to be ignored, but its inclusion in the criminal code creates problems. The investigation and prosecution of such cases ties up police (investigation itself is frequently "impractical") and clogs courts at the expense of their capacity to cope with more serious crimes. Sometimes attempts to enforce these laws are degrading or embarrassing for the police and raise troublesome legal questions for the courts.[36]

Occasionally the enforcement of these laws, the commission continued, has been unhappily associated with police, prosecutor, or court venality and corruption, leading to general disrespect for law. Arrest, conviction, and jail or probation rarely reform persons who engage in such behaviors, nor do they appear to deter potential violators. Continued reliance on criminal treatment for such offenders probably blunts community efforts to create more appropriate programs for the alcoholic, the homeless, the compulsive gambler, or the sexual deviate.

At the heart of some of the predicaments in which the criminal law finds itself has been the too ready acceptance of the notion that the way to deal with any kind of reprehensible conduct is to make it criminal. This is the crux of the issue generating widespread debate currently, with marijuana use or possession, homosexuality, and abortion prominent on the list of behaviors in question. Some argue that lowering the criminal bars against such behavior may be interpreted as license to engage in it. Others maintain that the limited tool of criminal law will work better against the most dangerous and threatening kinds of crime if it is confined to the kinds it can deal with most effectively. The relationship between law and morality is clearly the underlying issue. The 1966 President's Crime Commission settled for stating the issue and urged weighing carefully the kinds of behavior that should be defined as criminal.

The 1973 National Advisory Commission on Criminal Justice Standards and Goals called for criminal law revisions in every jurisdiction where such revision had not occurred within the preceding decade. The revisions should be complete rather than partial, and include procedural as well as substantive law. In its *Report on the Criminal Justice System*, the commission said:

> Law that prohibits conduct that a substantial minority, or majority, of the citizens finds tolerable or acceptable, could be considered for abolition, particularly if iden-

tifiable victims are not apparent. The objective should be a cohesive code that responds to current law enforcement needs—one that is free from vestiges of needs from a different era.[37]

Yale law professor Alexander M. Bickel is among those who assert that we "overuse criminal law as an instrument of regulation and the civil law suit as the basic, all-purpose instrument of social and individual justice."[38]

Jerome Skolnick regards overcriminalization as a significant element in police-community relations.[39] He holds that the enforcement of conventional morality typically produces two closely related consequences. One is a more threatening environment for the police officer. The other is the development of organizations for purveying forbidden goods and services. Legal moralism, Skolnick asserts, undermines the moral authority of the criminal law. He quotes an FBI agent's remark to the 1966 President's Crime Commission:

> The criminal code of any jurisdiction tends to make a crime of everything that people are against, without regard to enforceability, changing social concepts, etc. . . . The result is that the criminal code becomes society's trash bin. The police have to rummage around in this material and are expected to prevent everything that is unlawful. They cannot do so because many of the things prohibited are simply beyond enforcement, both because of human inability to enforce the law and because, as in the case of prohibition, society legislates one way and acts another way. If we would restrict our definition of criminal offenses in many areas, we would get the criminal codes back to the point where they prohibit specific, carefully defined, and serious conduct, and the police could then concentrate on enforcing the law in that context and would not waste its officers by trying to enforce the unenforceable, as is done now.[40]

Skolnick adds:

> If we could assume that we actually live in a society whose citizens subscribe overwhelmingly to a similar morality, *conventional* morality would indeed be, as the term suggests, *customary* morality. All evidence, however, is to the contrary. We are a nation of diversity, of ethnic differences, of regional differences, of rural-urban differences, of generational differences. We cannot coerce an entire nation to virtue as virtue is defined by those holding political power at any given time.[41]

University of California law professor Sanford H. Kadish writes in a similar vein:

> Excessive reliance upon the criminal law to perform tasks for which it is ill-suited has created acute problems for the administration of criminal justice. The use of criminal law to enforce morals, to provide social services, and to avoid legal restraints on law enforcement, to take just three examples, has tended both to be inefficient and to produce grave handicaps for enforcement of the criminal law against genuinely threatening conduct. In the case of morals offenses, it has served to reduce the criminal law's essential claim to legitimacy by inducing offensive and degrading police conduct, particularly against the poor and the subcultural, and by generating cynicism and indifference to the criminal law. It has also fostered organized criminality and has produced, possibly, more crime than it has suppressed. Used as an alternative to social services, it has diverted enormous law enforcement resources from protecting the public against serious crime. Finally its rise to circumvent

restrictions on police conduct has undermined the principle of legality and exposed the law to plausible charges of hypocrisy. Pressures to criminalize persistently block practical assessments of what the criminal law is good for and what it is not. Studies of the sociology of overcriminalization offer a means of understanding, and perhaps, to some degree, of controlling, this unfortunate phenomenon.[42]

In a definitive book on the subject, the late Herbert L. Packer of the Stanford University Law School took the same position as Kadish and Skolnick.[43] The book probes the rhetorical question: How can we tell what the criminal sanction is good for? Packer's analysis is highly systematic, beginning with the query: What are we trying to do by defining conduct as criminal and punishing people who commit crimes? To what extent are we justified in thinking that we can or ought to do what we are trying to do? Is it possible for us to construct an acceptable rationale for the criminal sanction enabling us to deal with the argument that it is itself an unethical use of social power? And if it is possible, what implications does that rationale have for the kind of conceptual creature that the criminal law is?

Packer proceeds from a discussion of such questions to others equally fundamental. For example, what do the rules of the game tell us about what the state may and may not do to apprehend, charge, convict, and dispose of persons suspected of committing crimes? Finally, Packer argues that we have overrelied on the criminal sanction and that we had better start thinking about how to adjust our commitments to our capacities, both moral and operational. In sum, Packer's thesis has to do with the uses of power:

> The criminal sanction is at once prime guarantor and prime threatener of human freedom. Used providently and humanely, it is guarantor; used indiscriminately and coercively, it is threatener. The tensions that inhere in the criminal sanction can never be wholly resolved in favor of guaranty and against threat. But we can begin to try.[44]

There are many signs of progress in dealing with overcriminalization. While omnibus revisions of the criminal code tend to bog down in legislative process in many states—usually because of a few highly controversial sections—piecemeal steps in the right direction are observable. For example, criminal sanctions for marijuana possession and use are widely being reduced, if not eliminated. Public drunkenness has been decriminalized in Michigan. The offense accounted for 11 percent of all arrests in the state and cost the state $4 million in 1971, or $111 per arrest. Decriminalization does not, however, remove social responsibility. Detoxification facilities and social services for alcoholics are generally inadequate, given the proportions of the problem, and cost considerations are crucial. But for drunks, treatment will undoubtedly prove to be a better social investment than incarceration.

THE COURTS AND THE PROSECUTORS

Some points regarding the exercise of discretion by prosecutors and judges have been discussed earlier in this chapter. A few additional comments should be added.

Various crime commissions have pointed to the manifold problems of our courts. There are judges who are ill-disposed and ill-trained to manage their extraordinary power. Sentencing in itself is always fair game for criticism, no matter what principles guide it. Some people doubt the wisdom of the jury system, at least some aspects of it. There are prosecutors and defense counsels who resort to obfuscation and legal chicanery. The sheer volume of cases, particularly in urban courts, has caused many observers to charge that justice is consistently and blatantly miscarried.

Concern for the Sixth Amendment's mandate for speedy trials has prompted legislation that establishes time limits in the federal courts and in the courts of an increasing number of states. The lower courts—the courts that dispose of misdemeanor cases and often process the first stages of felony cases—are in especially serious trouble. The 1966 President's Crime Commission had this to say about it:

> [This commission] has seen cramped and noisy courtrooms, undignified and per-
> functory procedures, and badly trained personnel. It has seen dedicated people who
> are frustrated by huge case loads, by the lack of opportunity to examine cases
> carefully, and by the impossibility of devising constructive solutions to the problems
> of offenders. It has seen assembly line justice.[45]

Convinced that a central problem of many lower courts is the gross disparity between the number of cases and the personnel and facilities available to deal with them, the commission specified some associated problems and then concluded, as the Wickersham Commission had said thirty years earlier, that the best solution to the problems of the lower courts would be the abolition of these courts. Short of this, it said:

- Felony and misdemeanor courts and their ancillary agencies—prosecutors, defenders, and probation services—should be unified.
- As an immediate step to meet the needs of the lower courts, the judicial manpower
  of these courts should be increased and their physical facilities should be improved
  so that these courts will be able to cope with the volume of cases coming before
  them in a dignified and deliberate way.
- Prosecutors, probation officers, and defense counsels should be provided in courts
  where these officers are not found, or their numbers are insufficient.
- The States and Federal Government should enact legislation to abolish or overhaul
  the justice of the peace and U.S. Commissioner systems.[46]

The entire machinery of justice has been so understaffed, underfinanced, cumbersome, and politically inspired that expediency has become its watchword. Yet it is also well to be wary of efficiency as an end in itself, because speedy judicial process sometimes thwarts justice and blunts the strategies of trial lawyership. There is considerable sentiment in this country for adopting certain features of the British system, for example: magistrates' courts; nonunanimous verdicts in jury trials; lower, relatively easily obtained bail; the British method of screening out frivolous appeals; and—as we earlier noted— the refusal of British courts to exclude evidence obtained through improper police methods. Many police officials feel that certainty of punishment is the most important crime deterrent and that the overwhelmed courts have made a farce of this idea.[47]

There is a variety of so-called diversionary programs in criminal justice, and we will return to this in a subsequent chapter. But prosecutorial pre-arrest diversion should be mentioned here as a type of program recently developed, often with the help of LEAA grants, illustrated by the Columbus, Ohio, night prosecutor project.[48] Instead of applying the typical arrest-jail-court procedure, criminal complaints involving interpersonal disputes—family arguments, landlord-tenant disagreements, neighborhood fights, and other conflicts among people who must continue to maintain close personal contact with one another—are diverted to a night prosecutor's "office trial," no later than a week after the offense. In effect, it is an administrative hearing involving all the parties, aimed at opening the channels of communication. Since 1972, when the program was initiated, only about 2 percent of the complaints have resulted in the filing of formal criminal charges and issuance of arrest warrants.

Another form of prosecutorial diversion is a program called the Citizens Probation Authority initiated some years ago in Genessee County (Flint), Michigan, by Prosecutor Robert Leonard. In its first three years, this program—subsequently copied in other places—guided 2,000 people through a probation procedure supervised by the prosecutor's office that saved them from formal litigation in court and from criminal records for their offenses.

As we have noted, plea bargaining is a widespread reality in legal processes, a routine enactment of prosecutorial discretion. For every ten cases that go to trial today, nine end earlier with a guilty plea resulting from some form of plea bargaining. In return, the prosecutor agrees to reduce charges, drop charges, or make an agreed-upon sentence recommendation to the judge. The trend is toward more openness about plea bargaining, and as this occurs, it may be predicted that some of its worst abuses will fade.

Critics, of course, call for abolition of plea bargaining. They say it is immoral because it coerces pleas from defendants who have a right to stand trial—or, at the other extreme, allows the guilty to escape the punishment they deserve. Defenders of the practice argue pragmatically that plea bargaining saves the system from complete breakdown and that the results are as fair as those of a trial. Without it, adjudicatory costs would skyrocket. Plea bargaining is frequently referred to as "assembly-line justice." Some idea of its magnitude was provided in a *New York Times* study of all 685 murder and manslaughter indictments adjudicated in New York City in 1973.[49] Almost eight of every ten defendants accused of homicide who pleaded guilty to a reduced charge were freed on probation or received a prison term of less than ten years. Of those receiving a maximum ten-year term, most would be eligible for parole in three years. Some 80 percent of the completed 1973 homicide indictments were determined by guilty pleas, almost always to a reduced charge.

The National Advisory Commission on Criminal Justice Standards and Goals decried plea bargaining in its 1973 report and called for its abolition by 1978. But the National Association of District Attorneys voted to support the practice. While abolition may be a tall order, there is little doubt that plea bargaining encourages public cynicism and disdain for criminal justice processes. Various efforts are under way to reduce its use and to regulate it by such safeguards as tougher policies, more careful screening of cases where the practice may be permitted, higher court review to assure that defendants have had no promise of leniency for pleading guilty, and a court rule that any negotiations between attorneys relating to cases scheduled for trial must be completed at least one week before the trial.[50] The controversy over plea bargaining is a consequence, we have noted, of greater openness regarding the legal and judicial system, another aspect of the accountability revolution of our time.

Another controversial question attracting debaters, pro and con, is the grand jury. The primary function of a grand jury, usually comprising twenty-three members, is to decide whether evidence presented to it by witnesses subpoenaed by the court and questioned by assistant district attorneys in its presence is sufficient to warrant an indictment. By law, the grand jury's work is conducted in secrecy, and this is one of many arguments used against it. The United States is one of very few countries retaining the grand jury system, which was abolished in England in 1933—where it originated over 800 years ago.[51]

LEGAL SERVICES FOR THE POOR AND POWERLESS

How does the criminal justice process look from the vantage point of the poor and powerless? In earlier chapters, we referred to the conflict-repression model of the criminal justice system advanced by Richard Quinney and others, and to the attitudes of minorities toward the police. How do the poor and powerless fare under the system?

Concern about this question originated with the birth of democratic government. In the United States, this concern appears to have become increasingly compelling in recent years. It has been integral to the civil rights movement and the war on poverty. The issue, simply stated, is to see to it that *everyone*—including the poor, the powerless, the black as well as the white, the nonreligious as well as the religious, the unbarbered as well as the barbered—receives fair and equal treatment in the processes of criminal justice.[52] This relationship between government and the individual is the essence of the free society.

Organized legal aid for the indigent grew commendably between 1965 and 1975. Through leadership, responsible research, unprecedented resources, and broad objectives, such organizations as the American Bar Association and the National Legal Aid and Defender Associations, the Vera Institute, the National Committee for Public Justice, the Legal Services program of the federal Office of Economic Opportunity, and Legal Aid societies in many cities all made notable contributions.[53]

Poor people are prone to legal trouble. In the legalities they face daily as parents, consumers, tenants, recipients of public assistance, and accused offenders, they are often defendants, rarely plaintiffs. When the late Senator Robert F. Kennedy addressed the University of Chicago Law School on May 1,

1964, he said: "The poor man looks upon the law as an enemy, not as a friend. For him, the law is always taking something away."

A National Conference on Law and Poverty, held in Washington, D.C., June 23–24, 1965, summarized the main characteristics of the problem:

> Poverty takes its toll in deteriorating human relationships. Poor families account for a disproportionate share of mental illness, alcoholism, drug addiction, illegitimacy, desertion and juvenile delinquency. Wife beating and child abuse are more frequent among the poor. Neglect proceedings are typical. All of these matters have legal assistance implications.
>
> The greatest material need of the poor is decent shelter. The poor inhabit the slums, and slum housing is not cheap. Welfare recipients spend the bulk of their allowances for rent and utilities, depleting food funds. Housing code violations are commonplace. Generally speaking, the legal rights of tenants in these circumstances are not well protected. Fundamental revision of antiquated landlord-tenant law is needed.
>
> Impoverished minority groups face legal obstacles arising from discriminatory practices that intensify their need for legal help. The right to equal opportunity must be tortuously defined by lawyers and courts in a variety of contexts.
>
> In consumer purchasing, the poor are often the victims of easy credit, high prices, legal threats, repossession, garnishment or its threat, and sundry unethical practices. Legal counseling is a much needed resource for the poor, and it is a practical way of imparting consumer education.
>
> For many of the poor who are recipients of welfare assistance (in the neighborhood of 15 million people), the welfare system is a maze of bureaucratic technicalities incomprehensible to anyone lacking legal training.
>
> The poor form the overwhelming percentage of the criminally accused. This speaks for itself in terms of its legal aid ramifications.
>
> Poverty breeds mental illness. Mentally ill patients frequently require legal assistance to protect their rights.[54]

The same report stated that the poor man is ruled by a legal system that he neither understands nor trusts. Often, the poor do not know that a lawyer can help. Or they do not know where or how to secure legal help. Or they find the lawyer too remote. Or they are afraid of reprisal.

Despite the advances made in legal services to the poor in recent years, the needs still far exceed what is available. Legal aid lawyers individually decide which cases to accept. Sometimes legal aid facilities shun publicity for fear of being taxed far beyond resources. Some organizations bar applicants by overly strict eligibility standards. Many legal aid offices exclude certain types of cases, for example, divorce, adoption, bankruptcy, civil mental commitment, and the like. To overcome the general indictment "too little and too late," a program of legal assistance for the poor should meet these qualifications:

1. Legal services must be accessible.
2. Legal services must be independent.
3. Legal services must be integrated with nonlegal services.
4. Legal services must be comprehensive.
5. Legal services must include preventive law, i.e., educate the poor to seek advice before crisis arises.
6. Legal services must be available to all who cannot afford to pay.[55]

Many states today have a system by which counties compensate attorneys who represent indigent criminal defendants in the courts. The basic methods used include the following:

1. Assigned counsel
   The judge appoints individual lawyers from private practice on a case-by-case basis. Compensation is based on a predetermined fee schedule or an hourly rate.

2. Public defender
   One or more salaried lawyers devote all or a substantial portion of their time to the defense of indigents.

3. Private defender
   Like the public defender, the private defender's office consists of one or more salaried attorneys who devote all or a substantial part of their time to the defense of indigent criminal defendants. But it is organized as a private association and is governed by a board of private citizens.

Each of these methods has its advantages and disadvantages.

The 1966 President's Crime Commission made some pertinent recommendations:

> The objective to be met as quickly as possible is to provide counsel to every criminal defendant who faces a significant penalty, if he cannot afford to provide counsel himself. This should apply to cases classified as misdemeanors as well as to those classified as felonies. Counsel should be provided early in the proceedings and certainly no later than the first judicial appearance. The services of counsel should be available after conviction through appeal, and in collateral attack proceedings when the issues are not frivolous. The immediate minimum, until it becomes possible to provide the foregoing, is that all criminal defendants who are in danger of substantial loss of liberty shall be provided with counsel.
>
> All jurisdictions that have not already done so should move from random assignment of defense counsel by judges to a coordinated, assigned counsel system or a defender system.
>
> Each state should finance assigned counsel and defender systems on a regular and statewide basis.[56]

Subsequent national commissions have voiced strong support of programs expanding legal services to the poor. Major responsibility for the development of such programs was placed with local bar associations, and law schools were urged to allow advanced students to provide legal assistance as part of their professional training. The Ford Foundation has provided generous grants to foster this cause. In *Tate* v. *Short* in 1971, the Supreme Court interpreted the equal protection clause of the Fourteenth Amendment to mean that no indigent may be imprisoned solely on account of his financial inability to pay a fine levied against him.[57]

Special attention in this matter has focused on the bail system, generally recognized as a rank injustice to the poor. In most county jails, as many as two-thirds of the inmates have not been sentenced. More than half have not been tried. Most simply lack the funds to post bond. The bail system aims at balancing the rights of the accused against the court's responsibility to ensure that the person appears for trial. The Bill of Rights states that "excessive" bail shall not be required and also stipulates the right to a speedy trial. But in actual practice, our jails are heavily populated with inmates without visible means of support.

The issue in the bail system is that financial means to make bond (or to be seen as a good risk by a bail bondsman) are not necessarily a fair and proper standard for determining which persons are dangerous to society or are unlikely to appear for later trial. The solution appears, therefore, to be refinement of the information system bearing on bail determinations. The pretrial release investigation and the development of more adequate court administration and information are key considerations, as indicated by the 1973 National Advisory Commission on Criminal Justice Standards and Goals.

High legal fees are a concern, too, of most middle-income Americans. There has been some talk of insurance similar to medical-hospital plans, and the deans of various law schools along with the American Bar Association are studying other proposals for lowering costs.

Obstacles to Legal Services for the Poor

Legal services for the poor invariably encounter obstacles. Some of the problems are suggested by the following examples:

> On September 22, 1970, the *New York Times* reported that representatives of leading lawyers' organizations had started a fight against a proposed regionalization of the federal program of legal services to the poor. The director of the Office of Economic Opportunity contested the position that such regionalization would emasculate the program. Some months earlier, private lawyers' groups had successfully joined with OEO to defeat a congressional effort to give a veto power over legal services programs to state governors.
>
> As of December, 1970, the OEO Legal Services program had grown to $60 million, employing 2000 lawyers in almost every state. It was handling over a million cases a year at a cost to the American tax-payer of $58 per case. But politicians and bureaucrats at various governmental levels were seeking to choke it off.[58]
>
> In February, 1971, George Washington University announced the discontinuance of its federally funded Urban Law Institute, described as the most effective clinical law education program in the country. The University gave as its reason the belief that its law school students should not practice law. The Institute had been involved in several controversial cases in Washington, D.C. The director of the Institute charged that the University had succumbed to political pressure, and added that it was part of a pattern of opposition against successful legal programs for the poor across the country.[59]

In the same month, the Supreme Court agreed to decide the question of whether poor persons prosecuted for petty offenses (misdemeanors) must be offered free legal counsel. The Court eventually ruled that a person may not be tried for *any* offense without counsel.[60] The Court had ruled eight years earlier that poor defendants were entitled to free counsel in felony cases (*Gideon* v. *Wainwright*, 1963). Of the eight million annual arrests for nontraffic violations, more than half are thought to involve poor people accused of petty offenses.

In March 1971, a bipartisan group of ninety-eight senators and representatives proposed that the embattled Federal Legal Services to the Poor program be permanently insulated from political pressures by the creation of an independent National Legal Services Corporation, to be funded by Congress and operated by an autonomous board of public and private members. The corporation would supplant and greatly enlarge the OEO Legal Services program.[61]

These examples are indicative of the constant political maneuvering that surrounds tax-supported programs to provide legal services for the poor. It is regarded by many as an aspect of "the welfare mess." Legal aid bureaus are perennially viewed as fair game for budget cutting, especially because such agencies have sometimes been involved in class action suits against government bodies.

Victims of Crime

The term "powerless" may be applied to the innocent victims of crime. This is a subject finally getting the attention it deserves in current criminal justice discussions. Numerous states have enacted legislation to compensate crime victims from public funds, and a federal scheme is under congressional scrutiny. Great Britain, New Zealand, Canada, Australia, and Sweden are among the countries that have such programs.

Encouraged by LEAA funding, crime victimization surveys have received unprecedented attention in the past few years. Data secured in these surveys are vital in the development of programs aimed at curbing crime. For instance, one significant discovery is that about three of every four victims of crime never report to the authorities. The reasons for this are numerous, but one is that victims see no benefit in reporting a crime. Some believe that nothing can be done (about 40 percent), some doubt that the incident is "important enough" (about 30 percent), some think the event is private or personal (about 5 percent), and some feel that the police will not want to be bothered (about 5 percent).[62]

The rights of suspects and defendants involved in criminal process are unquestionably important, and certainly merit the attention devoted to due-process considerations by the courts. Yet it is equally important, as is now being recognized, to protect the rights of the victims of crime. Because society as a whole is the indirect victim of crime, current insight acknowledges that we can best cope with crime by studying information provided by the direct victims.

SOME CONTROVERSIAL ISSUES

Most of the issues discussed to this point in this chapter are controversial to some extent. There are several additional "hardy perennials" of this nature that warrant mention here.

Entrapment

When, to make an arrest, police or other law enforcement officers, or agents working in their behalf, encourage the commission of a crime, this practice is known as *entrapment*.[63] Generally, it is frowned upon by American courts and has, in fact, been regarded as sufficient defense if there is good reason to believe the crime would not have been committed had it not been for such encouragement. The American Law Institute and the American Bar Association have each proposed a code of criminal justice administration that condemns police entrapment, without unrealistically opposing the use of informers.

The courts have argued that the law sullies itself when it induces someone to commit a crime. Further, the law should not act so as to tempt anyone, nor in such a manner as to invite blackmail, extortion, and bribery. Entrapment has been defended in cases involving illegal purchases and sales (narcotics, liquor, pornography, etc.); in prostitution and homosexual cases; and in political cases involving strikes, civil rights, antiwar and black militant actions, and student unrest. Edward Sagarin and Donal MacNamara contend that entrapment "constitutes a threat to the democratic process, tending to discredit otherwise legitimate social protest and to stay the hand of social change." Quoting former Chief Justice Earl Warren, "The function of law enforcement does not include the manufacturing of crimes."[64]

Stop and Frisk

Not so much in the news of late, but still an issue that keeps reappearing in constitutional law is stop and frisk. Several fairly recent statutes and court decisions—the most noteworthy of which are the New York state stop-and-frisk law, the Uniform Arrest Act, and the Model Code of Pre-Arraignment procedure—have given police the authority to use force in the practice of stop and frisk and to detain persons for investigation on grounds of less-than-probable cause. Stop-and-frisk legislation is applicable in two distinct situations: in instances of so-called preventive criminality, where an individual's demeanor and the accompanying circumstances justify a suspicion that he is about to engage in criminal activity; and in instances where the aim is to allow patrol officers to conduct investigations of persons they suspect have committed a crime.

Stop-and-frisk legislation has its roots in vagrancy and loitering statutes, and is subject to many of the same constitutional and practical limitations. The Fourth Amendment provides the principal constitutional standard that this type of legislation must meet. If the necessary detention is considered an arrest within the meaning of this amendment, any such police activity without probable cause will be unconstitutional. Lack of clarity in the distinctions between a detention and an arrest, and between a frisk and a search, render the regulatory statutes difficult to administer.

Society must run the risk of antisocial behavior in the interest of preserving the freedom of the individual. Further, the benefits resulting from the detention and frisking of suspicious persons may well be outweighed, as we have suggested earlier in this text, by an increase in tension between police and citizens, particularly citizens who are members of minority groups. Where authority is granted for apprehending persons suspected of having committed a crime, the present standard of probable cause should be retained. And forcing the police to conform to this standard will encourage improvement in methods of investigation.[65]

Preventive Detention

In late July 1970, President Nixon signed into law the District of Columbia Crime Bill. This bill contained several controversial sections, among which was the provision that judges would be allowed to jail defendants considered dangerous to society for as long as sixty days before trial. This clause was widely attacked as unconstitutional, and also criticized for its unsubstantiated assumptions, namely: (1) that the persons arrested for dangerous or violent crimes have a high propensity for arrest for subsequent offenses of a serious nature; (2) that when persons who are arrested for serious felonies are rearrested, it will be for an equally serious charge; and (3) that judges can accurately predict those who will be dangerous if released.

The National Council on Crime and Delinquency (NCCD) took a policy position opposing such legislation for these reasons:

1. Such legislation substitutes a presumption of guilt for a presumption of innocence.

2. Such legislation probably violates the Constitutional right to reasonable bail.

3. Such legislation contains an inherent danger of practical abuse. For example, there is an element of prejudice to defendants who are needlessly detained.

4. Such legislation undermines needed reforms in the system, by accepting pretrial detention because of the court's failure to provide speedy trials.

5. Typical preventive detention proposals provide for complex procedural safeguards which, if observed, would constitute a great additional burden on the courts.

6. Analysis of the data shows that the amount of dangerous crime prevented would at best be very small, whereas the damage to many nondangerous defendants and to correctional systems would be considerable.[66]

NCCD recommended the following procedures, in lieu of preventive detention:

1. Priority in trial should be granted upon the request of a prosecutor, in accordance with previously established court rules, without review by a judge.

2. The criteria and procedure should be formulated in any jurisdiction by the prosecutor, working with the court administrator, either a state administrator or an administrator for a district of general jurisdiction, and the controlling rules should be promulgated by the court.

3. Under these rules, crimes for which priority may be requested should be specified (a) by the nature of the crime charged, and (b) by elements that would be significant in identifying both dangerousness and likelihood of repetition.[67]

Increasing public concern about so-called career criminals has brought preventive detention to the forefront recently, in some localities. In Michigan, for example in the November 1978 election, voters cast a landslide verdict for a constitutional amendment granting authority to the courts to deny bail under certain circumstances involving violent crimes: murder, treason, armed robbery, criminal sexual assault, or kidnapping for extortion. It is of interest to note that, at the same time, Michigan voters also approved a proposal to prohibit the granting of parole to a prisoner convicted of certain crimes involving violence or injury to person or property until the minimum sentence has been served.

No Knock

Another controversial provision of the 1970 District of Columbia Crime Bill permitted police to obtain search warrants under which they could enter premises without announcing themselves if notice was likely to result in the destruction of evidence, to endanger the life of a police officer, or to permit an escape. This clause is popularly referred to as the *no-knock* clause.

Again, this section of the bill was harshly criticized on moral, practical, and policy grounds, and less so on constitutional grounds. Some critics claimed that many judges would grant search warrants almost automatically, and that there was no reason to think that they would not also grant no-knock permission in the same fashion, particularly in narcotics and gambling cases. The Comprehensive Drug Abuse Prevention and Control Act of 1970, signed into law by President Nixon in October of that year, provided for search warrants that specifically allowed enforcement officers to enter premises to be searched without notice, if there were probable cause to believe that the property sought would be destroyed or that notice would endanger someone's life or safety.

Some critics of the no-knock clause speculate that its actual effect may be to make the enforcement of narcotics laws more difficult because it encourages violators to resort to underground tactics. Clearly necessary are some guidelines to prevent misuse of the no-knock procedure. Some states, with New York again leading the way, had moved to statutory enunciation of such guidelines as early as 1964.[68]

The no-knock provision of the 1970 law was later repealed, in the light of some tragic police experience with it.[69]

Gun Control

Various presidential commissions in recent years—on crime, civil disorders, violence, and campus unrest—have made recommendations about the use of firearms, especially handguns, by private citizens. The push for federal and state controls has been pronounced, in the face of strong opposition by influential groups. Many progressive police administrators have joined in the plea for domestic disarmament.

Advocates of disarming the police, however, have been far fewer, and police officials themselves almost unanimously reject such action. The subject quickly generates highly emotional outbursts in this country, an interesting contrast with the situation in England, which has been a model for so much of American police organization and procedure, but where the cultural milieu is admittedly different. For the present, at least, it appears that we must settle for sane firearms policies for all law enforcement agencies, such as the guidelines recommended by the 1966 President's Crime Commission and generally reiterated by the 1973 National Advisory Commission on Criminal Justice Standards and Goals:

1. Deadly force should not be used against any suspect unless the arresting officer's safety or the safety of someone else is endangered.

2. Such force should never be used on mere suspicion that a crime has been committed.

3. Policemen should not fire on felony suspects when lesser force could be used.

4. Warning shots should never be used.

5. Any force, including deadly force, can be used by policemen to protect themselves or others.

6. Detailed written reports should be required on all discharges of firearms.[70]

Many police agencies actually operate with more stringent regulations than these, as a matter of policy.

Returning for a moment to the much more controversial question of gun control for society at large, Congress has, for several years, been trying to formulate acceptable regulatory legislation. It is estimated that there are approximately 50 million gun owners in the country, with 2½ million more each year. This statistic is said to have a gloomy relationship to crime and suicide statistics, and to the 27,000 fatal gun accidents occurring each year. Public opinion polls indicate that more than two-thirds of our citizens favor more effective gun controls, including registration of all firearms and licensing of all gun owners. However, past congressional efforts at control have proven ineffective. For example, the Federal Gun Control Act of 1968 banned the import of "Saturday night specials," but failed to ban the import of *parts*.[71]

While Congress has been stalling, several states and localities have adopted restrictive measures. The Ford administration was content to propose only a ban on the manufacture and sale of Saturday night specials, and the creation of a 500-man Treasury Department force to attack the black market in handguns in the nation's ten largest cities. Concurrently, several bills were introduced in the House of Representatives to *weaken* existing laws, and many more bills to *toughen* them—all the way to almost total prohibition of the manufacture, sale, purchase, and possession of handguns. Proposed legislation typically spanned the full range of views on the subject, and typically, nothing happened. The lobbying influence of the National Rifle Association and its allies on this issue makes the prospect for effective congressional action remote indeed.

In Michigan, where the so-called gun lobby is particularly potent, lawmakers have focused on increasing penalties for gun-related crimes, rather than on regulating the weapons themselves. Nationally, in 1973, someone used a gun in a crime every two minutes, for a total that year of 279,169 gun crimes, most of which involved handguns. Yet state experience with relatively tough controls, such as in New York, has not produced conclusive evidence that tougher controls necessarily add up to a significant reduction in gun-involved crime. Again, the fact that so many variables bear on the phenomenon makes it difficult to isolate any single factor. Nonetheless, public sentiment about the hand-gun situation has been such that tighter regulation is long overdue. The main goal of the gun lobby presently seems to be to salvage as many loopholes as possible.

SUMMING UP

This has been an extended chapter, touching upon selected aspects of the complex relationship of police, prosecution, and courts. The problems in this relationship reflect problems in the criminal justice system itself, which have been widely discussed by many observers in recent years. We have not under-taken to reflect all of this discussion, being content to highlight a few issues that seem especially important in community relations terms.

We have asked what it takes to make a true social system. We believe this has a good deal to do with a principle of interrelatedness, of interdependence —a basic principle running through all that we have said about police and the community. We identified some of the main factors that make the crimi-nal justice process dysfunctional as a system, stressing the idea of relation-ships. We reviewed various approaches to the systemic reform that seems more and more to be a common commitment of partisans of every vintage, al-though there is much disagreement on *how*, and some disagreement on *what*. We spoke of the merits of a pilot-program tactic for reform, exemplified by the Vera Institute in New York City.

Next, we considered more specifically some of the main burdens on the relationships of police, prosecution, and the courts, particularly as to the exer-cise of discretion and in regard to sentencing. As a strategy for coping with these problems, we suggested pluralistic planning, and noted how systems analysis can help provide data to define problems and facilitate discussion.

Our attention then turned to what Professor Herbert Packer called "the limits of the criminal sanction," and what is generally referred to as over-criminalization or legal moralism. This is the use of the criminal code to make a crime of everything people are against. Our difficulty in distinguishing between what is suited and what is ill-suited for criminal law complicates community relations for the entire criminal justice system. Related to this are procedural problems, such as volume of cases, plea bargaining, and misuse of judicial power.

We are especially interested in the question of legal services for the poor and powerless, our assumption being that one person's rights are as important as any other person's. Poor people are prone to legal problems, we observed, and, while acknowledging that notable progress has been made in legal services for the poor in recent years, we also noted that there is a long way still to go, and some signs of political opposition to going too far too fast. Finally, we briefly reviewed five controversial issues that merit attention in any contemporary text of this nature: entrapment, stop and frisk, preventive detention, no knock, and gun control.

A fitting close to this chapter is the following quotation from Harlan Cleve-land, presently the director of the Aspen Institute's Program in International

Affairs, from a speech delivered in Palo Alto to a joint meeting of the American Assembly and the American Bar Association:

> Whether we *will* in fact use our imagination for the humanistic management of interdependence, whether new styles of cooperative leadership will develop fast enough to govern a post-exploitive, post-trickle-down, post-patronizing world, are the central issues of survival and beyond. But at least they are riddles for the human race, not for nature or the gods, to decipher.[72]

Mr. Cleveland did not have criminal justice specifically in mind. But what he said is certainly applicable to it.

NOTES

1. Robert H. Scott, "Problems in Communication and Cooperation in the Administration of Criminal Justice," in A. F. Brandstatter and Louis A. Radelet, eds., *Police and Community Relations: A Source Book* (Beverly Hills, Calif.: Glencoe, 1968), p. 430. Reprinted by permission.

2. Ibid.

3. Elmer H. Johnson, "Interrelatedness of Law Enforcement Programs: A Fundamental Dimension," *Journal of Criminal Law, Criminology and Police Science* 60, no. 4 (1969):509–516. See also by the same author, *Crime, Correction and Society*, rev. ed. (Homewood, Ill.: Dorsey, 1969).

4. For a British expression of this point of view, see Patrick Arthur Devlin, "The Police in a Changing Society," *Journal of Criminal Law, Criminology and Police Science* 57 (July 1966): 124 ff.

5. Johnson, "Interrelatedness of Law Enforcement Programs," p. 510.

6. Ibid., p. 512. Reprinted by permission.

7. Ibid.

8. Ibid., p. 513.

9. Ibid.

10. Ibid., p. 514.

11. Ibid., p. 516.

12. Herman Goldstein, *Policing a Free Society* (Cambridge, Mass.: Ballinger, 1977), p. 93. Goldstein refers here to the comment of Kenneth Culp Davis, *Police Discretion* (St. Paul, Minn.: West, 1975), pp. 96–97. See also National Advisory Commission on Criminal Justice Standards and Goals, Standard 1.3, "Police Discretion," 1973; and American Bar Association Project on Standards for Criminal Justice, *Standards Relating to The Urban Police Function* (Chicago: American Bar Association, 1975).

13. Robert Martinson, "What Works? Questions and Answers About Prison Reform," *Public Interest*, Spring 1974, pp. 22–54.

14. Albert W. Alschuler, "Sentencing Reform and Prosecutorial Power: A Critique of Recent Proposals for 'Fixed' and 'Presumptive' Sentencing," in NILECJ, *Summary Report*, Special Conference on Determinate Sentencing: Reform or Regression, LEAA, U.S. Department of Justice, March 1978, pp. 59–88.

15. National Institute on Law Enforcement and Criminal Justice, *Summary Report*, Special Conference on Determinate Sentencing: Reform or Regression, LEAA, U.S.

Department of Justice, March 1978. See also Stephen P. Lagoy, Frederick A. Hussey, and John H. Kramer, "A Comparative Assessment of Determinate Sentencing in the Four Pioneer States," *Crime and Delinquency* 24, no. (October 4, 1978): 385–400.

16. Ibid., NILECJ, *Summary Report*, p. 1.

17. Norval Morris, *The Future of Imprisonment* (Chicago, Ill.: University of Chicago Press, 1974), p. xi.

18. C. S. Lewis, "The Humanitarian Theory of Punishment," in C. S. Lewis, *God in the Dock: Essays on Theology and Ethics*, edited by Walter Hooper (Grand Rapids, Mich.: Eerdmans, 1970).

19. Norval Morris and Donald Buckle, "Reply to C. S. Lewis," *20th Century: An Australian Quarterly Review* 6, no. 2 (1952): 20–26.

20. Norval Morris, *The Future of Imprisonment*, p. xi.

21. Ramsey Clark, *Crime in America* (New York: Simon and Schuster, 1970).

22. Isidore Silver, *Commonweal*, March 19, 1971, pp. 41–43. Reprinted by permission. Isidore Silver is chairman of the Department of Government and Economics at John Jay College of Criminal Justice in New York City.

23. Irving Reichert, in a speech to an Institute on Police-Community Relations held at the University of San Francisco, January 31, 1966.

24. *U.S. News & World Report*, March 31, 1975, pp. 28–32.

25. Ibid.

26. For a description of the Vera Institute approach and its early projects, see the testimony of the Institute's executive director, Herbert Sturz, before the Ribicoff Committee: U.S. Congress, Senate Committee on Government Operations, Subcommittee on Executive Reorganization, *Hearings: Federal Role in Urban Affairs*, part 13, pp. 2740–2757, 89th Cong., 2nd sess. (Washington, D.C.: U.S. Government Printing Office, 1967). For more recent reports, contact the Vera Institute directly. See also Jameson W. Doig, "Police Problems, Proposals, and Strategies for Change," "*Public Administration Review* 28, no. 5 (1968): 393–406.

27. Doig, "Police Problems, Proposals, and Strategies for Change," pp. 393 ff. Reprinted by permission.

28. Albert J. Reiss, Jr., "Professionalization of the Police," in Brandstatter and Radelet, eds., *Police and Community Relations*, p. 229.

29. Albert J. Reiss, Jr., and David J. Bordua, "Environment and Organization: A Perspective on the Police," in David J. Bordua, ed., *The Police: Six Sociological Essays* (New York: John Wiley & Sons, 1967), p. 36. Reprinted by permission of John Wiley & Sons.

30. Ibid., pp. 38–40. See also: V. A. Leonard, *The Police, the Judiciary, and the Criminal* (Springfield, Ill.: Charles C Thomas, 1969); National Council on Crime and Delinquency, *Model Rules of Court on Police Action from Arrest to Arraignment*, proposals by the Council of Judges, 1969.

31. Carl W. Hamm, "Pluralistic Planning within the Criminal Justice System," *Crime and Delinquency* 16, no. 4 (October 1970): 393. Reprinted by permission of the National Council on Crime and Delinquency.

32. Ibid., p. 402. Pfiffner called it "geopolitical planning."

33. Alfred Blumstein, "Systems Analysis and the Criminal Justice System," *Annals* 374 (November 1967): 92–100. Reprinted by permission.

34. Ibid., p. 94–95.

35. Ibid.

36. U.S., President's Commission on Law Enforcement and Administration of Justice, *The Challenge of Crime in a Free Society* (Washington, D.C.: U.S. Government Printing Office, 1967), pp. 126–127.

37. U.S., National Advisory Commission on Criminal Justice Standards and Goals, *Report on the Criminal Justice System* (Washington, D.C.: U.S. Government Printing Office, 1973), p. 177.

38. *New York Times*, October 22, 1970.

39. Jerome H. Skolnick, "The Police and the Urban Ghetto," *Research Contributions of the American Bar Foundation*, 1968, no. 3.

40. Jerome H. Skolnick, *Professional Police in a Free Society* (New York: National Conference of Christians and Jews, 1968), p. 16. Reprinted by permission of the National Conference of Christians and Jews.

41. Ibid.

42. Sanford H. Kadish, "The Crisis of Overcriminalization," *Annals* 374 (November 1967): 157. Reprinted by permission.

43. Herbert L. Packer, *The Limits of the Criminal Sanction*. See also Edwin M. Schur, *Crimes Without Victims* (Englewood Cliffs, N.J.: Prentice-Hall, 1965).

44. Packer, *The Limits of the Criminal Sanction* (Palo Alto, Calif.: Stanford University Press, 1968), p. 366.

45. President's Commission on Law Enforcement and Administration of Justice, *The Challenge of Crime in a Free Society*, p. 128.

46. Ibid., pp. 129–130.

47. See such additional references as Leonard Downie, Jr., *Justice Denied: The Case for Reform of the Courts* (New York: Praeger, 1971); Stephen Gillers, *Getting Justice: The Rights of People* (New York: Basic Books, 1971); Bruce Wasserstein and Mark J. Green, eds., *With Justice for Some* (Boston: Beacon Press, 1971).

48. John W. Palmer, "Pre-Arrest Diversion," *Crime and Delinquency* 21, no. 2 (April 1975): 100–108. See also American Bar Association, Project on Standards for Criminal Justice, *Standards Relating to the Prosecution Function and the Defense Function* (Chicago: American Bar Association, 1970), p. 246.

49. Selwyn Raab, *New York Times*, January 27, 1975, p. 1.

50. For a further discussion of plea bargaining, see Arthur Rosett, "The Negotiated Guilty Plea," *Annals* 374 (November 1967): 70–81.

51. David Rothman, "The Grand Jury vs. You," *Saturday Evening Post*, November 1974, pp. 40 ff.; Lloyd E. Mook, "The Grand Jury Is You," ibid., May–June 1975, pp. 34 ff.

52. In the summer of 1975, the Joan Little case in North Carolina attracted national attention because it dramatized the issues of racism, sexism, legal justice for the poor, jail conditions, and capital punishment.

53. For information on the first two of these organizations, see Don Hyndman, "The Rule of Law in the Republic," in Brandstatter and Radelet, eds., *Police and Community Relations*, pp. 1–7. For an article on the Legal Aid Society in New York City, see *Life*, March 12, 1971.

54. Paraphrased from Patricia M. Wald, *Law and Poverty: 1965*, edited by Abram Chayes and Robert L. Wald, prepared as a working paper for the National Conference

on Law and Poverty, cosponsored by the Attorney General of the United States and the Office of Economic Opportunity, Washington, D.C., June 23–25, 1965 (Washington, D.C.: U.S. Government Printing Office, 1965).

55. Ibid., pp. 64–67.

56. President's Commission on Law Enforcement, *The Challenge of Crime in a Free Society*, pp. 150–153.

57. *Tate* v. *Short*, 401 U.S. 395 (1971).

58. Terry Lenzner (former director of the OEO Legal Services program), *New York Times*, December 15, 1970, p. 45. See also *National Observer*, March 8, 1971, p. 5. Also see: "The Right to Counsel and the Indigent Defendant," a symposium in *American Criminal Law Review* 12, no. 4 (Spring 1975).

59. *New York Times*, February 23, 1971, p. 21.

60. *Angersinger* v. *Hamlin*, 407 U.S. 25 (1972); 92 S Ct. 2006, 36 L. Ed. 2d 530 (1072).

61. *New York Times*, March 18, 1971, p. 24. Nothing has happened in the implementing of this proposal.

62. U.S., National Advisory Commission on Criminal Justice Standards and Goals, "Victimization Surveying: Its History, Uses, and Limitations," Appendix A of *Report on the Criminal Justice System* (Washington, D.C.: U.S. Government Printing Office, 1973), pp. 199–206. See also Herbert Edelhertz and Gilbert Geis, *Public Compensation to Victims of Crime* (New York: Praeger, 1974).

63. Edward Sagarin and Donal E. J. MacNamara, "The Problem of Entrapment," *Crime and Delinquency* 16, no. 4 (October 1970): 363–378. Note that entrapment and setting a trap are distinct concepts. The latter is generally an acceptable police tactic. Entrapment is a *legal* concept: the person would not have committed the crime except for the encouragement of the police.

64. Ibid., p. 363; *Rittinour* v. *District of Columbia*, 163 A. 2d 588 (1960).

65. John J. Duffy, "Stop and Frisk: A Perspective" *Cornell Law Review* 53, no. 5 (1968): 899–915. See also U.S., President's Commission on Law Enforcement and Administration of Justice, *Task Force Report: The Police* (Washington, D.C.: U.S. Government Printing Office, 1967), pp. 38–41.

66. National Council on Crime and Delinquency, Board of Trustees, "Preventive Detention: A Policy Statement," *Crime and Delinquency* 17, no. 1 (January 1971): 1–8. Reprinted by permission of the National Council on Crime and Delinquency.

67. Ibid., pp. 2–3.

68. In New York State, Section 799 of the Code of Criminal Procedure, as amended.

69. Both the House and Senate repealed 21 U.S.C.A. 879 and its counterpart in the District of Columbia Code in 1974. These were the no-knock clauses. See 15 Crim. Law Rptr. 2460 (1974).

70. President's Commission on Law Enforcement, *The Challenge of Crime in a Free Society*, pp. 189–190.

71. Stephen Oberbeck, "Safer With a Gun? Don't Believe It!" *Reader's Digest*, February 1975, pp. 136–139 (condensed from an article in *Good Housekeeping*, March 1974).

72. *National Observer*, August 16, 1975. Reprinted by permission.

15

THE CRIMINAL JUSTICE SYSTEM: CORRECTIONS AND THE COMMUNITY

This chapter deals with the corrections aspect of the criminal justice system. Just as there is an abundance of literature dealing with problems of the police and other facets of the legal system, so the writings about the problems of correctional programs fill many library shelves. It seems that, although we know pretty well what the problems are, the debate is endless on what to do about them.

No attempt is made here to recapitulate any appreciable portion of what the many analysts have said about correctional maladies. Rather, we will highlight certain problems that seem particularly salient from a community relations standpoint. Inevitably, we will backtrack here and there to some matters discussed in the preceding chapter. Sentencing, for example, is multifaceted in its ramifications, and an analysis of it does not fall tidily into our chapter alignment.

THE CORRECTIONAL PROCESS

Historically, society has sought to deter crime through punishment and to redress wrongs against itself by exacting severe, sometimes barbarous penalties. In recent times, however, the criminal law has moderated vengeance and protected the accused against unjust and excessive punishment. Cesare Beccaria and others of the classical school of penology considered swiftness and certainty of punishment better deterrents than severity. A precise punishment for each offense became the goal. Gilbert and Sullivan parodied this principle in their operetta *The Mikado:*

> My object all sublime
> I shall achieve in time—
> To make the punishment fit the crime.[1]

Beginning in the 1700s, a series of reforms for offenders gradually evolved: separating children from adults and men from women, and developing the indeterminate sentence, probation, and parole.

The Declaration of Principles of the First Congress of Corrections in 1870 marked the beginning of the trend toward rehabilitation as a goal in corrections. For the next century, it was the rallying point for reform. From it evolved the concept of custody for treatment and the "medical model," the idea that convicted criminals can and should be treated as one would treat patients in a hospital.

Richard A. McGee, former director of corrections in California and current president of the American Justice Institute, put it this way:

> Man has never been pleased, in his saner and more thoughtful moments, with what he has had to do to carry out the sanctions of the penal law. And from the very beginning, this great new Republic of ours in the western hemisphere has generally frowned upon brutal, savage and unnecessarily severe punishments. . . .
>
> Since America has prized liberty so highly, it is only natural that it has always seemed to our leadership that the rightful punishment of an offender who has the high privileges of citizenship in a democracy should be the loss of his liberty.[2]

McGee listed several crucial questions regarding institutional confinement as a correctional procedure:

1. How much liberty should be taken from a man's life for one offense compared with another?

2. Which is the greater offense against society, the deed for which an offender is imprisoned, or the long imprisonment with the intention of eventual release but no preparation for that release?

3. How do we measure the waste of penal servitude in lost labor and human resources, and in the cost of operating custodial institutions?

McGee commented on the basic causes of the prison maladjustment inherent in the last question: inadequate financial support, official and public indifference, substandard personnel, enforced idleness, lack of professional leadership and professional programs, excessive size and overcrowding of institutions, political domination and motivation of management, and unwise sentencing and parole practices.

While McGee's questions are directed to only one aspect of *adult* correctional pathogenesis, they suggest some of the fundamental dilemma of corrections and community relations. It is somewhat like the dilemma of police and community relations. Just as the community has conflicts in what it expects the police to do, so it has conflicting ideas on what it expects of corrections. Is it a matter simply of punishing the offender for his wrongdoing? Or is it a matter, as McGee said, of exerting "every known skill we possess to bring about psychological and social changes in and with the offender, aiming at rehabilitation and acceptable adjustment as free and responsible persons?"[3] Actually, the juxtaposition of punishment and rehabilitation is an oversimplification—a point we shall take up later.

For centuries, punishment was considered the dominant purpose in dealing with the offender. He was required to "pay his debt to society." Beyond temporary control, this emphasis produced little more than hostility, perversion, and dehumanization. It certainly did not appear to have a deterrent effect upon criminal behavior. Indeed, one could argue that penal servitude itself was and is a significant cause of crime and other socially deviant activity. The distinction between punishment and penalty has never been clear. Emphasis shifted (at least in lip service) a century and a half ago to the reform of the offender— reform by means supplementary to incarceration itself—as a correctional objective. McGee urged that, while convicted offenders must be controlled, they must also "be trained, treated and readjusted to the fullest extent to which our knowledge and resources permit."[4]

McGee contended that rehabilitation as the primary aim in corrections has never been fairly tested.[5] Some of the reasons he gave were:

1. High initial cost.
2. Lack of skilled professionals.
3. Confusion in the public mind between rehabilitation and laxity or softness.
4. Lack of research as to the effectiveness of such programs.
5. Domination of correctional administration at the local and state levels by political influence, stultifying the development of enlightened, sustained leadership in the field.

McGee is one of many observers who feel that the correctional process is especially vulnerable to criticism where the short-term offender is concerned:

> The petty offender is not so much a menace to society as he is an expensive nuisance. We seem to have hung our hope over these many decades on the idea that if we harass these people enough, and throw them into jail often enough, and float them from town to town, that sooner or later they will see the light and become honest, upright citizens. Those of us who are in this work, whether we be police, correctional workers, social workers, psychologists, psychiatrists, or what-not, know that we are merely chasing this problem through a revolving door.[6]

The concept enunciated by McGee—indeed the entire medical model—is presently coming under sharp scrutiny and vigorous criticism. The medical model—the concept of rehabilitation—is being challenged as ineffectual. The National Council on Crime and Delinquency (NCCD) puts it this way:

> Does correctional rehabilitation 'work'? No other question is of greater urgency in corrections today. Far from a mere academic exercise, this issue has already captured the attention of legislators, political scientists and even the public at large. The debate on rehabilitation has been cited frequently in proposals to abolish parole, discard the indeterminate sentence, and restore punishment as the central function of the correctional system.[7]

Community-Based Correctional Treatment

Several forms of correctional treatment carried out by means of community resources have emerged in the nineteenth and twentieth centuries. The central idea, referred to in the corrections field as *community-based* correctional treatment, is that certain convicted offenders may, under some circumstances, be controlled and rehabilitated without being institutionalized. One form of this idea is *probation:* supervision under prescribed conditions in lieu of institutionalization, with the provision that, if these conditions are violated, the offender may then be committed to an institution. Another form is called *parole* for the adult offender, usually referred to as *aftercare* for juveniles. Parole may be defined as supervision in the community, following a period of institutional experience, under prescribed conditions which if violated may result in the subject's being returned to an institution as a parole violator. Other, newer community-related programs include work or study furloughs, halfway houses, and resident homes.

The arguments for one form or another of community-based correctional treatment are economically and socially impressive. But there are critics. Sharp-eyed analysts point to what they perceive as shortcomings in the administration, the judgmental features, and the supervisory aspects of these programs. Corrections professionals themselves are concerned with the inadequacy of standards to guide the courts in selecting persons for probation and to guide parole boards in selecting persons for release from institutions. Guidelines are needed by corrections professionals as they are by police, prosecutors, and sentencing judges, for the exercise of discretion. Concern is also shown for the size of caseloads for probation and parole officers that make effective supervision impossible, and for the absence of even minimal professional standards in many jurisdictions.

Probation and parole operate on the assumption that multiple community resources are available to assist in rehabilitation. For example, it is of cardinal importance that suitable employment be found for probationers and parolees. This requires the understanding cooperation of employers and labor unions. Sometimes clinical services are necessary for the emotionally maladjusted. Frequently, family and marital counseling are urgently needed. Police in the community must be close allies in the probation or parole processes, to avoid compromising the objectives. Social agencies and welfare and religious organizations are indispensable members of the community team, if these correctional measures are to work properly. Probation and parole failures are often the result of community indifference and inertia.

From outside the corrections field, increasing criticism is voiced by public, police, prosecutors, judges, and legislators. The public is frustrated, fearful, and angry. This fear is fanned by rising crime rates, the escalation of violence in our society, and the prominence given by the media to parole failures. Some police officers see offenders as a high-risk group and feel that the risk decreases as confinement increases. The overuse of probation and its use in doubtful cases by some judges has increased critical response from the police. Some prosecutors have a similarly critical reaction, especially to parole boards.

From these critics comes a move to eliminate indeterminate sentences and abolish or greatly restrict parole. This move is linked to the frustration voiced by inmates at the vagaries and uncertainties of the decisions of the releasing authority and the unproven value of "treatment" programs. Proposals also include mandatory prison sentences (some without parole) and restoration of capital punishment. We earlier reported what Michigan voters did in the 1978 election in eliminating good time for certain offenders and requiring service of the full minimum of indeterminate sentences.

A great deal of public misunderstanding surrounds procedures for securing release from correctional institutions. The protective function of parole is often lost from sight in the glare of publicity from parole failures. Granted the inability to predict human behavior with complete accuracy, it still seems better to use a period of supervised "convalescence" than to turn an offender loose without it. The Michigan Department of Corrections refers to this by the apt term "performance screening." Lee Rainwater's reference to the police, school teachers, and social welfare workers as "dirty-workers" might well include corrections personnel. And he says, "the silent middle class wants them to do the dirty work and be quiet about it."[8] In a comprehensive national study of American corrections in 1967, the report of President Johnson's Crime Commission said:

> Corrections remains a world almost unknown to law-abiding citizens, and even those within it often know only their own particular corner.[9]

Goals in Corrections

The question of goals has been pivotal to many of the problems in the corrections field. We might say that there is a kind of "hawk" and "dove" philosophy as to ends and means in this field, with shades of opinion between these extremes. As usual, the clash might be easier to reconcile were it not that there is something to be said on each side. The Johnson Crime Commission recognized this in a notable statement pertaining to goals in corrections:

> The task of corrections therefore includes building or rebuilding solid ties between offender and community, integrating or reintegrating the offender into community life—restoring family ties, obtaining employment and education, securing in the larger sense a place for the offender in the routine functioning of society. This requires not only efforts directed toward changing the individual offender, which has been almost the exclusive focus of rehabilitation, but also mobilization,and change of the community and its institutions. And these efforts must be undertaken without giving up the important control and deterrent role of corrections, particularly as applied to dangerous offenders.[10]

The emphasis in this statement upon the *community* aspects of corrections recognizes the connection between social forces and crime, systematically revealed in many studies, dating back to those by Clifford Shaw, Henry McKay, and their associates in the 1920s, and including others done more recently.[11] Theories of social causation for crime that support the emphasis on reintegration in corrections have parallels in other fields, for example, mental health. Treatment of the mentally ill has shifted significantly in recent years from institutional to community bases, and social psychiatry has become a professional specialty with important implications for corrections and other fields. There are many who see police and community relations as a problem in community mental health, or what is sometimes called *ecological psychology.*

President Johnson's Crime Commission pointed out that there is also a parallel in education. In an earlier era, slow learners were considered lazy; they were kept after school, birched, or rapped on the knuckles. Later, counselors and clinical workers were introduced into the school system to treat the problems of individual students. Today there is concern also for community factors, such as family disorganization, poverty, and racial discrimination, as influences upon scholastic motivation and achievement. New directions in correctional treatment today are not much different from these parallel developments. It is apparent that the mobilization of community institutions and resources necessary for anything approaching adequate community-based correctional treatment is a far larger task than corrections people alone can accomplish. Clearly, it requires broad social interests, with the prevention of recidivism as an important by-product. Evidence that these ideas are not purely utopian is provided by many current experimental programs.

The issue of correctional goals is not simply whether the methods amount to "coddling," but whether they ultimately make the community healthier by reducing the incidence of crime. The rehabilitation of offenders is a sensible way to go about doing this. Varying degrees and periods of incarceration are a sensible way to deal with certain offenders. Deterrence and control remain legitimate correctional functions. *The problem is that research and evaluation have so far not been sufficient to establish what methods work best for particular offenders.* As the Crime Commission stated it:

> It is no more logical . . . to suppose that various methods operate with uniform effect in deterrence than to suppose that any sort of rehabilitative treatment will work with all sorts of offenders. . . . For the most part, the choice of methods can be made meaningful only at the level of specific types of offenders and individual cases.[12]

What may be called the Great Divide in the correctional field today is fundamentally, then, an absence of consensus regarding goals. The 1974 annual report of the Michigan Department of Corrections expressed it nicely:

> This feeling of betrayal—that rehabilitation was supposed to work, but didn't—has resulted in several reactions. One says if rehabilitation doesn't work, then prisons are no good and should be abolished; the other says if prisons don't rehabilitate, then we shouldn't parole offenders who aren't rehabilitated.
>
> The first reaction—to abolish prisons—which is less likely to gain substantial support, ignores the fact that some individuals must be isolated from society because they are dangerous and violent. It offers no protection for the public.
>
> The second, which would lock up all prisoners longer, has gained more support, but it offers public protection only at an enormous human and economic cost.[13]

The report goes on to make a further, decisive point:

> As it stands now, the system neither allows nor demands responsible behavior. It was not set up to do that, but to treat a mass of people in the most economical way possible; this normally excludes any recognition of individual differences and needs.
>
> A system which differentiates between individuals and allows for inmate participation in the determination of what kinds of programs will be most relevant is more likely to provide the sort of test that approximates the outside world.[14]

Basic Assumptions

As we focus on community participation in correctional processes, some of our basic assumptions should be stated:

- It is "the community" that defines crime, through the instrument of law.
- The community also establishes priorities regarding crime—that is, the police, prosecutor, courts and corrections constantly study fluctuating community attitudes for what laws are to be enforced and how, which

offenders should be prosecuted, the type and severity of court sentences, and other related matters.

- The metropolitan areas where most of our people reside are polyglot amalgamations, with differing notions of law, crime, and enforcement. One police system (or one corrections system) may have great difficulties in its readings of what "the community" expects, because there is not clear consensus of expectations. Within a single state correctional system, for example, there must be considerable accommodation for differences in court sentences for identical offenses. The ambivalence of community attitudes is one of the reasons for these differences.

- The issue of correctional philosophy is not institutional *versus* community-based treatment. It is, rather, a matter of blending these approaches generally, and of choosing the most suitable and sensible approach for each individual.

PROBLEM AREAS IN CORRECTIONS AND COMMUNITY RELATIONS

Let us now consider more specific problems of corrections and community relations. Some of these have already been mentioned, but a more thorough discussion is in order.

Conflicting Community Expectations

The dissimilarities of various groups within a society foster dissimilar and conflicting ideas about the services that should be rendered by a public institution. We have already examined the implications of this point for the role of the police in today's society. Similar problems have developed in corrections, caused by conflicts in what society expects from correctional services.

At this point the picture presents conflicts and confusions not seen since the Declaration of Principles of 1870. Those goals represented a high-water mark with which most professional penologists agreed, however great the gap between principle and practice. That consensus is now subject to challenges of increasing magnitude and severity. These challenges come from three main sources: the public, professionals in various fields, and "ideologues." To examine the development of these differences requires tracing some tangled paths.

One challenge to the existing consensus is indignation against the rising rate of crime, especially violent crime. Coupled with this is a distrust of what is regarded by some as laxity, leniency, and disregard of public safety. As we have noted, this reaction is not confined to the general public but permeates the entire criminal justice field. Indeed, the division has always existed: the tide of support for punishment had only temporarily receded. Now it is rising again, as is evident in increased support for mandatory and longer prison sentences, in prohibitions against parole, and in consequently skyrocketing prison populations.

Due process (i.e., principles that limit governmental power to deprive a person of life, liberty, or property) is hardly new in the criminal justice system, but recent years have seen a special emphasis upon it well known to prosecutors, the courts, and the police, and lately evident in the field of corrections. At the same time, public concern about crime and order has increased. The implied conflicting community expectations are, as we have noted, a particular thesis in the writings of James Q. Wilson and Jerome Skolnick. Law-and-order proponents argue that too much stress on due process "handcuffs the police"; civil libertarians say that law-and-order is simply shorthand for fascism.

Some police officers tend to view probationers and parolees as poor risks, or "born losers," and sometimes feel frustrated "when justice is not done"; they are impatient with what they see as clemency, leniency, and soft-headedness. On the other hand, police often take a more lenient view of suspects who "cooperate" with the police, and of disposition of offenders by means of the negotiated plea. Corrections people may feel a particular case is a bad risk for society, while, under various pressures, prosecutors and judges may opt for a negotiated plea.

Such a case occurred in New York City in the summer of 1975. An eighteen-year-old youth committed four subway crimes at knifepoint, including one in which a woman was held hostage for an hour. Each of the first three offenses was reduced one degree on a negotiated plea. After many delays, the judge disposed of all offenses by placing the defendant on probation. The newspapers did not refer to any criticism by police but wrote that "several prosecutors and judges, informed of the outcome of the case, said that the sentence, while legal, was an abuse of the spirit of the Youthful Offender Statute."[15]

Conversely, an offender considered a poor risk by corrections workers may plead guilty through negotiation to a lesser charge. The court may then impose a substantial minimum, thus reducing parole eligibility when warranted. Differences among community attitudes toward crimes often cause serious disparity in crimes charged and sentences imposed. Generally, the charge and sentence vary in inverse ratio to the size of the community. Such practices engender conflict, confusion, and disparity within criminal justice.

Prevention of Anomie

We noted in the preceding chapter the concept of just desert. Now we introduce another element. By the penalties it exacts for crime, society maintains basic standards and upholds societal norms. When the power of social rule over individuals weakens, a state of "normlessness" is brought about. This is *anomie*, as first defined by the French sociologist Emile Dirkheim, and later amplified with special reference to crime causation by American sociologist Robert Merton.

We have noted that the criminal justice system must take punishment into account, in the sense of just retribution and not simply vengeance, and also the rehabilitation of the offender, looking toward his eventual return to the community. Now we see that the system must also take into account a third element: the prevention of normlessness—anomie—in a society. The consideration of anomie is illustrated by the weight that a parole board may ascribe to whether an inmate's crime has been "shocking to the conscience of society." Neither punishment nor rehabilitation may serve this end.

The public becomes frustrated at the apparent failure of social institutions to prevent crime. But as Michael Meltsner has put it, in the criminal process, it is generally only the correctional system, not the courts or the police, that has the capacity—and a small one at that—to rehabilitate and reform. At a time when crime is a matter of great public concern, the role played by the correctional system in determining whether offenders become useful citizens or recidivists is critical.[16] The same writer observes that the correctional process is perhaps most dangerous when it justifies itself as acting in the best interests of a defendant. The fact is that we do not really know enough about the effects of what we call treatment in corrections to predict what may best serve the defendant's interests.

Prosocial and Antisocial Attitudes of the Offender

Political regimes often protect themselves against whatever they determine to be excessive dissent. We have touched on the problem this produces for the criminal justice system in its handling of social unrest. Corrections is deeply implicated in this problem because it must deal with the casualties of social conflict. The crux of the issue for corrections is the question of how to differentiate among several types of prisoners who may commit identical crimes for different reasons. For example, to burn Selective Service files is arson. So is burning a supermarket in a riot. So is pyromania. So is arson for profit. The difficulty for correctional administration is to match the treatment with the individual problem, mindful that a central purpose in correctional treatment is to change antisocial attitudes and behavior to prosocial.

The standards for determining whether an individual's attitudes and behavior are sufficiently advanced in treatment to make him a good risk for release should, ideally, reflect societal norms. But when, through social upheaval, the norms become upset and society's distinctions between "antisocial" and "prosocial" behavior become ambiguous, how is corrections to draw a clear distinction between the two? If rehabilitation implies some sort of behavior norm as to what is antisocial and what is prosocial, whose behavior model is to be taken as antisocial, and whose as prosocial?

Again we see the basic problem of conflict in what the community expects from the criminal justice system. For the police or for the courts, the problems caused by this conflict are substantial. For corrections, they are even more formidable.

Political radicalization has become more commonplace in American prisons, meshing with the growing opinion among prisoners and outside radicals, including ideologically motivated lawyers and criminologists, that most crimes committed in the United States, particularly by minorities and poor whites, are essentially social and political in nature. This is so, the argument runs, because such crimes derive from sociological and political conditions. But there is a counterargument from those who say that a George Jackson is not so much a political prisoner as he is simply a menace to the rights, the property, and the lives of others who must be protected by whatever means are made necessary by the actions of the inmate.

Social Work and Corrections

Another problem has to do with social agency activities. Where *treatment* of juvenile and adult offenders begins, the criminal justice system comes face to face with social work. Probation and parole in particular, but institutional rehabilitation programs as well, reflect considerable social-work influence, observable in the professional training of corrections personnel. Philosophically, social work tends to view crime (and therefore correctional problems) as a social defect arising out of conditions of deprivation, neglect, abuse, and the like. There is, of course, much to be said for this view, and for the perspective that it suggests for *treatment*. However, corrections also has a responsibility for societal protection and security that carries connotations of control and restraint of offenders. The field of corrections, then, is oriented toward the demands of society, as well as toward the needs of the offender. For this reason, social work in corrections is a vital part of an interprofessional, interdisciplinary field, but its role should not be extended to the point of dominating change and improvement in a correctional system, with the assumption that social work "has all the answers."

Need for Independent Professionals

In some states, corrections—historically dominated by custodial goals—has developed into a monolithic bureaucracy. In other states, it is fragmented and piecemeal. Corrections has had a quasi-military character analogous to the police, with less flexibility than social work. Its professional organizations often function in a manner suggesting "company unions." Internal criticism has been rare, and outside intervention, even more so. What corrections needs is a solid body of independent professionals exercising a critical effect on the field, a kind of enlightened lobby of correctional personnel. To supply this need, the National Council on Crime and Delinquency is attempting to break the bureaucratic pattern with state-level citizen-participation councils. We shall have more to say shortly about the influence this could have in changing public attitudes toward corrections.

Lag of the Law

Another problem may be referred to as "lag of the law." We have alluded to the political dynamics of law making and law enforcing. Complex legislative and judicial processes are basically responses to public opinion, to the readiness of a substantial number of people to accept new concepts and changes in practice. Corrections is the last part of the criminal justice process to be scrutinized by the courts and by legislative bodies, because public pressures prescribe higher priority for other aspects. This is another way of saying that community relations is a particularly difficult task for corrections.

Due Process

The recent tide of emphasis upon due process in corrections is not, in itself, a problem in community relations, any more than is the similar emphasis in police work. Some police officers and corrections workers see this as a long overdue movement in what they deem the right direction. The *problem* is that not all police officers or corrections workers see it this way. Nor does the community. To cloud the corrections picture further, an outsider's assumption that the "doves" (treatment-minded personnel) approve of due process turns out not to be so at all. Some "hawks" defend due process beyond what some doves are willing to concede. These doves see "too much due process" or "too many legalisms" as inimical to treatment procedures. They hold that lawyers should not be permitted to invade the domain of professional correctional treatment; that allowing them to do so restricts the discretionary flexibility that correctional professionals should have. Yet some of the doves in corrections tend to make pretentious claims for their pet rehabilitation techniques, although these techniques may violate due process and are furthermore open to question because of inadequate substantiation of their effectiveness. In a community relations sense, the argument here is another commentary on freedom versus order.

This awareness of due process and the rights of the offender, which developed somewhat earlier in other branches of criminal justice, is now being emphasized in the field of corrections. For example, prisoner labor unions seeking recognition as inmate bargaining agents are today quite numerous. Several states have ombudsman systems in corrections, Michigan and Minnesota among them.

Further evidence of this trend is shown by the recent action of the Supreme Court. On June 29, 1972, in *Morrisey* v. *Brewer, Warden,* the United States Supreme Court overturned a U.S. Court of Appeals ruling that parole was only "a correctional device authorizing service of sentence outside the penitentiary." The Court spelled out requirements for parole revocation as *(a)* a preliminary inquiry near the alleged violation to determine whether there was probable cause to return the violator to prison; *(b)* a parole violation hearing in which the alleged violator was entitled to notice of the charges, witnesses for and against, and a written statement as to the evidence relied on and reasons for the decision. The Supreme Court specifically declined to consider the question of counsel and went on to say that it was not creating "an inflexible structure for parole revocation procedures." Here are some other examples of the growing awareness of due process and the rights of the offender:

> The Supreme Court has ruled that, under certain circumstances, state prison officials are subject to damage suits by inmates who are mistreated or arbitrarily punished without a hearing.[17]
>
> Clearer delineation, as for instance in New York State, of the conditions under which the board of parole or courts of sentence must restore the voting rights of

convicted offenders, and the conditions under which convicted offenders do not lose their right to vote. Indeed, a Bill of Rights for prisoners has been advanced by the Correctional Association of New York.[18]

While parole is discretionary (except [presumably] where denial is wilful or capricious), the trend today is toward making the actions of parole boards *visible and accountable*. Once parole is granted, it cannot be withdrawn without due process. In January, 1971, the New York State Court of Appeals ruled that parolees have a constitutional right to have their attorneys present at hearings weighing revocation of their paroles.[19]

The principle that inmates are not rightless is also being increasingly recognized in the policies and practices of correctional administrators. Once, when a prisoner was charged with an infraction of institutional rules, he was brought before a disciplinary board for a hearing, without an advocate. Nowadays there are prisons where an advocate system has been carefully developed to speak for the accused, although there are those who question the extent to which this is actually happening.

Balancing Rights

Some people believe that criminal justice has become too much concerned with the rights of the suspect and the convicted offender and not sufficiently concerned with the rights of the victims of crime. We have discussed this matter in other places in this text. A growing number of states are enacting laws providing for victim compensation, and federal legislation to compensate victims of criminal violence is no longer a dream.[20] A number of loopholes in criminal law appear to operate inequitably in favor of offenders. Several examples may be cited.

- The system of concurrent sentences in some states may not provide society with the protection it needs against the habitual offender. Sentences are often concurrent for a series of offenses committed prior to conviction as well as for those committed while on bond or probation. An individual convicted of stealing fifteen cars on different occasions could receive the same sentence, in effect, as an individual who steals one car. A cure for this problem could be to retain the minimum sentence but make the maximum cumulative to a reasonable limit. In its proposed Model Penal Code, NCCD sets this limit at thirty years, for the so-called dangerous offender.
- The mentally retarded person is not very well cared for by mental health programs, and even less so by the criminal justice system. Persons with subnormal intelligence who may be convicted of a crime are lost among the overlapping jurisdiction of the courts (under the concept of diminished capacity), corrections, mental health, and education.
- The "dangerous offender" poses a special problem. Again, a Catch 22 is involved. One school of thought points to the difficulty of predicting future dangerous behavior. Another stresses past performance as the best available indicator. Certain professional predispositions are discernible in these conflicting views.

- Police tend to see convicted offenders—especially those who have committed crimes of violence—as a demonstrably dangerous, high-risk group. Prosecutors, charged with representing the public, tend to view those whom they have not screened out or diverted as objects of prosecution. Yet faced with crowded calendars, insufficient staff, and the uncertainties of criminal trials, the prosecutor may opt for plea bargaining. The rationale contends that some punishment is better than none and may get the offender "off the street" for a while.

- An early parole, therefore, may seem to police and prosecutor as inconsistent with deterrence. A public frustrated, fearful, and resentful—faced with rising crime rates—tends to agree.

- Michigan's referendum of 1978 approved the elimination of good time credit from the minimum sentence of persons convicted of most crimes of violence and specifies that the minimum sentence must be served in full. However, *no* action was taken on the elimination of good time credit for the *maximum* sentence. Apparently, then, the maximum could expire before the minimum in certain cases, thus eliminating parole supervision—doubtless an unintended consequence.

- Michigan's mandatory gun law requires the imposition of a two-year prison sentence for crimes committed with a gun in possession. These two recent enactments combine to contribute to Michigan's rapidly rising prison population.

While in general principle we side with NCCD and with others who have been critical of preventive detention, there is another side of the matter with regard to the dangerous or habitual offender.[21] An alternative in certain circumstances might be the elimination of good time credit on the *maximum* sentence for certain classes of offenders—the dangerous, the habitual, and those committing offenses while on bond or probation. Assuming that these latter offenders were paroled, they should not be *discharged* until the expiration of the full maximum. This plan would not preclude release from parole *supervision* but presumably would allow apprehension of parole violators in appropriate circumstances.

Simplistic Approaches

Simplistic approaches, a phenomenon not unique to corrections, are another problem. One form is the "there ought to be a law" syndrome, about which we have previously commented. Another form is the "every man is an expert" approach, with everyone plugging his own pet remedy for complex social and personal pathology, where there is a dearth of balanced, coordinated, interprofessional, and interdisciplinary planning and research. Chief Justice Burger has hit a proper keynote in calling for a thorough rethinking of the American concept of justice:

We find lawyers and judges becoming so engrossed with procedures and techniques that they tend to lose sight of the purpose of a system of justice. We should stop thinking of criminal justice as something which begins with an arrest and ends with a final judgment of guilt. . . . Few things characterize our attitude toward prisoners and prisons more than indifference and impatience with the failure of the prisoner to return to society corrected and reasonably ready to earn an honest way in life. A large proportion of criminal offenders are seriously maladjusted human beings. And those who are not maladjusted when they go in are likely to be so when they get out.[22]

Jail Reform

No discussion of corrections problems can omit the need for jail reform, sometimes referred to as "the badlands of corrections." Richard McGee refers to the county jail as the "lowest form of social institution on the American scene . . . often more destructive than corrective." *Commonweal* magazine refers to "these sinks of despair and breeding ground for still more crime and violence." A national jail census was conducted by the federal government on March 15, 1970. On that day, there were 4,037 jails, in which 160,863 people were incarcerated. Some 500 jails still in use were built in the nineteenth century, and 6, in the eighteenth. The oldest working jail had been in use since 1705. One-quarter of all jail cells were more than fifty years old. On the day of this 1970 census, *some 83,000 (52 percent) of those held in jail had not yet been convicted of any crime.* Although 65,000 people were serving sentences in local jails, 10,000 of them for a year or more, most jails were equipped to do nothing but hold them behind bars for the duration of their sentences. Of the 3,300 jails in large communities, 85 percent had no educational or recreational facilities of any kind. About half lacked medical facilities, and about one-fourth had no facilities for visitors. In many of these institutions, the mentally disturbed, the hardened criminal, and the confused adolescent, the serious offender as well as the petty offender—and, overlapping these types, the tried and the not-yet-tried—were lumped together, often under conditions of overcrowding, filth, and degradation. The plight of our jails (with some notable exceptions) illustrates the patchwork-quilt approach to corrections and dramatizes the problems of our parallel but separate systems for attempting to treat felons and misdemeanants.[23]

Currently, national attention is focusing upon local correctional facilities, especially the jail. The National Institute of Corrections has launched a nationwide jailer training program at Boulder, Colorado. Federal courts, in a concern for due process and constitutional jails, have intervened in jail operations.

The regional jail concept looks like a step in the right direction but, by and large, the jail is an excellent place for community endeavor to concentrate in the corrections field—with prisons not far behind. Upheavals, riots, and rebellions in prisons and jails in the recent past may be the wellspring of hope for true reform. Unprecedented questions are being asked: for example, the extent to which the Bill of Rights applies to people behind bars; the Eighth Amendment's ban against cruel and unusual punishment; and whether people in jail awaiting trial should be given rights different from those of people in jail serving sentences. We commented earlier on the effects of a larger number of politically active, and angry, inmates in correctional institutions. Draft and drug offenses alone have accounted for a sizable portion of this increase in recent years. It appears that the higher the proportion of "political prisoners," such as in New York and California, the more public attention is drawn to what goes on behind the walls. David Rothenberg, executive secretary of the Fortune Society, an organization of former convicts and others seeking to create a greater public awareness of the problems of penal inmates, may have said it all: "Government responds not to problems but to pressures."[24]

Finances

Finally, but not least important, there is the problem of finances. Competition for the tax dollar being a main pressure point in political processes, we will settle for three observations:

- Prisons are often at the lowest priority in public budgets and outlays.
- Treatment is expensive. But we continue to try to find cheap ways to do it; for instance, in saying that volunteers save money, a good thing is favored for the wrong reason.
- In correctional treatment, because we are still not sure what works, requests for more dollars cannot be supported by adequate evidence that professional remedies are any better than popular, one-shot antidotes. In times of fiscal belt-tightening under the whip of taxpayer revolt, and indeed of some public delusion about "country club" correctional facilities, the outlook for more rehabilitative dollars is not bright, especially with the harder line regarding bail and good time.

Popular sentiment favoring stiffer sentences as the best answer to the crime problem calls for a word of caution. Few advocates of this policy are prepared to accept the financial tab for their ostensible remedy and fewer still are able to suggest ways of distinguishing between offenders for whom this prescription will work and those for whom it will compound the problem.

COPING WITH THE PROBLEMS

Having recited and commented on a rather long list of corrections problems with particular community relations importance, we should say something about coping with these problems. We shall suggest several general directions for coping and then pursue another more specifically, one that is probably no more important than the others, but too seldom analyzed.

Redesigning Prisons and Correctional Systems

Some obvious things have already been stressed, such as the necessity for revising the criminal code, reforming jail and prison conditions, and discovering ways for expediting justice procedures without reducing due process. Some authorities have urged a moratorium on building new prisons, but the current trend toward more and longer prison sentences makes this unlikely. The result is costly new prison construction.

The Michigan Corrections Department has recommended remodeling and breaking up big prisons into smaller units, with a population limit of 600. Also recommended are better diagnostic procedures to determine where new prisoners are to be placed to keep first offenders separated from confirmed criminals. Such proposals exemplify the possibilities in "inventing the future" of correctional systems. The state of Michigan has a model, medium-security prison in Muskegon, with built-in capability to research its problems.

Strengthening Social and Moral Values

Not quite so obvious, perhaps, and considerably more elusive and difficult to deal with concretely is the matter of strengthening our social and moral fabric. Basically, this is a question of values. We have in mind especially values bearing upon leisure time, personal privacy, emotional conflict in interpersonal relations, and such. We have in mind reducing social, economic, and political discrimination, and programs for eradicating poverty that transcend political partisanship. We have in mind a positive administrative philosophy in public affairs that rejects management by fiat in favor of policy making that genuinely involves people as full-fledged participants in the processes of government. To mention these things in these times may be viewed as preaching utopian platitudes, but we do it without apology.

Improving Corrections and Rehabilitation Processes

The Law Enforcement Assistance Administration (LEAA) of the United States Department of Justice and the program it currently and potentially encompasses represent an epochal breakthrough in the cause of an improved criminal justice system, across the board. Premised in large part on the work of the 1966–67 President's Crime Commission, LEAA promises a revolutionary departure from the patchwork approach. It seeks to deal with the criminal justice process as a whole by concerted efforts at the federal, state, and local levels—and at some points by a *regional* perspective that transcends traditional political boundaries. It fosters a continuing, consistent, critical examination of criminal justice processes, emphasizing research, planning, and persistent efforts to elevate professional standards. The LEAA has considerable political visibility, it has money, and while it also has its weaknesses and limitations, it is unquestionably the dominant contemporary force for change in the system.[25]

One encouraging development was the passage of the Federal Juvenile Justice and Delinquency Act of 1974. This act brought juvenile justice within the LEAA orbit, but in a way calculated to preserve the separate identity of juvenile procedures. To help bring a more coherent pattern to juvenile justice, the act created the office of Assistant Administrator for Juvenile Justice and Delinquency Prevention within LEAA, with responsibility for implementing policy objectives for all federal delinquency programs, including those outside LEAA. The act encouraged state and local governments to set up similar planning agencies by offering generous federal funding for juvenile programs to localities that do so. Nonetheless, the briarpatch of juvenile justice, state by state, remains largely as mind-boggling as ever.

Increasing Corrections Research

Several times we have mentioned correctional treatment approaches that are not yet proven. Exaggerated claims for this or that technique are common, as Chief Justice Burger has observed. Pointedly implied is the vast need for research in the corrections field. A good beginning has been made. Research can be one way for correctional administration to improve communication with the public. In a time of societal emphasis upon rationality and science, why should so much of correctional practice be based on hunch, myth, misconception, irrationality, and untested rules of thumb?[26]

Developing Community Resources

Logically, coping with problems of corrections and community relations requires the mobilization of community resources. This was a major recommendation of the 1966 President's Crime Commission, and LEAA has been pushing the idea enthusiastically. It is the foundation stone of NCCD's state citizen councils (in more than twenty states, at last count), a program that has had the generous support of the Ford Foundation.[27] The role of the volunteer in corrections is important. Volunteer group counseling, coaching, and instruction make a notable contribution.[28] Committees in communities close to correctional facilities are vital links in communications and community relations.

One important theme is a desirable blurring of the line between institutional and community treatment of offenders through such programs as work furloughs, educational work with inmates, and halfway facilities. Increased use of probation and parole is clearly a part of this picture also. Elmer K. Nelson of the University of Southern California makes a good point:

> In moving toward the increased use of community treatment, many problems must be overcome, including a lack of research information on the effectiveness of particular techniques; resistance to needed changes on the part of traditionalist staff and organizational systems; the difficulty of creating new and noncriminal identities for ex-offenders; and the problem of drawing community institutions into the task. The national attention which has been focused upon the needs of the correctional field has created an unprecedented opportunity to bring new resources and methods to the solution of these problems.[29]

LEADERSHIP IN THE CORRECTIONS FIELD

Having cited several general guidelines for coping with problems of corrections and community relations, we now deal with another at greater length. This is the question of leadership by correctional professionals in helping the public to know and understand the proper goals of correctional programs.

Difficulties of Leadership Development

We may say at the outset that the development of such leadership is not a simple task. Some reasons for this have been suggested by other writers.[30] We will suggest a few more.

Corrections professionals are, as a rule, cautious, almost shy. Public attitudes toward corrections explain this, in part. The public seems satisfied with mere tokenism and does not seem to care whether treatment works or not. To look at correctional programs carefully would turn up so many inadequacies that professionals in the field doubt that they themselves can do what they would tell the public ought to be done. In effect, corrections personnel are afflicted with a group inferiority complex. Also, conflicting aims and philosophies within the correctional field itself handicap community leadership by corrections personnel.[31]

The point at which some of the public do care about a correctional system is at the spreading belief that the system is failing, measured by such things as a particularly heinous crime committed by a person on probation or parole. What sometimes happens under such circumstances is that progressive steps in the field, of a type that moderate the revenge motive, are set back by what amounts to "backlash." Regressive steps are prompted by public turbulence. This is clearly not encouraging to forthright, progressive leadership in the corrections field.

Again, the question arises of what works and what does not work in correctional techniques and how success is to be measured. To what we have already said about this may be added the observation that the most promising programs are frequently expensive. Further, it should be observed that *scientific* tests of a program almost always fail to measure *humanitarian* efficacy.

The political sensitivity of corrections has been mentioned. Prison reform is frequently brought up in connection with political scandals, along with highway funds and police graft. It is a field in which survivors learn to play the game of political trade-off in harsh, pragmatic terms; and if they are idealists, as many corrections professionals are, they learn to live with frustration, heartrending disappointment, and tragedy.

Guidelines for Leadership

Leadership in community relations by correctional personnel, without which there is little hope for a brighter future in the field, can and must develop. Correctional personnel should welcome and encourage broad, critical review of the entire corrections bureaucracy. Needed is continuing, sustained evaluation, planning, and research, a way of removing politics from correctional work to a desirable, professional degree. This would educate the public far beyond ordinary public relations activity.

To clarify some implications of the previous paragraph, corrections should promote the idea that professionalism and bureaucracy are not identical but can be made compatible. Professional associations in the field of corrections should break away from the company union mantle and become more flexible within the system, that is, less rigidly intent on perpetuating existing practices. Professional schools for preparing correctional careerists, remembering that the public tends to turn to professional schools for *answers* and to bureaucracies merely for *explanations*, should recognize that their *critical* function is at least as important as their *educational* function.

Training and professional standards in corrections must continue to be elevated, while emphasizing a more sophisticated and sensitive handling of probationers, inmates, and parolees. The traditional distance between keeper and kept must be diminished. The movement toward upgrading correctional staffs, toward developing change agents in the system, is essential to reform and progress. Overly rigid civil service and labor union requirements can conceivably be obstacles in the professional development of corrections personnel. There is no reason professional associations and worker unions should not be able to coexist and, indeed, to complement each other. In fact, a union can be more inclusive in cutting across ranks and helping to unfreeze bureaucratic icebergs. But that a union and a professional association have different functions should be recognized and kept clear.

Commissions or committees appointed to look into corrections tend to focus on the particular rather than the general. The result is often to encourage the piecemeal, fragmented approach alluded to earlier, with each part of the system having its own goal ideas. A bar association committee for revising the penal code goes one way; an association of social workers goes another. The Joint Commission on Correctional Manpower and Training, authorized by Congress in 1965, started with the particular and became general in its scope. It made sweeping recommendations, but was commissioned for only three years.[32]

Corrections professionals must bring a *broad perspective* to the field and its community relations problems. The sheer enormity of the problem suggests "biting off manageable hunks," but the problems must be seen in their larger context. Rehabilitation, for example, demands a complex of community agencies and services far beyond the field of corrections. The interorganizational approach outlined by Elmer H. Johnson, referred to in the preceding chapter, is pertinent here. Corrections professionals should assist the community to go beyond the theory that to *name* the problem is, in itself, an important part of therapy. To name and to define the problem adequately is, indeed, a crucial step for the community in solving the problem. But if this process sputters and dies at the problem identification stage, as often happens, nothing materializes to resolve the problem.

In their responsibility to inform the public, corrections professionals would be well advised to stress the generic nature of the total field, rather than the public relations of any particular part of it. This follows from our previous point regarding a broad perspective.

Corrections shares with other social institutions the challenge of recognizing the difference between the creative and the imitative, and the need to know when to maintain the status quo and when to "rock the boat." What the public often gets is the reflection of bureaucratic judgment as to what the public wants, rather than what professionals in the system feel the public *ought* to want.

The fulcrum for change within correctional systems is *outside* the system. Therefore, corrections personnel must do more to discover how community and societal resources can be brought to bear on the problems of offenders, bearing in mind that *the community* is the corrective aspect of the correctional process.

Finally, corrections workers should keep their "client" relations prominently in the forefront of their attention. It is important to interpret to the client what's going on and why, just as it is in medicine and police service. In corrections, it is not always easy to determine who the client is. There is some argument about this in other public services; but in jails and prisons, few people perceive the client to be the prisoner. Most believe the client is society. This brings us back to the main question in corrections: What are we trying to do? Most proponents of rehabilitation say that we are trying to obtain greater opportunity and development for the individual offender, thereby defining the client. Others maintain that rehabilitation programs should give added protection to the public, to protect the community from criminality. This is another way to define the client. However, what helps the offender protects the community. The goal therefore should be to reintegrate the offender into the community whenever this can be done safely, whether through probation, prison, or parole.

RELATIONS WITHIN THE CORRECTIONS FIELD

Much that we have said bears directly or indirectly on relationships within the field of corrections. The nub of the problem of corrections is conceptual, very much as it is with the police in their relations with the community. It comes down to the question of how the corrections worker sees his role. This calls for more analysis.

Until lately, professional attention in corrections has focused on the medical model, which asserts that the offender's behavior can be modified through therapy, broadly defined. A utopian role conception portrays corrections workers using a variety of equipment and formulas to bring about remarkable reconstruction of "those who have gone wrong." A more realistic conception of role portrays them as social workers who are primarily troubleshooters and report writers. While the more sophisticated view—that of the corrections worker as an agent of change—is still the prominent view today, it is accompanied by a certain schizophrenic frustration. The worker feels caught between a rock and a hard place. The rock is the secure prison, isolating the offender from society. But the rock holds the prospect of the reformation of an earlier day or the rehabilitation of a more recent era. That prospect has been battered by the iconoclasts who say, in substance, "Rehabilitation does not work; the 'medical model' is not valid."

As if this battering were not enough, the corrections worker next feels the "double whammy" of due process. "Treatment may be okay, but it must be voluntary. Otherwise, inmates become actors—and parole boards become dupes." Thus speak the due processors. One would expect a corrections worker to become a disillusioned cynic or an indefatigable and deluded idealist. Or maybe he or she slogs along—doing the daily duty—hoping that the expert can illuminate the gloom and point to a better path. And the dilemma is complicated by the "hard-liners" who knew better all the time and the "caught-between" citizens who see crime and inflation as competing for first place in the litany of public woes.

Sometimes the correctional administrator who becomes the scapegoat of the correctional worker entertains no real hope that corrections can actually correct, but believes, rather, that the sooner an inmate can safely be released, the better will be his chances of recovery. Thus the practical-minded administrator who realizes the difficulty of securing additional resources, and distrusts the efficacy of what he has, may be more humane than the worker who insists upon conformity and participation in meaningless programs as the price of the inmate's freedom. The ostensible treatment process is often subverted when the "client" for whom change is possible perceives the techniques to be ineffective.

All the machinery of rewards and punishments in corrections reinforces conformity by convicted offenders, with the goals set by correctional workers. Prisoners are often forced to go through motions that have no meaning and to participate in programs that have no perceptible value for them. They do so because they believe their privileges and their ultimate freedom depend on it.[33]

Related to this is the conviction of some inmates that only poor people and other "rejects" go to jail or prison in the first place. Penal institutions have been largely class institutions; the current wave of agitation for reform no doubt reflects the fact that youth of upper- and middle-class backgrounds have recently tasted life behind the walls—on draft and drug charges and offenses related to civil rights and social protest activities. Criminologist Richard Korn spoke to this point in a paper prepared for the Joint Commission on Correctional Manpower and Training.[34] The notion that correctional treatment techniques amount to no more than "hocus-pocus" inspired by class-bound "do-gooders" is not conducive to a proper professional-client relationship.

The predicament of the correctional worker, then, is one fostered by conflicting community expectations, similar to the predicament of the police officer. Society resolves this predicament by seeking to sweep it under the rug, insisting that control and protection be of paramount concern in corrections. While criminal law and procedure move perceptibly toward moderation of the revenge motive with convicted offenders, there remain those who see the convicted offender as fair game for revenge. It may even be, psychologically, a means of avoiding guilt feelings for social disaster.

Karl Menninger asserts that we *need* crime. It is similar to our need for the religious to be holy for us, heroes to be brave for us, and government officials to exercise power for us. As Menninger puts it:

> We condemn crime; we punish offenders for it; but we need it. The crime and punishment ritual is part of our lives. We need crime to wonder at, to enjoy vicariously, to discuss and speculate about, and to publicly deplore. We need criminals to identify ourselves with, to secretly envy, and to stoutly punish. Criminals represent our alter-egos—our bad selves—rejected and projected. They do for us the forbidden, the illegal things we wish to do, and like scapegoats of old, they bear the burdens of our displaced guilt and punishment.[35]

Henry Wiehofen extends the point:

> No one is more ferocious in demanding that the murderer or rapist "pay" for his crime than the man who has felt strong impulses in the same direction. . . . It is never he who is without sin who casts the first stone. . . . A criminal trial, like a prizefight, is a public performance in which the spectators work off in a socially acceptable way aggressive impulses of much the same kind that the man on trial worked off in a socially unacceptable way.[36]

To which Jim Castelli adds:

> Our need for criminals extends to our classifying a man as a "criminal" and abandoning him simply because he is accused; that is the largest reason why 52 percent of all inmates [in jails] in America have not yet been to trial and are technically, constitutionally innocent.[37]

When the viewpoint just cited is placed beside another perception of the matter—the demands of retributive justice, to which we earlier alluded—it is easier to understand why corrections is more prone to human error than any other aspect of the criminal justice process. A saving feature is that fewer clients are involved in this part of the process, as compared, for instance, with police contacts. We have spoken of discretionary judgments by police officers on the street, pointing to these judgments as critical to the relationship of police and community. Now we point to the judgments, the human transactions, that are so much the substance of corrections. Who is competent to determine whom to confine, whom to release, when to release, and under what conditions to release? What most harms human welfare: to neglect the prisoner and leave him to the tide, or to try to help him by methods and programs so impoverished in dollars, creativity, evaluation, and other resources that no one really believes in their efficacy?

In the last twenty years of the twentieth century, corrections will be heavily involved in the sweeping changes ordained for criminal justice. Emphasis has shifted from the offender and his treatment to the process of criminal justice itself, the process that labels offenders, imposes penalties, and determines the extent of deviancy and the criteria by which deviance is defined.

The entire criminal justice process is being denounced by some scholars. Richard Quinney, for example, refers to it as "an order created for political purposes, to assure the hegemony of the ruling class."[38] This is a sobering analysis, one that students of criminal justice cannot ignore.

THE AIM OF CORRECTIONAL PROCESSES

Looking back over what we have said, several points deserve repetition, though perhaps in slightly different terms. Basically, there are two discernible views of correctional processes. One sees the prison as a place of confinement and control; a security institution for the protection of society. Some consider this a harsh and inhumane attitude; but remember, prisons were originally intended to be relatively more humane than other measures for dealing with criminals, for example, banishment, torture, mutilation, and hanging.

The second view sees the prison as serving more complex purposes: the protection of society, the deterrence of crime, and a means for the offender who wants to change his or her behavior. However, it is quite clear that such change is much more appropriate to the environment *outside* the prison: reform has always been more of an *external* than an *internal* process in corrections. It is largely a *community* determination. Probation, for example, was originally a volunteer movement, pioneered by John Augustus. Halfway houses are emerging as another community endeavor, often initiated by religious institutions. The challenge is to find the most favorable blend of custody and treatment for each individual. Today's *corrections specialist*, as found, for example, in pioneering programs in Michigan, finds his distinctive paraprofessional identity in this blend, a middle ground between hawk and dove.

One is reminded of Daniel Glaser's reference to the positive impact—that is, the influence of each upon inmate attitudes and behavior—of two types of institutional personnel: the traditional corrections officer and the work supervisor or foreman. The inmate has been in frequent contact with both of these persons; the reasons for their special influence are speculative. In any event, the relationship here has been an easy one, though within certain limits, taken against what Gresham Sykes calls "the culture of the yard."[39] The relationship between inmate and corrections personnel has, in the past, been subjected to rather strict administrative controls, lest it be interpreted as fraternizing. Recently, however, this hard line has been modified, after recognizing that a practice that may be undesirable 10 percent of the time may merit encouragement 90 percent of the time. The modern corrections specialist epitomizes this changing philosophy by injecting a humanizing element into institutional treatment.

The importance of such an element is appreciated when we reflect on how and why the prison becomes so repressive, to the point of working against itself. With administrative caution and societal security always the paramount themes, rules are made progressively, first prohibiting this and then that, until the very things that could be effective correctional tools are prohibited without explanation. The therapeutic community (or milieu therapy) developed by Dr. Maxwell Jones, an English psychiatrist, was an attempt to utilize the whole environment in the change process.[40] The modern corrections specialist is, in this sense, something of a therapist, working out basic relationships with inmates. But more than conventional therapy is applied. The total institutional situation is used as a kind of garden plot, in which the individual's growth may be carefully observed, evaluated, and guided.

Volunteers play various roles in correctional processes. One is a specific, nonpolicy role, such as coach, referee, entertainer, or friendly visitor. Another skates on the edge of policy through questions raised in discussion groups, counseling groups, and the like, which—in the partnership between the professional corrections worker and the volunteer—may emerge as questions or criticisms of policy. Then there is the member of the community at large who serves either in an advisory or in a policy-setting capacity as a member of a board or commission, for example, trade advisory councils to help resolve employment problems for released offenders. In its best aspects, this exemplifies corrections and community relations.

Community relations committees have recently begun to appear in correctional settings. Prison administrators usually spell out very carefully the limits of their policy making. Moreover, prison administrators tend to be wary of including inmates in institutional self-government; for instance, in prison councils aimed at sharing in making decisions or setting policy. Administrators are cautious and conservative because of a combination of forces inside and outside penal institutions, forces that seem to be allied. Radical or conflict criminology seems to lend support to the inmate's protest that he is a political prisoner. Forthwith, the correctional administrator may opt to "keep the lid on" as best he can, in a situation that is always potentially explosive. The less settled the larger society, the more likely that its "garbage can"—the prison—will be edgy. While the disposition to administrative wariness is not something on which corrections has a monopoly, there are certain features of it in corrections which stand out in times of general social turbulence. Norval Morris describes its distinctive nature:

> What happens is that the inmate invests ordinary criminal activity with the idea that he is part of political change. That way you end up with the absurdity that killing a policeman or robbing a store is somehow a political act. The common criminals have never been on the cutting edge of any revolutionary movement. Nor are they now. They are being used, and misused, by some elements of the New Left. But it is important to understand how blacks come to see all of this. They see that prisons are disproportionately black and run by whites. They come to view the American prison system as meaning simply blacks locked up by whites. This is the kind of thing that feeds this rhetoric of revolution, and ultimately the violence. What we have now in our prisons is the fusing of the ideology of the political prisoner with the technology of the common criminal. It is an explosive mixture.[41]

In community relations terms, there is a kind of paradox in all this. Correctional endeavors desperately need community support. But unsettled conditions and catastrophic happenings in prisons frighten the community away. There are, no doubt, in police and correctional work, situations too awesome, too technically demanding, too harrowing to be left to anyone other than seasoned professionals. On the morning after the Attica uprising, the volunteers for work inside the prison included those who sought to exploit the situation to their particular advantage. And there were those who came to investigate, to study, or to minister to human needs. Those who did not come included some who were not so much frightened away as they were inclined to be "turned off" by such a tragedy and to interpret it as substantiating the view that a prison is a human waste-pile best kept out of sight. In any event, the effect—at least temporarily—was to curtail much of the community intercession that the situation so urgently required.

Good community relations is not merely a matter of good will and cooperative effort. While good will and good intention are certainly valuable assets, responsible community relations also require *knowledge* and *understanding* of situations and problems. In short, interprofessional approaches imply mutual respect for what has to be *learned* in a given professional field. Law, for example, has traditionally been thought of in our society as fundamentally committed to fair play. Yet it is conceivable that the parole process can be made so legally complex and technical as to blur the distinction between one who has not yet been convicted of a crime and one who, having been convicted, is now a candidate for parole.

Parole violation raises another question. Parole is a privilege that can be granted or withheld. But once the prisoner has been granted parole, he may be said to have a vested right of which he should not be deprived arbitrarily and without due process. No one, for example, has an *absolute* right to a driver's license or to the practice of law, but *once these privileges have been granted*, they cannot be denied summarily. Thus runs the emerging new theme in the parole field.

The central consideration is that of the rights of the parolee. Some of those who resist due process do so for fear that a parole hearing will become a repetition of a criminal trial. There is a distinction—not clearly drawn currently—between what due process of law means in court activity at the point of criminal trial proceedings, what it means in parole board activity at the point of consideration for release from a penal institution, and what it means in a parole board hearing in the case of a returned parole violator. Such a distinction is important in countering simplistic positions that hamper communication on vital questions.

With LEAA and companion influences in recent years, unprecedented attention has been devoted to the need for overhauling long-standing practices in criminal justice processes. These are some important recommendations carrying special weight for corrections:

1. Unification of corrections systems on a state-wide basis, including adult and juvenile facilities, jails, probation, institutions, and parole.

2. Elimination from the criminal code of victimless crimes such as sexual activity between consenting adults, simple drunkenness, and gambling.

3. Elimination of status offenses for juveniles (e.g., truancy, running away, and incorrigibility).

4. Implementation of the concept that the criminal justice system should be the last resort for social problems, and the institution should be the last resort for correctional problems.

5. Recognition that the criminal justice system in general and corrections in particular can reduce crime but not the social ills and inequities that produce it.

6. Revisions based on an awareness that corrections inherits the effects of any inefficiency, inequity, or improper discrimination that may have occurred earlier in the criminal justice process.

7. Efforts to modify the wide separation between the police and corrections elements of criminal justice, both in sequence and in attitudes toward offenders. Police are closer to the victim, the witnesses, and the public; corrections workers are closer to inmate needs for humane treatment and rehabilitation. Understandably, these differences can cause conflict.

8. Realization that the courts have greatly extended their concern with the legal rights of offenders in both juvenile and adult corrections.

9. Diversion of offenders from the criminal justice system when consistent with lower costs, better service to the offender, and no increased risk to society.

10. Avoidance of undue delays in trials and prolonged, unnecessary detention by improving cooperation within the criminal justice system.

11. Elimination of the "nine-to-five syndrome" in corrections work—in institutions as well as in probation and parole.

12. Introduction of order and rationality into current chaotic sentencing practices.

13. Reform of bail practices and reduced reliance on money bail, including greater use of ROR (Release on Own Recognizance) and the deposit of 10 percent of the bond by the accused in lieu of using bondsmen.

15. Emphasis on "a change in the offender's relation to the community" (the so-called reintegration model) rather than a change in the offender himself (the medical model). Recognition of the ineffectiveness of the reward-punishment approach to changing the offender's behavior.

16. Further development of misdemeanant probation services, including pre-sentence investigations.

17. Operation of local jails and other misdemeanant institutions as part of a unified corrections system, with eventual removal of law enforcement personnel from correctional duties.[42]

THE IMPACT OF SOCIAL REVOLUTION ON CORRECTIONS

Earlier parts of this text have been devoted to various aspects of the social revolution of the 1960s pertaining to police and community relations. We have looked at the great changes in social ethics and modes of conduct that have shaken the state of affairs in a variety of startling ways and have brought on new styles of behavior, many of which clash with existing laws. Police and corrections personnel find themselves turning to criminal law as a means of forestalling change that they judge to be too drastic to allow.

In the forefront of the movement for change in social ethics are those whom we tabbed earlier as prosocial. The prosocial groups are challenging society to live up to its pronouncements, to bring its performance more in harmony with its proclaimed creed. The antisocial groups would overthrow existing values by any available means—some even by violence—to correct the ills of society. Prisoners from both the prosocial and the antisocial groups, as well as other groups, see themselves as victims of an unjust social and political structure and identify themselves as political prisoners.

That these crosscurrents inevitably accelerate to a point of collision is illustrated by the Soledad Seven in California and the Attica revolt in New York. A double-barrelled kind of action occurs: a takeover by rioting, seizing cellblocks, taking hostages, and so on from within a penal institution, which is not a new element, and a reinforcement by dissident elements outside the institution, which is the new development. The general social climate of war, as exemplified by airline hijackings, the kidnap-murder of various government leaders, the seizure of hostages, bombings, bizarre and bloody Mansonian orgies, and the like, is such that it would be surprising if the most violent of men—those in prison—did not react explosively. In this sense, Attica floodlighted the kind of violence that is increasing on the national and international scenes. What appeared to be reasonable concessions to the inmates were negated by two nonnegotiable items: the question of immunity for crimes committed and the question of sanctuary and transportation to another country.

The community relations implications of the Attica phenomenon were both stark and subtle. To illustrate, Ramsey Clark wrote in the *New York Times:*

> Attica reminds us how quickly America resorts to violence and how little we revere life. We created the "Big House," knew of the inhumanity there and waited for the recurrence of death and destruction that was bound to come. When the crisis arose we accepted, perhaps wanted, official violence to smash the prisoners we hated and feared. . . . Attica shows again America's reliance on violence as a problem solver. [43]

Writing in the same newspaper, former California Governor Ronald Reagan expressed another view:

> Rhetoric to the contrary, a criminal who holds a knife to the throat of a captive is not an ambassador with diplomatic immunity. Unless we recognize this, if we accept the falsehood that violence, terror and contempt for the moral values of our society are acceptable methods of seeking the redress of grievances, then we will all become prisoners. [44]

THE EFFECTIVENESS OF REHABILITATION

The effectiveness of treatment in reducing recidivism is being sharply questioned by the public and by many professionals. In 1967, Robert Martinson, Judith Wilkes, and Douglas Lipton were commissioned by Nelson Rockefeller, then governor of New York, to survey the prevailing forms of correctional treatment with the aim of recommending the most appropriate for reducing the high rates of recidivism. In a speech before a workshop of the 105th Annual Congress of the American Correctional Association in August 1975, Dr. Martinson said that of the 231 research reports on correctional treatment found to be the best available up to 1967, none provided conclusive evidence that any particular mode of treatment had a decisive effect in reducing recidivism. Martinson went on to criticize those who would misuse the tentative knowledge he and his colleagues had provided in the survey to push their favorite programs. He noted that the corrections field is "already groaning under the weight of fadism, charlatinism, tons of fake research and mountains of badly allocated funds." [45]

Martinson observed that "the idea that 'nothing works' has assumed the status of one of the Ten Commandments. To assert that reform is a flop is utter nonsense, since it would make the tough line in corrections the critics want to push a flop too. . . . The canons of proof are not suddenly going to relax because one particular perspective has been found wanting. [The hard-liners] must be required to provide the public and . . . criminal justice with clear, solid evidence that their proposals are superior to those we have now." [46]

Martinson pointed out that there is clear and unmistakable evidence that one can teach an illiterate to read in prison, impart vocational skills, and change attitudes, and that group counseling improves the institutional climate. If these measures do not have the additional effect of reducing recidivism, one should not blindly assume that nothing works. One should first ask why these and similar measures produce changes at one level and not at another.

To those who would use the survey findings as justification for advocating the elimination of probation or parole, Martinson spoke pointedly:

> The survey indicates that *small* case loads are not effective for reducing recidivism and that, in general, supervision of the kind we now give is not an effective treatment when compared to mere placement on probation or parole. . . .
>
> Because there is no measurable treatment effect on recidivism does not mean it makes no difference to overall crime rates whether you have these systems or abolish them. That is an absurd conclusion. . . . Nobody knows what would be the effect [were probation and parole abolished]. . . . It would be the height of folly to abolish the only living, viable alternative to the cage without finding out what the effects are likely to be. Probation and parole are our only workable alternatives to prison and to abolish them would further reduce our limited options when in fact these options must be increased.[47]

Martinson continued:

> We in criminal justice are living through one of the greatest intellectual crises of our generation. The end of the age of treatment is upon us and the prospect of what to do next and how to do it is somewhat dismal. The ideas of the prison reformers of the 19th century have been played out to their end and they are exhausted. The inmates know this and the public are beginning to suspect it. Already the politicians are tooling up to provide us with instant solutions that will solve nothing. The public is clamoring for a reduction in crime and Congress will provide billions. . . .
>
> We must see what levers to pull, what the trade-offs are, and most of all we must stop believing that the mysterious entity called Corrections [will] ever be able to reverse the social processes that provide us with the intake for our system. It is only hard facts, knowledge which will provide us with a realistic perspective so we can resist the fads and fashions that run through this field.[48]

As a sequel to the New York survey report, Federal Bureau of Prisons Director Norman Carlson was quoted as saying:

> The unfortunate truth of the matter is that we don't know very much about the causes and cures for crime. For a long time we said we did—or kidded ourselves that we did. But I think a new sense of reality is sweeping over the entire criminal justice of this country.[49]

POLICE AND CORRECTIONS

Basically, the relationship between the police and corrections exhibits another role conflict. In the classic delineation of police responsibilities (protection of life and property, apprehension of criminals, preservation of peace, prevention of crime), the specific criminally related activities are investigation and apprehension. As we have noted, the police are confronted with a phenomenon in statistical attrition where crime is concerned:[50]

- Only a certain percentage of crimes committed are reported.
- Only a certain percentage of crime perpetrators are detected.
- Only a certain percentage of those arrested are prosecuted and go to court trial.
- Only a certain percentage of those tried are convicted and sentenced.
- Many of those convicted and sentenced plead guilty to a lesser charge.

By the time corrections enters the picture, either through imprisonment or probation, some police are already predisposed to feel that justice has not been adequately vindicated. Their view of corrections may be, "We catch 'em; you let 'em go!" To police who think in such terms, the increased use of probation, the indeterminate sentence, and the presumption of parole at some point are evidences of leniency. Other police are not opposed to the principle of parole but think it is used too frequently, too lightly, and for the wrong people. In presentence reports, it is not uncommon to find police recommendations strongly favoring incarceration in preference to probation, with longer minimum sentences suggested, an attitude revealed in the IACP (International Association of Chiefs of Police) national survey of the police and their opinions.

In criminal investigation work, the police logically tend to concentrate their efforts where the practical odds seem to point—the prior offenders. The data on such individuals is known: fingerprints, modus operandi, haunts and hangouts, and background. Add to this the considerations that those who have served time are seen as relatively poor social risks: prisons do leave disfiguring or crippling wounds. Moreover, there is often broader legal authority to arrest probationers and parolees believed to be in violation.

The police view of probation and parole officers is ambivalent. Sometimes they are seen as allies, for instance, as sources of investigative evidence or information. At other times they are seen as fostering aims that conflict with police aims, for instance, premature release, "soft" treatment, and such. Generally, the police are more militarily organized and oriented than is corrections. In corrections, lateral movement of personnel is much more accepted than it is in police work. The police are "out-professionalized" by corrections, in that less educational preparation is required of the police. The police officer as pragmatist, sometimes cynical, is apt to regard corrections people as naïve, as believers in rehabilitative fantasies that too often fail to work in the real world. As these police officers see it, the police must handle the problems resulting from failures of the corrections system, and dealing with "hardened criminals" is difficult and dangerous.

These generalizations about the police and corrections must be qualified to allow for many shades of difference in individual opinions on both sides. Some probation officers still work at their job with surveillance as a primary orientation, although this is waning. Conversely, there are police officers whose work, for example, with juveniles, would meet the highest standards of probation. Reciprocal stereotyping here does not make for any more positive relationships than in any other brand of we-and-they differentiation.

Another problem in the police-corrections relationship bears on the use sometimes made of individual parolees by the police. To assist the police in investigations, the parolee may be cajoled or frightened into the role of an informer or an undercover agent. Correctional workers generally take a dim view of this practice for several reasons, one being that it tends to lead the parolee to believe that he should enjoy special privileges. Trust versus gullibility is an issue with a very fine line of distinction in correctional work. If cynicism gets to a point of blocking trust, treatment cannot work. But a realistic middle ground is difficult to find. Police are apt to see correctional people as a bit gullible for tending to rely too much on trust; and at the same time, the correctional worker may pin too much hope on the efficacy of the correctional process. Add to this the consideration that the police tend to see the public as the client and the criminal as the adversary; whereas the corrections worker tends to see the offender as the client, and those who would inhibit his release at the appropriate time as the adversary. And within institutions the treatment-custody dichotomy often casts corrections officers as the police force of the prison.

Also pertinent in the police-corrections relationship is our discussion in the preceding chapter of the exercise of discretion, by the police, by the courts, and by parole boards. Recall additionally our comments on the indeterminate sentence and its alternatives, mandatory and presumptive sentences.

PROSECUTORS, COURTS, AND CORRECTIONS

The criminal court and its ancillary functions powerfully affect corrections in many ways, some quite apparent, others less so. While we indicated some of these crosscurrents earlier, further comments are in order.

The Prosecutor

The prosecutor must act with due consideration both for the protection of society and for the rights of the defendant as he approves arrest warrants, determines the category of crime with which the wrongdoer is charged, decides what cases to prosecute or drop *(nolle prosequi)*, and negotiates guilty pleas. Although made with the approval of the judge, his decision may be the crucial one in determining whether the defendant is to receive probation or, if sentenced to confinement, is to go to a local institution or a state prison.

Setting bail is a matter on which the prosecutor may wish to present arguments to the court. Pretrial confinement is a problem receiving particular attention. It burdens most heavily the young and the poor, for they are predominantly the ones who must idle away time awaiting trial in overcrowded cells, endangered by other inmates, while the prosperous, the respectable, and the organized crime offenders are enjoying the freedom provided by bail. In the attention lately focused on ways of releasing suspects awaiting trial, the long-known but little-used practice of release on recognizance has come into prominence. The Vera Institute made a study showing that selected offenders released on recognizance had a better record of appearing for trial than run-of-the-mill offenders admitted to bail.

The case of the parole violator has a special place in the prosecutor's decision on cases to be tried or dropped. A parolee who violates his parole by committing a new crime could serve the new and the old sentence at the same time. In fact, if the remainder of the first sentence exceeded the maximum of the new sentence, the new sentence could expire while the violator served the original. Under such circumstances, prosecution for the new sentence has little practical value. However, to prevent confusion or claims by the parolee that he was acquitted, the reason for not prosecuting the crime should be recorded. If this were done, the task of the releasing authority would be simplified and clarified; but the decision is the prosecutor's.

The prosecutor will sometimes present a recommendation for sentence that reflects the views of the police as well. The prosecutor may plead for leniency where the offender has cooperated by turning state's evidence, by pleading guilty, or by assisting police through clearing cases.

Lastly, the prosecutor may make known to corrections his views on early parole. Occasionally, he will intervene on behalf of an inmate who has assisted the prosecution; more often, if queried, he will leave the decision to the releasing authority. Frequently, too, he voices an objection to early parole.

Views concerning eligibility for parole vary widely among police, prosecutors, judges, corrections workers, and various segments of the public. Probation gains increasing acceptance, perhaps at the expense of parole, for the more promising cases are skimmed off, leaving a poorer residue. The differing views arise largely from the different roles played by the various professionals involved. Local courts, prosecutors, and police serve as a check upon the centralized parole process. The courts say that the standards of the community against the violator must be stoutly maintained, and those who threaten these standards must be kept out of circulation through substantial sentences. Negotiated pleas may result in heavier minimum sentences (presumably to counterbalance the shortened maximums), leaving less flexibility for parole. Some courts are reluctant to lessen the minimum by early paroles, perhaps distrusting parole leniency or prison population pressures. Authorities responsible for release, in turn, chafe against the inflexibility that curbs the release of inmates whose attitudes have changed and who lose ground when confined too long after adjustment begins to take place. Parole boards, from the state's vantage point, are confronted with the parodox of disparate sentences from different courts and communities.

Since the *Gideon* v. *Wainwright* decision, the right to counsel of indigents accused of serious crime has become well-nigh universal. That right has been extended to parole violators charged with minor offenses for whom a conviction could revoke their parole. The right to counsel for *any* offense, the penalty for which includes confinement, was extended by the U.S. Supreme Court in June 1972 in *Angersinger* v. *Hamlin*.[51]

On July 26, 1972, the Michigan Supreme Court held in *People* v. *Tanner* that a sentence of 14 years and 11 months to 15 years was not an indeterminate sentence as provided by law. The court did not adopt the American Bar Association's standard of a minimum of no more than one third the maximum. Instead, it specified that a minimum of more than two-thirds would *not* be an indeterminate sentence. The court opined that with good time allowances, its rule reasonably approximated the ABA standards.[52]

Ultimately, executive clemency is the means of overruling the decisions both of the courts and releasing authorities. Even here, such clemency is modified by statute and usually requires investigation and recommendation by the parole board. In all circumstances, chief executives move with caution, conscious of community sentiment, the inequity of the offender's position, and the inequity to others similarly situated.

The Sheriff

The sheriff is an arm of the court as well as a law enforcement officer. In addition to his enforcement duties, he is custodian of those awaiting trial and those serving a jail sentence. We have noted the antiquity of many jails and the inadequacies of the jail system. The fact remains that the sheriff is the local penal administrator, and no system of corrections is complete without recognizing the part played by local correctional facilities. Prolonged confinement in overcrowded facilities with little or no program is an injustice, especially because it falls with greater frequency upon the young, the indigent, and the minority group member.

The Judge

The trial judge not only presides, he decides. His assurance that guilty pleas are properly and fairly given, that charges are correctly drawn, that only proper evidence is received, that juries are correctly charged, and that verdicts are consistent with the weight of evidence is crucial to the administration of justice. To the community, the essential features are often blurred by what may seem excessive technicalities that defeat justice. The right of the public to know and the right of the defendant to be tried by court and jury rather than by the press are somewhat inconsistent, as we shall see in the next chapter. Witnesses and jurors alike may be frustrated by harassment and delay. All these people are part of the nontechnical community at large, whose confidence in justice is eroded by overtechnicality or unnecessary delay.

Close attention is being given by court administrators to notification of attorneys and witnesses to ensure that trials proceed on schedule, with a minimum of delay and inconvenience. Many police officers feel that they are often "had" in the liberties that courts take with their time. Incidentally, the one-day, one-jury concept is being tried in numerous jurisdictions, in an effort to diminish juror disgruntlement regarding forced idleness for protracted periods, including off-the-job penalties.

The scales of justice are not evenly balanced. In the defendant's favor rests the formidable weight of reasonable doubt. To it are added the weights of protection against unlawful search and self-incrimination. Add to these fundamental legalities the problems of time-consuming jury selection, the technicalities of motions and pleas, and the formal rules of evidence. These are the fine meshes through which the defendant's guilt is screened. A prosecutor is not to be blamed if he argues against probation and for a stiff sentence. The police officer whose professional investigation convinces him of a guilt that cannot be proven beyond a reasonable doubt by competent evidence may feel an understandable frustration when, thwarted in telling what he knows, he sees the guilty set free. Nor is the community at large immune to such feelings of frustration.

What might be said here regarding sentencing and currently shifting sands in that reference has been covered in the preceding chapter. There is, as we said, more and more support for sentencing guidelines.[53]

Corrections System

When the verdict is in, or the guilty plea accepted, the work of corrections begins. The blindfold is removed from the eyes of justice, and she sees the defendant for what he has been and what he may become as the probation officer presents the facts of the defendant's background in the presentence investigation. The judge selects the means he believes most likely to produce good results for the community as well as the offender. It is in the sentencing process that the trial court stands on the border of corrections. Here, in felony cases at least, the court usually has available a probation officer. The latter develops the presentence investigation—the social and criminal history and a suggested disposition. A variety of sentencing patterns exist, and alternative dispositions are increasing; but basically, it is the judge who determines whether a defendant will go to prison and, if so, for how long. And the presentence investigation is his principal tool for making that decision. The investigation, in addition to the information on the defendant's background, reflects community attitudes, including the views of the prosecutor and often of the police.

The traditional confidentiality of the presentence investigation is now being challenged. Several jurisdictions are giving defense counsel access to that report in the sentencing process, to increase the chances for fairness. However, those who seek to preserve confidentiality fear that reprisals may result and sources of information may dry up. If the defense counsel has access to the report, the responsibility for protecting confidential portions of the report will be increased.

The probation officer is a direct corrections arm of the court. It is he who supervises the offender and initiates violation hearings. The defendant should be entitled to an advocate, a counsel for defense, who will point out any deficiencies in the report and argue for any favorable dispositions, for example, probation instead of imprisonment. But in doing so, the defense counsel should remember that the question of guilt has already been decided.

The appellate court, the court of last resort in criminal justice, determines the rules by which the system operates. These rules are made in individual cases, but the merits of the person are not the point: the *principle* is. Thus, a persistent or even a dangerous offender may be the occasion for a sweeping reform in the criminal law. Miranda was a convicted burglar, but his case became a benchmark against self-incrimination without due warning.

An appellate court decision does not permit administrative problems to excuse the denial of improvements in the administration of criminal justice. The legal principle embodied in the case is the overriding consideration. The administrator must clean up the havoc that the hurricane of a decision may wreak. New resources may be required, legislation enacted, or even constitutional amendments sought. The appellate court is not indifferent to the problems created, but does not permit them to thwart justice.

The two main exits of the institutional process of corrections are parole and discharge at the expiration of sentence. Parole boards have had virtually unlimited discretion within sentencing limits. Parole board members come from a variety of backgrounds and have different perspectives and criteria. Just as discretion has been critically analyzed in the preceding phases of criminal justice, so has parole discretion come under scrutiny. A study on parole guidelines has been developed for the United States Parole Commission.[54]

The increasing interest of the court in the corrections process has already been described. The emphasis has been upon due process, not only in preconviction matters but also in probation, imprisonment, and parole. There is presumably a delicate and intricate interplay among the various forces in criminal justice agencies. Instead of being defensive about the role of corrections, and instead of resisting interference with correctional procedures, the corrections professional would be well advised to be the one to inform the other criminal justice agencies, in particular the courts, of the deficiencies of his own field so that the courts, especially, can be cognizant of the better as well as the poorer correctional practices. Moreover, corrections should set its own house in order and not leave it to the courts to do so.

DIVERSION

Among criminal justice professionals, there has been much attention in recent years to various types of so-called diversionary programs. To divert means to turn aside, to deflect in another direction. As applied to crime, there is *primary* diversion, meaning measures taken to prevent initial contact with criminal justice process, and *secondary* diversion, meaning measures taken to prevent further contact following one or more experiences. Obviously, the latter focuses on recidivism, or repeated offenses. The relationship between diversion and crime prevention is intimate, and so is the relationship between diversion and community responsibility.

Diversion is another of the many subjects mentioned in this text that deserve volumes in their own right. The term is used to cover programs with widely diversified functions; for example:

1. Primary diversion can be accomplished by wholesome family, educational, and religious influence—or by any number of other community resources (recreation, sports, neighborhood youth resources centers, PAL, etc.).

2. The exercise of police discretion is diversionary when the decision is not to invoke criminal process, but to refer a youth back to family or community, or simply to drop the case.

3. Pretrial diversion occurs when, rather than proceeding with charges in criminal court, it is decided at the pretrial stage to deal with the case in some other way. This might also be called prosecutorial diversion.

4. Alternatives to imprisonment can be diversionary. These include absolute or conditional discharge, restitution, fines, suspended sentence, probation, community service orders, partial detention in a community-based residence (halfway house), and parole release.[55]

To lessen or minimize contact between the offender and the criminal justice system is, thus, one of the chief purposes of secondary diversion. The "absorption of crime by the community" is a phrase that captures the key idea. Restraint in the use of criminal law is another way to put it. Discretion in handling individual situations is a presupposition of any diversionary program.

Diversion raises numerous questions that will have to wait upon future experience for reliable answers. One common attitude is that diversion is simply a new term for "soft" treatment of criminal offenders. This attitude once again reflects the fallacy of trying to conceive of remedies for crime in terms of simplified slogans. A more rational approach is to recognize that diversionary programs will not solve all of the problems that lead people to commit crimes. Yet there is growing disappointment with overreliance on criminal law as a means for dealing with social problems. In this sense, decriminalization is a kind of diversion. There is also a growing realization that rehabilitation does not work for every criminal either. Sentencing must increasingly take into account not only the offender, but the community and the victim of crime as well. The Law Reform Commission of Canada states this neatly in its working paper on diversion:

> There is a need to examine diversion then, not only because it is already upon us and is often the norm but also because diversionary practices can give rise to greater satisfaction between victims and offenders. The general peace of the community may be strengthened more through a reconciliation of the offender and the victim than through their polarization in an adversary trial. To put the matter another way, there is a need to examine diversion at this time if only to discover again that there is much value in providing mechanisms whereby offenders and victims are given the opportunity to find their own solutions rather than having the state needlessly impose a judgment in every case.[56]

UNRESOLVED PROBLEMS OF CORRECTIONS

In a scatter-fire way, we have touched on a number of unresolved problems in corrections. The challenge is not to find problems in this field, but to reach agreement on the solutions. Two lengthy chapters, replete with rhetoric about problems in a system, should come to a point of summary. In no particular priority, then, here are summarized the main unresolved problems.

1. The need to coordinate the branches of the correctional system. Far greater coordination is needed throughout the correctional process: between state and local factions, between the police and courts and corrections, between the machinery for dealing with felonies and that for dealing with misdemeanors, and between all these and the community. The objective in this is *not* to create another super bureaucracy, but to move toward a true system, an integrated mechanism like a watch, with each part having a distinct function, yet being interrelated with all others.

2. The need to equalize rights in the jail-bail system. The person awaiting trial is subjected to the inequities of the jail and bail system, the so-called economic basis of justice, and the degradation—especially when one has not yet been found guilty of a crime—of confinement. The jail is aptly called the number one corrections problem.

3. The need to reconcile the rights of offender and community. The increasing attention to *due process* in the field of corrections has pointed up our failure to reconcile the protection of society with the rights of the individual offender. Maintaining order and control among men and women—some of whom are dangerous—in a prison, while at the same time recognizing and respecting their rights as persons is difficult, perhaps impossible. Sometimes the imposition of intricate legal and judicial machinery under these circumstances actually has the effect of sabotaging correctional management and treatment, as lawyers invade a territory in which they are professional strangers.[57]

4. The need to improve evaluation procedures and techniques. As in other fields, corrections suffers from *a deficiency of evaluation* of its efforts. Because we can prove so little about correctional methods, we have an oversupply of unfounded claims for one technique or another, of professional guesswork, and of tokenism. We are not sure what personnel and resources are needed to do a job so haphazardly defined. Consequently, there is a lack of candor in relations between corrections and the public. Failure is camouflaged as something for which neither corrections nor the community is to blame. There are signs that the LEAA, the NCCD, and the American Correctional Association, taking cues from two Presidential Crime Commissions, are pressing for much more sophisticated evaluation of correctional activities.

5. The need to balance public security with offender treatment. The hue and cry about the medical model and the indeterminate sentence does not invalidate the concept of *voluntary* treatment. It questions only the relationship of *involuntary* treatment to release. Corrections needs an expansion of opportunities for self-improvement, coupled with performance screening through graduated release under supervision. The public would be better protected than by the presumed alternative of flat time. Both the offender and society could benefit.

6. The need for *inmate involvement*. While recognizing the problems of management and security peculiar to a corrections setting, ways should be found to improve communications. We are not suggesting inmate self-government, but staff and inmate cooperation in working out programs and problems. Experience has shown that inmates have constructive views that merit consideration.

7. The need to *extend the corrections day*. Too often constructive programs stop at 4:30 or 5:00 P.M., when many of the institutional staff go home.

8. The need to curb abnormal behavior. A prison is an abnormal social environment. Small wonder, therefore, that inmates find outlets in deviant and devious ways. The problems of homosexuality, drug addiction, and alcoholism inside prison walls beg for more imaginative approaches than have so far been tried. Coeducational prisons and connubial visits are current experiments.

9. The need to equalize application of the law. Corrections is often blamed unfairly for the problem of *inequity in sentencing*. In fact, the corrections problem here is that it must cope with such widely diversified judicial interpretations of what constitutes equitable application of the law. The indeterminate sentence is coming under increasingly heavy criticism in several states, particularly California, which pioneered legislation on it in 1917 and enlarged it into a total system in 1942. Such a sentence is designed to prevent courts from imposing harshly unequal penalties for similar crimes, to avoid fixed penalties under an inflexible penal code, and to ensure that release reflects the readiness of the offender to reenter society. Critics of the indeterminate sentence charge that a prisoner languishes behind bars for years beyond the date when he normally could expect parole, for such things as minor infractions of prison rules, attitudes considered negative by correctional authorities, or a lack of interest on the part of the inmate in so-called rehabilitation programs. Such prisoners are said to be ripe for bitterness, frustration, violence, and rebellion.

10. The need to develop *ancillary services* and service to inmate families. Smaller institutions are needed, closer to the community. Maximum security institutions should not be concentrated in remote areas.

11. The need to develop and explore new *theories of crime causation* and treatment. The term *treatment* should not be shunned, but the treatment process should be voluntary wherever possible.

12. The need to develop procedures and programs for the *mentally retarded*.

13. The need to expand *furlough* and *conjugal visitation* programs.

14. The need to emphasize the use of regional facilities for misdemeanants and to diversify felony institutions and programs.

CURRENT DIRECTIONS IN CORRECTIONS

The current unrest in our culture affects corrections in several ways. First, the civil rights movement has forced increased emphasis upon due process in criminal justice and, most recently, in corrections. This emphasis may further relax unreasonable restrictions on the personal freedoms of inmates; it may allow, for example, uncensored mail (already a practice in Michigan and elsewhere), receipt of publications heretofore deemed unsuitable by cautious officials, and greater freedom in grooming and dress.

Second, the rapid rise to power of ethnic minorities in the wake of civil rights advances is bolstering strenuous efforts to recruit minority-group members for corrections work. Racial tensions growing out of rising racial consciousness must be dealt with affirmatively. This question is at the heart of community relations.

Third, corrections workers need to "get with it" in understanding where corrections clients "are at." Careful education and constant communication is needed to develop tact, tolerance, and understanding. Conventions are not as important as the human values and aspirations from which they grow. Values do not change: the forms of their expressions do.

The American Friends Service Committee proposes several changes,[58] including the following:

· Abolishing indeterminate sentences
· Reducing the number of crimes (eliminate "victimless crimes")
· Applying criminal law uniformly
· Making treatment programs voluntary
· Recognizing prisoners' human rights and civil liberties
· Enlisting the community in the reintegration of prisoners

Others, such as the National Council on Crime and Delinquency, would also abolish such victimless crimes as drunkenness, prostitution, drug addiction, gambling, and homosexuality, and concentrate resources on crimes against other persons and their property. Still others criticize the heaping of penalty on penalty until the result can be measured in sentences hundreds of years long.

Tragedy spotlights needs. Reforms follow. Some are placebos, others untested theories. Many prescriptions are good but insufficient, others are unrealistic, some even harmful. "Yesterday's wisdom is today's common sense and tomorrow's folly," said an East Lansing clergyman in a recent sermon. But the memory of the public is short, and its fancies are fickle. The professional bureaucrat is forced to hitch the team of theory and practice and drive it down the road of the future. Let us see where some of the recommended routes might lead.

Eliminating the Indeterminate Sentence

Often bitterly criticized by inmates, the indeterminate sentence is seen by them as a device by means of which authorities lengthen prison terms at their own discretion without possibility for challenge. The inmates' demand is for *determinate* sentences. When and if this happens, one can predict that the injustice of "everyone alike who meets a legal definition" will resurface. The presumptive sentence is preferable.

Let's take a look at the pros and cons. The opponents of the indeterminate sentence argue that uncertainty of the length of the sentence constitutes cruel and inhuman punishment. Behaving himself ever so correctly or engaging in programs ever so diligently, the inmate cannot be sure what behavior will result in his release. Opponents argue further that decisions are arbitrary, biased, and unfounded. The values involved and the terms describing them are vague, subjective, and individualistic.

It is a commonly held thesis that an inmate's good conduct in prison does not mean good behavior in the community. The concept of paying a debt to society has two fallacies: first, under this theory, punishment becomes a "pound of flesh"; second, the penalty, exacted in terms of time incarcerated, becomes the factor that permits the inmate to ignore the need for change. The penalty is seen as part of a calculated risk. Readiness for release becomes irrelevant. And how is the penalty fixed? Clearly, by the criminal code. Yet the code cannot predict human behavior, or evaluate change, or differentiate among persons who commit similar crimes. In short, the fixed sentence makes individualized treatment impossible. The result of eliminating the indeterminate sentence could land heavily on the lesser offender and less heavily on the major offender.

What would be the effect of the determinate sentence upon plea bargaining? One can postulate that, in many cases, the inexperienced offender would more readily admit to serious charges while the experienced offender would plea bargain for lesser charges. As often happens, the question is better than the answer and raises issues that need more careful responses than so far proposed.

Making Treatment Available but Voluntary

Several criticisms are leveled at treatment in correctional institutions: first, that treatment is inadequate; second, that results are not well observed or reported; third, that effects upon postrelease behavior are unpredictable; finally, that an individual is forced to "knuckle under" by submitting to an invasion of his privacy as a person. He should, according to this theory, be able to choose between seeking such treatment or having his parole status determined without it.

Much more is needed by way of treatment—both in quantity and in quality—for which more money is essential. More careful evaluation of such treatment is indispensable. The voluntary nature of such treatment cannot be answered by a simple yes or no. Some kinds of treatment are more necessary than others. The child molester, the sadistic rapist, and the narcotic addict require treatment. If the offender will not accept it or cannot benefit from it (or cannot demonstrate change by other means), the alternative may be longer sentences.

But now desert—a proportionate relationship between the crime and the punishment—conflicts with public protection predicated only upon past behavior. We see the probability of increased plea bargaining or the reluctance of juries to convict where extenuation exists or the penalty seems grossly disproportionate. Remember the mandatory life sentence for fourth felony convictions.

In addition, we see the need for some sentence adjustment by either sentence review procedure, a releasing authority, or some other as yet unperceived means.

We also see the need for continued executive clemency. But pressed to its outer limits, such clemency argues for the retention of parole boards. Moreover, the public protection inherent in parole is not sufficiently recognized. Put in its baldest terms, some form of conditional release does provide for the extension of performance screening and the reincarceration of the parolee who significantly demonstrates his commitment to further crime.

Finally, we consider the question of good time, also now under challenge. We believe it is a valuable control mechanism in prison management. Perhaps it is used too much. We believe it should be retained, even if modified, and we further believe that some recognition and reward should be given for efforts at self-improvement, even though the motive may be self-serving.

Recognizing the Human Rights and Civil Liberties of Prisoners

Courts are now turning attention to the penal process. Once convicted, with appellate procedures exhausted, the probationer, prisoner, or parolee has been largely without redress within the legal limits of sentence, provided constitutional rights were not denied. Now the corrections system is being called into account at many points. The confidentiality of the presentence investigation is under challenge. How can a convicted person defend himself against unknown charges or unfavorable opinions obtained from undisclosed persons? Must a prisoner accept all administrative decisions about his care, custody, and treatment with no possibility of examination by an independent body? Is the decision of the releasing authority immune to inquiry? Can a parole, once granted, be revoked without a hearing? Are attorneys or witnesses, or both, to be permitted at parole interviews? Is a corrections agency obliged to provide the treatment that has been diagnosed as necessary? These and other questions are emerging; some, especially in the parole revocation process, have already been adjudicated in important aspects. Visibility and accountability, to use Fred Cohen's phrase, are new words in the lexicon of corrections.[59]

These changes are warmly welcomed by many corrections workers and greeted with caution and skepticism by others. Two observations seem relevant. First, skeptics fear that a judicial review of administrative decisions will paralyze the system and prematurely free dangerous criminals. This fear seems excessive. The alternative is to leave decisions unexamined and unchecked. Procedures can be developed that will safeguard prisoners' rights without defeating good administration. The court is simply examining the reasonableness and legality of administrative decisions.

Second, lawyers need to develop greater expertise in corrections matters. A parole violation hearing is not the place to retry questions of guilt or innocence earlier determined by a court. Moreover, lawyers need to develop canons of ethics that apply to the confidentiality of information, such as that contained in a presentence investigation. By so doing, the lawyer can defend his client against unjust or unfounded speculations without revealing sources. Moreover, the offender whose status is the subject of an appearance or inquiry is entitled to know the factors considered in arriving at a decision. How else can he effectively plead his case or know how to correct his deficiencies? Admittedly, skill and will are required to achieve just decisions that also serve the goals of treatment without undue encumbrance or delay.

Enlarging the Role of the Community in Returning Prisoners to Normal Life

Community rehabilitation assistance—already begun in important areas (community corrections centers, to name but one)—is urgently needed.[60] The blurring of the distinction between the prison and the community is manifested in work-release programs, furloughs, and overnight visits by inmates' spouses. These important steps are present now in token form. They should be expanded to meet the needs of inmates in all jurisdictions.

But the role of the community should be seen in broader terms. Crime destroys community. The idea of *community* presupposes commonly held goals, an openness, and an interrelatedness. Interrelatedness assumes equal respect for the rights of others. Criminal law is based upon consensus. The essence of criminal law is the invocation of sanctions. When the fabric of society is ripped by dissension, or when a substantial minority disagrees with a criminal sanction, self-enforcement breaks down, and law is either unenforceable or ignored.

Basically, then, criminal law *is* community relations. Criminal justice is the process by which those who violate society's minimum standards are identified, penalized, and redirected. It is the *community* that must open its ranks to the violator if he is to be restored to full membership.

SUMMING UP

The focus of this extensive chapter has been corrections and the community. Its emphasis is what the community can and must do if *correcting* criminal and delinquent behavior is to be undertaken seriously; its plea is that *community* can provide the correctional element in corrections. A dozen problem areas are identified in corrections-community relations. Then several general strategies for coping with these problems are suggested, with special attention to the development of professional leadership in the corrections field.

The complicated question of the ends of the correctional process is reviewed, set side by side with the impact of social change on corrections today. Such analysts as Robert Martinson have said that the age of treatment in the corrections field has ended, and no one seems sure of what to do next or how to do it. Yet there appears to be greater and greater reliance upon community-based correctional programs, exemplified by the many forms of diversion. The unresolved problems of corrections are numerous; again, a dozen or so are listed, and constructive future directions are recommended.

NOTES

1. *The Mikado*, Act II.

2. Richard A. McGee, "The Administration of Justice: The Correctional Process," in A. F. Brandstatter and Louis A. Radelet, eds., *Police and Community Relations: A Source Book* (Beverly Hills, Calif.: Glencoe, 1968), p. 415. Reprinted by permission. The other ideas attributed to McGee in this section are based on the same article, pp. 414–435.

3. Ibid., p. 417.

4. Ibid.

5. William Raspberry of the *Washington Post* (October 29, 1971) refers to "the counterproductive ambivalence involved in simultaneous punishment and education."

But he goes on to reflect that separation of the two functions causes problems as well. See also "Assessment of Attica: A Symposium," in Louis A. Radelet and Hoyt Coe Reed, *The Police and the Community: Studies* (Encino, Calif.: Glencoe, 1973), pp. 224–254.

6. McGee, "The Administration of Justice," p. 419.

7. Robert Martinson, Ted Palmer, and Stuart Adams, *Rehabilitation, Recidivism, and Research* (Paramus, N.J.: National Council on Crime and Delinquency, 1976).

8. Lee Rainwater, "The Revolt of the Dirty-Workers," *Transaction*, November 1967, p. 2.

9. U.S., President's Commission on Law Enforcement and Administration of Justice, *Task Force Report: Corrections* (Washington, D.C.: U.S. Government Printing Office, 1967), p. 1.

10. Ibid., p. 7.

11. For example: Clifford R. Shaw, et al., *Delinquency Areas: A Study of the Distribution of School Truants, Juvenile Delinquents, and Adult Offenders in Chicago* (Chicago: University of Chicago Press, 1929); Edwin H. Sutherland and Donald R. Cressey, *Principles of Criminology*, 8th ed. (Philadelphia: J. B. Lippincott, 1970).

12. President's Commission on Law Enforcement, *Task Force Report: Corrections*, p. 16.

13. Michigan Department of Corrections, Preface to "Annual Report," mimeographed (Lansing, Mich.: Department of Corrections, 1974).

14. Ibid. See Karl Menninger, *The Crime of Punishment* (New York: Viking Press, 1966).

15. *New York Times*, August 25, 1975.

16. Michael Meltsner, "The Future of Correction: A Defense Attorney's View," *Crime and Delinquency* 17, no. 3 (July 1971): 270.

17. *Sostre* v. *Oswald*, 404 U.S. 1049 (1972).

18. *NCCD News*, May–June 1971.

19. *NCCD News*, March–April 1971. See also Milton Burdman, "The Conflict Between Freedom and Order," *Crime and Delinquency* 15, no. 3 (July 1969): 371–376.

20. *NCCD News*, March–April 1971. In the eighteenth century, Cesare Beccaria made a fatal error in ignoring the victims of crime; he assumed that a criminal act injures only the state. This oversight was written into Anglo-American jurisprudence.

21. Refer to our discussion of this in chapter 13. The position taken by the National Council on Crime and Delinquency on preventive detention appears in *Crime and Delinquency*, January 1971, pp. 1–8.

22. *Time*, March 2, 1970.

23. *Commonweal*, February 26, 1971. See U.S., Department of Justice, Law Enforcement Assistance Administration, *National Jail Census, 1970*, National Criminal Justice Information and Statistics Service, Series SC-No. 1 (Washington, D.C.: U.S. Government Printing Office, 1971).

24. *New York Times*, December 3, 1971, p. 41.

25. By its nature, LEAA is a *political* entity, and the political waters around it are inevitably turbulent at the moment, there is considerable Congressional disenchantment with its accomplishments.

26. See *Crime and Delinquency* 17, no. 1 (January 1971). The entire issue is devoted to articles about research in corrections.

27. See *Citizen Action to Control Crime and Delinquency* (New York: National Council on Crime and Delinquency, 1968).

28. LEAA, Technical Assistance Division, U.S. Department of Justice, *Guidelines and Standards For the Use of Volunteers in Correctional Programs*, Stock No. 2700-00236 (Washington, D.C.: U.S. Government Printing Office, 1972).

29. Elmer K. Nelson, Jr., "Community-Based Correctional Treatment: Rationale and Problems," *Annals* 374 (November 1967): 82–91. Reprinted by permission.

30. See *Annals* 376 (January 1969). The theme of this issue is "The Future of Corrections."

31. An interesting example of this type of conflict is described by Elmer H. Johnson in "Report on Innovation—State Work-Release Programs," *Crime and Delinquency* 16, no. 4 (October 1970): 417–426.

32. The final report of this commission was issued in November 1969; its numerous impressive publications may be secured from the American Correctional Association, 4321 Hartwick Road, Suite L-208, College Park, Md. 20740.

33. Inmate frustration with this kind of program was particularly dramatized in the Attica, New York, prison tragedy of September 1971.

34. Available from the American Correctional Association. See note 32 for address.

35. Menninger, *The Crime of Punishment*, pp. 153–154.

36. Henry Wiehofen, as quoted by Jim Castelli in "The Year of the Prisons," *Commonweal* 94, no. 21 (September 21, 1971).

37. Jim Castelli, "The Year of the Prisons." Reprinted by permission.

38. See Richard Quinney, *Critique of Legal Order.*

39. Daniel Glaser, *The Effectiveness of a Prison and Parole System* (Indianapolis, Ind.: Bobbs-Merrill, 1964); Gresham Sykes, *The Society of Captives: A Study of a Maximum Security Prison* (Princeton, N.J.: Princeton University Press, 1958).

40. Maxwell Jones et al., *The Therapeutic Community: A New Treatment Method of Psychiatry* (New York: Basic Books, 1953).

41. Norval Morris, "Reform: It Must Come," *Life* 71, no. 13 (September 24, 1971): 36. The syndicated columnist, Ralph de Toledano, wrote in October 1971 that he had a document in his possession proving that the Attica riot was "the opening gun of a national campaign built around the demand that by July 4, 1976, all of the prisoners in all U.S. prisons must be released and the prisons abolished." (*Lansing* (Mich.) *State Journal*, October 12, 1971.)

42. These recommendations are all contained in U.S., National Advisory Commission on Criminal Justice Standards and Goals, *Report on Corrections* (Washington, D.C.: U.S. Government Printing Office, 1973). See also National Council on Crime and Delinquency, "Model Act for the Protection of Rights of Prisoners," *Crime and Delinquency* 18, no. 1 (January 1972): 1–14.

43. *New York Times*, September 30, 1971.

44. *New York Times*, October 7, 1971.

45. Robert Martinson, as quoted in *Corrections Digest*, September 3, 1975, p. 4.

46. Ibid.

47. Ibid., pp. 5–6. Reprinted by permission.

48. Ibid.

49. "Big Change in Prisons: Punish—Not Reform," *U.S. News & World Report*, August 25, 1975.

50. See Jerome H. Skolnick, *Justice Without Trial: Law Enforcement in Democratic Society*, 2nd ed. (New York: John Wiley & Sons, 1975).

51. *Angersinger* v. *Hamlin*, 407 U.S. 25; 92 S. Ct. 2006, 32 L. Ed. 2d 530 (1972).

52. *People* v. *Tanner*, 387 Mich. 683 (1972). The Court (in 1972) could not foresee what would later happen to good time, by voter mandate in the 1978 referendum.

53. Leslie T. Wilkins, Jack M. Kress, Don M. Gottfredson, Joseph C. Calpin, and Arthur M. Gelman, *Sentencing Guidelines: Structuring Judicial Discretion*, LEAA, National Institute of Law Enforcement and Criminal Justice, U.S. Department of Justice, Stock No. 027-000-00583-7 (Washington, D.C.: U.S. Government Printing Office, 1978). For an illuminating, thoroughly documented, and comprehensive discussion of current sentencing controversies, see Marvin Zalman, "The Rise and Fall of the Indeterminate Sentence," *Wayne Law Review* (Wayne State University School of Law, Detroit) 24, nos. 1 and 3 (1977–78).

54. Don M. Gottfredson, Leslie T. Wilkins, Peter B. Hoffman, and Maurice H. Sigler, "The Utilization of Experience in Parole Decision-Making," Summary Report of the Parole Decision-Making Project, U.S. Board of Parole, on a grant from the National Institute of Law Enforcement and Criminal Justice, LEAA, administered by the National Council on Crime and Delinquency, 1974; Lucille K. DeGostin and Peter B. Hoffman, "Administrative Review of Parole Decisions," *Federal Probation* 38 (June 1974): 24; Don M. Gottfredson, Peter B. Hoffman, Maurice H. Sigler, and Leslie T. Wilkins, "Making Paroling Policy Explicit," *Crime and Delinquency* 21 (1975): 34.

55. See: Canada, Law Reform Commission, *Working Paper 7, Diversion* (Ottawa: Canada Law Reform Commission, 1975).

56. Ibid., p. 23.

57. See Sol Rubin, "Needed—New Legislation in Corrections," *Crime and Delinquency* 17, no. 4 (October 1971): 392–405.

58. American Friends Service Committee, *Struggle for Justice: A Report on Crime and Punishment in America* (New York: Hill and Wang, 1971).

59. Fred Cohen, *The Legal Challenge to Corrections: Implications for Manpower and Training* (Washington, D.C.: Joint Commission on Correctional Manpower and Training, 1969); see also NCCD, "A Model Act to Provide for Minimum Standards for the Protection of Rights of Prisoners," *Crime and Delinquency* 18, no. 1 (January 1972): 4–14.

60. See the monograph series on crime and delinquency topics of the National Institute of Mental Health; for example, *Community-Based Correctional Programs: Models and Practices*. In the same series is *Crime and Justice: American Style*, by Clarence Schrag, a comprehensive overview of literature and research bearing on the entire criminal justice system.

16

THE MEDIA

In chapter 8, we looked briefly at police and community relations as a *communications* problem. This suggests intermediary forces or instrumentalities—the media of communication or of public information—whose primary function is to convey messages and interpretations back and forth between "sender" and "receiver." Much of this is done, in public affairs, by newspapers, magazines, books, other formats of the written word, and by television and radio, referred to generally as "the media." Clearly, public opinion about crime and criminals is influenced substantially by the powerful forces of the media. What the police and other criminal justice entities do and how they do it are subject to constant monitoring by the media.

Indeed, in a broader sense, in democratic societies where the media are not captives of government, relationship problems between governmental bodies and the media are endemic to political processes. Conflict of interest is, to some degree, embedded in this relationship, and it is perfectly normal and generally healthy in terms of the common good. If the newspapers and other media were not "policing" the police and other governing factions, if they were not channeling information and interpreting messages between criminal justice agencies and the public, they would be shirking a vital responsibility and would be open to serious criticism.

THE COMPLICATED RELATIONSHIP BETWEEN THE POLICE AND THE MEDIA

The relationship between a police organization and newspapers or television stations can become so complicated that strong feelings and positions crystallize on either side. The cultivation by the police of good relations with the media is an important means of good public relations. It is a good way to keep the public informed of what is going on in a police department and why. But when a police department hedges on publicity, or a newspaper or other medium violates what the police view as the ethics or ground rules of reporting crime news, problems arise.

Such clashes occur most frequently when the police deem it necessary to withhold information from the media because the release of certain information would thwart police objectives. It can also happen when the media get on the spoor of what they sense to be misconduct or corruption within a criminal justice agency. For whatever reasons, the impression may be created that somebody is not playing fair with the media, which the media have a habit of translating into the accusation of not playing fair with the public. Yet, it may well be that, because of the circumstances, full disclosure of all available information is *not* in the best interests of either the criminal justice agency or of the public.

Thus, the dialogue between a particular police department and particular newspapers or television stations may become quite caustic. Administrative judgments on withholding information are occasionally questioned by the media, and their questions transmitted to the public—to the possible disadvantage of the administrator. Because he cannot explain his decision without disclosing information that he believes is best withheld, his terse "no comment" may be interpreted as pugnacity or evasiveness. This dilemma of police-media relations is a typical one in police administration.

The media may also face a dilemma. A newspaper and a radio or television station are ordinarily profit-making enterprises. They also have responsibilities to the public interest. Whatever dilemma arises from these partly conflicting objectives is reconciled by the decisions of those who rule such enterprises and is recognized by the public only in somewhat detached notions as to what constitutes a "responsible" newspaper or television station. Public tastes and tolerances in such a matter are as varied and fickle as in the choice of toothpastes. Clearly, the public interest is not always best served by the profit-making policies or practices of the media. Among other things, this principle of the public interest might—more often than it does—call into question a newspaper's use of such slogans as "the public's right to know" in a manner suggesting a right as unquestionable as that of life itself. From time to time, one suspects that the newspaper is really using an excuse for doing, in the name of the public interest, what best serves its profit motive.

So we have a dilemma on the police side of the relationship, and a dilemma on the media side. And as Winston Churchill might have put it, we also have a conundrum within the dilemma. For the newspaper, in a highly competitive market, often finds its premium story to be what the police (or the prosecutor, or the court) are most reluctant to disclose. This dual dilemma and the conundrum constitute the essence of the relationship problem of the police and the media—of criminal justice and the media. The ramifications touch on such matters as the fierce competitive dynamics within the media world, the deadline, sensationalism and so-called yellow journalism, the scoop, free press versus fair trial, and disclosure of information sources.

THE DISCLOSURE OF INFORMATION

When, therefore, the discussion turns to issues in police-media relations, there is no escaping the larger context of these issues. The conflicts of interest involved are, at once, as ancient and as current as democratic government. Take the central question of public access to information about governmental operations. As John Steele has stated:

> This conflict often pits the President and the Executive Branch against Congress, regulatory agencies against consumer interests, bureaucrats against environmentalists, Congress against the voter, the courts against the bar and, at times, the news media against all of them.[1]

With respect to what he called "a current cliché from the political lexicon—the people's right to know," Steele observed:

> The Constitution, as it happens, does not provide for any such right. The courts, moreover, have never interpreted the First Amendment—which prohibits Congress from abridging freedom of speech or the press—as requiring the Government to make unlimited disclosures about its activities.[2]

Steele further asserted that an uncurbed right to know eventually collides dramatically with what might be called the right *not* to know. Many historians, philosophers, political scientists, and even a few journalists have conceded that there must be some limit to the right of the public to have information about government. By the same token, the right of the government to maintain secrecy must also be restricted. As James Russell Wiggins, former editor of the *Washington Post*, put it: "We can give up a little freedom without surrendering all of it. We can have a little secrecy without having a Government that is altogether secret. Each added measure of secrecy, however, measurably diminishes our freedom."[3]

So the question is: How much secrecy? Under what specific conditions, and by whose judgment, may government officials operate "on and off camera"? Inquisitive news people, as well as inquisitive congressional and private investigators, have turned up some appalling incidents of bare-faced news control by government in recent years. No one seems to be willing to confess that he knows much about criteria for such control. In fact, sometimes the justification for secrecy seems to be no better than apathy or red tape, or splendid evidence of the effectiveness of special interest lobbies and pressure groups. Congress has passed little legislation relating to the disclosure of official information in the public interest. The Freedom of Information Act of 1966 has proved inadequate, because it exempts such areas as national defense and foreign policy. A congressional study reported that the media made little use of it during the first four years of operation, although commercial interests did.

The media, of course, are also subject to criticism. One criticism of the media is that they are, at times, too considerate of the sensibilities of government officials who try to manage the news. The abuse of trust where privileged information has been made available has also occurred. For instance, liberties are sometimes taken with informational release deadlines: "Not to be released prior to 12:01 A.M." on such and such a date. More serious breaches of confidence occur under competitive duress. So it is that we have another two-sided street here, calling for *balance* in carefully worked-out ground rules and guidelines, while recognizing that excesses on either side threaten rights best safeguarded by a kind of constructive, creative tension in the relationship. The challenge is again to turn indigenous conflict to constructive ends, to "structure" the relationship by voluntary guidelines, to maximize cooperation and minimize vituperation, in the public interest.

Senator Daniel P. Moynihan contributed a helpful analysis several years ago. Writing about the changing relationship between the Presidency and the press, he identified five causes:

1. The journalistic tradition of muckraking—the exposure of corruption in government or of the collusion of government with private interests—while still

very much alive in the reportorial spirit, is giving way to what Lionel Trilling calls "the adversary culture" as an element in journalistic practice. Common to both, however, is a mistrust of Government.

2. Journalism has become, if not an elite profession, then at least a profession attractive to elites. The political consequence of the rising social status of journalism is that the press grows more influenced by attitudes genuinely hostile to American society and American government.

3. Washington reporters depend heavily on more or less clandestine information from Federal bureaucracies which are frequently, and in some cases routinely, antagonistic to Presidential interests. When the bureaucracies think their interests are threatened, they often turn to the press. Both bureaucrats and journalists "stay in town"; Presidents come and go.

4. Questions of objectivity are often raised in reporting the statements of public figures. While the tradition in journalism is to print "the news," whether or not the reporter or the editor or the publisher likes it, there is a rub when it comes to a question of whether an event really is news—or simply a happening, staged for the purpose of getting into the papers. The issue, then, is: what is journalistic objectivity, and what is merely an excuse for avoiding judgment? If it becomes clear that someone is lying or "playing games," why print it—or at least, why print it on the front page?

5. Finally, and most important, there is the absence in American journalism of a professional tradition of self-correction—a mark of any developed profession. Honest mistakes ought to be seen as integral to the process of advancing the field. But journalism will never attain to any such condition.[4]

Moynihan summarized his views by saying that he wished to emphasize two points: (1) that in the eyes of the media in a democracy, it is hard for government to succeed, even when it has indeed done so; and (2) the conditions are thus set for protracted conflict in which the government "keeps losing." And this Moynihan identified as a serious matter of national morale. By way of resolving the issue, he called for a better balance. He seemed to admit, implicitly, that there was another side to the argument, but he did not spell it out. Perhaps, he said, some sort of national press council, of a type earlier proposed by Norman Isaacs, a working journalist, and even earlier by Robert M. Hutchins and his Commission on Freedom of the Press, would help. But Moynihan backed off and contended that such a council would be the wrong thing to create in this country at this time; there is, he asserted, "a statist quality" to many of the existing press councils abroad. He thought the American press should become much more open about acknowledging mistakes. As for government, he observed that misrepresentations of government performance should never be allowed to go unchallenged:

> The culture of disparagement that has been so much in evidence of late . . . is bad news for democracy. . . . Where is . . . socially responsible criticism to come from? Or rather, where is it to appear in a manner that will inform and influence the course of public decision-making?[5]

GOVERNMENT POWER VERSUS MEDIA POWER

In 1734, John Peter Zenger was accused of libel and jailed for printing repeated attacks in his weekly paper on the colonial governor, William Cosby. A jury finally acquitted him after long deliberation, helping to establish the right of newspapers to criticize the government. Subsequently, this principle was further enshrined by the journalistic activities of Ben Franklin, Tom Paine, and many others.

Our discussion to this point is not very difficult to translate into the narrower terms of police-media relationships, or of criminal justice-media relationships. The larger drama being enacted is the jousting of Big Government and Big Media.

The gravity of the issues in this drama is beyond question. While government (the police and the criminal justice system are favorite targets, but not, by any means, the sole ones) appears to be more than ever the object of public criticism, the news media also seem to be under attack. Generally, the charge against the media is bias. The specifics vary. The poor and the nonwhite accuse the media of unfair treatment. Minorities have long since had their own newspapers, magazines, and radio stations; and alienated groups have had their underground press. These media are especially critical of the police. Blue-collar descendants of European immigrants are saying that they are not fairly treated by the media. Young radicals proclaim that the popular media distort their image. The police often accuse the media (as in Chicago in August 1968) of prejudiced reporting, and sometimes of "stoking the fires of unrest." In 1969 the National Commission on the Causes and Prevention of Violence stated that "a crisis of confidence exists today between the American people and their news media."[6] The Kerner Commission devoted considerable attention to media reporting, charging that the media had failed to communicate adequately on race relations and ghetto problems, and had failed further to bring more blacks into journalism.

In short, the so-called credibility gap in the relationship between government and citizens seems to be matched by the credibility gap between the media and "the masses." One explanation for the gap in the recent past has been the apparently increasing political polarization of the nation. People "strike out," as Mark Arnold phrased it, "at the messenger who delivers the bad news."[7] Another explanation is distortion of the news by the media, through editorial bias, economic or political pressure, and so on. Still another explanation is the charge that the media have not adapted well to the times, and they have failed to identify for themselves a constructive role in interpreting social change and social conflict. Indeed, there are charges that the media aggravate social conflict by their definition of what constitutes news and by various journalistic tactics that place undue—and sometimes distorted—emphasis on selected aspects of news stories. Newspapers appear, however, to be moving away from the "shotgun" approach, the front-page buildup, with splashy pictures and box scores of the latest riot news. Dramatic but meaningless predictions have also largely disappeared. But serious problems remain. Glaring instances of inaccuracy, exaggeration, distortion, misinterpretation, and bias still occur in all types of news media, as pointed out by the U.S. Commission on Civil Rights.[8] Unprofessional news reporting and unprofessional police behavior represent two sides of what is often unprofessional police-media relations.

Americans, it seems, are viewing or hearing the news more and liking it less.

There is obviously enormous power represented by approximately 1,750 daily, 575 Sunday, and 8,000 weekly newspapers; 150 general editorial magazines; 6,400 radio stations; and 850 television outlets. The wear-and-tear of competition, increasing publication and circulation costs, the frantic pace of life, and growing public disenchantment with the quality of news reporting are among the factors influencing the media. Politicians, in typical fashion, have moved with what they perceive as a rising tide of criticism directed against the media, and have sought to exploit it for their own political advantage.

Some observers who see these signs as threatening the survival of a free press point to various indications of what they interpret as government intimidation of the media. There is concern that distrust of the media apparently increases with education and income level. We have discussed at length the police role predicament in today's society. The media also have a pressing role dilemma. They are expected to stand apart from the society, in a kind of dispassionate, objective, watchdog fashion—despite their other role as members of society, with their own intrinsic pressures and prejudices. To this extent, the similarity in the role predicament of police and press is striking. There are also some differences.

The dramatic events following the Watergate break-in undoubtedly revealed many of the seamier aspects of the battle between government and the media. At the same time, however, they also called attention to the watchdog and reporting roles of the media. Media coverage of Watergate was a massive example of the media "riding herd" on government—"doing our job," as media people like to say.

THE BALANCE OF POWER

It is not unusual, of course, for big-power economic or political confrontations to largely ignore the interests of third parties. Labor-management strife is one illustration. The Cold War in international relations was another. Big Media versus Big Government appears to be another. The third party, generically, is the public, which directs accusations of a credibility gap against both media and government. Where there is power, there is always the question of control. In this confrontation, it is a question of control of the media by the government, or control of the government by the media. Put another way, the ultimate conflicts of interest must be controlled through a negotiated balance of power, lest the conflicts destroy the system or the society.

Because this discussion pertains to the police-media relationship, it may seem to be ranging pretty far afield, but in fact we are very much on target. The point bears repeating that the contact of patrol officer and news reporter on the street or in the stationhouse is a microcosm of a larger, complex issue, an issue that is very hot in our time.

In a recent book, John Hohenberg refers to the tendency in public discourse to blame every problem on a "a crisis of confidence" in the institutions of democratic society. Under these circumstances, he says, "when it is difficult for either the governors or the governed to find anybody, outside each other, to blame for their troubles, a certain amount of critical fallout is bound to descend on the press."[9] Some of this is the result, Hohenberg asserts, of the independent newspaper's contention that it is the principal common medium for discourse between the American government and the American people. Therefore, when the communication channels get clogged, the medium must be prepared to take some of the blame. Hohenberg writes:

> What it all comes down to, in reality, is whether the daily newspaper, as presently constituted, is capable of publishing the news at the same time it is trying to get at the truth. The public, as is evidenced by the widespread use of the phrase "newspaper talk," long ago recognized that the two functions were not necessarily identical. . . . Of course the truth is hard to come by in the complicated modern world. But neither the elite of democratic governments nor the paladins of the press can shrug off public dissatisfaction by pleading that the job is difficult and perhaps even impossible to do to everyone's satisfaction. Two thousand years ago, nobody was satisfied, either, with Pontius Pilate's crafty evasion, "What is truth?"[10]

The historical specter of abuse of media power in this country is conveyed through dim memories of William Randolph Hearst and Orson Welles's portrayal in *Citizen Kane*. However, John Tebbel expresses doubt that the power of the press today is controlled by big owners like the late Lord Thomson of Fleet Street (who was virtually unknown to most Americans of any age, yet who owned many newspapers in America), or Arthur Ochs Sulzberger, president and publisher of the *New York Times*, or Samuel I. Newhouse, a retiring figure known to few outside the industry. Tebbel thinks that Robert R. McCormick and Roy Howard were the last of the "press lords."[11]

Newspapers today derive their power, Tebbel believes, from what they print. Gone is the day when a publisher and his paper could be a decisive factor in political fortunes; political editorials are read and heeded only where a paper's constituency is already largely in agreement. But this does not mean, Tebbel cautions, that newspapers are without any political influence. They do provide a sounding board for many viewpoints, and they do help to crystallize public opinion on the important issues of the day. Government would hardly be so concerned with the media if the assumption were that the media have little influence with voters and taxpayers. The danger, in Tebbel's view, is this:

> The press might slip into the unrestrained advocacy [which makes] it a mere propaganda instrument and therefore utterly unreliable as a purveyor of news. . . . Just as the idea of a university as an instrument of social change instead of an intellectual laboratory is being widely advocated, so too can we expect a further steady push by those who insist that a newspaper should have the same kind of public utility. . . . More and more, the real power of the press today emerges as a conveyor of information that government and others would like to withhold from the public if that were possible, so that they might exercise their own power without undue interference. . . . The public frequently does not agree with the information the newspapers provide, but that is immaterial. What is important is that the information is provided, without interference, so that the public can interpret it, argue about it, and act upon it if it chooses. That is, and always has been, the true mission of the press in our kind of democracy.[12]

Tebbel's remarks naturally lead one to consider questions of journalistic ethics. Debate on this topic is just one aspect of the current public debate on the ethics of politicians, lawyers, judges, and other public officials. The ethical questions being asked of the media include these: Is a story true? Is it fair? Is it biased? Is it an unjustified intrusion into someone's privacy? Is the "reliable source" really reliable? The answers are elusive, but every day thousands of reporters, editors, and publishers implicitly answer these questions by writing the news, each guided by his or her own list of dos and don'ts.

Michael T. Malloy, writing in the *National Observer,* came to this tentative conclusion:

> So our ethical problems . . . seemed often to boil down to the contradictory professional tasks we set ourselves. To televise reporters who are "involved" yet "objective." To report the facts but not neglect the deeper "truth." To explain complex stories but do it in 90 seconds. To make hard subjects easy and dull ones interesting. To give our audience what it wants and what we (arrogantly?) think it needs.[13]

BIAS AND THE MEDIA

Charges of bias invariably come from those who disagree with a position taken. Seldom do we hear anyone say: "I disagree, but it's fair." What we said about perception in chapter 8 is relevant to all of this. Different ways of seeing an issue or problem should be described as just that, more often than not, thereby avoiding use of the personalized invective conveyed by the charge of bias. The difficulty with this, in human transactions, is that sometimes deliberate distortion (bias) does occur. An ultimate absurdity is reached when an investigation to determine whether there is bias is conducted by, let us say, a committee or commission of "impeccable credentials," only to have its report branded as "biased."

What are some specifics of the charges of biased reporting directed at the media? We cannot offer an exhaustive listing, nor do we argue the merits or demerits of any of these allegations; but the following are indicative of contemporary "free swinging" allegations:

- Reporters today are disproportionately "dogmatic liberals" with a strong "leftward bias" and "a set of automatic reactions" that incline them to "oversimplify" the news. As a result, U.S. journalism is out of touch with the American mainstream.[14]
- The media are unduly subservient to the pressures of advertisers.
- The media are unduly subservient to the pressures of politicians.
- Local media depend too much for news coverage and editorial position on hookups with national networks.
- The media all but ignore stories that challenge their basic editorial positions on favored candidates or proposals.
- The media use chauvinistic criteria in judging what is news.
- The media stress spot reporting, usually confined to the unexpected or the unusual. They neglect perspective reporting. (Example: In the campus unrest of a few years ago, the 5 percent of students who rioted on campus were news; the 95 percent who did not were perspective.)

- The media emphasize tragedy, conflict, disorder, the bizarre, and the like in their reporting and tend to neglect joy, cooperation, peace, good works of ordinary people, and so on. The media are more interested in problems than in solutions, in destruction than in construction, in reaction than in action, in fights than in civil dialogue, in irresponsibility than in responsibility, and so on.

- The media distort by telling only part of a story, by promoting a particular viewpoint, or by slanting a story by headlines or by position in the paper.

- The Kerner Commission said that the media made a real effort to report factually the 1967 disorders, but had failed to report adequately on the causes and consequences of civil disorders and the underlying problems of race relations. Racial bias in one form or another is a frequent criticism of the media.

- Media reporters sometimes side with protesters and demonstrators, thereby embarrassing the police and making the police task more difficult.

- The media sometimes stage news events.

- Interpretive reporting tends "to widen the credibility gap," merely revealing the prejudices of the reporter.

- The media are fascinated with glitter and glamor at the expense of significance.

- The media often label people with convenient, stereotypic terms.

Such a litany of allegations against the media may strike some readers as bias in itself. Although the subject is touchy enough to set off such responses, the list is presented here to provoke discussion of particulars, rather than generalizations. As in a court of law, the key question is: What is the evidence?

By way of swinging the pendulum of the discussion, let us turn again to John Tebbel for a look at the other side. He muses that critics of the press are usually just as wrong in their complaints about what the papers *do* print as they are about what they think *ought* to be printed. As he states it: "Critics in high places, particularly, make generalized assertions of no validity whatever as though they were fact."[15]

Tebbel conducted a modest sampling of prominent dailies across the country, deliberately excluding New York and Washington papers (lest the survey be considered biased!), to determine what, if any, basis in fact there was for some of the main criticisms. He found that the charge that the front pages are filled with crime and violence was without factual basis. So was the charge that the papers feature mostly local news. So was the charge that newspapers do not print good news, or that they are filled with trivialities. So was the charge that the papers offer only the publishers' opinions. It is now common, Tebbel found, for newspapers to present a broad range of opinion in the editorial section, often spread across two facing pages. Tebbel also discovered that the papers he surveyed run many nonviolent stories about nonviolent people preoccupied with worthwhile, nonviolent activities.

Someone would no doubt suggest that Tebbel is a biased reporter who set out to prove what he already believed. Perhaps our discussion would be more productive if we turned to some concrete—and complex—issues.

THE COURTS AND THE MEDIA: THE RIGHTS OF REPORTERS

In recent years, the courts (the Supreme Court in particular) and the media (newspapers in particular) have been engaged in an intriguing tug-of-war regarding constitutional rights. One of several specific issues highlighted pertains to the rights of reporters.

While there are those always willing to cheer for the adventurer who takes on "the stiff-necked" media in "open combat," there are also those who take a dim view of such things as the use of government subpoenas to uncover sources of press information about radical organizations, or the infiltration of the Saigon press corps by military agents posing as reporters, or the use of a congressional subpoena to persuade a national television network to submit any and all material connected with the production of a documentary "that provoked Big Brother in Washington," as one newsmagazine put it. An interesting case to review is that of *New York Times* reporter Earl Caldwell.

The trouble began in October 1969, when four Chicago newspapers, NBC News, and *Time, Life,* and *Newsweek* magazines were subpoenaed to produce files, photographs, film, and even reporters' notebooks dealing with a four-day rampage by the SDS Weathermen in Chicago. In early February 1970, CBS News disclosed that it had been subpoenaed for all film that had been shot for a program on the Black Panthers. Then the government ordered black reporter Caldwell to surrender "all notes and tape recordings" of his interviews with Black Panther leaders, in particular an interview with David Hilliard, who was charged with threatening President Nixon's life.[16]

So the issue was joined: freedom of the press, resting on protection of confidential information and sources, versus the obligation of every citizen to serve as a witness in support of law and judicial process. But in this case, the issue was complicated by the outrage of news people at the sheer number and catch-all nature of the subpoenas, and further by the application of such governmental tactics to reporters covering the politics of protest and violence. The CBS network pleaded that what may have been orthodox procedures for news-gathering years ago were obsolete today. When, for example, a news source is a pot-smoking young activist who confidentially outlines his plan for a rally that may produce violence, the reporter's duty is not so clearly apparent, whether or not he sympathizes with the source or the cause. But prosecutors and defense counsels for indicted activists have learned that reporters often possess vital information. As *Newsweek* stated it:

> Hauled into court under a subpoena and threatened with contempt proceedings if he doesn't talk, the newsman finds himself caught between the law, his professional ethics and his responsibilities as a citizen. . . . Only thirteen [seventeen, as of May 1971] states have statutes protecting a reporter's confidential relationships, and attempts to get such a nationwide law through Congress have failed.[17]

The *New York Times* initially provided legal counsel for Caldwell. Then Attorney General John Mitchell announced that some of his subordinates had gone too far and that he would meet with the offended editors and try to work out a mutually satisfactory set of ground rules. Caldwell's trial in San Francisco Federal District Court was pressed, although the court stipulated that Caldwell could not be compelled to disclose confidential information from his interviews with Black Panther party leaders "unless the government could prove there was no other way of obtaining the same information on a matter of 'national interest'."[18] Caldwell appealed, but at this point the *Times* indicated that it would not take part in the appeal.

In November 1970, the Ninth Circuit Court of Appeals quashed the federal subpoenas that had been served on Caldwell and vacated a contempt-of-court citation against him, and in so doing sharpened the focus on a journalist's hitherto ill-defined privilege under the First Amendment. In its decision, this court said:

> The very concept of a free press requires that the news media be accorded a measure of autonomy. To convert newsgatherers into Department of Justice investigators is to invade the autonomy of the press by imposing a governmental function upon them. To do so where the result is to diminish their future capacity as newsgatherers is destructive of their public function. . . . The need for an untrammeled press takes on special urgency in times of widespread protest and dissent. In such times, the First Amendment protections exist to maintain communication with dissenting groups and to provide the public with a wide range of information about the nature of protest and heterodoxy.[19]

Caldwell had been prepared to go to jail. His own lawyers held that his chances of acquittal were poor. The general principle enunciated by the court in this particular case would have to be developed in later cases. From a journalistic vantage point, the decision was a landmark. But it was not the end of the case. In May 1971, the U.S. Supreme Court agreed to hear a further appeal in the case, pressed by U.S. attorneys wanting the court to compel Caldwell to testify. In June 1972, the Supreme Court ruled, in a five-to-four decision, that journalists have no First Amendment right to refuse to tell grand juries the names of confidential sources of information. But it could be predicted that the matter would not be allowed to rest at that.

At its annual meeting in the spring of 1971, the American Society of Newspaper Editors discussed the need for national legislation to protect reporters from court procedures aimed at forcing them to disclose news sources. Particular alarm was voiced regarding the recent "epidemic" use of the subpoena. It was charged that "lazy" law enforcement officials were using the subpoena to try to force the press to do their investigating. Attorney General Mitchell was commended for his efforts to develop guidelines. But most people at the convention still thought that freedom of the press was in grave jeopardy, under the threat of the subpoena. The problem of television and radio news gatherers was considered especially acute because the stations operate under government licensing. Richard L. Tobin wrote in *Saturday Review:*

> As every newspaperman knows but won't always admit out loud, protection of a source of news can be used as an excuse or a crutch or, worse, to rationalize a point neither necessarily true nor useful to the general public. . . . All the same, despite

an occasional racket, such as the hiding behind the shield of news source immunity by an amoral journalist, the ASNE's drive for a Federal law to protect reporters from court procedures trying to force them to disclose their sources of news does make sense professionally. For if every legitimate source of information knew that he or his journalist friend might be hauled into court for questioning, or even jailing, not many headlines would be written or broadcast except for cut and dried events covered in routine fashion, and the traditional investigative role of the press would fade forever.[20]

Commonweal commented:

The public information media are a long way from perfect, and nothing should be allowed to obscure this fact. But there is nothing wrong with the press and television that can be cured by the heavy hand of Washington either, and this is an even more basic truth.[21]

In mid-1971, the case of the Pentagon papers again raised the same issues. As Jude Wanniski put it in the *National Observer:*

The disclosures leave in their wake a host of far-reaching inquiries about the nature of government itself; about the war-making power of the Executive Branch in a representative government; about the methods of decision-making; about the inherent strain in a superpower democracy between the need for an informed public and national security requirements for secrecy in foreign affairs.[22]

There are abundant signs that tension between the courts and the media has increased recently. The question of the confidentiality of sources continues as a major bone of contention. Since 1972, forty to fifty reporters have been held in contempt of court for refusing to divulge information. A notable, recent case involved another *New York Times* newsman, M. A. Farber, hit by a New Jersey court with a stiff fine and six months' jail sentence for refusing to turn over materials, even under subpoena, to the attorney for the defendant in a murder trial. The *Times* was also cited and slapped with a heavy fine. The case provided a dramatic showdown between the First Amendment guarantee of a free press and the Sixth Amendment right to a fair trial. The core question is clearly critical in constitutional law.

In 1972, the Supreme Court decided in the Branzburg case that a reporter who witnessed a crime must testify before a grand jury, as anyone else. Following that case, many states passed laws shielding reporters from disclosing information in legal proceedings. But judges, as exemplified in the New Jersey case (where there is such a law), have sometimes ignored the statute and ordered reporters to divulge information, evidently on the ground that "it was not the State asking for information to prove guilt but a defendant asking for information to prove innocence."[23] The argument is, in effect, that the rights of the defendant take precedence. The newspapers' position hinges on resistance to being turned into an investigative arm of the government—and on the right of the public to be informed.

The courts, and the Supreme Court in particular, seem to be saying that the media have no more rights than anyone else, under the Constitution. The public's right to know is not absolute and, indeed, is nowhere stated, as such, in the Bill of Rights. By the same token, media people have the same obligations as anyone else called upon to act as a witness in a trial, and fulfilling such obligations does not transform them into government investigators.

The Supreme Court refused to review the *Times*-Farber case. But no one interpreted this as an end to the issue. The question of whether the apparently increasing strife between the courts and the media will abate remains unanswered. It should be recognized that recent Supreme Court decisions which appear to strain the relationship pertain to new questions and are not reversals of earlier decisions. The court seems to be nudging the media toward reexamination of their responsibilities toward society.[24] But Katherine Graham, board chairman of the *Washington Post*, has commented: "The real world in which we work is neither evil nor heroic. It is the same environment of conflict, ambiguity and hard choices that mark most enterprises in our time. In that real world, our responsibilities are not often as obvious as you might think."[25]

RELATED QUESTIONS

There are some recent developments regarding several related questions, of sufficient importance to our subject to report briefly:

- In June 1976, the Supreme Court virtually outlawed "gag" orders by judges seeking to prevent excessive or inflammatory publicity that might endanger a defendant's right to a fair trial. The use of such orders to silence the press had risen sharply in the preceding decade. The ruling grew out of a press challenge to the sweeping order of a Nebraska judge in a widely discussed trial of a mass murderer. The Supreme Court held unanimously that the press, generally, could not be prevented or delayed from publishing whatever information it secured in the courtroom. It also pointed out that a judge had other means of silencing prejudicial publicity, such as sequestering the jury and changing the location of a trial.[26]

- Law enforcement officials armed with warrants were permitted, as a result of a Supreme Court decision in late May 1978, to conduct surprise searches of newsrooms, seeking information about possible crimes by third parties. The case involved a 1971 police search of the offices of Stanford University's student newspaper.[27]

- Amendments to the Freedom of Information Act, in 1975, made it possible for citizens, businesses, and the media to obtain, upon request, information previously hidden in government files about individuals and organizations, for example, in records of the FBI and CIA. Surprisingly, the media have not made extensive use of the act, apparently because of apprehension as to what the courts might rule in questions of privacy and libel.

- Further, in a 1978 decision, the case involving San Francisco's public television station KQED and a question of access to the Alameda County jail, the Supreme Court said that the media had no more First Amendment rights to enter a public facility than any private citizen.[28] In effect, the

Court seemed to be suggesting that, once the media have information, it may be published; but the government is not obliged to give the media unique access to it.

- In early 1976, the celebrated case of CBS television newsman Daniel Schorr limelighted the issue of reporters' rights. CBS suspended Schorr for leaking a classified House intelligence report. When CBS itself refused to broadcast the report, Schorr released it to the *Village Voice*, a New York City paper. He described his action as an "inescapable decision of journalistic conscience."[29]

The free press–fair trial tug-of-war has a long history in American constitutional law.[30] The Presidential Crime Commissions have stressed the vital role of the media in the administration of justice. Reporting maintains the public knowledge, review, and support, said President Johnson's Crime Commission, so necessary for the proper functioning of the courts. Critical inquiry and reporting by the media on the operation of the courts can prevent abuses and promote improvements in any part of the justice system. On the other hand, a fair jury trial can be held only if the evidence is presented in a courtroom, not in the press, and only if jurors come to their task unprejudiced by publicity. The commission recommended setting standards for releasing news:

> Police, prosecutors, bar associations, and courts should issue regulations and standards as to the kinds of information that properly can be released to the news media about pending criminal cases by police officers, prosecutors, and defense counsel. These regulations and standards should be designed to minimize prejudicial statements by the media before or during trial, while safeguarding legitimate reporting on matters of public interest.[31]

The difference of opinion regarding live television coverage of trials finds many lawyers who are opposed on the ground that "the search for truth is difficult enough without putting it on stage."[32] Canon 35 of the *Canons of Judicial Ethics* of the American Bar Association has banned the filming of judicial proceedings, based on a fear that cameras, cables, lights, and technicians might constitute an intolerable courtroom distraction that could influence the behavior of participants in a trial and affect its outcome. But the ABA today appears to be softening its position, while the Judicial Conference— which makes the rules for federal courts and is chaired by Chief Justice Warren Burger, who opposes TV in the courtroom—is expected to maintain its negative posture on the question. As of spring of 1978, these seven states permitted televised trials, under strict rules: Alabama, Colorado, Florida, Georgia, Texas, Washington, and Montana. The argument, pro and con, remains lively.

In Michigan, the state supreme court has adopted a revised code of ethics that forbids the release by attorneys and prosecutors of statements to the press that might influence the outcome of pending cases. The change in the lawyer's code of conduct, the first since 1935, reduces forty-seven canons to nine restrictions on press coverage of criminal trials, including these:

- Statements cannot be made concerning the identity, testimony or credibility of a prospective witness.

- Statements cannot be made concerning the results of any tests or the objection of the accused to submit to examination or tests.

- Statements cannot be made revealing the prosecutor's opinion as to the guilt or innocence of the accused.

- Statements cannot be made concerning the character or prior criminal record of the accused.

- Statements cannot be made concerning the possibility of a plea of guilty or to the acceptance of a lesser charge.

In a provocative 1977 article, Macon (Georgia) Junior College criminal justice Professor George Mettler argued that the constitutional guarantee of a fair trial is the direct and primary responsibility of the judicial system, not of the news media. It is up to the judiciary, not the press, to ensure that a defendant's rights are safeguarded. Mettler wrote:

> Judges, then, must maintain control of trials in their court and cannot be heard to cry foul if and when the news media makes their jobs difficult. Their jobs ought to be difficult. And if ever it is otherwise, then our liberties are indeed in jeopardy.[33]

VIOLENCE AND THE MEDIA

As chairman of the 1947 Commission on Freedom of the Press, Robert M. Hutchins said that "the relative power of the press carries with it relatively great obligations." Many people today are gravely concerned about what they regard as the failures of our social institutions, and among them are many who point to the media as a prime example and the chief cause of much that has seemingly gone wrong with other institutions. Louis Harris polls have lately reflected declining public confidence in the media. Sex, sadism, and violence in magazines and newspapers, on the radio and television, and in the movies are often pointed to as symptoms of deteriorated values and coarsened public taste. Individuals and agencies disagree widely and sharply about the effects of certain subject matter—for example, of violence on television—upon children and adults. The protest against violence on television—clearly related to so many manifestations of violence on the social scene (civil disorder, terrorism, crime, delinquency and more serious crimes by juveniles, and so on)—was organized in the 1960s.

We observed earlier that violence has been prominently ingrained in the American *ethos* from the beginning of our history. The encounters between the early settlers and the Indians were hardly a form of nonviolent social protest. The "winning of the West" was not inspired by a philosophy of live and let live. The games played by the older generation as children could not be blamed on television, for there was no such thing; but the silent and later sound movies most vivid to us prompted our quarrels about who would be Tom Mix, Buck Jones, or Tim McCoy. And it wasn't a tea party that we had in mind; we sometimes used "bee-bees" in our air rifles, and we weren't hunting for sparrows!

Graphic violence abounds in great literature. In nature, it is an important part of life. In human affairs, so is evil. But if evil or violence are featured, emphasized, held up as models of behavior in a multitude of ways, there will inevitably be social agitation for controls of one kind or another, premised upon concern for society's survival. *Sesame Street* and *Mister Rogers' Neighborhood* forthwith emerged and joined *Captain Kangaroo* on television in a tone of sensitivity, gentleness, compassion, and loving understanding of living things, and, not least of all, of self and other people. For this, too, is telling it like it is. As Margaret Culkin Banning has put it:

> We need candor. But we should not confuse frankness with only the uncovering of lewdness, violence, and despair. Frankness should also expose loyalty, gentleness, courage, and love for they too exist and have a right to be shown on the screen and in the pages of books.[34]

Eliot Daley, speaking as a parent, zeroed in on television violence with the observation that the *average* child sees 12,000 TV deaths before he is fourteen years old. What is real to these children? Daley asks. Far too many programs, he believes, convey the idea that the manipulation of persons through deceit, guilt, pseudo-humor, or brute force is legitimized by the eventual getting of one's way. Small wonder that today's children are masters of manipulation. Daley thinks that the underlying difficulty for most young viewers is that programming directed at them is really adult fare presented in juvenile dialect. But children have not sampled enough reality in the world at large to be able to put cartoon violence in a context where it can be funny.[35] Daley goes on:

> Ordinarily, the young viewer watches virtually in vain for *alternatives* to a violent expression of hostility or aggression. None are needed apparently, since there is a seemingly limitless warehouse of willing victims and an incredible quality and variety of violence. Worse, there is a total tolerance and total absence of condemnation of violence. Not a voice is raised to suggest the limited appropriateness of violence as a human-relations skill. . . . Nowhere does the violence-as-a-problem-solver thesis come a cropper.[36]

The National Commission on the Causes and Prevention of Violence concluded that television was loaded with violence; that it was teaching American children moral and social values "inconsistent with civilized society." The commission marshalled some frightening statistics to bolster this charge, and contended that the vast majority of experimental studies bearing on the question have found that observed violence stimulates aggressive behavior. The commission was careful to point out that it did not see television as a principal cause of violence in society. But it is, the commission insisted, a contributing factor. Television entertainment based on violence may be effective merchandising, but it is, the commission opined, "an appalling way to serve a civilization—an appalling way to fulfill the requirements of the law that broadcasting serve the public interest, convenience and necessity."[37]

The commission approached the question of television violence with great care, at pains not to make television a scapegoat. It recognized that violence is a complex phenomenon, with complex causes.

A task force report of 613 pages, prepared for the same commission under the direction of a former Justice Department attorney, Robert K. Baker, and a Seattle sociologist, Sandra J. Ball, was published in January 1970, but did not have the endorsement of the full commission. This study contended that the news media in general contribute to violence in America by failing to report thoroughly on the social problems that lead to disorders, violence, and confrontations. This, in effect, repeated what the Kerner Commission had said. The task force report described the news media as oversensitive to outside criticism and then continued:

> The news media can play a significant role in lessening the potential for violence by functioning as a faithful conduit for intergroup communication, providing a true marketplace of ideas, providing full access to the day's intelligence, and reducing the incentive to confrontation that sometimes erupts in violence. That is a subtle and uncertain mission.[38]

Sometimes, said the report, the press is unjustly blamed for violence. Some groups do use the media to exploit their goals. But it should be remembered, the task force observed, that violence is not necessarily aimed at gaining media attention. Further, groups engaging in violence are likely to have their message lost because of the media tendency to focus on the violence to the exclusion of the message. Moreover, resorting to violence is often a political instrument used to provoke the police and, as in the case of campus disorders, to incite to radical action large numbers of students sympathetic to the radical goals who would ordinarily reject radical tactics.

The task force recommendations included more self-examination by the media, more interpretative reporting on social ills, tighter guidelines for the coverage of disorders, the establishment by news organizations of internal appeal boards to hear citizen complaints about coverage, better relations between the press and minority groups, and a press council independent of the media and government as a public watchdog for all news outlets. The report concluded:

> The last generation of reporters concentrated on reporting objective physical happenings—telling the reader what he saw with his own eyes and heard with his own ears. The next generation must concentrate on describing what somebody else thinks. . . . The government can no more legislate good journalism than it can legalize good manners. More important than the adoption of specific suggestions is that each news organization make an independent determination of what is significant.[39]

Writing in the *New York Times*, William V. Shannon quoted the British critic, T. R. Fyvel: "Professional television pressures work constantly towards portraying action and not thought, personalities and not issues, what is visually happening and not the boring explanations why." Shannon laments the effects on children of watching television three to four hours a day throughout their growing years (one-quarter of all children watch it more than five hours daily), especially those of shortened attention-span and passivity. He objects to entertainment that provides instant gratification with no effort or imagination, whose sole effect is "to subvert education and malnourish the mind."[40]

The entire area of the role and responsibility of the media in social conflict has not been much explored in our society. The questions involved are loaded with cross-purpose dilemmas not easily reconciled. The basic issue is the question of journalistic ethics. Example: Do you exacerbate racial trouble by reporting it, or mislead your readers by pretending it doesn't exist? John Hughes, editor of the *Christian Science Monitor*, writes: "Readers are being turned off on newspapers that keep telling them, 'Here's what the situation is—and isn't it awful?' "[41]

Suppose that surveys say that there is an audience for crime stories. Should the media pander to the audience? Take the recent rash of police and detective programs on television. Two *Wall Street Journal* writers, Ethan Katsh and Stephen Arons, both assistant professors in the Legal Studies Program at the University of Massachusetts at Amherst, spent three months watching randomly selected television police programs in an attempt to determine whether television police obey the law, and to discover what message about law was being transmitted to viewers. They found that almost every episode of almost every police show contained one or more violations of the Fourth, Fifth, or Sixth Amendment guarantees of freedom from unreasonable search and seizure, the right to due process, and the right to counsel. They found further that many viewers failed to detect blatant police-state tactics. They concluded that, if police shows are in any sense morality plays, the message communicated is that evil may be subdued by state-sponsored illegality. In short, the end justifies the means.[42]

In a California case decided in 1978, NBC-TV was sued for $11 million on the grounds that a 1974 program (a movie entitled *Born Innocent*) had led directly to the rape, four days later, of a nine-year-old girl by three girls and a boy, on a San Francisco beach. The case was dismissed because the plaintiff could not prove intentional incitement. A key argument for the defense was that, although speech that intentionally incites violence is not protected by the First Amendment, drama or news reports that portray violence *are* covered.[43]

The role of the media with regard to terrorism is a matter meriting special study. There is little doubt that the media can be a tool of terrorists, and indeed that "the meanings of ordinary words and phrases can be deftly contorted to advance political ideologies."[44] The essential point for our purpose is expressed as follows by T. K. Fitzpatrick:

> The media must not be the dupes of the radical script writers, nor should they be the mouthpiece of government. There is a mean. Law enforcement and the media cannot be locked in combat. Law enforcement has to realize the function of the media is to report the news, and hopefully not alter it. The media must be cognizant of the very real danger of glorifying the terrorist.[45]

On the same theme, Yonah Alexander writes:

> . . . to terrorists, an extensive coverage by the media is the major reward and . . . they willingly or unwillingly become tools of the terrorist strategy, and that advertising terrorism increases the effectiveness of its message through repetition and imitation. [Another problem] concerns the vital importance of protecting the "people's right to know" and of a free press in open societies. A related critical issue is the relationship between the media and police agencies. . . . The important question, then, is how can the media in a democratic society devise new methods of fair reporting of terrorism without jeopardizing their responsibilities to the public and

without adversely affecting the management role of law enforcement officials in handling terrorist incidents?[46]

Alexander proposes a number of considerations for research on the matter, looking toward improvement in "the management of terrorist activities by both the media and criminal justice processes."

THE POLICE-MEDIA RELATIONSHIP OF THE FUTURE

To blame the media alone for violence obviously makes no more sense than to blame the police. Occasionally, under particular circumstances, imprudent or even unethical media (or police) action may trigger mayhem, but usually the causes go much deeper. Hatred and hopelessness are not manufactured by the media or by the police, though they may play a part. Who trusts whom? This is a key question in a social milieu that reveals its attitudes by the commonplace use of such terms as "watchdog," "bullshit," "Orwellian," "rip-off," and "conniving bastard."

As we said at the outset of this discussion, the fundamental issue is as old as the free society. Alexis de Tocqueville referred to it this way:

> In this question, therefore, there is no medium between servitude and license; in order to enjoy the inestimable benefits that the liberty of the press ensures, it is necessary to submit to the inevitable evils that it creates.[47]

Are the media more the builders or the disrupters of democracy? Sometimes one, sometimes the other. Just as police departments do, they make mistakes. Who trusts whom? Frank admission that none of us is omnipotent is a good beginning, if one is intent upon improving relationships with anyone.

We have suggested the complexity of the causes and effects of violence. Likewise complex has been the evolution of the government-media relationship in our society. Police-press relations is one among many vessels on a currently turbulent lake. The television program *The Selling of the Pentagon* and the Pentagon papers were sails on another boat on the same lake. Watergate turned out to be a major craft. Government surveillance by wiretap or various other techniques is another very large vessel that includes in its cargo a variety of governmental activities calculated to cope with dissent, protest, and revolutionary plot, especially at times when such social swells sweep the lake. Free press and fair trial constitute another substantial boat on the same lake. So do the protection of privacy and, at the same time, the protection of the rights of reporters and the public in handling police information.

For the police officer, these big issues are telescoped in matter-of-fact questions. For example, he asks: If only a small part of the allegations about violence that have been made against television are valid, why is it that anyone would seriously suggest that police should be disarmed? Why should a police officer put his life on the line as a first tentative step in a grand strategy of defusing our society? It's not unlike international disarmament. Who takes the initiative? Where and how does the building of mutual trust begin? Not with crooks and terrorists, surely. But just as logically, then, not with "crook catchers" either.

So it is that we eventually come to the kind of question that police, news reporters, and many others can study together: What produces violence or crime or social revolution in the first place? Not the police, alone—nor news reporters, alone—nor anyone else, alone. And so on. One risks sermonizing and oversimplification by pursuing such reasoning too far.

Much can be done to establish police-media relations on a mutually beneficial plane, despite (or better, because of) the inevitable conflict of interests. Every urban police agency and the local media should have worked out a modus operandi, more or less effectively, in the form of "ground rules," "working principles," "guideposts," or "guidelines."[48] The 1966 President's Crime Commission implied that the police-press relationship may thrive better when cooperative efforts have a specific focus—organized crime, for example, about which the commission recommended, among other things:

> All newspapers in major metropolitan areas where organized crime exists should designate a highly competent reporter for fulltime work and writing concerning organized criminal activities, the corruption caused by it, and governmental efforts to control it. Newspapers in smaller communities dominated by organized crime should fulfill their responsibility to inform the public of the nature and consequence of these conditions.[49]

Some may disagree with the details of this recommendation, but the basic message of police-media cooperation is clear.

Speaking to the 1976 annual meeting of the International Association of Chiefs of Police, then Los Angeles Police Chief Edward M. Davis made some suggestions as to how he felt police-media relations could be improved:

1. By development, on both sides of the relationship, of an "open system," as opposed to a "closed system."

2. By reducing antagonism on each side. One way to do this is to work on a perspective of helpfulness to each other, as opposed to a combative stance.

3. By letting each other do the job each is expected to do, and facilitating this, rather than by being obstructionist.

4. By a presumption of good faith, reciprocally, and by efforts to improve, on each side, what might be called line-and-staff communication.

5. By eradicating impressionistic reporting, "manufactured" news and politicized, "hit man" journalism.[50]

Evidently, Chief Davis had in mind that the mutual stake of police and media is the survival of free society.

SUMMING UP

In this chapter we have seen that many of the issues that generate tension between the police and the media are part of a larger context. Disclosure of information is frequently the bone of contention, as suggested by recent Supreme Court decisions which have been resisted by the media. The Court seems to be saying that the media have no more rights than anyone else, under the Constitution.

The free press-fair trial argument continues to enliven court-media relations, as it has throughout constitutional history. The subject of violence on television also generates spirited public discussion, with no sign of decisive evidence on either side of the issue.

NOTES

1. John Steele, "The People's Right to Know: How Much or How Little?" *Time*, January 11, 1971.

2. Ibid.

3. Quoted by John L. Steele in *Time*, January 11, 1971, p. 16.

4. Daniel P. Moynihan, "The Presidency and the Press," *National Observer*, March 29, 1971, p. 22 (first appeared in *Commentary*, March 1971). Reprinted by permission.

5. Ibid.

6. U.S., National Commission on the Causes and Prevention of Violence, Preface, *Report of Task Force on the Mass Media*, Staff Study Series, vol. 9 (Washington, D.C.: U.S. Government Printing Office, 1969).

7. Mark R. Arnold, "The News Media—Besieged by Critics," *National Observer*, July 6, 1970.

8. *Civil Rights Digest* 4, no. 1 (Winter 1971).

9. John Hohenberg, *The Best Cause: Free Press—Free People* (New York: Columbia University Press, 1970).

10. John Hohenberg, "The Free Press Is on Trial," *Saturday Review*, April 14, 1970, p. 109. Reprinted by permission. See also Harry S. Ashmore, "Government by Public Relations," *Center Magazine* 4, no. 5 (1971), pp. 21–28.

11. John Tebbel, "Press Power Revisited," *Saturday Review*, June 13, 1970, pp. 53–54.

12. Ibid., p. 54. Reprinted by permission.

13. Michael T. Malloy, "A Rainbow of Gray," *National Observer*, June 26, 1975. Reprinted by permission.

14. Howard K. Smith, ABC newsman, as reported in *Newsweek*, March 9, 1970, p. 84.

15. John Tebbel, "The Stories the Newspapers *Do* Cover," *Saturday Review*, April 11, 1970, p. 66.

16. *Newsweek*, February 16, 1970, pp. 55–56. The charge against Hilliard was dismissed in early May 1971 because of a technicality in the use of wiretapping by the government to secure some of the evidence.

17. *Newsweek*, February 16, 1970, pp. 55–56. Copyright © 1970 by Newsweek, Inc. All rights reserved. Reprinted by permission.

18. *Newsweek*, May 11, 1970, p. 74.

19. *Newsweek*, November 30, 1970, p. 87. Copyright © 1970 by Newsweek, Inc. All rights reserved. Reprinted by permission.

20. *Saturday Review*, May 8, 1971, pp. 45–46. Reprinted by permission. See also Richard L. Tobin, "Reporters, Subpoenas, Immunity, and the Court," *Saturday Review*, December 11, 1971, pp. 63–64; Nat Hentoff, "A Deepening Chill," *Commonweal* 95, no. 21 (February 25, 1972): 486–488.

21. *Commonweal* 94, no. 9 (May 7, 1971): 206. Reprinted by permission.

22. *National Observer*, June 21, 1971. Reprinted by permission.

23. *Newsweek*, August 7, 1978, p. 87, and *U.S. News & World Report*, August 14, 1978, p. 27.

24. Philip B. Kurland, in *U.S. News & World Report*, October 9, 1978, pp. 71–72.

25. As quoted in *U.S. News & World Report*, August 2, 1976, p. 20.

26. *Nebraska Press Association* v. *Stuart*, 427 US 539 (1976); and *U.S. News & World Report*, August 2, 1976, p. 23.

27. *Zurcher* v. *Stanford Daily*, 23 Cr L. 3061, May 31, 1978. In December 1978, the Carter administration proposed legislation that would give news organizations broad protection against police searches. If enacted, such legislation would supersede the Supreme Court's decision in the *Zurcher* case.

28. *Houchins* v. *KQED, Inc.*, 23 Cr L. 3164, June 26, 1978.

29. Associated Press release, February 24, 1976.

30. For a representative reference, see Fred S. Siebert and George A. Hough, III, *Free Press and Fair Trial* (Athens: University of Georgia Press, 1971). See also Louis A. Radelet and Hoyt Coe Reed, *The Police and the Community: Studies* (Encino, Calif.: Glencoe, 1973), pp. 195–211.

31. U.S., President's Commission on Law Enforcement and Administration of Justice, *The Challenge of Crime in a Free Society* (Washington, D.C.: U.S. Government Printing Office, 1967), p. 138.

32. Edward Bennett Williams, "What's Needed to Speed Up Justice?" *U.S. News & World Report*, September 21, 1970.

33. George B. Mettler, "The Fair Trial—Free Press Controversy," *Criminal Justice Columns* (Allyn and Bacon/Holbrook Press, October 1977), pp. 1 ff.

34. "Sex and Violence in Movies, Books, TV—Helpful or Harmful?" *Family Weekly*, January 11, 1970.

35. Eliot A. Daley, "Is TV Brutalizing Your Child?" *Look*, December 2, 1969, pp. 99–100.

36. Ibid.

37. As reported in "TV Violence: 'Appalling'," *U.S. News & World Report*, October 6, 1969, pp. 55–56. See also University of Chicago Center for Policy Study, *The Media and the Cities*, edited by Charles U. Daly (Chicago: University of Chicago Press, 1968).

38. National Commission on the Causes and Prevention of Violence, *Mass Media and Violence* (Washington, D.C.: U.S. Government Printing Office, 1969).

39. Ibid.

40. *New York Times*, September 3, 1975, p. 35.

41. As quoted in *U.S. News & World Report*, August 2, 1976, p. 24.

42. *Wall Street Journal*, July 22, 1975, p. 14.

43. *Time*, August 21, 1978, p. 85.

44. T. K. Fitzpatrick, "The Semantics of Terror," *Security Register* 1, no. 14 (November 4, 1974): 21–23.

45. Ibid., p. 23.

46. Yonah Alexander, "Terrorism, the Media and the Police," *Police Studies* 1, no. 2 (June 1978): 45–52.

47. Alexis de Tocqueville, *Democracy in America*, translated by Phillips Bradley (New York: Knopf, 1944), vol. 1, p. 184.

48. For example, the New York City Police Department as described by Patrick V. Murphy (when he was Deputy Chief Inspector in 1965) to the National Institute on Police and Community Relations at Michigan State University. See Murphy's "Police-Press Relations," in A. F. Brandstatter and Louis A. Radelet, eds., *Police and Community Relations: A Source Book* (Beverly Hills, Calif.: Glencoe, 1968), pp. 435–440. See also C. P. Corliss, *Guideposts to Reporting Spot News Happenings in the Los Angeles Megalopolis* (Hawthorne, Calif.: Butler Data Systems, 1969).

49. U.S., President's Commission on Law Enforcement, *The Challenge of Crime*, p. 208. For a series of articles on police-press relations of a more practical nature, see "Guidelines," *Police Chief* 39, no. 3 (March 1972): 62 ff. Also see Marianne Fisher "Police and the Press—A View from the Outside," ibid. 42, no. 3 (March 1975): 66.

50. Edward M. Davis, Workshop on "Freedom of Information: Rights vs. Responsibilities," *The Police Yearbook: 1976*, published by the International Association of Chiefs of Police, pp. 113–115.

17

POLITICS AND THE POLICE

In chapter 4, we spoke of several interlocking social systems involving the police. We have discussed the criminal justice system and the social institutional system. Now we will look at the political-governmental system.

In the first chapter of this text we said that, in democratic society, policing is a public, political function. This statement has implications inviting more explicit attention and is the theme of this chapter.

What the police are, what they do, and what is expected of them, how well or how poorly they fulfill these expectations, what can be done to improve police services—these are, in considerable measure, political questions. They are also in some sense sociological, social psychological, and economic questions, depending on the eye of the beholder. Historically, however, policing has tended to be viewed primarily as a political institution, inextricably tied to the function of governing through the executive responsibility for enforcement of laws enacted by legislatures and interpreted by courts. Given this orientation, it is surprising that police and community relations programs have devoted so little specific attention to the political aspects of police work.

Perhaps one reason so little attention has been devoted to the political aspects of police work is that community relations has a certain idealistic flavor to it, as we suggested earlier. Idealists sometimes find it difficult to bridge the gap between what might be and what is. Yet every important issue in criminal justice is as much a political issue as it is a community issue. Policing is a public, political function.

POLITICAL POLICING

A lot of public confusion has been generated by such slogans as "Take the police out of politics" and "The police must not play politics." If the slogans are interpreted to mean partisan political activities, or use of a police department and officers as pawns of political machines and bosses, or as instruments of political chicanery of one kind or another, then such slogans are quite sensible. Police agencies have notoriously been integral to political spoils systems; and at least one political scientist, James Q. Wilson, has argued effectively that this has not been all bad.[1] What seems at first blush to be a simple question— Should the police be separated from politics?—turns out to be, in the face of such arguments as Wilson's, a rather complicated matter.

In other than a partisan, political sense, it seems clear that the police have a perfectly legitimate, respectable, and indeed indispensable political role to play. Because of public confusion about politics and the police, discussion of any respectable interpretation of the matter has been almost entirely avoided. This reluctance may be attributed, to some extent, to the use of the police by political regimes to forcefully perpetuate themselves. This tyrannical use of police force has not been unusual in political history, and still happens today in so-called police states. However, it is time to stop thinking of the police and their political relations only in terms of clandestine activity.

Police service is plainly in the realm of public administration, by its nature political. There was a period in the history of this country when there were pretensions about detaching administration from politics, but we seem to be pretty well past this nonsense now. Similarly, there was a time when it was proposed that professionalized police should be divorced from politics, as the slogans proclaimed. This, too, is nonsense.

The best of police chiefs, by any professional criteria, rather frequently lose their jobs through the stratagems of political maneuver. The community "out there" is constituted of citizen taxpayers who vote, attend public hearings, speak their piece, sign petitions, write letters to the editor, and do many other things that kick up political dust. A police agency that pretends to carry on as if all this is not really happening is in for a sad awakening. Therein hangs the message: community relations *is* political policing, in a very good and sound sense in an open society.

There are, to be sure, some important distinctions to be made. The basis of social control is *authority:* the right to command, take action, and make final decisions. As we have said, authority has a moral quality, what some authors refer to as the *mandate,* coming from the community. *Politics* is a process of making authoritative decisions, decisions that command assent. *Power* implies force or coercion: as Banton puts it, *B* does what *A* commands because he is fearful of the consequences of noncompliance. Banton's distinction between police authority and police power applies as well to government (or politics) at large.

The police must, we have stressed, be responsive and accountable to the community. To be so, the police must be able to distinguish between corrupting political pressures and the needs of the larger community. In an era in which private and factional interests are everywhere being presented and pressed in a manner either ignoring the public interest altogether, or gratuitously assuming that private and public interests are coterminous, the distinction is, in fact, often difficult to draw. The International City Management Association deals with the point as follows:

> The complexities of the police function in the environment in which policing occurs place great pressure on the police administrator to maintain a balance between professional competence and responsiveness to legitimate political pressures which are reflective of the needs of the community. The police chief must have a basic commitment to maintaining a position of neutrality when political issues are involved. Within the context of accountability through the political process, the chief must insure that partisan interests are separated from community priorities.[2]

The term *politics* has many definitions. It is not the same as government. John Pfiffner, whose field is public administration, defines it somewhat differently from Michael Banton, whose field is social anthropology. Pfiffner says that politics is the process by which contesting forces vie for favorable outcomes on decisions. Thus, to him, power (politics) and authority (government) are not the same. Nor are *policy* (the product) and politics (the means).

John Norton and Gregory Cowart observe that there is no political way of patrolling a police beat. While this statement may be true in a literal sense, patrol activity, they insist, "embraces political concerns" in many ways. For instance, there is the question of one-person or two-person units. Tied to this question are numerous considerations, all more or less political.[3] We have referred often to the *politics* of discretion in police patrol, for it pertains to the use and control of power, power delegated by the community.

So it is time to forget the taboos against open discussion of politics and the police. To expect the police in democratic society (or any other society, for that matter) to be nonpolitical is like expecting presidents, governors, mayors, and city councils to be nonpolitical. The key question is this: What is and what is not legitimate, functional, publicly beneficial political activity by the police? It was generally conceded, to point to an example, that the late O. W. Wilson accomplished wonders in professionalizing the Chicago Police Department while he was superintendent. But he was appointed to the position by the late mayor, Richard J. Daley. Whatever happened there came about as a result of an obvious harmonizing of the requirements of professional police service and practical politics. The terms and conditions of one system were apparently satisfied within the terms and conditions of another system, not without some conflicts certainly, but Wilson and Daley found a way to "live together." Politics and policing are, in fact, integral.

THE ROLE QUESTION AGAIN

Inescapably, we must return again to the matter of police role. As earlier implied, and as James Q. Wilson emphasizes repeatedly, the role question is, at heart, a *political* question. Police officials count votes, just as Supreme Court justices do. Consensus is a political phenomenon. William Westley, James Sterling, and others tell how police officers size up their reference groups and reach decisions on how to act depending upon how they weigh factors of influence and power in the community. We have quoted the British Royal Commission in its statement regarding the process of seeking and securing middle-ground positions when faced with alternative extremes. As we have suggested, to survive as a police administrator these days, or as any kind of public administrator, requires deft political skills.

Wilson contributes this pertinent comment:

> The American police officer finds himself today on the grinding edge between the need to maintain his authority on the street and the increased community pressures against that authority. A police force may improve greatly because of professionalization, but if at the same time the popular image and authority of the police officer have deteriorated, the two changes may cancel each other out, producing no net gain in police morale and creating a continuing police problem. In order to maintain morale, the officer may have to rely increasingly on police doctrine, a perhaps exag-

gerated conception of the rightness of what he is doing, and a contempt for both the criminal and hypocritical noncriminal elements of the population. Under such pressures, it is not surprising that many police officers have shown themselves amenable to extremist political positions.[4]

In the matter of the police role predicament, Wilson's is mainly a political analysis. In his consideration of three styles of policing (watchman, legalistic, and service), he states that the particular style that prevails in a particular community is not explicitly determined by community decisions, although a few of its aspects may be so determined. In Wilson's language, "the police are in all cases being governed by it."[5] He goes on to say that the police do not distinguish to any great extent among issues that are actually quite different in principle, whether it be a city manager's efforts to reform the department, a council member's efforts to name a new deputy chief, or a civil rights organization's efforts to establish a civilian review board. All such issues are interpreted by police as a struggle by "outside forces" for control of the department, and all officers see them all as "politics."

Wilson's general conclusion is that understanding the political life of a community will not provide an adequate explanation of existing police policies. To a considerable extent, such policies are left to the police themselves. Many segments of the community apparently prefer not to push their own interests unless a crisis develops. There may be public pressure for the police to "do something" about some problem. But *what* to do and *how* to do it is left to the police. Again Wilson comments:

> Police work is carried out under the influence of a *political culture*, though not necessarily under day-to-day political direction . . . with respect to police work—or at least its patrol functions—the prevailing political culture creates a "zone of indifference" within which the police are free to act as they see fit.
>
> The most important way in which political culture affects police behavior is through the choice of police administrator and the molding of the expectations that govern his role.[6]

In sum, Wilson's position is that the community ("political culture") influences law enforcement in a broad sense, but this influence is ordinarily indirect and indecisive. Many people feel that any kind of an alliance with the police spells trouble. The vast majority of citizens prefer to "keep their distance" from the police. They seem content to leave policing to the police. An officer signals trouble, to be avoided if possible. Thus, serious efforts to ally police and community more closely require ambitious public, *political* education as an integral part of problem-solving projects.

Edward Banfield and James Q. Wilson pointed to another basic aspect of the politics-police integration. The police play a subtle role in preserving and protecting a particular life-style or environment in a community.[7] Law is, after all, a reflection of societal values; and so, too, is what is defined by law as crime. Law making is a fundamental political process; so, too, is law enforcement. Eugene Czajkoski has stated the point in this way:

> Looking over the multifarious aspects of criminological interest, it is easy to perceive subjects well beyond the reach of quantitative and allegedly valueless investigations.

The very concept of "justice" is a humanistic value . . . the radical criminologists and the critical criminologists, oftentimes referring to principles higher than those articulated in the criminal law, are applying an ideological tool in order to disagree. Challenges of substantive laws, different views as to the seriousness of crimes and demurrers on the appropriateness of punishment are all within the scope of value operation.[8]

Obviously, Czajkoski is speaking about the "stuff" of politics in a pluralistic democracy, in effect, the value clashes bearing on criminal justice processes. Not only is policing politically saturated, but so are all other parts of the multiple systems in which the police are positioned. In chapters 14 and 15, we touched on some of the political factors that prominently grace current issues in adjudication and corrections. Norval Morris and Gordon Hawkins have developed a comprehensive plan that they guarantee would reduce crime substantially.[9] They assert that it is not lack of knowledge but rather a failure of *political* responsibility that supports our "luxuriant" crime rates. Hence, their program "is directed to the politicians and to the concerned citizens who are responsible for them." The main features of their program are:

1. Decriminalization of such "crimes" as public drunkenness, possession of any drug, gambling, disorderly conduct and vagrancy, abortion, and sexual behavior between consenting adults.

2. The professionalization of the police, along lines Morris and Hawkins prescribe in detail.

3. Overhaul of the entire corrections system, including abolition of the money bail system, community-based treatment of offenders in the vast majority of cases, reduction of the size and number of prisons, creation of integrated state jail systems, and greater use of probation and parole.

4. Elimination of juvenile status offenses.

5. More adequate psychiatric and psychological treatment of offenders.

FORMS OF POLITICAL POLICING

Even to use the term "political policing" turns many people off. They tend to see politics in a negative way and have trouble acknowledging that there may be such a thing as good and necessary politics in police service, as well as in other activities at city hall. Are there corruptive and highly undesirable aspects or forms of political policing? Surely there are. Back in 1931, members of the Wickersham Commission must have had this in mind when they spoke of "taking the police out of politics." They were concerned about graft and complicity of the police with political corruption. They were concerned about the police as crooks and captives of political hoodlums. They were concerned about the police perceived by the public as hapless, or at best amusing, symbols of political debauchery.

Another negative or undesirable form of political policing occurs when local mores are enshrined in ordinances or statutes that run counter to the law as interpreted at a higher level. The police then enforce the ordinance or statute "no matter what the Supreme Court says," and the local courts go along. Years ago, in the matter of racial segregation, this was referred to as "interposition." It involves a type of political policing that poses difficult choices for the police, as "rock-and-a-hard-place" value conflicts always do.

Still another form of political policing, rapidly gaining momentum, is that represented by police unionization. From the 1919 Boston police strike to the recent past, police fraternal organizations functioned in part as unions, while resisting every move to call them that. During this period, the idea of collective bargaining rights for police officers was strongly rejected by the public. This attitude has changed, and the political "clout" of police line organizations is observable today in well-planned and well-financed lobbying, so-called "job actions"—because the strike is still anathema in public opinion—and various other activities associated with what has come to be called *blue power*. [10]

Then there is what we may label the administrative form of political policing, with the administrator playing the essential role of "stumping" for desired organizational goals. This includes good relationships with decision makers in government: mayors, city managers, city councils, and the like. It also includes influencing public opinion so that important gains can be made in the quality of police work. We called this *community leadership* in an earlier discussion. Obviously, there is nothing wrong with this type of political policing: it is the very essence of public administration.

Our discussion will benefit from further probing of the administrative and unionization forms of political policing.

ADMINISTRATIVE POLITICKING

A good example of the administrative style of political policing is described in chapter 2 of the *Task Force Report: The Police* of the 1966 President's Crime Commission. The commission pointed to the increasing need for a deliberative planning process for developing policies to guide and control police officers in dealing with the wide variety of situations that require the exercise of some form of police authority. The commission observed, however, that police administrators have been generally reluctant to develop policies for dealing with crime and potential crime situations. Several reasons for this were suggested, all with political implications. [11]

The commission emphatically recommended that the police must assume a larger role in the development of law enforcement policies:

> The "administrative process" and administrative flexibility, expertise, and, most important, administrative responsibility are as necessary and as appropriate with respect to the regulation of deviant social behavior as they are with respect to other governmental regulatory activity. This seems perfectly obvious. Yet the common assumption has been that the police task is ministerial, this perhaps reflecting an assumption that administrative flexibility and "the rule of law" are inconsistent. This assumption seems invalid. The exercise of administrative discretion with appropriate legislative guidance and subject to appropriate review and control is likely to be more protective of basic rights than the routine, uncritical application by police of rules of law which are often necessarily vague or overgeneralized in their language. [12]

Mature participation of police as a responsible administrative agency—along with prosecutors, legislatures, and courts—in the development and execution

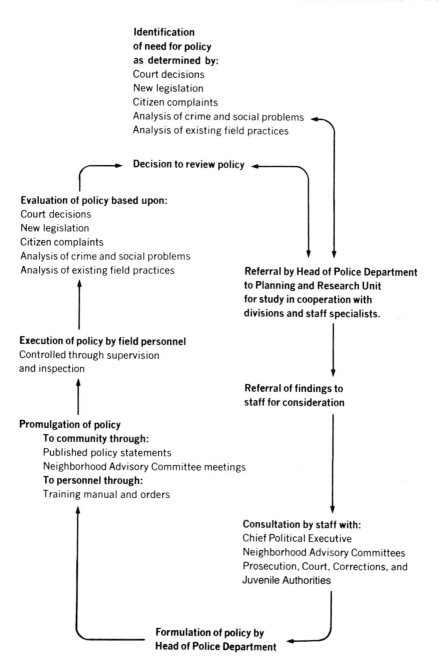

**Identification
of need for policy
as determined by:**
Court decisions
New legislation
Citizen complaints
Analysis of crime and social problems
Analysis of existing field practices

Decision to review policy

Evaluation of policy based upon:
Court decisions
New legislation
Citizen complaints
Analysis of crime and social problems
Analysis of existing field practices

**Referral by Head of Police Department
to Planning and Research Unit
for study in cooperation with
divisions and staff specialists.**

Execution of policy by field personnel
Controlled through supervision
and inspection

**Referral of findings to
staff for consideration**

Promulgation of policy
　To community through:
　Published policy statements
　Neighborhood Advisory Committee meetings
　To personnel through:
　Training manual and orders

Consultation by staff with:
Chief Political Executive
Neighborhood Advisory Committees
Prosecution, Court, Corrections, and
Juvenile Authorities

**Formulation of policy by
Head of Police Department**

FIGURE 17-1. Formulation and execution of police policy.

of enforcement policies is clearly political policing of a largely unprecedented nature. Few police executives would call this recommendation ill-advised, inappropriate, or untimely. Policy development is a complex responsibility requiring fresh insights, police leadership, personnel, training, and organization, as pointed out by the commission in charts such as that shown in figure 17-1.[13]

In discussing police organizational objectives, the 1973 National Advisory Commission on Criminal Justice Standards and Goals advocated politically sensitive administrative principles:

> All goals and objectives, agencywide and unit, should be directly responsive to community needs. Normally, if problem definition and analysis have been adequate and alternative solutions carefully screened, responsiveness to community needs can be achieved. . . . Obtaining input from within the agency requires an atmosphere that encourages all employees, regardless of rank, to submit ideas.[14]

The Political Issue: Power

Government, the function of political institutions, is the exercise of power. The police are regarded by the community as an instrument of this power. The problem of police and community relations, simply stated, is that some people are dissatisfied with the manner in which the police use power. This defines the problem in political terms, but we should be mindful that there are also sociological, psychological, and other complementary definitions of the problem. The prevalent tension, however, pertains to *what* the police do with their delegated power, and *how* they do it. As various observers have said, the means required to achieve police goals may conflict with conduct prescribed for the police as legal actors. Some argue for more power and freedom for the police to operate, in a loose construction of the law, as we have seen. Others argue for more control and restriction to compel the police to function under a strict construction of the law.

The practical political situation is the aim of various individuals and factions to control the police by standards favorable to the interests of a few, conflicting with a more general interest. This is the heart of politicking. The outcomes of political process make it inevitable that police policies and procedures will be, in some degree, obstructive to what some individuals and groups in the community regard as their best interest. So it is with every public policy decision in democratic society.

Speaking on the topic "Police Education and Training" at a symposium at Tufts University on the subject of Law and Disorder, Professor Robert Sheehan of Northeastern University's Law Enforcement faculty said:

> There has . . . been a traditional political resistance to educating the police. The root of this resistance lies deeply imbedded in what seems to me to be a prevailing, but rarely stated, political attitude that if the police are encouraged to become professional, and thus are made more effective, they will become a much less controllable arm of the executive branch of government and hence less amenable to the interests of political influence that almost always lead to partial rather than impartial enforcement of the law.[15]

The essential *political* issue, then, in the relations of the police and the policed in a democratic society is the balance of power and restraint. As Frank Remington has remarked, this issue is particularly difficult for governmental agencies such as the police, who find themselves caught between those who desire change and those who resist change.[16] Elaborating on the legitimacy of the police administrative-political role, Elmer H. Johnson asserts that police professionalization has been impeded by the conferring of appointments as political reward, by the consequent uncertainty of job tenure, by the undermining of personnel standards, by the preservation of the myth that specialized competence is not necessary for law enforcement, and by the erosion of ethics. However, Johnson points out that these consequences of partisan politics do not justify the belief that a police agency can ignore the importance of developing and maintaining relationships with the political structure of which it is part:

> As a public administrator, the police executive must be skillful in maintaining relationships within the community power structure whereby the resource needs of his agency are made known to decision-makers, resource allocations obtained, and police problems communicated in a style conducive to obtaining community support. In terms of this responsible version of political skill, the limitation of law enforcement to "real" crime will have little effect toward reducing the difficulties encountered by the executive.[17]

This view of the legitimate political role of the police administrator is consistent with Johnson's emphasis upon the interrelatedness of police work and the activities of other social institutions in the community, including political institutions, that we discussed in chapter 14. One implication of such a view of police-political relations is the recognition that the possibility of change, of reform in policing and in the criminal justice system, is basically a *political* question.

In plain language, effective police (or public) administration depends on winning support for needed resources and needed changes. It depends on vote-getting in legislative bodies. It depends on selling one's program, often in competition for scarce dollars with other agencies of government. There is nothing mysterious or clandestine or reprehensible about this, and there is no reason for police officials to be apologetic or embarrassed about it. To be defensive tends to perpetuate ugly connotations of political policing of a type that cannot and should not be defended. Indeed, one of the strongest arguments that can be mounted for an effective police public relations program, in very practical terms, is exactly what we have been suggesting: the police are an integral *part of* the community, not a discrete entity. In the political sense, therefore, the police "must have the votes" in order to accomplish their mission, the very nature of which is a political determination. In a sense, to advocate "taking the police out of politics" is similar to advocating that civil disobedience should be declared illegal.

Several undercurrents in this discussion may be detected. One is Banton's distinction between police power and police authority. Chester I. Barnard drew the same distinction when he said that "authority becomes viable only through the acceptance of those exposed to it." Another point is equally basic: empirically, politics and administration are inseparable. It is also true that politics and power go together, especially if we adopt the definition of politics that was given earlier in this chapter. Floyd Hunter referred to power as a necessary function of society and defined it as the actions of some men going about the business of moving other men to act in relation to themselves or in relation to organic or inorganic things. Power centers on decision making, said Hunter, and on seeing to it that necessary things—"power functions" delegated to specific persons—get done.[18]

One of the most interesting events to observe, in point of politics and the police, is what happens when there is a change in the position of chief executive of a sizable department. Should a big city promote a new chief from within or open the competition to candidates from around the country? Such a question is a political acme. Part of the debate centers on whether civil service, initially intended to separate the police from politics, has really been such a good thing after all. Opinion is sharply divided.[19]

Another example of high-level police political skirmishing pertains to the apparently widening split between police administrators associated with the Police Executive Research Forum and the International Association of Chiefs of Police (IACP). Members of the Forum are also members of IACP. The Forum charges that IACP is dominated by chiefs of very small police agencies. IACP has denied the charge. The real issues at stake in this choosing up of sides, with political power as a necessary means, pertain to fundamental questions in law enforcement and criminal justice.[20]

The Classical Theory of Police Organization

One such fundamental question is how best to organize a municipal police department. John Angell is interested in the translation of theories of power, politics, and public administration to police organizations. He observes that the structures of most modern American police organizations are rationalized, hierarchical arrangements that reflect the influence of classical organizational theory as delineated by Max Weber.[21] The salient features of these structures, Angell says, are:

1. Formal structures are defined by a centralized hierarchy of authority.
2. Labor is divided into functional specialties.
3. Activities are conducted according to standardized operating procedures.
4. Career routes are well established and have a common entry point; promotions are based on impersonal evaluations by superiors.
5. Management is conducted through a monocratic system of routinized superior-subordinate relationships.
6. Employee status is directly related to their positions (jobs) and ranks.[22]

Angell believes that these characteristics result in a firmly established, impersonal system in which most of the employees and clients are *powerless* to initiate changes or to arrest the system's motions. He raises serious questions on the adequacy of this bureaucratic model in the modern police agency. It creates problems, he contends, in police and community relations, in employee morale, and in communication and control—all documented by the 1966 President's Crime Commission. The concern of police administrators for efficiency and economy (a basic goal of classical organization theory) has caused some lack of concern for side effects detrimental to community relations. Moreover, Angell feels that classical organization concepts do not facilitate adequate flexibility in policy—with which, for instance, to meet legitimate needs and values of particular subcultures or groups. Angell has another criticism:

Classical theory also supports police reformers who insist that police departments be isolated from politics. As police departments become more refined and move nearer their goal, they move further away from another basic goal of democracy— guaranteeing every citizen access to and influence with governmental agencies. Under a highly developed police bureaucracy, nearly all citizens view their police department as essentially beyond their understanding and control. Where the police department is a highly-developed, traditional bureaucracy, its structure and its philosophical underpinnings will eventually cause the organization to become socially irrelevant and ineffective. This situation, in turn, will have a profoundly damaging effect upon police and community relations.[23]

Thus, Angell traces citizen reluctance to get involved with the police to the mystique of classical organization structure. Further, Angell argues that such structuring tends to support a perpetual state of low morale among employees of bureaucracies. Weber himself condemned this aspect of bureaucracy. Angell points to increased police activism and the police unionization movement as indicative of this problem. He predicts that these are trends toward employee engagement in decision-making processes that are unlikely to cease.

Another Angell argument against classical bureaucracy is its long-recognized problem of internal communication and control. The chief administrator seldom gets a true picture of what is going on in the department. The assumption that formal authority to command can force compliance from subordinates is everywhere being questioned today. As Chester Barnard put it, "Authority rests with subordinates rather than with the supervisor."[24]

The Environing System

Albert Reiss and David Bordua discuss the "environing system" of the metropolitan police. They say that the central meaning of police authority itself is its ability to manage relationships. This is their description of police-community interaction in pragmatic, political terms:

> Directing traffic, investigating complaints, interrogation, arresting suspects, controlling mobs and crowds, urging prosecutors to press to drop charges, testifying in court, participating with (or battling, as the case may be) probation officers in juvenile court, presenting budget requests to the city council, pressing a case with the civil service commission, negotiating with civil rights groups, defense attorneys, reporters, irate citizens, business groups, other city services, and other police systems—even such an incomplete list indicates the probable values of a perspective that emphasizes transactions and external relationships. The list also indicates something else of considerable significance. All of these transactions can be and often are antagonistic ones.[25]

Reiss and Bordua further reflect that modern metropolitan police agencies exist only because communities are legally organized. In effect, the police are called upon to *mediate* between the urban community and the legal system. This describes rather starkly the police-government linkage. Some of the questions that we have discussed in earlier chapters have their foundation in this linkage: for example, the position of the police in the legal order, that is, their relation to prosecutors and the courts; police administrative strategies for manipulating the image of crime in the community and measurements of police "success"; and problems of internal relations and morale in police agencies brought about by either or both of the factors just mentioned.

Reiss and Bordua end their analysis with a consideration of civil accountability, command, and control in police organizations, in a manner paralleling Angell's approach. They refer to police literature stressing command as the basis of control. In Weberian terms, the police department "as an order" is legitimated by the principle of command, with a correlative attitude required by those subject to it. Commitment to obedience, in this sense, is a sign of membership. The classical status reward is honor. Joining these segments of classical administrative theory, Reiss and Bordua emerge with this synthesis:

> In the case of the American municipality, police chiefs . . . are politically accountable officials who ordinarily stand or fall with the fortunes of their civilian superiors. . . . Given the often controversial nature of police work and the often irrational and unpredictable nature of political fortunes in municipal government, the American police chief who is responsible to a politically elected official comes close to the position of a "patrimonial bureaucrat," in Weber's terms. His tenure as chief, though not necessarily his tenure in the department, depends on continuing acceptability to the elected official(s). . . .
>
> Given strict accountability plus insecurity of tenure, we can expect a kind of obsession with command and a seemingly irrational emphasis on the twinned symbols of the visibility of the commander and the obedience of the force. Some of the rhetoric of command in the police literature likely arises from an attempt to protect the chief by the compulsive effort to overcontrol subordinates, almost any of whom can get him fired. This amounts to saying that as civil superiors increase the formal accountability of the police chief *without changing* the tenure features of the role, the increasing bureaucratization of the police stressed by J. Q. Wilson leads to the development of an organization animated by a principle of the commanding person. This "personalized subordination" to the hero chief can become an operating, if not a formal, principle of organization.[26]

Reiss and Bordua add that increased professionalization can be an accommodation to such a situation, aimed not at control of the force but at control of the mayor by changing the grounds of accountability. Perhaps it is difficult, they conclude, to have a professionalized police force without having a professionalized mayor.

RELATIONS BETWEEN POLICE AND LOCAL GOVERNMENT

The Reiss-directed University of Michigan study for the 1966 President's Crime Commission considered the police and their relations with local government and its legal system.[27] Police officers in the cities studied were asked about their views of the efforts of local government to deal with crime. Most officers did not believe that their local government had done much, although Chicago officers were far more supportive of the job that local government had done to deal with crime than were officers in Boston and Washington, D.C. Forty percent of the officers believed that local government had made it harder for the police to do their work. However, only 20 percent in Chicago believed this, while 50 percent of the officers in Washington, D.C., and 30 percent of those in Boston believed it. The police officers complained that local government interfered with police powers and that officials were too critical of the police department.

It should be noted that state legislatures across the country have assumed a new look in recent years from several standpoints. Reapportionment has ended the domination of rural areas and tipped the balance of power in favor of suburbia. Staff and technical assistance has been expanded; legislative salaries and facilities have been improved. The assemblies meet more often, and for longer sessions, handling far more bills. The proportion of women in their membership has been doubled, and the proportion of blacks has been tripled. The occupational makeup of the typical state legislature is much more diversified, with fewer farmers and lawyers and more businessmen, teachers, and even students. The trend is toward younger lawmakers. There is some indication that traditional business and industrial lobbies have lost some of their clout, and broad-based interest groups have begun to rival them. These trends obviously have important political implications, which prudent police administrators are well advised to study.

The Hatch Act has severely limited the political activities of federal government employees, and it has been copied at the state and local levels and applied to police officers, along with other governmental employees. But in recent years the blue power movement has challenged such restrictions on police political activity.[28] The history of the restrictions goes back many years, embedded in civil service reforms aimed at flagrant abuses arising from political patronage. The Hatch Act was a 1939 chapter in this history. Its coverage was expanded in 1940. Strict rules grew out of major scandals of the past. But by 1966, the appointment by Congress of a Commission on Political Activity of Government Personnel was a tipoff that the pendulum had begun to swing. Yet most police departments today still retain many restrictions on political activity by police officers. While some such restrictions are clearly necessary, relaxation of overly rigid rules seems in order, in light of changing social conditions. There is no reason police officers should be emasculated citizens.[29]

BLUE POWER

Our attention now turns to political policing as represented by police line organizations, what has come to be called blue power. The politicization of the police, in this sense, is a phenomenon of increasing importance; and in some respects we would say that it is as legitimate, as inevitable, and probably as desirable in the long run as the administrative politicization discussed above. It is epitomized in the police unionization movement that has grown out of fraternalism.

Do police officers have the right to organize for the purpose of collective bargaining? Is this desirable? On the face of it, the answer to these questions today would have to be affirmative. Jerome Skolnick writes that the American police officer is overworked, undertrained, underpaid, and undereducated.[30] Moreover, Skolnick continues, officers' jobs are increasingly difficult, forcing them into the almost impossible position of repressing the demands of various groups for social and political change. In this role, they are unappreciated and, at times, despised. Their difficulties are compounded by a view of social protest that gives little consideration to the effects of such factors as poverty and discrimination, and all but ignores the possibility of legitimate social discontent. This view invariably attributes mass protest to a conspiracy of some sort, promulgated by agitators, often called Communists, who mislead otherwise contented people. To the extent that this view exists among the police, it leaves them ill-prepared to understand or to deal with dissident groups.

Consequently, Skolnick avers, many police officers have been frustrated, alienated, and angry. They have turned to militancy and political activism. They have protested via slowdowns and other such actions ("blue flu"), often of questionable legality, directed toward material benefits, or changes in governmental policy ("take the handcuffs off the police"), or changes in internal organizational procedures. Direct police challenges to departmental and civic authority have followed recent urban disorders, and criticisms of the judiciary have escalated to "court-watching" by the police. What were once strictly or largely police fraternal associations have become more and more potent political organizations, more and more in the character of unions, more and more vociferous toward police management and municipal management on questions of power and control.

In short, the police have emerged as a self-conscious, independent, political force. In many cities and states, the police lobby has become quite influential. Yet the courts and the police are still expected to be politically "neutral," lest public confidence in the legal system be impaired. The result is that a kind of masquerade goes on, with police unions not overly anxious for the public to know much about their political activities or influence. Police fraternal organizations remain resistant to being called unions, and a strike is referred to as a "job action" or "blue flu." In terms of community relations and public attitudes, police unions tend to come across as surreptitious, and the view of them that is often reflected by police administrators, understandably, does little to improve the union image.

There have been instances in recent years, in more than one place, where blue power has been coupled in the public mind with police violence in handling mass protest. References to a "police state" have appeared, as exemplified by the following tract by W. H. Ferry:

> It is instructive to note the extent to which this power already is beyond the control of elected officials. This power appears more and more to reside in the police trade unions—the police benevolent and fraternal organizations. These unions are increasingly dictating to mayors and police commissioners what the police will and will not do: the weapons they will use, the circumstances under which they will use them, the methods to be employed with suspects or crowds. In many cities, the police are already in a state of near revolt against their elected superiors, and this mood is encouraged by the police unions. It need scarcely be said that these unions are conservative and self-interested. These organizations naturally favor strongarm over non-violent methods, direct action against conciliation, station-house confessions to the laborious job of proving criminal acts, the judgment of the man on the beat over the judgment of his civilian superiors. . . . I hazard the opinion that these unions will prove the most intractable and dangerous to the general welfare of any in the nation's history.[31]

Ferry is not generally anti-union in his sociopolitical views. But he takes a strong position against police unions, some may say too strong. His is by no means a lone voice expressing concern, not so much about police unions per se as about manifestations of police power that provoke the ugly epithet "police state." As another example, Edgar Z. Friedenberg wrote:

> The law enforcement process is thought of as democratic, as more democratic than the law itself, since the courts are dominated by smooth-tongued lawyers, while the police represent—and indeed, act out—the anxieties and sentiments of the populace as well as, and often rather than, the commands of the law. Where the two are in conflict, the police remind individuals that they have overstepped the social norms. The victims may win on appeal, but it takes a decade and costs a fortune. Police action, rather than conviction in court, is the real sanction.
>
> To criticize law enforcement as a social function, rather than to direct one's complaints to specific abuses, is therefore to challenge the democratic process itself. The socially acceptable response, instead, is to say that the law should be changed, but the police must be obeyed till it is. In practice, even this is more than an angry and hostile community will often tolerate.[32]

In the same vein is the view of Ed Cray, who has been associated for some years with the American Civil Liberties Union in Southern California:

> From city to city, the authority of elected officials varies inversely with the control maintained by ranking police officers. . . . In the face of threats, real and imaginary, the police have openly girded themselves with a newfound armor—political influence, supported by public fear of rising crime rates and ghetto rebellion. . . . Law enforcement is testing its political muscle, emboldened by the easily sensed mood of a public demanding domestic tranquility at any price. The police claim they can provide instant peace of mind—the slogan is "law and order" and until their campaign collapses in futility, they will muster ever greater support. And with that support, the police will push even harder for complete control of law enforcement.[33]

Many police react to such statements heatedly, accusing the authors of sharp-tongued extremism. A more balanced perspective may be obtained by recalling what retired New York City Police Inspector William P. Brown has said about the pressures that have moved the police toward "their own councils," which we cited in an earlier chapter. In the same article, Brown wrote:

> The police administrator . . . must ask the more difficult questions of how one deals with political realities, how one controls the police themselves in trying to effectuate a humane and yet practical policy of enforcement in such delicate areas as those involving race relations.[34]

While he was on leave several years ago from his position as an Indiana University associate professor of police administration, serving as commissioner of public safety in Utica, New York, Hillard Trubitt analyzed the situation in a somewhat broader context. The police in a community, he said, are usually mirrors of the entire local government approach to city problems. It is true, he continued, that the police traditionally rely on old, established methodology and doctrine not geared to contemporary problems. But generally the police are no worse in this regard, and sometimes they are much better, than "their parent governmental entities" in their failure "to perceive the difference between form and substance." Trubitt maintained that the essential problem is an overregard for procedural regularity and not enough regard for the primary objectives. As he put it, "the goal of police service is peace and order, not bureaucratic game playing."[35]

The politics of police line organizations is not confined to the Fraternal Order of Police, the Policemen's Benevolent Association, and the like. Racial and ethnic police organizations, such as the Guardians Society and other black police officers' groups, are concerned with using the dynamics of power in police agencies to protect the interests of their members. It is hardly news that political and social polarization on racial or ethnic grounds exists *within* big-city police forces. As a matter of fact, some think that, as the numbers of black and other minority police grow, internal tensions within urban police agencies will be exacerbated. While it is difficult to imagine that in the near future organizations such as the Guardians will gain sufficient membership to become bargaining agents, unquestionably their political influence has definitely been felt in many big-city departments. The National Council of Police Societies was formed in 1971 as a central coordinating and communicating forum for local and state black police officers' groups.[36]

This minority clustering within the police world evidences the same political savoir faire observable in the Black Caucus formed in the House of Representatives during the 92nd Congress. A few years ago, such a development would have been unthinkable. *Washington Post* reporter William Raspberry commented that this Black Caucus represented something truly special and unprecedented in the realm of national politics. It was, he said, a recognition that black people face some rather special problems, for which they should have special interest representation. At the same time, however, it was also a recognition that to work for the best interests of black people does not necessitate working *against* the best interests of white people. The congressional Black Caucus and the black mayors of large cities require political coalitions with white to build the consensus that makes social problem solving possible. Chicano political and social action organizations have also multiplied rapidly in recent years. Indeed, as we observed in chapter 10, charges of police brutality from Spanish-speaking Americans seem to be multiplying, as the United States Commission on Civil Rights has pointed out.

POLICE CONSERVATISM

As with all political issues, there are liberal and conservative views of the issues in law enforcement and criminal justice. We have earlier referred to the clear dominance of the conservative position, within the ranks of police and corrections. Political analysts find nothing surprising about this. The critics, however, tend—with occasional exceptions—to be of more liberal political persuasion, again not surprisingly. Reform comes slowly and grudgingly, in part because conservatives are most often in control of the political decision-making apparatus, and they require a lot of convincing! As we say, "This is the way it is," and there is much to be said for playing it conservatively where the politics of crime and criminals is concerned.

While conservatism is deeply ingrained in the values of the police occupational subculture, it is important to recognize that the social and political views of officers vary considerably. There are shades of liberalism as well as shades of conservatism on every issue that affects police work. Arguments among officers are sharp and constant. Will more higher education affect this situation in the future? There is little evidence that it has made much difference to date. But there are more basic questions being asked today regarding higher education for police officers. One is well advised to take a conservative stance in speculating about the future.

On social and political issues, Nelson Watson and James Sterling found that the police do tend somewhat toward a conservative position, but it is by no means as consistent, or as extreme, as some observers have suggested. Seymour Lipset also makes this point:

> In evaluating the disposition of the police to participate in the radical right, it is important to note that only a minority of the police are involved in most communities. Most police, though relatively conservative and conventional, are normally more concerned with the politics of collective bargaining, with getting more for themselves, than with the politics of right-wing extremism.[37]

POLICE UNIONS

The movement of the police to form unions has been part of the broader surge of unionization among municipal employees. Police unions existed prior to 1960, but recent years have witnessed their unprecedented growth, coupled with increased legal recognition of their right to exist and to bargain collectively. Hugh O'Neill of Columbia University writes:

> One of the most important developments on the urban political scene over the last decade has been the rapidly increasing strength and militancy of municipal employee unions. These organizations have become new centers of power in the cities. They have used their power to influence not only the terms and conditions of employment, but major policy decisions as well. And with increasing frequency they have demonstrated the effectiveness of their "ultimate weapon," the disruption of vital municipal services.[38]

Historically, the American Federation of Labor was not eager to organize police unions because the police were considered enemies of organized labor. The AFL changed this policy in 1919, probably influenced by the success of British police unions. The Boston police strike occurred in September 1919, and was broken by Massachusetts Governor Calvin Coolidge and the troops he summoned. This action wiped out police unionism for a time. A period of several decades followed when police organization assumed the form of benevolent and social societies, but even these were prohibited in some places.

With the Franklin D. Roosevelt era, the American Federation of State, County, and Municipal Employees (AFSCME) came into being. Police unionism still remained dormant, however, until the 1940s. By 1944, the AFSCME reported that locals made up entirely of police had been organized in twenty-eight cities. By 1946, this had become forty-nine locals, but still represented only a minor number of police departments. In the 1950s, public-employee unions, plagued by the Communist bugaboo, experienced some growing pains, but the 1960s brought a great surge in such unionization.

Late in the sixties, an AFL-CIO committee recommended that a national police union be chartered. In November 1969, representatives of police organizations from twelve cities met in Omaha and drafted a constitution for the International Brotherhood of Police Officers. This constitution contained a no-strike clause, but one official of the new group remarked, "A job action is not a strike."[39]

The AFL-CIO Executive Council was in no hurry to decide whether to charter the new union. The president of the National Fraternal Order of Police, which does not see itself as a union although it negotiates contracts, declared that police officers should not be permitted to join a union. President George Meany of the AFL-CIO announced that the labor federation would not issue a charter for a police union unless there was widespread national interest. But the Omaha-drafted constitution of the fledgling organization was, nonetheless, approved by seventy-five delegates attending a May 1970 convention in Washington. Still another organization, the International Conference of Police Associations, met in St. Louis in December 1970, with leaders of 135 local police associations attending. In addition, rumors that the Teamsters had decided to enter the police unionization field proved to be well founded, and the Teamsters have in fact done so. Indeed, the field today is rather chaotic, with rival unions competing with each other and little progress being made in efforts to organize statewide or form national coalitions based on minimal cooperation.

Public employee unions have become more aggressive in recent years. Teachers, for example, have been in the headlines constantly. With teachers, the issue is no longer the right to organize or to bargain collectively. The issue is the right to strike. A few years ago, this question was not seriously considered. Today, there are signs that in some states a limited right to strike has been conceded to teachers, and the goal now is legislation to control the duration and conditions of strikes (deadlines for negotiation, binding arbitration, and the like). This concession seems to have followed the recognition that teachers do strike under some circumstances, in spite of laws prohibiting it. So why not settle for laws that aim to regulate it? Leaving the matter to the courts has not worked out very well, because of conflicting judicial decisions. At the federal level, congressional committees have been hearing arguments and counterarguments, from teacher and public-employee lobbyists and from such organizations as Americans Against Union Control of Government, focusing on proposals to guarantee the right to collective bargaining for all teachers and other public employees.

What has been happening with teachers is also indicative of the situation with other public employees. In one city, the sanitation people take the initiative; in another city, the fire fighters are the vanguard. So-called job actions are commonplace. Prison or jail personnel, nurses at hospitals and mental institutions, office clerical workers, parks and welfare employees, doctors staffing public hospitals, and, of course, police officers—walkouts by all of these and others are regularly featured in the news, with wages the predominant issue. The six-day New York City police strike of January 1971 was a particularly dramatic case in point, with fire fighters and sanitation workers poised to join hands with the police wildcatters. O'Neil points out one of the sources of this militancy:

The final source of aggressiveness among municipal unions that might be mentioned is the generally militant attitude that in the 1960's seemed to be part of the national character. When acts of civil disobedience become everyday occurrences, the fact that public employee strikes are illegal is not enough to prevent them. When society as a whole becomes politicized, public employees become willing to take advantage of their monopoly in the provision of vital public services to achieve political ends that appear to them every bit as vital. This development has added a new and difficult dimension to the business of governing cities.[40]

Inflation and job security considerations are important elements in most labor disputes involving public employees. Job security is especially important to teachers, because many school boards are trying to tighten budgets by reducing personnel. In addition, the fiscal predicaments of many metropolises are highlighted by the public-employee bargaining crises. New York City has provided the premier example, but the same problems are well known in other cities. The Citizens Budget Commission of New York City reported that the rate of increase of city workers' total pay, pensions, and other benefits has averaged 10½ percent a year over the past ten years. But the sanitation workers said that this statistic merely revealed how little they were being paid a decade ago!

The crux of the matter is that the potential tax income of central cities has been decreasing for years, for well-known reasons. However, the need for public services, such as hospitals, welfare, fire fighting, and police, has substantially increased in the inner city, and so has the cost of such services. Economic recession and inflation, of course, aggravate the situation. Proposition 13 in California, and its counterparts elsewhere, do not promise better days ahead, fiscally speaking, for public services of any kind. Every politician, liberal or conservative, has joined the chorus of voices calling for lower taxes and less government spending. The implications do not augur well for labor-management negotiations in police organizations in the days ahead.

The dilemma that government units face with regard to public-employee unionization is how to recognize the right to organize and bargain without recognizing the right to strike. The Department of Labor reported that, in the decade between 1964 and 1974, the number of public employees belonging to unions doubled, at all levels of government. Antistrike laws and penalties do not seem to work. Professor Jack Stieber of Michigan State University believes that public services should be classified three ways: (1) services most essential to public safety—police, fire, corrections; (2) services that can be interrupted for a limited period but not indefinitely—sanitation, public utilities, and schools; and (3) services that can sustain work stoppages indefinitely—parks, road maintenance, and municipal offices. Stieber looks to compulsory, binding arbitration as the ultimate recourse in the first category, to court injunctions in the second category, and to bargaining until settlement in the third category.[41] Irwin Ross has also outlined some basic requirements for a solution to the problem:

No legislation and no impasse-breaking mechanism will prevent *all* strikes. But a realistic plan that allows the right to strike under circumstances where the community can afford it, and provides a viable alternative where strikes must be prohibited, would seem to come closest to squaring the interests of public servants with the rights of the public that they serve.[42]

In recent police strikes, both actual and threatened, wages and fringe benefits have been the standard issues. This was true of the 1975 disputes in New York City, Albuquerque, and San Francisco. However, some disputes have involved other interesting issues as well. In Detroit, for instance, there was the matter of which officers would be laid off because of the financial squeeze: white, male officers with seniority, or black or women officers hired more recently under an affirmative action program. A rather complicated compromise agreement was worked out, encouraged by a federal district court ruling favorable to those hired under affirmative action. The NAACP and the AFL-CIO were on opposite sides of this question. Incidentally, it was not helpful to the police-union cause in Detroit to have inebriated police demonstrators involved in scuffles, or in San Francisco to have police strikers who violated court orders and walked picket lines armed with revolvers—only to receive total amnesty in the end.

In Detroit, another hotly debated question was whether police officers should be required to reside inside the city limits. This issue pitted the basic personal rights and attitudes of individual officers against police effectiveness and community relations, and raised the larger issue of white flight to the suburbs and its implications for the city's future. The dispute was referred to arbitration panels under a crossfire of pro and con opinion from the Detroit Police Officers Association (DPOA, who felt that officers should be able to live wherever they wished), Mayor Coleman Young, the Guardians Society, and the city council. An existing ordinance prohibited city employees from living beyond city limits, but an earlier ruling of the Michigan Supreme Court had made the question subject to contract negotiations, and the DPOA contract was due to expire in June 1976. One observer put the matter this way: "It will take very persuasive evidence for the panel to change the residency rule, and [the evidence] just ain't all that persuasive."[43] In September 1975, the arbitration panel found in favor of the existing ordinance barring out-of-city residency. Binding arbitration is the last step in grievance procedure in the vast majority of police labor contracts today. The open shop is a rarity.

The question of police officer affiliation with national unions is sticky, in part because of national security considerations. The courts have tended to support legislative efforts to circumscribe police unionization.[44] In the matter of the strike, this is particularly clear. And in some states, even the right to collective bargaining has not been recognized. While the U.S. Bureau of the Census reported that, in 1976, roughly 55 percent of people working for local and county police departments belonged to some kind of union or association (52 percent of state police employees), the police union movement remains basically conservative. One reason for this is the absence of a unified organization, although several national labor unions have police affiliates.[45] One of these, to whom more and more police seem to be turning because of its acknowledged economic and political clout, is the International Brotherhood of Teamsters.

Teamster officials claim that they bargain on behalf of 15,000 police officers in about 225 municipalities, most of them suburban and rural.[46] In some places, just the threat of "bringing in the Teamsters" has won significant gains for embattled officers. Michigan is the Teamsters' home state; they will accept workers as members from almost any field. In fact, it is charged by Teamster opponents that their real aim is to organize all public employees. In a January 1977 decision, the Virginia Supreme Court ruled all public employee unions invalid.[47] It should be noted that prison guards and other security personnel have also gravitated to the Teamsters in recent years. A 1977 U.S. Supreme Court decision went against the right of state prisoners to unionize.[48]

Critics of the "teamster cop" trend point to the potential for conflict of interest. They also stress the corrupt record of the Teamsters, harking back to the McClellan hearings of the late 1950s. Control of the police by labor racketeers, hoodlums, and mobsters is predicted by Teamster adversaries. But the government has no clear idea of how much organized crime exists in unions because no effort has been made to find out since the McClellan Committee investigation.[49]

DEALING WITH POLICE UNIONS

A police management philosophy for dealing with unions has been emerging. As early as 1971, then Dayton Police Chief Robert Igleburger and his training director, John Angell, asserted that police administrative opposition to police unions had become pointless. Police executives are faced, they said, with the necessity of dealing with such organizations in good faith. They advocated flexible managerial philosophy and skills, illustrated by the systems concepts of Talcott Parsons and Edward Shils. This theory portrays an organization as a cluster of interacting positions and roles, defined by reciprocal behavior expectations. The essential task of the administrator is the intermediary role, to facilitate role consensus among supervisors, middle managers, the employee union, and the city administration.[50]

In such an intermediary role, emphasis is upon the need for flexibility and willingness to modify and redefine positions and to consider alternatives. In short, the administrative role, according to this theory, requires positive *political* skills and strategies. Igleburger and Angell applied this principle to the specifics of policy development and staff development, and to establishing an information system inside and outside the department. They also showed its use in establishing effective grievance procedures, in the process of negotiation itself, and in the implementation of the contract after a settlement has been reached. Their article concluded on this note:

> In dealing with the union, the administrator must insure his employees and their union fair treatment and due process, but he must also be concerned about protecting the interests of citizens, legislators, his supervisors, and his managers. To adequately fulfill these obligations, the chief must view himself as an intermediary between these various significant groups and individuals who are concerned with the outcome of the collective bargaining process. A prerequisite to the competent fulfillment of this position is a realistic approach to collective negotiations through the use of rational techniques and strategies.[51]

The key question that police unions raise, especially in the mind of the police manager, is control of the department. In a 1972 article, then Detroit Police Commissioner John Nichols stated it bluntly:

> So for those of you who feel that unionism has no designs on management prerogatives, no desire for power, no intentions to covertly or overtly control the organization, forget it. Just as other labor organizations are encroaching on the management level, so shall police unions. . . .[52]

Meantime, government management generally is preoccupied with the need for budget squeezing in every possible way, with stretching available funds to provide more and better public services. This is the essence of recent attention to public sector productivity. Where police services are concerned, the unions clearly must be party to any serious effort of this type. They must be recognized, and their legitimate rights must be recognized. The adversary element in labor-management relations must be turned to constructive ends. Not only should police unions be "lived with" or tolerated, but the basis for collaboration should be broadened. The matter of productivity is an appropriate focus for this collaboration.[53]

NEIGHBORHOOD GOVERNMENT

In chapter 13, we discussed the question of neighborhood and community control of the police, a discussion that is relevant in the context of this chapter. The basic issue is how to govern the urban monstrosity. Is a New York City or a Los Angeles governable under today's conditions? How is big-city government to be made responsive to the needs of the governed? Whose police department (or school system) is it, fundamentally? Accountability and responsiveness are the current code words.

Such questions are clearly political. A public administrator might say that the big puzzle is how to decentralize functions or services while maintaining necessarily centralized authority, which is the way James Q. Wilson states it. Neighborhood meetings in which mayors, city managers, and council members mix with grass-roots people have become commonplace. Neighborhood advisory groups for various municipal departments—schools, police, parks, sanitation, and others—are no longer novel. Pertinent questions to ask regarding such groups are: Who sets them up? Who determines their membership? Who belongs, and whom do the members represent? What real power or influence do they have?

The key idea is *control*, political control. And in a democratic society, political control is a relative thing, with many built-in safeguards against its becoming absolute. This means that political control is divisible: it comes down to such questions as how much, by whom, and subject to what review. In the typical metropolis, a maze of governmental boundaries criss-cross the city— police districts, school districts, sanitation districts, health, zoning, planning, fire—all different, some political, some administrative, some simply historical. This is further complicated by recent Model Cities areas, urban renewal sections, task force zones, economic opportunity pilot neighborhoods, and what have you.

How far should we go with neighborhood government in large cities? If government becomes more splintered and fragmented than it already is, what about the efficiency of its delivery system, its services to its clients? If 62 or 122 neighborhood police departments were to be created in New York City, how would they cope with crime and disorder that are not so neatly arranged? It would seem that if the desired goal is more citizen participation in decision making and policy setting in police departments and school systems, complete administrative autonomy at the neighborhood level is *not* the best way to achieve it. In fact, administrative trends in police work today run counter to such fragmentation.

Citizens should certainly play a stronger role in influencing police organizational goals, policies, and procedures. But because police work is increasingly a professional art calling for special training, experience, and knowledge, important distinctions must be drawn between the police role and the citizen role in the partnership we have been emphasizing. Granting that "community control" has been exploited as a slogan in the urban confrontations of recent years, the best argument for it is not the possibility that it may really happen—although the Berkeley, California, referendum in April 1971 was certainly instructive in this regard—but in the reminder that change of some sort is needed in present structures and ways of doing things. Somehow these social structures, exemplified by police departments and school systems, must become more "tuned in" to all segments of the community they serve. Bureaucracies tend to avoid making controversial decisions, if possible; more localized accountability means that agencies will be watched more closely and their actions will, therefore, be more responsive to community needs.

John Angell has shown that the major pragmatic question for a police administrator, from a professional and ethical standpoint, is to whom or to what he should be responsive. Angell analyzes police administrative responsiveness to judicial influences, public influences, legislative influences, and organizational influences and suggests some guidelines for administrative survival in each of these references:

> Responsiveness in the final analysis is an expected and legitimate means of accumulating and maintaining power in a democratic society, and a police administrator must learn to use it effectively. What does it matter if he organizes his area of responsibility in perfect compliance with the classical theory [Weberian], if in the process he does not properly respond to the public and its values and, as a result, loses its confidence and support? He may be successful when evaluated in the light of classical organizational theory, and yet a failure when evaluated on his ability to meet public expectations. These latter criteria may have the most important effect on his ability to remain in his position.[54]

Participative democracy can be ruinous in political dynamics if every faction or group stubbornly insists on having all of its way on any given conflicting issue, with threats of "going to court" and other "muscle" as the price of resisting its terms. To make our system work, there is a point where compromise and consensus are essential, for the public interest. There are some indications that we are losing sight of this vital principle, in a time when "me first" seems to have become so widespread a motto.

JUVENILE JUSTICE AND POLITICS

The problems of the juvenile justice system are, as we have said repeatedly, among the most exasperating in the legal order. At least one recent work has defined the issue in unequivocal political terms, thereby pinpointing our theme in this chapter:

> A central difficulty is that of introducing into law enforcement and the administration of justice a real, not hypothetical, balance of power between individuals who are on the receiving end of justice and the officials who administer it. The crucial task will be that of building a public policy which both recognizes and understands the inherent conflicts of interest between those groups and collectivities in society against which the law is enforced and those in whose name and for whose benefit it is enforced.[55]

One of the authors of the foregoing extract, John Martin of Fordham University, presents the same thesis in another publication. The real problem, he says, lies in the very way the institutions of the juvenile justice system are organized, in the specification of their goals, and in the manner in which they function. Far more is entailed than crowded court calendars, huge caseloads, legally trained judges, the lack of trained caseworkers, and lack of money. Martin writes:

> Much more crucial to a fuller understanding of the situation is an appreciation of the narrow ideological and theoretical foundation upon which the juvenile justice apparatus rests. The system is grossly conservative in that it accepts little or no active responsibility for winning social justice for the children with whom it deals. It remains wedded to the idea that what is wrong in delinquency is limited to that which is presumed to be wrong with the youngster himself or with his family.[56]

While Martin was speaking in particular of the juvenile justice system, his language seems to apply to the criminal justice system in general:

> Far deeper organizational difficulties also exist which may prove to be far more significant than any of its other characteristics for understanding the unfairness and injustice which taint the system. Essentially the problem boils down to this: When decisions about the lives and careers of powerless people and their children are made by a large and remote bureaucratic system, which by design has made very little provision for establishing a balance of power between the two camps, unfairness and injustice inevitably follow.[57]

Martin is not content with generalized criticism. He examines specifically what he perceives as the central imbalance of power inherent in the system. He recognizes and documents the point that sociopolitical power has long been acknowledged as a useful line of analysis in describing delinquency. But he contends that it has not been expressed emphatically enough in recent treatises, which have tended to stress an *order model* of society, as distinct from a *conflict model*. Martin asserts that perhaps the outstanding characteristic of the juvenile justice system is that it is constructed on order model lines, reinforced by the ideology, theory, and treatment ideals of the mental hygiene movement, "with scarcely a thought given to the consequences of the political imbalances which may flow from such arrangements."[58]

FREEDOM AND ORDER

In the rhetoric of political philosophy, the fundamental question is the relationship between individual liberty and collective security, between freedom and order. To be concrete, the syndicated newspaper columnist, Sydney Harris, holds that the most dangerous and widespread fallacy of our time has been successfully prompted by the advocates of "police power." They have persuaded the public, Harris feels, that the effectiveness of law enforcement increases as due process of law is diminished.

Harris points out that this is not true, has never been true, and can never be true. The real effectiveness of law enforcement, he continues, depends upon two factors only: the degree to which the public respects the law, and the degree to which law enforcement officers perform their duties fairly and honestly. Crime rates, he says, are everywhere lowest where these two conditions obtain, and highest where they do not. Harris continues:

> Crime is lowest in those countries where the public knows that the police are not corrupt or the agents of political forces; where the administration of justice is swift, certain, and equitable; where police and prosecutors are not permitted to conspire in the withholding of evidence unfavorable to their case; where the poor defendant has as much pre-trial protection as the rich one.
>
> And crime is highest—as in the U.S.—where the opposite conditions are rife: where the police are regarded with suspicion and distrust; where the administration of justice is slow, capricious, and weighted heavily against the poor and the ignorant; where prosecutors are more concerned with "making a record" than representing the people; and where defendants who cannot make excessive bail are kept locked up for months.[59]

Jerome Hall's formulation follows:

> This general problem has sometimes been formulated in terms of an *opposition* of values—security *versus* civil liberty. On the surface, at least, it may seem persuasive that if any and all controls and methods of securing evidence are used, order and security can be more effectively preserved. So, too, at first blush it seems almost axiomatic that the exercise of liberty necessarily involves the risk of disorder. But if the inquiry is considered not abstractly, but with reference to our society, opposing security to liberty is irrelevant. Harsh methods of control and democracy are incompatible, so that the question becomes simply the survival of democratic society. Thus, the basic postulate: A democracy, like all other societies, needs order and security; but it also and equally requires civil liberty.[60]

Our entire criminal justice system is a testing ground for the tension that must be maintained between freedom and order. It is not the only such testing ground, but the question arises explicitly in rules applied to persons accused of crime and those "accused" of mental illness. The boldest statement of the case is that letting a murderer go unpunished is better than risking a sociolegal structure under which an innocent man may lose his freedom.

On the other hand, concern is sometimes expressed that the protection of individual freedom may have come to outweigh the common good. For example, Professor Fred Inbau of the Northwestern University Law School said this in 1961, and has frequently expressed the same point of view since:

We are not only neglecting to take adequate measures against the criminal element; we are actually facilitating their activities in the form of what I wish to refer to as "turn 'em loose" court decisions and legislation. To be sure, such decisions and legislation are not avowedly for the purpose of lending aid and comfort to the criminal element, but the effect is the same. It is all being done in the name of "individual civil liberties." . . . We can't have "domestic tranquility" and "promote the general welfare" as prescribed in the Preamble to the Constitution when all the concern is upon "individual civil liberties." . . . Individual civil liberties, considered apart from their relationship to public safety and security, are like labels on empty bottles.[61]

Time magazine commented on this issue as follows:

The Warren Court's application of most Bill of Rights safeguards to all criminal defendants now seems as self-wounding to the nation's highest tribunal as it then seemed vital to American justice. By overlooking the real fears of a crime-ridden society, the court made itself a political target, which in turn encouraged police evasion of its rules, the very official lawlessness that it had aimed to curb in the first place.[62]

One's perspective on the fundamental issue is sharpened by hearing a different drummer. Here, then, is what former Attorney General Ramsey Clark has written on the matter:

The dialogue over the proper limits of police action and barely relevant court rulings consumes most of the emotion and much of the energy that could be constructively used to strengthen the system of criminal justice. . . . The resulting diversion of attention, emotionalization of concern and polarization of attitude damage the system of criminal justice. Those who . . . protest their willingness—even desire—to sacrifice freedom on the altar of order add immeasurably to the burdens of achieving excellence in the performance of criminal justice agencies and commitment to eradication of the underlying causes of crime. . . .

There is no conflict between liberty and safety. We will have both, or neither. You cannot purchase security at the price of freedom, because freedom is essential to human dignity and crime flows from acts that demean the individual. We can enlarge both liberty and safety if we turn from repressiveness, recognize the causes of crime and move constructively. . . . The government of a people who would be free of crime must always act fairly, with integrity and justice.[63]

Peter Schrag summarized our view of the issue in an editorial in the *Saturday Review:*

Too many national politicians have welcomed the confusion between dissent and crime, and . . . through the crime issue, they have launched a coordinated and consistent assault, not on thieves, rapists and murderers, but on minorities, political critics, and the weakest individuals in the society. The target is social and cultural deviance, not criminality. . . . At the same time, disregard of the more fundamental causes of disorder and injustice is likely to exacerbate "crime" and produce pressure for still more repressive laws. The failure of the nation to support the most hysterical politicians of law and order in 1970 provides what may be the last and best opportunity for a reasonable discussion of the issues. If not, it could be the fire next time.[64]

Neither freedom nor security (order) can be absolute. As Clark says, these principles are interdependent in the service of justice. The art of governing in a democratic society, he argues, involves judgments that must be made. In theory, in any given judgment, voting produces two positions: winners and losers. In actuality, the process requires compromise, negotiation, accommodation, and all such strategies and tactics for achieving political consensus.

True, we hammer out decisions through processes that are sometimes brutal, sometimes contrived or manipulated, and more often than not, inefficient. And we have reason to speak of "dirty politics." But political processes in the free society, with their culmination in government by consensus, accurately reflect human relations. Whether in a family or in international relations, it is consensus that keeps things running. How to achieve it by means that weigh all views of an issue, but ultimately submit to the necessity for decision making, represents the true test of whether we can keep things running.

SUMMING UP

Policing in a democratic society is a public, *political* function. Police-community relations is basically a matter of practical politics, and is much better understood in such terms than in terms of the run-of-the-mill programs of recent years. No matter how "politics" is defined, the notion of "taking the police out of politics" is absurd.

These are the prevailing ideas of this chapter. In a time of unprecedented attention to police accountability and responsiveness to the community, the politics of police-community relations is plainly of vital interest. Some observers hold that rising crime rates are a sign of political irresponsibility.

Various forms of "political policing" are considered in this chapter, with special attention given to the political aspects of public (police) administration. The essential political issue in the relations of the police and the policed in a democratic society is the balance of power and restraint. Blue power, as reflected in the increasing "clout" of police unions, poses some as yet unanswerable questions for police-community relations. Is neighborhood control of the police the way to go? Experience with it in analogous circumstances, such as New York City's public schools, suggests the need for careful evaluation before we proceed in such a direction.

NOTES

1. James Q. Wilson, "The Police and Their Problems: A Theory," *Public Policy*, Yearbook of the Harvard University Graduate School of Public Administration (Cambridge, Mass., 1963). Reprinted by permission.

2. International City Management Association, *Local Government and Police Management* (Washington, D.C.: ICMA, 1977), p. 37.

3. John J. Norton and Gregory G. Cowart, "Assaulting the Politics/Administration Dichotomy," *The Police Chief* 45, no. 11 (November 1978): 26–28. See also William Ker Muir, Jr., *Police: Street Corner Politicians* (Chicago: University of Chicago Press, 1977).

4. James Q. Wilson, "The Police and Their Problems," p. 101. See also Wilson's *Varieties of Police Behavior: The Management of Law and Order in Eight Communities* (Cambridge: Harvard University Press, 1968).

5. Wilson, *Varieties of Police Behavior,* p. 230. See also James Q. Wilson, *City Politics and Public Policy* (New York: John Wiley & Sons, 1968).

6. Wilson, "The Police and Their Problems," p. 233.

7. Edward C. Banfield and James Q. Wilson, *City Politics* (Cambridge, Mass.: Harvard University Press, 1963), p. 18.

8. Eugene H. Czajkoski, "Comment Involving the Humanities in Doctoral Education in Criminology and Criminal Justice," *Journal of Criminal Justice* 6, no. 3 (Fall 1978): 196.

9. Norval Morris and Gordon Hawkins, *The Honest Politician's Guide to Crime Control* (Chicago: University of Chicago Press, 1969).

10. See U.S., President's Commission on Law Enforcement and the Administration of Justice, *Task Force Report: The Police* (Washington, D.C.: U.S. Government Printing Office, 1967), chap. 7, pp. 208–215. See also Louis A. Radelet and Hoyt Coe Reed, *The Police and the Community: Studies* (Encino, Calif.: Glencoe, 1973), pp. 212–223.

11. President's Commission on Law Enforcement, *Task Force Report: The Police,* p. 17.

12. Ibid., p. 18.

13. Ibid., p. 26.

14. U.S., National Advisory Commission on Criminal Justice Standards and Goals, *Report on Police* (Washington, D.C.: U.S. Government Printing Office, 1973), p. 50.

15. Quoted in *Atlantic,* March 1969, p. 130.

16. Frank J. Remington, "Social Change, the Law and the Common Good," in A. F. Brandstatter and Louis A. Radelet, eds., *Police and Community Relations* (Beverly Hills, Calif.: Glencoe, 1968), pp. 235–236.

17. Elmer H. Johnson, "Interrelatedness of Law Enforcement Programs: A Fundamental Dimension," *Journal of Criminal Law, Criminology and Police Science* 60, no. 4 (December 1969): 510–511. Reprinted by permission.

18. Chester I. Barnard, *The Functions of the Executive* (Cambridge, Mass.: Harvard University Press, 1960), pp. 163–169. Floyd Hunter, *Community Power Structure* (Chapel Hill: University of North Carolina Press, 1933). See also C. Wright Mills, *The Power Elite* (New York: Oxford University Press, 1956).

19. Rob Wilson, "In L.A., the New Chief Had the Inside Track," *Police Magazine* 1, no. 2 (May 1978): 23–27.

20. *Law Enforcement News* 4, no. 18 (October 23, 1978): 1.

21. John E. Angell, "Toward an Alternative to the Classical Police Organizational Arrangements: A Democratic Model" (monograph, School of Criminal Justice, Michigan State University, 1970). See Max Weber, *Essays in Sociology,* translated and edited by Hans Gerth and C. Wright Mills (New York: Oxford University Press, 1958); also see Reinhard Bendix, *Max Weber: An Intellectual Portrait* (Garden City, N.Y.: Doubleday, Anchor Books, 1962).

22. Angell, "Toward an Alternative."

23. Ibid. See also Alan A. Atshuler, *Community Control* (New York: Western Publishing, 1970); Milton Kotler, *Neighborhood Government* (New York: Bobbs-Merrill, 1969).

24. Barnard, *The Functions of the Executive*, pp. 172–175.

25. Albert J. Reiss, Jr., and David J. Bordua, "Environment and Organization: A Perspective on the Police," in Bordua, ed., *The Police: Six Sociological Essays* (New York: John Wiley & Sons, 1967), p. 26. Reprinted by permission of John Wiley & Sons.

26. Ibid., p. 52.

27. U.S., President's Commission on Law Enforcement and Administration of Justice, *Field Surveys III, Studies in Crime and Law Enforcement in Major Metropolitan Areas* (Washington, D.C.: U.S. Government Printing Office, 1967), vol. 2, sec. 2, pp. 94–100.

28. The constitutionality of a New York State law prohibiting police officers from engaging in political activities was challenged in the State Supreme Court by the Nassau County Patrolmen's Benevolent Association in the spring of 1969. The suit was not upheld.

29. See Allan D. Hamann and Rebecca Becker, "The Police and Partisan Politics in Middle-sized Communities," *Police* 14, no. 6 (1970): 18–23. Reprinted by permission of Charles C. Thomas, Publisher.

30. U.S., National Commission on the Causes and Prevention of Violence, *The Politics of Protest: Violent Aspects of Protest and Confrontation* (Washington, D.C.: U.S. Government Printing Office, 1969), pp. 201–217.

31. W. H. Ferry, "The Police State, American Mode" (Starr King Commencement Speech, Unitarian Church of Berkeley, California, October 10, 1969).

32. Edgar Z. Friedenberg, "Hooked on Law Enforcement," *Nation*, October 16, 1967. Reprinted by permission. See also: William W. Turner, *The Police Establishment* (New York: G. P. Putnam's Sons, 1968).

33. Ed Cray, "The Politics of Blue Power," *Nation* 208, no. 16 (April 21, 1969): 493–496. Reprinted by permission. By the same author, *The Enemy in the Streets: Police Malpractice in America* (New York: Doubleday, Anchor Books, 1972).

34. William P. Brown, "Mirrors of Prejudice," *Nation* 208, no. 16 (April 21, 1969): 500. Reprinted by permission.

35. Hillard J. Trubitt, "Going by the Book," *Nation* 208, no. 16 (April 21, 1969). See also Thomas R. Dye and Brett W. Hawkins, eds., *Politics in the Metropolis*, 2nd ed. (Columbus, Ohio: Charles E. Merrill, 1971).

36. At a Philadelphia meeting in June 1971, this organization, claiming to represent 25,000 black police officers, voted to oppose using black officers as undercover agents to investigate politically oriented cases in black neighborhoods. The 220 delegates from fifteen cities also agreed to support the formation of civilian police review boards and pledged to take action against any law enforcement officer who abuses any citizen. The organization also voted to encourage at least two years of college education for police officers, to favor human relations training for all police officers, and to oppose the indiscriminate use of stop-and-frisk and preventive detention laws. (Reported by the Associated Press, June 16, 1971). See Alex Poinsett, "The Dilemma of the Black Policeman," *Ebony* 26, no. 7 (May 7, 1971): 122–131.

37. Seymour Martin Lipset, "Why Cops Hate Liberals—and Vice Versa," *Atlantic* 223 (March 1969): 81. Copyright © 1969 by The Atlantic Monthly Company. Reprinted by permission.

38. Hugh O'Neill, "The Growth of Municipal Employee Unions," in *Unionization of Municipal Employees*. Reprinted by permission from *Proceedings of the Academy of Political Science* 30, no. 2 (1970): 8. A one-day strike in June 1971 of New York City

bridge operators and some 6,000 other municipal workers was referred to by a union official as the "biggest, sloppiest, nastiest" strike in the city's history.

39. *New York Times*, November 3, 1969.

40. O'Neill, "The Growth of Municipal Employee Unions," p. 13.

41. Jack Stieber, *Public Employee Unionism: Structure, Growth, Policy* (Washington, D.C.: Brookings Institution, 1973), chap. 8.

42. Irwin Ross, *Reader's Digest*, July 1975, p. 45.

43. *Detroit Free Press*. See James P. Gifford, "Dissent in Municipal Employee Organizations," in *Unionization of Municipal Employees*, pp. 159–172; and Ewart Guinier, "Impact of Unionization on Blacks," ibid., pp. 173–181.

44. V. A. Leonard and H. W. Moore, *Police Organization and Management*, 3rd ed. (Mineola, N.Y.: Foundation Press, 1971), p. 30.

45. Tim Bornstein, "Police Unions: Dispelling the Ghost of 1919," *Police Magazine* 1, no. 4 (September 1978): 25–29.

46. Allan Dodds Frank, "When All Else Fails, Call the Teamsters," *Police Magazine* 1, no. 4 (September 1978): 21 ff.

47. Ibid., p. 34.

48. *Jones* v. *North Carolina Prisoners' Labor Union, Inc.*, 45 L.W. 4820, June 23, 1977.

49. *U.S. News & World Report*, May 8, 1978, p. 83.

50. Robert M. Igleburger and John E. Angell, "Dealing with Police Unions," *Police Chief* 38, no. 5 (May 1971): 50–55; Talcott Parsons and Edward Shils, eds., *Toward a General Theory of Action* (New York: Harper & Brothers, 1962).

51. Igleburger and Angell, "Dealing with Police Unions," p. 55. Reprinted by permission of the International Association of Chiefs of Police, Gaithersburg, Maryland.

52. John F. Nichols, "Management and Legal Aspects of Police Strikes," *The Police Chief* 39, no. 12 (December 1972): 38–43.

53. See John A. Grimes, "The Police, the Union, and the Productivity Imperative," in *Readings on Productivity in Policing* (Washington, D.C.: Police Foundation, 1975), pp. 47–85.

54. John E. Angell, "Responsiveness—An Obligation and a Technique of the Police Administrator," *Police Chief* 26, no. 3 (March 1969): 22–26. Reprinted by permission of the International Association of Chiefs of Police, Gaithersburg, Maryland.

55. John M. Martin, Joseph P. Fitzpatrick, and Robert E. Gould, *The Analysis of Delinquent Behavior: A Structural Approach* (New York: Random House, 1970). See also Howard James, "Children in Trouble: A National Scandal," *Christian Science Monitor*, 1969.

56. U.S., Department of Health, Education and Welfare, Youth Development and Delinquency Prevention Administration, Social and Rehabilitation Service, *Toward a Political Definition of Juvenile Delinquency*, by John M. Martin (Washington, D.C.: U.S. Government Printing Office, 1970), pp. 1–2.

57. Ibid., p. 2.

58. Ibid.

59. Sydney Harris, "Police Power Not the Answer," *Lansing* (Mich.) *State Journal*, November 25, 1970.

60. Jerome Hall, "Security and Civil Liberty," *Indiana Law Journal* 28, no. 2 (1953). Reprinted by permission.

61. Fred E. Inbau, "Public Safety v. Individual Liberties," *Police Chief* 29, no. 1 (January 1962): 29–33. Reprinted by permission of the International Association of Chiefs of Police, Gaithersburg, Maryland.

62. *Time*, June 21, 1971.

63. Ramsey Clark, *Crime in America* (New York: Simon & Schuster, 1970), pp. 251–254. Reprinted by permission.

64. Peter Schrag, "The Law-and-Order Issue," *Saturday Review,* November 21, 1970. Reprinted by permission.

18

CRIME PREVENTION

Often today, when one mentions police and community relations, the reaction suggests something that has become "old hat." While it is not difficult to locate places still ten years or more behind the times, where community relations are only now being discovered, most police agencies take their extensive community relations activities for granted. In many cities, the nomenclature has changed: activities once called community relations are now called "community-based crime prevention," or the like. Another change is evident in college courses, where the emphasis today tends to be on *criminal-justice* and community relations, rather than on the narrower police-community relations. These changes beckon for analysis.[1]

In practical terms, police and community relations are still defined today largely as police and minority groups, police and racial tensions, police and the disaffected, and so on. To the extent, therefore, that the social revolution of the 1960s is regarded as the bad news of a yesterday best forgotten, police-community relations tend to be seen in the same vein. The subject was never popular with some rank-and-file police officers. The very term conjures up either police-citizen street confrontations too psychologically draining to be relished, or public relations activities carried out by police agencies "to project a good image." In either event, community relations are not top priority. When budgets are cut, community relations "gets the axe" early.

REVIEWING THE POLICE-COMMUNITY RELATIONS CONCEPT

Seeing police-community relations in too narrow a perspective is not a new development, as we have observed in earlier chapters. This is one significant reason so many police people are "turned off" by the term and the ideas it conveys. Yet these same people feel that community relations cannot and must not be ignored, or even publicly disparaged. So the lip service continues strong, especially when Law Enforcement Assistance Administration (LEAA) grants have been available to support programs, albeit not necessarily under the specific heading of community relations. Call the project "conflict management," "crisis intervention," "psychological-stress training," or "community-based crime prevention," and the odds for funding are better. Moreover, if the scope of the project is "the system," rather than just the police, and if the grant application is generously sprinkled with terms such as "technical assistance" and "delivery system," the chances for a funded project skyrocket.

There is probably no serious damage done by such charades, particularly when many police officers react more favorably to conflict management or community-based crime prevention, for example, than they would to police-community relations. But we should remember that the earliest organized big-city police-community relations programs, such as the often-copied St. Louis project, made community-based crime prevention their primary purpose as early as 1956. The prevalent concept of police-community relations that developed in the ensuing years, especially during the turbulent 1960s, has obscured this original rationale, lately rediscovered.

It is of interest to note that current reports and articles in British sociological journals indicate that British police administrators favor a broad definition of the police role. Sir Robert Peel would have applauded this philosophy, quite consistent with his principles for metropolitan policing.[2]

POLICE-COMMUNITY RELATIONS AND CRIME PREVENTION

We are back to the role question again. The reference is British, but its American application is not difficult to formulate. Both the 1966 President's Crime Commission and the 1973 National Advisory Commission on Criminal Justice Standards and Goals referred to community stabilization (the quality of life) as the condition that is ultimately jeopardized by crime, and viewed increased crime as the inevitable result of faulty relations between police and community. From this point of view, ends and means in police service fall into place. Stated starkly, it comes to this: the only way to cope successfully with the so-called crime problem is through the development of more effective police–criminal-justice–community collaboration. Sherlock Holmes would call this basic principle "elementary." It is the fulcrum of any serious attempt to prevent crime or to cope with it; it is likewise the fulcrum of any serious effort toward positive police–criminal-justice–community relations. This is, once again, the central thesis of this text.

Can crime be prevented? There are those pragmatists who are dubious. They hold that very little serious crime can be prevented, that it is more a matter of trying to contain it as best we can, of keeping the loss of life and property as low as possible, and that any goal beyond this is naive idealism. This philosophy need not detain us long. Can crime be entirely eliminated? Clearly not. Is it possible to control it, contain it, reduce the number and gravity of its occurrences? Clearly it is, given certain conditions. Why argue about such a point? When we say "prevention," we mean it in this sense.

Next question: Would anyone or any group *oppose* the prevention of crime? Obviously, yes—individuals and interests who profit from it. If those who insist that crime does not pay were altogether correct, there would be no crime. Depending upon the particular delinquent or criminal, the payoff for crime may be psychological or political or economic, or a combination of any of these. "Take a chance; you won't get caught!" "What's the matter—chicken?" "What's the difference; nobody cares!" These are typical verbalizations associated with delinquent and criminal behavior. Each expression has a note of cynicism that often is coupled with fear or threat. One effect is a prevailing attitude in society that not much can be done to deal with crime and criminals.

Yet public opinion polls indicate that the community favors crime prevention by a clear margin when asked to rate the importance of the police functions of prevention and criminal apprehension. Many police departments, however, act as if they are not listening. They say that they cannot give more attention to preventing crime because they are too busy apprehending criminals. When they are brought to task for their dismal record in apprehensions and clearances, they claim that they are kept too busy "doing social work." They establish crime prevention units as "fringe benefits" with LEAA grants, then report later—as the grant runs out—that the crime prevention program must be terminated because funds are exhausted. The community—if it is indeed aware of the existence of the project—permits this to happen without the protest it deserves. This common occurrence is much less the result of a fatalistic attitude regarding the inevitability of crime than it is of an outrageous default in police-community relations. There are even those in police circles who have insisted that there is little or no connection between the crime prevention unit and the police-community relations unit. This spurious reasoning is convenient when the department has received separate grants to support each unit.

Michael Banton has a pertinent comment:

> To interpret the objective of crime prevention in a way that makes sense throughout today's police service is a difficult task because it is not easy to reward men for successful preventive actions; the task also gets entangled with the problems of the extent to which the detective branch should be organizationally separate. But if progress could be made on this front it would ease the doubts of the men at the bottom who wonder if they should be acting as social workers when serious crime is increasing. To prevent crime the policeman needs to know and be at the service of all sections of society. If his role is defined in these terms it will resolve the major problem in the way police approach community relations.[3]

As a social anthropologist, Banton stresses that the reinforcement of *informal* controls on individual behavior is the most vital way to reduce the incidence of crime. "Compliance with most laws," he asserts, "does not depend upon the likelihood of their being enforced, but upon an acceptance of informal norms and a concern for the feelings of others."[4] Banton also laments the tendency to place major responsibility for crime prevention with the police. He believes that the crime prevention work of the police can only be meaningfully discussed in the wider context of "criminal policy." This means public policy pertaining to crime and criminals. The formation of such policy, not yet evident in any country, would require—Banton argues—the participation of all social institutions with responsibilities toward the public peace.[5] He has in mind local and national crime prevention councils.

DEFINING THE CRIME PROBLEM

If one is to consider what can be done about crime, a good place to begin is to study how the problem is defined. In the United States, we rely heavily on so-called Uniform Crime Reports (UCR). The data for these reports are gathered through a procedure initiated by local police agencies, who report monthly to state police agencies, who in turn report to the Federal Bureau of Investigation. The FBI publishes these statistics quarterly and annually. Much has been said and written in recent years about the shortcomings of the procedure and the data. We will not review all of that here. Suffice it to say that a recent LEAA national study puts *unreported* crimes at two to three times the number of reported crimes. So the extent and gravity of the crime problem, one may safely conclude, is considerably greater than our standard index suggests.

In recent years, another useful crime indicator has emerged from LEAA-sponsored victimization studies. These studies have been important as a basis for estimates of unreported crime. By using established sampling techniques geared to Census Bureau polls, LEAA was able to report, for example, that Miami and Washington, D.C., had the lowest proportion of crime victims among the thirteen cities surveyed in 1973, and that San Francisco and Minneapolis had the highest. Yet the astute analyst must again be wary lest he be deceived by the statistics.[6]

The early victimization surveys, dating back to the first—done by the 1966 President's Crime Commission—have given way to annual reports, called the National Crime Survey, which provides an abundance of statistical information on victims, offenders, and crime characteristics, based on a large national sampling of citizens and businesses.[7] Thus, in the statistical sense, we know much more today about crime in this country than UCR reports encompass.

The mass circulation news media, including television, have devoted considerable attention to crime. One opinion is that the media themselves contribute to the problem, but this is controverted by another view that emphasizes the positive benefits in public education and constructive political action that are traceable to the media. The apparently increasing gravity of the problem of serious crime in recent years has certainly been underlined for public attention by such headlines as: CRIME UP 17% IN PAST YEAR; ROBBERIES UP 255% IN 14 YEARS; AGGRAVATED ASSAULT UP 153% ; U.S. MURDER RATE SOARS; VIOLENT CRIME RISING STEADILY.[8]

All of the currently available crime statistics focus on easy-to-measure crimes by individuals, rather than on white-collar or corporate crime, thereby fostering the stereotype that the prototype criminal is young, male, black, urban, and poor. Yet, as Edwin Sutherland and Donald Cressy and others have pointed out for years, fraud—which is difficult to detect or measure accurately—is the most prevalent crime in America. Incidentally, there is no such thing as *the* crime problem: crime is multifaceted, not a single entity.

Improved methods of gathering, recording, and reporting crime data have resulted in useful refinements in our understanding of the crime problem. At the same time, they invite extensions of crime research. In this sense, methodological improvements in gathering crime data have somewhat furthered our insight into criminal patterns, but, in a larger sense, they force us to realize the limits to the types of questions that can be answered by statistics.

Transitory though the statistics are, however, here are some recent examples of the "ball park" of crime in this country:

- Suburban crime is up 20 percent; rural crime is up 21 percent. One theory on this is that crime crackdowns in the cities force the problem out to suburbia and beyond. Another theory is that more rural crimes against property are reported because more rural residents have insurance these days. Still another view is that rural law enforcement has been short-changed in federal largesse. In suburban communities, shoplifting is particularly widespread, and much more of it goes undetected. Moreover, how much of it is pilferage by store employees is impossible to estimate. Burglary, vandalism, and bike theft are other significant suburban crimes.

- Almost half the serious crimes are committed by juveniles or young adults. Juvenile crime has risen by 1,600 percent in twenty years. More crimes are committed by children under fifteen than by adults over twenty-five. Of those arrested for street crimes, excluding murder, 75 percent are under twenty-five.

- The murder rate is going up, the suicide rate is down in general, but up for high school and college age youth. More than 40 percent of all murders occur inside a home. About 94 percent involve murderers and victims of the same race. The murder rate for black men is ten times greater than that for white men. There appears to be no significant correlation between the death penalty and the homicide rate.

- About 70 percent of all adults imprisoned for serious crimes are repeat offenders.

- The number of women committing serious and violent crimes is increasing rapidly. The dominant trend in female crime is toward property and "white-collar" offenses, notably burglary, robbery, larceny, embezzlement, and fraud.

- White-collar and business crime are increasing. Ralph Nader is among those who have said that there seems to be less concern about corporate crime on the part of law enforcement agencies than there is about "crime in the streets." Kickbacks are a white-collar crime with a roughly estimated "take" of anywhere between $5 billion and $20 billion a year in the U.S. The consumer pays the bill. Add to this the bill for shoplifting, pilferage, and hijacking, threats to kidnap, etc.[9]

- An estimated 4,580 Bibles were stolen from New York hotel rooms in one recent year. Stripping hotel or motel rooms of television sets, towels, and other room accessories is commonplace. Stealing blankets from airlines is likewise no novelty.

· Burglaries in our cities occur at a rate defying even minimal police attention. The recovery of stolen goods is a rarity. Burglars depend upon readily available "fences." This may be their vulnerable point, and perhaps the key to a strategy for dealing with this crime.

The actual rate of crime in a community—reported or unreported—does not necessarily correspond to citizen attitudes about crime. The public may under- or overestimate the scope of the problem, and public opinion about it is easily manipulated by police handling of statistics and by the media.[10] In any event, public attitudes and perceptions about crime are an important political reality, even when these attitudes are based more on emotion than on fact. When more than half of the people polled say that they feel more uneasy on the streets than they did a year ago, police administrators had better pay attention. Every year since 1970, almost 70 percent of the respondents in a Louis Harris survey have asserted that "our system of law enforcement does not discourage people from committing crimes." Approximately 30 percent have listed stricter law enforcement and severer penalties as the best way to prevent crime. Fewer than 50 percent have said that the police are doing a good job. More than 50 percent feel that the courts are too lenient. Older residents generally tend to feel more apprehensive about crime. Blacks are much more apt than whites to feel that their vicinities are unsafe.

The close kinship in the public mind between the crime rate and the quality of life in a community has been suggested by many studies, for example, one in Detroit by the University of Michigan Survey Research Center:

> Omnipresent concerns about public safety have a strong influence on how satisfied people are with their neighborhoods and with their communities. It is unlikely that a person who considers his environment to be a dangerous one can at the same time express very much satisfaction with that environment. Indeed, we find that one of the strongest influences on how satisfied a person says he is with his community is his perception of how safe that community is.[11]

The victims of crime have been receiving more attention lately, and no discussion of public attitudes toward crime is complete without the reflection that more crime means more victims of crime. Compensation for crime victims is costly. More and more states have established crime victims' compensation programs. Perhaps it is not an idle hope that a larger number of crime victims, and cash payments to an ever larger proportion of them at taxpayer expense, will result in less public complacency and increasing pressure to do something about it. A complacent public has often been pointed to as the most significant factor in a worsening crime situation.[12]

The increase in criminal violence and terrorism is, of course, a worldwide phenomenon. But in a provocative, recent book, Charles Silberman analyzes it domestically, especially in racial terms.[13] While marveling that there has been so little black violence over this country's history, he attests that there has been a decided upswing in it during the recent past. This, he explains, has been the result of a breakdown in traditional cultural controls, with the exodus of middle-class blacks from ghettos. Leadership roles left vacant by this "erosion of authority" were filled by lower-class toughs, fifteen to twenty-four years of age, angry, frustrated, and heavily unemployed. Hispanics have been comparatively less violent because of differences in history and culture.

In the second part of his book, Silberman discusses criminal justice processes, in the course of which he makes some startling statements.[14] He holds that criminal sentencing is remarkably similar in any particular court system; that plea bargaining has been an essential and appropriate means to settle criminal cases for the past century; and that the guilty do *not* escape punishment, as many other observers claim. Still, Silberman maintains, that "the courts convey an aura of injustice that undermines respect for law." He made his six-year study with Ford Foundation support. Short of the elimination of poverty and discrimination as an ultimate, utopian approach to violent crime, he advocates such measures as punishing violent teen-age criminals by adult standards and giving judges more options in sentencing.

THE CAUSES OF CRIME

What causes crime? This question has triggered many an argument, many a lengthy discourse, and many an apology for not being able to provide a simple response. Because crime itself is not a homogeneous category, the search for univariate explanations is senseless. It may be that everything that needs to be said, or that can be said, about the causes of crime has been said. The complexity of defining crime, as suggested in the preceding discussion, is matched by the complexity of identifying its causes, *in the particular instance*. We will settle for some limited commentary.

To begin with, and repeating a basic point, crime is defined as a kind of human behavior that is *deviant* by certain established standards of authority in society. All behavior obviously has causes, more or less identifiable. Criminal behavior has been studied from countless experiential and academic vantage points. Thus, its causes are often categorized: physiological, psychological, medical-psychiatric, political, economic, sociological, familial, educational, and so on. In recent years, there has been a tendency for more analysts to examine the yardsticks themselves, as we have noted. For example, for years Marvin Wolfgang has been a leader among those who take a critical view of crime statistics.

Now and then, there is a fresh insight. Characteristically, new insights complicate what once appeared to be self-evident. To illustrate this point, the neat categories of crime causes are disturbed by the observation that agencies ostensibly created to control crime are themselves significant contributors to the problem. To say this in an open forum is to unleash a storm of uptight, defensive reactions. Yet there is considerable evidence to support the charge. Police corruption, for instance, is probably one of the causes of a specific type of crime. John Gardiner has made the point that "the first precondition for corruption is a substantial conflict over the goals of the legal system."[15] Conflict over goals makes a social system dysfunctional, which in turn accounts for some measure of recidivism. Many people are convinced that prisons cause more repeated crime than they deter, and in some quarters parole is said to be a failure because premature releases cause recidivism.

It is also disturbing to observe that constructive efforts to thwart crime—by more effective police activity, or by more effective police-community coopera- tion in crime-coping programs—will probably produce *more*, rather than less, reported crime in the short run. Again, such a statement draws attention to the yardsticks for measuring crime. For politicians—and for police people who are at the mercy of politicians—simple truths of this nature are anathema. Apparently, it is felt that instructing the public to think sensibly about crime is a task for neither politician nor police official. Both insist that something *must* be done about crime, without taking the trouble to think clearly about it; and to this extent, they each contribute to public confusion, frustration, and ap- prehension.

Another point is that the homilies from attorneys general, prosecutors, judges, police executives, and other high-level officials imploring the public to do something about crime often fail to specify what it is that the public should do. For lack of guidelines, many people concoct their own private campaign against crime, such as buying guns or installing some bizarre contraption for snaring burglars. Where is the leadership to come from if we are serious about community-based crime prevention? Clearly, it must come from the police and other criminal justice people. And it must be a brand of leadership far surpass- ing the common practice of scapegoating within the system: the police citing lenient courts or easy parole as the villain, judges suggesting that the police see only the punishment side of sentencing, and prosecutors asserting that rehabilitation of offenders is a flop.

It is instructive to examine the Gardiner principle cited earlier in relation to the yardsticks of crime measurement. Peter Manning has done this. He begins with the proposition that, to the degree that police agencies lack a legitimated mandate on which there is widespread consensus, they will tend to direct energy either into dramatization of their effectiveness or into repressive ac- tions in attempts to expand their mandate. Most police work is administrative, Manning writes, and therefore not publicly visible. So the police tend to look for what can be dramatized in their activities; for example, they use crime statistics as a symbolic barometer of their effectiveness. This is especially true when the crime rate goes down. It soothes the public into believing that the police protect life and property, and thus are entitled to public trust. This then becomes their *mandate* to maintain the image of "crook catchers." Manning continues:

> Where public disagreement is high, where the laws are numerous and under direct public criticism (e.g., crimes without victims, especially drug laws), where local government is under question, and the linkage between the local government and the police is directly and mutually agreed upon, repressive action will tend to occur.[16]

Manning's analysis unveils five additional propositions in stepping-stone fashion, each of which he clarifies by examples and research citations:

1. To the degree that dramatic aspects of policing become the dominant concern of the police and the public, ceremony replaces instrumentalism and police work becomes redundant: it simply reaffirms other modes and forms of social control. The idea of community leadership goes down the drain.

2. To the degree that instrumentalism replaces the ceremonial features of police work, the degree of sanctity of moral rules that they convey will be reduced. In time, coercion replaces consensus on the police mandate and its legitimation.

3. If the conceptions of policing provided by the police themselves are legitimated by public consensus, then police action frees itself from the community in which it is rooted and may establish its own norms and values.

4. To the degree that formally constituted control agencies are faced with a paradox between what is formally expected of them in the community and what is possible, they will tend to retreat from a collective definition of morality, the law, and social order.

5. The greater the gap between the moral standards of the community and the police culture, the greater the growth of cynicism among the police, and the greater the corruption and the number of internal disciplinary violations.

Stated succinctly, Manning argues that the police are caught between their rhetoric and the reality that there is very little crime that they can control, solve, or investigate completely.[17] Lest this seem anti-police in orientation, another way to put it is simply to say that police behavior must be understood in its linkage with their social or environmental context, as we have earlier suggested.[18]

At the outset of this discussion of the causes of crime, reference was made to the conventional wisdom regarding the categories of causes. The current widespread pessimism about the prospects for curbing crime is related to the lack of substantiation for the conventional wisdom about causes. Solid research is sparse. In an atmosphere of uncertainty, frustration and pessimism flourish. Because we are so unsure about causes, we are similarly unsure about remedies. The question of capital punishment exemplifies the point. How about swiftness and severity of punishment? Same problem. Recent concern about the effect of unemployment and economic depression on the rate of certain crimes has caused the same division of opinion. Academics have insisted that the relationship is more complex and ambiguous than popular and news-media speculation concede.[19]

Another question of recent concern is whether layoffs of police officers as a result of fiscal distress, in New York City and elsewhere, affect crime rates. Police union spokesmen say they do, of course, but many criminologists and some police administrators have been skeptical, asserting that too many other factors influence the situation. This could mean that there may be such an effect, but it cannot be measured, a problem not uncommon in any study of human behavior.

Another example of cause-and-effect difficulties in trying to understand crime and how to control it has been provided by a Kansas City study of police patrol patterns, sponsored by the Police Foundation. This well-known study indicated that sharp reductions or increases in patrol had little effect on crime, arrests, or police response time.[20] The study has been widely criticized, especially by police officials, but this is not surprising when long-revered operational assumptions are called into question.

Indeed, the director of the Kansas City study, George Kelling, has subsequently written that the strategy of preventive patrol has not only failed to demonstrate its effectiveness in controlling crime but has also created the worst possible situation: an ineffectiveness which alienates citizens.[21] He indicates that studies of police response time show this factor also is ineffective when measured by apprehensions.

How does one go about researching the questions involved in the study of crime causes? The scarcity of valid research is certainly understandable. Take, for instance, a question such as this: To what extent would legislation banning or restricting the use of handguns affect the rate of certain crimes? Again, there is a lot of opinion on both sides of this question, as well as a lot of legislative lobbying. How would one take hold of this question in research that would be acceptable to all sides? One might well respond that research could not be initiated unless such legislation were selectively tried, thus creating experimental and control situations. Generally speaking, social research lacks such sophisticated public legitimation in our society.

So it is that scholarly consideration of the causes of crime turns up endless questions for which adequate answers are not available. Some questions appear to be unresearchable. Yet this is no argument against doing whatever research that *can* be done to extend our knowledge. As an example, the Police Foundation supported a Wayne State University doctoral study of what was called "the Detroit factor"—murder.[22] The study focused on the year 1974, when there were 801 homicides in Detroit. In these cases, 642 victims were black, 153 were white, and 6 were Mexican American. There were 371 killings in homes, and 175 in the streets. Handguns were used in 440 cases, shotguns in 110, rifles in 72, and knives in 133. Nearly half of those involved in the homicides (both victims and perpetrators) had criminal records. And so on. This is useful information, a product of research, and it leads to specific questions to be pursued in further research. We are doing a better job of gathering data, and this is good. But we are not doing much research on the big question, why specific individuals commit specific crimes. The primary reason seems to be that such research is very difficult and very expensive to do.

THE CITIES: ECONOMIC AND SOCIAL PROBLEMS

Clearly, the causes of crime are both individual and social. This is where the arguments begin: What proportion of each? The usual response is that no generalization is possible: it comes down to the particular person and the particular circumstances. Whatever weight may be placed upon individual responsibility for behavior, psychological processes do not operate in a vacuum.

One must consider the social environment if one is to understand why people act as they do. That is, if one is to try to understand the causes of crime, one must look at the social circumstances in which it occurs. Historically, increased crime has been seen as one of the telling signs of a deteriorating social environment. If 70 percent of our population reside in urban concentrations and an abundance of certain types of crime appear to be similarly located, one is inclined to infer some kind of simple correlation. However, it must be remembered that correlation and causality are not the same.

Much has been said and written about "the plight of our cities." New York City's problems have dramatized it, but many of our big cities are similarly afflicted. Some are constantly on the brink of social and financial disaster. Not only is the quality of the physical environment in danger, but, even more profoundly, so is the quality of human relations. Interpersonal and intergroup contacts and transactions are too often depersonalized and desensitized, communities are becoming atomized, and so on. The sheer banality of everyday affairs in the typical metropolis breeds a special style of behavioral defense and compensation. A list of specifics is not necessary; such a list has been provided by many analysts. News magazines frequently feature "the urban crisis."[23] It was sheer irony that, in New York City's crisis, the list of possible economy measures included the closing of all but one of the city's zoos, its radio and television stations, and the *abolition of its Human Relations Commission*.

What causes crime and what is happening to our cities are parallel rails of the same track. This sounds like the old refrain that crime can best be managed by reducing poverty, elevating general educational achievement, renewing decayed housing, organizing block clubs, and setting up counseling centers for wayward youth. In short, it sounds like what James Q. Wilson would describe as "suburbanizing the slums." To do all these things might well have a wholesome effect in crime terms, although the evidence is by no means clear and unmistakable. But argument about this is irrelevant because our main concern about crime and the city is the more devastating consideration expressed as follows by Wilson:

> Predatory crime does not merely victimize individuals; it impedes and, in the extreme case, even prevents the formation and maintenance of community. By disrupting the delicate nexus of ties, formal and informal, by which we are linked with our neighbors, crime atomizes society and makes of its members mere individual calculators estimating their own advantage, especially their own chances of survival amidst their fellows. Common undertakings become difficult or impossible, except for those motivated by a shared desire for protection.[24]

This is the essence of the relationship between crime and the quality of life. Wilson takes the point to its zenith:

> What constitutes the "urban problem" for a large percentage (perhaps a majority) of urban citizens, is a sense of the failure of community. By "community" I do not mean, as some do, a metaphysical entity or abstract collectivity with which people "need" to affiliate. . . . When I speak of the concern for "community," I refer to a desire for the observance of standards of right and seemly conduct in the public places in which one lives and moves, those standards to be consistent with—and supportive of—the values and life styles of the particular individual. . . . Viewed this way, the concern

for community is less the "need" for "belonging" (or, in equally vague language, the "need" to overcome feelings of "alienation" or "anomie") than the normal but not compulsive interest of any rationally self-interested person in his and his family's environment.[25]

The objectives of soundly conceived programs in police-community relations focus on *community* in precisely this sense. Cooperative ventures to do something about crime thereby fall into place as part of police-community relations. Ideally, their very process should be an *acting out* of community.

Lewis Mumford, a master of the study of urban life, concludes one of his best-known volumes in this manner:

> The final mission of the city is to further man's conscious participation in the cosmic and the historic process. Through its own complex and enduring structure, the city vastly augments man's ability to interpret these processes and take an active, formative part in them, so that every phase of the drama it stages shall have, to the highest degree possible, the illumination of consciousness, the stamp of purpose, the color of love. That magnification of all the dimensions of life, through emotional communion, rational communication, technological mastery, and above all, dramatic representation, has been the supreme office of the city in history. And it remains the chief reason for the city's continued existence.[26]

COPING WITH CRIME: WHAT'S BEING DONE?

Our commentary to this point on the definition and causes of crime brings us to the question of what can be done about it. Because we will be discussing programs in subsequent chapters, our intention here is not to list or describe approaches, although we will cite some to illustrate a point. Mainly, however, we will stay in the analytical vein.

There have been innumerable approaches to crime and criminals in recent years, many with the label "community-based crime prevention," virtually all as a result of LEAA funding. Whatever may be said for or against these programs in the sense of their impact on crime—and it's anybody's guess—it may be observed that their priority is at least politically astute. With public opinion polls since 1965 pointing to crime as the biggest problem in our cities, crime prevention and control have received unprecedented political interest. Nonetheless, crime increased 115 percent between 1965 and 1975.

Why is crime a political football? The reasons for this are fascinating. They involve, in roughly equal parts, three interdependent considerations:

1. Criteria set in law, along with theological-psychological aspects of human nature, guarantee that crime will always exist as a behavioral phenomenon, regardless of the programs formulated to combat it. Any problem that cannot, by its nature, be entirely solved, no matter what is done, makes a good political issue in a democratic society.

2. Any problem that has been insufficiently researched to establish any professional or public consensus about its causes lends itself to freewheeling political manipulation. Any approach may have merit, yours as well as mine, because no one is sure.

3. Under circumstances created and cultivated by the two preceding considerations, the politics of crime becomes a game of avoiding the changes and reforms that might conceivably make the greatest difference. By focusing on peripheral issues, those who have a stake in the current system divert attention from the relatively drastic changes that would get at the heart of the matter.

"Blue Ribbon" Commissions

One tool of political hoodwinking is the "blue ribbon" commission, committee, or panel. This includes all the specially mandated presidential and national crime commissions, as well as the state and local counterparts that make studies, surveys, and "unbiased investigations" into crime and what should be done about it. These commissions generally produce slick, magazine-style reports, financed by tax dollars, and packed with recommendations for revamping the machinery of criminal justice. Knowledgeable people spend countless hours on such public-spirited endeavors, seeking innovative goals and standards to be implemented by executive and legislative officials whose stratagems can be understood only by those who are familiar with political conduct. Thus reports of blue ribbon bodies are, more often than not, mere relief for political pressure, rather than practical blueprints for solving problems. Pragmatists may not even take the time to read the reports.

One example will suffice to illustrate the "blue ribbon" process. In Michigan, the Office of Criminal Justice estimates that there are slightly more than 500 law enforcement agencies. Of these, 37 percent (185) have five men or fewer and 73 percent (365) have twenty or fewer. Management experts claim that it takes twenty persons to operate a seven-day, twenty-four-hour police service with reasonable efficiency. It should not require a blue ribbon commission to determine that the majority of citizens in Michigan are not adequately protected. Those disposed to commit crime are fully aware of this fact. But efforts to consolidate police services, as clearly should be done, encounter stubborn political resistance fueled by law enforcement lobbies, whose primary interest is to protect the status quo.

Newsletters, press releases, and "white papers" for semipopular reading are often instruments of the political game. A typical story might read:

> The State Criminal Justice Planning agency today announced the award of thirty-five grants totaling $2,601,723, mainly to improve anticrime operations—including Operation Identification, neighborhood watch groups, and police agency crime prevention units.

How much of what kind of crime do these programs prevent? What do we learn from them about the nature and causes of crime that might be more generally applied? Rarely are there satisfactory answers to such questions, or are these questions even asked. Project evaluations required by LEAA are frequently done in a cursory way by the project staff, whose chief interest is in laying the groundwork for another grant. The overriding tendency is to keep the taxpayers placated, and to be prepared with an impressive recital of programs when asked what is being done. The unspoken hope is that very few will ask what *effect* these programs have. But to avoid embarrassment if and when this question *is* asked, there are complicated statistical responses that will make the questioner sorry he pushed it so far.

One major difficulty with politically determined programs of crime control, perhaps largely because they *are* political, is their tendency to apply blanket solutions to complex problems. For example, take the current swing away from rehabilitation of offenders toward harsher treatment: mandatory and stiffer sentences, greater reliance on incarceration and less on probation, tougher parole practices, limits on plea bargaining, and the like. These "get tough" prescriptions are merchandised as *the* answer to crime, without regard for the important differences in offense, law, circumstances, and offender that would be revealed in effective presentence investigation. The political approach to crime control frequently treats all alike; there is no patience with individuality. It ducks the hard questions and the delicate and vital distinctions by invoking a single, all-purpose remedy.

This matter of penalties for offenders is part of what many observers perceive as the heartbeat of criminal justice processes: sentencing. In a sense, sentencing is the climax. An individual has been found guilty in a court of law, and now the question is: What penalty? The judgment involved is human, subject to infinitely many influences even under the best circumstances. The essential problem in sentencing is disparity: when like individuals committing like offenses are treated differently. Inevitably, one influence is the value system of the judge, the way he weighs the elements of sentencing: protection of society, deterrence (general and individual), rehabilitation, and retribution. These elements are clearly conflicting. A different mix is called for in each case, and this cannot be reconciled with the pressures of political expediency. What frequently emerges is branded as *bias*, from one viewpoint or another. There are, of course, bigoted and otherwise incompetent judges. But the charge of bias is not confined only to them.

Whether justice is done in court, therefore, is as much a question of values as is the decision of the court under scrutiny. This indicates the community dimension of what the courts do, especially in the sentencing of offenders, neatly summarized by Columbia University's Willard Gaylin:

> When serious criminals go unpunished, when minor offenses are excessively punished, when a chosen group receives lesser punishment or a despised group more punishment, it threatens all of us in that society, even the lawabiders. It corrodes the basic structural prop of equity that supports our sense of justice. An excessive disparity in sentencing threatens that kind of breakdown.[27]

Program Effectiveness

How effective are various crime-fighting programs? Because sound program evaluation is so difficult, personal opinions are often taken as "authoritative." Just as often, the evidence is lacking, or questionable at best. Again, this invites political game playing.

Let's consider some examples. Do police helicopters have an impact on crime? Departments so equipped are sure these machines make a difference. Pasadena Chief Robert McGowan, tracing a ten-year experience with helicopter patrol operation, points out that major crime in that city has inched up barely one percent during that period, as compared with more than 100 percent in the seven prior years.[28] But there can be no assurance that it was the helicopter that accomplished this. No one knows what would have happened without it. And how about cost effectiveness?

Another department, the U.S. Park Service Police in Washington, has revived the police horse, for the advantages of high visibility, effective crowd control, better park and shopping center surveillance, and—most of all—good public relations. It seems to be a minor trend. In 1970, about forty police jurisdictions had mounted units. In 1974, more than fifty did, and this has more recently gone past seventy.[29] What's the verdict on horses? The reports are mixed, but it appears that the main assets are in traffic control and public relations, not in crime prevention.

The Los Angeles Police Department is using undercover bikers as a tactic for random patrol and for dealing with specific crimes.[30] Other departments are doing the same, persuaded by the low-cost, crime-deterrent appeal. The telephone emergency services operation identified as 911 has been initiated in many areas. Whether its advantages will justify its costs remains to be seen.

How about special anticrime strike units? Plainclothes officers riding in unmarked cars is one common pattern for combating "street crime." To build cases against syndicate gambling, drug trafficking, loansharking, and fraud schemes, more complicated special units are required, usually operating at the state or national levels. In New York City, the police have used as many as 250 taxicabs in their "Yellow Cab brigade," with seemingly notable success. The cruising cab has a driver and one or two police officers as passengers. In 1974, more than half of the 24,000 felony arrests by undercover police officers in New York City involved a taxi in some way. In Detroit, two special squads concentrated on underworld murders and on killings connected with another crime; in 1975, homicides in Detroit were down 20 percent from 1974.

The take-home car program of the Indianapolis Police Department was developed a decade ago on the premise that a marked police car on routine patrol is a crime deterrent. The objectives of the program were not achieved, and it ended in the summer of 1977. But no one is sure that the program itself really failed because many contingencies (variables) made specific assessment impossible.[31]

An LEAA-funded felony project in Bellingham, Washington, failed in its primary objective because, as an evaluation report indicated, "it spread itself too thin."[32] While there were some bright spots, for example, an increase in burglary clearances, the major difficulty with the project was that it "overstepped its original parameters."

In Albuquerque, New Mexico, Crime Stoppers is a privately financed project that offers rewards of up to $1,000 for information that leads to felony indictments, and additional rewards for courtroom testimony that results in felony convictions.[33]

We mentioned earlier the Kansas City Preventive Patrol study that has brought into question some long-held beliefs regarding the relationship between police patrol tactics and crime. Another Kansas City study has more recently undermined some long-held beliefs about the relationship between police response time and crime.[34] This LEAA study concluded that rapid police response does not lead to an arrest or the availability of witnesses in a large proportion of serious crime; that the time taken by a citizen to report an incident largely predetermines the effect of police response in those few serious crimes which could be affected by rapid police response; and that police response time is not strongly associated with citizen satisfaction but rather citizen satisfaction is dependent on whether citizens perceive response time to be faster or slower than they expect.

So it is that developing research, sometimes with results highly unpopular with most police administrators, may yet prove its worth. It encourages experimentation with new methods and examination of "sacred cow" assumptions. It stimulates better management, not least of all fiscal management. The name of the game these days is productivity![35]

There is no question that the American police, by and large, have tried many new techniques, have vastly improved their operational efficiency, and have substantially upgraded their training and education. One reason crime rates have soared is that the police are making more arrests, a point often overlooked. As we have noted in earlier chapters, the typical police officer feels that the public leaves too much of the crime-fighting job to the police. Further, he or she feels that the major difficulties in criminal justice processes are in the courts and corrections, partly because of the overburdening that results from more efficient police work. Many civilians sympathize with this police view.

However, the pattern of police progress has been extremely erratic, depending on where one looks. Progress in one sector is matched by the fears, insecurity, and politics in another sector. For example, using team policing as a method of patrol organization to increase effectiveness in coping with crime appears to be working well in some cities, but it is sharply condemned when broached in others. This is because making team policing work requires a basic shift in the locus of power in a police agency, something few agencies are prepared to face.

THE COMMUNITY DIMENSION

Because the causes of crime spring from all of a community's social institutions, it follows that crime-coping activities should be just as comprehensive. Presumably this simple logic requires constant reenforcement, for too many people are inclined to see crime as a problem solely for the police and the courts. It is similar to the problem of poverty in this respect. Few people think they cause it; therefore, it must be somebody else's business to deal with it. It is said that we hire functionaries to do society's "dirty work." A social problem has to affect many people before it becomes *everybody's* business. We might hope that this is what has begun to happen with the crime problem. In the past few years, undoubtedly due in part to the influence of LEAA and several national commissions, citizen responsibility and action to curb crime has received unprecedented attention.

Much has been accomplished in the way of public education. There is no need here to recite the list of dos and don'ts for homeowners, apartment dwellers, automobile owners, vacationers, and the rest.[36] The program generally called Operation Identification is widely known and utilized. Citizens who report tips or suspicious circumstances to the police are paid cash rewards or carry membership cards and lapel buttons for CHEC—Citizens Helping to Eliminate Crime—or a similar organizational title and credential. Neighborhood Watch, COP (Community Oriented Policing), Lady Beware, and Citizens' Alert are familiar tags for programs that are common in the United States and Canada. Block watching, crime prevention vehicles, architecturally secure buildings, new types of alarm systems, watchdogs, Operation Whistlestop—these are among the many trappings of the current community crime prevention emphasis. In some cities, but not enough, groups have formed to attempt to secure jobs and equal rights for released prisoners. Other groups work to remove certain crimes from the criminal code. The trend toward consumerism sheds new light on potential fraud. Community demands for a disclosure of personal finances on the part of candidates for public office help to forestall repeated Watergates. Some of the programs engage civilians in activities too close to vigilante tactics to be palatable to even the most frustrated police officers, and some raise provocative questions as to whether the police or the citizens should be credited with apparent decreases in crime. But the results of the citizens' movement against crime, which even the FBI promotes, appear to be substantial in many places.[37] Major cities throughout Canada have extensive programs of this kind, with strong governmental and police agency backing.[38]

Surveillance of neighbor on neighbor (Nosy Rosy) is, to be sure, a delicate enterprise and can easily create more problems than it solves. Some training for participants is a good idea, and close liaison with the police is essential, provided that the police themselves are properly sensitive to the Bill of Rights. Court watching is another kind of action employed by some citizen groups, sometimes as a method of pressuring judges to toughen sentences. This, too, can be ill-advised. Court monitoring can serve a socially worthwhile purpose, but not when it is based upon a single-theory answer to the crime problem. As a general principle for citizen action, it should be remembered that various measures that may curb crime may also destroy liberty and community.

The 1973 National Advisory Commission on Criminal Justice Standards and Goals divided its work into several areas with a task force in each area, as was done by the 1966 President's Crime Commission. One task force focused on community crime prevention. Its report is a treasury of information, recommendations, and suggestions relative to citizen action programs.[39] In concluding an appendix to the report, the task force said:

> As someone once remarked, "Law enforcement is not a game of cops and robbers in which the citizens play the trees." Unfortunately, there are still too many trees. If

crime reduction is to become anything more than wishful thinking, citizens must care enough to devote energy, money, and—most of all—themselves to the fight for positive results.[40]

In many communities, the results of citizen action have been slow to show up in the statistics, and discouragement has set in. Often it is difficult to secure citizen interest initially. The widespread charge is "public apathy." There are a number of reasons for public apathy, particularly when the subject is crime and involvement with "the law." Fear of retaliation is one reason frequently mentioned. So is the time it takes and the inconvenience. "Just plain dangerous" is another explanation. These and other more or less standard reasons for non-participation are familiar, and more or less justified in the particular case. However, there are sometimes more subtle factors in the situation, such as these:

1. The attitude may be one better characterized as bitter or "turned off," rather than as apathetic. The contacts of some citizens with the police, and sometimes the courts, have left them adamantly opposed to any kind of cooperation, assistance, or collaboration. They feel that there is no way, judged by their own experience or by that of a close friend or relative, in which they can bring themselves to trust the system. Some have become involved, for example, as informers, only to be subjected to intolerable, petty police harassment.

2. Some citizens feel strongly that, unless substantial reforms take place in the way the police and the courts see and do their jobs, there is no point in becoming involved in efforts to resist crime. As with the first point above, the logic may not be entirely immune to criticism, but if we wish to understand these attitudes, the question of whether we agree or disagree with them is not central.

3. The police and the courts tend to nurture a certain mystique about their work, where citizens are concerned. The "apathetic community" is, for them, a convenient scapegoat to blame for crime. On the other hand, they insist, citizens should not get *too* involved in crime-fighting efforts, lest they become a nuisance and interfere with the work of the "professionals." This mystique is closely related to what James Q. Wilson has called "syndicalism": the rise in power of organizations of police and corrections officers and the continued power of tenured judges "constituting a serious impediment to progress [because of] decisions unduly influenced by the organized interests of those whose behavior is to be changed."[41]

Someone might say that the police and the courts have no monopoly on public mystique. Lawyers, the clergy, medics—and even auto mechanics—are reluctant to share what they know with "amateurs."

The various forms of diversion, which we discussed in an earlier chapter, are of course germane to the matter of community responsibility for crime and criminal justice processes. It should be recalled also that school-centered programs (police-school liaison or resources officer, Officer Friendly, etc.) have delinquency prevention as a prominent purpose.

The following concerns about community involvement in crime prevention should be noted:

1. Concern regarding excesses by vigilante-type citizen patrols bent on self-defense.

2. Concern regarding citizen groups functioning independently of the police organization.

3. Concern regarding the "Nosy-Rosy" syndrome in neighborhood surveillance.

4. Concern regarding efforts that are deficient in planning, management, and evaluation.

5. Concern regarding the possibility that citizen involvement may not have staying power.

6. Concern regarding fragmented programs that champion single dimension approaches, as against coordinated, comprehensive impacts.[42]

SOME CONCLUDING POINTS

A chapter in which there has been so much critical comment owes it to the reader to conclude with something constructive. A good way to begin is to understand that controlling crime means affecting human behavior. Crime control is social control, in its sociological meaning. Therefore, the approaches must be many and diverse, because the causes of behavior, including behavior deemed deviant, are many and diverse. Behavior is also, in some degree, unpredictable; it does not submit to strict cause-and-effect patterning.

From such elementary principles, one can draw important implications for dealing with criminal behavior. One is that crime is, to some extent, inevitable, in the way that sin in the theological sense is inevitable. Another implication is that the causes of aberrant behavior in particular individuals are not always easy to fathom; therefore, we do not understand the causes of crime as well as we would wish. Pertinent research is badly needed. Further, we have too long looked for the causes of crime in characteristics of the individual offender, rather than in the sociopolitical context in which he behaves. One further implication is that the sociologists, psychologists, psychiatrists, family and school counselors, social workers, and the many others who have had something to say about the causes—and remedies—of delinquent or criminal behavior are not, collectively, idiots. We mention this because such epithets frequently spark the arguments about, for instance, the relative merits of "hard" versus "soft" approaches to the problem.

A good start in a public policy to cope with crime would be to eliminate from the criminal code the accumulation of offenses that should not be there. We have discussed this in earlier chapters, but it bears repetition here. To accomplish this is a challenge to both public education and political process. Norval Morris and Gordon Hawkins have boldly described a cure for crime, arguing that we know much more about it than we are willing to admit. They grant that crime, like disease, is not in any final sense soluble. But they insist that it can be subjected to effective control.[43] The decriminalization of public drunkenness, or of gambling, is not a panacea, yet any such move is important in light of the proportion of police cases involving these behaviors.[44] Decriminalizing drunkenness does not, of course, wipe out the community responsibility to deal with it. But it does put treatment in more appropriate hands.

This author is inclined to be more concerned with what the criminal justice system should be doing than with what other disciplines and fields might contribute. In this vein, the cardinal reality is the fragmentation and dysfunction-ality of criminal justice processes, the "nonsystem" character of these process-es. In the context of this chapter, it may be plainly stated that the dysfunction is itself a significant contributor to the crime problem, specifically to repeated crime. Several examples will serve to support this point:

- Roughly 70 percent of adults imprisoned for serious crime have been in jail before.
- Offenders serving time in county jails are usually incarcerated for less than a year. In recent years, the jail population in Michigan, for example, has increased approximately 10 percent annually. Over the same period, crime rates have skyrocketed.
- Syndicated columnist Chuck Stone wrote in May 1975:

  I would suggest that the greatest increase in crime which is now occurring in low-income ghettoes is related proportionately to the severity of police brutality and judicial abuse suffered by those communities. As ghetto residents experience an arithmetic increase in official dehumanization, they respond with a geometric increase in negative feelings toward the one system which stands between them and the law of the jungle.[45]

- The Attica prison riot of September 1971 left 39 inmates and prison em-ployees dead, 89 others wounded, with subsequent investigations involv-ing 1,200 inmates and close to 1,000 law enforcement officers. A three-volume report of a six-months' investigation by Bernard S. Meyer, a re-tired New York State Supreme Court justice, was presented to Governor Hugh Carey late in 1975. Meyer was "critical of just about everybody who had anything to do with the Attica prosecution" and charged that "the state has dealt unfairly with the inmates and affirmative action is neces-sary to correct the situation." Meyer pointed to the fact that grand juries had charged 62 inmates in 42 indictments with 1,289 crimes, but only one state trooper had been indicted for reckless use of a shotgun during the facility's retaking.[46]

- Between 1971 and 1974, England conducted a thorough review of its crim-inal court procedures, resulting in a new system far more fluid than the old. Britain's stress on relatively quick disposition of court cases has been maintained. This example shows that reform can be accomplished.[47]

Perhaps the National Advisory Commission on Criminal Justice Standards and Goals made the point best. The commission referred to Criminal Justice Systems 1 and 2. System 1 is the series of agencies: police, prosecution, the courts, and corrections. System 2 includes "many public and private agencies and citizens outside of police, courts, and corrections [who] are—or ought to be—involved in reducing and preventing crime, the primary goal of criminal justice."[48] The commission continued:

The debate over criminal justice has . . . been sharpened by frequent intramural conflicts among the components of the Criminal Justice System 1.[49]

The report then quoted the 1966 President's Crime Commission:

Police, court and corrections officials all share the objective of reducing crime. But each uses different, sometimes conflicting methods and so focuses frequently on inconsistent subobjectives. The police role, for example, is focused on deterrence. Most modern correctional thinking, on the other hand, focuses on rehabilitation and argues that placing the offender back into society under a supervised community treatment program provides the best chance for his rehabilitation as a law-abiding citizen. But community treatment may involve some loss of deterrent effect, and the ready arrest of marginal offenders, intended to heighten deterrence, may by affixing a criminal label complicate rehabilitation. The latent conflicts between the parts may not be apparent from the viewpoint of either subsystem, but there is an obvious need to balance and rationalize them so as to achieve optimum overall effectiveness.[50]

This analysis suggests that criminal justice efforts should be concentrated on improving operating relationships within the system, and that such improvement will have a salutary effect on the reduction of repeated crime. Generally speaking, police, prosecutors, judges, and corrections personnel do not talk with one another on a regular, systematic, civilized basis about the issues that divide them. This must change. They might begin by discussing roles and goals, with a view to eventually establishing consensus on the local level about future guidelines for dealing with crime more effectively and justly.

Too idealistic? Then let us propose how the community might help. The method we propose is essentially democratic and political; it treats the community as part of the system, not as an element beyond its perimeters. This is done by bringing political pressure to bear on criminal justice functionaries, aimed at persuading them to change the manner in which they handle their jobs. Indeed, this is the traditional way in which reform takes place in any facet of democratic society. The so-called new criminology and its principal spokesman, Richard Quinney, feel that such reform is not possible.[51] More optimistic about the possibility for change is Herbert S. Miller of the Georgetown University Law Center, who writes:

> There are several keys to effective change in the criminal justice system. First, it is important for citizens to gain entree into the system. Second, the understanding they gain can result in pressure for changes in the system. Third, once judges, lawyers, and jailers see that effective work is being done by citizens, the groundwork is established for cooperative effort to change the system.[52]

It may be noted that diversionary programs, which are now receiving increased attention, have the effect of encouraging and facilitating cooperation, collaboration, and mutual assistance among the various components of the system and their supportive social agencies. Diversion encourages the system to become more functional, it encourages the community to participate in criminal justice processes, and it also encourages the courts to adopt sounder sentencing principles.

In addition to intrasystem cooperation, an effective criminal justice policy also requires cooperation between the practitioners and theoreticians, the "doers" and the "thinkers." If such collaboration could become cross-agency and cross-professional on the one side, and at the same time cross-disciplinary on the other side—on the obvious premise that each side desperately needs the other—significant progress will be made in understanding and probably in reducing crime.

In 1972, psychotherapist H. Jon Geis declared that ideas about how to influence human behavior effectively must clearly be fundamental to any program of crime prevention. This is a point which this chapter has stressed, and we conclude on that note. Speaking of the police, Geis said:

> If one would argue that the role of the police worker desirably ought to include changing rather than simply maintaining and apprehending the potential or actual anti-legal citizen, then the insights and techniques of psychology, psychotherapy, psychoanalysis and related disciplines ought to be incorporated in job functions and in selection and training procedures.[53]

Suppose that crime prevention, then, were *really* to become the primary mission of the police and of other criminal justice agencies. Geis poses this prospect. When one stops to think about it and realizes what it would mean in terms of standards for recruitment of personnel, training and education, promotions and incentive systems, and all other organizational and functional aspects—indeed, even for the criteria of productivity and successful performance—one wonders why we delay any longer in adopting such a preventive criminal justice policy.

James Q. Wilson gives us the finishing touch:

> In the next ten years, I hope we can learn to experiment rather than simply spend, to test our theories rather than fund our fears. This is advice, not simply or even primarily to government—for governments are run by men and women who are under irresistible pressures to pretend to know more than they do—but to my colleagues: academics, theoreticians, writers, advisers. We may feel ourselves under pressure to pretend we know things, but we are also under a positive obligation to admit that we do not know and to avoid cant and sloganizing.[54]

SUMMING UP

Since 1955, police-community relations programs in this country have frequently referred to crime prevention as an important objective. It's logical that police-community partnership in problem solving should center on efforts to prevent or control crime; but during the 1960s, police-community relations programs were actually much more concerned with the prevention or control of riots. Only recently has there been a strong trend toward community-based crime prevention, yet the basis of crime prevention in police-community relations has yet to be acknowledged.

This chapter strongly advocates crime prevention as a peg on which to hang police-community relations activities. The police sometimes admit that they have little chance of containing crime without community assistance. Soliciting community involvement in crime prevention belongs to the "soft" side of police work, to be sure, yet Sir Robert Peel advocated such involvement in his first principle for metropolitan policing.

How crime is defined is a first consideration for students of crime prevention. The next step is to understand the multiple forms of crime and its multiple causes. The complexity of these issues makes it possible for the police to dramatize their efforts to cope with crime—for example, by using crime statistics as a symbolic barometer of police effectiveness. This encourages the public to feel protected and to trust the police. The police, in turn, take this trust as a mandate to maintain their image as "crook catchers"—the "hard" side of police work, which accounts for only 15 to 20 percent of patrol time in urban localities.

So this chapter brings us back once again to the fundamental role dilemma of the police. What is being done in crime prevention is difficult to measure because the yardsticks for such measurement lack consensus. Effective community cooperation with the police may cause crime rates to rise rather than fall, at least in the short run. A good start would be to make criminal-justice processes more functional—that is, to reduce the abrasive relationships among the police, the prosecutors, the courts, and corrections.

NOTES

1. See Louis A. Radelet, "Police and Community Relations—At This Point in Time," *Police Chief* 41, no. 3 (March 1974): 24–33.

2. Michael Banton, "The Definition of the Police Role," *New Community* 3, no. 3 (1974): 164–171. Much of this issue is devoted to articles on police and community relations.

3. Ibid., p. 171.

4. Michael Banton, "Crime Prevention in the Context of Criminal Policy," *Police Studies* 1, no. 2 (June 1978): 3. Copyright © 1978.

5. Ibid., p. 9.

6. Associated Press release, July 1, 1975.

7. U.S. Bureau of the Census, *Criminal Victimization in the United States, 1976*, National Criminal Justice Information and Statistics Service, LEAA, 1978.

8. See, for example, "The Crime Wave," *Time*, June 30, 1975; and "Violence in America—Getting Worse?" *U.S. News & World Report*, December 11, 1978. Also *Report on Torture* (London: Amnesty International, 1973). See also *National Observer*, July 12, 1975.

9. *U.S. News & World Report*, June 16, 1975.

10. See Terry V. Wilson and Paul Q. Fuqua, *The Police and the Media* (Boston: Little, Brown Educational Associates, 1975).

11. "Public Safety," in *Quality of Life in the Detroit Metropolitan Area*, University of Michigan Institute for Social Research, Survey Research Center (Ann Arbor, Mich., 1975).

12. U.S. Bureau of the Census, *Oakland (CA)—Public Attitudes About Crime* and *San Francisco (CA)—Public Attitudes About Crime*, National Criminal Justice Information and Statistics Service, LEAA, 1978.

13. Charles E. Silberman, *Criminal Violence, Criminal Justice* (New York: Random House, 1978).

14. Review by Jerrold K. Footlick, in *Newsweek*, October 23, 1978, p. 134.

15. John A. Gardiner, "Law Enforcement Corruption: Explanations and Recommendations," in Lawrence W. Sherman, ed., *Police Corruption: A Sociological Perspective* (Garden City, N.Y.: Doubleday, Anchor Books, 1974), p. 316.

16. Peter K. Manning, "Dramatic Aspects of Policing: Selected Propositions," *Sociology and Social Research* 59, no. 1 (October 1974): 22. The list following the quote is paraphrased from the same article. Much of this and related articles by Peter Manning is incorporated in his *Police Work: The Social Organization of Policing* (Cambridge, Mass., MIT Press, 1977).

17. Peter K. Manning, "The Police and Crime: Crime and the Police," *Sociologische Gids* (edited by Maurice Punch), May 1978.

18. D. H. Bayley, *Police and Society* (Beverly Hills, Calif.: Sage, 1977).

19. See, for example, Tom Wicker, "Jobs and Crime," *New York Times*, May 13, 1975; U.S. Bureau of the Census, *Capital Punishment 1977*, National Criminal Justice Information and Statistics Service, LEAA, 1978: A. Blumstein, J. Cohen, and D. Nagin, eds., *Deterrence and Incapacitation—Estimating the Effects of Criminal Sanctions* (National Academy of Sciences, 1977); and Center for the Study of Democratic Institutions, *Crime and American Society* (1978).

20. See George L. Kelling et al., *The Kansas City Preventive Patrol Experiment: A Summary Report* (Washington, D.C.: Police Foundation, 1974).

21. George L. Kelling, "Police Field Services and Crime: The Presumed Effects of a Capacity," *Crime and Delinquency* 24, no. 2 (April 1978): 177.

22. James D. Bannon, "Assaults upon Police Officers: A Sociological Study of the Definition of the Situation" (Ph.D. dissertation, Wayne State University, 1976); Marie Wilt, "Towards an Understanding of the Social Realities of Participants in Homicides" (Ph.D. dissertation, Wayne State University, 1974).

23. For example: "Cities in Peril," *U.S. News & World Report*, April 7, 1975; "How New York City Lurched to the Brink," *Time*, June 16, 1975; "New York's Last Gasp?" *Newsweek*, August 4, 1974.

24. James Q. Wilson, *Thinking About Crime* (New York: Basic Books, 1975), p. 21.

25. Ibid., p. 24.

26. Lewis Mumford, *The City in History: Its Origins, Its Transformations, and Its Prospects* (New York: Harcourt, Brace & World, 1961), p. 576.

27. Willard Gaylin, *In the Service of Their Country (War Resisters in Prison)* (New York: Viking Press, 1970).

28. Robert H. McGowan, "Police Helicopters." A series of three articles appearing in *The Police Chief*, February, March, and April 1978.

29. Robert Carney, "The Return of the Horse," *Police Magazine* 1, no. 1 (March 1978).

30. Don Bernstein, "The Bike Patrol," *Police Magazine* 1, no. 1 (March 1978).

31. David M. Hanley, "Take-Home Car Program and Its Effects on Crime," *The Police Chief* 45, no. 5 (May 1978).

32. *Law Enforcement News*, October 23, 1978.

33. Bruce Cory, "Stop, Thief!" *Police Magazine* 1, no. 4 (September 1978).

34. LEAA, *The Kansas City Police Response Time Study*, 1978. Note, also, the press release on the Kansas City police response time study, by the Police Executive Research Forum, Washington, D.C., commending LEAA for this study.

35. Kevin Krajick, "Does Patrol Prevent Crime?" *Police Magazine* 1, no. 4 (September 1978). See also J. M. Tien, J. W. Simon, and R. C. Larson, *An Alternative Approach In Police Patrol—Wilmington Split-Force Experiment*, National Institute

of Law Enforcement and Criminal Justice, LEAA, 1978; and David K. Wasson, *Community-Based Preventive Policing,* Office of the Solicitor General of Canada, 1977.

36. Such information is available in newspapers and magazines; for example, see "Spiraling Crime—How to Protect Yourself," *U.S. News & World Report,* November 24, 1975; T. Schiffman, *Protect Yourself!* (Washington, D.C.: High Street Press, 1977). The June 1978 issue of *The Police Chief* contains numerous articles on private security and crime prevention.

37. See Gary T. Marx and Dane Archer, "Citizen Involvement in the Law Enforcement Process," *American Behavioral Scientist* 15, no. 1 (September–October 1971). This article evaluates citizen self-defense groups.

38. Canadian Criminology and Corrections Association, *Crime: A Community Responsibility,* October 1976. See also J. C. Hacker, *Prevention of Youthful Crime—The Great Stumble Forward* (Agincourt, Ontario, Canada: Methuen, 1978).

39. U.S., National Advisory Commission on Criminal Justice Standards and Goals, *Report on Community Crime Prevention* (Washington, D.C.: U.S. Government Printing Office, 1973).

40. Ibid., p. 325.

41. Wilson, *Thinking About Crime,* p. xviii.

42. Panel Discussion on "Citizen Participation in Crime Reduction" (John C. Klotter and others), *The Police Yearbook, 1978,* International Association of Chiefs of Police.

43. Norval Morris and Gordon Hawkins, *The Honest Politician's Guide to Crime Control* (Chicago, Ill.: University of Chicago Press, 1970).

44. See F. J. Fowler, Jr., T. W. Manglione, and F. E. Pratter, *Gambling Law Enforcement in Major American Cities—Executive Summary* (LEAA, 1978); and Diane Casbeer, "The Impact of Decriminalization of Public Intoxication in New York State," *The Police Chief* 45, no. 4 (April 1978).

45. *Lansing* (Mich.) *State Journal,* May 1, 1975 (originally appeared in *Philadelphia News*). See also Howard Zinn, *Justice in Everyday Life: The Way It Really Works* (New York: William Morrow, 1974).

46. Bob Buyer, "Attica: Blame for Lawmen, but no Coverup," *National Observer,* January 3, 1976. See also Louis A. Radelet and Hoyt Coe Reed, *The Police and the Community: Studies* (Encino, Calif.: Glencoe, 1973), pp. 224–253.

47. Interview with Lord Widgery, Lord Chief Justice of England, in *U.S. News & World Report,* January 27, 1975.

48. U.S., National Advisory Commission on Criminal Justice Standards and Goals, *Report on Criminal Justice System* (Washington, D.C.: U.S. Government Printing Office, 1973), p. 1.

49. Ibid.

50. U.S., President's Commission on Law Enforcement and Administration of Justice, *Task Force Report: Science and Technology,* p. 53.

51. Tony Platt, "Street Crime—A View From the Left," *Crime and Social Justice,* Spring–Summer 1978.

52. Herbert S. Miller, "The Citizen's Role in Changing the Criminal Justice System," *Crime and Delinquency* 19, no. 3 (July 1973). See also Alexander B. Smith and Arthur Niederhoffer, "The Psychology of Power: Hubris v. Chutzpa in the Criminal Court," ibid.: 406–413.

53. H. Jon Geis, "The Policeman of the Future: A Psychotherapist's View of Tomorrow's Policeman as Human Relations Expert and Psychologically-Skilled Interventionist-Activist" (paper presented at the Second Inter-American Congress of Criminology in Caracas, Venezuela, November 19–25, 1972).

54. James Q. Wilson, *Thinking About Crime*, pp. 208–209. Copyright © 1975 by Basic Books, Inc. Publishers, New York. Reprinted by permission.

SUMMARY OF PART 4

The five chapters in part 4 come under the miscellaneous caption Other Important Considerations. The first two chapters take up relationships within the criminal justice system: police-prosecutorial-court relations, and corrections-community relations. Then comes a chapter devoted to media relations, another on the politics of policing, and finally a chapter dealing with crime prevention, especially in terms of community responsibility.

The police are part of several interlocking social systems. One of these, called the *criminal justice system*, is usually described as including the police, the prosecutor, the courts, and corrections, with other social institutions and agencies playing important supportive roles. Evidence is mounting that the criminal justice system in our country does not work very well and that it may, in reality, be a nonsystem. Because any social system is a human invention relating people in different parts of a whole process, its dysfunctionality invariably raises questions about relatedness, coordination, and teamwork.

If, then, the criminal justice system is in some measure dysfunctional, what are the main reasons for this? We identified a half dozen problems pertaining to:

- The age of offenders
- The youthful offender
- The two-track, nonunified approaches to felonies and misdemeanors
- The opposing philosophies (therefore conflicting goal delineation) among practitioners within the system
- The differing theories of the causes and responsibility for crime
- The problems of professional education and training

In the most general terms, coping with these problems requires that the criminal justice system function more effectively as a system; that is, relationships within the system, and between all parts of the system and the community it serves, must be strengthened. Only a concept of relations that can be described as interorganizational, intergroup, interinstitutional, interprofessional, and interdisciplinary will enable us to deal with complex, interlacing problems—such as crime—in these times. Such problems have a network of causes; their solutions require a network approach.

Looking specifically at police-prosecutor-court relationships, we focused on what we called *jurisdictional disputes*. Whenever a number of roles enter into the decision-making process for any one case and several professional competences compete in its handling, conflicts occur. In these cases, police are often viewed as less professional than other professionals in the system. Moreover, they are sensitive to being treated as adversaries by prosecutors and judges in trial proceedings, and to having no say about the disposition of cases that they themselves introduce into the system. Police express resentment sometimes by accusations that they are being "handcuffed" by certain court decisions, that their rights are given far less attention than the rights of the accused, and that "no one cares about cops anyhow."

We reviewed some of the recommendations of various national commissions bearing on the operation of the criminal justice system. We referred to the noteworthy pilot projects of the Vera Institute, and to the purposes of the National Council on Crime and Delinquency. A broad perspective is needed, and the need was illustrated by what we called *pluralistic planning* for dealing with the problems of criminal justice. *Systems analysis* is an example of how science and technology can contribute to systemic improvement in criminal justice.

A fundamental question to be faced in any study of the criminal justice system is the question of how crime is defined. What specific behaviors has our society proscribed in the criminal code? An improvident and excessive use of the criminal code to perform tasks for which it is ill-suited has created acute problems for the criminal justice system. One problem—the sheer volume of cases flooding the system—in itself contributes to the finger-in-the-dike mentality toward controlling crime and to the frustrations that lead to scapegoating, in and out of the system. Pressures to criminalize, to try to solve all problems by making this or that behavior illegal, persistently block objective assessments of what is the proper use of criminal law. In short, overcriminalization is often at the root of criminal justice–community relations.

Next, we examined the class-bound nature of our criminal justice system through its attitudes toward legal services for the poor and the politically powerless. The poor are ruled by a legal system they neither understand nor trust, and we summarized some of the current efforts to alleviate inequities in the system, none of which can boast of smooth political sailing. Five issues in contemporary criminal justice–community relations have sometimes been quite controversial: entrapment, stop and frisk, preventive detention, no knock, and the use of firearms by police.

Corrections and community relations problems discussed here are no easier to solve than other problems we have considered. Stressing community endeavor in the correctional process as our special interest, we undertook an annotated enumeration of a dozen problems and then suggested several guidelines for coping with them. One in particular, the development of corrections leadership, would go far toward educating the community and elevating the standards of correctional programs. Coordination throughout the correctional process would be improved by the development of better relationships within the field of corrections, and between corrections and the police, the courts, and the community.

Systemic relations in criminal justice depend a great deal on public attitudes, public expectations, and public education. The role of the media is of obvious importance in such matters, so our attention turned next to relations between the police (and other criminal justice agencies) and the media of mass communication and public information: newspapers, magazines, television, radio, motion pictures, and the like. An inherent element of conflict of interest was observed in this relationship as we viewed the media in its watchdog function in democratic society. Helping to "keep the police honest" is a function with adversary connotations; in this sense, it may be argued that the police-media relationship should not, ideally, be too close. Rather, it is a matter of making the relationship of agencies with conflicting interests as cooperative and mutually supportive as possible, by developing ground rules.

The broader, deeper issue in police-newspaper and criminal justice–media relations is power versus power: Big Government versus Big Media. This issue has been dramatized over the years by clashing constitutional principles invoked in free press versus fair trial donnybrooks, and more recently by various cases straining court-media relations.

By what generally acceptable standards is media reporting to be measured and judged? What is bias? What is truth? Should a newspaper merely report the news or does it have some obligation to the public to seek out truth? What should be the role of the media in monitoring social conflict? What, for example, is the responsibility of the media in the violence phenomenon? These are a few of the difficult questions in the discussions of what amounts to media-community relations in today's society, a subject too rarely studied in all our preoccupation with other social institutions.

Although policing is a public, *political* function in a democratic society, there seems to be some reluctance to talk about the police and their political relationships. The assumption in recent years has been that the higher the degree of professionalism achieved by the police, the farther removed from political influence they will be. Thus, we hear slogans such as "take the police out of politics." Of course, in one sense, this idea of separating policing from politics is a very good thing, indeed. In another sense, it is pure hogwash.

We differentiated among several types of "political policing," holding that the police cannot be divorced from the basic political processes that create their function and monitor it.

Most troubles in police and community relations arise from questions of control of police power—of holding the police accountable to *all* of the community—the powerless as well as the powerful. Accountability is a political matter, and so is its complementary side in police and community relations: winning public support for what the police need in the way of resources to do their job, and for the changes that should be made in the way they go about doing it. The classical organizational and functional model of most police agencies is often an obstacle to the playing out of accountability to the community. Police responsiveness to community needs, therefore, requires that the classical administrative, quasi-military model undergo major modification.

How far should police officers be permitted to go in the realm of practical politics? Statutory and policy limits on this question are universal: the argument today is that these limitations may be too stringent. Police militancy at the line level is on the increase, and there is no sign that it will subside. Police unions are here to stay, and blue power mocks the diehards who decry the politicization of the police. The big question is: Will police unions and blue power become allied with the cause of criminal justice reform and go beyond the immediate aims of financial and personal security and protection of police officers? Political cleavages also occur *within* police ranks, as exemplified by the various racial, ethnic, and religious societies and organizations that attract police membership.

The consideration of the police and their political relations takes us back again to the fundamental tension between freedom and order. The question is: How can power be better balanced between those who administer justice and those who are its presumed beneficiaries?

Our discussion of crime prevention began by considering the ways in which the crime problem is defined. The shortcomings in these methods were mentioned, with special attention to the consequent skewing of public perceptions and attitudes about crime. The politics of coping with crime was of particular interest to us as we considered the questions of causes and remedies. Our focus was on criminal justice processes, and again on dysfunctionality as a contributing factor to the problem of repeated crime. Therefore, we concluded, a solid step toward the goal of more effective control of crime—a significant element in a community's quality of life—would be to make the parts of the criminal justice system more truly *systemic*. To accomplish this will require political pressure from a community that is better educated and more motivated to become involved than at present. Rising crime rates and correspondingly more crime victims may provide the stimulus for unprecedented citizen action.

PART **5**

Programs

19

PROGRAMS OF THE PAST

Every problem, no matter how difficult, has its solution. This is a belief that has been thoroughly ingrained in the American ethos, a belief often noted by foreign observers, but one that has not always helped Americans to understand other cultures. However, some people say that some social problems have become literally insolvable. They insist that there will always be poor people, physically and mentally handicapped people, dishonest and selfish and irresponsible people, bigoted people, ignorant people, "fatcat" people, scheming people, indifferent and apathetic people, people who will be people.

In a sense, "people problems" are inevitable. But to assert that *nothing* can be done, not even in resourceful, indomitable America, invites argument. Some say that our cities have become unlivable and ungovernable, and that the problems are overwhelming. They claim our big cities are beyond salvaging.

The problem of police-community relations receives a similar defeatist response from some. These observers feel that *power* is the issue in police-community relations, and that nobody gives up power voluntarily. All the recent attention to police and community relations is viewed as a mere charade, because nobody wants to do anything about the real problems. People cannot be forced to love what they hate, and a lot of people hate cops. Or, there is the argument that those who hate cops don't believe in our system of government anyhow, so why worry about it?

The counterargument is, of course, that every problem, no matter now difficult, has some kind of a solution *provided* that enough people care and decide that change is necessary. It has been said with some insight that our problems are not nearly as insolvable as those who profit by perpetuating them pretend. How can people be motivated to care?

A text of this kind may tend to foster frustration because it focuses on human relations problems and frequently resorts to such phrases as "this problem is further complicated by . . ." and "the popular view of this situation is a gross oversimplification." We keep repeating that problems must be adequately defined, giving due weight to diverse viewpoints, if there is to be any hope for solution. Many people just aren't that much interested. They are impatient with the democratic problem-solving process: they want instant answers. They complain: "Why do we have to take time for all this? Everybody knows what the problem is. Let's get on to the solution." They usually mean by this that they have their own solution, and they want others to accept or endorse it.

The pragmatists among us preach that problems are solved only to the extent that people feel like actual or potential victims of the problem and decide to do something about it. Differences are then reconciled and turned into assets, coalitions are developed, consensus is achieved. Plainly, this is a somewhat cynical view of problem solving. In effect, it is a political approach in which such things as brotherhood, the Golden Rule, and saintly concern for others are "nice," but not particularly utilitarian.

Out of this hodge-podge of varying views and rationalizations for solving or not solving social problems, a great number and variety of police–community programs relations have been mounted, going back to the 1940s. Details about these programs of the past have faded in importance, and there is little point in recounting them here. Instead, this chapter contents itself with general descriptions of the main types of such programs.

PRELIMINARY POINTS ABOUT PROGRAMS

During the fifties and sixties, it was widely assumed that programs and solutions for police and community relations problems were one and the same. There is reason to doubt that this is really so. Because programs of this kind have not, for the most part, been carefully evaluated—beyond the feedback that convinces program planners that their efforts are appreciated by the participants—we do not know very much about what happens as a result of well-intentioned program efforts. There is no harm, of course, in people feeling good about a meeting or conference they have attended. But does it make a difference in what they think and in what they do? This is, after all, the crucial question, and one not easy to answer in the typical police and community relations program. Thus, we suggest that to equate programs with solutions to problems is too grandiose an assumption.

Another questionable assumption has been that big problems require big programs for solution. Sometimes, the programs become so complicated and so bureaucratic, so filled with politicking and with "busy work" as an end in itself, that we lose sight of the problem that the program was supposed to solve. We forget that simple, routine acts of police officers and citizens, on a one-to-one basis, still constitute the basic metabolism of police and community relations. As Norman Cousins, editor of *Saturday Review*, once put it: "To hold out a helping hand to a fellow human being who is in need may not represent universal regeneration. But it does happen to be individual responsibility at its best."

Another important point has to do with the *process* of community problem solving. As we have indicated, there is a good deal to be said for the idea that the process is in itself a significant part of the solution. A shorthand way to suggest this is to say that *community* is both an end and a means. We have noted that functional breakdowns in social systems are the result basically of interrelationship problems. So the key is to mend the relationships.

Do programs matter? Can programs be made to count? Unquestionably, much depends on how the goals of a given program are set. As an example, the aims of some so-called human relations training programs for police officers have been stated so as to suggest nothing less than haloed monks as the ultimate product. Or the stated purpose of a given institute on police and community relations gives aid and comfort mainly to those who believe in the possibilities of paradise this side of Valhalla. One of the problems of evaluating such programs is in the implied need to measure what cannot be measured. The objectives of programs should be realistically cast. It is not a question of ambition or virtue. It is simply a matter of stating program goals so that what happens can be measured.

In the most general terms, what are some things that could be done to alleviate police-community relations tensions? One could

1. Revise the criminal code to reduce overcriminalization and legal moralism.

2. Modify the organizational models of police and criminal justice agencies, in tune with community consensual role delineations, better to harmonize social control with social change, to improve responsiveness and community support.

3. Eliminate racism of whatever color or auspices, along with its fellow travellers, poverty and squalor.

Plainly, these are vast goals. One program more or less will not make that much difference. These are long-range goals, for programs collectively. But it is not racism in Afghanistan that we have in mind. It is the racism, the criminal code, the police organization as near to us as *Mytown, U.S.A.*, although in our world today, what happens in one part of it affects all of the rest.

We shall review six types of programs of the past:

1. Police training programs
2. Police-community relations institutes
3. Metropolitan programs
4. School programs
5. Public information and public relations programs
6. Special purpose programs

POLICE TRAINING PROGRAMS

When we speak of police training programs, we mean systematic preservice or in-service instruction for police officers in such areas as human relations, intergroup relations, interpersonal relations, police-community relations, police–minority-group relations, race relations, the social psychology of police work, the sociology of the police, crisis intervention, social-conflict management, and the like. As we explained in chapter 1, such instruction was the earliest type of police and community relations program to develop historically. We explained why this was so. Often instruction of this kind has been part of a broader police training program.[1]

The first question faced by police trainers in programs of this type is about objective. Is the instruction aimed at changing attitudes, or is it aimed at changing behavior—and is this really a tenable distinction? In concrete terms, is it proper to say to police trainees, "We don't care about your personal prejudices in racial matters. What we care about is that you *behave* as a professional police officer, no matter what your personal attitudes may be"? This position, closely akin to the stance that police officers will enforce a law whether they personally agree with it or not, has been taken by countless police trainers. From the standpoint of the integrity of training and educational pedagogy, this question of attitude and behavior is tricky. To split the two may be opportunistic, short-run strategy; in the long run, as with the parallel rails of a train track seen at a distance, they appear to fuse into a single entity.

An important pedagogical question is whether instruction in community relations is most effective if presented by separate courses and topics, or by integration into regular training courses and topics. This is an old question in the field, going back to early experiments with teacher training in human relations. The argument has never been settled. Probably the best answer is that a combination of both approaches is best: some aspects of the material should be taught separately, for instance, the psychological dynamics of prejudice and rumor; and other aspects should be integrated, for instance, in teaching police field practices. Closely akin to this, pedagogically, is the importance in training programs of clarifying basic conceptual confusions: for instance, the relationship of community relations and public relations; of community relations and race relations or minority-group relations; and the distinction between *preventive* police work in community relations and *tactical* police work in handling civil disturbances.

Human relations training for police, as with school teachers and others, is not simply a matter of what is taught in a given curriculum, no matter how imaginative it may be in content or method. Ideally, it is an emphasis, an orientation in all aspects of the given organization or type of activity. A good teacher of astronomy can teach the subject with a human relations slant. Good teachers of police management courses can teach the subject similarly, espousing management theory that is human relations oriented.[2]

The methods of police training in general have, until recently, relied heavily on traditional patterns: lecture and lesson plans, with limited opportunity for questions and discussion. Today, however, police training seems to be gradually breaking away from the past and beginning to try techniques long since adopted in other educational spheres. Police trainers have lately discovered teaching methods that combine the affective and cognitive dimensions of learning. We are seeing more use of graphic aids, more role playing and simulation, more group discussion and case analysis.

The pooled resource approach to police training was novel in the 1950s, when community-relations subject matter was not being given much attention. The director of the National Conference of Christians and Jews (NCCJ) in New Jersey at that time, Howard Devaney—himself a former police officer— devised an interesting method to get the job done. He conducted forty to fifty Police Institutes on Community Relations, as he called them, in that state over a period of ten years. A given police agency, in Elizabeth or Newark or Trenton or Paterson, would agree to host such an institute, with the sessions usually taking place in a local high school, and NCCJ footing the bill. As many as fifteen or twenty police departments within a radius of fifty miles would, by enrolling several officers each in the institute, build a class of approximately seventy-five trainees, all experienced police officers. Sessions would be held one afternoon a week for six weeks, three hours for each session, with each session featuring a single consultant-lecturer or a panel on a different facet of police and community relations. The usual format was an hour of presentation, an hour of discussion in small groups, and an hour of general feedback with the speaker or panel. The Devaney model was subsequently copied in other places. But standardized program "packages" are difficult to design because of local variations in the determining circumstances.[3]

Teaching social science to police officers has its perils, as any experienced instructor knows. A doctoral study done by Dr. Geraldine Michael at the University of Missouri at Kansas City analyzed the results of a general education social science program for a police training unit.[4] This program was based on six questions:

1. Do police officers make the most appropriate instructors for police training units?

2. Can the behavior of police officers in actual working conditions be predicted during training?

3. Are field supervisors' evaluations of officer performance of any utility?

4. Can the traditional norms and values of police officers as reflected in various reports and public complaints be modified by an overall program of classroom instruction and situational training?

5. Can a training program help reduce the widely noted difference between stated police philosophy and actual police officer behavior?

6. Can one obtain effective criteria for assessing a good officer?

This study recommended (1) that criteria be established for appropriate and inappropriate behavior by police officers, (2) that evaluation procedures for police officer behavior be continuous and constant and not depend upon traditional field supervisor evaluations, (3) that the question of using only police officer instructors in training units be systematically investigated, (4) that guidelines for recruitment, training, and placement be established, (5) that existing police-community relations programs be carefully evaluated, and (6) that selective as well as general recruitment for police service be initiated.

Specific Training Techniques.

Several of the newer approaches to police training call for some explanation. There is programmed instruction, situational training, sensitivity training, and case analysis. So-called *programmed instruction* involves a philosophy of education with a long history. In the past twenty-five years, it has been extensively used in schools, industry, and the military. It is being pushed currently by some police training leaders. Programmed instruction puts learning in an ordered sequence of stimulus items, each of which brings forth a specified response from the student.[5] Students are enabled to advance in small steps at their own paces. Their responses are reinforced by immediate feedback. This leads students from what they know toward what they are expected to learn in a given program. The technique is better suited to some types of subject matter than to others; for example, mathematics is easily taught through programmed instruction. Social science material is more difficult to teach in this way. Programmed instruction has its critics who scoff at "teaching machines" and such, but its possibilities have been recognized in all phases of police training.

Again, what is sometimes called *situational training* is not unique to police instruction, but variations of it are being used in some police academies. In college programs, it is referred to as work-study, with Antioch College as the model. Field training, *practicum*, field trip observation, apprenticeship, and internship are all terms and approaches sharing a common educational philosophy: to provide some in-situation (on-the-job) learning experience for the student or trainee. Professional and vocational schools in particular are likely to use some techniques of this kind, and police academies have long had their internship aspects.

Case analysis, or *situational analysis*, appears to be an especially productive training technique in community relations. Experiments with it are still too few, however, because it is regarded as too expensive and too time consuming, and requires instructional skills that are not thought to be widely available. The American Institutes of Research and the Quaker Project in Community Conflict of the American Friends Service Committee have been among those fostering *critical incident analysis*, originally developed by John Flanagan of the University of Pittsburgh as a technique in conflict management. Simulated situations enacted through role playing or on film are among the tools of this approach, an approach that has spawned several variations in the search for new and better ways of coping with embattled urban relationships.

Crisis intervention and *conflict management* have, in some places, become ways of referring to police training that in the past was called human relations or community relations. Specialized training for police officers in family crisis intervention was pioneered by City College of New York psychologist Morton Bard, working in a New York City precinct. The concept has been broadened to include such matters as consumer protection and landlord-tenant relations, for example, in the Oakland, California, Police Department. The conflict management approach to police-community relations developed in the Dayton Police Department in the late 1960s, as a Law Enforcement Assistance Administration (LEAA) pilot.

Also developing in 1960s police community-relations training was so-called *sensitivity training*, already a recognized method in other fields. The term has been used loosely for a great deal of educational and psychological counterfeiting, indeed for a time was viewed as a panacea for all manner of police and community friction. In some quarters, sensitivity training (confrontation or encounter group or T-group) was regarded as Communist-inspired in something of the same fashion as John Dewey's ideas on "progressive education" in an earlier generation.

Sensitivity training involves learning that stresses the affective dimension: feelings are facts. It employs empathy-building, projective techniques more or less bordering on group therapy, depending upon the given situation. Under amateur direction, it is certainly *not* therapeutic, and indeed may be a means of compounding problems. One difficulty is that too many amateurs and charlatans regard themselves as competent enough to sell their services as consultants to police departments, school systems, and community organizations, and then proceed to do much damage for which sensitivity training in general is blamed. Properly understood, this should be the business of reputable professionals only, who know *what* they are doing, and *why* they are doing it, and are able to explain it in simple terms to anyone asking questions.

Sensitivity training for police officers and other citizens, as a technique to improve police and community relations, has been conducted in numerous cities in recent years. It has been fostered by various educational consulting agencies whose personnel often includes university professors, and by some colleges directly, all interested in sharing in the federal and state grants recently available to police departments wishing to bolster their community relations programs. The nature of the technique is such that it is difficult to describe in a manner that can be taken as representative. Social-psychological game theory plays a prominent part in sensitivity training. One problem with game theory is the difficulty people have in transferring the lessons of the game to human conflicts in the real world. The game tends to be more fun, something of an escape mechanism.[6]

Fred Ferguson, the former police chief in Riverside and Covina, California, has been an enterprising innovator in his experimentation with several different kinds of sensitivity experiences in training personnel of his department. One project was known as *Operations Empathy—Skid Row*, in which police Officers spent a day or two playing the part of skid row inhabitants. Dressed accordingly, with shopping bags containing collected junk or a bottle of wine, they were sent into a community where they were unknown. Several were apprehended by police officers and learned swiftly how it feels to be a derelict on the receiving end of justice. Another well-known Ferguson exercise put police officers in jail in a neighboring county for a weekend and included being booked, fingerprinted, mugged, deloused, and dressed and treated as jailbirds.[7]

Sensitivity training may have useful shock value, but skilled direction must keep it from becoming merely the application of gimmicks for the purpose of manipulating human behavior or subjecting it to pseudoscientific testing and observation.[8] There is, however, a proper place for psychological and psychiatric techniques in police personnel practices. Psychological testing and psychiatric evaluation of police candidates is no longer considered bizarre, and some departments have adopted continuous, in-service group psychotherapy, individual therapy interviews, and emotional stress evaluations of persons promoted to supervisory positions.[9] Much has been said about police officer overreactions in tense community incidents, and about training police for "affective disengagement." So-called stress training is no longer uncommon for police officers, by itself or as part of broadly based training in interpersonal and intergroup relations. Emotional equilibrium in police work is a treasure that can be discovered through the use of established technical methods under skilled professional guidance. If it is possible for the military services to prepare personnel to withstand prisoner-of-war brainwashing if captured by the enemy, it should be possible to prepare police patrol officers to withstand the indignities to which they are occasionally subjected. But the heavy punching bag in the precinct station may still be a good idea.[10]

Specialized Training Program

Once the many general police-training programs in human or community relations emerged, some with a more specific focus followed. Examples include police-media relations; police-Indian or police-Spanish-speaking or police-Puerto Rican relations; police handling of campus disorders; relationships within the criminal justice system; the police role in labor-management disputes; and police handling of the mentally abnormal. Occasionally, a plea has been made by special interests for police training in dealing with homosexuals and transsexuals. Today, some police departments also have squads or units specially trained to deal with family crises, consumer fraud, and landlord-tenant disputes, as part of a general administrative emphasis on conflict management, as we have noted. Special training for police officers to cope more effectively with psychological stress is also much in current vogue, and some departments have special units for dealing with abused and battered wives.

Police Attitude Toward Training

Not everyone takes easily to education and training, police officers included. When the subject is human relations, those with experience in police training programs in human relations are prepared for special resistance. Trainee reactions are frequently so negative and hyper-critical that the question arises whether there may be reasons for it beyond what might be termed "normal bitching."

Psychologist Robert Shellow looked into this question a few years ago with police from the Washington, D.C., area who underwent special training for coping with anticipated problems in connection with the 1963 civil rights march on Washington. Shellow observed the pattern of grousing about the training, the trainers, the "agitators," and such, and checked to determine whether this verbalized resistance seemed to affect the later performance of the officers. His conclusion was that it didn't seem to. Rather, the officers' performance suggested that the training had been effective, despite their negative verbalizations.[11]

Harold Silverman reported no serious resistance to the human relations instruction he provided in the Dayton Police Department, but Arthur Niederhoffer pointed out that, while students of police academy training may be oriented to the social and behavioral sciences, the rookie is introduced to human relations on the job by an older patrol officer who presumably "knows the score." Such informal instruction frequently erodes the idealism of the academy. Both John McNamara and James Sterling made similar points in their studies of police recruits in training.[12]

In a 1970 University of California doctoral dissertation, Thomas A. Johnson reported his study of police resistance to community relations in the Denver Police Department. Johnson showed that a direct relationship between the goals of a police organization and resistance to police-community relations is revealed in the enactment of a patrol officer's role. Johnson contended that patrol officers enacted their role more in response to the nature of a situation classified as emergency, than to a situation classified as criminal or noncriminal. What this means is that where organizational goals are broad and general, patrol officers perceive efficiency as the primary goal, often at the expense of community relations goals. Moreover, Johnson found that police administrators tend to minimize organizationally induced role conflict. As he says,

> as long as there continues to exist the basic incongruity in what policemen are recruited to do, and in fact rewarded to do for the actual work being performed, there will always remain as a constant factor a high degree of perceived role conflict by members of the organization and a concomitant degree of citizen alienation from both the organization and its personnel.[13]

Johnson observed that officers did not deny the importance of improved police-community relations. They simply did not conceive of it as part of their primary role. To them it was not *real* police work. It was Johnson's opinion that defects in the structure and organization of municipal police agencies led to this problem. The correction of these defects would, he thought, make a significant difference in police officer attitudes and behavior. Johnson concluded that the norms, mores, and values of the patrol officer subculture within the larger police subculture were frequently incompatible with the normative value structure of other components of the police organization. Not only did this help explain resistance to police-community relations, he asserted, but it also provided a framework for analyzing the resistance of patrol officers to organizational change in general.

Negative police reaction to human relations training is also, in part, the harvest of unimaginative, unproductive instructional methods and techniques. As Donald Bimstein has written, effective police training cannot rely on procedures used successfully only with children. The average police trainee is a mentally and emotionally mature person. He has the incentive to learn more about his job, but not to the extent of withstanding a procession of lengthy and dull lectures on what he should do or believe. He is pragmatic in his desire for knowledge: he wants instruction that is clearly and concretely job related. Lectures may provide valuable information, but as a pedagogic method the lecture is a relatively ineffective way to influence attitudes or to teach skills and processes. The student must be more personally engaged—talking, questioning, practicing, suggesting, arguing, discussing, teaching—anything but passively auditing. Fortunately, more and more police training facilities are recognizing this elementary fact and moving toward improved methods of teaching. The need for improved methods is related also to the application of a need-determination process that more closely and realistically relates police officer training to identified organizational needs.[14]

Improved training methods are also placing more emphasis on the evaluation factor. Alert training instructors are keenly interested in feedback from trainees on the quality of the instructional and educational programs. LEAA investments in police training projects require increasingly careful, objective evaluation. The National Center on Police and Community Relations at Michigan State University completed a rather complex evaluation (mentioned earlier) of an in-service human relations training program in the Muskegon Police Department.[15] Sketchily described, the main results were the following:

1. The training program failed to increase the percentage of police officers seeing their primary role as peace officers rather than as law enforcers.

2. The percentage of police officers indicating some negative feeling toward blacks slightly increased rather than decreased during the training period. The percentage of officers registering negative feeling toward Mexican Americans decreased.

3. The training program substantially improved officer attitudes toward welfare and probation workers, slightly improved attitudes toward the county department of social services, and slightly worsened attitudes toward the antipoverty program.

Another finding in the study was that more than three-fourths of the patrol officers and one-third of the departmental supervisors felt that they received little or no benefit from the classroom training sessions, which relied principally on lecture. The training program was designed and conducted by the state civil rights commission. Initially, it was deemed to be a notch or two higher on a figurative ladder of sophistication than many similar programs.

Evaluation of Police Training Programs

Police training programs in human relations (community relations, intergroup relations, police-minority relations, social and behavioral science) have suffered from certain shortcomings. Here is a summary developed by the Urban Task Force in Pittsburgh:

1. Imprecisely stated goals and unrealistic expectations.

2. Insufficient active support for programs and program goals on the part of high-ranking police officials. There has been much lip service and not enough real commitment.

3. Failure to recognize that a training program requires support from *all* aspects of organizational philosophy and role conception. Too often, human relations training (as with community relations units) has been window dressing detached from the main thrust of organizational priorities.

4. Lack of sophisticated educational methodologies.

5. Lack of on-going consultation between police officers and program personnel in planning and implementation—in short, poor feedback.

6. Little correlation between curricula and the day-to-day realities of the police function, even in programs using sophisticated techniques.

7. Insufficient means for the reinforcement of new learning following the completion of training sessions.

8. Little planning for fitting human relations training (or other types of police-community relations for that matter) into changing police agency operations.

9. Little use of the research findings and observations that appear in studies of police work and police-community relations, including the pertinent recommendations of several recent federal commissions.

10. Basic resistance to organizational change, and undue devotion to practices and procedures geared to horse-and-buggy communities.

11. Insufficient community participation in planning and implementing training programs.

12. Lack of systematic evaluation of the results of training programs.[16]

POLICE-COMMUNITY RELATIONS INSTITUTES

The term *police-community relations* originated with institutes, beginning with the one at Michigan State University in 1955, since copied or paralleled in many similar endeavors across the country. Through the years, the National Conference of Christians and Jews has been the most active sponsoring and promotional agency for such programs. Although many programs have been local in focus, there have also been annually repeated institutes at the state and regional levels. Today there are still several national institutes, although the one at Michigan State is no longer held. All of this has been discussed in chapter 1, including the purposes, assumptions, and key concepts of such institutes.[17]

Key Ideas of Institutes

An institute on police and community relations is based on the following assumptions:

1. Special human relations training for the police is vital. Police officers also need the educational experience of meeting with other citizens of diversified backgrounds, to discuss issues and problems of common concern and to participate in teamwork approaches to solving these problems.

2. Crime prevention can be and frequently is the primary purpose of teamwork approaches. Mutual understanding and respect may be heightened as a by-product of such problem-solving efforts.

3. Coordination and cooperation within the criminal justice system may be encouraged as a result of such joint endeavors.

4. Tensions between the police and minority groups are basically manifestations of conflict in the relationship between the powerful and the powerless, in political and economic terms. Race in itself is merely a convenient label for other inequities. Therefore, real change in police-minority relations depends. greatly upon change in the larger political, economic, and social spheres.

5. Change in police and community relations depends also upon sorely needed revisions of existing criminal codes, especially with respect to so-called victimless crimes. Change also depends upon considerable attention to the role dilemma of the police and other criminal justice agents, coupled with drastic modifications in the structural and functional organization of police agencies, to align them more closely with community needs in changing times. Two key items in this are responsiveness to the community and appropriate control of police behavior.

No single institute can possibly encompass all of these ideas. Yet they are not nearly as "radical" today as they seemed even ten years ago. Gradually we are beginning to realize that there is much more to good police-citizen relations than mere public relations to improve the police image, however important doing so may be. We are beginning to recognize that the ultimate goal is stable community life and a just social order, as the 1966 President's Crime Commission and later national commissions emphasized. Such a goal, under current conditions, is quite beyond the reach of bumper stickers and law-and-order sloganeering.

Strengths and Weaknesses

Institute-type programs in police and community relations have had both strengths and weaknesses.

Strengths

- Projects aimed at improving police and community relations have been promoted.
- Honest communication has occurred in these settings, with some genuine dialogue and introspection, some worthwhile ventilation of doubts and fears, interchange of ideas, empathy, etc.
- Some responsible community action has resulted from these institutes, implementing the principle of total community responsibility for efforts to solve problems and to cope with crime.
- Police have been helped to see the diversity of the community, and elements of the community have been helped to see the police in human terms.
- Overt expressions of prejudice and of outright hostility have probably become less blatant.
- The professionalization of the police as well as interprofessionalism have been encouraged, and to some extent have been more carefully analyzed.
- Some impetus has been provided for analyzing interrelationship problems in a social systems perspective—for example, the context of the criminal justice system.

All of these statements are carefully qualified generalizations. There is ample substantiating evidence, though it has not been systematically nor scientifically gathered. The same may be said for what follows.

Weaknesses

- These conferences, as do all conferences, revolve around the spoken word; and while talk is a form of action, many variables determine the degree to which talk helps to solve problems. Its value should not be lightly dismissed, yet sometimes mere talk may substitute for solving problems.
- Who are the people participating in such conclaves? From what backgrounds do they come? For whom do they speak? Sometimes the participants are more academics than they are adversaries. Go-to-meeting people go to meetings; others stay home with the problems.

- We know too little about what happens as a result of such institutes. Evaluation of attitude and behavior changes has generally not been done—and it is extremely difficult to do.

- Educational conferences rarely involve or produce a consensus commitment to political action aimed at correcting social problems. Resolutions are usually as far as they go, if that far, and often difficulties arise in continuity and follow-through. There is a window-display aspect of such conferences, perhaps with limited, politically symbolic effect, but not always focusing on what is most wrong, for the tendency is to focus on issues where power is not in contest, thus avoiding political realities. Exemplifying this is a failure frequently observed in academic civil rights discussions in recent years: failure to understand the real meaning of organized violence as a substitute for "normal" political process—in short, the dynamic relationship between violence and social reform.

Extending the last point a step further, conferences dealing with social pathology provide a kind of psychological release valve for societal guilt. Burton Levy has referred to police-community relations as "a million-dollar Brotherhood Week operation where the parties involved in the dispute are often not named, where the symptoms and causes are frequently not discussed, and where most of the participants are hostile and defensive."[18] Levy may overstate the case a bit, but he goes on to say that there are two key questions that should be discussed frankly in any conference designed to reduce the hostility between blacks and police:

1. What steps can be taken within the bureaucratic framework to ensure that the police officer on the street is more likely to take the proper action in contact with black citizens?

2. Given the historical relationship and experience, how do you convince the black community that law enforcement in that community is wholeheartedly attempting to be absolutely fair and nondiscriminatory?

Another weakness is that too many conferences of this nature fail to engage the participants meaningfully in determinations of the program. Program design often is an elitist function, and the participants do not identify with it as their handiwork or as meeting their particular needs.

Institutes on police and community relations, or some variation of this theme, are still being held and are still regarded by many as eminently worthwhile. Now generally less popular than in the sixties, such institutes have been a very important part of the educational advancement of the cause.[19]

METROPOLITAN PROGRAMS

Lee Brown has classified police-community relations programs in large cities into four types: (1) externally oriented, (2) youth oriented, (3) service oriented, and (4) internally oriented. Brown distinguishes these four types of programs as follows:

- Externally oriented programs are generally developed by specialized police-community relations units in a police department and are directed toward the general public or various enclaves in the community.

- Youth oriented programs are directed mainly at youth in the community.
- Service oriented programs are aimed primarily at the alleviation of social problems.
- Internally oriented programs are operated on the premise that every police officer is a police-community relations officer and stress officer-on-the-beat efforts to create good relationships.[20]

The Saint Louis Model

The Saint Louis Metropolitan Police Department was the first in a major city to establish a police-community relations division, doing so in 1957, after two years of preparatory work in the department and in the community, spearheaded by the National Conference of Christians and Jews and its Saint Louis Committee for Better Police-Community Relations and continued as chairman until 1974 of what came to be called the Saint Louis Council on Police-Community Relations. This was a voluntary, independent, self-constituted advisory body to the police-community relations division of the police department.

Each of the nine police districts had a police-community relations committee. A district police-community relations officer worked with the district committee as the representative of the district commander. The district committees functioned with a constitution and by-laws, elected their own officers, and conducted a variety of projects and activities through their subcommittees. Any citizen residing in the district could belong to a district committee. A patrol area leader had membership recruitment as one important duty.

One of the functions of a district committee was receiving and referring citizen complaints directed against the police. But the primary purpose of the entire program was crime prevention, in effect, teamwork between police and citizens in projects and programs aimed at heading off crime and thereby maintaining more livable, stable neighborhoods. A half-dozen storefront centers of the police department scattered throughout the city provided a facility for residents to seek police assistance conveniently: bases for all manner of social services.[21] The police-community relations division of the police department was staffed by a combination of sworn and unsworn personnel and was directly accountable to the chief of police and the Board of Police Commissioners.

Police–Community Relations Units and Storefront Centers

Two common features of metropolitan programs have been a police-community relations unit within a police department, and neighborhood storefront centers, usually in lower class, deteriorating, high crime areas. During the 1960s, these centers came to be looked on as standard earmarks of an urban police agency that was serious in its community relations purposes. The President's Crime Commission devoted rather enthusiastic attention to these features of a "good" program.

On the face of it, the logic for establishing such a unit seems impregnable; however, form is not necessarily substance. A police-community relations unit in a department, whatever it may be called, may make sense—but only under certain conditions. One condition is that such a unit should not be a facade for doing nothing. Another is that such a unit should not excuse personnel not specifically assigned to it from meeting their share of the total community relations responsibility. Some police-community relations units carry on a cornucopia of "busy work" activities involving many people in the community, but never really level with citizens about substantial issues. In effect, the unit joins the establishment: not to do so creates difficult problems within the department, or between the department and other governmental or community echelons.

Semantics have figured in the matter because attitudes make terminology important. As "police-community relations" has become old-hat and has declined in popularity, departments have adopted such terminology as *critical incident* or *tension control*, or *conflict management*, or *crisis intervention*. It is no longer "community relations," but "community affairs" or "community involvement." The semantics have become more sophisticated and, in a few departments, so have the working concepts, the functional charts, and the personnel deployment and training. But still, in too many departments, semantics is a means of deluding the public into believing that big things are happening when in fact it's "business as usual." In such departments, the byword with many officers is, "I don't want any John Q. telling me how to do my job." A police-community relations unit in such a department, by whatever label, is eyewash. And many groups in the community see it as exactly that.

A word of sympathetic understanding is due the police officers who are assigned to police-community relations units. The attitudes of some other officers in the department, including some at the supervisory and command levels, make their lot unhappy indeed. We alluded earlier to the relationship between such attitudes and the basic role predicament of the police. This may explain it philosophically, but it fails to provide much relief for the police officers who are victimized by this brand of internecine warfare. Their problems constitute another way of indicating that police-community relations units, as such, need to be more carefully evaluated than has been generally done to date. Their existence in a department does not mean that the department's community relations house is necessarily in order.

As for the storefront centers, the idea again is certainly laudable. But again, there are divided opinions, with evidence to bolster both critics and supporters. As Glen D. King of the International Association of Chiefs of Police has astutely observed.

> Viewing . . . the storefront operation as basically a public relations activity will . . . likely doom it to failure. The police administrator must clearly distinguish between public relations programs, which are designed to interpret law enforcement programs and practices to the public, and community relations programs which must be designed to provide an improved level of service.[22]

In short, a storefront center or substation can be as much a masquerade as a police-community relations unit. The basic idea is sound; what matters is the way it is used.

Crime-Buster Programs

Detroit, along with other big cities, has had its so-called crime-buster program. In Detroit, it was called STRESS, meaning "Stop the Robberies, Enjoy Safe

Streets." STRESS was the subject of considerable controversy. Similar programs, though with different names, exist in many cities, from New York City to Washington, D.C., to Philadelphia to Dade County, Florida, to Cleveland to Kansas City (Hot-Spot Squad) to Houston to Los Angeles. These programs operate through a presumably well-trained, well-selected unit of police officers designed to deal tactically with crime in the streets, that is, crime in the process of being committed. In Detroit, the unit focused on robberies, using such techniques as decoy police officers.

These "safe streets" programs are open to the same questions that arise with saturation patrol in high-crime areas. But the critics have been cautious, for they realize they are dealing with a mixed broth. Black citizens in big cities are interested in programs intended to contain crime in the neighborhoods where blacks reside in large numbers, simply because they are the chief victims of such crime. So they are inclined to be somewhat tolerant of experiments that promise to serve this purpose, while at the same time retaining some skepticism. In the first eight months of the STRESS program in Detroit, eleven persons—ten of them black—were killed by STRESS units. One police officer lost his life, and thirty-eight were wounded. Forthwith, the Michigan Civil Rights Commission threatened an investigation and called for the program to be eliminated.[23] Both the National Association for the Advancement of Colored People and the Black Panthers agreed that STRESS tactics were unacceptable.

Such programs as Operation Crime Stop, Stamp Out Crime (San Diego), and CHEC (Citizens Helping to Eliminate Crime) encourage citizens in many cities to assist the police directly in the apprehension of lawbreakers and "suspicious persons."[24] For the most part, such programs rely upon the telephone (e.g., Dial-a-Cop). Critics of these programs refer to vigilantism, to Orwellian connotations, and to the tendency for suspicious persons to be black, poor, young, and the like.

The hiring of private security patrols by residents of a particular block or neighborhood to protect life and property is a variation on the same theme. These guards are civilians, usually uniformed but unarmed, and lacking police powers. Their mere presence is believed to deter crime. Their main job is to telephone the police when necessary, and they are warned not to interfere in domestic quarrels.

Electronics also help in police-citizen cooperative crime control, as illustrated by the Community Radio Watch Program of Rochester, New York.[25]

Evaluation of Metropolitan Programs: A Summary

There are both strengths and weaknesses of metropolitan programs in police and community relations.

Strengths (according to the advocates of such programs)

- Programs have helped to build mutual trust, credibility, and better communication, have improved police intelligence with respect to community attitudes, and have assisted the police in conducting investigations.

- Many citizens have been enlisted in partnership with the police in coping with crime.
- Police-public relations, especially with youth, and police-media relations have been improved.
- Intercultural understanding has been enhanced and has helped to reduce racism by forcing a reexamination of fundamental attitudes.
- Programs have helped establish police liaison with many community groups, including extremist groups.
- Interagency and interprofessional cooperation have been encouraged.
- Police-school cooperation has improved.
- Assistance for many people in need of jobs, health services, and many other services has been provided, especially through storefront centers.
- Programs have helped to control rumors.
- Programs have helped to stabilize neighborhoods and to restore pride among residents.

Weaknesses (according to the critics of such programs)

- Programs have not done much to curb crime. (The problem is an old one in program evaluation: we don't know what would have happened if the program did *not* exist.)
- Programs have not gone beyond window-dressing and public relations activities.
- "The right people," "grass roots people," etc., have not been reached.
- Programs have not been supported by total commitment throughout police agencies; they have been regarded as a secondary function of low priority.
- Programs have lost sight of genuine police work. The problem is to maintain police identity and, at the same time, win the confidence of community groups. Deviation from standard police practices makes social workers of the police—at least so the critics allege. Critics add that this isolates a community relations unit from the remainder of the department.[26]
- Community relations workers in a police agency sometimes engage in formal complaint machinery or internal investigations. This turns them into "snitchers" and "head-hunters" and adds to their role ambiguity.[27]
- Police intelligence is sometimes overemphasized in investigations, making stool pigeons of citizens and jeopardizing the civil rights of informers as well as of suspects.
- Programs cultivate only citizens who are already disposed to be friendly toward the police, sometimes for reasons of personal aggrandizement.
- Programs sometimes operate with inadequately trained community-relations personnel. As a simple example, many speak only English, and many of these do not understand the idiom of the streets and the ghetto.
- Such programs attract those looking for a forum to vent their hostilities against the police.

- Few *real* changes have resulted from the programs: police officers and police departments have not changed much, many laws are still on the books that shouldn't be, and racism is still rampant.

One cannot sit in judgment on the merits of these opinions. There are plenty of advocates, police and nonpolice, for each point. Much depends upon what one wants to prove. If one is anti–community relations, he will find evidence for the weaknesses. If one is pro–community relations, he will find evidence for the strengths. As James Q. Wilson has observed, we are talking at and past one another, and the real issues are largely lost in rhetoric.

SCHOOL PROGRAMS

Police-School Liaison Programs

Police and community relations programs and programs concerned with youthful attitudes and behavior are often thought of as synonymous. One reason is that the adult planners of such programs frequently regard "problems of youth" as a fitting subject for inter-professional dialogue. Another reason is the increasing incidence of juvenile delinquency and of crimes committed by young people. Still another reason is the hope that things will be better in the future in police-community relations, and with respect to social problems in general, if we concentrate on proper teaching of today's youth. "They will do better than we have done" is a typical expression of this notion.

Many programs and projects aimed at combatting or preventing youthful crime do have some police-community dimensions. Program objectives commonly stress that respect for law and authority (and for the police, courts, etc.) is attitudinal insurance against delinquent behavior. Some police agencies combine police-community relations and youth services in one unit. A similar idea has inspired the community services or crime prevention units of other police agencies. As we have noted, some departments feel that crime prevention is a more appropriate social responsibility for them than community relations per se. While this is fencing with semantics to some extent, one is well advised not to argue the point so long as the job gets done. Actually, the police have been engaged to a limited degree in crime prevention, and more in delinquency prevention programs, since the turn of the century. Juvenile aid units date back to the 1930s.

Among many types of programs of this general nature, an especially interesting one is called police-school liaison. The essence of it is to place a police officer on duty in a school. The idea originated in England.[28] In this country, Flint, Michigan, is recognized as a pioneer developer of such a program, beginning in 1958.[29] Salient features of the Flint program were these:

- The police officer, called *police counselor,* is assigned to a junior or senior high school. He is also responsible for elementary schools in that area. (Flint public schools operate on a community school pattern.)
- The officer, in plain clothes, is not responsible for enforcing school rules and regulations. His main concern is with behavior of a predelinquent or delinquent nature. But he also exercises some secondary functions in

career counseling, in rapping with students, and in helping to develop friendly attitudes toward police.

· Decisions to refer a case are made by a counseling team at the school, of which the police counselor is a member.

Rather impressive results, as represented by delinquency statistics, have been claimed for the Flint program, although there are those who remain skeptical. The plan has been imitated in numerous other cities, with some variations. Tucson, Arizona, for instance, adopted it beginning in 1963, with the officer stationed in school in full uniform, the idea being to encourage youth to see police officers as friendly helpers. The question of whether the officer should be in uniform has provoked much argument. In Tucson, the police officer alone made the final decision on referrals of problem cases. The Tucson program was threatened by legal suit in 1968, when the Arizona Civil Liberties Union charged that it was mainly a police intelligence operation that deprived students of their civil rights.

Police-school liaison programs have both staunch advocates and strong critics. June Morrison has lined up the arguments on each side as follows:

Pro

· School administrators are generally favorable in their views of the program. So too are police administrators.

· Police officers in such programs believe that goals are being met in a very satisfactory manner, in terms both of youthful attitudes and of delinquency.

· Statistics seem to show that the program does make a significant difference in delinquency and youthful crime. While the results of program evaluations are circumspectly interpreted (and it is difficult to learn exactly what has been studied, by whom, and how), the statistical evidence of apparent success is persuasive.

· Faculty and youth themselves are generally favorable in their views of the program. The same appears to be true with parents, though there are exceptions with all three groups.

Con

· Police officers in these programs are sometimes not adequately trained for their duties in school counseling.

· The program injects primitive attitudes into the treatment of children.

· Attitudes of youth toward police are not being changed in a positive direction.

· The program takes manpower away from police activities that should have priority.

· Interrogation and investigation by police officers in the program jeopardize the civil rights of students.

· Police officers are used as school disciplinarians, which should not be their function.

· The program carries with it an Orwellian atmosphere of youth under con-

stant harassment and surveillance. It establishes "a network of informers."

- The program encourages the misuse of educational process for police purposes.[30]

Some of the objections to the program can and should be met by procedural
guidelines and safeguards, for example, in such matters as interrogating students and notifying parents. A central question in police-school liaison programs is again the question of role. To the extent that they are convinced that
liaison programs help to control delinquency and crime, police administrators
are likely to be in favor of them. So the question is not so much whether the
police ought to have a role in the programs as it is the ambiguity of the police
officer's role in the school setting. Some of the forementioned arguments
against the liaison-type program reveal other important points that should be
resolved. One may well ask, for example, whether police officers in the school
setting should be in uniform and whether they should be armed.

Defining the role of the school liaison officer means coming to grips with the
central questions: What is it, exactly, that the police officer is there to do? Does
a uniform—or a gun—contribute to this purpose? These are not easy judgments to make in our society today, and the answers to these questions would
probably differ according to particular community conditions and attitudes.
The ultimate aim by one role definition is summed up in the Tucson statement
of purpose:

> The School Resource Officer Program is a cooperative effort of the public schools and
> law enforcement agencies to develop an understanding of law enforcement functions
> and to prevent juvenile delinquency crime.[31]

If a community is to consider such a program, all parties concerned should
have the opportunity to speak their piece and to be fully informed about what is
to be done, why and how, and with what procedural guidelines. This is not a
matter for unilateral, arbitrary policy setting by police or school administrators. Discussions leading to a decision should enlist the police, appropriate
governmental leaders and bodies, juvenile court people, school administrators
and faculty, certain social agencies, civil rights and due process organizations,
students and parents, and every other interested citizen and group. The students and parents, who are pivotal figures in the aims of the programs, are
most likely to be forgotten in this process. Initiators of the programs must take
the time and the means necessary to ensure that the base of opinion and
consultation is as broad as possible and that information about such programs,
where they presently exist, is available for reference.

A national Institute on Police and School Liaison programs was convened
under the sponsorship of the National Conference of Christians and Jews in
Atlantic City, December 5–8, 1971. The participants in the institute came from
seventeen states and the District of Columbia. They represented all sections of
the nation, from the East Coast to California, and from New England to the
deep South. The participants were police, educators, and high-school students,
plus a few additional persons who represented both public and private human-
relations agencies. A total of 185 persons took part in the deliberations.

The following is a résumé of the basic agreements hammered out in over

4,600 man-hours of discussion in plenary sessions, task forces, and caucuses. Unanimity was not achieved on any issue, but broad areas of consensus emerged as follows:

1. As a matter of principle, it was agreed that the police should not occupy full-time, regular staff roles in the schools. Their presence in the schools on any such basis is viewed as indicative of the failure of the society at large to fulfill its primary obligations to its younger citizens. However, because the police *are* serving in a variety of roles in many schools throughout the nation, the Institute turned its attention to ways in which their presence could be most creatively and constructively put to use.

2. Police should not be called to serve as school security guards, except in the most extreme emergency situations. The police should not be viewed as the first line of defense against disorder and should be called only as a last resort after all other measures have failed. After the emergency has abated, the police as an enforcement agency should be removed from the school premises as quickly as possible. Their continued presence tends to exacerbate the tensions they were called in to control, and inhibits an educational process.

3. On the other hand, the police would be welcomed into the schools by both students and administrators as liaison officers acting in an educational and counseling role. The Institute, therefore, recommended that all high schools seek to adopt a school liaison officer program.

4. Liaison officers should be authorized, sworn members of the major law enforcement agency operating in the jurisdiction in which the high school is located. Under the command of either the juvenile bureau or the community relations bureau of their department, they would be assigned to full-time duty working with students in cooperation with school authorities. It was emphasized that:

   a. The liaison officer should not be regarded as a law enforcer in the school. It was agreed, however, that if a violation of the law occurred within his immediate view, it would be necessary for him, as a police officer, to take appropriate lawful action. If a violation were to take place where he was not present, it would be preferable for the school authorities to determine, in consultation with the liaison officer, the proper course of action. If the incident is deemed to be one that the officer can deal with on a discretionary basis, he should do so. If there are grounds for legal custody, other police officers should be called in to make the arrest. While it must always be understood that the liaison officer is a police officer, his relationship with the students should not be jeopardized by giving them reason to believe that his role in their school is mainly one of surveillance and enforcement.

   b. The liaison officer should not be called upon to take over the responsibility for maintaining discipline in the school. This is a task for the administration and the students themselves. Principals and teachers should not abdicate their responsibilities for order maintenance by calling on the liaison officer to enforce school policies and regulations. To do so would be to reinforce the already too prevalent image of the police as a repressive force rather than a helpful resource.

5. The visual image of the liaison officers in the school—how they should dress, whether they should be armed—was the subject of much thought and discussion. The final recommendations reflected mutual concessions:

a. *Dress.* The majority preference was civilian attire for liaison officers while on the job in the school, but many police officers felt that liaison personnel should be in uniform. As a compromise solution, it was agreed that civilian dress with a sports blazer and an identifying pocket patch insignia would be appropriate most of the time, but that periodically, perhaps once a week, liaison officers should wear their regulation uniform so that their identity as police officers would not be lost.

b. *Arms.* If the law or department policy required that all officers wear side arms, it was agreed that (1) when the regulation uniform was worn, the gun could be visible, and (2) when civilian attire was worn, the gun should be as inconspicuous as possible. The students and many of the police believed that, if possible, the weapon should be kept locked in the liaison officer's office during his period of duty on school property.

6. The role of the liaison officer was defined as combining three functions: counselor, resource person, and educational aide. The functions were outlined as follows:

a. *Counselor.* Police, students, and educators alike felt that the liaison officer could make an important contribution as a resident friend, counselor, and listener to youth with personal problems. The role was likened by some to that of an ombudsman, to whom the students could turn for help and guidance.

In this role, the liaison officer should cooperate closely with, and not conflict with, authorized guidance counselors in the school. It was felt, however, that because most guidance counselors are so overburdened with testing, curriculum adjustment, and long-range planning for student welfare, they do not have the time to deal with the kinds of daily personal matters that the students might take to the liaison officer, and they would welcome help in this area.

b. *Resource and referral.* The liaison officer should be well acquainted with the kinds of help available to young people with special problems and refer them to the local resources that can aid them in matters beyond his or her depth to solve. This helping function would frequently be on a "shared client" basis with the school guidance counselor.

c. *Educational aide.* The Institute recommended that the liaison officer serve an educational function by helping to create and conduct courses of study designed to acquaint students with the American system of justice and the ways in which it operates on the local level and touches their lives.

These courses should be electives, but should earn credits. They should be developed cooperatively by the educators and the police and conducted under a team-teaching system. The courses should be designed to make use of a wide range of community resources and to put emphasis on group-process techniques, instead of lecture methods, with as much student participation as feasible.

7. With respect to the qualifications of the person for this kind of job, it was agreed by the Institute that:

a. The liaison officer should have at least two years of college training or the equivalent experience.

b. He or she should be a volunteer for the job, for only an officer who really wants this kind of responsibility is qualified to handle it.

    c. He or she should receive specialized training both before and during the assignment, with emphasis on adolescent psychology.

8. Other recommendations pertaining to the liaison officer were the following:

    a. The students should be given a voice in the selection of the officer assigned to work in their school.

    b. Wherever feasible, it would be better if liaison officers were residents of the community in which the school is situated. The students, however, said they were more interested in the attitude that officers brought to their assignments than they were about where the officers lived. "We don't want a cop in the school; we want a friend. And if he's a friend, we don't care where he grew up," was the way one young man stated it.

    c. The liaison officer should have an office in the school and be available to the students on a daily basis.

    d. He or she should be considered a part of the educational team and be included in all faculty conferences and consultations.

    e. It was emphasized that beyond regular duty in the school, the liaison officer should participate in extracurricular and community affairs and conduct regular meetings with parents, individually as needed and in groups.

9. The opinion of many of the Institute participants, cutting across police-youth-educator lines, was that the best police-school liaison program in the world would be worthless if the students' experience with the police outside the school setting contradicted the trust relationship established by the program. It was recommended, therefore, that *all police* working in the district in which the school is located be required to make periodic visits to the school and, under the aegis of the liaison officer, participate in rap sessions with the students. This kind of exchange, it was believed, would help to achieve better understanding on both sides.

10. All three groups attending the Institute—police, students, and educators—agreed that a police-school liaison program should not be undertaken without adequate advance planning and delineation of goals and roles. Police, students, and educators should work together to establish the guidelines under which the program is to operate, and matters of students rights, educational prerogatives, and police responsibilities must be understood in advance by all concerned.[32]

Other School Programs

There are many different types of police-school cooperative programs, as we have said. Some examples are driver education in high schools, traffic and bicycle safety programs, the Officer Friendly, Patrolman Bill, and other political socialization projects to which we referred in chapter 12. Add to these such activities as a Police-Community Relations Youth Council (Saint Louis), Teenage Traffic Court, Career Days, Operation Blue Star (Des Moines), Police Partners (Philadelphia), Teen Post and School Contact programs (San Diego), Police-Public School Cadet (Flint), Police Youth Service Corps (Pontiac, Michigan), police junior-aide programs, police cruiser tours, shoplifting and theft prevention lectures, junior crime prevention projects, student symposia on law and order, youth protection instruction and narcotic education, and many more.

Whatever the program worked out with the collaboration of appropriate community groups, students, parents, and others, it is clear that school systems and police departments must get together in furthering their common purposes. Persons concerned with police-community relations and school-community relations have much to learn from each other, for they share common objectives. In the past, police and schools have tended to go their separate ways, each insisting that there be no interference from the other. While the need for clear role delineation for each institution becomes more compelling as collaboration and cooperation increase, there is no justification in today's society for continuation of the separatist pattern.

Law and Order in the Schools

Large numbers of today's youth do not conform to traditional controls, in or out of school. Problems of discipline loom large in and around classrooms, especially in the heterogeneous inner city. Teachers and administrators from "good" backgrounds are faced with grave difficulties in understanding and adjusting to pupil behavior perceived as antischool or antiteacher, if not antisocial. Some of this behavior is due to personality and some to environmental factors, but there is little question that it is sometimes technically criminal, sometimes dangerous, and always frightening. Many school systems are, therefore, increasing their protective and security personnel in order to enforce order and discipline, and in so doing are encountering some negative community reaction to "cops in the corridors."[33]

The maintenance of order is vital in a school setting. Wide agreement on such a generalization contrasts with wide disagreement on what constitutes order, whether it is more or less important than (or different from) freedom to learn, and in any case, how it is best achieved. To be specific, what difference may there be between the school's approach to discipline and order with lower-class Puerto Rican children and that with middle-class WASP children? Here is one comment on such a question:

> Many contemporary "disadvantaged" children, while feeling limited in upward economic and social mobility and limited in world-view, sense a greater freedom to express, and often act out, a generalized personal and collective rage at traditional and adult institutions. . . . The fact that must be dealt with is that if anger, hostility, frustration, or disenchantment are accompanied by invective or physical attack upon school personnel, fellow students, or property, the optimum atmosphere for teaching or learning rapidly deteriorates.[34]

Something must be done, then, to control bedlam and terror in the school. It is to be hoped that this can be accomplished without appreciably sacrificing teaching resources to monitoring resources. How? More student participation in the governance of schools seems to be part of the answer and more community participation in the governance of schools, another. Programs that help to bridge the cultural and social gulf between teachers and pupils are still another part of the answer.[35] Improving the quality of instruction may help.

Ultimately, however, the question may be when to bring in the police. First, we may say, *certainly not until after a great deal of reflection by school personnel.* Calling in the police to handle school disorder is very often an easy cop-out, although it is conceded that community pressures sometimes force this action when it is imprudent. Here again, a great deal of community education is required, preferably *before* a crisis develops. Panic takes over when a crisis occurs and impairs clear thinking. An increase in police or security personnel in schools does not really get at the base of the problem; it merely consoles those who are content to deal with symptoms. As Wendell Roye points out:

> Security forces secure, protect, monitor, control, intimidate, and repress. Remediation . . . is not the primary function of police, in hallways or elsewhere. . . . Employment of uniform, club, badge, gun, and the other paraphernalia of law enforcement to make teenagers walk straight and quietly down a school hallway is demeaning to the officer, insulting to the children and their families, and of questionable overall merit or effectiveness. Finally, uniformed guards in great number in a school are a clear indication that the institution is proceeding in fear and failure.[36]

This is not to argue that there is *never* a time and circumstance when a police officer is plainly needed in the school for the specific purpose of maintaining order or of invoking criminal process. But we believe that this should not be the first move when things get out of hand. One problem with the police-school liaison program, as we have stated, is the role ambiguity of the police officer in the school. Because he or she is on the scene and on the school staff, it is easy to rely on that officer as a kind of symbolic deterrent in disciplinary upheavals. The image of the officer then comes through to students as a tyrant, rather than as a helper, counselor, confidant, and friend. To be sure, the officer must occasionally make arrests in the line of duty. Parents, too, must sometimes punish children. But few parents wish to be perceived by their children as mainly punishers. Punishment is not so much discipline—though it is frequently regarded as such—as it is a sign of a breakdown in order-thinking, order-abiding behavior. When a police officer makes an arrest to restore order in a school, a lot of things have probably gone wrong.

School and police officials need to join in cooperative endeavors apart from dealing with crisis. Many school administrators think of calling the police only when events are beyond them. Many police officials think of preventive work in schools as "social work." Somehow, these attitudes must change. The appropriate time for school-police collaboration is in the absence of crisis, when joint resources can be brought to bear on the *prevention* of crisis. Such a strategy also helps to improve attitudes toward the police within the school, because the officer is more apt to be viewed as a helper and resource person, not as a disciplinarian.

PUBLIC INFORMATION AND PUBLIC RELATIONS PROGRAMS

Police agencies today are doing many things for the purposes of public information and public relations, far more than ever before. Certainly this is necessary and important, but there is no escaping the truism that the best public relations is that of rendering good police service. In business and industry, a quality product is the best advertising. In police work, as in other kinds of public service, taxpayers measure quality by what happens when they need the service.

But the taxpayer does not always *call* for police service. Sometimes it is thrust upon him. Even so, arresting an individual for just cause is regarded as a service to many. This is the idea of "the common good." But because most taxpayers are not quite so philosophical about it, the actions of the police become a target of public concern. As we have observed more than once, they *do* make arrests, they *do* put people in jail, they *do* sometimes inconvenience one's schedule. This makes public relations for a police agency a bit more complicated than it is for, say, a tourist bureau. With the police, there are similarities to public relations for medics and hospitals. The service provided may be a good thing in the long run, indeed even indispensable, but it isn't likely to get rave notices while the operation is in progress.

Because public ignorance and apathy with respect to police activities and criminal justice problems are generally acknowledged, public information and public relations efforts merit considerably more attention than has been assumed in the past. It is not merely the amount, but the *quality* of the public information and public relations endeavors that must be examined. As with railroad passenger service, the endeavors may be calculated to *discourage* public interest. Annual reports of police departments frequently appear to be so calculated, as we have noted. Indeed, there is even a theory that the police have not welcomed public attention because it might expose widespread corruption. Yet it is interesting to study police officer rationalizations for corruption, which invariably implicate "the public." A companion theory, earlier noted, is the belief of some officers that professional police officers should not submit their deportment to review by uninformed, unprofessional citizens. Police resistance to public relations and public education tends to confirm the idea that they have something to hide, and to that extent it makes the notion of a "professional" police officer amusing in the public view.

In chapter 2, we listed some examples of the public relations and community service activities being carried on by police agencies. One curious point regarding public relations for the police is the stress on selling police officers as *human beings*, which is clearly aimed at counteracting whatever tendency there may be for the public to see the police officer as repressive, punitive, and therefore *inhuman*. So public relations features "the human side" of the officer: most police are honest, trustworthy, empathetic, compassionate, helpful—and possess other such Boy Scout attributes.[37] Another public relations pitch proclaims that police officers are fair, firm, objective, courageous, not easily swayed, and vigilant in enforcing the law. There is just a trace of the superhuman in the image projected to the average citizen, who wants to believe that those who protect his life and property are a shade less susceptible to human foibles than he is. Many current police scenarios on television play on this theme, which we will leave to social psychologists to analyze.

The mixed role of the police is central to their public relations strategies. Depending on the audience, the images projected must truly be plural: the officer is helper, friend, and service oriented in one projection; the officer is guardian, protector, and fearless enemy-of-crime in another projection. Police public relations must play to all audiences and their diversified expectations. The problem is that the expectations are not simply diversified but are, to some extent, *conflicting*. This is no great problem in a police department prepared to provide a diversity of services to meet these expectations and to project correspondingly diverse images in its public relations. But for a large city department set on a single style of service and a single image projection, some public relations difficulties are predictable. It is the same old point: pluralistic communities require pluralistic police services.[38]

The most elaborate public relations schemes and projects are no substitute for quality performance by the individual police officer in contacts with clients. To emphasize the positive helps to cushion the negative and prohibitive in what a police officer must sometimes do. Television, radio, the newspapers and newsmagazines, departmental newsletters, advertisements, and the like directed to public education and information, can be important instruments and allies of police public relations.[39] Public education in matters of great interest to the police depends on the police taking the initiative. The case for recognition of the police as professionals rests significantly on the quality of their public educational efforts. A reverse aspect of this is education of the police by the various publics. A true professional is prepared to listen as well as to tell.

SPECIAL PURPOSE PROGRAMS

Some programs in police-community relations do not fit neatly into the categories we have discussed because they are designed to serve special needs in different communities. Some of these programs are of the past; some still go on. Following are some brief descriptions:

- Several cities (San Francisco and Atlanta, among others) have assigned police officers to full-time duty in job opportunity and job training centers in economically depressed areas, with particular attention to assisting those released from correctional institutions in locating and qualifying for jobs. The idea started with OEO-antipoverty programs and had crime prevention as its main purpose.

- Some years ago, New Orleans instituted what was called the Police Foundation, an organization of local business executives seeking to raise funds by public solicitation to help defray tuition costs for local police officers attending local colleges. This should not be confused with the Ford Foundation–supported Police Foundation, which operates at the national level, mainly as a catalyst for experimentation and change in police organization and practices.

- Clergy-police relations have been brightened by such projects as a Philadelphia program in which clergy of varying denominations rode the "red cars" with police officers on an eight-hour shift; by the 77th Street Interdenominational Clergy-Police Council that grew out of the 1965 Watts riot in Los Angeles; and by a clergy-initiated referral service in Washington, D.C., in which delinquent youth are sent to certain ministers for help in solving their problems. Church groups have also opened storefront clinics for narcotics addicts and halfway houses for released prisoners. They have initiated such social services programs as FISH, and have been active in some communities in setting up crisis-counseling centers. In Pittsburgh and in fourteen other cities in the five jurisdictions of the

United Methodist Church, someone in the local church started placing priority for church action in the relationship between the community and the police. The projects are linked together through the Board of Christian Social Concerns and the Women's Division of the Board of Missions, with special funding from the Fund for Reconciliation. In each city, the task force is ecumenical.

- Boston police districts have had community relations workshops similar to those in Chicago, sponsoring various programs such as helping applicants to prepare for police entrance examinations.

- The effectiveness of group discussion in mitigating police-resident hostility in an urban ghetto has been studied.[40]

- The National Association for Mental Health, Inc., publishes an excellent, succinct training booklet for police officers entitled *How to Recognize and Handle Abnormal People*, written by Robert A. Matthews, M.D., and Loyd W. Rowland, Ph.D.[41]

- The San Jose, California, Police Department uses public-service time for regularly scheduled Spanish-language radio broadcasts to the 50,000 Mexican Americans residing in that city. The programs provide information about the police and about various service agencies, including probation, parole, legal aid, state employment, and the like.[42]

- Good police-community relations are effected not only by the initiative and activities of police agencies, but also by the initiative and activities of community organizations of many kinds. Illustrations: bicycle safety projects of service clubs; leaflet and poster projects; traffic safety and crime prevention films, speakers, panels, exhibits, fairs, billboards, etc.; home safety and pedestrian safety campaigns; drinking-driving-drugs programs. Several years ago, the Illinois Chamber of Commerce sponsored an excellent statewide project dedicated to better police service and police-community relations.

- In many cities, an elaborate rumor control network has been developed. In Los Angeles, for example, there is a police rumor control center in each of the seventeen divisions.

- At one time, all new police officers in Atlanta were assigned to the Crime Prevention Bureau (another name for a police-community relations unit) for several weeks, until the police training school was ready to accept them. Young officers were sent into the community with experienced officers and familiarized with the people and their problems. Every police officer hired in Dayton for a time served initially as a community service officer, assigned so he would *not* be teamed with a veteran patrol officer.

- In St. Louis, the Police Junior Aide project has been a coordinated effort of the Police Department, the YMCA, and the Metropolitan Youth Commission, dating back to the summer of 1967. Thirty-six boys, aged fourteen and fifteen, were hired in poverty areas to work with the police in non-dangerous tasks. Some of the boys were predelinquents. The program helped to curb delinquent behavior, but did *not* change the attitudes of the participants toward the police.

- Increase in the incidence of conflict with the law on the part of the Canadian Indians and Eskimos prompted a survey study by the Canadian Corrections Association (1967) to seek solutions to the problem. A selected field staff visited communities in urban, rural, and remote areas of the provinces. The law enforcement, judicial, and correctional processes were evaluated, as they related to these minority groups.[43]

- The Positive Action for Youth (PAY) program has been operating in Flint, Michigan, community schools since the fall of 1966, with support from the Mott Foundation. The program involves male juvenile probationers, their peers, teachers, and parents, and offers group counseling, work experience, family counseling, supportive action, and individual counseling directed to *all* family problems, not merely to the needs of the program participants. Somewhat similar are Youth Services Bureaus located in community centers, demonstrating that public and private organizations can cooperate to establish services for delinquent youth.[44]

- To improve the police officer's knowledge and appreciation of community relations and to demonstrate how the officer can develop support from the community, the Community Relations Orientation for Police (CROP) program was established in Philadelphia. It provides training sessions and discussions of police-community relations goals and problems.[45]

- The Cincinnati Police Department has experimented successfully with a summertime Tension Alert Unit in its Community Relations Bureau. School Resources Officers, free for the summer, worked in teams of two, in uniform, walking the streets in heavily populated neighborhoods, talking to people and reporting any symptoms of potential tension or trouble. In New York City, the Preventive Enforcement Patrol (PEP) is a special squad of black and Puerto Rican police officers who live and work in Harlem, free from routine calls so they can concentrate on personalized preventive patrol.

- An institute centering on tensions between white and black police officers in large urban departments was held in Detroit in the spring of 1972, cosponsored by the Guardians Society, New Detroit, the Detroit Police Department, the Center for Urban Affairs, and the School of Criminal Justice of Michigan State University.

- The Birmingham, Alabama, Police Department has a guidebook called *Answers to Issues* covering in brief form many questions about police procedures.

- An art exhibit in New York City's 32nd Precinct featured art work done by police officers and children of the neighborhood.

SUMMING UP

A National Association of Police Community Relations Officers was formed in 1969, with its membership composed of police officers working in this field and other concerned citizens. It is appropriate to conclude this chapter with this association's statement of the objectives of a good police-community relations program.

1. To initiate continuing programs aimed at fostering and improving police services, communicating, reducing hostilities, and ferreting out areas of tension and their causes in the total community.

2. To assist the police and total community in acquiring the special skills and knowledge to meet the pace of social change.

3. To assist in defining the police role in society.

4. To establish a reciprocal line of communication and responsiveness between the police department and the public.

5. To instill in every policeman the proper attitude toward, and appreciation of, good police-community relations.

6. To enhance the community's understanding of the functions of the police, and to aid the police in understanding the needs and aims of the community.[46]

The association goes on to say that the following should *not* be part of the objectives of police-community relations programs:

1. Police-community relations units should *not* serve as intelligence units of the police department, or work in an undercover capacity.

2. Police-community relations personnel should *not* be used as a tactical force in enforcement eventualities.

3. Police-community relations units should *not* handle matters normally assigned to an internal affairs unit.

4. Police-community relations should *not* be a "cooling" unit, acting as a pacifier between those in positions of responsibility and the community. It should pursue just and tangible solutions to problems.

5. A police-community relations unit should *not* be used as a vehicle of token appeasement for poor police practices.

The association's central theme is this:

> Those police administrators who fail to recognize the importance of police-community relations programs will fail to achieve what should be the ultimate aims of law enforcement.[47]

Police-community relations programs, as understood in the recent past in this country, began with police training courses in human relations during World War II. Institutes on police-community relations were initiated, beginning in 1955 with the first national institute at Michigan State University, which was widely copied in subsequent years. Programs tailored to large metropolitan centers emerged from these institutes. School-related projects of considerable diversity developed, directed to improve the attitudes of youth toward the police and other authority figures. There have also been many public information and public relations activities initiated by police and other criminal justice agencies in recent years. Notable too are programs with a specific objective, such as police–Puerto Rican relations, police–Chicano relations, and police–Native American relations. This chapter has touched on all these and on other programs of the past.

NOTES

1. A panoramic survey of police training programs in the community relations field as of 1966 was provided in two reports of the President's Commission on Law Enforcement and Administration of Justice, *Task Force Report: The Police* (Washington, D.C.: U.S. Government Printing Office, 1967), pp. 175–178, and *Field Surveys V, A National Survey of Police and Community Relations,* prepared for the commission by the National Center on Police and Community Relations, Michigan State University School of Police Administration and Public Safety (Washington, D.C.: U.S. Government Printing Office, 1967), pp. 209–225. Some typical programs are described in Louis A. Radelet and Hoyt Coe Reed, *The Police and the Community: Studies* (Encino, Calif.: Glencoe, 1973), part 5.

2. The literature of intergroup education in schools dates back thirty years or more. As one example, see Hilda Taba, Elizabeth H. Brady, and John T. Robinson, *Intergroup Education in Public Schools* (Washington, D.C.: American Council on Education, 1952).

3. The Riverside County project is described in an informative manual developed by the Riverside County Allied Law Enforcement Agencies (Box 512, Riverside, California) under the direction of Riverside County Sheriff Ben J. Clark. An excellent example of standardized training guidelines is *Police-Community Relations,* California State Peace Officers' Training Series, no. 79 (Sacramento: California Community Colleges Bureau of Vocational-Technical Education, 1968).

4. Geraldine Michael, "Social Science Education for Police Officers," *Police Chief* 38, no. 6 (June 1971): 56–61. Reprinted by permission of the International Chiefs of Police, Gaithersburg, Maryland.

5. See Harry W. More, Jr., and John T. Nesbit, "Programmed Instruction for Law Enforcement," *Police* 14, no. 2 (1969): 16–23. This article includes a bibliography on the subject.

6. For more on sensitivity training, see Radelet and Reed, *The Police and the Community: Studies,* pp. 275–280.

7. This course was devised and conducted by Creative Management Research and Development, a nonprofit organization. For information on the approach of another agency, Community Confrontation and Communication Associates, see Fletcher Knebel, "A Cop Named Joe," *Look,* July 27, 1971. See also Deborah Johnson and Robert J. Gregory, "Police-Community Relations in the United States: A Review of Recent Literature and Projects," *Journal of Criminal Law, Criminology and Police Science* 62, no. 1 (March 1971): 94–103; L. Deckle McLean, "Psychotherapy for Houston Police," *Ebony* 23, no. 12 (October 1968): 76–82. A Grand Rapids project was conducted by Scientific Resources, Inc., of Union, New Jersey, now defunct. For a critical view of sensitivity training, see W. Cleon Skousen, "Sensitivity Training—A Word of Caution," *Law and Order* 15, no. 11 (1967): 10 ff.

8. See M. Lakin, "Some Ethical Issues in Sensitivity Training," *American Psychologist* 24, no. 10 (October 1969): 923–928.

9. For example, see Edward E. Shev and James Wright, "The Uses of Psychiatric Techniques in Selecting and Training Police Officers as Part of Their Regular Training," *Police* 15, no. 5 (1971): 13–16.

10. There is an abundance of current articles dealing with police officer stress training. For example, see the April 1978 issue of *The Police Chief* 45, no. 4. See also John Blackmore, "Are Police Allowed to Have Problems of Their Own?" *Police Magazine* 1, no. 3 (July 1978): 47 ff.

11. Robert Shellow, "The Training of Police Officers to Control Civil Rights Demonstrations," in Arnold M. Rose and Caroline B. Rose, eds., *Minority Problems* (New York: Harper & Row, 1965): 425–430.

12. Harold Silverman, "Police Attitudes Towards Community Relations Training," *Police Chief* 35, no. 6 (1968): 57–59; Arthur Niederhoffer, *Behind the Shield* (Garden City, N.Y.: Doubleday, Anchor Books, 1969); John H. McNamara, "Uncertainties in Police Work: The Relevance of Police Recruits' Background and Training," in David J. Bordua, ed., *The Police: Six Sociological Essays* (New York: John Wiley & Sons, 1967); James W. Sterling, *Changes in Role Concepts of Police Officers During Recruit Training* (Washington, D.C.: International Association of Chiefs of Police, 1972).

13. Thomas A. Johnson, "A Study of Police Resistance to Police-Community Relations in a Municipal Police Department" (Ph.D. dissertation, University of California School of Criminology, 1970). See David H. Bayley and Harold Mendelsohn, *Minorities and the Police: Confrontation in America* (New York: Free Press, 1969), for further information on the same departmental situation.

14. Donald Bimstein, "Improving Departmental Training Programs," *Police* 15, no. 5 (1971): 22–25. See James H. Auten, "Determining Training Needs," ibid. 15, no. 1 (1970): 25–28; also see "PCR—Preparing Officer and Department," *Police Chief* 42, no. 3 (March 1975): 46–56. For several years, the March issue of this publication has had police and community relations as a theme, with many information articles in each issue.

15. Knowlton W. Johnson, *Examining Behavior and Perceptions*. See also Charles R. Taylor and John R. Kleberg, "A Decade of Police Training in Illinois: A Basic Police Training Course Evaluation," *Police* 13, no. 4 (1969): 28–34.

16. Summary developed by Urban Task Force, Episcopal Diocese of Pittsburgh. Also see Craig Parker, Jr., Sandra C. Reese, and James Murray, "Authoritarianism in Police College Students and the Effectiveness of Interpersonal Training in Reducing Dogmatism," *Journal of Law Enforcement Education and Training* 1, no. 1 (September 1971); Bruce T. Olson, "Some Social-Psychological Sources of Tensions on Police Basic Training," ibid.

17. See Louis A. Radelet and Hoyt Coe Reed, *The Police and the Community: Studies*, pp. 260–274.

18. Michigan, Commission on Civil Rights, *One Basis for Social Violence: Police-Negro Tensions*, by Burton Levy (Detroit: n.d.).

19. For a discussion of some of the merits and demerits of institutes on police and community relations, see Victor G. Strecher, "Police-Community Relations, Urban Riots, and the Quality of Life in Cities" (Ph.D. dissertation, Washington University, St. Louis, 1968).

20. Lee P. Brown, "Typology: Orientation of Police-Community Relations Programs," *Police Chief* 38, no. 3 (March 1971): 16–21. Reprinted by permission of the International Association of Chiefs of Police, Gaithersburg, Maryland.

21. A number of articles describing the St. Louis program in detail appeared in *Police Chief* 32, no. 3 (March 1965).

22. Glen D. King, "Storefront Centers," *Police Chief* 38, no. 3 (March 1971): 31. Reprinted by permission of the International Association of Chiefs of Police, Gaithersburg, Maryland. See also Ned O'Gorman, "Storefront," *Columbia Forum* 13, no. 3 (1970): 5–11.

23. As reported by Agis Salpukas, *New York Times*, December 14, 1971.

24. Indianapolis pioneered a program of this type called "Crime Alert," which has received considerable acclaim. Numerous other cities have picked up the idea.

25. Hal Wand, "Extra Eyes and Ears for a Police Department," *Police* 13, no. 4 (1969): 96–98.

26. Skolnick, "The Police and the Urban Ghetto," pp. 15–17.

27. Theodore L. Rankin, "PCR—Fact or Farce?" *Police Chief* 38, no. 3 (March 1971): 62–64.

28. A Liverpool City Police Liaison Officer Scheme was initiated in 1951. This program has been criticized on the grounds that the police officers assigned to schools have lacked training in social groupwork or casework, and that the police have injected punitive and inflexible attitudes into the treatment of children. See *The Police and the Children* (Liverpool, England: Office of the Chief Constable, 1962).

29. The Flint program is described in Louis A. Radelet and Hoyt Coe Reed, *The Police and the Community: Studies*, pp. 269–274. U.S., President's Commission on Law Enforcement and Administration of Justice, *Task Force Report: The Police* (Washington, D.C.: U.S. Government Printing Office, 1967) describes many types of school programs in which police participate. See also William B. McClaran, "A New Home . . . A New Approach," *Police Chief* 42, no. 3 (March 1975): 20.

30. Our analysis of police-school liaison programs relies heavily on June Morrison's article, "The Controversial Police-School Liaison Programs," *Police* 13, no. 2 (1968): 60–64. Reprinted by permission of Charles C Thomas, Publisher.

31. From a brochure published by the Tucson Police Department.

32. *NCCJ Hot Line*, 4, no. 4 (January 1972). Reprinted by permission of the National Conference of Christians and Jews.

33. In our discussion here, we rely heavily on Wendell J. Roye, *Law and Order in Classroom and Corridor*, Tipsheet No. 6, National Center for Research and Information on Equal Educational Opportunity (New York: Columbia University Teachers College, 1971). See also "Violence in the Schools," *U.S. News & World Report*, April 14, 1975.

34. Roye, *Law and Order*, p. 2.

35. See Frank Reissman, *The Culturally Deprived Child* (New York: Harper and Row, 1962). Also see Arthur L. Stinchcombe, *Rebellion in a High School* (New York: Quadrangle Books, 1964); *The Problem of Discipline/Control and Security in Our Schools*, Position Paper No. 1, Educational Advisory Committee of the National Urban League (1971).

36. Roye, *Law and Order*, p. 6.

37. George H. Savord, "Selling Law Enforcement to Your Public," *Police* 13, no. 6 (1969): 6–11. See also Jerry Marx, *Officer, Tell Your Story: A Guide to Police Public Relations* (Springfield, Ill.: Charles C Thomas, 1967); and Richard L. Holcomb, *The Police and the Public* (Springfield, Ill.: Charles C Thomas, 1969).

38. Jean Anderton and Fred Ferguson, "Police-Community Relations Coffee Klatch Program," *Police* 13, no. 5 (1969): 19–22.

39. John P. Howard, "Integrating Public Relations Training for Police Officers," *Police* 7, no. 1 (1962): 57–58. See Walter Grauman, "Lights! Camera! Action! The Role of Television in Law Enforcement," *Police* 12, no. 6 (1968): 81–83; and Thomas J. Hardesty, "Ads for a New Image," *Police Chief* 38, no. 2 (February 1971): 14.

40. Paul D. Lipsitt and Maureen Steinbruner, "An Experiment in Police-Community

Relations: A Small Group Approach," *Community Mental Health Journal* 5, no. 2 (April 1969): 72–80. See also Rachel Davis DuBois and Mew-Soong Li, *Reducint Social Tension and Conflict Through the Group Conversation Method* (New York: Association Press, 1971), and Burton Levy, "Cops in the Ghetto: A Problem of the Police System," *American Behavioral Scientist* 2, no. 4 (1968): 31–34.

41. The NAMH address is 10 Columbus Circle, New York, N.Y. 10019.

42. J. Ross Donald and Louis Cobarruviaz, "Eliminating the Language Barrier," *Police Chief* 38, no. 6 (June 1971): 8.

43. *Indians and the Law* (Ottawa: Canadian Corrections Association, 1967).

44. Michael N. Canlis, "Tomorrow Is Too Late," *California Youth Authority Quarterly* 21, no. 1 (1968): 9–16.

45. Harry G. Fox, "Community Relations Orientation for Police in Philadelphia, Pennsylvania (CROP)," *Police Chief* 35, no. 6 (1968): 22–26.

46. *Get the Ball Rolling* (Washington, D.C.: National Association of Police Community Relations Officers, n.d.).

47. Ibid.

20

PROGRAMS OF THE PRESENT

The six kinds of police and community relations programs described in the preceding chapter are as much programs of the present as of the past. There is probably more police training in this type of subject matter going on currently than ever before—although in some places, there is none, or not enough. Institutes are still being staged. Metropolitan projects are plentiful, though many are not of the same specific character as in the past. School programs of many varieties, including police-school liaison and Officer Friendly, are thriving. And in the publications and special purpose categories, there is no shortage of activity. The personalities and labels change, fresh thinking keeps a cutting edge on program planning, but the issues and problems remain pretty much as they have been—a little less severe, perhaps, here or there, yet still requiring undiminished "care and feeding."

LEARNING FROM THE PAST

Our intention in this chapter is to review programs of the present, mainly to identify new features and new approaches. Our basic question in the chapter is this: What have we learned from program experiences of the past that is being applied to programs of the present? There seems to be no better response to this question than a panoramic litany of notations and comments, almost as if jotted in the margin of a theatrical playbill. Some of the key labels for current programs of interest to students of police–criminal justice–community relations are these: community-based crime prevention; crisis intervention and management, with particular reference to family crisis (battered wives or abused children) and to psychological stress experienced by police officers; diversionary programs of one kind or another; 911 emergency services; team policing (or community-based preventive policing); and programs focusing on relationships within the criminal justice "family." In what follows, we will arrange what we have to say in the order suggested by the above listing, then go beyond it with brief comments on several other pertinent developments.

COMMUNITY-BASED CRIME PREVENTION

What we have to say on this has largely been said in chapter 18. Only a few additional points come to mind:

- Law Enforcement Assistance Administration (LEAA) grants have created crime prevention units in many police agencies. Questions: How much actual community participation is there in the projects developed by and through these units? Many appear to be preoccupied with gadgetry, rather than with involving citizens. What happens to the activity when the grant runs out? Do evaluations show that the activity has really affected crime? How and by whom was the evaluation made?

· Experience in a number of cities indicates that police service aides (paraprofessionals) can be "introduced and integrated" into established police organizations and that they can handle numerous service calls as well as, or better than, sworn officers.[1] The paraprofessional can be *cost effective.* Perhaps the service aide should more generally be a first step in the career ladder of a police officer. Police unions will have to be made allies in fostering this idea. In any event, the paraprofessional represents an important program for continued testing and evaluation, looking possibly to more general adoption of the idea.

· The practice of maintaining separate police-community relations and crime prevention units in the same agency is indefensible and should be eliminated. Call it by whatever name seems to be most prudent in particular circumstances, just so the functions of community relations and crime prevention are not separated. Citizen involvement is the only route there is to preventing crime.

CRISIS INTERVENTION

The movement of police agencies toward crisis intervention training and special units has been noted earlier in this text. To cope more effectively with family crisis situations has been a principal purpose, although some attention has been devoted also, by some departments, to landlord-tenant encounters and to consumer protection. Currently, the problems of battered wives and abused children have received special attention from many agencies. We touched on these matters briefly in chapter 12.

The traditional police stance regarding domestic violence in general and battered wives in particular was to treat each instance as a private crisis.[2] Police officers knew such cases to be extremely dangerous and knew also that they were not trained to cope with them. But police attitudes and practices in this matter are slowly changing. Specialized training in the techniques of dealing professionally with cases of wife abuse are beginning to appear, oriented to the understanding and skills proper to the police job, *not* designed to transform police officers into clinicians or psychiatric social workers. The International Association of Chiefs of Police is encouraging this development.

As to child abuse, the questions facing the police are again those of specialized training, and whether special units should be established, as in 1976 in the Baltimore County Police Department.[3] A key point in police handling of these crisis situations is the necessity for carefully worked out cooperative guidelines with other professionals and social agencies, so that competencies and "jurisdictions" are clear.[4]

What may be called the other side of the coin in crisis intervention currently has to do with the problems of psychological stress for police officers. Many recent programs have taken this focus. An International Law Enforcement Stress Association has been formed, which publishes a quarterly.[5] Hans Selye, president of Montreal's International Institute of Stress, writes:

> Being a policeman automatically involves shift work, long working hours, constant fear and anticipation of danger and death, actual confrontations with injury and violence as well as prejudice, suspicion and hostility by the public at large, which invariably causes disillusionment and disappointment in the job itself. These are the typical stressors inherent in police work, and in large measure they are responsible for the stress diseases that are so common in this group.[6]

Among the police agencies that have developed a stress reduction program, the Boston Police Department has been a pioneer. Wives and husbands of police officers are frequently involved in such programs. Commander Richard Caretti of the Detroit Police Department's Personnel Bureau regards psychological stress as a management problem as well as a personal problem for affected officers.[7] He calls for improved psychological services to officers in all departments. A stress awareness training unit is part of the general training curriculum of the Federal Law Enforcement Training Center. Morton Bard believes, however, that we still have a long way to go in research on this subject, although at last it has been identified as an area of concern.[8] The earliest program efforts were directed toward the alcoholic officer and encountered considerable resistance. Perhaps programs of the future will go beyond mitigating stress effects in individual officers and will concentrate to a greater extent on work conditions and the organizational environment. It may be that what most needs changing is the organization mold.[9]

DIVERSION

Again, we have discussed diversionary programs and the diversionary philosophy at some length in chapter 15. What needs to be reemphasized is the community dimension, the very heart of diversion. Diversionary programs of any kind lay responsibility squarely on the local community in dealing with juvenile and adult offenders. Moreover, the benefits of diversion include economies of time and of prosecution, smaller court backlogs, more time for the police and other criminal justice agents to spend on dangerous and habitual offenders, and smaller jail populations—plus the provision of needed rehabilitative services on an individual basis. Sound programs help to resolve problems of substance abuse, unemployment, lack of education, and social instability. Timely intervention can be a significant deterrent to criminal behavior.

Little wonder that diversionary programs of one kind or another have been gaining momentum generally. Strongly advocated by the Presidential Crime Commissions of recent years, these programs have some kinks that need to be worked on. One is that there are too many definitions of diversion. Another is the old trouble with program evaluation. Yet another is the necessity for care in protecting the due process rights of individuals involved. It must be remembered that diversion is not simply release. Diversion, properly done, means *work, help, service.*[10]

911 EMERGENCY SERVICES

In recent years, especially since the Criminal Justice Standards and Goals Commission encouraged it in 1973, there has been progress in many parts of the country toward full-fledged establishment of the so-called 911 emergency services system, a single, centralized, computer-assisted communication and dispatch center for all emergency services within a designated area, such as one or several counties. The system centralizes functions while maintaining local administrative control of police, fire, ambulance, and other services involved. All the arguments for and against consolidation of such services have been part of the story of slow and erratic progress on this subject. It dramatizes many of the typical difficulties that must be "hassled out" in the development of community action programs.

This is not the appropriate place for a discussion of the technical complexities of a 911 system. But one of the interesting arguments has been on the question of whether there should be civilian representation on the policy-making bodies of 911 systems. How "political" should such bodies be? To whom should they be accountable? Another interesting question hinges on how 911 systems are to be evaluated? How is cost effectiveness to be demonstrated? How, in this regard, should public relations benefits be weighted?

TEAM POLICING AND ALTERNATIVE PATROL PATTERNS

At first glance, the question of how a police agency deploys its personnel—more specifically, what pattern or operational plan it utilizes for its patrol function—does not appear to be a *programmatic* matter in police and community relations. On second thought, however, it emerges as perhaps the most basic of all programs. For it is in routine patrol activities that police and policed come into the most frequent, most proximate contact, and it is here that the real testing of the relations most consistently occurs. The prime target of most of the programs is the patrol sector. So the question of what is happening here currently is quite relevant.

In general, this is a period of unprecedented experimentation with a wide variety of patrol patterns. The pages of police periodicals are generously devoted these days to descriptions and analyses of one type of operational design or another. Tables of organization are under painstaking scrutiny by police managers set to discover what works best under the generally accepted mandates of management by objectives and cost effectiveness. The governing question is how to provide better service to the community for less money.[11]

Perhaps the most prominent—and many would say the most promising, from the community relations standpoint—of the various patrol alternatives proposed and implemented in recent years has been team policing. This term has been used to refer to a variety of patterns such that what is called team policing in one place is quite different from what is called by this name in another place. Actually, team policing presupposes a philosophy of policing which holds that the primary mission is to prevent crime. This philosophy also rests on a high level of communication and understanding between the police and the public.

Properly understood, team policing has six key elements: (1) geographic stability of assignment; (2) decentralization of authority; (3) emphasis on crime prevention; (4) emphasis on community relations; (5) mechanisms for effective internal police department communication; (6) reduced reliance on the use of specialists.[12]

John Angell's impatience with classical organizational structure in municipal police agencies, which we discussed in chapter 17, led to his proposal of an organization model with three primary sections: general services, coordination and information, and specialized services.[13] All supervisory positions, as traditionally defined, would be abolished; military ranks and titles would not be used. He defined the control system as checks and balances in which one section of the organization would have authority in one instance, another section would have authority in another instance, and the third section in a third instance. The general services section would consist of teams of generalists decentralized to work in a small geographic area. The coordination and information section would be centralized and might even be regional or statewide. This section would encompass what are now called administrative and staff functions. The specialized services would contain those activities currently classified as line units, for example, investigative, juvenile, and traffic functions.

Operationally, Angell's basic unit is one usually referred to as the generalist-specialist combination in team policing. In it he saw these expected advantages:

1. It should improve employee morale and effectiveness because it eliminates formally assigned supervision.

2. It gives citizens more influence in policy decisions. Because policies would be more flexible, it should provide more socially relevant police service.

3. It increases the professional standing of the generalist without damaging the status of the specialist.

4. It destroys the formal classical hierarchy and thereby provides employees with the authority and responsibility necessary for attaining professional status. It facilitates citizen involvement and organizational responsiveness.

Quite plainly, such a model—which Angell subsequently implemented as a consultant to the Holyoke, Massachusetts, Police Department—requires substanial changes in management philosophy and in police training. As Angell foresaw, the plan requires attitude changes at all levels of an organization. The crux of these attitudinal shifts pertains to the manner in which power is distributed in a police organization. And it is here that team policing has encountered its most formidable opposition.

As Angell, Lawrence Sherman, and others early warned, resistance by police management to team policing has impeded adequate testing of the concept. Managers have a habit of insisting on the retention of administrative control of patrol operations, and team policing is perceived by many as threatening to this prerogative. Indeed, to make it work properly, team policing does require significant modifications in power relationships. Angell claims that the effectiveness of his model would be enhanced by (1) formally establishing a more logical definition of the police role to make it consistent with actual police duties and responsibilities, (2) classifying the police as a human service agency rather than a criminal justice agency, (3) integrating police officers and human service workers in community teams assigned to neighborhoods, and (4) centralizing and merging police staff services with nonpolice governmental staff services at the local or regional level. [14]

Well over a hundred cities have tried some form of team policing. But the trials have been short-lived in most. Lawrence Sherman's 1973 study of team policing, for the Police Foundation, focused on seven cities: Dayton, Detroit, New York City, Los Angeles, Holyoke, Syracuse, and Richmond, California. [15] Only Los Angeles and Syracuse have retained the plan. A 1977 survey of team policing in nineteen cities, done jointly by the National Sheriffs Association and LEAA, turned up mixed evidence of success and failure. [16]

Perhaps the best-known team policing project in the country has been the Police Foundation's pilot in Cincinnati, called COMSEC, Community Sector Team Policing. The project ran from 1973 to 1977 and was carefully evaluated by the Urban Institute. The results were not all that exciting. Police-community relations, already good, improved slightly. Burglaries were reduced; other Part I crime categories (the most serious crimes, as categorized in the FBI *Uniform Crime Reports*) remained about the same. Police officer enthusiasm cooled, after hitting a high in the early stage of the project, because of a feeling that top administration was lukewarm.

A more recent Urban Institute evaluation of team policing efforts in Boulder, Colorado; Elizabeth, New Jersey; Multnomah County, Oregon; Hartford, Connecticut; Santa Ana, California; and Winston-Salem, North Carolina, indicates that there are advantages and disadvantages, and that team policing does not appear to make much difference. [17]

Pushed as it has been by national crime commissions and widely viewed as an innovative approach to police patrol organization as well as to police-community relations, team policing today is apt to be greeted with shrugs in something like the way the high school All-American football player turns out to be a disappointment as a halfback at dear ole' Siwash. Yet team policing may merit more of a chance to prove itself than it has had, especially if George Kelling is accurate in his diagnosis of the problem:

> . . . team policing represents a real threat to police departments' formal and informal power distribution. While officers can mobilize considerable enthusiasm for such attempts, organizational decentralization threatens established and entrenched interest groups which have considerable power inside the organization, often control employee organizations, and, in the case of detectives, often have important ties with the press and politicians.
>
> [A second] factor is that present police orientation around rapid response to service calls is essentially incompatible not only with team policing but also with almost every other approach which emphasizes planning of "out-of-service" activities. [18]

David Anderson puts Kelling's first point this way:

> The real issue is power. If police administrators are serious about giving captains and lieutenants full authority over a neighborhood, if they are serious about giving sergeants and patrol officers the right to participate in decision making, then they are talking about taking power away from some people and granting it to others. And that rarely happens without a battle in organizations like police departments.[19]

Lawrence Sherman referred to team policing as "a major revolution" and added that many attempts at revolution fail.

The central problem is complicated, but in its bare-bones essentials, it comes to this: no chief at central headquarters feels that he or she should rest the reputation of person and department on decisions made at the neighborhood level by sergeants, lieutenants, or patrol officers, acting autonomously. By the same token, police employee organizations will not stand still for administrative sanctions directed against officers whose decisions are second-guessed by higher-level supervisors and managers.

Many departments are experimenting with novel plans for patrol organization and personnel deployment. Often these schemes include team policing aspects, though called by some other name. The so-called split-free concept is one example. Another is what is called PBO, Policing By Objectives.[20]

SUPERVISION AND DECENTRALIZATION

Considerations relative to both supervision and decentralization of police operations are central in a discussion of team policing. Some brief comments about each are in order.

It is obvious that policies and regulations in a police agency are only as effective as supervisors make them. Middle management is frequently singled out for special attention in police-community relations programs because sergeants, lieutenants, and captains in larger departments possess crucial authority and influence with respect to the impact of high-level policies and pronouncements. In considerable measure, the entire "system" of police work revolves around supervision. It is here that the community relations orientation gets its decisive test. If the supervisory attitude is that "it's a lot of crap," this attitude will be communicated to line personnel. Such an attitude is more often conveyed subtly than explicitly, especially in organizations where the attitude runs counter to stated policies. Police officers do not find it difficult to sense supervisory attitudes and priorities. They quickly learn how to play the game in pleasing their immediate superiors. There is, of course, nothing about this that is unique to police work.

In short, as V. A. Leonard has stressed, no organization can rise higher than the quality of its supervisory personnel.[21] Often, as we have noted, the difficulty has been to get patrol officers to take community relations seriously. The attitudes of supervisors are of great influence here. With team policing, sergeants are clearly sergeants, with special authority, but the system encourages full participation of patrol officers in decision making and in goal and priority setting. The sergeant has one vote, as have other team members. This system requires that middle managers exhibit unusual qualities and that they maintain close contact with what's happening in their area. The plan fosters initiative in all team members, and the generalist-specialist concept tends to rotate leadership functions according to the situation.

Variations on team policing democratize police organizations and bring them closer to the people. One variation is functional decentralization. The idea is similar to that advocated for the public schools, with the same rationale. It is synonymous with the concept of neighborhood control.

As we have noted, David Bordua and John Angell are among those favoring a combination of centralization and decentralization in metropolitan police organization. James Q. Wilson agrees, believing that the authority that governs the police should not be dispersed, but that police functions can and should be decentralized. This, he argues, is a vital distinction, as we noted in chapter 13.

> Precinct commanders in a decentralized department would have greater freedom of action and more control over their patrolmen; precinct commanders in a dispersed department would surrender that control to whatever constellation of political forces the neighborhood might produce.[22]

That Wilson has his finger on a key point is indicated by the testimony of Dr. Kenneth B. Clark in May 1972 to the State Board of Regents in New York. Dr. Clark, noted psychologist and president of the Metropolitan Applied Research Center in New York City, charged that school decentralization in that city was failing to improve the quality of education because neighborhood boards were more interested in power than in better schools. Coming from a leading figure in the movement for decentralization of schools, this was newsworthy. Dr. Clark further stated:

> I do not see that we have kept—or the local boards have concentrated on—quality and methods for raising quality as much as they have concentrated on power, actions, control of finances.[23]

New York City was divided into thirty-one community school districts after the state legislature passed the School Decentralization Act of 1969. The community school boards were elected by the registered voters in each district. These boards, comprising unpaid members, were given the power to select and assign personnel in the elementary, intermediate, and junior high schools within their boundaries. They also had power, within overall limits set by the Board of Education, over the allocation of virtually all funds spent in the schools. Dr. Clark did not recommend the abandonment of the decentralization plan, but he did urge that efforts be made to make it more effective as a means of improving educational quality. City School Chancellor Harvey Scribner said that the plan needed more time for proper testing. Mayor John Lindsay declared that the city's decentralized school boards had brought a new vigor to the whole process of achieving quality education but that it was too soon to make a final judgment. Detroit's more recent experience with decentralized school boards has certainly not added up to improved educational quality.

Until recently, police administrators were extremely reluctant to acknowledge that a metropolitan police agency actually worked with a different style precinct by precinct, depending on the "style" of a neighborhood: cultural, ethnic, racial, social class, and so on. That it was so was privately conceded. Painstaking studies of what the police do and how they do it, neighborhood by neighborhood, has in the recent past produced data indicating the great disparity in neighborhood conditions within a single metropolitan organizational jurisdiction. In New York City, for instance, there are wide differences in the ability of individual precincts to arrest criminals. A *New York Times* study revealed that:

> In one Harlem precinct with 53,351 residents, there were 105 criminal homicides in 1971. In a precinct in Kew Gardens, Queens with 162,802 residents, there was one homicide. For 1971, the homicide rate in Central Harlem was 328 times as high as the homicide rate in Kew Gardens.

> The robbery rate of the Manhattan West Side's 20th Precinct was twice as high as the East Side's 19th Precinct.

> The rate of reported burglaries was 31 percent higher in Greenwich Village than the average rate in eight of the city's worst slum precincts.[24]

Such statistics require careful interpretation and raise more questions that need to be answered. Aside from the speculation such surveys engender as to the causes of the findings, the case for diversification in police style and resources from precinct to precinct, and perhaps even within precincts, is fortified. Simply in terms of deployment of manpower, the implications are obvious. The study also showed sharp police performance variations by precincts, measured by the relative success of the police in making arrests. But of course this is a precarious basis on which to judge police efficiency, because many variables must be considered.

Implementing the concept of functional decentralization in metropolitan police organizations can provide more effective service, as well as improve police and community relations at the neighborhood level. This is not a new discovery. The St. Louis district police-citizen councils were created for this purpose in 1956. It should be recalled that this program was primarily geared to citizen involvement with the police in crime prevention and neighborhood improvement, not simply to foster better relationships or to elevate the public image of the police.

It should be stressed that administrative consolidation of police activities in metropolitan areas does not necessarily mean that police-citizen rapport should be strained by poorer or more impersonal service. On the contrary, as the London and Toronto examples are often cited as indicating, administrative centralization and functional decentralization with strong community rapport seem quite compatible. The experience in many cities with team policing also bolsters this point. Again, St. Louis is a good place to look for documentation.[25]

POLICE TRAINING AND EDUCATION

New approaches to police tasks, such as that exemplified by team policing, involve rather drastic adjustments in police training. This may be the crucial factor in the success or failure of an experimental program, although there are other factors of great importance.

As we have emphasized in earlier chapters, the substance and techniques of police training are largely dictated by the conception of police role. Role concept is also decisive in responding to the question of the values of higher education for police officers and the question of what type of college education is best for police purposes. In the matter of training, Hans Toch, J. Douglas Grant, and Raymond Galvin have an interesting observation:

> Police training in general is starting to reflect the newly adopted service orientation. The best police training programs have previously emphasized the development of technical competence in crime control and strict discipline, often through the application of stress techniques, and the majority of them still do, but there is a growing awareness of the need to improve their abilities in coping with people problems. Where casual community relations presentations were once offered, depth analyses are now given, stressing the acquisition of a concrete understanding of the various police clients and their unique problems.[26]

LEAA has spent vast sums of tax money in recent years to bolster police training and education. LEAA and Police Foundation studies have raised pointed questions about the quality and value of many training and college educational programs. It seems likely that the results of these studies, cresting in 1979, will be observable shortly. Some college programs, especially of the two-year kind, are likely to fold, while others will undergo severe modification. Arguments regarding what police training and education programs should be or do will continue so long as there are arguments regarding what the police should be or do.

Perhaps the inevitable debates focusing upon certification and accreditation will eventually prove to be beneficial as a force for achieving greater consensus, simply as a necessary strategy of survival for criminal justice higher education. It is not unusual for a cross-disciplinary field of scholarly inquiry to encounter difficulty in the traditional academic setting. What is everybody's business becomes nobody's business! Thus there is a surge to establish criminal justice as a kind of unique discipline in itself, with an academic identity in its *blend* of relevant disciplines and in its particular *focus* on issues and problems integral to crime and criminal processes.

But this is not the proper place for any extended discussion of such questions. It is no service to the field to treat these questions in a cursory and cavalier manner. The discussion these days is not as to whether the police and other criminal justice careerists need training and education. That question is pretty well settled. The continuing disagreement has to do with the shape and content of training and education, the thrust of each, and the relationship between the two. The argument is especially spirited where police training and education are concerned. It is an important argument in current police and community relations programs because it revolves around the fundamental dilemma of police role.[27]

POLICE MANAGEMENT AND POLICY

No program in police-community cooperation has a chance to succeed without positive and honest commitment to it by police administrators. The gap between pronouncement and practice must be eliminated. The retired executive director of the International Association of Chiefs of Police, Quinn Tamm, said it well:

> The police chief who does not include a greater sensitivity to community needs as a part of his basic philosophy of law enforcement is now out of step with the times. . . . They [police-community relations programs] are beneficial insofar as they reflect desire on the part of the police to provide as great a level of service as possible to the citizen. They are useless to the extent that they attempt to distract attention from basically improper police practices in daily operations.[28]

Chief Howard Earle of the Los Angeles County Sheriff's Department put it this way:

> Police-Community Relations is a field as rife with social dissension as any endeavor in the history of man. And whether they know it or not—or like it or not—peace officers spend a lot more time engaged in police-community relations activities than they suppose.[29]

Administrative commitment is generally reflected in organizational policy. Community relations is, in this respect, a *management* concept. What is "in the book" in the way of written requirements, rules, regulations, procedures, general and special orders pertaining to community relations? Policies ought to make clear what management expects from all employees, including supervisors. Nothing should be left to chance or taken for granted. It would be refreshing to find more criminal justice agencies with a policy statement reading: *This department is firmly committed to the Bill of Rights of the U.S. Constitution. All personnel will be held to this in their behavior.*

As Herman Goldstein has pointed out, police policy manuals should go beyond the ordinary rules of conduct regarding drinking on duty, absence from post, accepting gifts, and the like. Policy should also be a management tool in the control of discretion out on the street, albeit not so rigidly as to circumscribe imprudently the latitude needed by an officer to be effective in dealing with people, nor to make the department overly vulnerable to civil suits encouraged by "overwriting" policy.[30]

Police violence, as William Westley recognized years ago, has profound implications in a democratic society. It represents political autocracy, with all the horror that this conjures up in the memories of those who have experienced it, and those who know it only vicariously. Certainly the rising incidence of attacks on police officers must be condemned and curbed. But, as Tom Wicker has said in the *New York Times*, "Neither that fact nor public concern about other forms of disorder justifies the police or any level of government in using whatever means they choose to maintain order." Wicker goes on to say:

> When authority itself is guilty of an unjustified and illegal act, it not only commits a crime, it brings the law and those sworn to uphold the law into the scorn and disrepute of those who ought to respect it. A law is not only broken but respect for *all law* is undermined. . . . nothing could contribute more to an *atmosphere of lawlessness* than a widespread belief that law enforcement officers themselves are corrupt or brutal or unjust, and that government permissiveness allows them to go unpunished for it—even encourages them. And it is in an atmosphere of lawlessness that violence is most likely to proliferate.[31]

Something should be said about the rather-too-popular administrative tactic of dodging the issues in public communications. For example, suppose an accusation is made by a public figure that the police are not doing very well in curbing the drug traffic or gambling. Forthwith, the police chief holds a press conference in which he vigorously denies the charge, citing statistics to show that the police department made X percent more arrests or conducted Y percent more raids this year than last year. The upshot of this defense is at least twofold: (1) it contributes to the defensive posture of the police, and (2) it fails to place the responsibility for the problem where it really belongs—with the community and its ambivalent attitudes about drugs or gambling.

The administration of police agencies is subject to four crucial influences: judicial, public, legislative, and organizational. Responsiveness and accountability are attuned to these influences. John Angell has suggested certain guidelines in each of the four spheres. In the public sphere, for example, Angell notes that the police administrator needs to be flexible enough to change programs or redirect methods when community pressures indicate a need for change. He should be prepared with alternatives in the event of public resistance to a particular way of dealing with a problem or situation.[32]

All bureaucratic organizational structures have inherent problems of public responsiveness and accountability. The complicated structure itself is conducive to a hide-and-seek game of shifting responsibility from desk to desk and office to office. "Oh, that's not our job—you'll have to see so-and-so." People get tired of trying to chase down the ultimately responsible party. In large police organizations, as in large universities, necessarily bureaucratic, it is presumed, because of practical considerations, responsiveness and accountability to the community must be explicitly and deliberately cultivated and emphasized in administrative philosophy and actions. These qualities must be made more than mere abstractions.

Indiana University's Workshop in Political Theory and Policy Analysis, and the team of Elinor and Vincent Ostrom in particular, have contributed generously in recent years to research and analysis of public administration topics, with special attention to police organization and responsiveness. Elinor Ostrom calls for a reexamination of current assumptions about institutional design:

> We must learn to understand the operation of complex, and at times, seemingly chaotic, police institutions. We must stop assuming that complex arrangements are automatically inefficient. On the other hand, we need not start assuming that complex institutions are automatically efficient. The critical problem is to develop a reliable theory of institutional design which will enable us to predict the range of likely consequences to flow from the establishment of a particular mix of institutional arrangements for the provision of a particular set of goods and services in a particular environment. Until a more reliable theory of institutional design is developed, further reforms using the traditional ideology are liable to increase the unresponsiveness of urban police institutions.[33]

The interest in civilian review boards and community control in recent years is symptomatic of bureaucratic problems. At issue is the fuller development of constructive participation of citizens in public affairs, in the face of increasing bureaucratization, depersonalization, and mechanization of governmental institutions. The depreciation of public confidence in governmental activities in recent years has not bypassed law enforcement. Yet the interest in civilian review boards seems to have faded since the peak of urban strife in the 1960s, perhaps in part because some of the weaknesses of such boards have become better known. Undoubtedly, however, the threat of their imposition prompted some police reforms.

Richard Chackerian and Richard F. Barrett of Florida State University refer to attacks from several directions on the idea of professionalization of the police. One is the charge that professionalization "merely provides the conditions for the protection of the police, rather than insuring increased police commitment to equity and fairness in enforcing the law."[34] James Q. Wilson's comment about protecting the practitioner from the client rather than the client from the practitioner will be recalled. The implication is that, while professionalism implies the application of technical standards widely accepted in police circles, these standards are not necessarily related to the public interest.

Chackerian and Barrett also refer to attacks on police professionalism made by those advocating neighborhood control. They might well have added civilian review boards. The idea here is that equity and effectiveness in police service result in favorable citizen evaluations of the police. However, it is the socially homogeneous neighborhood that becomes the context for developing the specific standards of equity and effectiveness, rather than the police organization itself or a larger political unit. Professional and community standards should be harmonized, and the uniqueness of neighborhood life-styles must be taken into account. Chackerian and Barrett have validated the following hypotheses in their research:

1. High evaluations of police performance by citizens are positively associated with low crime rates, high arrest rates, and citizen perception of equity in law enforcement.
2. Professionalism is associated with low crime rates, high arrest rates, and citizen perception of equity in enforcement.
3. Professionalism is positively associated with high evaluation, but this association will be stronger in socially homogeneous communities than in heterogeneous communities.

They go further in arguing also that evaluations of the police might be less a consequence of police effectiveness than an expression of an extremely diffuse sense of access to government. Their hypotheses in this respect are:

1. A high sense of access to government will be positively related to high evaluations of law enforcement.
2. Professionalism will be unrelated to evaluations if the effects of access are controlled.

It may be recalled that we commented earlier on the difficulty of distinguishing public attitudes toward the police from public attitudes toward government in general. Credibility—or the absence of it—is comprehensive.

All police managers acknowledge that it is exceedingly difficult to build a good relationship between police and community under circumstances in which the police are unworthy of public respect. As we said at some length in an earlier chapter, graft, corruption, and other unethical and illegal practices in police work are inevitably police-community relations concerns. The Knapp Commission in New York and similar investigations in other cities have been reminders that police corruption is certainly of current relevance. It ought to be a matter of concern in many cities, as Albert Reiss has suggested in *The Police and the Public*. He claims that extensive corruption exists in almost every major and in many medium-sized police departments in the country.

Almost daily, newspaper accounts of kickbacks, shakedowns, and perjury implicate police officers. Curiously, investigations are often inspired by newspaper or television allegations, as was true of that conducted by the Knapp Commission. The tie between police corruption and organized crime is widely recognized. Many observers believe that much corruption is still undiscovered.[35]

What is not always so sharply stressed in publicity about police graft is its link with the community. Bribery of a police officer is an illustration. For every officer who is offered a bribe, there is a "law-abiding citizen" offering it. This does not, of course, excuse the behavior of the officer who accepts the bribe, but it does suggest that police corruption is a problem with a broader base than is usually assumed.

Yet in matters of police corruption, there is an inevitable management responsibility. It is clearly underlined by Richard Dougherty:

> New York, with its Broadway flair for public confession and self-flagellation, is not unique in the matter of police corruption. Indeed, it may be stated as an axiom that no illegal activity which is dependent on a sizable retail trade can operate in any city without the cooperation of crooked cops. However much the folks in Seattle, New Orleans, Philadelphia . . . would like to think otherwise, so long as anyone can buy a drink after hours, put down a bet with a bookmaker, patronize a whorehouse, or buy narcotics, some part of what he pays will find its way into the pockets of police.[36]

There have long been those who have dismissed the problem of police corruption rather lightly by citing the old saw: there are a few rotten apples in every barrel. But there have also been those with a ready rebuttal. For instance, it has been pointed out that corruption cannot exist without the cooperation of the "honest" cop. The police subculture, especially that of patrol officers, which supports the concept of "covering up for your buddy," is stacked against the honest cop who informs on his crooked partner. Corruption cannot exist on a widespread basis without officers in general knowing about it. The honest cop can stop it. Unless and until he does, the plaintive cry from police officers that the reputation of all is being blackened by a few will not find many sympathizers.

In testifying before the Knapp Commission, Sergeant David Durk of the New York City Police Department said that he and Officer Frank Serpico knew nothing about corruption that was not known to every officer. Not to know was, they stated, to be either blind or incompetent. Durk went on to observe that, to him, police corruption was an attack on "a way of life, on the rule of law, and on the vocation of policing." The real price, he added, was "not free meals, but broken homes in dying neighborhoods, and a whole generation of people being lost." He concluded:

> Responsibility must also be fixed outside the Police Department, against all the men and agencies that have helped bring us to our present pass, against all those who could have helped expose the corruption but never did. Like it or not, the policeman is convinced that he lives and works in the middle of a corrupt society, that everybody is getting theirs and why shouldn't he, and that if somebody cared about corruption, something would have been done about it a long time ago.[37]

THE POLICE-COMMUNITY RELATIONS UNIT

Many police organizations in recent years have made a police-community relations unit part of their structure. The Law Enforcement Assistance Administration has provided funds to establish such units in many departments of varying size and circumstances across the country. Specialists in the field of police and community relations have encouraged this trend. The titles and some other features of these units differ somewhat: Crime Prevention Bureau, Community Affairs Division, Community Services Division, Conflict Management Division, and so on. But the essential idea is pretty much the same. The term police-community relations is now regarded as old hat in some quarters, and some critics newly arrived in the field have been quite uncomplimentary regarding early approaches. New euphemisms are thought to be improvements on older ways of saying things.

By and large, however, the police-community relations unit in a police department has come into vogue, and something should be said for its advantages and disadvantages. One general criticism has been mentioned several times: such units are sometimes more form than substance, more interested in public relations gimmicks than in solid, issue-related programming, more devoted to political and administrative gamesmanship than to genuine commitment—part of a strategy to divert public attention from what really needs to be done to effect significant change. Our response to this criticism is that the critics are often correct.

Another related problem is the negative attitudes of many officers in the ranks toward the police-community relations unit and personnel assigned to it.[38] As we have said before, this hostility can be substantially reduced, if not eliminated, by proper administrative tactics and community support. It should again be emphasized that effective community relations is a theme that should orchestrate the entire police organization, and not merely a special unit therein. This means more than the slogan "every officer a police-community relations officer." It means that every action in every part of the organization must be community conscious. Sir Robert Peel said it well: the police are the public, and the public are the police.

The prime purpose of a specialized unit in a department should be the facilitation and coordination of community relations activities in all aspects of the organization, and particularly at the level of patrol operations. Such a unit will always be "walking uphill," however, in a police organization that has adopted it purely as a window-dressing device, using easily obtained federal funds. Indeed, Charles Reasons and Bernard Wirth have stated:

> It may be that such units will have difficulty making any gains in rapport externally without losing ground within the department. Unit survival may necessitate pleasing all parties except those for whom the units were ostensibly established, e.g., disaffected and antagonistic youth and minorities.[39]

POLITICS AND POLICE-COMMUNITY RELATIONS

If, indeed, politics is the basic lubricant of police-community relations, one way or another, what political realities of special note appear on the current scene? There are two such realities, each meriting brief comment. One is police unions; the other is taxes.

Our discussion of unions in chapter 17 referred to their rather spectacular surge in the past two decades, to a present position of unquestionably strong political power in law enforcement administration. One is struck by the similarities in the patterns of diverse opinion that exist among police officers and among college professors as to whether unionization (of either) is a good thing. The majority of police administrators and the majority of college administrators take a dim view of the unionization movement. This is hardly surprising. It appears, however, that relatively few administrators of either type have had time to study the factors, in and out of their organizations, that have produced the unionization phenomenon. One might speculate as to the effect it would have if these factors were carefully identified and fashioned into administrative programs designed to cope with the needs and sentiments thus exposed.[40]

Those who favor police unionization claim it will bring benefits in influencing judicial and legislative actions affecting police powers, in public information, in promoting unity among officers and improving morale, and of course, in making common cause regarding financial betterment. Few advocates of police unions are specific in what they think unions will do for professional growth in other than economic terms or in improvement of police service to meet community needs. The advantages of unionization are generally delineated much more in what it will do for police officers than in what it will do for society. What most needs to be shown, perhaps, is how the good of one may well be the good of the other. It is in this sense that police unionization poses a police-community relations puzzle, as yet unresolved.

Opponents of police unions claim that such organizations concentrate power into relatively few hands, that they increase the possibility of police strikes and job actions, that unionization tends to deprive police administrators of essential administrative prerogatives and autonomy, and further that it alienates police and community. It seems clear that *power* is the key idea among both proponents and opponents, accurately reflecting the context of our times.

Police unions are, at base, more political entities than economic, though these two aspects are inevitably intertwined. The rhetoric of police unions features such terms as votes, bargaining, coalitions, caucus, deals, contracts, job actions, "calling the shots," prime target, lobbying, and the like. This is a relatively new language in police work, and it is too soon to tell what it will mean. Police officers—even those who pay their dues and are classified as union members—are sharply divided on the matter. But they do tend to close ranks when a subject such as civilian review boards comes up. After all, "professionals" should have some autonomy. But then, why do "professionals" need a union? Is it to protect the practitioner from the client? If so, then who protects the client from the practitioner?

What has happened in recent years relative to police unionization must be seen in the larger context of unprecedented organization of public employees generally. The Teamsters are an example. Some observers believe that the Teamsters see police unionization as incidental to their organizing larger groups of public employees. In any event, collective bargaining rights for the police are no longer much contested, even though the ultimate strike weapon is everywhere denied by law. Police unions are still "Balkanized," and tend to be rather conservative when compared with the mainstream of the American labor movement.[41]

Tax rebellion, exemplified by California's Proposition 13, and fiscal insolvency at the municipal level, exemplified by the city of Cleveland, are current happenings that are likely to influence the dynamics of police unionization considerably. The prospect is for increasing political "muscle" from police unions, which will be substantially strengthened to the degree that there is greater coordination of efforts. Some of this coordination will probably be with other public employee unions.

Reductions in police agency budgets resulting from taxpayer revolts will ultimately mean cutbacks in such functions as training and—quite predictably—community relations. The unions will strongly resist cutbacks in personnel. Under such pressure, police managers will look elsewhere in their budgets for "expendable" items. The outcome may be that important gains made in recent years, in such matters as police training and in police-community relations, will be lost. Union resistance to budget cuts for such purposes is unlikely. The resistance will have to come from the community.[42]

USE OF DEADLY FORCE

Numerous police officials have spoken for federal and state firearms control, especially in the use of handguns. The murder-by-gun rate in the United States is 35 times higher than in West Germany or Britain, and more than 300 times higher than in Japan—all strong gun-control nations. Police Foundation President Patrick V. Murphy has written:

> Statistics reveal that about 25 percent of all violent crimes in the country involve the use of firearms. Furthermore, guns are the weapons used in 65 percent of all murders. Logic tells us that a decrease in the availability of guns would necessarily achieve a decrease in the number of violent crimes, and experience in the few areas where effective gun control has been enforced confirms this expectation. We cannot be equivocal with the present increase in violent crimes and the increase at an even more rapid rate of crimes involving guns. To control crime in this country, we must control firearms.[43]

The polls indicate that a clear majority of the American people support Murphy's position. The continuing argument pertains to how much control, at what level of government, and how to make a control system work. Powerful lobbying interests stand in opposition to controls. Progress in tightening regulations and laws is measured in small steps. For example, in March of 1978, the U.S. Department of the Treasury proposed new regulations to make it easier to identify firearms used in crimes and to trace the flow of firearms used for illegal purposes. The intent was to improve the federal government's ability to carry out its regulatory responsibilities under the Gun Control Act of 1968. Specifically, the proposed regulations would have required that unique serial numbers be stamped on every firearm by the manufacturer, that all thefts of firearms be reported to the Bureau of Alcohol, Tobacco and Firearms (ATF), and that quarterly reports be made to ATF on all sales or other dispositions of firearms among licensed manufacturers, importers, and dealers.[44]

The use of deadly force by police officers remains a live issue. It is one of the most sensitive points of controversy in police-community relations. A deadly force investigation by police agencies is handled with all the care of a homicide investigation. Standard operating procedures for doing so exist in all sizable departments, hand-in-hand with firearms use policies. Peter Donnelly has identified an important consideration:

> What may be legally justifiable may be unacceptable in a practical social context. Therefore, many departments are restricting firearms use to situations involving armed felons, while statutes may allow such force to be used against escaping felons. The police administrator would do well to keep abreast of case law regarding use of deadly force. What may be legally justifiable may also expose a police department to civil liability in the eyes of a jury.[45]

MISCELLANEOUS PROGRAM NOTATIONS

Perhaps we have strayed a bit from the theme of this chapter: programs of the present. Yet the discussion has dealt with matters highly pertinent to that theme. Nonetheless, a few miscellaneous program notations may be in order.

Among the Exemplary Projects for 1978 of LEAA's National Institute of Law Enforcement and Criminal Justice were these:

- *The Baton Rouge, Louisiana, Stop Rape Crisis Center.* While similar projects exist now in many cities, the Baton Rouge center was cited because it varied significantly from others. It operates as a section of the District Attorney's office. Its emphasis is on coordination of police and social services. Local judges collaborate in a system of "vertical prosecution," thus minimizing the burden on the victim. The medical community provides free services to victims. Trained volunteer counselors staff the twenty-four-hour crisis telephone line. Annual operating costs are kept below $40,000.

- *The Community Crime Prevention Program in Seattle.* This program involves residential security inspection, property marking, block watches, and informative materials—plus careful coordination, the commitment of full-time staff, the cooperation of the Seattle police, and the cultivation of a sense of community in the neighborhoods.

- *Volunteer Probation Counselor Program in Lincoln, Nebraska.* This program is for high-risk probationers, misdemeanants aged 16 to 25 with an average of 7.3 previous arrests and convictions.

- *One Day/One Trial Jury System, Wayne County, Michigan.* This system taps seven times as many citizens for jury duty, makes better use of their time, and saves money for the courts.

- *The Public Defender Service (PDS) of the District of Columbia.* PDS provides quality representation to the indigent defendant from arrest to release.

- *Montgomery County, Maryland, Work Release/Pre-Release Center (PRC).* PRC helps to ease the transition from incarceration to freedom by assuring that its clients have employment, housing, and cash savings at the time of release.

- *Community-Based Corrections Program, Polk County (Des Moines), Iowa.* Coordinates four services for defendants and convicted offenders: pretrial release on own recognizance, pretrial supervised release, probation, and residence at Fort Des Moines, a correctional facility offering work and educational release.

- *Community-Based Adolescent Diversion Project, Champaign-Urbana, Illinois.* A cooperative program of the University of Illinois and the local communities. It involves juvenile offenders assigned to student volunteers.

The heavy reliance of successful programs on volunteers is noteworthy. It appears that volunteers in the community are playing a more and more decisive role in criminal justice processes, especially in diversionary projects of varying kinds. The VIP (Volunteers in Prevention, Prosecution, Probation, Parole, Prisons) division of the National Council on Crime and Delinquency (NCCD), out of modest origin in Royal Oak, Michigan, has established a National Center for Criminal Justice Voluntarism at the University of Alabama, with a grant from the Kresge Foundation. The W. K. Kellogg Foundation is supporting a national training program for volunteers in criminal justice, coordinated by VIP-NCCD. An annual forum for such volunteers is co-sponsored by the National Association of Volunteers in Criminal Justice and the Volunteers in Courts and Corrections Association.

PROGRAM EVALUATION

All program planners and managers are haunted by the requirements of evaluation. Through the years, in police and community relations programs, evaluation has been conducted far more in quantitative than in qualitative terms. How many institutes or workshops? How many participants? How many cities or states represented? How does this compare with last year and the year before that? How many repeaters? How many speeches to service clubs? How many church meetings? How many school visits? And so on.

Such information is not without value. But it can be deceiving. It can lull programmers into false assumptions. It tends to emotionalize and sentimentalize ideas as to what particular programs accomplish. If people "feel good" or "get a lift," the conclusion is drawn that significant, lasting change has taken place. Most of the time, this is an illusion. "Feeling good" about a program is quite acceptable. But if the prime purpose is to change attitudes, or to induce behavior modification, or to inspire alterations in the organization of a police department, "feeling good" may be a somewhat less than satisfying outcome.

One reason police-community relations programs have so rarely been qualitatively evaluated is that it is very difficult to do. When program objectives speak of change in attitude or behavior, checking the results is not easy. Perhaps the most perplexing part of it, typical of all behavioral research, is the control of variables in before-and-after testing. But the difficulties in program evaluation begin earlier. In many instances the obstacle is in the way the goals of the program are stated—if they *are* stated. The decisive question is whether progress toward the goal is actually measurable. Often the "change-the-world" language employed by human relations program planners in goal statements leaves evaluators cold. Evaluation is often treated, under these circumstances, as a kind of frill, a purely academic exercise.

Program evaluation is a big subject, and we must limit what we say about it here.[46] However, the following basic points should be stated:

- The first step in program evaluation is to identify the component parts of the evaluation process: objectives, programs, standards, and methods. In effect, this can be translated as: What is it that the program is intended to accomplish? What is the specific substance of a program that it seems may achieve this (model)? What testing criteria will disclose the extent to which the program meets its objectives? What methods of testing (instruments) will produce the desired evaluation data?

- Evaluation should be built into program design and process, from the initial stage. It should be integral to the process, not an afterthought, an end in itself, nor merely a device to accommodate funding agencies who insist on it. Ideally, evaluation feedback should occur as the program progresses, rather than after its completion—the point being to try to improve productivity while there is still a chance.

- In comparing two or more programs, it is obviously essential that the four parts of the evaluation process be as nearly identical as possible. This is the important matter of control of variables, and it has other ramifications—for instance, if a comparison is to be made between programs in two or more communities, two or more neighborhoods or precincts, the situations to be compared should be as nearly alike as possible. Frequently, a "control group" is incorporated in the evaluation—a place where there is no program—as a check against outcomes in places where there is a program.

- Further, regarding comparative study, it should be noted that program features may vary—for example, in measuring the effects of alternative programs—but the objectives, the standards, and the evaluation methods should *not* vary.

- Program evaluation should be related as closely as possible to the needs of practitioners in a given field. This means that, ideally, practitioners as well as theoreticians should participate in joint planning of programs, with due attention to evaluation as part of such collaboration. In short, the ultimate measure of the worth of program evaluation should be *utility*.

- Behind goal delineation in a given program lie certain values and assumptions that should be carefully and painstakingly examined for bias. This is more difficult to do than to state the objectives, but the unstated values slant the objectives, and there is sometimes a great difference between the underlying values of the program architects and those of the program recipients. Unless such differences are carefully identified, evaluative research can be a nightmare.

- There are various levels of program goals, such as short-range, long-range, immediate, etc. Effective evaluation requires that these be properly distinguished.

- Program goals are, as we have said, frequently stated in global terms. They are also often stated in such idealistic terms as to be unmeasurable. Idealism is not to be faulted, but it complicates program evaluation. The emotional element in both goals and results is difficult to measure and therefore difficult to evaluate.

- Fixing the target audience for a program is another vital aspect of evaluation. "Anybody can come" may be good public relations for a program, but it hardly facilitates evaluation. Who is to be affected by the program? Programs with "something for everybody" usually turn out to be disappointing to all.

- Process evaluation is as important as content or methodological evaluation. To explain: a group begins, let us say, by identifying and defining a problem. It proceeds to a diagnosis of causes, thence to designing a program to remedy the matter. This program has a certain content and certain methods. But the best programs are not totally successful, and the worst may not be total flops. Which parts worked and why? Which parts failed and why? Process evaluation attempts to identify the conditions resulting in success or failure—what helped and what hindered.

- There is a cost accounting aspect to program evaluation—the ratio between what was given up and what was gained—how much return for the investment made. "Cost" in this sense is not simply a question of money. It includes such considerations as time, energy, man-hours, psychic expense, and emotional drain.

- The public is a major hindrance in program evaluation. Reports that do not fit public biases are promptly blasted and laid to rest on the shelf. If a program is deemed good by the public, contrary evidence is not apt to be welcomed.

- Because politicians are responsive to public biases, and politicians sometimes influence funding agencies, the latter are not always friendly toward
objective evaluation. Sometimes the sponsor of a program is eager for an
evaluation, provided there is assurance that the results will support what
he has already decided.

- Occasionally, evaluators themselves handicap their own efforts. There is
such a thing as a *strategy* of effective evaluation, which avoids many of the
common pitfalls. People feel threatened by evaluations of their performance. It is important that they be made to feel part of the process itself—in
effect, so they may be assisted in discovering for themselves how performance may be improved. The more evaluation is self-oriented in this sense,
the better.[47]

The final report of a police-community relations project called PACE, based
in San Francisco, contained some critical assertions of interest to evaluators of
programs in this field, reflecting more the frustrations of evaluation efforts
than empirical evidence to support some of the points:

- In effect, the term police-community relations is useless; it is useless operationally; it is useless administratively; and it is useless from an effectiveness point of view. This is because historical and contemporary evidence
indicates that traditional police-community relations efforts have borne
very little fruit in improving the police-community relationship.

- People want respect and efficient service, nothing more and nothing less.
Any police activity designed to achieve these objectives is very likely to
meet with substantial success.

- Police-community relations programs that foster mutual respect and more
effective crime prevention and control are appealing to those who historically and presently have rejected programs labeled as police-community
relations. These programs are appealing because they are responsive to
the self-interest of both the police establishment and the white majority
community.

- The severe inequities that exist in law enforcement and the administration
of justice system and the need for change are recognized and supported by
[only] a small percentage of people. The majority of people feel no need to
know more.

- Police-community relations has traditionally been defined in terms of
police-minority relations, which is a limited and unrealistic definition.

- Police departments and other city agencies do not *plan* but *react*—react to
pressure.

- Program "effectiveness," measured with relevant and meaningful criteria,
is not a value endorsed by most people. Organizational survival and effectiveness often are clashing values, and survival usually wins.[48]

Another project report of special interest in program evaluation is that of the
Washington, D.C., Pilot Precinct. Following are some highlights from a report
about that program:

Police-community relations is a power relationship consisting of three interrelated dimensions: efficiency, responsiveness, and representativeness.

The conflict over how to improve police-community relations is often based on different judgments of how improvement can best be achieved. One group stresses greater professionalization of the existing police force; another group stresses changing police policies and structures to permit greater citizen participation in and control over law enforcement.

The essential problem is to determine which attitudes and behaviors of police officers are correctable by in-service training and which changes need to be made at a broader institutional and personnel level.

The community *must* be a core part of any effort to improve existing relationships.

Police officers are happier with training units stressing technical professional efficiency than they are with training units stressing personal responsiveness to citizens.

Efforts to improve police-community relations cannot be limited to bettering the quality of police services. Police-community relations improve when local citizens not only have access to power positions vital to police selection and decision making, but when they actually obtain some control over these two power dimensions.[49]

SUMMING UP

The ultimate message of this text is that the community has basic responsibility for, and must play a decisive role in, *coping with crime* and in all aspects of criminal justice processes preoccupied with *juvenile and adult offenders*. An appropriate concluding thought for this chapter comes from James Vorenberg of the Harvard Law School, who was director of the 1966 President's Crime Commission:

> It is increasingly clear that the police, the courts, the prisons, and the correctional services generally are engaged in what, at best, is a holding action. . . . this means that until we are willing to give poor people a stake in law and in order and in justice, we can expect crime to increase. The best hope for crime control lies not in better police, more convictions, longer sentences, better prisons. It lies in job training, jobs and the assurance of adequate income; schools that respond to the needs of their students; the resources and help to plan a family and hold it together; a decent place to live; and an opportunity to guide one's life and to participate in guiding the life of the community.[50]

NOTES

1. James M. Tien and Richard C. Larson, "Police Service Aides: Paraprofessionals For Police," *Journal of Criminal Justice* 6, no. 2 (Summer 1978): 117–131.

2. Joan Potter, "Police and the Battered Wife: The Search for Understanding" and others articles on the same subject, *Police Magazine* 1, no. 4 (September 1978): 40 ff.

3. Richard Steen, "Child Abuse Units in Law Enforcement," *The Police Chief* 45, no. 5 (May 1978): 38–39. See also International Association of Chiefs of Police, *Police Perspective in Child Abuse and Neglect*, a training manual, 1977.

4. See Raymond F. Shelton, "An Effective Way to Establish Rapport With Service Agencies in the Community," *The Police Chief* 45, no. 11 (November 1978): 36–37.

5. Publisher: Gibson Graphics, Inc., Bedford, Mass. 01730.

6. Hans Selye, "The Stress of Police Work," *Police Stress* 1, no. 1 (Fall 1978): 7.

7. Richard Caretti, "Improving Psychological Services to Police Officers: A Management Problem," *Police Stress* 1, no. 1 (Fall 1978): 15–16.

8. As quoted by John Blackmore in "Are Police Allowed to Have Problems of Their Own?" *Police Magazine* 1, no. 3 (July 1978): 48.

9. Ibid., quoting George Kirkham, p. 55. The April 1978 issue of *The Police Chief* (vol. 45, no. 4) contains numerous articles on police officer stress and includes descriptions of various existing programs attempting to cope with it.

10. See Dale M. Rothenberger and Jack R. Shepherd, "Police Juvenile Diversion: A Summary of Findings," *The Police Chief* 45, no. 6 (June 1978): 74–77.

11. See Daniel J. Bell, "Management By Objectives and the Police Administrator," *The Police Chief* 45, no. 12 (December 1978): 66–67.

12. David K. Wasson, *Community-Based Preventive Policing* (Ottawa, Ontario, Canada: Research Division of the Office of the Solicitor General, 1977).

13. John E. Angell, "Toward an Alternative to the Classical Police Organizational Arrangements: A Democratic Model" (monograph, School of Criminal Justice, Michigan State University, 1970.)

14. John E. Angell, "An Exploratory Study of Changes Accompanying the Implementation of a Community-Based, Participatory Team Police Organizational Model" (Ph.D. dissertation, Michigan State University, 1975).

15. Lawrence W. Sherman, Catherine Milton, and T. Kelly, *Team Policing* (Washington, D.C.: The Police Foundation, 1973).

16. William G. Gay, H. Talmadge Day, and Jane P. Woodward, *Team Policing in the United States* (Washington, D.C.: U.S. Government Printing Office, LEAA and the National Sheriffs Association, 1977).

17. In this summary of experiences with team policing, we are reflecting David C. Anderson in his article, "Getting Down With the People," *Police Magazine* 1, no. 3 (July 1978): 5 ff.

18. George L. Kelling, "Police Field Services and Crime: The Presumed Effects of a Capacity," *Crime and Delinquency* 24, no. 2 (April 1978): 179. Kelling refers to the Dallas experience with team policing, which dramatizes his first point "in detailed and stark terms."

19. Anderson, "Getting Down With the People," p. 12.

20. Anthony Vastola, "Police Patrol Systems: A Need For Alternatives," *The Police Chief* 46, no. 9 (September 1977):77 ff.; and by the same author, "Policing By Objectives: An Alternative Patrol Model," *The Police Chief* 45, no. 12 (December 1978): 53 ff.

21. V. A. Leonard, *Police Organization and Management* (New York: Foundation Press, 1964). All standard texts on police supervision make the same point.

22. James Q. Wilson, "Controlling the Police," *Harvard Today*, Autumn 1968.

23. Reported by Emanuel Perlmutter, *New York Times*, May 8, 1972.

24. David Burnham, *New York Times*, February 14–15, 1972.

25. Anderson, "Getting Down With the People." The entire article focuses on St. Louis.

26. Hans Toch, J. Douglas Grant, Raymond T. Galvin, *Agents of Change: A Study in Police Reform*, a Schenkman Publication (New York: John Wiley & Sons, 1975), p. 10.

27. See Lawrence W. Sherman and the National Advisory Commission on Higher Education for Police Officers, *The Quality of Police Education* (San Francisco: Jossey-Bass, 1978); Gordon E. Misner, *Criminal Justice Education: A Profile* (Academy of Criminal Justice Sciences, 1978); various articles dealing with police training and education in *The Police Chief* 45, no. 8 (August 1978).

28. Quinn Tamm, editorial, *The Police Chief* 38, no. 3 (March 1971).

29. Howard H. Earle, "Police-Community Relations: The Role of the First-Line Peace Officer," *Police* 14, no. 1 (1969): 23.

30. Herman Goldstein, *Policing a Free Society* (Cambridge, Mass.: Ballinger, 1977), pp. 122–124.

31. Tom Wicker, *New York Times*, October 25, 1970.

32. John Angell, "Responsiveness—An Obligation and a Technique of the Police Administrator," *The Police Chief* 36, no. 3 (March 1969): 22–26.

33. Elinor Ostrom, "Community, Public Service and Responsiveness: On the Design of Institutional Arrangements for the Provision of Police Services" (paper prepared for a New Political Science panel at the annual meeting of the American Political Science Association, Chicago, August 29 to September 2, 1974).

34. Richard Chackerian and Richard F. Barrett, "Police Professionalism and Citizen Evaluation," *Governmental Research Bulletin* 9, no. 1 (January 1972), Institute for Social Research, Florida State University.

35. As reported by David Burnham in the *New York Times*, January 28, 1972. It was Burnham's revelations in April 1970 that led to the appointment of the Knapp Commission. Burnham was a member of the staff of the 1966 President's Crime Commission.

36. Richard Dougherty, "The New York Police," *Atlantic* 229, no. 2 (February 1972): 10.

37. As quoted in *NCCJ Hot Line* 4, no. 5 (February 1972).

38. Lee P. Brown provides an able assessment of the problems of police-community relations units in U.S., Department of Justice, Law Enforcement Assistance Administration, National Institute on Law Enforcement and Criminal Justice, *Police-Community Relations Evaluation Project*, Final Report, Grant NI-075 (Washington, D.C.: U.S. Government Printing Office, 1971), pp. 175–198.

39. Charles E. Reasons and Bernard A. Wirth, "Police-Community Relations Units: A National Survey," *Journal of Social Issues* 31, no. 1 (1975): 27–33.

40. John C. Meyer, Jr., "Both Sides Now: Police Opinions of the National Police Union," *Police Chief* 39, no. 4 (April 1972): 68–75. See also Norman S. Goldner and Ronald Koenig, "White Middle-Class Attitudes Toward an Urban Policemen's Union: A Survey of a Problem in Community-Police Relations," *Crime and Delinquency* 18, no. 2 (April 1972): 168–175.

41. Tim Bornstein, "Police Unions: Dispelling the Ghost of 1919," *Police Magazine* 1, no. 4 (September 1978): 25.

42. See Earl W. Robitaille, "Tax Revolt, The Police Function and Police Training," *The Police Chief* 45, no. 11 (November 1978): 24–25.

43. Patrick V. Murphy, "Social Change and the Police," *Police* 16, no. 7 (March 1972): 64. Reprinted by permission of Charles C Thomas, Publisher.

44. See General Accounting Office report, *Handgun Control Effectiveness and Costs*, issued February 6, 1978, which deals with the relationship between handguns and violent crimes.

45. Peter J. Donnelly, "Investigation of the Use of Deadly Force," *The Police Chief* 45, no. 5 (May 1978): 26.

46. See Lee P. Brown, "Evaluation of Police-Community Relations Programs," *Police* 14, no. 2 (1969): 27–31.

47. These points regarding program evaluation rely in large part on Roger O. Steggerda, "Principles and Guidelines in Evaluative Research" (monograph, School of Criminal Justice, Michigan State University, 1972).

48. Paraphrased from Terry Eisenberg, Robert H. Fosen, and Albert S. Glickman, *Project PACE: Police and Community Enterprise (A Program for Change in Police-Community Behaviors)*, Final Report, prepared under a grant from the Ford Foundation (Washington, D.C.: American Institutes for Research, 1971). See also *Learning to Cope with C.O.P.S.* (New York: National Conference of Christians and Jews, 1972), a pamphlet based on the PACE report.

49. Rita Mae Kelly et al., *The Pilot Police Project: A Description and Assessment of a Police-Community Relations Experiment in Washington, D.C.* (Washington, D.C.: American Institutes for Research, 1972). An interesting exchange of views by Robert Shellow and Rita Mae Kelly as to the merits of the Washington project evaluation was offered in the *Journal of Social Issues* 31, no. 1 (1975): 87–94 and 95–98. See also Ralph G. Lewis and Jack R. Greene, "Implementation Evaluation: A Future Direction in Project Evaluation," *Journal of Criminal Justice* 6, no. 2 (Summer 1978): 167–176.

50. As quoted in *NCCJ Hot Line* 4, no. 4 (January 1972).

21

PROGRAMS OF THE FUTURE

An obvious remark with which to begin this chapter is that it is much easier to describe and analyze programs of the past and present, in any field of study, than it is to recommend or predict programs of the future. Still, by what we have said about the past and present, some recommendations for future programs have been implied, if not explicitly stated.

GUIDING PRINCIPLES FOR PROGRAMS

It may be helpful at this point to list a few of the guiding principles for police and community relations programs, looking ahead:

- Police-community relations programs should take into account (more than they have, to date) the practical political factors bearing on problems and the possibilities of resolution. The politics of police-community relations needs greater emphasis.

- Improving the police image with various sectors of the community may be a worthwhile secondary goal in programs, but it should not be featured as a primary purpose. Likewise, it should be recognized that the popularity of police officers is not a program objective of major importance, however gratifying it may be as a by-product.

- The definition of community relations as a combination of public relations, community services, and community participation seems to be as viable a theoretical construction as ever, although one or the other will be stressed at a given time and place.

- Police-community relations programs must discover ways to hear the messages of those in a community who are not joiners and who should not be compelled to join an organization or attend meetings as the price of being heard.

- Community elements must become more articulate in their expectations of services from the police and assume a larger share in determining police role and such associated considerations as police policy delineation, structural and functional organization of police agencies, citizen complaint procedures, police recruitment standards, training content and methods, and the like. These matters must not be left solely to the discretion either of police and public administrators or of police unions, by reason of community default.

- It would help the police greatly if a larger community consensus could be secured as to which is to have priority: the protection of individual rights or the apprehension of criminals. The issue in this is not the propaganda line, "soft on crime." The issue is whether a free society is to become no more than a mere propaganda line.

- Voices from the community should be just as quick to commend police action when it deserves commendation as to criticize where it deserves criticism. If community-sensitive police behavior helps to fortify credibility and trust in "the system," then by the same token citizen assistance to a police officer helps to strengthen his or her belief in the integrity of civic responsibility.

- Community forces should influence police organizations to confine the functions of police-community relations units (whatever they may be called) to identification of conflict, planning for conflict control, and public information. To mention one of the major abuses of this principle, such units should *not* be citizen complaint bureaus, nor carry on internal investigations in the manner of so-called gumshoe squads. This is not to say that a citizens' complaint bureau may not be vital. It is simply a matter of keeping conflicting functions from snarling role definitions and job specifications.

- Police and community relations as a field of study and social action should be thought of in broader terms. It should not be just another name for public relations, nor should it mean solely race and minority group relations, nor should it isolate the police from the larger social systems of which they are part. The problems and issues in this field must be seen as pieces in a larger jigsaw.

- No particular formula for good police-community cooperation can be applied in all communities. While there are general trends, problems and programs will have distinctive local features simply because the relevant conditions vary. "Package" programs are like nonprescription patent medicines.

- Community leaders should recognize the important difference between an advisory body of citizens for a police department and a so-called civilian review board. It is not a question of one's being better than the other. Each has a purpose, and each operates differently. A citizens' advisory committee is set up mainly to provide a police agency with information and recommendations reflecting as wide a spectrum of community opinion as possible. A civilian review board is an adjudicatory body dealing with complaints. It conducts hearings and functions in a quasi-judicial manner. An effective advisory group may help to make a review board unnecessary, but there are situations in which police relations with the community have deteriorated to the point where a review board is seen as the only answer. In such an unhappy state of affairs, a review board probably won't do the job either.[1]

- Many community organizations should consider inviting police participation in their activities. Numerous groups have overlooked this, or have decided on their own that the police would not be interested. For some activities, this may be true, but a principle of appropriateness should be applied. Interagency relationships are an integral part of police and community relations.

- Education of school children in matters of law enforcement, legal institutions, social control and the police part in it, and problems of the criminal justice system is a very significant aspect of the total community task. Happily, the development of curriculum units of instruction dealing with law and justice, and training junior and senior high school teachers to teach them, has become a major emphasis of the American Bar Association and the National Council for Social Studies.

- It is as important to be precise in goal delineation for a given program as it is to be precise in problem definition. Neither of these is done very well in the vast majority of social action undertakings, and the results are correspondingly blighted.

The key to community action is increased community education and participation. How is this to be achieved? What is it that moves people to care? Various social organizers and planners have become more or less famous for their ideas on this question. Ralph Nader is a contemporary "institution" reminding us that most people will do almost anything to avoid making waves, and the late Saul Alinsky, widely known organizer of community action groups, said that middle-class Americans considered direct, controversial statements as "boorish and uncultured." To avoid conflict and controversy is widely regarded as a virtue. Yet Alinsky believed that conflict was the essence of a free and open society. It has been, he often declared, "the matrix of every new and good idea" in America. Alinsky's career was dedicated to organizing the "wave-makers," to create a unified force—he called it "fun," "adventure," "exhilarating."[2] The Naders and the Alinskys are not popular with the establishmentarians.

COMMUNITY ACTION

It will be recalled that in chapter 2 we discussed the Sherif principle of superordinate goals as applied to community problem solving. Police and community relations programs have sometimes been billed as "an interprofessional approach to community problems." The central idea has been explained by Robert Trojanowicz:

> One of the major considerations when attempting to initiate community development programs is to understand how two or more interest groups can have sufficient convergence of interest or consensus to agree on common goals which will result in program implementation. Each group involved and interested . . . must be able to justify and, hence, legitimize the common group goal within its own pattern of values, norms, and goals.[3]

This theory, which has a long history in community organization and community development, lends itself nicely to police and community relations. The logical primary focus (convergence of interest) is the crime problem as it affects the quality of life in our communities. Particularly in planning of prevention programs, this problem is a natural for community action. Approaches to it could help heal relationship difficulties, especially those in community-police interaction. The possibilities for interagency cooperation and coordination are beyond calculation. As a monstrous social problem, crime makes interprofessional and cross-community action mandatory. Richard Myren has expressed the thought this way:

> Crime must be put into its context of general social deviance and the relationship of that deviance to conformity; criminal justice agencies, such as police departments, must be put into their context of the general criminal justice system; our criminal justice system must be put into its context of general social control mechanisms, both formal and informal. Failure to focus on context has led to distortions responsible for at least a substantial part of the difficulty that crime is causing in America today.[4]

Coping with crime through community involvement, as stressed in chapter 18, is a laudable slogan for a sound program in community-police partnership. Some of the assumptions in such a program would be:

1. As Peel said, the general enforcement of community standards is conducted more by the community itself than it is by law enforcement officers.

2. Coordinated efforts to deal with complex problems require effective communication among the parties cooperating in the effort.

3. The different parties will have different experiences with the problem; therefore, they will tend to define it in somewhat different ways. Each party should have full opportunity for input.

4. Effective problem solving through community action begins with education of the partners in the effort: fact finding, surveys, research, etc. However, data collection should not become an end in itself.

5. It is appropriate for a police agency to play a pivotal role in coordinated crime prevention programs. In fact, this provides such agencies with the opportunity to work at their most neglected function, in the only way in which it can be done—in league with community institutions and organizations.

It will do no harm to mention again the importance, in police-community relations terms, of proceeding to decriminalize certain crimes. Professors Alexander Smith and Harriet Pollack of New York City's John Jay College of Criminal Justice pinpoint the issue well:

> Possibly because we live in an era that has seen great changes in public mores in a relatively short time, we have too many laws that the police are attempting to enforce and the courts to handle that large segments of the public simply will not obey. . . . There is something very frightening to most people in advocating repeal of morals laws. It is as though, by advocating repeal, the conduct that heretofore has been forbidden is being endorsed. Nothing could be further from the truth. In repealing morals laws, the legislature is not proposing that people become immoral; it is simply declaring that the criminal sanction will no longer be used to enforce a

particular mode of conduct. . . . The unpalatable truth is that passing a law does not mean that it will be obeyed or that it can be enforced. Conversely, the repeal of a law does not necessarily mean an increase in undesirable conduct.[5]

It also bears repeating that decriminalizing selected offenses does not eliminate social responsibility. Substituting a public health approach for criminal procedures in dealing with public intoxication, for example, makes the challenge of rehabilitating inebriates no less demanding. As Paul Friday has pointed out, decriminalization and detoxification must be linked.[6] In the long run, the problem requires more emphasis on prevention.

Another issue affecting the future of police-community relations is the question of civil liability for inadequate police training, which the federal courts explored in the aftermath of the 1970 Jackson State College tragedy. The ancient common law rule known as the doctrine of sovereign immunity is rapidly disappearing in modern jurisprudence. This makes it imperative that police administrators be aware of what the courts are doing regarding the daily activities of police officers. For instance, in the use of deadly force, the responsibility for adequate training of officers in the use and care of firearms is quite clear, as is the civil liability of police officers and their employers. Other issues that are particularly sensitive to court decisions are the misuse of arrest powers and malicious prosecution flowing from it; invasion of privacy; negligence in the reasonable protection of life and property; and negligence in the operation of a police vehicle. Little wonder that police departments are increasingly exacting in the legal training of officers and are moving toward more reliance on legal advisers.[7]

There is a popular American fable that money alone will solve most social problems. This delusion is often applied to the crime problem. There is no question, of course, that programs in criminal justice often starve for lack of adequate financing. Neither is there any question that the Law Enforcement Assistance Administration (LEAA) has provided financing for new and existing programs. But because such funding is necessarily a political procedure, LEAA authorities have tended to interpret results in such statistical terms as a reduction in crime rates. We have been told that helicopters, radio communication, and data processing systems help to reduce crime. No doubt these claims have some validity. The productivity of mechanical and electronic devices is easily measured. But the productivity of a neighborhood citizens' council in its efforts to stabilize family life is much more difficult to weigh. Politicians cater to a public that wants results interpreted in "hard, cold facts."

The point is that there is more to solving the crime problem than money. Unlimited LEAA funds and more street lights, more police, more police cars, more helicopters, and more hardware of other types are vain investments unless ways can be found to involve people of all kinds in understanding and combatting crime. This is a hackneyed point, surely, and therefore it is commonly ignored. Can it be made to work? There is evidence to suggest that it can.

Take what is called community-based treatment in the corrections field. We discussed this concept at some length in chapter 15. Only a beginning has been made in exploring noninstitutional correctional programs as alternatives to incarceration. Community resources for such programs are only beginning to be identified and harnessed. The potential for interagency cooperation and coordination in diversionary programs can only be imagined. What communities *are* doing is clearly far less than what they *can* do, or even what they *should* do, but there are signs that progress is being made in new directions in the field of corrections. The point is best made by referring to concrete examples of the possibilities for the future, as afforded by current programs.

In Toronto, 30,000 citizens of Police Patrol Area 5411 have an opportunity to determine whether they can handle neighborhood crime better than the police and the courts. An "average urban" neighborhood of ninety-six blocks was chosen to test new concepts in Canadian criminal law. The aim is to discover whether mediation and counseling can take the place of arrest and trial in dealing with certain minor crimes.[8]

In the experiment—sponsored by the Canada Law Reform Commission, a governmental body—petty thieves can pay for what they steal instead of serving a jail term. Domestic brawls are dealt with by neighbors and volunteers. The police continue to patrol and handle serious crimes. But by police decision, minor crimes are turned over to one of the project workers. One purpose of the program is to encourage citizens to say what they think the laws of the future ought to be. The program has other features underscoring the responsibility of "average citizens" to participate appropriately in coping with crime.

Many police agencies today are experimenting with alternatives to traditional arrest procedures—with noteworthy implications for community relations. Perhaps the best-known experiment of this type is the procedure permitting officers to release misdemeanants at the scene of arrest if the surrounding circumstances indicate that there is no need to transport an arrestee to the police lockup for detention or to require posting of a bond. The traditional procedures are used only when field release of the arrestee is adjudged to be inappropriate. This alternative procedure, endorsed by several presidential commissions and now enacted into legislation in several states, is likely to spread. The results of the so-called citation procedure, to date, are encouraging. Continued evaluation of such experiments is urgently needed.[9]

As a result of a combination of various police department measures and steps taken by other community agencies in Washington, D.C., an astonishing crime rate was reduced dramatically over a two-year period.[10] A significant aspect was a narcotics treatment program heavily geared to methadone. A new approach to the problem of narcotic addiction became federal policy with the passage of the Narcotic Addict Rehabilitation Act of 1966. Under the provisions of this act, known as NARA, narcotic addicts are civilly committed to a federal program that provides them with treatment, followed by supervised aftercare in their own community for up to three years.

An extension of the federal policy encourages the development of community-based treatment and rehabilitation services wherever they are needed throughout the country. These services eliminate the need for narcotic addicts and other drug dependent persons to be hospitalized at great distances from home. They also offer addicts and drug users treatment, aftercare, and rehabilitation in their own communities; permit them to continue education or employment or resume it soon after; and reduce disruptions in personal and family life.

At first glance, programs of this nature may seem far removed from police and community relations. But further thought suggests that drug abuse is closely associated with crime, indeed with organized crime, and clearly requires community teamwork, along with participation of the police and other criminal justice agencies.[11] Police-community relations program planners have done far too little with this type of approach.

The national crime commissions of the recent past generated some systematic and scientific studies of public attitudes toward crime. Information of this kind is, in the long run, nearer to the center of the target than is data revealing what burglar alarms apparently do to reduce crime.

Leading figures in and out of police work continue to plead for better interagency cooperation and coordination in community action aimed at crime and other social problems. The yawning reaction is frequently, "So what's new?" A typical unarguable statement is this, by 1972 IACP President George A. Murphy, chief of police in Oneida, New York:

> The time for direct communication with our colleague agencies in the criminal justice system is now. We must meet and learn from each other. And together we can identify and act upon the common problems which confront us all. Through such interaction, we can forcefully meet the problems of antiquated laws, probation and parole inequities, poor enforcement, irresponsive institutions, and the myriad of other challenges that obstruct the war on crime.[12]

One would be hard pressed indeed to locate a criminal justice spokesperson who opposes cooperation, collaboration, and teamwork across the board of criminal justice processes. The declarations of this principle are abundant. Pricking the skin of these testimonials, however, reveals all sorts of reservations, qualifications, and conditions, generally translatable in the expression "protecting our turf." So we hear the banality, "It was a good idea—but it didn't work!" Too often this means that a new approach threatens interests long protected. If business and industry, science and technology handled innovative ideas in the manner of criminal justice (and some other branches of the so-called public sector), the horse and buggy would still be widely regarded as "radical enough."

It is encouraging to note the signs of increasing cooperation between the academic and operational sides of criminal justice. These signs include more college education for more police officers, more operational-academic consultation on research undertakings, and more concern for the relevance of training and education for operational requirements.

Planning as an administrative requisite has only recently become institutionalized in police work. The value of systems analysis has been recognized, but its possibilities in operational and developmental problem solving have not yet been perceived.

Michael Banton believes that internal relations in a police department are closely connected with external relations between police and public. In other words, problems of police-community relations are often an extension of relationship problems within police organizations. He is concerned about what he calls "a crisis of authority" in many large American municipal police departments, centering on the question of who shall define the police role. It is a struggle, as Banton sees it, between the "bosses" and the workers, the latter being represented by increasingly powerful police unions.

Behind the disputes in labor-management relations, he observes, is a difference of opinion as to what the job is all about. Men on the street think that the bosses are out of touch with changed circumstances. One difference of opinion pertains to the "war on crime," and it illustrates the point. The younger officers think it necessary to have as many men as possible in cars on the streets. To them, this is real police work, much more exciting and "professional" than engaging in "social work." But if the priority is to reduce crime, greater efforts by the police alone are not the major requirement. Rather it is a matter of training police officers to appreciate, Banton points out, "that one of the most important aspects of their job is encouraging public cooperation and eliciting information." The decisive insight is in recognizing the difference between a too narrow or too superficial perception of the job and a broad-based, community-oriented view of it. The internal division on this point, within police ranks, is projected today into problems of external relationships. It is unquestionably a key element in police and community relations.

The syndicated columnist Sydney J. Harris has Banton's analysis in mind, it appears, as he writes:

> Police officials will admit that public cooperation is the prime ingredient in the effectiveness of a police force. The people must recognize the legitimacy of the power they have delegated to the police; when they do not, civil order collapses and laws are broken without any sense of shame or guilt or indignation about lawbreakers.
>
> "All authority is moral," . . . Nowhere is this plainer than in the performance of police duties and the public response. Crime will not drop—no matter what harsh Draconic measures we take—until and unless trust and respect for the police are restored in the slum communities. As always, this political problem rests on a moral base.[13]

PUBLIC POLICY

It is gradually dawning on criminal justice administrators that they are engaged in a vitally important facet of public policy formation, that having to do with crime and criminals. Somehow it seems that the managerial position in this field has not previously been accorded such prestige. Full understanding of what it means, specifically as to what criminal justice administrators can give and take in the process of public policy development, is still to be achieved. The status is so novel that its nuances are not altogether appreciated.

One insight that should soon emerge is the recognition that criminal justice public policy formulators might learn much from their counterparts in other realms, even realms that appear initially to be only remotely related to criminal justice. It is not simply a matter of developing a kind of cross-disciplinary, truly systemic perspective in public policy development among the police, prosecution, the courts, and corrections, vital though this is. The plea here is to go beyond this, to a cross-disciplinary perspective in a larger context. The plea is that criminal justice decision makers, in public policy terms, should and must "tune in" to the thinking, the experience, and the perspective of decision makers in other areas. Public health, energy, environmental protection, business and industry, the media, education, social services—these are some of the areas that come to mind. Public policy pertaining to crime and criminals is far too important and too complex to be left solely to the "inner circle." It will benefit immensely in the years ahead from steps taken to open itself to what may be learned from sources "outside the fold." At the same time, in appropriate reciprocity, criminal justice leaders will be sharing their experience with others who, in the past, have tended to see criminal justice as a private, closed preserve.

PROCESS AND PRODUCT

We have mentioned several times that "good" police relations with the community is a process that is, in large part, the product. It is, in this sense, similar to "good" administration—of a police department, a business, a university. The Theory X and Theory Y philosophies of administration make the point clear. *The process is vital to the product.* The same may be said about coaching a football team, or developing a successful community action strategy. Yes, for a business, selling the product with a profit is important. Containing crime and preserving the peace is important for the police agency. Turning out educated graduates is important for the university. Winning is important for the football team. Solving a problem is important in community action.

The question is, however, how best to engage people to attain any particular goal? Take the football team. One big challenge of coaching is that of persuading players to relate to one another *as a team*, with all-out commitment to a goal. The *process* is of cardinal importance. So it is in community action to solve problems. And if the problem is essentially a relationship problem, the process even more proximately is the point.[14]

AMERICAN POLICING IN THE TWENTY-FIRST CENTURY

The homily-like tone of the preceding sections should not suggest that we are naïve concerning the essentially political context of public policy formulation and of the problem-solving process in criminal justice–community relations. Idealism is tempered by realism. David Farmer, director of the Police Division of the National Institute of Law Enforcement and Criminal Justice, LEAA, strikes this very note in his projections for American policing in the twenty-first century.[15]

It is unlikely, says Farmer, that the United States will have a national police force. Second, he considers it also unlikely that the current "atomistic" system of local police departments—more than 17,000 in the country—can survive. As a commentary on the confusion wrought by this proliferation of police agencies, he recalls that the 1966 President's Crime Commission *estimated* that there were 40,000 police departments in the United States, the point being that no one knows for sure!

Farmer goes on to express the hope that police agency functions will be more precisely defined by the year 2034. He looks for more police attention to white-collar crime. It is also probable, he thinks, that the service functions of police will be emphasized. He sees it as likely that "more effective organizational arrangements" will be made for the educated police officer, this as a result of community pressures for better service. More women officers will also push this trend. The general duty officer will better fit David Bordua's model of a "community manager" type. Police executives will be better selected and trained. There will be radical restructuring, already under way, of "police field service delivery systems," with recent studies on such matters as preventive patrol, response time and criminal investigations already having called long-standing operational assumptions into question. Changes in operational patterns will demand accompanying managerial adjustments. The most significant pressure point will be the perfection of police performance evaluation, hand in hand with more sharply defined functions.

Clearly, as Farmer concludes, such a level of achievement by 2034 will require substantial advances in research, as well as in action. More will be said about this shortly. Farmer quotes Herman Goldstein's statement that "the whole reform movement in policing has been short-sighted in focusing almost exclusively on improving the police establishment without having given adequate attention to some serious underlying problems that grow out of the basic arrangements for policing in our society."[16] Goldstein is not alone in this stance, but he has been consistently articulate about it for some years. So his ideas about effecting changes in policing command wide attention and respect.

Goldstein leaves no question about where he stands in the matter of the goal of police reform. "The ultimate objective of all efforts to improve the police," he says, "is to increase their capacity to deliver high-quality services to the citizenry and to equip them to do so in ways that are consistent with and support democratic values."[17] The main needs in the years immediately ahead, Goldstein believes, are to clarify the police function, to develop alternatives to criminal process, to recognize and structure police discretion, and to improve systems for achieving political accountability and for controlling police conduct. The process of change, he argues, will be more than merely "a strategy for police administrators" alone. It will require initiative by a combination of forces *external* to police departments: legislatures, other governmental administrators, the courts, the media, the universities, the community. And the support of police unions will be critical. Goldstein spells out specific responsibilities for each of these forces.[18] His summary statement goes directly to our central theme:

> In the end, however, it is not the attitude of the police administrator and his agency, nor of the legislature or other government agencies, that will determine the nature and rate of change in the police. The position of these forces and the degree to which they succeed in achieving their objectives will be determined by the interest and support of the community.[19]

ANOTHER VIEW

Robert Fogelson is less sanguine than Goldstein on the subject of police reform.[20] Fogelson portrays the reform movement as dating back two decades or so and as making good progress, until the demand for community control came out of the black power development of the 1960s. This, he asserts, "posed a severe threat to the on-going campaign for police reform." Mainly, the demand for community control generated apprehension among businessmen, lawyers, academics, public officials, police chiefs, and "other upper-middle and upper-class Americans who were impressed with the reform movement and committed to its principles."[21] Right-wingers saw community control of the police as Communist-inspired. Moderates saw it, Fogelson opines, as injecting politics into policing, lowering police efficiency, and fostering urban apartheid. The advocates of community control voiced counterarguments. The upshot, Fogelson concludes, has been a kind of stalemate in which the police reform movement has been stalled, and he does not think that matters are likely to change much in the foreseeable future. As Fogelson puts it:

> According to public opinion polls, most Americans think that the police are doing a pretty good job. Of the rest of the citizens, few are so dissatisfied that they are inclined to support community control or, for that matter, any fundamental overhaul of the structure, personnel, and function of their police departments.[22]

It could be, of course, that events in some big-city police departments have already gone past Fogelson's melancholy assessment of the reform outlook. Farmer and Fogelson certainly have different perceptions of what is happening and of twenty-first century indications. In reviewing the Fogelson book, Michael O'Neill writes:

> A gloomy forecast. . . . But it makes sense only if you believe that politics follows philosophy. If you consider, on the other hand, that politics always follows power, and that philosophy serves only to explain and justify what politics has done, then it's simply not convincing.[23]

TIME FOR A SHIFT IN EMPHASIS

We have cited the Police Foundation's George Kelling several times. Reviewing the research to date pertaining to the police function and such police activities as preventive patrol, rapid response, team policing, and investigations (the same points of reference to which Farmer refers)—and also the advances in police technology—Kelling concludes that the emphasis on crime-related tasks has failed to achieve significant crime-reduction goals.[24] Moreover, he feels that this emphasis may have exacerbated problems of police-citizen alienation and citizen fear of crime. Kelling reflects that the police can have only a limited influence on crime. What does this mean, he asks, for the development of future plans, styles of policing, strategies, and research innovation? Kelling responds to the question:

> Briefly, the critical need is to improve the quality and quantity of police-citizen interaction. This must be a central task, not for the purpose of improving the police

image but rather to encourage the normal social control exercised by a healthy community. The police must be seen as only an aid to the community, as the community itself deals with social problems. The police certainly are essential, but *policing* is too important to be left to the police alone. . . . we should declare a ten-year moratorium on technology and concentrate hard on learning what it is that the police should—and can—do.[25]

IN THE SAME VEIN

If the Kelling message for the future is to be taken seriously, it follows logically that programs of the future—aimed at more and better community participation in policing and other aspects of criminal justice process—should profit from the lessons of past programs. Georgette Bennett-Sandler has addressed herself to this topic.[26] She identifies several problems that have emerged, she believes, in programs of the past twenty years ostensibly fostering citizen participation in policing:

1. The conflict between the openness demanded by citizen participation and the traditional secrecy of the police.
2. The contradiction between police as an autonomous profession and a publicly accountable agency.
3. The problem of representativeness of the citizens who participate, and of the police agency itself.
4. The mutual distrust that exists between police and segments of their clientele.
5. The marginal nature of the programs that have developed.

In earlier chapters, we have dealt with aspects of several of these problems. But Bennett-Sandler provides a tidy summary and adds some perceptive commentary, for example: ". . . what makes the police-client relationship unique is that, unlike the other professions, it is the client who gives the practitioners their mandate, while at the same time having no choice in practitioners. . . . Police authority over their clients is a perpetual loan." Police power, she writes, is "a public loan, not a private right."[27]

On the point regarding representativeness, Bennett-Sandler says what we have said, in her own way:

"Responsible" often means agreement with police and affiliation with some formal community organization. Thus, the very groups which need to be targeted are, in effect, further alienated. . . . the most hostile groups are often the ones most affected by police policies, and at the same time, the ones with the least input into these policies.[28]

Her analysis of the marginality of community relations programs in police departments deals with the problems of special units and what constitutes "real" police work. The "social work" connotation is bolstered by the community action–community organization approach to programs, implying that police officers charged with special responsibilities to initiate and monitor such programs possess the particular skills required to do so effectively. In fact, most officers with such assignments lack such skills, and police training in this field has not done much to meet this need. As Bennett-Sandler observes: ". . . while community organizing is a clear deficiency in police programs, it is not at all clear that police are either functionally or politically suitable to undertake such a task."[29]

CRIMINAL JUSTICE RESEARCH

The days of "seat-of-the-pants" or "out-of-the-vest-pocket" administration of police and other criminal justice agencies is pretty well past. Hit-or-miss approaches to the responsibility will simply not do in today's world. This means that *research* is the key word in criminal justice, looking to the future to know better exactly *what* we are doing, *how* to do it, and *why*. It is not that there has been an absence of applicable theory. Regarding the nature and causes of crime, for example, sociology alone has supplied libraries of theory. We know a lot about crime as a collective phenomenon, yet at the same time very little about it in specific, individual cases. Moreover, because what we are studying is behavioral, what appeared to be sound theory yesterday is often challenged by new insights, new discoveries. In criminology today, conflict-oriented theory, for instance, is a formidable challenge. Paul Friday has captured the idea neatly:

> The political turmoil in the United States during the 1960's led many to re-evaluate the role and function of law. Subsequently, there developed a re-analysis of the definition of crime, an urging for a de-mystification of the law and, in response to the over-criminalization of prior times, an urging for decriminalization. The emphasis shifted, essentially, to the "other side" of criminology, looking at the system and its abuses instead of simply looking at the offender and his abuses.[30]

Friday goes on to say that conflict criminology changed the question from the who and why of crime, to why one group and not another is selected for prosecution. Conflict or radical criminologists suggest that the answer lies in the structure of the legal system.[31] The political nature of the new criminology may be seen in the issues currently surrounding criminological research. The focus has shifted to the *structure* of society and of the legal system. Friday summarizes the situation:

> At the present time, criminologists who hold to consensus assumptions cannot effectively deal with analysis of necessary structural changes which may affect crime. Those who adhere to the conflict assumptions consume their energies on restating power positions and the development of criminal law and have no opportunity (nor even desire) to affect social policy.[32]

The dilemma of each camp, Friday argues, is evident. The traditionalists in criminology are struggling within the system for input into policy, but are confined to making recommendations which fail to deal with the "root causes" of crime. Conflict criminology holds that the causes are integral to the system itself, therefore makes little policy impact. Marvin Wolfgang, not a radical, points to the future in research: "We have focused long enough on the offender and his weaknesses. It is time we look to ourselves—to this chaotic, decaying, degrading system and indict it for its failures."[33]

Peter Manning has described the situation as follows:

> In the last ten to fifteen years, the criminal justice 'system' . . . has become as much created as creator. It has been newly shaped. . . . It has become increasingly dependent on federal funds and structuration. . . . The research apparatus has eroded many of the previous assumptions about crime itself, about what can and should be done about it, what to do with, for and about criminals, and how the information relevant to each of these questions ought to be gathered and applied. . . . The system has created knowledge by which others outside can evaluate it, and now is facing new interpretations of its own mission.[34]

With the recently augmented knowledge base, Manning reasons, the actions of criminal justice agencies will be increasingly reflected back upon them. Correspondingly, they will shed their aura of secrecy, mystique, and mythology, as viewed by the public. The paramilitary organizational model, for example, is reinforced in the public view of the police so long as crime-stopping and crook-catching are viewed as the main tasks. But as research discloses that the police actually spend only a small portion of their time in crime work and that "preventive patrol" yields very little in the way of leads or arrests, questions of better resource allocation and of alternative patrol patterns and organizational models are raised.[35] Clearly, Manning and Kelling are on a similar track.

Manning concludes by identifying some of the major research issues meriting attention that cut across criminal justice components:

1. The development of more precise measures of production, for the courts, corrections and police.

2. Much of police work is situationally-determined, one of the difficulties in performance evaluation. So-called "human factors" reduce the impact of technological innovations—for instance, in intelligence-information systems. This is also an obstacle in the development of generalized theory in the field. Research is needed for "detailed knowledge and contextualized information on which situational rationality can be based."

3. The "war on crime" metaphor should be researched to determine the validity of the present evidence that the primary determinants of criminal justice practice are "not such vague legalisms as THE LAW, POLICIES AND PROCEDURES, or PUBLIC OPINION, but the demands of organizational survival, of careerism and self-protection, and expediency."

4. Comparative and cross-cultural research is needed on such key questions as police organization, the deterrent effects of laws and sanctions, conflict resolution by non-legal means, decriminalization, and economic crime.[36]

COMMENCEMENT

The end of such a text as this is ideally more in the nature of a beginning—a commencement. The motif should be, "On with the work to be done."

Police and community teamwork in dealing with problems, of which better relationships are a by-product, is basically an exercise in participative democracy. Its chances of success, measured by effective problem solving, are about as good as our commitment to act on what we believe in theory. It is a mistake either to overestimate or to underestimate the possibilities. Few of us, in the course of a lifetime, succeed in living up to our capacity for good. As David Twain, Eleanor Harlow, and Donald Merwin observe:

> We can no longer afford to be complacent about our failure to deal effectively with crime, urban disorders, mental illness, addiction, educational failure, and all the problems which accompany poverty and social alienation. The blame—if any can be found—must be very broadly placed. Human problems elicit emotional and subjective, not scientific responses. Social institutions and formal organizations become rigid and resist change. Few individuals are completely open to new ideas or to changes in daily routine. Inertia and habit are basic facts of human existence. It requires determination and a strong sense of purpose to work toward a long-range goal of rational action through the building of knowledge.[37]

Can "me-first" thinking of what Christopher Lasch has called the "culture of narcissism"[38] sabotage our motivation to want to get involved in any cause-related program "for the common good"? Undoubtedly, this is quite possible. Then we should understand what Irving Louis Horowitz wrote in the aftermath of the Attica prison riot:

> Perhaps it is simply time to recognize the universal truth: that freedom is not confined to those outside of prison, nor is slavery a necessary consequence of being inside. The prisoners have already articulated a sense of doing for themselves what must be done. Perhaps it is time for the rest of the American population to redefine its own goals in such a way as to recognize that freedom or slavery is less a consequence of being inside or outside prison walls than it is of one's place in the social order.[39]

Abraham Maslow has said that when one's only tool is a hammer, every problem looks like a nail! It is time for criminal justice to go beyond this perspective.

NOTES

1. A brief summary of the alternatives is given by William C. Berleman in "Police and Minority Groups: The Improvement of Community Relations," *Crime and Delinquency* 18, no. 2 (April 1972): 160–167.

2. See Saul Alinsky, *Reveille for Radicals* (New York: Random House, 1969).

3. Robert C. Trojanowicz, "Police Community Relations: Problems and Processes," *Journal of Criminology*, February 1972, Trojanowicz bases his theory on ideas developed by Christopher Sower et al., *Community Involvement* (Glencoe, Ill.: Free Press, 1957). Sower calls it the "normative sponsorship theory."

4. Richard A. Myren, "A Context for Crime," *Police* 13, no. 1 (1968): 4. Charles C Thomas, Publisher.

5. Alexander B. Smith and Harriet Pollack, "Crimes Without Victims," *Saturday Review*, December 4, 1971.

6. Paul C. Friday, "Issues in the Decriminalization of Public Intoxification," *Federal Probation* 42, no. 3 (September 1978): 33–39.

7. For an analysis of this matter, see Douglas M. Walters, "Civil Liability for Improper Police Training," *Police Chief* 38, no. 11 (November 1971): 28–36.

8. Reported by Frank Drea in *National Observer*, June 10, 1972.

9. See Mark Berger, "The New Haven Misdemeanor Citation Program," *Police Chief* 39, no. 1 (January 1972): 46–49.

10. Herbert Miller, "Reversing the Crime Trend," *Police Chief* 38, no. 7 (July 1971): 48–50.

11. See Richard H. Blum, "Drugs, Behavior, and Crime," *Annals* 374 (November 1967): 135–146; U.S., Department of Justice, *Horatio Alger's Children*, by Richard H. Blum et al. (Washington, D.C.: U.S. Government Printing Office, 1972).

12. Editorial, *Police Chief* 39, no. 1 (January 1972): 8. Reprinted by permission of the International Association of Chiefs of Police, Gaithersburg, Maryland.

13. Sydney J. Harris, "Police Power Waning," *Lansing* (Mich.) *State Journal*, May 3, 1972.

14. See Jack David et al., "Police-Community Relations: A Process, Not a Product," *The Police Chief* 43, no. 3 (March 1976): 16 ff.

15. David Farmer, "The Future of Local Law Enforcement in the United States: The Federal Role," *Police Studies* 1, no. 2 (June 1978; published in England and the United States, in the United States by John Jay Press, New York, N.Y.): 31–38.

16. Herman Goldstein, *Policing A Free Society* (Cambridge, Mass.: Ballinger, 1977), p. 8.

17. Ibid., p. 307.

18. Ibid., chap. 12.

19. Ibid., p. 329.

20. Robert M. Fogelson, *Big-City Police*, an Urban Institute Study (Cambridge, Mass.: Harvard University Press, 1977).

21. Ibid., pp. 299.

22. Ibid., pp. 300–301.

23. Michael W. O'Neill in a review of the Fogelson work, *Journal of Criminal Justice* 6, no. 2 (Summer 1978): 178–180.

24. George L. Kelling, "Police Field Services and Crime: The Presumed Effects of a Capacity," *Crime and Delinquency* 24, no. 2 (April 1978): 173–184.

25. Ibid., p. 184.

26. Georgette Bennett-Sandler, "Citizen Participation in Policing: Issues in the Social Control of a Social Control Agency" (unpublished monograph, June 1976).

27. Ibid.

28. Ibid.

29. Ibid.

30. Paul C. Friday, "Changing Theory and Research in Criminology," *International Journal of Criminology and Penology* 5 (1977): 159–170.

31. Friday cites Richard Quinney, *Critique of the Legal Order* (Boston: Little, Brown, 1970).

32. Ibid., p. 165.

33. Marvin Wolfgang, "Making the Criminal Justice System Accountable," *Crime and Delinquency* 18 (January 1972): 15–22.

34. Peter K. Manning, "The Reflexivity and Facticity of Knowledge: Criminal Justice Research in the Seventies," January 1979. Prepared for the *American Behavioral Scientist* 22, no. 6 (July–August 1979), a special issue edited by Gil Geis; the article appeared on pp. 1–20.

35. Ibid.

36. Ibid.

37. David Twain, Eleanor Harlow, and Donald Merwin, *Research and Human Services: A Guide to Collaboration for Program Development* (New York: Jewish Board of Guardians, 1970), p. 93.

38. Christopher Lasch, *The Culture of Narcissism* (New York: Norton, 1978).

39. "Alias 'Mad Bomber Sam'," *Commonweal* 96, no. 14 (June 16, 1972): 327–331.

SUMMARY OF PART 5

In part 5, we have discussed programs aimed at bringing about improvement in the relations of criminal justice agencies and the community. One chapter was devoted to programs of the past, some dating back a quarter of a century or more. A second chapter focused on programs of the present; a third indulged in some projections for future programs.

Initial police-community relations efforts date back to the World War II period. Due mainly to demographic trends, particularly the migration of southern blacks to northern and western big cities, concern grew about the possibility of racial turmoil in which the police would find themselves playing a key peace-making role. So the first programs undertook police training in what amounted to the social psychology of racial and cultural conflict, with such typical titles as "The Police and Minorities" or "The Police and Racial Tensions."

A decade later, at the time of the Supreme Court's decision in the school desegregation cases, a second phase of programs emerged, this time with the umbrella label of "Police and Community Relations." Institutes, pioneered at Michigan State University, attracted police and community leaders from many states and countries and came to be copied and repeated at numerous universities. Metropolitan programs developed out of the institutes, as early as 1956 in St. Louis. Programs especially directed at youth began to appear, many of them in the school setting. Other special-purpose projects centered on such matters as police and Spanish Americans or Puerto Ricans or native Americans, police-media relations, police and the mentally abnormal, and the like.

It is probably safe to say that police agencies today generally give much more attention to public relations and public information than a few years ago. "Getting the word to the public" has come to be recognized as a priority administrative responsibility, and the function is being carried out in myriad ways. For perhaps too many police departments, public relations and community relations mean the same thing. They never go beyond activities designed by the department to make the department look good. They have not discovered that there is a significant difference between *looking* good and *being* good.

The best public relations for a police organization is the quality of the services it renders to the community. Apprehending those who commit crime is one of these services. Preventing crime is another. Both of these services are utterly dependent on community trust and assistance. And crime, just as civil disorder, is much better prevented than dealt with after the fact. Crime prevention and police-community relations are, to a large extent, complementary causes. They can be reversible ends-and-means, and the potential in this vein has just lately been realized.

In the chapter dealing with programs of the present, we attempt to set down some indications of learning from the past. Because police-community relations is not a popular label in some places, the current shorthand is often "community-based crime prevention." The Law Enforcement Assistance Administration (LEAA) has generously funded programs with a variety of labels, with the common denominator of community responsibility and participation in criminal justice activity of one kind or another. Diversionary projects are an example.

Crisis intervention is another common name for the special attention currently focused on the police in their mediation function, in such matters as family crisis, landlord-tenant encounters, and consumer protection. Special attention is also being directed to the appropriate police role in cases of abused children and battered wives. Also related to this is unprecedented concern about psychological stress in police work, with much literature and special training devoted to it.

Team policing and alternative patrol patterns in police operations are currently undergoing study and experimentation. Effective delivery of services to the community is the goal, and closer police-community collaboration is increasingly seen as the essential means to achieve that goal. Involved also are high priority considerations of crime prevention and improved productivity in dollar terms, with taxpayer revolt prominently in administrative minds.

Brief comments are made in the chapter regarding current police training and education, police management and policy vis-à-vis community relations, politics and the same framework, and use of deadly force. The chapter concludes with a section dealing with program evaluation.

The final chapter plays the perilous game of looking ahead to future programs, with some suggestions for desirable emphasis. What should be done in programs having a criminal justice–community relations focus must necessarily be seen in the larger context of what should be done with a broader base. In the police realm, for instance, research needs pertaining to the role of the police, to the structuring of police organizations, to patterns of patrol operation, or to functional decentralization—to mention a few of the likely prospects—will have clear implications for police-community relations. Some of the research needed in the police area should have significant implications for other areas of criminal justice.

Quoting from several well-placed and well-respected criminal justice analysts, we implicitly associated ourselves with what they have said about future needs in this field. In capsule, the position we take is that studies in recent years have added abundantly to knowledge and empirical data regarding police work and other criminal justice processes. We have learned enough to know that some of the traditional assumptions and "conventional wisdom" are vulnerable in the face of critical appraisal. It may be confidently expected that this trend will continue and, indeed, that it will gather momentum in the years ahead. While the prognostications for police and criminal justice in the early twenty-first century are not universally optimistic, the reality of rational assessment cannot be denied. This, in itself, is cause for celebration.

SUGGESTED READINGS

Titles have been selected to include most of the books cited in the notes as well as relevant new publications chosen from the lists of over four hundred publishers. Titles that do not clearly suggest content have been annotated. Articles from periodicals have been omitted, because they are often difficult for students to locate, and because we wanted to keep this list to a reasonable length. The selections are arranged according to the parts of the text, for readers who wish to pursue specific subjects.

PART 1. THE SCOPE OF THE PROBLEM

Annotated

Brill, Naomi I. *Working With People: The Helping Process.* 2nd ed. Philadelphia, Pa.: Lippincott, 1978. Treats the basic attitudes and skills for human services in socialization—working with children, the aged, the poor, and minorities, individually or in groups—and stresses accountability.

Forst, Martin L. *Civil Commitment and Social Control.* Lexington, Mass.: Lexington Books, 1978. Concludes that civil commitment is being used increasingly on persons previously subject to criminal sanctions and is now a major form of social control in America: the criminalization of civil commitment.

Gross, Hyman. *A Theory of Criminal Justice.* New York: Oxford University Press, 1978. Lawyers, legislators, judges, police, and citizens will find here a blueprint of criminal justice in tune with liberal democracy. Illuminates legal riddles of the ages, explaining the moral underpinnings on which criminal law rests, exploring controversial points in depth.

Manning, Peter K., and John Van Maanen, eds. *Policing: A View from the Street.* Santa Monica, Calif.: Goodyear, 1978. Eighteen articles on urban policing from the ethnographer's perspective. Several previously unpublished papers. Bibliography of field studies.

Mayhall, Pamela D., and David P. Geary. *Community Relations and the Administration of Justice.* 2nd ed. New York: John Wiley & Sons, 1979. Stresses the importance of understanding human beings in police-community relations, and its practical potentials. New materials on the young, the elderly, and the police. Student oriented.

Murphy, Patrick V., and Thomas Plate. *Commissioner: A View from the Top of American Law Enforcement.* New York: Simon and Schuster, 1977. In this autobiographical account, Murphy (former head of police in New York, Detroit, and Washington, etc.) illuminates the problems, structure, and realities of enforcement in the United States today. He questions the basic assumptions of American police work which satisfy none.

Niederhoffer, A., and E. Niederhoffer. *Police Family: From Station House to Ranch House.* Lexington, Mass.: D. C. Heath/Lexington Books, 1978. Difficulties encountered by police families, including excessive jealousy of wives, high divorce rates, and problems of children. Also sections on community relations, police management, and personnel administration.

Ostrom, Elinor, Roger B. Parks, and Gordon Whitaker. *Patterns of Metropolitan Policing.* Cambridge, Mass.: Ballinger, 1978. Identifies and describes patterns of organizing and setting policies for all sizes of police departments, suggesting those appropriate for various types of communities, including auxiliary delivery patterns.

Schwartz, Alfred I., Alease M. Vaughn, and Joseph S. Wholey. *Employing Civilians for Police Work.* Washington, D.C.: The Urban Institute, 1975. Indicates the benefits of civilian employees in terms of reduced training costs, release of officers from routing tasks, and improved community services. Assesses the risks of such practices.

Shalala, Donna. *Neighborhood Governance: Issues and Proposals.* New York: American Jewish Committee, n.d. A review of the literature on the reorganization of government on the neighborhood level.

Thorns, D. C. *Quest for Community.* New York: John Wiley & Sons, 1976. Examines local authority housing estates, redevelopment schemes, multistory complexes, suburbs and commuter villages, new towns, squatter areas not part of a planned city structure, and ideologically based communities of religious or other groups.

Williams, Robin M., Jr. *Mutual Accommodation: Ethnic Conflict and Cooperation.* Minneapolis, Minn.: University of Minnesota Press, 1978. Asks how social change occurs and what strategies are best suited to produce desired outcomes. States that such strategies are now available in terms of schools and racial desegregation. Illustrates basic concepts of conflict and settlement.

Witt, James W. *The Police, the Courts and the Minority Community.* Lexington, Mass.: Lexington Books, 1979. Looks at the training and supervision of police personnel and the functional aspects of our criminal justice system.

Unannotated

Anonymous. *Citizen Action to Control Crime and Delinquency.* New York: National Council on Crime and Delinquency, 1968.

Atkins, Burton, and Mark Pogrebin. *Invisible Justice: Discretion and the Law.* Cincinnati, Ohio: Anderson, 1978.

Banton, Michael. *The Policeman and the Community.* New York: Basic Books, 1964.

Bard, Morton. *Family Crisis Intervention: From Concept to Implementation.* New York: City College Research Foundation, 1974.

———. *Training Police as Specialists in Family Crisis Intervention.* Washington, D.C.: U.S. Government Printing Office, 1970.

Bassiouni, M. C. *Citizen's Arrest: Law of Arrest, Search and Seizure for Private Citizens and Private Police.* Springfield, Ill.: Charles C Thomas, 1977.

Becker, Harold K. *Police Systems of Europe: A Survey of Selected Organizations.* Springfield, Ill.: Charles C Thomas, 1973.

Bent, Allen E., and Ralph A. Possum. *Police, Criminal Justice and the Community.* New York: Harper & Row, 1976.

Block, Peter B., and Deborah Anderson. *Policewoman on Patrol: Final Report*. Washington, D.C. Police Foundation, 1974.

Block, Peter B., and D. Specht. *Neighborhood Team Policing*. Washington, D.C.: U.S. Government Printing Office, 1973.

Bordua, David J., ed. *The Police: Six Sociological Essays*. New York: John Wiley & Sons, 1967.

Brandstatter, A. F., and Louis A. Radelet, eds. *Police and Community Relations: A Source Book*. Beverly Hills, Calif.: Glencoe, 1968.

Broderick, John J. *Police in a Time of Change*. Morristown, N.J.: General Learning Press, 1976.

Brown, John, and Graham Howse, eds. *Police in the Community*. Lexington, Mass.: Lexington Books, 1975.

Burpo, John H. *The Police Labor Movement: Problems and Perspectives*. Springfield, Ill.: Charles C Thomas, 1971.

Cain, M. E. *Society and the Policeman's Role*. London: Routledge and Kegan Paul, 1973.

Cohen, Robert, Robert P. Sprafkin, Sidney Oglesby, and William Claiborn, eds. *Working With Police Agencies*. New York: Human Sciences Press, 1976.

Cohen, Alvin W., ed. *The Future of Policing*. Beverly Hills, Calif.: Sage, 1978.

Cohn, Alvin, and Emilio Viano, eds. *Police-Community Relations: Images, Roles and Realities*. Philadelphia, Pa.: Lippincott, 1976.

Conrad, John P., ed. *Evolution of Criminal Justice: Guide for Practical Criminologists*. Beverly Hills, Calif.: Sage, 1978.

Cray, Ed. *The Enemy in the Streets: Police Malpractice in America*. New York: Doubleday, Anchor Books, 1972.

Cromwell, Paul F. *Police Community Relations: A Guide to Strengthening Police Relations with the Public*. Santa Cruz, Calif.: Davis, 1978.

Cromwell, Paul F., Jr., and George Keefer. *Police-Community Relations*. 2nd ed. St. Paul, Minn.: West, 1978.

Davis, Kenneth Culp. *Discretionary Justice*. Baton Rouge, La.: Louisiana State University Press, 1969.

———. *Police Discretion*. St. Paul, Minn.: West, 1975.

Drapkin, Israel, and Emilio Viano, eds. *Victimology: A New Focus*. Lexington, Mass.: Lexington Books, 1974. Vol. 1, *Theoretical Issues*, 1974. Vol. 2, *Society's Reaction*, 1974. Vol. 3, *Crimes, Victims and Justice*, 1975. Vol. 4, *Exploiters and Exploited*, 1975. Vol. 5, *Violence and Its Victims*, 1975.

Evans, Margaret, ed. *Discretion and Control*. Beverly Hills, Calif.: Sage, 1978.

Farmer, Richard E., and Victor A. Kowalewski. *Law Enforcement and Community Relations*. Reston, Va.: Reston, 1976.

Fink, Joseph, and Lloyd G. Sealy. *The Community and the Police—Conflict or Cooperation?* New York: John Wiley & Sons, 1974.

Garofalo, James. *Public Opinion About Crime: The Attitudes of Victims and Nonvictims in Selected Cities*. Washington, D.C.: U.S. Department of Justice, LEAA, 1977.

Geary, David Patrick. *Community Relations and the Administration of Justice*. New York: John Wiley & Sons, 1975.

Goldsmith, Jack, and Sharon G. Goldsmith. *Police Community—Dimensions of an Occupational Subculture.* Pacific Palisades, Calif.: Goodyear, 1974.

Goldstein, Herman. *Policing a Free Society.* Cambridge, Mass.: Ballinger, 1975.

Greifer, Julian, ed. *Community Action for Social Change: A Casebook of Current Projects.* New York: Praeger, 1974.

Haynes, William D. *Stress Related Disorders in Policemen.* Palo Alto, Calif.: R & E Associates, 1978.

Hill, M. J. *Partners: Community Volunteer and Probationer in a One-to-One Relationship: Project Evaluation.* Nome, Alaska: Division of Corrections, 1972.

Johnson, Knowlton W. *Police Interagency Relations: Some Research Findings.* Beverly Hills, Calif.: Sage, 1978.

Judge, Anthony. *A Man Apart: The British Policeman and His Job.* London: Arthur Barker, 1972.

Kelly, Rita Mae. *On Improving Police-Community Relations: Findings from the Conduct and Evaluation of an OEO-Funded Experiment in Washington, D.C.* Washington, D.C.: American Institutes for Research, 1972.

Kline, Paula. *Urban Needs: A Bibliography and Directory for Community Centers.* Metuchen, N.J.: Scarecrow Press, 1978.

Klyman, F. I., and F. B. Hannon. *Police Roles in a Changing Community: A Community Relations Planning Guide for Law Enforcement Agencies.* Wichita, Kans.: Wichita State University Press, 1973.

Kroes, William H. *Society's Victim—The Policemen: Analysis of Job Stress in Policing.* Springfield, Ill.: Charles C Thomas, 1977.

Kuykendall, Jack L. *Community Police Administration.* Chicago: Nelson-Hall, 1975.

Lane, Roger. *Policing the City: Boston 1822–1885.* Cambridge, Mass.: Harvard University Press, 1967.

Lee, W. L. Melville. *A History of Police in England.* London: Methuen, 1901.

McEvoy, Donald W. *The Police and Their Many Publics.* Metuchen, N.J.: Scarecrow Press, 1976.

McGillis, Daniel, and Joan Mullen. *Neighborhood Justice Centers.* Washington, D.C.: U.S. Department of Justice, LEAA, 1977.

Malinowski, Bronislaw. *Crime and Custom in a Savage Society.* Cambridge, England: Routledge and Kegan Paul, 1966.

Manning, Peter K. *Police Work: The Social Organization of Policing.* Cambridge, Mass.: MIT Press, 1977.

Morris, Lynn, et al. *Program Evaluation Kit.* Beverly Hills, Calif.: Sage, 1978. 8 vols. Written under the auspices of the Center for the Study of Evaluation at UCLA Graduate School of Education. The volumes are:
  1. *Evaluator's Handbook*
  2. *How to Deal with Goals and Objectives*
  3. *How to Design a Program Evaluation*
  4. *How to Measure Program Implementation*
  5. *How to Measure Attitudes*
  6. *How to Measure Achievement*
  7. *How to Calculate Statistics*
  8. *How to Present an Evaluation Report*

Muir, William Ker, Jr. *Police: Streetcorner Politicians*. Chicago: University of Chicago Press, 1978.

National Institutes of Mental Health. *Community-based Correctional Programs*, 1971.
——— . *Correctional Treatment in Community Settings*.
——— . *Crime and Delinquency Research* (in Europe).
——— . *Crime and Justice: American Style*, 1971.
——— . *Diversion from the Criminal Justice System*, 1971.
——— . *Function of Police in Modern Society*.
——— . *Instead of Court: Diversion in Juvenile Justice*.
——— . *Juvenile Court: A Status Report*, 1971.
——— . *Perspectives on Deterrence*.
——— . *Police, Prisons and Problem of Violence*.
Rockville, Md.: National Institutes of Mental Health.

Niederhoffer, Arthur. *Behind the Shield: The Police in Urban Society*. Garden City, N.Y.: Doubleday, 1967.

Niederhoffer, Arthur, and Abraham S. Blumberg, eds. *The Ambivalent Force: Perspectives on the Police*. 2nd ed. New York: Dryden Press, 1976.

Olmos, Ralph A. *An Introduction to Police-Community Relations: A Guide for the Pre-Service Student and Practicing Police Officer*. Springfield, Ill.: Charles C Thomas, 1974.

Ostrom, Elinor, and William H. Baugh. *Community Organization and the Provision of Police Services*. Beverly Hills, Calif.: Sage, 1973.

Pfiffner, John M. "The Function of the Police in a Democratic Society," *Occasional Papers: Center for Training and Career Development*. *School of Public Administration*, University of Southern California, Los Angeles, 1967.

Platt, Robert M. *The Concept of Police-Community Relations*. Kendale, Tex.: Criminal Justice Press, 1973.

Potholm, Christian P., and Richard E. Morgan, eds. *Focus on Police: Police in American Society*. Cambridge, Mass.: Schenkman, 1976.

Preiss, Jack J., and Howard J. Ehrlich. *An Examination of Role Theory: The Case of the State Police*. Lincoln: University of Nebraska Press, 1966.

Radelet, Louis A., and Hoyt Coe Reed. *The Police and the Community: Studies*. Encino, Calif.: Glencoe, 1973.

Reith, Charles. *British Police and the Democratic Ideal*. London: Oxford University Press, 1943.

Ross, Murray G. *Community Organization: Theory and Principle*. Rev. ed. New York: Harper & Brothers, 1955.

Ruchelman, Leonard. *Who Rules the Police?* New York: New York University Press, 1973.

Sanders, I. T. *The Community*. 3rd ed. New York: John Wiley & Sons, 1975.

Schwartz, Ira M., Donald R. Jensen, and Michael J. Mahoney. *Volunteers in Juvenile Justice*. Washington, D.C.: U.S. Department of Justice, LEAA, 1977.

Schwartz, Richard D., and Jerome H. Skolnick. *Society and the Legal Order*. New York: Basic Books, 1970.

Shellow, Robert, and Morton Bard. *Issues in Law Enforcement*. Reston, Va.: Reston, 1976.

Skolnick, Jerome H. *Justice Without Trial: Law Enforcement in Democratic Society.* 2nd ed. New York: John Wiley & Sons, 1975.

———, ed. *Police in America.* Boston: Little, Brown Educational Associates, 1975.

———. *Professional Police in a Free Society.* New York: National Conference of Christians and Jews, 1975.

Stein, Maurice. *The Eclipse of Community: An Interpretation of American Studies.* Princeton, N.J.: Princeton University Press, 1960.

Sterling, James W. *Changes in Role Concepts of Police Officers During Recruit Training.* Washington, D.C.: International Association of Chiefs of Police, 1972.

Strecher, Victor G. *The Environment of Law Enforcement: A Community-Relations Guide.* Englewood Cliffs, N.J.: Prentice-Hall, 1971.

Swanson, B. E., and E. Swanson. *Discovering the Community: Comparative Analysis of Social, Political and Economic Change.* New York: John Wiley & Sons, 1977.

Territo, Leonard, C. R. Swanson, Jr., and Neil C. Chamelin. *The Police Personnel Selection Process.* Indianapolis, Ind.: Bobbs-Merrill, 1977.

Toch, Hans, J. Douglas Grant, and Raymond T. Galvin. *Agents of Change: A Study in Police Reform.* New York: John Wiley & Sons, 1975.

Trojanowicz, Robert C., and Samuel L. Dixon. *Criminal Justice and the Community.* Englewood Cliffs, N.J.: Prentice-Hall, 1974.

U.S., President's Commission on Law Enforcement and Administration of Justice. Reports listed are available from the U.S. Government Printing Office, Washington, D.C.

> *Field Surveys IV. The Police and the Community: The Dynamics of Their Relationship in a Changing Society.* Prepared for the commission by the University of California School of Criminology, Joseph D. Lohman and Gordon E. Misner, 1967.

> *Field Surveys V. A National Survey of Police and Community Relations.* Prepared for the commission by the National Center on Police and Community Relations, Michigan State University School of Police Administration and Public Safety, 1967.

> *The Role of the Police.* Prepared for the Commission by Richard A. Myren, 1967.

Washington, D.C., Metropolitan Police Department. *Evaluation Design: Use of Women for Patrol in the District of Columbia Police Department.* Washington, D.C.: Metropolitan Police Department, 1972.

Watson, Nelson A. *Police-Community Relations.* Gaithersburg, Md.: International Association of Chiefs of Police, Research, Development and Planning Division, 1966.

Watson, R. A. *Promise and Performance of American Democracy: With Coverage of State and Local Governments.* 3rd ed. New York: John Wiley & Sons, 1978.

Westley, William A. *Violence and the Police.* Cambridge, Mass.: MIT Press, 1970.

Whisenand, Paul M., James L. Cline, and George T. Felkenes. *Police-Community Relations.* Pacific Palisades, Calif.: Goodyear, 1974.

Wilson, James Q. *Varieties of Police Behavior: The Management of Law and Order in Eight Communities.* Cambridge, Mass.: Harvard University Press, 1968.

Wright, Burton, and Vernon Fox. *Criminal Justice and the Social Sciences.* Philadelphia, Pa.: W. B. Saunders, 1979.

Ziegenhagen, Eduard A. *Victims, Crime and Social Control.* New York: Praeger, 1977.

PART 2. PSYCHOLOGICAL CONSIDERATIONS

Alex, Nicholas. *Black in Blue: A Study of the Negro Policeman.* New York: Appleton-Century-Crofts, 1969.

────── . *New York Cops Talk Back: Study of a Beleaguered Minority.* New York: John Wiley & Sons, 1976.

Allport, Gordon. *ABC's of Scapegoating.* Freedom Pamphlet. New York: Anti-Defamation League of B'nai B'rith, 1948.

────── . *The Nature of Prejudice.* New York: Addison-Wesley, 1958.

Allport, Gordon, and L. Postman. *The Psychology of Rumor.* New York: Henry Holt, 1947.

Anderson, Mary A. *Women in Law Enforcement.* Portland, Oreg.: Metropolitan Press, 1974.

Baldwin, James. *Nobody Knows My Name.* New York: Dial Press, 1961.

Berrien, Frederick M., and Wendell Bash. *Human Relations: Comments and Cases.* 2nd ed. New York: Harper & Brothers, 1957.

Cohen, Jozef. *Sensation and Perception.* Eyewitness Series in Psychology. Chicago: Rand McNally, 1969.

Ellison, Ralph. *The Invisible Man.* New York: Random House, 1952.

Gibson, James J. *The Senses Considered as Perceptual Systems.* Boston: Houghton Mifflin, 1949.

Gourley, G. Douglas. *Public Relations and the Police.* Springfield, Ill.: Charles C Thomas, 1953.

Heston, Margaret. *Feelings Are Facts.* Intergroup Educational Pamphlet. New York: National Conference of Christians and Jews.

Katz, Judy H. *White Awareness: A Handbook for Anti-Racism Training.* Norman, Okla.: University of Oklahoma Press, 1978.

Knopf, Terry Ann. *Rumors, Race, and Riots.* New Brunswick, N.J.: Transaction Books, 1975.

Marx, Gary. *Protest and Prejudice: A Study of Belief in the Black Community.* New York: Harper & Row, 1967.

Quinney, Richard. *Critique of Legal Order.* Boston: Little, Brown, 1974.

Regoli, R. M. *Police in America.* Washington, D.C.: University Press of America, 1977.

Sherman, Lawrence W. *Controlling Police Corruption: The Effects of Reform Policies* (Summary Report). U.S. Department of Justice, LEAA, 1978.

Sutherland, Edwin H., and Donald R. Cressey. *Criminology.* 10th ed. Philadelphia, Pa.: Lippincott, 1978.

Trager, Helen G., and Marian R. Yarrow. *They Learn What They Live: Prejudice in Young Children.* New York: Harper & Brothers, 1952.

Wambaugh, Joseph. *The New Centurions.* New York: Dell Books, 1970.

────── . *The Blue Knight.* New York: Dell Books, 1972.

────── . *The Onion Field.* New York: Dell Books, 1973.

────── . *The Choirboys.* New York: Dell Books, 1975.

Wambaugh, Joseph. *The Black Marble.* New York: Dell Books, 1978.

Watson, Nelson A., and James W. Sterling. *Police and Their Opinions.* Washington, D.C.: International Association of Chiefs of Police, 1969.

Wolfe, Joan L., and John F. Heapy. *Readings on Productivity in Policing.* Washington, D.C.: Police Foundation, 1975.

Yefsky, Sheldon, ed. *Science and Technology in Law Enforcement.* Chicago: Thompson, 1967.

Zinn, Howard. *Justice?* Boston: Beacon Press, 1978.

PART 3. SOCIOLOGICAL CONSIDERATIONS

Annotated

Abadinsky, Howard. *Social Service in Criminal Justice.* Englewood Cliffs, N.J.: Prentice-Hall, 1979. Written to help officers further understand the functions of, and be able to work with, social agencies for referral purposes. Includes charts and other aids and an extensive bibliography.

Alexander, Yonah, and Seymour Finger, eds. *Terrorism: Interdisciplinary Perspectives.* New York: John Jay Press, 1978. Covers the effects of terrorism deemed most pertinent today: role of the media, international dimensions, and legal aspects. Overview by Baljit Singh of Michigan State University.

Ambrosino, Lillian. *Runaways.* Boston: Beacon Press, n.d. Why young Americans run away, what their problems are, and how communities can help or provide for them.

American Civil Liberties Union. Series of handbooks on civil rights. New York: Avon Books. n.d. Includes titles on rights of veterans, hospital patients, gay people, aliens, mental patients, mentally retarded, reporters, the poor, students, candidates and voters, military personnel, suspects, women, teachers, prisoners, young people, and nonsmokers.

Ayars, Albert L., and John M. Ryan. *The Teenager and the Law.* North Quincy, Mass.: Christopher, 1978. Written by a school superintendent and a lawyer, the book is directed to the 30 million youths of America to help them understand the relation of laws to their everyday lives. Develops understanding and respect for rights and responsibilities in terms of their freedom, safety, property rights, and opportunities.

Blum, Jeffrey D., and Judith E. Smith. *Nothing Left to Lose.* Boston: Beacon Press, n.d. Illuminating case studies of "street people" who found help in voluntary community counseling centers.

Bowker, Lee H., et al. *Women, Crime and the Criminal Justice System.* Lexington, Mass.: Lexington Books, 1978. Comprehensive look at female criminal behavior and the treatment of women in the criminal justice system. This book covers frequency and types of crime, comparative international crime rates, and the victimization of females by criminals.

Cottle, Thomas J. *Children in Jail.* Boston: Beacon Press, 1978. About the 600,000 Americans between the ages of 12 and 17 in jails the majority of whom are in for status offenses. Personal realities are brought out in poignant conversations.

Falkin, Gregory P. *Reducing Delinquency.* Lexington, Mass.: Lexington Books, 1979. Evaluates the cost of various criminal justice policies and simulates their effects on crime reduction and other criminal justice goals.

Gorham, William, and Nathan Glazer, eds. *The Urban Predicament.* Washington, D.C.: The Urban Institute, 1978. Presents original research of twelve experts in urban affairs on finance, housing, crime, education, and transportation. Examines most significant trends and underlying forces, and predicts what can reasonably be expected in the future.

Hamparian, Donna, et al. *The Violent Few: Study of Dangerous Juvenile Offenders.* Lexington, Mass.: Lexington Books, 1978. Reports the results of a cohort study of juvenile offenders, each of whom was arrested at least once for a crime of violence.

Holmstrom, Lynda L., and Ann W. Burgess. *Victim of Rape: Institutional Reactions.* New York: Halsted Press & Wiley Interscience, 1978. In-depth account of the devastating effects of institutional processing of the rape victim and what our institutions (hospitals, courts, etc.) can do about it.

Mann, Michael. *Workers on the Move: The Sociology of Relocation.* New York: Cambridge University Press, 1973. A study of factory relocation and worker migration, based on original survey research. Tables, map.

Martin, J. P., ed. *Violence and the Family.* New York: Halsted Press & Wiley Interscience, 1978. Examines the reality of family violence in personal, psychological, and sociological terms, describing the policies and practices that may help prevent or mitigate the sufferings of the victims. Also, suggestions for public policy.

Mauss, Armand L., and Julie Camille Wolfe, eds. *This Land of Promises: The Rise and Fall of Social Problems in America.* Philadelphia, Pa.: Lippincott, 1977. Presents the perspective that social movements are closely related to, and even reenforce, social problems. Relates crime to inequality, sex, drugs, protest, and environment.

Radzinowicz, Sir Leon. *The Growth of Crime: The International Experience.* New York: Basic Books, 1977. The first authoritative attempt to take an international comparative look at every aspect of crime and enforcement. Warns that nowhere does the justice system work well, but warns also that most reforms suggested today have failed to work elsewhere, and that the worldwide problems of crime may be beyond the scope of criminal justice systems anywhere.

Rosen, Lawrence. *The Delinquent and Non-delinquent in a High Delinquent Area.* Palo Alto, Calif.: R & E Research Associates, 1978. In this study the author utilized 921 black males in a high delinquent area of Philadelphia to support his conclusions. The purpose of the study was to determine whether the variables that had been used successfully in the ecological analysis of delinquents could also be used successfully to distinguish delinquents from nondelinquents in a high delinquent area.

Sadoff, Robert L., ed. *Violence and Responsibility: Individual, Family and Social Aspects.* New York: Halsted Press & Wiley Interscience, 1978. A collection of ideas on the causes and concerns of violence viewed from the perspectives of psychiatrists, a neuroligist, criminologist, historian, law professor, judge, and a forensic psychiatrist.

U.S. Government Printing Office. *Black Crime.* Washington, D.C.: U.S. Government Printing Office, 1977. Item no. 146X8 (Order no.: J 1.2B 56 S/N 027-000-00658-2). Papers from a symposium of top-ranking black police officials exchanging opinions about the problems of crime in the black community. Conference held September 7–9, 1976.

Woodson, Robert L., ed. *Black Perspectives on Crime and the Criminal Justice System (A Symposium by the National Urban League).* Boston, Mass.: G. K. Hall, 1977. Black American criminologists discuss the issues as they relate to blacks' experiences in United States. Includes papers by Dr. Benjamin Carmichael, Alex Swann, and John O. Boone.

Unannotated

Alinsky, Saul. *Reveille for Radicals.* New York: Random House, 1969.

Allinson, Richard. *Status Offenders and the Juvenile Justice System: An Anthology.* Hackensack, N.J.: National Council on Crime and Delinquency, 1978.

Bartollas, C., S. J. Miller, and S. Dinitz. *Juvenile Victimization: The Institutional Paradox.* New York: John Wiley & Sons, 1976.

Basham, Richard. *Urban Anthropology: The Cross-Cultural Study of Complex Societies.* Palo Alto, Calif.: Mayfield, 1978.

Bassiouni, M. Cherif. *International Terrorism and Political Crime.* Springfield, Ill.: Charles C Thomas, 1975.

Bayley, David H., and Harold Mendelsohn. *Minorities and the Police: Confrontation in America.* New York: Free Press, 1969.

Bell, J. Bowyer. *A Time of Terror: How Democratic Societies Respond to Revolutionary Violence.* New York: Basic Books, 1978.

Black, Algernon D. *The People and the Police.* New York: McGraw-Hill, 1968.

Borland, M., ed. *Violence in the Family.* Atlantic Highlands, N.J.: Humanities Press, 1976.

Bouma, Donald. *Kids and Cops.* Grand Rapids, Mich.: Wm. E. Eerdmans, 1969.

Burt, Marvin R., and Ralph R. Balyeat. *Comprehensive Emergency Services System for Neglected and Abused Children.* New York: Vantage Press, 1977.

California Commission on Peace Officer Standards and Training. *Project Star: Impact of Social Trends on Crime and Criminal Justice.* Santa Cruz, Calif.: Davis, 1976.

Carlton, D., and C. Schaerf. *International Terrorism and World Security.* New York: John Wiley & Sons, 1975.

Center for Research on Criminal Justice. *The Iron Fist and the Velvet Glove: An Analysis of the U.S. Police.* Berkeley, Calif.: Center for Research on Criminal Justice, 1975.

Center for the Study of Democratic Institutions. *Civil Disobedience.* Santa Barbara, Calif.: Center for the Study of Democratic Institutions, 1966.

Ciminillo, Lewis H. *Violence and Vandalism in Public Education.* Danville, Ill.: Interstate, 1977.

Coleman, James S. *The Adolescent Society.* New York: Free Press, 1971.

Community Research Applications. *Child Abuse and Neglect Programs—Practice and Theory.* Washington, D.C.: Superintendent of Documents, 1977. Stock no. 017-024-005659-0.

Conrad, John P., and Simon Dinitz. *In Fear of Each Other: Studies of Dangerousness in America.* Lexington, Mass.: Lexington Books, 1977.

Cottle, Thomas J. *Busing.* Boston: Beacon Press, 1978.

Crites, Laura, ed. *The Female Offender.* Lexington, Mass.: Lexington Books, 1977.

Curtis, Lynn A. *Violence, Race and Culture.* Lexington, Mass.: Lexington Books, 1975.

Davis, Samuel M. *Rights of Juveniles: The Juvenile Justice System.* New York: Clark Boardman, 1974.

Dollard, John. *Caste and Class in a Southern Town.* New Haven, Conn.: Yale University Press, 1937.

Duberman, Lucille. *Social Inequality: Class and Caste in America*. Philadelphia, Pa.: Lippincott, 1976.

Edwards, George. *The Police on the Urban Frontier: A Guide to Community Understanding*. New York: Institute of Human Relations Press, American Jewish Committee, 1968.

Ehrlich, Paul, and Shirley Feldman. *The Race Bomb: Skin Color, Prejudice, and Intelligence*. New York: Ballantine Books, 1978.

Eldefonso, Edward, and Walter Hartinger. *Control, Treatment and Rehabilitation of the Juvenile Offender: Basic Perspectives*. Encino, Calif.: Glencoe, 1975.

Elliott, John D., and Leslie K. Gibson. *Contemporary Terrorism: Selected Readings*. Gaithersburg, Md.: International Association of Chiefs of Police, 1978.

Ernst, Robert T., and Lawrence Hugg. *Black America: Geographic Perspectives*. Garden City, N.Y.: Doubleday, 1975.

Evans, Alona E., and John F. Murphy, eds. *Legal Aspects of International Terrorism*. Lexington, Mass.: Lexington Books, 1978.

Festinger, Leon. *A Theory of Cognitive Dissonance*. Palo Also, Calif.: Stanford University Press, 1957.

Fogel, David. "*. . . We Are the Living Proof . . .": The Justice Model of Corrections*. Cincinnati, Ohio: W. H. Anderson, 1975.

Fogelson, Robert M. *Big-City Police: An Urban Institute Study*. Cambridge, Mass.: Harvard University Press, 1977.

Fortas, Abe. *Concerning Dissent and Civil Disobedience—We Have an Alternative to Violence*. New York: New American Library, Signet Books, 1968.

Friday, Paul C., and V. Lorne Stewart. *Youth Crime and Juvenile Justice*. New York: Praeger, 1977.

Ganz, Alan S., Hans W. Mattick, Kenneth J. Northcott, and Jerome H. Skolnick. *The Cities and the Police*. Chicago: University of Chicago Round Table, 1968.

Glueck, Sheldon, and Eleanor Glueck. *Of Delinquency and Crime: A Panorama of Years of Search and Research*. Springfield, Ill.: Charles C Thomas, 1974.

Gruber, Alan R. *Children in Foster Care: Destitute, Neglected, Betrayed*. New York: Human Sciences Press, 1978.

Hahn, Paul H. *The Juvenile Offender and the Law*. 2nd ed. Cincinnati, Ohio: W. H. Anderson, 1978.

Hahn, Paul H., and R. W. Holland. *American Government: Minority Rights versus Majority Rules*. New York: John Wiley & Sons, 1976.

Huber, Joan, and Paul Chalfant. *Sociology of American Poverty*. Norristown, N.J.: General Learning Press, 1974.

Jessor, Richard, and Shirley L. Jessor. *Problem Behavior and Psychosocial Development: A Longitudinal Study of Youth*. New York: Academic Press, 1977.

Johnson, Thomas. *Introduction to the Juvenile Justice System*. 2nd ed. St. Paul, Minn.: West, 1979.

Kephart, William M. *Racial Factors and Urban Law Enforcement*. Philadelphia: University of Pennsylvania Press, 1957.

Kett, Joseph F. *Rites of Passage: Adolescence in America, 1790 to the Present*. New York: Basic Books, 1977.

Klein, Malcolm W., ed. *The Juvenile Justice System*. Beverly Hills, Calif.: Sage, 1976.

Kluchesky, Joseph T. *Police Action on Minority Problems.* New York: Freedom House, 1946.

Koestler, Frances A. *Runaway Teenagers.* New York: Public Affairs Pamphlets, 1977.

Krisberg, Barry, and James Austin, eds. *The Children of Ishmael: Critical Perspectives on Juvenile Justice.* Palo Alto, Calif.: Mayfield, 1978.

Lee, Alfred McClung, and Norman D. Humphrey. *Race, Riot: A Study of the Detroit Riot.* New York: Octagon Books, 1967.

Lineberry, W. P. *Struggle Against Terrorism.* Bronx, N.Y.: H. W. Wilson, 1977.

Lipsky, Michael, and David J. Oldon. *Riot Commission Politics: The Processing of Racial Crisis in America.* New Brunswick, N.J.: Transaction Books, 1976.

Locke, Hubert G. *The Detroit Riot of 1967.* Detroit, Mich.: Wayne State University Press, 1969.

McCaghy, C. H. *Deviant Behavior—Crime, Conflict and Interest Groups.* Riverside, N.J.: Macmillan, 1976.

Malielski, S. J., Jr. *Beleaguered Minorities.* San Francisco, Calif.: W. H. Freeman, 1973.

Montagu, Ashley. *Statement on Race.* 3rd ed. London: Oxford University Press, 1972.

Mumford, Lewis. *The City in History: Its Origins, Its Transformations and Its Prospects.* New York: Harcourt, Brace & World, 1961.

Owens, Charles E., and Jimmy Bell. *Blacks and Criminal Justice.* Lexington, Mass.: Lexington Books, 1977.

Parry, Albert. *Terrorism: From Robespierre to Arafat.* New York: Vanguard Press, 1977.

Parsons, Talcott. *The Social System.* New York: Free Press, 1951.

Patterson, Franklin K. *The Adolescent Citizen.* Glencoe, Ill.: Free Press, 1960.

Petersen, Gene, Laura M. Sharp, and Thomas Drury. *Southern Newcomers to Northern Cities.* New York: Praeger, 1976.

Ransford, Edward. *Race and Class in American Society: Black, Anglo, Chicano.* Cambridge, Mass.: Schenkman, 1977.

Read, Frank T., and Lucy McGough. *Let Them Be Judged: The Judicial Integration of the Deep South.* Metuchen, N.J.: Scarecrow Press, 1978.

Reed, Thomas. *Perspectives on the Police-Juvenile Problem.* St. Paul, Minn.: West, 1979.

Rose, Arnold M., and Caroline B. Rose, eds. *Minority Problems.* New York: Harper & Row, 1965.

Ross, John Michael. *Resistance to Racial Change in the Urban North.* Cambridge, Mass.: Ballinger, 1975.

Sagarin, Edward, ed. *Deviance and Social Change.* Beverly Hills, Calif.: Sage, 1977.

Sellin, Thorsten, and Marvin Wolfgang. *The Measurement of Delinquency.* Montclair, N.J.: Patterson Smith, 1977.

Senn, Milton. *A Study of Police Training Programs in Minority Relations.* Los Angeles: Law Enforcement Committee of the Los Angeles County Conference on Community Relations, 1952.

Servin, Manuel. *An Awakened Minority: The Mexican Americans.* 2nd ed. Encino, Calif.: Glencoe, 1974.

Simon, Rita James. *Women and Crime*. Lexington, Mass.: Lexington Books, 1975.

Simpson, George E., and Milton Yinger. *Racial and Cultural Minorities*. Rev. ed. New York: Harper & Brothers, 1953.

Smith, Mark H., Jr. *Urban Education, the Black Child and You*. Morristown, N.J.: General Learning Press, 1976.

Staples, Robert. *Introduction to Black Sociology*. New York: McGraw-Hill, 1976.

Tellmann, Kathie S., et al. *Diversion, Delinquency and Labels*. Lexington, Mass.: Lexington Books, 1979.

U.S. Commission on Civil Rights, *The State of Civil Rights*. Washington, D.C.: U.S. Government Printing Office, February 1978.

———. *Social Indicators of Equality for Minorities and Women*. Washington, D.C.: U.S. Government Printing Office, August 1978.

U.S. National Advisory Commission on Civil Disorders. Reports listed are available from the U.S. Government Printing Office, Washington, D.C. *Report of the National Advisory Commission on Civil Disorders* (Kerner Report), 1969. *Supplemental Studies for the National Advisory Commission on Civil Disorders*, 1968.

Vorrath, Harry H., and Larry K. Brendtro, eds. *Positive Peer Culture*. Chicago: Aldine, 1974.

Warrior, Betsy, ed. *Working on Wife Abuse*. Cambridge, Mass.: Betsy Warrior, Publisher, 1978.

Weckler, J. E., and Theo E. Hall. *The Police and Minority Groups*. Chicago: International City Managers Association, 1944.

Weston, Paul B., and Kenneth M. Wells. *When the Marching Stopped—An Analysis of the Black Issues of the '70s*. New York: National Urban League, 1974.

Wilkerson, Albert D., ed. *The Rights of Children*. Philadelphia, Pa.: Temple University Press, 1974.

Wilkinson, Paul. *Terrorism and the Liberal State*. New York: Halsted Press, Division of John Wiley & Sons, 1978.

Willie, Charles V. *Black/Brown/White Relations: Race Relations in the '70s*. New Brunswick, N.J.: Transaction Books, 1976.

Wintersmith, Robert. *Police and the Black Community*. Lexington, Mass.: Lexington Books, 1974.

Wright, Sam. *Crowds and Riots: A Study of Social Organization*. Beverly Hills, Calif.: Sage, 1977.

PART 4. OTHER IMPORTANT CONSIDERATIONS

Annotated

Bequai, August. *Organized Crime*. Lexington, Mass.: Lexington Books, 1979. Case histories explain specific forms of organized crime, such as gambling, fencing, loan-sharking, drugs, and political corruption.

Blomberg, Thomas G. *Social Control and the Proliferation of Juvenile Court Services*. Palo Alto, Calif.: R & E Research Associates, 1978. Indicates ways in which expansion of court services for juveniles may produce more effective client treatment by juvenile courts.

Braswell, Michael. *Cases in Corrections*. Santa Monica, Calif.: Goodyear, 1979. Supplement for upper-level justice and corrections courses. Examines full scope of professional and nonprofessional roles in corrections problems. Also for in-service training.

Buckley, Marie. *Breaking Into Prison*. Boston: Beacon Press, n.d. Ways that concerned citizens and communities, by working both inside and outside prison walls, can effect more humane prison life and inspire reform.

Chang, Dae H. *Crime and Delinquency*. Cambridge, Mass.: Schenkman, 1977. This mini-text adopts a cross-national perspective on how other countries (some underdeveloped) and ours handle crime and delinquency problems.

Clinard, Marshall B. *Cities With Little Crime*. New York: Cambridge University Press, 1978. Compares crime data from Switzerland, Sweden, and other European countries showing relationships of policy-oriented recommendations in the fields of criminal justice, urban and political decentralization, nationalization of criminal codes and gun control legislation, and crime rates.

Crime Prevention Library. *Understanding Crime Prevention*, vol. 1. Lexington, Ky.: National Crime Prevention Institute Press, 1978. A professionally written overview of the crime prevention field that presents the knowledge of crime prevention in a systematic, comprehensive fashion. Includes three chapters on community involvement in prevention.

Dodge, Calvert R. *World Without Prisons*. Lexington, Mass.: Lexington Books, 1979. Focuses on alternatives to incarceration in the United States, Canada, and Western Europe. Includes historical background of prisons, the community approach to resocialization of criminals, prison management, and a discussion of the future of prisons and alternatives.

Gillers, Stephen. *Getting Justice: The Rights of People*. Bergenfield, N.J.: New American Library, n.d. A noted civil rights attorney describes an individual's legal guarantees, tells how authorities try to circumvent them, and explains what one must do to protect these rights. Introduction by Ramsey Clark.

Greenberg, David F., ed. *Corrections and Punishment*. Beverly Hills, Calif.: Sage, 1977. Essays that assess ways in which prisons are affected by society at large; the social structure, functions, and processes of prisons through which they change. Treats failures of rehabilitation, growing militancy of prisoners and their unionization, and impact of recent policy decisions.

Johnson, Elmer Hubert. *Community-Based Corrections in Western Europe*. Carbondale, Ill.: Center for the Study of Crime, Delinquency and Correction, 1974. A review of penal reform written following a visit to eight Western European countries in 1972.

Jones, David Arthur. *Crime Without Punishment*. Lexington, Mass.: Lexington Books, 1979. Discusses the plea-negotiating process and emphasizes how the majority of crimes committed by sophisticated offenders go unpunished.

McKelvey, Blake. *American Prisons: A History of Good Intentions*. Montclair, N.J.: Paterson Smith, 1977.

March, Ray A. *Alabama Bound*. University, Ala.: University of Alabama Press, 1978. Not for the squeamish. A first person oral history of three generations of personnel in Alabama prisons, indicating "cruel and unusual punishment" and the effects on inmates, by a professional investigative reporter.

Meiners, Roger E. *Victim Compensation*. Lexington, Mass.: Lexington Books, 1978. Covers the legal background, various cost estimates, and recent relevant legislation.

Newman, Graeme. *The Punishment Response*. Philadelphia, Pa.: Lippincott, 1978. Discusses the historic habit of man of punishing social, legal, and religious violators of laws and customs and the various justifications for doing so, even when they are mere rationales.

Parizeau, Alice, and Denis Szabo. *The Canadian Criminal Justice System*. Lexington, Mass.: Lexington Books, 1977. The only complete summary of the Canadian criminal justice system. Notes, tables, figures, bibliography, and index.

Powis, David. *Signs of Crime: A Field Manual for Police*. New York: John Jay Press, 1978. Tells the thousand and one ways a constable or police officer can spot criminals, the result of thirty-one years of experiences on the street.

Prassel, Frank N. *Criminal Law, Justice and Society*. Santa Monica, Calif.: Goodyear, 1979. Upper-level text for Law Enforcement/Criminal Justice majors; supplement to Penal Law and Criminology courses. Basic concepts, definitions, historical internation precedents, and cases.

Punke, Harold H. *Education, Lawlessness and Political Corruption in America*. North Quincy, Mass.: Christopher Publishing House, n.d. An authority on law enforcement probes the reasons for, and the problems surrounding, lack of order and political corruption in America, and offers plausible alternatives to existing practices.

Reiner, Robert. *The Blue-Coated Worker.* New York: Cambridge University Press, 1978. Considers British police unionization, based on interviews of officers of a large city force. The book suggests the contradictory position of police as a political institution and cites sources of support for unionism.

Rhodes, R. P. *The Insoluble Problems of Crime*. New York: John Wiley & Sons, 1977. Candid analysis of the political realities of today's criminal justice system. Discusses practical solutions and describes how to measure success or failure.

Sheleff, Leon S. *The Bystander: Behavior, Law and Ethics*. Lexington, Mass.: Lexington Books, 1978. Examines the legal rights and duties of the bystander, the ethical issues, and the need for changes in the law.

Solomon, Hassim M. *Introduction to Community Corrections*. Boston: Holbrook Press, 1976. Treats innovative programs in community corrections, probation/parole, and institutions, both adult and juvenile, from across the nation. Includes many teaching aids; instructor's manual available on adoption.

Strickland, Katherine G. *Correctional Institutions for Women in the United States*. Lexington, Mass.: Lexington Books, 1979. Reports that the relatively small number of female offenders has greatly influenced the size and structure of women's correctional institutions.

Tyrnauer, Gabrielle, and Charles Stastny. *Who Rules the Joint?* Lexington, Mass.: Lexington Books, 1979. The reforms and revolutions of the post World War II era have given rise to a new kind of prison culture and new breed of leader in prison society. This book traces the political and sociopsychological development of these changes and provides an in-depth study of experiment with reform.

Wasserstein, Bruce, and Mark J. Green. *With Justice for Some*. Boston: Beacon Press, n.d. Failures of the American legal system to provide justice for the variously underprivileged.

Unannotated

Akers, Ronald L., and Edward Sagarin, eds. *Crime Prevention and Social Control.* New York: Praeger, 1974.

Allen, Harry E., and Clifford E. Simonsen. *Corrections in America: An Introduction.* 2nd ed. Encino, Calif.: Glencoe, 1978.

Alper, Benedict S. *Prisons Inside-out: Alternatives in Correctional Reform.* Cambridge, Mass.: Ballinger, 1974.

Andenaes, Johannes. *Punishment and Deterrence.* Ann Arbor: University of Michigan Press, 1974.

Anonymous. *Call for Citizen Action: Crime Prevention and the Citizen.* Washington, D.C.: National Criminal Justice Reference Service, 1974.

Bacon, G. Richard, et al. *Struggle for Justice: A Report on Crime and Punishment in America.* New York: Hill & Wang, 1975.

Banfield, Edward C., and James Q. Wilson. *City Politics,* Cambridge, Mass.: Harvard University Press, 1963.

Barnard, Chester I. *The Functions of the Execution.* Cambridge, Mass.: Harvard University Press, 1960.

Bartollas, Clemens, and Stuart J. Miller. *Correctional Administration: Theory and Practice.* New York: McGraw-Hill, 1978.

Bent, Allen Edward. *Politics of Law Enforcement: Conflict of Power in Urban Communities.* Lexington, Mass.: Lexington Books, 1974.

Bequai, August. *White-collar Crime.* Lexington, Mass.: Lexington Books, 1978.

Blumstein, Alfred, and Daniel Nagin, eds. *Deterrence and Incapacitation: Estimating the Effects of Criminal Sanctions on Crime Rates.* Washington, D.C.: National Academy of Sciences, 1978.

Carroll, Leo. *Hacks, Blacks and Cons: Race Relation in a Maximum Security Prison.* Lexington, Mass.: Lexington Books, 1974.

Chicago Center for Police Study. *The Media and the Cities.* Chicago: University of Chicago Press, 1968.

Clark, Ramsey. *Crime in America.* New York: Simon and Schuster, 1970.

Cohen, Fred. *The Legal Challenge to Corrections: Implications for Manpower and Training.* Washington, D.C.: Joint Commission on Correctional Manpower and Training, 1969.

Cole, George F. *Politics and the Administration of Justice.* Beverly Hills, Calif.: Sage, 1973.

Conrad, John P., and Milton G. Rector. *Should We Build More Prisons?: A Debate between Conrad and Rector.* Hackensack, N.J.: National Council on Crime and Delinquency, 1977.

Cortner, Richard C. *The Supreme Court and Civil Liberties Policy.* Palo Alto, Calif.: Mayfield, 1976.

Denfield, Duane. *Streetwise Criminology.* Cambridge, Mass.: Schenkman, 1974.

Dougherty, Richard. *The Commissioner.* Garden City, N.Y.: Doubleday, 1962.

Downie, Leonard, Jr. *Justice Denied: The Case for Reform of the Courts.* New York: Praeger, 1971.

Dye, Thomas R., and Brett W. Hawkins, eds. *Politics in the Metropolis.* 2nd ed. Columbus, Ohio: Charles E. Merrill, 1971.

Edelhertz, Herbert, and Gilbert Geis. *Public Compensation to Victims of Crime.* New York: Praeger, 1974.

Feldman, M. Philip. *Criminal Behavior: A Psychological Analysis.* New York: John Wiley & Sons, 1978.

Fleming, Macklin. *Of Crimes and Rights.* New York. W. W. Norton, 1978.

Fosdick, Raymond. *American Police Systems.* New York: Century, 1920.

Fretz, Donald R. *Courts and the Community.* Reno, Nev.: National College of the State Judiciary, University of Nevada, 1973.

Gaines, Larry K., and Truett A. Ricks. *Managing the Police Organization: Selected Readings.* St. Paul, Minn.: West, 1978.

Galaway, Burt, Joe Hudson, and C. D. Hollister, eds. *Community Corrections: A Reader.* Springfield, Ill.: Charles C Thomas, 1975.

Gammage, Allen Z., and Stanley L. Sachs. *Police Unions.* Springfield, Ill.: Charles C Thomas, 1972.

Gardner, Erle Stanley. *Cops on Campus and Crime in the Streets.* New York: William Morrow, 1970.

Giallombardo, Rose. *The Social World of Imprisoned Girls.* New York: John Wiley & Sons, 1974.

Glaser, Daniel. *The Effectiveness of a Prison and Parole System.* Indianapolis, Ind.: Bobbs-Merrill, 1964.

Goldfarb, Ronald. *Jails: The Ultimate Ghetto in the Criminal Justice System.* Garden City, N.Y.: Doubleday, 1976.

Goldfarb, R. L., and L. R. Singer. *After Conviction.* New York: Simon and Schuster, 1975.

Goldstein, Herman. *Police Corruption: A Perspective on Its Nature and Control.* Washington, D.C.: Police Foundation, 1975.

Gurr, Ted Robert, et al. *Politics of Crime and Conflict: Comparative Study of Four Cities.* Beverly Hills, Calif.: Sage, 1977.

Hermann, Michele D., and Marilyn G. Haft. *Prisoners' Rights: Theory, Litigation, Practice.* New York: Clark Boardman, 1973.

Hoenberg, John. *The Best Cause: Free Press—Free People.* New York: Columbia University Press, 1970.

Hudson, Joe, and Burton Galaway. *Considering the Victim: Readings in Restitution and Victim Compensation.* Springfield, Ill.: Charles C Thomas, 1974.

Hunter, Floyd. *Community Power Structure.* Chapel Hill: University of North Carolina Press, 1953.

Ianni, Francis A. J. *Black Mafia—Ethnic Succession in Organized Crime.* New York: Simon and Schuster, 1975.

Igleberger, R., G. Pence, and J. Angell. "Changing Urban Police: A Practitioner's View." *Innovation in Law Enforcement.* Criminal Justice Monograph. Washington, D.C.: U.S. Government Printing Office, 1973.

Inciardi, James A., and Anne F. Pottieger. *Violent Crime: Historical and Contemporary Issues.* Beverly Hills, Calif.: Sage, 1978.

International City Management Association. *Local Government and Police Management*. Washington, D.C.: International City Management Association, 1977.

Jarvis, Dwight C. *Institutional Treatment of the Offender*. New York: McGraw-Hill, 1978.

Jones, David Arthur. *Crime and Criminal Responsibility*. Chicago: Nelson-Hall, 1976.

Jones, Ralph T. *City Employee Unions, Labor and Politics in New York and Chicago*. Cambridge, Mass.: Ballinger, 1975.

Juris, Harvey A., and Peter Feuille. *Impact of Police Unions: A Summary Statement*. Washington, D.C.: National Criminal Justice Reference Service, 1974.

———— . *Police Unionism; Power and Impact in Public Sector Bargaining*. Lexington, Mass.: Lexington Books, 1973.

Kalish, Carol B. *Crimes and Victims: A Report of the Dayton–San Jose Pilot Survey of Victimization*. Washington, D.C.: National Criminal Justice Reference Service, 1974.

Kalmar, R. *Child Abuse—Perspectives on Diagnosis, Treatment and Prevention*. Dubuque, Ia.: Kendall Hunt Publication Co., 1977.

Kelly, William, and Nora Kelly. *Policing in Canada*. Toronto, Canada: Macmillan, 1978.

Kerper, Hazel B., and James Kerper. *Legal Rights of the Convicted*. St. Paul, Minn.: West, 1974.

Kiester, Edwin, Jr. *Crimes With No Victims: How the Law Wastes Police Resources*. New York: American Jewish Committee, n.d.

Killinger, George G., and Paul F. Cromwell, Jr. *Introduction to Corrections: Selected Readings*. St. Paul, Minn.: West, 1978.

Kotler, Milton. *Neighborhood Government*. New York: Bobbs-Merrill, 1969.

Kratcoski, Peter C., and Donald B. Walker. *Criminal Justice in America: Process and Issues*. Glenview, Ill.: Scott, Foresman, 1978.

Krohn, Marvin D., and Ronald L. Akers, eds. *Crime, Law and Sanctions*. Beverly Hills, Calif.: Sage, 1978.

Leonard, V. A. *Police Organization and Management*. New York: Foundation Press, 1964.

Lewis, Marlin, Warren W. Bundy, and James Hague. *Introduction to the Courts and Judicial Process*. Englewood Cliffs, N.J.: Prentice-Hall, 1978.

Lippman, Walter. *Public Opinion*. New York: Harcourt Brace, 1922.

McArthur, A. Verne. *Coming Out Cold: Community Re-Entry from a State Reformatory*. Lexington, Mass.: Lexington Books, 1974.

McDonald, William F., ed. *Criminal Justice and the Victim*. Beverly Hills, Calif.: Sage, 1976.

McLeary, Richard. *Dangerous Men: The Sociology of Parole*. Beverly Hills, Calif.: Sage, 1978.

Maddox, Charles W. *Collective Bargaining in Law Enforcement*. Springfield, Ill.: Charles C Thomas, 1974.

Martinson, Robert. *Rehabilitation, Recidivism and Research*. Hackensack, N.J.: National Council on Crime and Delinquency, 1976.

Masotti, Louis H., and Robert L. Lineberry. *The New Urban Politics*. Cambridge, Mass.: Ballinger, n.d.

Menninger, Karl. *The Crime of Punishment*. New York: Viking Press, 1968.

Mettler, George B. *The Fair Trial—Free Press Controversy*. Boston, Mass.: Allyn & Bacon, Holbrook Press, 1977.

Miller, Stuart A., Simon Dinitz, and John P. Conrad. *The Dangerous Offender and the Police*. Lexington, Mass.: Lexington Books, 1978.

Mills, C. Wright. *The Power Elite*. New York: Oxford University Press, 1956.

Milton, Catherine. *Women in Policing*. Washington, D.C.: Police Foundation, 1972.

Moos, R. H. *Evaluating Correctional Community Settings*. New York: John Wiley & Sons, 1975.

Morris, Norval, and Guy Hawkins. *The Honest Politician's Guide to Crime Control*. Chicago: Chicago University Press, 1969.

New York State Special Commission on Attica. *Attica: The Official Report*. New York: Bantam Books, 1972.

Orland, Leonard. *Justice, Punishment, Treatment—The Correctional Process*. New York: Macmillan, 1973.

Palmer, John W. *Constitutional Rights of Prisoners*. Cincinnati, Ohio: W. H. Anderson, 1972.

Poulos, John W. *The Anatomy of Crime*. Mineola, N.Y.: Foundation Press, 1975.

Radzinowicz, Sir Leon, and Marvin Wolfgang. *Crime and Justice*. 2nd rev. ed. 3 vols. New York: Basic Books, 1977.

Reckless, Walter C. *The Crime Problem*. 5th ed. Santa Monica, Calif.: Goodyear, 1973.

Reppetto, Thomas A. *The Blue Parade*. 100D Brown Street, Riverside, N.J.: Free Press, 1979.

Ruchelmen, Leonard. *Police Politics: A Comparative Study of Three Cities*. Cambridge, Mass.: Ballinger, 1974.

Rudovsky, David. *The Rights of Prisoners*. New York: Avon Books, 1973.

Schafer, Stephen. *The Political Criminal*. New York: Free Press, 1974.

Schur, Edwin M. *Crime Without Victims*. Englewood Cliffs, N.J.: Prentice-Hall, 1965.

Schur, Edwin M., and Adam Begau. *Victimless Crimes*. Englewood Cliffs, N.J.: Prentice-Hall, 1974.

Siebert, Fred S., and George A. Hough, III. *Free Press and Free Trial*. Athens: University of Georgia, 1971.

Silberman, Charles. *Criminal Violence/Criminal Justice*. New York: Random House, 1979.

Singer, Richard G., and William J. Statsky. *Rights of the Imprisoned*. New York: Bobbs-Merrill, 1974.

Sink, John M. *Political Criminal Trials*. New York: Clark Boardman, 1974.

Skolnick, Jerome. *The Politics of Protest*. New York: Simon and Schuster, 1969.

Sparks, R. F., H. G. Glenn, and D. J. Dodd. *Surveying Victims: Measurement of Criminal Victimization, Preceptions of Crime, and Attitudes to Criminal Justice*. New York: John Wiley & Sons, 1977.

Stewart, V. Lorne, ed. *The Changing Faces of Juvenile Justice*. Vol. 2 of Monographs of the United National Crime Prevention and Criminal Justice Branch. New York: New York University Press, 1978.

Stieber, Jack. *Public Employee Unionism: Structure, Growth Policy*. Washington, D.C.: Brookings Institution, 1973.

Strick, Anne. *Injustice for All: How Our Adversary System of Law Victimizes Us and Subverts True Justice.* New York: Penguin Books, 1978.

Sykes, Gresham. *The Society of Captives: A Study of a Maximum Security Prison.* Princeton, N.J.: Princeton University Press, 1958.

Uhlman, Thomas M. *Racial Justice: Black Judges, Black Defendants, and the American Legal Process.* Lexington, Mass.: Lexington Books, 1979.

U.S. National Advisory Commission on Criminal Justice Standards and Goals. Reports listed are available from the U.S. Government Printing Office, Washington, D.C.
A Call for Citizen Action: Crime Prevention and the Citizen. 1974.
A National Strategy to Reduce Crime. 1973.
Report on Community Crime Prevention. 1973.
Report on Corrections. 1973.
Report on the Criminal Justice System. 1973.

U.S., President's Commission on Law Enforcement and Administration of Justice. Reports listed are available from the U.S. Government Printing Office, Washington, D.C.
The Challenge of Crime in a Free Society. Commission report. 1967.
Crimes of Violence. Prepared for the commission by Marvin Wolfgang. 1967.
Field Surveys I. Report on a Pilot Study in the District of Columbia on Victimization and Attitudes Toward Law Enforcement. Prepared for the commission by the Bureau of Social Science Research, Inc. 1967.
Field Surveys II. Criminal Victimization in the United States: A Report of a National Survey. Prepared for the commission by the National Opinion Research Center, University of Chicago, 1967.
Field Surveys III. Studies in Crime and Law Enforcement in Major Metropolitan Areas. 2 vols. Prepared for the commission by the University of Michigan, Albert J. Reiss, Jr., and associates.
Task Force Report: Corrections. 1967.
Task Force Report: The Courts. 1967.
Task Force Report: The Police. 1967.
Task Force Report: Science and Technology. 1967.

Viano, Emilio. *Criminal Justice Research.* Lexington, Mass.: Lexington Books, 1975.

Whisenand, Paul M., and R. Fred Ferguson. *The Managing of Police Organizations.* 2nd ed. Englewood Cliffs, N.J.: Prentice-Hall, 1978.

Williams, L., and Mary Fish. *Convicts, Codes and Contraband: The Prison Life of Men and Women.* Cambridge, Mass.: Ballinger, 1974.

Wilson, James Q. *Thinking About Crime.* New York: Basic Books, 1975.

Wilson, Terry V., and Paul Q. Fuqua. *Police and the Media.* Boston: Little, Brown Educational Associates, 1975.

PART 5. PROGRAMS

Annotated

Alper, Benedict S., and Lawrence T. Nichols. *Doing Justice: By the Community.* Lexington, Mass.: Lexington Books, 1979. Describes neighborhood justice programs, such as diversion, mediation, arbitration, restitution, victim compensation, and advisory sentencing procedures.

Bakal, Yitzhak, ed. *Community-Based Alternatives to Correctional Settings.* Lexington, Mass.: Lexington Books, 1978. Describes programs designed to replace the present system of corrections, with emphasis on closing down institutions in Massachusetts. Assesses strengths and weaknesses of alternative programs, including Outward Bound.

Cox, Steven M., and John J. Conrad. *Juvenile Justice: Guide to Practice and Theory.* Dubuque, Iowa: Wm. C. Brown, 1978. Comprehensive text, in lay terms. Provides insights into causes of delinquencies, procedures for handling, and the juvenile law itself. Discusses police, courts, and agencies involved.

Drummond, Anthony Dean. *Riot Control.* New York: Crane, Russak, 1975. Concerned with averting riotous situations. Covers psychology of crowds and rioters, their motivation, how they are led, and techniques employed by government agencies around the world in riot control.

Gottfredson, Don M. *Guidelines for Parole and Sentencing.* Lexington, Mass.: Lexington Books, 1978. Develops model prisoner placement programs for structuring and controlling discretion in such decisions.

Jeffery, C. Ray. *Crime Prevention Through Environmental Design.* Beverly Hills, Calif.: Sage, 1977. Maintains that ways must be found to deal with crime before it occurs. Indicates the weaknesses of police, courts, etc., for deterrence and presents models for innovation.

Johnson, E. H. *Evaluating Work Release as a Community-Based Strategy.* Carbondale, Ill.: Center for Study of Crime, Delinquency and Corrections, 1971. Based on *Work Release: Factors in Selection and Results* (see below).

———— . *Work Release: Factors in Selection and Results.* Carbondale, Ill.: Center for Study of Crime, Delinquency and Corrections, 1969. Data on males in North Carolina program (1957–1963) to test effectiveness of work release as measured by comparison of prisoners who have and have not been on parole.

———— . *Staff Looks at Community-Based Corrections.* Carbondale, Ill.: Center for Study of Crime, Delinquency and Corrections, 1972. Considers staff recruitment and attitudes regarding community-based corrections, and relationships between community centers and prisons.

Lemert, Edwin M., and Forrest Dill. *Offenders in the Community: The Probation Study in California.* Lexington, Mass.: Lexington Books, 1978. Shows that probation reduces state costs by halting the spiral of increased commitments and ever greater capital construction projects.

Nagel, S. S. *Modeling the Criminal Justice System.* Beverly Hills, Calif.: Sage, 1977. Examines law enforcement, police, and court operations for community variables in crime control and cost effectiveness. Analyzes models and alternatives.

National Institute of Law Enforcement and Criminal Justice. *NCJRS Selected Bibliographies.* Washington, D.C.: National Institute of Law Enforcement and Criminal Justice, 1978. Pamphlet. Available from Document Loan Program, Box 6000, Rockville, Md. 20850. Gives brief lists of references under such headings as Basic Sources in Criminal Justice, Community Crime Prevention, Evaluation, Recidivism, Team Policing, Terrorism, Victim Compensation, and White-Collar Crime.

Parsole, Phyllida. *Juvenile Justice in Britain and the United States.* Boston: Routledge and Kegan Paul, 1978. Establishes points of contact and differences between the systems, showing a common concern with welfare and community involvement. Discusses the possibilities for new forms of treatment.

Romig, Dennis A. *Justice for Our Children*. Lexington, Mass.: Lexington Books, 1977. Describes 170 controlled experiments on delinquent youth rehabilitation, evaluating each to formulate an ideal model. Includes an examination of the major components of the criminal justice system: diversion, probation, community resident programs, institutions, and parole.

Ruth, Henry. *Research Priorities for Crime Reduction Efforts*. Washington, D.C.: The Urban Institute, 1977. Statistically examines current trends in crime, reports the most significant current trends in research, and suggests areas for future research, including decriminalization of certain types of behavior.

Sorrentino, Anthony. *Organizing Against Crime: Redeveloping the Neighborhood*. New York: Human Sciences Press, 1977. Documents a movement demonstrating how, with local help and professional aid, neighborhood residents can play a meaningful role in changing social situations that cause delinquency.

Wheeler, Gerald R. *Counter Deterrence: Report on Juvenile Sentencing and Effects of Prisonization*. Chicago: Nelson-Hall, n.d. Based on a national survey, reviews major assumptions about juvenile sentencing and parole supervision as a deterrent to crime and delinquency. Makes specific recommendations for viable alternatives to present policy of counterdeterrence.

Wycoff, Mary Ann, and George L. Kelling. *The Dallas Experience: Organizational Reform*. Washington, D.C.: Police Foundation, 1978. Some of the proposed programs were not a success. Others worked well and continue to improve the department. The concepts of decentralized neighborhood stations and generalist/specialist team policing were never tried. But the educational level, the selection, and the training of officers have been improved greatly.

Unannotated

Allen, Harry, and Richard Seiter. *Community Based Corrections*. Philadelphia: W. B. Saunders, 1979.

Anonymous. *Dade County Safe Streets Unit Project*, Final Report. Dade County, Fla.: Public Safety Department.

Anonymous. *Philadelphia Neighborhood Youth Resources Center*. Washington, D.C.: U.S. Printing Office, 1975.

Bakal, Yitzhak, ed. *Closing Correctional Institutions: New Strategies in Youth Services*. Lexington, Mass.: Lexington Books, 1973.

———. *Hard-core Delinquents and Their Treatment*. Lexington, Mass.: Lexington Books, 1978.

Bakal, Yitzhak, and Howard W. Polsky. *Reforming Juvenile Corrections: Alternatives and Strategies*. Lexington, Mass.: Lexington Books, 1978.

Block, Irvin. *Gun Control: One Way to Save Lives*. New York: Public Affairs Committee, 1976.

Brown, Lee P. *Police-Community Relations Evaluation Project*, Final Report, Grant NI-075. Washington, D.C.: U.S. Government Printing Office, 1971.

Butler, Dodie, Joe Reiner, and Bill Treanor. *Runaway House: A Youth-run Service Project*. Rockville, Md.: National Institutes of Mental Health, 1974.

Carney, Louis P. *Corrections and the Community*. Englewood Cliffs, N.J.: Prentice-Hall, 1977.

Carter, Robert M., and Malcolm M. Klein, eds. *Back on the Streets: The Diversion of Juvenile Offenders*. Englewood Cliffs, N.J.: Prentice-Hall, 1976.

Cirel, Paul, et al. *Community Crime Prevention Program: An Exemplary Project* (Seattle, Washington). Washington, D.C.: U.S. Department of Justice, Law Enforcement Assistance Administration, 1977.

Clifford, William. *Planning Crime Prevention*. Lexington, Mass.: Lexington Books, 1976.

Cramer, James A., ed. *Preventing Crime*. Beverly Hills, Calif.: Sage, 1978.

Eisenberg, Terry, Robert H. Fosen, and Albert S. Glickman. *Police-Community Action: A Program for Change in Police-Community Behavior*. New York: Praeger, 1973.

Empey, Lamar T. *The Silverlake Experiment: Testing Delinquency Theory and Community Intervention*. Chicago: Aldine, 1971.

Fox, Vernon. *Community-Based Corrections*. Englewood Cliffs, N.J.: Prentice-Hall, 1977.

Fuqua, P., and J. V. Wilson, *Terrorism—The Executive's Guide to Survival*. Houston, Texas: Gulf, 1978.

Gay, William G., et al. *Issues in Team Policing: A Review of the Literature*. Washington, D.C.: U.S. Department of Justice, 1977.

Gay, William G., H. Talmage Day, and Jane P. Woodward. *Team Policing in the United States*. Washington, D.C.: Law Enforcement Assistance Administration and National Sheriffs Association, 1977.

General Accounting Office report. *Handgun Control Effectiveness and Costs*. Washington, D.C.: U.S. Government Printing Office, 1978.

Getz, William, Allen Wiesen, Sue Stan, and Amy Ayers. *Fundamentals of Crisis Counseling: A Handbook for Crisis Intervention*. Lexington, Mass.: Lexington Books, 1974.

Hermann, Robert, Eric Single, and John Bosto. *Counsel for the Poor: Criminal Defense in Urban America*. Lexington, Mass.: Lexington Books, 1977.

International Association of Chiefs of Police. *Police Perspective in Child Abuse and Neglect, A Training Manual*, 1977. Gaithersburg, Md.: International Association of Chiefs of Police, 1977.

International Halfway House Association. *Guidelines and Standards for Halfway Houses and Community Treatment Centers*. Washington, D.C.: National Criminal Justice Reference Service, 1973.

Jones, Maxwell, et al. *The Therapeutic Community: A New Treatment Method of Psychiatry*. New York: Basic Books, 1953.

Jorgensen, James D., and Ivan H. Scheirer. *Volunteer Training for Courts and Corrections*. Metuchen, N.J.: Scarecrow Press, 1973.

Kassenbaum, Gene, et al. *Contracting for Correctional Services in the Community*, vol. 1. Washington, D.C.: U.S. Department of Justice, Law Enforcement Assistance Administration, 1978.

Kelling, George L., et al. *The Kansas City Preventive Control Experiment*. Washington, D.C.: Police Foundation, 1974.

Kelly, Rita Mae, et al. *The Pilot Police Project: A Description and Assessment of a Police-Community Relations Experiment in Washington, D.C.* Washington, D.C.: American Institutes for Research, 1972.

Killinger, George G., and Paul F. Cromwell, Jr. *Corrections in the Community: Alternate to Imprisonment.* 2nd ed. St. Paul, Minn.: West, 1978.

Klotter, John C., et al. "Citizen Participation in Crime Reduction." In *Police Yearbook,* 1978. Gaithersburg, Md.: International Association of Chiefs of Police.

Law Enforcement Assistance Administration, Technical Assistance Division, U.S. Department of Justice, *Guidelines and Standards for the Use of Volunteers in Correctional Programs.* Washington, D.C.: U.S. Government Printing Office, 1972.

Lohman, Joseph D. *The Police and Minority Groups.* Chicago: Chicago Park Police, 1947.

Loomis, Charles P., and J. Allen Beagle. *A Strategy for Rural Change.* Rev. ed. Cambridge, Mass.: Schenkman, 1975.

McCrea, Tully, and Don M. Gottfredson. *Guide to Improved Handling of Misdemeanant Offenders.* Washington, D.C.: National Criminal Justice Reference Service, 1973.

McGruder, John L., Nancy Beran, and Harry E. Allen. *The Community Reintegration Centers of Ohio: A Three-year Evaluation.* Columbus: Ohio State University Press, 1975.

McPartland, James M., and Edward L. McDill, eds. *Violence in the Schools: Perspectives, Programs and Positions.* Lexington, Mass.: Lexington Books, 1976.

Maher, George F. *Hostage: A Police Approach to Contemporary Crisis.* Springfield, Ill.: Charles C Thomas, 1977.

Mangold, Margaret E. *La Causa Chicano: The Movement for Justice.* New York: Family Services Association of America, 1973.

Marx, Jerry. *Officer, Tell Your Story: A Guide to Police Public Relations.* Springfield, Ill.: Charles C Thomas, 1967.

Misner, Gordon D. *Criminal Justice Education: A Profile.* New York: Academy of Criminal Justice Sciences, 1978.

Morris, Norval. *The Future of Imprisonment.* Chicago: University of Chicago Press, 1974.

National Council on Crime and Delinquency. *A Halt to Institutional Construction in Favor of Community Treatment.* An NCCD Policy Statement. Hackensack, N.J.: National Council on Crime and Delinquency, 1972.

———. *Instead of Prison.* Hackensack, N.J.: National Council on Crime and Delinquency, 1973.

Nejelski, Paul, et al. *Diversion in the Juvenile Justice System.* Hackensack, N.J.: National Council on Crime and Delinquency, 1976.

Police Foundation. Reports listed were published by the Police Foundation, Washington, D.C.
Cincinnati Team Policing Experiment. 1977.
Dallas Experience: Organizational Reform. 1978.
Domestic Violence and Police: Detroit & Kansas City. 1977.
Performance Appraisal in Police Departments. 1977.
Police Chief Selection: Handbook for Local Governments. 1976.
Police Personnel Exchange Programs, Bay Area. 1976.
Team Policing: Seven Case Studies. 1973.
Police and Interpersonal Conflict: 3rd Party Intervention Approaches. 1976.

Portune, Robert G. *Changing Adolescent Attitudes Toward Police.* Cincinnati, Ohio: W. H. Anderson, 1971.

Priestino, Ramon R., and Harry E. Allen. *The Parole Officer Aid Program in Ohio: An Exemplary Project.* Columbus: Ohio State University Press, 1975.

Pursuit, Dan G., et al. *Police Programs for Preventing Crime and Delinquency.* Springfield, Ill.: Charles C Thomas, 1972.

Rembar, Charles. *Removing Politics from the Administration of Justice.* Washington, D.C.: U.S. Government Printing Office, 1974.

Rothman, J., J. G. Erlich, and J. Teresa. *Promoting Innovation and Change in Organizations and Communities: A Planning Manual.* New York: John Wiley & Sons, 1976.

Rowat, Donald C., ed. *The Ombudsman.* Toronto: University of Toronto Press, 1965.

Saltman, Juliet. *Open Housing: Dynamics of a Social Movement.* New York: Praeger, 1978.

Sandu, Harjit S. *Modern Corrections: Offenders, Therapies and Community Reintegration.* Springfield, Ill.: Charles C Thomas, 1978.

Schwartz, Alfred I., and Sumner Clarren. *The Cincinnati Team Policing Experiment: A Summary Report.* Washington, D.C.: The Urban Institute, 1977. Available only from the Police Foundation, Washington, D.C.

Scott, Joseph E. *Ex-Offenders as Parole Officers.* Lexington, Mass.: Lexington Books, 1975.

Scull, Andrew W. *Decarceration: Community Treatment of the Deviant.* Englewood Cliffs, N.J.: Prentice-Hall, 1978.

Segal, Steben P. *The Mentally Ill in Community-Based Sheltered Care: Study of Community Care and Social Integration.* Somerset, N.J.: Wiley-Interscience, 1978.

Sherman, Lawrence, Catherine Milton, and T. Kelly. *Team Policing: Seven Case Studies.* Washington, D.C.: Police Foundation, 1973.

Siegal, Arthur L., et al., *Professional Police Human Relations Training.* Springfield, Ill.: Charles C Thomas, 1963.

Simpson, Antony E. *Guide to Library Research in Public Administration.* New York: Center for Productive Public Management, John Jay College of Criminal Justice, 1977.

Sower, Christopher, et al. *Community Involvement.* Glencoe, Ill.: Free Press, 1957.

Steggert, Frank X. *Community Action Groups and City Government.* Cambridge, Mass.: Ballinger, 1975.

Taba, Hilda, Elizabeth H. Brady, and John T. Robinson. *Intergroup Education in Public Schools.* Washington, D.C.: American Council on Education, 1952.

Tien, J. M., et al. *An Alternative Approach in Police Patrol—Wilmington Split-Force Experiment.* Washington, D.C.: National Institute of Law Enforcement and Criminal Justice, Law Enforcement Assistance Administration, 1978.

Trojanowicz, Robert C., and John M. Trojanowicz. *Community Based Crime Prevention.* Santa Monica, Calif.: Goodyear, 1975.

U.S. Department of Justice, Law Enforcement Assistance Administration, National Institute of Law Enforcement and Criminal Justice. *Improving Police-Community Relations.* Prepared by R. Wasserman, M. P. Gardner, and A. S. Cohen. Washington, D.C.: U.S. Government Printing Office, 1973.

U.S. Department of Justice, Law Enforcement Assistance Administration. *Training Police as Specialists in Family Crisis Intervention.* Washington, D.C.: U.S. Government Printing Office, 1973.

Vera Institute of Justice. *Programs in Criminal Justice Reform: Ten Year Report.* New York: Vera Institute of Justice, 1972.

Von Hirsch, Andrew. *Doing Justice: The Choice of Punishments.* Report of the Committee for the Study of Incarceration. New York: Farrar, Straus and Giroux, 1976.

Wasson, David K. *Community-Based Preventive Policing.* Ottawa, Canada: Office of the Solicitor General of Canada, 1977.

Wenk, Ernst A., ed. *Delinquency Prevention and the Schools.* Beverly Hills, Calif.: Sage, 1975.

Whisenand, Paul M. *Crime Prevention.* Boston: Hollbrook Press, 1978.

Wickwar, Hardy. *The Place of Criminal Justice in Development Planning.* Vol. 1 of Monographs of the United Nations Crime Prevention and Criminal Justice Branch. New York: New York University Press, 1977.

Wilkins, Leslie T., et al. *Sentencing Guidelines: Structuring Judicial Discretion.* Law Enforcement Assistance Administration, National Institute of Law Enforcement and Criminal Justice. Washington, D.C.: U.S. Department of Justice, U.S. Government Printing Office, 1978.

Woodward, Bob, and Carl Bernstein. *National Strategy to Reduce Crime.* New York: Avon Books, 1974.

Zinn, Howard. *Justice in Everyday Life: The Way It Really Works.* New York: William Morrow, 1974.

INDEX